1985
YEARBOOK
OF
SCIENCE
AND THE
FUTURE

1985
YEARBOOK
OF
SCIENCE
AND THE
FUTURE

Encyclopædia Britannica, Inc.
Chicago

Auckland   Geneva   London   Manila   Paris   Rome   Seoul   Sydney   Tokyo   Toronto

The University of Chicago
The Yearbook of Science and the Future
is published with the editorial advice of the faculties of
the University of Chicago.

1985
YEARBOOK OF SCIENCE AND THE FUTURE

CONTENTS

Feature Articles

Agricultural scientists are studying the potential usefulness of many species of plants that until now have been neglected. Among the most promising are the perennial prairie grasses, which might prove to be easily and economically grown sources of food.

Many of the animals native to the tropics offer the people of those underdeveloped regions great potential sources of meat, milk, and labor. They provide viable alternatives to imported temperate-zone livestock, which have not been able to flourish in the heat and humidity of the equatorial regions.

The Soviet Union inaugurated the space age in 1957 with the launch of Sputnik. Today, despite technological shortcomings and disastrous setbacks, Soviet space planners continue to move doggedly toward a number of significant goals, including a manned space station, a space-shuttle transportation system, and the capability of conducting warfare from orbit.

As increasingly large space stations are developed, the possibility of performing a variety of industrial operations in them becomes greater. Among the enterprises that would benefit most from the environment of space is the purification and separation of materials.

Manned spacecraft and unmanned satellites equipped with powerful sensing equipment are making discoveries that are revolutionizing our ideas about the oceans.

The volcanic explosion of El Chichón in Mexico in 1982 was one of the latest of the major eruptions that have sent huge quantities of ash and dust into the Earth's atmosphere and stratosphere. The extent to which these events affect climate and other conditions on the Earth is the subject of intense scrutiny by scientists.

Submersible craft exploring the deep ocean have found remarkable areas on the seafloor where extremely hot, mineral-rich water flows upward through cracks in the Earth's crust. These hydrothermal vents are surrounded by dense and unique assemblages of marine life.

Lightning on the Rails

by Lucia S. Turnbull

Trains presently in service in Europe and Japan whisk intercity passengers along at speeds of 125–170 miles per hour. Their technology as well as such advanced concepts as magnetic levitation are under study by transportation planners around the world.

Richly appointed deluxe passenger train, part of the Baltimore and Ohio Railroad's popular Royal Blue line, operated between Washington, D.C., and Jersey City, New Jersey, at the turn of the century. Within a few decades its likes were gone, as competition from other forms of transport compelled railroads in the U.S. and other developed nations to seek more limited and specialized niches.

LUCIA S. TURNBULL, *a Project Director for the Office of Technology Assessment of the U.S. Congress, completed a study of advanced rail technology in 1983.*

Illustrations by John Zielinski

Mention "railroad," and for many people the word conjures visions of the glorious technology of a bygone century—a century of steel when reliable, low-cost railways dominated overland transport of both freight and passengers, crossed the Siberian wastes, opened up the American West, created industrial tycoons, and greatly advanced the Industrial Revolution throughout much of the world. In the early 1900s, a scant 100 years from its origins, the railroad reached maturity, particularly in the developed countries where the growth and sophistication of road, air, pipeline, and ship transport soon would begin to restrain and modify the further development and commercial role of rail technology.

Those halcyon days of the "iron horse" may bring twinges of nostalgia to railroad buffs, but they have little cause to inspire mourning, for the railroad continues to thrive in various forms. In many nations it is still the primary all-purpose land carrier. In others it has specialized, depending upon social, industrial, and geographical opportunities and constraints, and has encouraged a specialized technology, one commonly and strongly influenced by the importance of speed.

Some recent history

While the evolution of the railroads from mine trolleys occurred under private ownership, by the time the United Kingdom nationalized its railways after World War II, only Canada and the U.S. had any substantial private ownership. In the U.S., with far the greatest railroad mileage on Earth, it was all private, though regulated by government. There, shortly after the war, the railroads began petitioning the federal Interstate Commerce Commission to drop their passenger routes and concentrate

10

on the more profitable freight ones. In 1971 Amtrak, a quasi-public corporation subsidized by federal funds, was created to take over intercity passenger rail transport, thereby virtually eliminating the private sector. By contrast, in Europe and Japan, with histories of nationalized transport systems, tight geographical boundaries, and dependence on expensive foreign energy, the need for passenger trains continued and led to the search for better ways of moving people faster. Consequently Japan, France, and Great Britain are now leaders in high-speed intercity passenger rail, while Japan and West Germany continue to pursue advanced ground-transport technologies, particularly magnetic levitation (maglev).

Japan has by far the greatest experience with high-speed trains, having inaugurated its first route in 1964 with totally new tracks and vehicles. Its Shinkansen (literally "new trunk line"), or Bullet train, system carries 125 million passengers annually; it operates more than 275 trains daily at speeds of 130 mph or more (100 miles is about 160 kilometers). France has developed what in the early 1980s was the fastest passenger train service in the world—its 170-mph *Train à Grande Vitesse* (TGV; "high-speed train") connecting Paris with Lyon. For the TGV the French constructed new rail line in rural areas between cities and used existing track in urban areas around Paris and Lyon. Unlike France and Japan, Great Britain chose to use existing tracks and to upgrade its diesel and electric equipment to achieve speeds of 125 mph. These trains, commonly referred to as High Speed Trains (HST's), operate over six mainline routes in Britain. In the mid-1980s the British also continued work on their Advanced Passenger Train (APT), which is designed to take curves at higher speeds on existing track.

Swift foals of the iron horse, high-speed passenger trains of the 1980s have emerged from a technology guided by numerous social, economic, and geographical factors and strongly influenced by a desire to move people from place to place as quickly as possible. Japanese Bullet trains (above left) await duty at a rolling stock base outside Tokyo. TGV train car (above) nears completion at a French construction facility.

11

American Metroliner train, a consequence of the High-Speed Ground Transportation Act of 1965, was developed as a demonstration project for the Northeast corridor to prove the viability of intercity passenger train service in the U.S. Built from available technology during the late 1960s, the multiple-unit railcars could reach speeds of 160 mph.

U.S. interest in high-speed rail and advanced ground-transport technology was kindled in 1964, during a time when both passenger and freight rail systems were facing major economic problems. Policymakers saw the Northeast corridor, the system of routes connecting densely populated Washington, D.C., New York City, and Boston, as the most likely candidate for high-speed rail transportation. However, the priority given to economic recovery of the freight rail system and the need for stabilizing the passenger network—the creation of Amtrak—led to upgrading existing equipment of the Northeast corridor rather than developing the high-speed rail line initially envisioned.

Today continuing developments in foreign high-speed rail and maglev are reawakening American interest in rail technology. U.S. government and business leaders in a position to influence policy are taking a hard look at many questions: How well do these high-speed technologies really work? Under what circumstances—geographic, economic, and societal—are they most appropriate? How much do they cost? Who should or could pay for them? And where do they fit in among the priorities defined by societal and transport needs? A major source of information, both for the U.S. and for other nations with similar interests, lies in the international experience of the past two decades.

Each country involved with high-speed rail applications and research has set its own goals and steered its own course accordingly. Nevertheless, all share in common a perception of the importance of speed and see a future role for railroads and advanced ground technology in intercity transport.

The American priority: resuscitating passenger rail

A year after American planners began studying the feasibility of high-speed trains for the Northeast corridor, the U.S. Congress passed the High-Speed Ground Transportation Act of 1965. Private railroads were still operating, and losing money on, passenger rail service. The new legislation included provisions for government research and development (R and D), demonstration programs, and data-gathering efforts. From the early 1950s until the passage of the act, no new intercity railcars had been designed or developed in the U.S. The showpiece of the government-sponsored demonstration effort was the Metroliner program for the Northeast corridor, which was intended to prove that a viable market existed for intercity passenger train service. The project was not a new technology development program but used multiple-unit electric railcars designed and built from available technology to achieve speeds as high as 160 mph.

Inaugurated in 1969 and initially operated by the Pennsylvania Railroad under government contract, the Metroliner demonstration encountered numerous technological difficulties as well as management problems resulting from mergers, bankruptcy, and subsequent reorganization of the corridor passenger service under Amtrak, which happened while the demonstration was taking place. Despite these problems the Metroliners attracted and maintained high ridership along the Washington–New York

12

corridor while ridership on every other passenger route in the nation continued to decline. In 1972 Amtrak incorporated the Metroliners into its routine service.

In addition to the Metroliner program the High-Speed Ground Transportation Act also prompted an R and D program in advanced technology for high-speed intercity transport. Research first focused on examining a variety of technology options and later emphasized development in tracked air-cushion vehicles, magnetic levitation, and linear induction motors. The U.S. contributed substantially to international research efforts in maglev and linear induction motor propulsion systems before the programs were terminated in the mid-1970s.

With the reorganization of the passenger rail system into Amtrak in 1971 and the collapse of Northeast and Midwest freight railroads in the early 1970s, the U.S. government opted to revitalize the freight rail system, stabilize the passenger network, and upgrade the Northeast corridor. Work on the corridor is slated to finish in 1985 at an appropriated cost of $2,190,000,000, or about $4.8 million per mile of line. (All but 156 miles of the 455-mile corridor is electrified.) At that time trains will speed along corridor sections at 125 mph and make 30 round-trips daily between Washington and New York City, with one-way trip times of 2 hours 39 minutes. In 1983 ridership between Washington and New York was approximately six million. Improvements include centralized traffic control and major use of concrete ties and continuous welded rail to improve ride quality and reduce maintenance.

U.S. cities tend to be farther apart and their population densities lower than those of many other industrialized countries having smaller land masses. As a result air and road vehicles dominate the U.S. intercity travel market. Interest in new rail technologies is increasing, however. Several regions in the U.S. have expressed interest in high-speed rail or maglev technology, some of which are progressing with engineering and market feasibility studies.

Amtrak's Northeast Corridor Improvement Project makes use of a 1½-mile-long series of machines that replaces old wooden ties with concrete ones (above left), installs continuous rail, cleans and restores stone ballast (above), fastens the rails to the ties, and aligns the track. This upgrading, scheduled to finish in 1985, will allow train speeds of 125 mph along some corridor sections, permitting one-way trip times of 2 hours 39 minutes between Washington and New York City.

13

Japanese Bullet trains (above) pass one another along elevated sections of two recently completed lines. The track on the left connects Omiya, a suburb of Tokyo, with Niigata, 168 miles distant; the other, 289 miles long, ties Omiya with Morioka. Engineer (top right) mans his post in the cab of a Bullet train, while businessmen relax and confer in a dining car (bottom right).

Japan: a demography built for speed

The Japanese National Railways (JNR) inaugurated its Shinkansen service on Oct. 1, 1964. Planning for the system's first section began in 1958, and construction of the 320-mile Tokyo–Osaka line, which serves the key industrial and socioeconomic belt of the nation, was completed in 1964.

Japan's island and mountain terrain, its dense population, and its dependence on imported petroleum and other raw materials have helped stimulate high-speed rail development. About 120 million people live on Japan's 146,000 square miles, with one-sixth of the land mass arable (1 square mile = 2.59 square kilometers). Tokyo, the largest city, with a population of 8.1 million, averages 27,100 people per square mile. By comparison, California has the same land area but only 24 million people. Los Angeles, the largest city, has a population of 7.5 million in the standard metropolitan statistical area; the population density of the city center is only 6,300 people per square mile.

In planning the Shinkansen system JNR engineers realized they had reached ridership capacity on the existing narrow-gauge track (3½ feet between inside faces of the rails). Their basic plan included laying of totally new standard-gauge (4 feet 8½ inches) double track. Conventional rail lines would serve only local stops and freight traffic.

The first Bullet trains between Tokyo and Osaka made 60 round-trips daily, cutting travel time between the cities from 6 hours 30 minutes to 3 hours 10 minutes. Following the first year's success, train service was

14

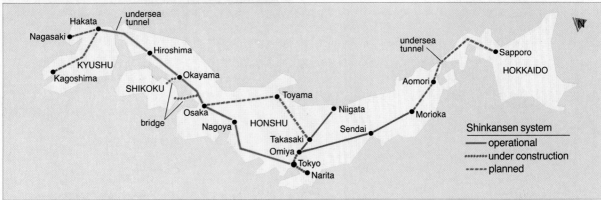

increased to 110 round-trips daily. Ridership on conventional routes declined about 20% before stabilizing, and air traffic between points along the route diminished significantly and ceased altogether between Nagoya and Tokyo. JNR completed two southern extensions to the Tokyo–Osaka route in 1972 and 1975. The first connected Osaka with Okayama and added 100 miles to the system. The second added another 246 miles and connected Japan's main island, Honshu, to Kyushu, tunnelling under the Kanmon Strait, and connecting Tokyo with Hakata (Fukuoka) on Kyushu.

Once the southern links were completed, the Japanese began expanding to the north. Two new sections opened in 1982, one connecting the Tokyo suburb of Omiya with Morioka, the other connecting Omiya with Niigata. Omiya, about 50 miles from Tokyo, will eventually be linked to the main Shinkansen system in Tokyo. In 1983 the Shinkansen system totaled 1,127 miles.

By early 1984 the Shinkansen system was operating more than 275 trains daily, including express service between principal stations. Maximum train speed is 130 mph, though JNR plans to raise it to 140 mph. Annual ridership in 1981, before the opening of the northerly lines, was 125 million passengers, with an average travel distance of 208 miles per passenger.

The Shinkansen system is largely built on concrete slab along dedicated right-of-way and is all-electric. A Bullet train consists of either 12 or 16 cars depending on the route and accommodates from 885 to 1,483

First morning train of the Tokyo–Osaka run departs the yard (top left). This line, the oldest in the Shinkansen system, opened in 1964. From a computerized control center in Tokyo (top right) teams of dispatchers continuously monitor and direct all aspects of Shinkansen operations including passenger information, train movements, railcar assignments, power supply, signaling, communications, and maintenance. Route map (above) gives the status of Shinkansen lines planned, under construction, and in operation as of early 1984.

15

Plow-equipped Bullet train (top left) clears its own path over snow-covered tracks in northern Japan. Along sections experiencing especially heavy snowfall, sprinklers spaced about 20 feet apart melt snow from the tracks with a spray of preheated, recycled water (top right). Work nears completion on the 33-mile-long Seikan tunnel under the Tsugaru Strait (above left); when finished it will link the islands of Honshu and Hokkaido by Bullet train. Because of Japan's mountainous terrain almost 32% of the Shinkansen system consists of tunnels (above right). This construction experience has made Japanese engineers world leaders in advanced tunneling technology.

passengers. Each car is propelled by four axles driven by individual electric motors that draw power from overhead wire supplying 25 kilovolts of 50- or 60-hertz, single-phase AC current.

The topography and weather of the Japanese islands spurred JNR to develop advanced technology features, among them a snow-melting system on open tracks in northern sections, where accumulated snow can reach 13 feet (four meters) during the winter. This equipment automatically detects the beginning of a snowfall and sprays water to melt the snow on the tracks. In addition, special coverings were built over tracks between mountain tunnels to protect them from being blocked by heavy snow or avalanches. In areas of lighter snowfall, snowplows installed on trains are sufficient. At switches (turnouts) installed devices melt the blocks of snow that fall from trains. All underfloor equipment is encased to prevent snow adhesion, and air intakes for cooling and ventilation are equipped with centrifugal snow-air separators.

The system also uses earthquake detection equipment that senses seismic activity and automatically stops trains. In addition, special detectors are placed at selected locations 25–65 miles from the track along certain coastal routes to sense undersea quakes so that train speeds can be reduced before the shock waves actually reach the track.

The islands and mountainous terrain presented problems in building tunnels and bridge systems. More than 493 miles or 44% of the en-

16

Photos, Orion Press

tire system consists of tunnels, bridges, and viaducts, which required substantial advances in engineering methods. The longest completed undersea tunnel in the Shinkansen system between Tokyo and Hakata is the Shin Kanmon tunnel, approximately 11.6 miles long. The newest undersea tunnel, planned for a northern section, is the Seikan tunnel under the Tsugaru Strait between Honshu and the northernmost island of Hokkaido. When completed, it will run 33 miles, the longest such ever attempted. An overland tunnel, the Daishimizu tunnel in northern Japan, was completed in 1979 along a distance of more than 13 miles.

Cost of the earlier Shinkansen lines was about $20 million per mile. Estimates for the two newest routes fall between $30 million and $40 million per mile. The high ridership on the Tokyo–Osaka route is unparalleled anywhere in the world, thus making the Shinkansen essentially a fast mass-transit system between cities.

In its two decades of operation the Shinkansen system has maintained a perfect record of no passenger fatalities. Traffic control is fully computerized; an automatic train control system sets the maximum speed for each train depending on the location of other trains and various safety-related factors and automatically slows any train that exceeds the set limit. The Shinkansen's meticulous maintenance program includes nightly routine maintenance and a special seven-car multipurpose inspection train for checking track and electric facilities.

The Shinkansen's enviable safety record owes much to a rigorous maintenance program conducted at numerous rolling stock bases along its routes. The base at Sendai (above left) covers nearly 57 acres; its teams of technicians (above) are equipped to perform all prescribed levels of maintenance, including complete disassembly for general inspection.

17

British work on high-speed passenger trains has been guided by the decision to produce new equipment that can operate on existing track. One approach still under development, the Advanced Passenger Train (right), employs a tilt-body suspension system that allows a safe, comfortable ride through sharp turns. The British High Speed Train (below right) emerged during the 1970s from efforts to upgrade existing rolling stock. A Canadian tilt-body train, called the Light Rapid Comfortable (below), has been placed in service in Canada's passenger rail fleet.

The U.K.: capitalizing on existing track

In 1967, as a result of research in the dynamic interaction between track and vehicles and fearing an increase in competition from road and air travel, British Rail decided to design a high-speed vehicle suitable for use on existing track. Planners had initially considered totally new high-speed systems but had rejected the idea because of anticipated environmental opposition and high construction costs. In examining the existing network they found that more than half the track system had relatively sharp curves. Average speeds on conventional trains, therefore, were being held down by the maximum speed traveled through curves.

Initial research focused on development of the Advanced Passenger Train (APT), which in principle would reduce trip times by raising both maximum speed and curve speed. To minimize the discomfort that riders experience during sharp, high-speed turns, British Rail explored methods for tilting the railcar body into the curve by means of an active roll suspension. Thus another, more general name is associated with APT's—tilt-body trains. Original APT plans called for a vehicle designed to run at 155

18

mph on existing track, to negotiate curves 40% faster than conventional trains, and to use existing signaling systems.

Fierce air and road competition prompted British Rail to upgrade existing locomotives and trailer cars to operate at maximum speeds of 125 mph (compared with the then-current maximums of 85–115 mph) while it developed the longer term APT. These near-term refinements led to the High Speed Train. In 1976, HST train sets—each consisting of two diesel locomotives and five cars with seating for 450—were placed in revenue service over six mainline routes in Great Britain and met with immediate success. In the first four years of service ridership between London and Bristol increased by 40%, between London and Leeds by 14%, and overall by an estimated 30%. The decisions that led to the HST suited existing conditions in Great Britain, for the rail system was well established and located in fairly densely populated areas (London's population density is 11,100 people per square mile). Installing new track, the cost of which could have been prohibitive, was not chosen.

Like the British, the Canadians have also been developing tilt-body equipment, commonly referred to as Light Rapid Comfortable (LRC). Two Canadian tilt-body cars were leased and tested by Amtrak in the United States but ultimately were not purchased because of maintenance costs and lack of compatability with other Amtrak equipment. In the mid-1980s Canadian firms were actively refining their equipment, and Via Rail, Canada's passenger rail system, was using the new LRC's in its fleet.

As of the early 1980s technical and commercial problems in tilt-body equipment remained to be solved. Judged from the experience, maintenance costs appeared high, and the reliability of the tilt mechanism was still an issue. Nevertheless, the British plan to have APT equipment in revenue service by 1990.

France at 170 mph

The French National Railways (SNCF) first considered building a high-speed passenger line in 1967 in order to ease traffic problems on the Paris-to-Lyon route, which serves an area in which 40% of the French population lives. Two tracks had been carrying as many as 260 trains a day, and SNCF had the options of increasing the number of tracks, rerouting freight trains in order to accommodate passenger traffic exclusively, or constructing a new high-speed passenger line.

When SNCF opted for the last, the matter was referred in 1969 to a government task force, which recommended turbine-powered trains. Further efforts, however, were not undertaken until the energy crisis of 1973, when a newly appointed committee recommended electric trains. Following approval by the French Cabinet, construction on the line started in December 1976. Development of the electric railcars began earlier, and a prototype appeared in 1974. In a test run in May 1976 a single electric railcar achieved a speed of 188 mph; another test in February 1981 produced a speed of 235 mph, a world record. Maximum speed during normal service is about 170 mph.

Revenue service on the *Train à Grande Vitesse* began in September

High power and a large proportion of driving axles allow the French TGV to negotiate grades as steep as 3.5%. This capability helped hold down construction costs for the Paris–Lyon line by eliminating the need for tunnels along its 250 miles of new double track.

SNCF

19

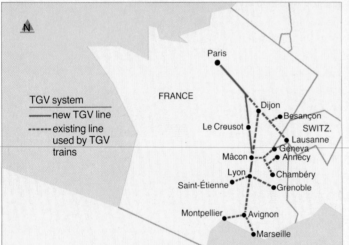

TGV system
—— new TGV line
------ existing line
used by TGV
trains

Long, straight stretches of dedicated track in rural areas (top) permit the TGV to approach speeds of 170 mph during normal service. The new track also has reduced the travel distance between Paris and Lyon by 55 miles. Map (above) depicts TGV lines as of early 1984. Control-room dispatchers working in the Gare de Lyon station in Paris (above right) monitor the Paris–Lyon line.

1981. In its first 16 months of operation ridership reached ten million, and SNCF projects 20 million riders annually by 1987. In early 1984 TGV trains departed Paris and Lyon every hour.

Costs totaled about $1.5 billion—about $4 million per mile—including land acquisition, roadbed, track, signaling, electrification, and the purchase of 87 train sets, each comprising two power cars and eight trailer cars and seating as many as 386 persons. Of this amount $420 million went for laying about 250 miles of double track and 25 miles of single track. Cost of the 87 train sets was about $475 million.

To hold down costs, to increase and improve service to feeder lines, and to avoid technological problems, planners decided to integrate the TGV into existing lines. This eliminated the need for building completely new rail lines, as in Japan, and avoided heavy construction costs in and around urban areas. New, dedicated lines were constructed in rural areas and designed so that trains could travel at steep gradients (as great as 3.5%, or 3½ feet vertically per 100 feet horizontally), thus

20

eliminating tunnels and reducing the need for bridges. Furthermore, the dedicated rural tracks shortened the route between Paris and Lyon from 320 miles to 265 miles. The new lines are specially designed to high-speed standards: gentle curves, long straight runs of track, and switches that allow speeds as high as 120 mph. The trains are electrified by way of overhead wire carrying 25-kilovolt, 50-hertz, single-phase AC current, with provisions made for operation from 1.5-kilovolt DC current to allow access to Paris and Lyon on existing tracks.

Each of the ten-car train sets is expected to run between 280,000 and 300,000 miles per year, with all maintenance confined to one facility outside Paris. Lightweight construction has reduced wear on the tracks, and new line is carefully maintained to standards required for high-speed operation. SNCF officials report that fuel consumption is less per seat-mile than on the conventional trains displaced by the TGV. In the mid-1980s consideration was being given to a second TGV line between Paris and Bordeaux.

Common scenes from a TGV run include the engineer's post in the lead power car (top left); a train bar (center left), open throughout the trip for purchasing sandwiches, packaged meals, and drinks; and the TGV station at Lyon (top right). Construction proceeds on a TGV power car at the Alsthom-Atlantique plant in Belfort, France (above left). Track-laying machine (above center) emplaces concrete ties and continuous welded rail on new TGV line. High-speed switch (above right) allows TGV trains to change tracks at 120 mph.

Maglev times two

Research in such technologies as tracked air-cushion vehicles, magnetic levitation, and linear induction motors began in the late 1960s and early 1970s in Japan, the United States, Canada, Great Britain, and West Germany. Drawing from these first efforts, R and D concentrated on magnetically levitated cars propelled by linear synchronous motors. Such vehicles literally float on a magnetic cushion and are pushed or pulled along their track, or guideway, by waves of magnetic forces. Of the countries originally interested, only Japan and West Germany continued their efforts for high-speed intercity applications, although others including the U.S. pursued maglev research in the 1980s for low-speed urban use. Two different maglev systems, based on either magnetic attraction or magnetic repulsion, were initially explored in both Japan and West Germany. Each country settled on a different system to develop.

Repulsion or electrodynamic maglev, being developed in Japan, makes use of the fact that like poles of magnets repel one another. Along the bottom of each train car are niobium-titanium wire coils constantly bathed in liquid helium that is kept within a few degrees of absolute zero by an on-board cryogenic refrigerator. At this temperature each coil becomes superconducting; once a current begins to flow around the coil it does so indefinitely, making the coil a powerful and highly energy-efficient electromagnet. The guideway for the train is U-shaped, and embedded along its base are unenergized wire coils. As the train's superconducting magnets pass over, their magnetic fields induce electric current in the guideway coils, creating electromagnets having the same polarity as the moving electromagnets. The resulting repulsion lifts the train to a maximum of four inches (ten centimeters) above the guideway. The faster the train's superconducting magnets are moving, the more powerful the repulsion. In fact, levitation is achieved only at speeds above 50 mph; rubber wheels support the train at lower speeds.

The linear synchronous motor that propels the Japanese maglev operates on the same principle as an ordinary electric motor, in which a movable magnetized portion, the rotor, is spun by the rotating magnetic field set up by surrounding stationary coils, the stator. In the maglev system the train itself becomes the "rotor," but it moves linearly rather than rotates; the stator has been opened up from its conventional cylindrical shape and is laid flat along the guideway. In practice, the train's on-board levitation magnets interact with conventional electromagnets lining the sides of the guideway. The guideway magnets are energized in a way that sends traveling waves of alternating magnetic polarity down the guideway, pushing and pulling the train's magnets and thus the train along with them. Among unique technological features of the Japanese system are its superconducting magnets, the compact refrigerator used to cool the magnets, and the specific linear motor design.

In April 1977 the Miyazaki Test Track opened, and by 1979 a Japanese maglev test vehicle had achieved speeds of 320 mph on the 4.5-mile track. In the mid-1980s Japan intended to build a larger test facility and to continue development work. Planners envision maglev trains

Maglev trains under development in Japan and West Germany are propelled by linear synchronous motors, which depend on the interaction of arrays of electromagnets aboard the train and along the guideway (facing page, upper diagram). Whereas the polarities of the train's magnets are kept fixed, the guideway magnets are energized with alternating current, which causes their polarities to reverse repeatedly. As the train moves forward, north and south poles of the train's magnets perpetually experience the pull of opposite polarities just ahead of them in the guideway as well as the push of like polarities from behind. (Lower diagram) Levitation systems for West German and Japanese maglevs are compared. In the West German attraction system, electromagnets on winglike extensions of the car body are drawn upward toward iron bars in the T-shaped guideway rail, while separate magnets on car and rail are used for propulsion and guidance. In the repulsion system being pursued in Japan, superconducting electromagnets on the train pass over coils in a U-shaped guideway, inducing a field in the coils that repels the train's magnets and pushes the train upward. Propulsion and guidance are provided by interaction of the train's magnets with magnets along the sides of the guideway. Unlike the West German maglev, which can levitate while motionless, the Japanese maglev depends on forward motion for levitation and rolls on rubber wheels until it achieves "lift-off" speed.

operating in commercial service at a top speed of about 300 mph, which would enable passengers to make the Tokyo–Osaka trip in less than an hour and a half.

West Germany chose to develop an attraction or electromagnetic maglev system, which exploits the attractive force exerted by a magnet on ferromagnetic materials like iron. The sides of each train car are built with winglike projections that extend downward and under the edges of a large, broad, T-shaped guideway rail. Attached to the tips of the "wings" and facing up toward the underside of the rail are conventional iron-core electromagnets. When energized from batteries aboard the train, these magnets are drawn upward toward iron bars in the rail, lifting the car about a half inch (a little more than a centimeter) off the rail; proper spacing is maintained by precise control of the energizing current. In this system suspension is independent of speed, and the vehicle can levitate at rest. Similar to the Japanese system, electromagnets on the train and along the guideway form a linear synchronous motor for propulsion.

West German scientists and engineers began research on both repulsion and attraction systems in the early 1970s, but by 1977 they had chosen the latter because it appeared to offer the greater cost advantage. Work began that same year on a test vehicle for display at the Hamburg Transport Exhibition in 1979. During that event a maglev vehicle accommodating 70 passengers operated at speeds of 47 mph on a 0.6-mile track.

In 1984 West German engineers were completing a 20–30-mile test

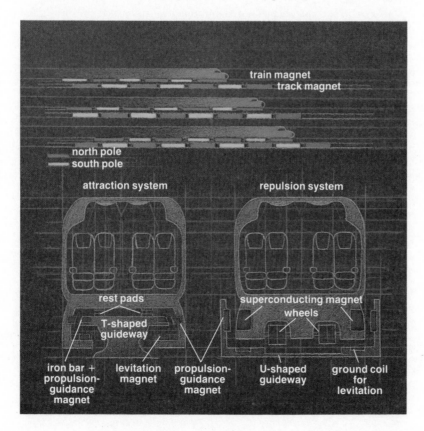

facility at Emsland in Lower Saxony near the Dutch border. Tests were under way on two 200-passenger vehicles that were first expected to achieve sustained speeds of 200 mph and later 250 mph. The ultimate goal was to demonstrate a level of performance and reliability suitable for revenue service. Because there are fewer new technological developments in the attraction system, it is likely to be ready for application sooner than Japan's repulsion system. The comparative advantages of the two approaches are as yet uncertain.

Although there appear to be no unsolvable technical obstacles in either approach, some experts believe that substantial development work still is needed for their complex power and control systems. Some R and D also remains on the superconducting magnets and refrigeration for the Japanese system.

There are several questions of safety, reliability, and cost to be answered about these maglev systems. For example, can the small gaps between train and guideway be maintained in the face of wind resistance, unpredictable gusting, and sudden pressure changes at tunnel entrances and exits? Could passengers experience harmful or unpleasant side effects from the powerful magnetic fields employed, or could damage be done to audio and video tapes and electronic equipment carried aboard? Will areas around maglev routes be subjected to electromagnetic interference? Can suitable emergency and safety procedures for the public be developed? Once maglevs are placed in service, can they be maintained efficiently and economically?

The principal advantages cited for maglev trains are the presumed lowered maintenance costs due to friction-free suspension systems and fewer moving parts, improved productivity as a result of higher speeds,

Two- and three-car experimental maglev vehicles (right and above) undergo tests at the Japanese National Railway's Miyazaki Test Track. In the photo at right, both the reddish-orange ground coils for levitation and the white propulsion/guidance coils can be seen within the guideway.

Japanese National Railways; (inset) Hisashi Morokawa

(Left) Internationaler Verkehrsnachrichten-und Bilderdienst; (right) Konsortium Magnetbahn Transrapid—Interfoto Pressebild

enhanced safety since derailment is theoretically more difficult, and lower noise and vibrational effects than conventional or high-speed rail systems. Whether these benefits can be achieved and whether conditions are such as to make maglev systems attractive are yet to be determined. Both Japanese and West German developers, however, are confident about the future and see a place for maglev trains in the world market.

The future

From this review of past and present it appears that high-speed ground transport will remain an attractive form of intercity travel in the future. But the specific technologies chosen and the extent of their adoption will vary with the conditions of each country.

A report dating from the early 1960s on the future of the British passenger rail system suggested that the logical approach to shaping any rail system is to determine its distinguishing characteristics and to determine under what conditions these characteristics make it the best available form of transport. Historically, rail passenger services have been distinguished by operation of dedicated tracks that permit running large, high-capacity vehicles. Given the existence of competition from other transportation systems and the wide range of travel distances—from a few miles to thousands of miles—speed also becomes an important characteristic. Questions pertinent to the future include: Into what niche does high-speed rail or maglev ground transport fit in transportation systems? What effect will the current explosive growth of electronic communication and information systems have on travel? And what world events might alter the course of or need for fast ground transport systems?

In 1983 *U.S. Passenger Rail Technologies*, a report prepared by the U.S. Congressional Office of Technology Assessment (OTA), suggested that the routes where U.S. high-speed rail application would be most useful included those between cities having both high populations and high population densities; between cities having mass-transit feeder systems and where strong reasons exist for travel from one to another; and between

Advanced West German maglev (above) glides over its T-shaped track at the Emsland test facility. The wraparound extensions below the car body contain the train's levitation and propulsion magnets. In 1979 the West German Transrapid 05 (above left) carried thousands of passengers on maglev rides during a transportation fair in Hamburg.

25

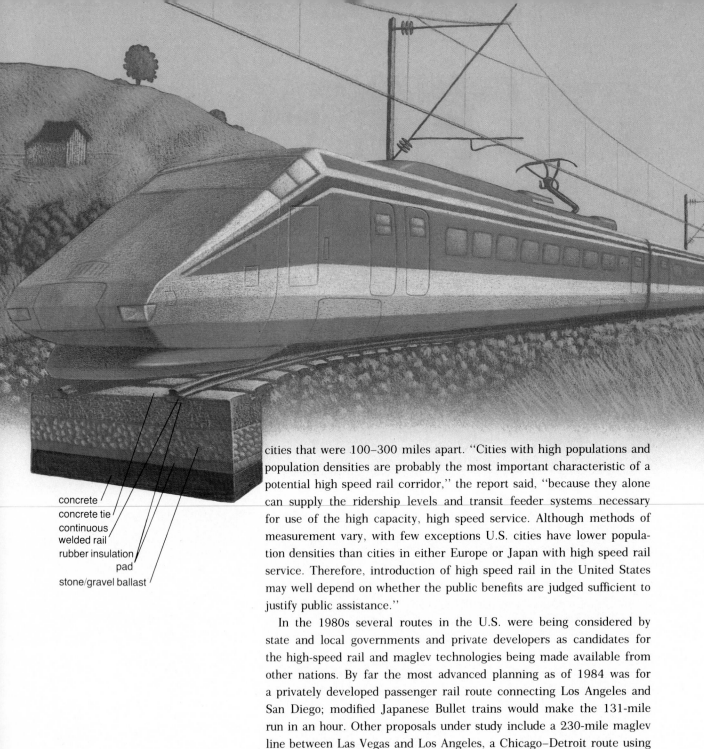

concrete
concrete tie
continuous
welded rail
rubber insulation
pad
stone/gravel ballast

cities that were 100–300 miles apart. "Cities with high populations and population densities are probably the most important characteristic of a potential high speed rail corridor," the report said, "because they alone can supply the ridership levels and transit feeder systems necessary for use of the high capacity, high speed service. Although methods of measurement vary, with few exceptions U.S. cities have lower population densities than cities in either Europe or Japan with high speed rail service. Therefore, introduction of high speed rail in the United States may well depend on whether the public benefits are judged sufficient to justify public assistance."

In the 1980s several routes in the U.S. were being considered by state and local governments and private developers as candidates for the high-speed rail and maglev technologies being made available from other nations. By far the most advanced planning as of 1984 was for a privately developed passenger rail route connecting Los Angeles and San Diego; modified Japanese Bullet trains would make the 131-mile run in an hour. Other proposals under study include a 230-mile maglev line between Las Vegas and Los Angeles, a Chicago–Detroit route using either upgraded existing line or a new system, a New York City–Montreal link based on the French TGV, and a Florida corridor connecting Tampa, Orlando, and Miami.

Anyone seeking federal funding for high-speed or maglev projects in the U.S. will confront stiff competition. For the remainder of the 1980s, according to a report prepared by the Congressional Budget Office, the U.S. government will need to supply $13 billion annually, or $91 billion total, to maintain the country's road system alone. Most of the nation's urban transit and bus networks operate at significant losses, and subsi-

(Opposite page and below) Based on information obtained from the American High Speed Rail Corporation

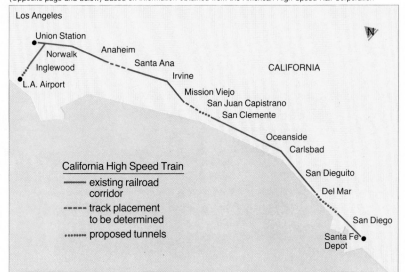

Los Angeles

Union Station

Norwalk

Anaheim

Inglewood

Santa Ana

L.A. Airport

Irvine

CALIFORNIA

Mission Viejo

San Juan Capistrano

San Clemente

Oceanside

Carlsbad

California High Speed Train

——— existing railroad corridor

- - - - track placement to be determined

·········· proposed tunnels

San Dieguito

Del Mar

San Diego

Santa Fe Depot

Artist's conception (facing page) details a modified Bullet train under consideration for a high-speed rail link connecting Los Angeles and San Diego, California. Track design for the run, shown in cross section, incorporates advanced features. The proposed route (left), put forward by the American High Speed Rail Corp. of Los Angeles, would generally follow existing railroad rights-of-way and would include a segment connecting downtown Los Angeles with its major airport.

dizing Amtrak cost $735 million in 1982. Although the U.S. freight rail system has begun economic recovery, much needed modernization of the national air traffic control system looms on the horizon.

In Japan planned extensions of the Shinkansen system appear to be facing stiff economic scrutiny. According to a recent report government subsidies to the JNR totaled about $6 billion. Whether Japanese lawmakers believed that the public benefits of employment and improved transport system capacity merited continued construction was still an uncertainty in early 1984. As a leader in rail technology, however, Japan hopes to introduce its skill and knowledge in world markets. The Tokyo–Osaka route may well be the scene of inaugural service for Japanese maglev trains, but probably not until the early 1990s. Before then Japanese policymakers will have to face the difficult question of whether the benefits of the even higher speeds of maglev justify replacing the most successful high-speed rail route in the world.

Although French plans include a TGV route between Paris and Bordeaux, the increased traffic is expected to be insufficient to pay interest charges on the investment. SNCF officials may consider actual construction only if the government agrees to offset interest costs. Great Britain hopes to be running its APT's on existing routes before the 1990s if commercial viability and technical problems can be resolved. When West Germany's maglev trains see service may depend on the time needed to successfully test the system. German engineers hope to have maglev considered in their country's 1985 strategic transportation planning. West German officials are also actively marketing their system in the U.S.

During the next several years the world's industrialized nations will be pondering questions of importance to the future of high-speed train technology. Whether Japanese Bullets will be rocketing from Los Angeles to San Diego in 1990 or West German maglevs whisking commuters between Frankfurt and Paris before the end of the century may well hinge on how those questions are anwered.

In the face of fierce competition passenger rail continues to strive for the speed and efficiency that will allow it to remain an attractive form of intercity travel in the future.

© René Burri—Magnum

27

SECRETS from the FALLEN STARS

by Stephen P. Maran

Newfound meteorite specimens from Antarctica and increasingly powerful analytical techniques are improving our knowledge of the solar system and its ancient "birth." Some meteorites may even have come from the Moon and Mars.

Meteorites, rocks of stone and metal that have fallen from space, have been studied scientifically for more than a century. Not long ago the discovery of a meteorite was a rare, unpredictable event, subject to the fortunes either of finding a previously fallen meteorite by sheer accident or of observing a fall and then locating where it landed. During the past decade, however, deliberate searches have turned up a large number of meteorites in Antarctica, where natural glacial and meteorological processes have concentrated the rocks in localized regions. In addition, scientists have devised new methods for collecting meteoritic dust in the atmosphere as well as new techniques of analysis. Consequently, current studies are yielding important information about the ancient parent bodies from which meteorites are derived and the nature of the solar nebula, the cloud of gas and dust from which the Earth's solar system formed. A handful of unusual meteorites even seem to be rocks that were knocked off the surfaces of Mars and the Moon and later fell to Earth.

The Antarctic bonanza

Scientists first realized that Antarctica was a meteoritic treasure trove after a team of Japanese investigators happened upon several meteorites atop the ice while exploring the Antarctic ice cap in 1969. Since finding even a single meteorite had been a rare event, it was first thought that these specimens were all scattered fragments of a single stone that had broken up in the atmosphere. Further study, however, revealed that the meteorites were of several different types. In the next few years other Japanese expeditions found even more meteorites on the ice cap, and since 1975 U.S. expeditions making use of helicopters and snowmobiles have searched selected regions with great success. Between 1969 and early 1984 about 7,000 specimens had been collected from Antarctic survey areas totaling less than a thousand square kilometers. Because meteorites often break up when they fall, the 7,000 specimens must correspond to a much smaller number of distinct meteorites, perhaps 100–1,000. These numbers can be compared with an estimated 50,000

STEPHEN P. MARAN is a Senior Staff Scientist in the Laboratory for Astronomy and Solar Physics. NASA-Goddard Space Flight Center, Greenbelt, Maryland

(Overleaf) Illustration by Jane Meredith

Wind-whipped ice crystals dance across an Antarctic ice field (facing page), pelting the campsite of a U.S. meteorite search team. This scouring action, which can erode the ice surface at a rate of five centimeters (two inches) per year, is responsible for exposing meteorites that have fallen and become buried in the glacial ice. (Left) Search team members equipped with snowmobiles and Nansen sleds conduct a final check before setting out across the ice.

specimens collected from all the rest of the Earth during the past century or so, which correspond to about 2,000 distinct meteorites. Clearly there are far more meteorites per given area in some parts of Antarctica than in any other known location.

The fact that elsewhere on Earth meteorite specimens found near each other are almost always fragments of a single original rock suggested that local forces at work on the Antarctic ice cap concentrate unrelated meteorites. The process, according to geologist William Cassidy of the University of Pittsburgh, involves both wind and ice. Elsewhere on Earth meteorites are lost in the sea, destroyed by erosion and weathering on land, or buried by geologic processes. On the ice cap they are covered by falling snow, which eventually becomes ice. As the ice slowly flows downhill from the high Antarctic plateau toward the sea, it carries meteorites that have fallen over large areas and over long intervals of time like stones on a great glacial conveyor belt. Where the ice runs up against the buried slopes of coastal mountains, it and the meteorites within

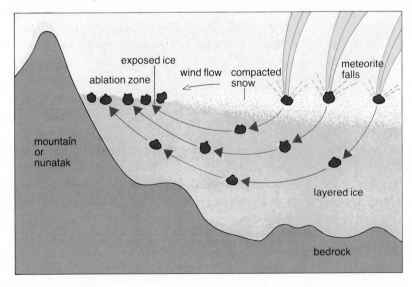

Meteorites that fall at different times and places on the Antarctic ice cap are soon buried in snow, which eventually becomes compacted to solid ice under the weight of new snow accumulation above. As the ice slowly flows from the inland regions of the continent down to the sea, it carries the meteorites along like a giant conveyor belt. Where mountains or isolated outcroppings of bedrock (nunataks) impede the flow, the ice and its entrained meteorites well up against the barrier. There strong, persistent winds erode the ice, leaving one meteorite after another on the surface.

(Left) NASA/JSC; (right) William A. Cassidy

A stony meteorite (above), resting exactly as it was first found on the Antarctic ice, is photographed together with a field numbering device and a scale for determining approximate size. It will then be transferred to a Teflon bag, sealed inside a second bag, and shipped frozen to a laboratory at NASA's Johnson Space Center in Texas for further study. (Above right) Scientists conducting a meteorite search by helicopter prepare to collect a specimen that was spotted from the air.

slowly accumulate. There fierce Antarctic winds scour the ice, eroding layer after layer and exposing meteorites on the fresh surface. Further scouring exposes rocks that fell in the more distant past, since these are usually buried under more ice. Moreover, a meteorite buried in the ice is protected from most weathering processes, including the action of liquid water. Thus, the large number of meteorites found in Antarctica results from unique conditions for concentration and preservation.

Rare Antarctic finds

Given the volume of Antarctic meteorites for study, it is no surprise to find a few rare specimens among them. The deep-freeze conditions, however, help raise those odds considerably since certain meteorites may be rare not because they are unusual in space but because they tend to deteriorate rapidly on the Earth. For example, an uncommon but important type of meteorite, the carbonaceous chondrites, is known to be very fragile. They break up in the air and upon hitting the ground and may crumble if not handled with great care. Most of the non-Antarctic specimens of these stones were actually seen to land—like the Allende meteorite that fell in Mexico in 1969—and were collected soon thereafter by or with the aid of eyewitnesses. By contrast, a large fraction of the much sturdier iron meteorites have simply been found by chance. In most regions of the world local weather and geologic conditions, which an iron meteorite might survive for centuries, will disintegrate a carbonaceous chondrite if it is not soon found.

Carbonaceous chondrites are of great interest to researchers because of the large meteorites (i.e., all but meteoritic dust) they are the most primitive, showing the least effects of the geochemical reactions, igneous activity, and other processes that took place on their parent bodies. Consequently they give important clues to the nature of the ancient solar nebula before it was substantially altered by planetary processes. Only about three dozen carbonaceous chondrites, however, some consisting of many individual fragments, had been collected around the world prior to

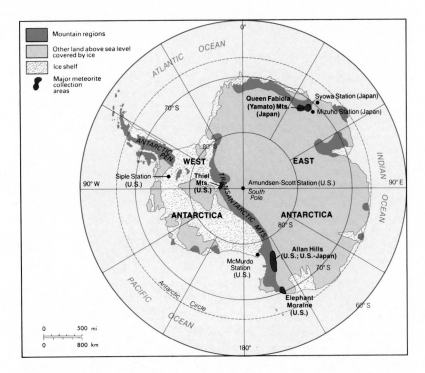

Map locates collection sites for the majority of the 7,000 meteorite specimens discovered in Antarctica between 1969 and 1984. Each of the collection areas lies at the edge of an ice field whose flow is blocked by mountains. Before 1969 Antarctic explorers had found only four meteorites, three of them on rocky ground where they may have fallen directly. Polished section (below), measuring ten centimeters (four inches) across, is of an iron meteorite found at Allan Hills—only the second iron known to contain diamonds. The tiny diamond crystallites, which occur in clumps within the large dark inclusion in the lower right, may have been formed during a violent collision in space. Another Allan Hills specimen, ALHA 81005 (bottom), is strongly suspected of originating on the Moon.

1978. About 40 carbonaceous chondrites have been found in Antarctica in recent years, and unlike most of the earlier specimens, they all fell and became preserved many years before they were discovered.

The Antarctic also has yielded other rarities including an iron meteorite that is only the second one known to contain diamonds; a rare type of achondrite (stone meteorites that lack the rounded mineral inclusions, or chondrules, characteristic of the great majority of meteorites); and the stone ALHA 81005 (the letters are an acronym for the Allan Hills region of Antarctica where it was discovered), which seems to have come from the Moon. Although radioactive dating of meteorites from around the world consistently reveals that they are about 4.6 billion years old, there are nine known exceptions, called SNC meteorites, which are "only" about 1.3 billion years old. Two of these nine oddities, specimen numbers ALHA 77005 and EETA 79001 (from the Elephant Moraine), are Antarctic finds.

Natural forces may concentrate and preserve meteorites in Antarctica, but luck plays a role, too. ALHA 81005, perhaps the most unusual meteorite ever found, is a stone about three centimeters (hardly more than an inch) in size and less than 32 grams (a little over an ounce) in weight. Each year expeditions search the Antarctic ice during the austral summer, departing before severe weather sets in. ALHA 81005 was discovered on Jan. 18, 1982, the final day of the 1981–82 field season, at the far point of a 30-kilometer (19-mile) snowmobile traverse made in unfavorable weather and just before the explorers turned back to camp. More than a dozen research groups that subsequently examined its crystallography, petrology, chemical composition, thermoluminescence, magnetism, and other physical properties found that it is almost indistinguishable from many of the Moon rocks collected by Apollo astronauts but is unlike any

(Top) Roy Clarke, Smithsonian Institution; (bottom) NASA

33

NASA/JSC

Member of a meteorite expedition team operates a drilling rig to obtain core samples of the Antarctic ice cap. Shipped frozen to laboratories in the U.S. and elsewhere for analysis, ice cores yield information about deposition and erosion rates, thereby aiding studies of meteorite concentration processes at work in the ice. Ice cores also contain micrometeorites, which allow scientists to compare meteoritic dust falling on the Earth today with material that fell many years ago.

(Facing page) WB-57F aircraft operated by NASA (top left) carries gear for collecting micrometeorites in a rectangular pylon mounted on the bottom center of each wing. The meteoritic dust is captured on scrupulously clean, oil-coated plastic flags, which are deployed individually from air-tight recesses in the pylon (top right) after the aircraft reaches high altitude, typically 19 kilometers. In the laboratory each exposed plate is examined under a microscope (bottom right), and dust samples are picked off with a fine needle and transferred to a mount. Scanning electron micrograph of a micrometeorite particle (bottom left) reveals a long mineral "whisker," a clue that the particle may have condensed in space directly from a gas. Another micrometeorite (bottom center) comprises metal mounds of nickel-iron alloy on glassy spheres; its appearance suggests that it was rather strongly heated during atmospheric entry. By contrast, much of the meteoritic dust that falls on the Earth undergoes little alteration from frictional heating and probably appears much as it would if it were collected in space.

other meteorite or any Earth rock. Yet the Apollo specimens were brought back in space vehicles, while ALHA 81005 clearly made it to the Earth on its own. The most reasonable explanation is that a large meteorite struck the Moon, ejecting into space some pieces of the lunar surface. At least one piece eventually fell on Antarctica, perhaps in several fragments, of which one survived as ALHA 81005. (In early 1984, Japanese scientists presented strong evidence that a second Antarctic find, Yamato 791197, from the Yamato Mountains region, also originated on the lunar surface.)

Micrometeorites

The smallest meteorites, known as interplanetary dust or micrometeorites, are particles that continually drift down through the atmosphere from space. This material is especially important to scientists because it contains what may be pristine samples of mineral grains that condensed in the solar nebula. Collecting equipment mounted on high-flying jet aircraft—primarily U-2 and WB-57F craft operated by the U.S. National Aeronautics and Space Administration (NASA)—currently constitutes the best method for gathering the dust. When sampled at lower altitudes or on the ground, micrometeorites are hard to isolate from the terrestrial particles and contaminants with which they are mixed.

To snare micrometeorites from an aircraft cruising at about 19 kilometers (12 miles) altitude, a collector plate coated with a sticky silicone oil is mounted on each wing. Many of the particles obtained in this way are truly extraterrestrial as shown by their relatively high content of iridium, an element that is much more prevalent in meteorites than in Earth rocks. They also contain atoms of the noble gases helium, neon, and argon in proportions characteristic of gases implanted by the solar wind, a continuous outpouring of atomic particles from the Sun.

An estimated 10,000 tons of micrometeorites—each typically ten micrometers (four ten-thousandths of an inch) in diameter and weighing

34

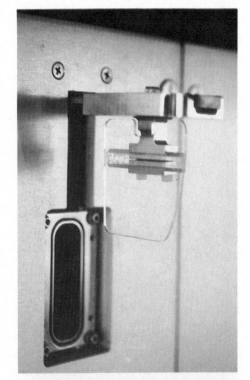

about a billionth of a gram—rain down on the Earth in a year. Although only an infinitesimal fraction is captured in an aircraft flight, the knowledge gained from the tiny samples is significant. Laboratory analyses indicate that many micrometeorites, more fragile and primitive even than carbonaceous chondrites, are porous aggregates of smaller mineral grains. Under the electron microscope individual grains of the mineral enstatite (typically less than one micrometer in size) take the shapes of whiskers and platelets, forms characteristic of solid particles that have condensed directly from a gas, without passing through the liquid state. Such vapor-phase condensation is exactly the process by which dust grains are believed to form in the atmospheres and winds of red giant stars and in interstellar dust clouds of our Milky Way Galaxy. Vapor-phase condensation is also thought to have occurred in the solar nebula. In a recent electron microscope study a micrometeorite was found to contain the substance epsilon iron-nickel carbide, a metal-carbon material that probably formed at low temperature in a gaseous environment. The epsilon particle may well be a surviving dust grain from the solar nebula.

Some micrometeorites have been found to have a high content of

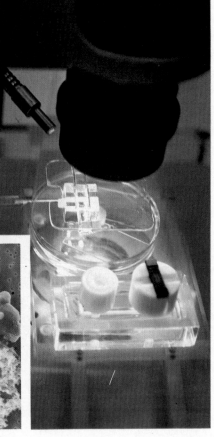

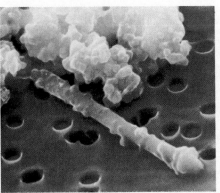

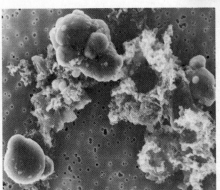

(Left, center) Donald E. Brownlee, University of Washington; (right) NASA/JSC

Stephen J. Edberg

Micrometeorites are thought to be debris from comet tails, dust that condensed on the outskirts of the solar nebula and became frozen in the icy cometary heads. Comet West (above) is shown as it appeared in the western U.S. sky in 1976.

deuterium, a heavy isotope of hydrogen. This is noteworthy because radio telescope observations of gas clouds in the Milky Way show that many have a very high deuterium content. Carbonaceous chondrites also have enhanced deuterium, confirming that the solar nebula contained some of the same material observed today in interstellar space.

Even in entering the Earth's atmosphere micrometeorites are less altered than ordinary meteorites. The surface of a typical high-density meteorite reveals that the outer layer melted due to frictional heating in the atmosphere, but no such effect appears in most of the porous, low-density micrometeorites collected in the stratosphere, where they must be almost exactly as they are in space. Further, some micrometeorites have a high sulfur content; if they had melted, much of this volatile element would have vaporized and escaped. The primitive nature of micrometeorites and their freedom from the effects of atmospheric heating explain why they tell investigators so much about the circumstances that prevailed at the birth of the solar system.

Micrometeorites are generally thought to be debris from comet tails, a theory that helps explain why the dust particles are virtually unprocessed. Comets are largely chunks of dusty ice that formed on the frigid outskirts of the solar nebula. When a comet nears the Sun, solar radiation vaporizes the outer layers of ice, and the embedded dust particles are blown outward by the escaping gases and swept backward by the pressure of sunlight to form the comet's tail. Micrometeorites, trapped in the cometary ice for billions of years after formation, were preserved much like the Antarctic meteorites. Ice cores from Antarctica yield preserved micrometeorites as well, allowing investigators to compare dust falling on the Earth today with that which fell many years ago. A recent core study verified that micrometeorites that fell in 1833, a year in which occurred one of the largest meteor showers in recorded history, have the same structural forms as micrometeorites falling to Earth today.

Laboratory methods pay off

New analytical methods, some of which were originally developed or perfected for studying the Moon rocks brought back by Apollo astronauts, are augmenting older techniques for gleaning precious information from meteorites. Even meteorite handling procedures have benefitted from the Apollo program. For example, meteorites collected in Antarctica are bagged in inert plastic and shipped in freezer chests to a NASA laboratory in Houston, Texas. There, in a clean, pure-nitrogen atmosphere, they are handled, weighed, and measured by technicians working through glove boxes that prevent skin or breath contact and consequent contamination. Even the sawing of sample stone slices is done in nitrogen-filled handling chambers.

Electron diffraction, one of the newer technologies being used to probe meteorites, makes use of electrons that are beamed through or reflected from the surface of a meteorite crystal. The transmitted or reflected particles form a pattern that reveals properties of the specimen, including details of the crystal structure and the nature of trace substances.

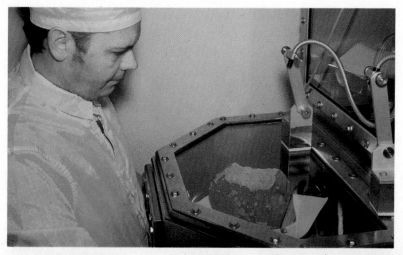

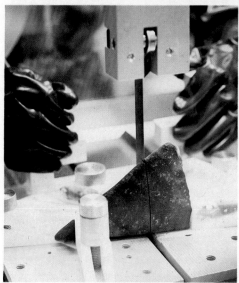

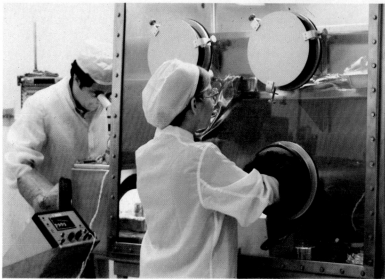

Borrowing from handling procedures developed for Moon rocks brought back by Apollo astronauts, scientists at the Johnson Space Center (left) study Antarctic meteorites through a nitrogen-filled glove box, which prevents deterioration and contamination of the specimens. This special handling also allows for weighing meteorites (center right) and sectioning them on a band saw equipped with a diamond-edged blade (center left). Working through a glove box a NASA geochemist (top) examines the Antarctic specimen EETA 79001, which once may have been part of the surface of the planet Mars.

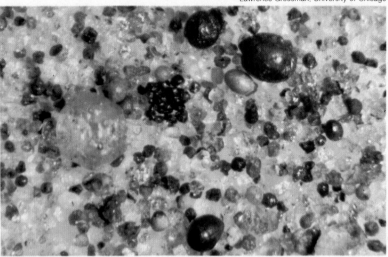

Chondrules from the Murchison meteorite, a carbonaceous chondrite, appear as light and dark rounded grains amid other loose mineral fragments following a laboratory procedure in which water and repeated freeze-thaw cycles are used to break down small chips of specimen into a coarse powder. The freed chondrules, which are thought to have formed separately from molten droplets during the birth of the solar system, then can be picked out with forceps and examined individually. In one kind of analysis a single chondrule is broken in two; one half is viewed in a scanning electron microscope to determine the identity of the minerals in the chondrule and their relative arrangement, while the other half is subjected to neutron activation analysis to identify the elements present and determine their amounts.

In electron microprobe analysis an electron beam stimulates X-ray emissions from atoms in the meteorite sample. The X-rays are produced at specific wavelengths, which tell investigators what atoms produced them. Comparison of X-ray emissions from the meteorite with those from standard samples of known composition reveals what elements are present in the meteorite and in what relative amounts.

Neutron activation is valuable in verifying that the tiny particles collected by aircraft are in fact micrometeorites and not just terrestrial dust or chemical residue from rocket exhausts, a common particulate at high altitudes. In this method sample particles are sealed in a quartz tube and irradiated by neutrons for many days. The neutrons are absorbed by the nuclei of atoms, some of which are transmuted into short-lived radioactive isotopes. As the isotopes decay, they emit gamma rays that are counted with sensitive detectors. From the count rates of gamma rays at different energies physicists can determine the chemical composition of the specimen.

Stepped combustion is used to study carbon-bearing meteorites to determine which components contain enhanced or depressed amounts of specific isotopes of carbon. The sample is exposed to oxygen and heated in stages of increasing temperature. The carbon associated with specific components of the meteorite sample burns preferentially at different temperatures, since differing grain size and crystal structure make some components less resistant to heating than others. The burning carbon combines with oxygen to form the gas carbon dioxide. The gas collected from burning at a chosen temperature is analyzed by mass spectrometry, discussed below, to determine the relative amounts of the isotopes carbon-13 and carbon-14.

A similar process, stepped heating, is used to evaporate other meteorite specimens to determine the respective chemical composition of components, or phases, of a given meteorite that were formed at different temperatures. The phases corresponding to the lowest temperatures of mineral formation produce the gases that evaporate from the specimen during the earlier steps of heating, while the more refractory phases that formed at high temperatures yield the gases released from the specimen in the later steps of heating.

A key point is that most meteorites are breccia, conglomerates of fragments of various preexisting rocks on the parent bodies or on smaller objects that eventually came together to make the parent bodies as they accumulated from the solar nebula. Usually a lab study is directed at one particular component of a meteorite specimen, and it is desirable to locate and extract a sample of that component while preserving as much as possible of the remainder of the specimen. The latest method for minimizing unnecessary damage takes a leaf from the modern surgeon's book: the technique of computed X-ray tomography. A small meteorite is scanned with X-rays while mounted in each of several different orientations. Computer processing then produces cross-sectional images that map the locations of distinct mineral components within the specimen. Recognizing the desired component and knowing its location, the scientist can play surgeon, extracting it in the least damaging manner.

Some older technologies continue to yield important information on meteorites. Mass spectrometry is used to study ionized gas that is released by a meteorite sample when heated in a flame. The gas passes between the poles of a magnet, whereupon each ion (electrically charged atom or molecule) of the gas follows a curved path that depends on its mass and electric charge. This process separates the different types of ions, allowing chemists to identify them and measure their relative amounts in the meteorite.

Careful inspection under the microscope is still an important method. For example, although a meteorite's chondrules often have well-defined borders, inspection of some stone meteorites reveals chondrules with blurred borders that seem to blend into the surrounding matrix. Sharp borders reveal that chondrules cooled rapidly from the molten state, while blurred borders suggest that the stones may have been reheated at some time after they formed or that they slowly cooled from a high temperature while buried within their parent bodies.

The ages of a meteorite

A mineral crystallizes from the molten state with a known, characteristic chemical composition. Then, over time, atoms of radioactive isotopes of rubidium, uranium, potassium, and other elements originally in the mineral—called parent isotopes—decay into atoms of other elements—daughter isotopes—at known rates. (The isotopes of a given element have the same number of protons in their atomic nuclei but differ in the number of neutrons.) Therefore, the age of a meteorite, defined as the time since its minerals crystallized, can be determined by measuring the relative numbers of parent and daughter atoms in its constituent minerals. The older the meteorite, the fewer parent isotope atoms and the more daughter atoms. This strategy, one of several included under the general term radioactive dating, reveals that most stone meteorites formed about 4.6 billion years ago at the birth of the solar system. These

A cross-sectional X-ray image of a small piece of the Allende meteorite (below), made with a computed tomographic (CT) scanner, is compared with the cut face of the specimen after it was sliced through the same plane as the scan (bottom). Recently applied to meteorite studies, CT scanning offers a way of probing a sample nondestructively to locate areas of interest.

Photos, John P. Testa, Jr.

39

stones are several hundred million years older then the most ancient rocks known on Earth.

Other aspects of the history of meteorites are inferred by radioactive dating. For example, iron meteorites have ages as much as 800 million years less than the 4.6-billion-year stone meteorites. This difference suggests that the deep interiors of the parent bodies, where iron and other heavy elements became concentrated, remained hot enough to keep iron molten as long as 800 million years after the bodies formed. Sometimes such an event as the collision of a parent body with another object caused enough heating to melt or partially melt some minerals but not others. The radioactive clocks of the minerals that melted would be reset, since fresh crystals with the characteristic initial composition would form as the molten rock cooled. In the minerals that did not melt, the radioactive processes would continue their original countdown from 4.6 billion years ago. Thus, radioactive dating can tell both when a meteorite formed and when its parent body was subjected to an event that produced melting.

While buried in their parent bodies, which could have had diameters as large as hundreds of kilometers, the rocks that became meteorites were shielded from cosmic rays, the high-energy atomic nuclei that bombard the solar system from all directions in space. Even after the parents were broken up, all but the outer few meters of large rocks were likewise shielded. But once further disintegration produced pieces less than a few meters in size, cosmic rays penetrated extensively. Bombardment with these energetic nuclei transformed some elements into other isotopes, notably of the gases helium, neon, and argon, that are not characteristic of the minerals. By measuring the amounts of these cosmogenic isotopes in a meteorite, scientists can determine its cosmic-ray exposure age: the time that elapsed between its fragmentation down to a size of a few meters or less and its arrival on Earth, where the atmosphere provided a new shield from cosmic rays. Cosmic-ray exposure ages determined in this way range from about 20,000 to 100 million years for most stone meteorites and as high as a billion years for irons. If all of the parent bodies broke up at roughly the same time, this difference in exposure

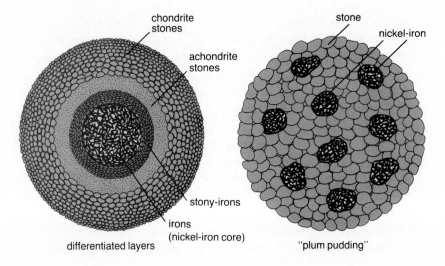

chondrite stones

achondrite stones

stone

nickel-iron

stony-irons

irons (nickel-iron core)

differentiated layers

"plum pudding"

(All photos except bottom) Jeffrey K. Wagner; (bottom) Jeffrey Kurtzman, Arizona State University

ages means that the fragile stones disintegrate in space faster than the irons, presumably from collisions.

Radioactive dating can even tell when a meteorite landed on Earth. If a cosmogenic isotope is radioactive, then the number of its atoms in a meteorite will decrease after the meteorite lands, since there are no more cosmic ray impacts to replenish the supply of that isotope. The time since the meteorite fell can be calculated from the relative amounts of the cosmogenic parent and daughter atoms. Terrestrial ages rarely exceed several thousand years for stone meteorites found outside Antarctica, but those preserved in Antarctic ice are as old as 800,000 years. Such ancient falls offer the possibility in future work of searching for systematic differences among meteorites that fell in different eras. The oldest meteorite that was actually seen to fall, probably in AD 861, resides in a Shinto shrine at Nogata, Japan. The next oldest, its fall dated with certainty at Nov. 16, 1492, came down at Ensisheim, Alsace, and is kept there in the town hall.

Parent bodies

As shown by measurements of their cosmogenic isotopes, meteorites have existed in space as small bodies over quite a range of times. Before that the majority seem to have been parts of asteroids, destined to be chipped off during collisions and sent into orbits that intersected the orbit of Earth. The few meteorite orbits that have been determined from an analysis of photographs of meteor trails have an aphelion—or most distant point from the Sun—within the asteroid belt, between Mars and Jupiter, suggesting an asteroidal origin. Since all but the largest asteroids are thought to be the fragmented remains of still larger masses, the parent bodies of meteorites and asteroids are apparently one and the same. A once controversial theory, now gaining support, holds that some small asteroids that are not part of the asteroid belt are the remains of comets that have lost their volatile materials and that these asteroids are the parent bodies of some of the stone meteorites. In 1983 the Infrared Astronomy Satellite (IRAS) discovered an asteroid that seems to be the remnant of the vanished comet that produced the Geminid meteor shower. (It should be noted that the annual meteor showers such as the Perseids and Leonids result from the passage of the Earth through trails of debris left by comets as they orbit the Sun. These small fragments almost always burn up completely before they reach the Earth's surface and thus rarely produce meteorites.)

The wide differences in composition and density among meteorites suggest that many of their parent bodies differentiated, like the Earth, into a metallic core and rocky outer layers. The most dense meteorites, the irons, presumably come from the central cores of such parent bodies, although some investigators have suggested they formed in great metal lumps dispersed throughout the parent body interiors, as though they were plums in a pudding. The concept of a metallic core surrounded by great layers of stone is supported by studies of the crystalline structure of certain nickel-iron alloys in the irons. Many of these structures are typical of crystals formed in a slowly cooling and hence presumably well-insulated melt.

Meteorites that are mixtures of stone and iron probably formed in regions of the parent bodies where the lighter stone of the outer layers came in contact with the molten metal. These stony-irons are rare, perhaps because the boundary regions where they formed were thin. Achondrites, stone meteorites that lack chondrules, contain less volatile material than other stones and are more heavily processed. They may have formed in the layers just above those of the stony-irons, where the achondrites were subjected to more heat and compression than the rock in layers above. The stones called ordinary chondrites, even less processed than achondrites, are the most common meteorites even though they deteriorate significantly in space. Thus, the bulk of a meteorite parent body may have consisted of the layers of rock that became ordinary chondrites, located above the achondrite source region. Carbonaceous chondrites may have come from the cooler surface layers, where planetary forces did the least processing.

The foregoing is an illustrative model, based on clues from many different meteorites. It attributes each major class of meteorite to a different region of a single type of parent body. The real situation was probably more complex, some meteorites being produced in different types of parent bodies. For example, if extinct comets are a type of parent body, the meteorites derived from them are probably all ordinary and carbonaceous chondrites.

Seasonings in the solar nebula

Advanced laboratory techniques are enabling investigators to unlock many of the secrets of primitive meteorites. Components of carbonaceous chondrites have been found to contain matter that seems to have been formed in stars that predated our Sun. Stellar winds and explosions may have blown that ancient stardust across the wide gulf of interstellar space so that it enriched the solar nebula. There is evidence for matter that formed in the nuclear furnaces of supernovas, red giant stars, and perhaps others. In addition, the studies offer suggestions about the event that triggered the solar nebula to condense into the Sun and planets as well as about the energy source that melted the interiors of the meteorite parent bodies.

42

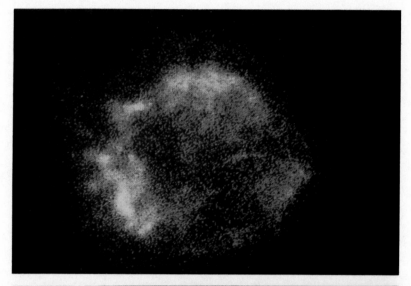

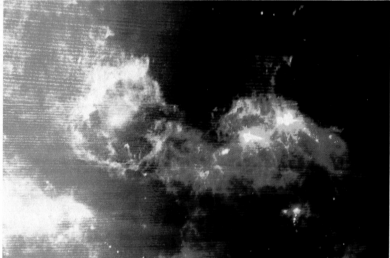

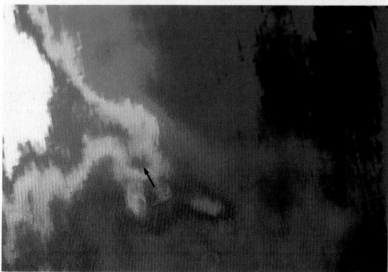

X-ray view of the Cassiopeia A supernova remnant (top) reveals the expanding cloud of debris from a star that exploded in the latter half of the 17th century. Evidence from meteorites together with theories of star formation suggest that a similar supernova event more than $4\frac{1}{2}$ billion years ago not only enriched the solar nebula with ancient stardust but actually triggered its condensation into the Sun and planets. The condensation of stars from interstellar clouds is a process that can be seen and studied even today. The constellation of Orion (center), shown in several color-coded infrared wavelengths recorded by the Infrared Astronomical Satellite (IRAS), possesses regions of star formation within the large red-hued area in the right half of the image, known as the Orion molecular cloud. Barnard 5 (bottom), another cloud believed to be a stellar nursery, has been shown by IRAS imaging to include a newborn star no more than 100,000 years old (arrow), one whose nuclear furnace has not yet ignited. Estimates of the object's mass hint that it may be much like the Sun was in an early stage of formation.

(Top) Smithsonian Astrophysical Observatory; (center, bottom) JPL/NASA

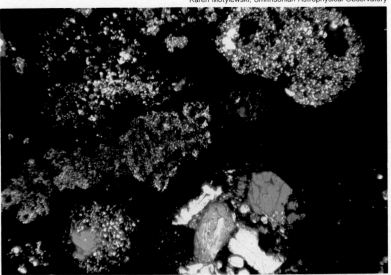

Thin section of a piece of the Allende meteorite viewed under the microscope in polarized light includes some of the meteorite's more scientifically important components. The dark background comprises the carbon-containing material that characterizes the stone as a carbonaceous chondrite, while the rounded multicolored objects are chondrules. The elongated, amoebalike object in the left center of the image represents a type of inclusion that shows isotopic ratios unlike those of matter from the Earth or Moon, in accord with the idea that the solar nebula was laced with matter from ancient stars.

Astrophysicists have concluded that although the two lightest elements, hydrogen and helium, were created in the big bang at the dawn of the universe, the heavier elements and additional helium must have been made later by nuclear reactions in stars. Today, within the Sun, such a process of nucleosynthesis is turning hydrogen to helium. A few billion years from now the Sun will swell and become a red giant star, much larger and more luminous but with a cooler surface. Within red giants helium is built up into carbon, nitrogen, and oxygen. Accepted physical theory states that the internal nuclear furnaces of stars can build elements of increasing atomic weight up to iron. In addition, it is thought that a chain of reactions called the s-process, believed to occur in red giants and perhaps also in novas, produces certain isotopes of even heavier elements. (Novas are explosions that occur on the surfaces of small, dense stars called white dwarfs in gas accumulated from larger companion stars.) In 1983 a Nobel Prize for Physics was awarded to William Fowler of the California Institute of Technology for his work on the processes of nucleosynthesis in stars.

On red giants and most other stars, stellar winds are constantly blowing the stellar gases into space. Massive stars and some binary systems (two stars orbiting each other) undergo extremely powerful explosions called supernovas in which whole stars are disrupted, spewing the earlier products of their nuclear furnaces into space. In addition, most of the known elements heavier than iron, which are not created within a star in its stable phase, are made in the supernova explosion itself. Thus the supernova liberates lighter elements that were created during a star's long life as well as heavier elements that were made as it underwent explosive death.

The radioactive isotope aluminum-26 (^{26}Al), which decays to the isotope magnesium-26 (^{26}Mg), is absent both in meteorites and in Earth and Moon rocks today. Once it is made, its decay rate is such that half of a given quantity disappears in only 720,000 years (its half-life). Thus

44

nearly all the ^{26}Al that might have been present in the solar nebula must have vanished after a few half-lives elapsed. Along with ^{24}Mg and ^{25}Mg, ^{26}Mg is a stable isotope. The relative proportions of the three magnesium isotopes in Earth and Moon rocks are well known. Some meteorite components, however, have excess ^{26}Mg, *i.e.*, amounts larger than those usually present, relative to the other two magnesium isotopes. This excess is identified as the daughter product of radioactive ^{26}Al.

Because according to astrophysical theory a supernova is the only likely source for ^{26}Al in space, the excess ^{26}Mg in meteorites implies that a supernova exploded near the solar nebula within one or two ^{26}Al half-lives before solidification of the minerals that show excess ^{26}Mg today. The aluminum probably condensed onto dust grains in the supernova debris before reaching the solar nebula. Otherwise, were the aluminum still a gas, it would have mixed uniformly into the nebula such that meteorites would not have more ^{26}Mg than Earth and Moon rocks.

Theorists believe that the condensation of stars from interstellar clouds is triggered in many cases by shock waves from violent events in the Galaxy, including supernovas. The probability that a supernova explosion will occur in such a small region as the vicinity of the solar nebula in an interval of a few million years or less is very small. This reasoning suggests that it is no coincidence that the nebula that gave rise to the solar system was enriched by ^{26}Al from a supernova. Indeed, the solar nebula might not have condensed at all were it not for the shock wave from the supernova. Furthermore, it seems likely that enough ^{26}Al was present shortly after the meteorite parent bodies formed so that the heat released by radioactive decay was enough to melt and differentiate their interiors.

Independent laboratory experiments on carbonaceous chondrites reveal clear traces of the *s*-process, the chain of nuclear reactions that builds heavy elements in red giants and perhaps in novas. For example, stepped heating of material from the Murchison carbonaceous chondrite, which fell in the Australian state of Victoria in September 1969, showed a component of the meteorite to be enriched in certain isotopes of xenon but deficient in others, in accord with theoretical calculations of isotopic abundances produced by the *s*-process. Likewise, the abundances

Microscopic mineral inclusion found in the Allende meteorite (below right) appears to be an aggregate of original solid particles that condensed at high temperature from the solar nebula and may represent one of the oldest unprocessed mineral structures in the solar system. Under the electron microscope a thin section of the Murchison meteorite (below left) shows some of the fine- and coarse-grained carbon-bearing material that has been found to contain anomalous ratios of xenon isotopes as well as enrichments of carbon-13. The pattern of isotopic abundances present in the Murchison meteorite is consistent with theoretical predictions of the way elements are synthesized in red giant stars and possibly in novas.

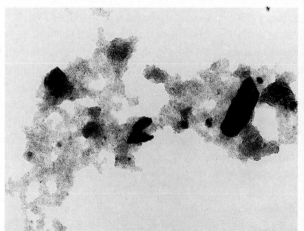
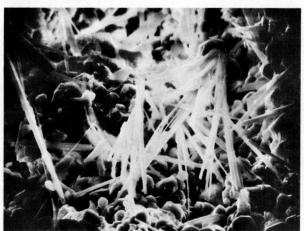

(Left) Mitsuo Ohtsuki, University of Chicago; (right) photo, I. D. Hutcheon; courtesy, Lawrence Grossman, University of Chicago

of seven neodymium isotopes found in a component of the Allende carbonaceous chondrite follow just the pattern expected for nucleosynthesis by the s-process. The presence of other isotopic enrichments further support the idea that red giants, novas, or both contributed their dust to the solar nebula.

Rocks from the Red Planet

As mentioned above, nine stones, the SNC meteorites, can be dated no older than 1.3 billion years, indicating that they formed from a magma that recently. Further, the radioactive clocks of some minerals in the SNC meteorites were reset only about 180 million years ago, and the presence of a glassy mineral called maskelynite indicates that this event was due to a powerful impact. The parent bodies of the vast majority of meteorites cannot be the source of the SNC meteorites, for they formed about 4.6 billion years ago and no longer had molten interiors after 800 million years.

The chemical composition of the SNC meteorites is unlike that of other meteorites or of Moon rocks, although there are some resemblances to terrestrial igneous rock. Nevertheless, the presence of cosmogenic isotopes and trapped gases from the solar wind, plus some real chemical differences from all known Earth rocks, rules out the Earth as the source. (They were not, for example, thrown off the Earth by some process, exposed to the solar wind and cosmic rays, and then returned to Earth.) A large asteroid that was rendered partly molten by a collision with another large body is one suggested source of the SNC meteorites, but this idea lacks any real supportive evidence.

The most likely source of the SNC meteorities appears to be Mars. There are large volcanoes on its surface, and some parts of the volcanic terrain were molten relatively recently, as shown by the small number of impact craters compared with other regions of Mars. Also, there are chemical similarities between SNC meteorites and Martian soil samples that were analyzed by the two Viking lander spacecraft in 1976.

Calculations indicate that the SNC meteorites could not have been shot out into space from Martian volcanoes; there would not have been enough energy for the rocks to attain escape velocity. The impact of a large meteorite could provide the energy to knock chips off the Martian surface and into the solar system, but such a collision would totally melt or even vaporize the ejecta and not simply reset some of their radioactive clocks. A better solution is a grazing impact. Calculations by Laurence E. Nyquist of the Johnson Space Center in Houston, Texas, indicate that a grazing strike by a large meteorite could propel some Mars rocks into space without melting them.

A long-standing objection to the idea that material can reach the Earth from Mars has been that Mars is much farther than the Moon, yet no Moon rocks are found on Earth. Why should Mars rocks get into space and land on Earth when Moon rocks do not? The nearly unanimous agreement that meteorite ALHA 81005 is of lunar origin now seems to eliminate this objection.

The Antarctic meteorite EETA 79001 is one of nine stones, called the SNC meteorites, that appear to have solidified from molten rock no earlier than 1.3 billion years ago, or nearly 3 billion years after the parent bodies of the vast majority of meteorites had completely cooled. The most attractive explanation is that these rocks came from Mars, having been propelled into space by the grazing strike of a large meteorite.

Meteorites and life

Studies of meteorites within the past few years have revealed a remarkable content of organic molecules, including many amino acids. In living matter amino acids are the building blocks of proteins, the basic stuff of life. According to a recent report from John R. Cronin and Sandra Pizzarello of Arizona State University, 52 different amino acids have been positively identified in the Murchison carbonaceous chondrite, of which 33 are not found on Earth. Moreover, the chemicals adenine, guanine, cytosine, thymine, and uracil have all reportedly been found in this meteorite. Of these molecules the first four are the building blocks of the DNA molecule, the storehouse of genetic information, while the fifth is a component of RNA, another fundamental constituent of life. At the present time there is no evidence that meteorites are derived from objects where life existed. Eventually, however, they may help explain how life arose on the Earth and perhaps elsewhere in the universe.

FOR ADDITIONAL READING

  William A. Cassidy and Louis A. Rancitelli, "Antarctic Meteorites," *American Scientist* (March–April 1982, pp. 156–163).

  Ian Halliday and Bruce A. McIntosh, *Solid Particles in the Solar System* (D. Reidel, 1980).

  P. W. Hodge, *Interplanetary Dust* (Gordon and Breach Science Publishers, 1981).

  Robert Hutchison, *The Search for Our Beginning* (British Museum and Oxford University Press, 1983).

  Roy S. Lewis and Edward Anders, "Interstellar Matter in Meteorites," *Scientific American* (August 1983, pp. 66–77).

  D. W. Sears, *The Nature and Origin of Meteorites* (Oxford University Press, 1978).

GIANT
VOIDS
IN THE
UNIVERSE

by Robert P. Kirshner

*New observations have revealed enormous
regions in space that appear to contain
little or no matter. This discovery has
far-reaching implications for theories
of the evolution of the universe.*

The simplest and most compelling modern pictures of the universe describe a homogeneous, smoothly expanding space that originated in the Big Bang about 20 billion years ago and whose fate hinges on a delicate balance between the motion of expansion and the attraction of gravitation. While this picture is beautiful in its simplicity, and powerful in its predictions, it misses out on all the fun of the real universe, which is richly populated with delightful inhomogeneities. Distinct planets, particular stars with familiar and romantic names, and individual galaxies are familiar objects in the cosmos. The galaxies are gathered into clusters, and recent work shows that the clusters themselves are connected by strings of galaxies into superclusters and separated by yawning voids that can be 350 million light-years across. (A light-year is the distance that light can travel in one year, about 6,000,000,000,000 miles.) These extreme departures from the prevailing uniformity reveal the distribution of matter in the universe and provide clues to the nature of the Big Bang.

Though one can observe these inhomogeneities, the idea that the universe is homogeneous on the largest scales is important enough to have a name: the Cosmological Principle. On small scales one piece of the universe is not like another; our Galaxy is not identical to M31, and a cluster of galaxies is not like a void. The scales of structure and individuality extend up to distances of a few hundred million light-years. Yet on the largest scales, a few billion light-years, astronomers believe that the universe is the same everywhere. Fog is like that: made up of individual water droplets when observed on a small scale, but smooth and uniform when seen on larger scales.

This paradox of a lumpy and interesting universe that averages out to become a simple one on large scales is the result of recent observations with new and powerful instruments. Understanding the origin of the

ROBERT P. KIRSHNER is Chairman of the Department of Astronomy and Director of the McGraw-Hill Observatory at the University of Michigan, Ann Arbor.

M31, the Great Nebula in the constellation Andromeda, is about 900,000 light-years distant and shines with the combined light of 40,000,000,000 stars like the Sun.

Edwin Hubble and his associates used new telescopes in the 1920s to determine that the spiral nebulae are distant stellar systems as large as our Milky Way galaxy.

voids and filaments of galaxies has brought new ideas from the arena of particle physics into the cosmological discussion.

Distances, recession, and the expanding universe

The story starts in the opening decades of this century with the discovery of the distances to galaxies. Using the new 60-inch and then 100-inch telescopes at Mount Wilson Observatory in California, Edwin Hubble and his associates established that the spiral nebulae were really distant stellar systems as large as our own Milky Way galaxy. The nearest big galaxy is M31, the Great Nebula in the constellation Andromeda, and Hubble's estimation, based on the apparent brightness of a particular type of variable star found within that galaxy, was that this system is about 900,000 light-years away and shines with the combined light of about 40,000,000,000 stars like the Sun.

Hubble's early explorations were severely limited by the great distances between the galaxies. Precisely because the distances are so large, the stars that Hubble used as distance indicators appear extremely faint, even in nearby systems, and are completely indistinguishable in distant galaxies. While Hubble and his modern successors did develop a system of distance measures based on brighter objects, such as the brightest stars in galaxies, exploding stars, and eventually the galaxies themselves, the uncertainty increased with each step so that serious workers disagree on the distance scale by a factor of two.

During the same era Vesto Slipher at the Lowell Observatory in Flagstaff, Arizona, was measuring another property of galaxies, their motions. Through extremely difficult observations of the spectra of light from galaxies, Slipher found that most galaxies were moving away from ours, and that some were moving at remarkably high speeds. The velocity of this recession causes a shift toward the red end of the spectrum in the light received from a galaxy. Hence, the recession velocity is often called the redshift. Slipher's measurements were used by Hubble to demonstrate one of the most remarkable facts about the universe. Combining his own distance estimates with Slipher's velocities, Hubble found that the recession velocity of a galaxy was just proportional to its distance from the Earth. This fact needed an explanation. If one accepts the Cosmological Principle, then it follows that our view of the universe is not unique or special but must be the typical view that an observer on any galaxy would enjoy. The problem then becomes one of developing a picture of the universe in which every galaxy would see its neighbors receding, and see the more distant galaxies moving away more rapidly.

Fortunately, such a picture is not as difficult to comprehend as it might seem and has a simple connection to physical theory. If one imagines that the whole universe is expanding, and that expanding space carries the galaxies along with it, then Hubble's relation between recession velocity and distance follows naturally. By analogy, one can imagine a giant jungle gym with observant six-year-olds on each rung. If one then imagines that the jungle gym doubles in size, each climber will see his neighbors moving away as the whole system grows. The child one rung away will double his distance and appear two rungs away. During the same time period the child ten rungs away will move to twenty, and so his recession velocity will be ten times larger than that of the first child. In fact, every observer will have the same view: nearby neighbors moving away slowly and distant ones receding more rapidly. Hubble's observation about the galaxies is exactly reproduced by this simple expanding grid. Thus the interpretation of Hubble's observation that is consistent with the Cosmological Principle is not that our galaxy is particularly repellent but that space itself is expanding—that we live in an expanding universe.

Redshifts are related to distance, according to Edwin Hubble's concept of an expanding universe. The velocity of recession from the Earth of a galaxy causes a shift toward the red end of the spectrum in the light received from that galaxy. Thus, the galaxies that are farthest away reveal the largest redshifts and are receding the fastest. The vertical arrow indicates the position of the element calcium in the fuzzy spectrum of the Virgo galaxy. The horizontal arrows show the calcium redshift, which becomes greater as the galaxies are more distant.

Galaxies   Redshifts

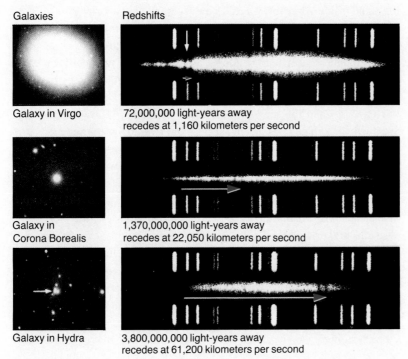

Galaxy in Virgo

72,000,000 light-years away
recedes at 1,160 kilometers per second

Galaxy in
Corona Borealis

1,370,000,000 light-years away
recedes at 22,050 kilometers per second

Galaxy in Hydra

3,800,000,000 light-years away
recedes at 61,200 kilometers per second

Mount Wilson and Las Campanas Observatories, © Carnegie Institution of Washington

Gravity and the future of the universe

This view is not just a crafty metaphor created to fit the data. It also has a deep foundation in physical theory. In the same years that the distances and motions of the galaxies were being measured, Albert Einstein was developing a new theory of gravity, the General Theory of Relativity. Several applications of Einstein's revolutionary views to astronomical problems demonstrated that his new theory agreed with the observations better than the predictions based on classical Newtonian gravitation. Einstein also investigated the effects of gravitation on the universe as a whole. He found that the universe could be expanding or contracting, but did not have a natural way to remain static. In an ironic twist Einstein did not then predict that the universe would be expanding or contracting. Instead, he distorted his theory by adding in an extra term to the equations, the "Cosmological Constant," which made static universes a mathematical possibility. Other workers explored the details of expanding universes, however, and by the 1930s it was widely recognized that the best theory of gravitation, General Relativity without modification, could account for the observations of Hubble and Slipher and make definite predictions about the geometry and fate of the universe.

The universe has been expanding for a long time, and so in the distant past the cosmos must have been a denser place, and possibly a hot one. In 1965 Arno Penzias and Robert Wilson, working at Bell Laboratories, detected radio emission coming from all directions that looked exactly like cooled radiation from a hot Big Bang. This discovery provided a picture of a hot Big Bang roughly 10 billion to 20 billion years ago that began the expansion of the universe as we know it. The background radiation detected by Penzias and Wilson is exceptionally smooth, showing the same brightness everywhere to an accuracy of 1 part in 10,000. This indicates that the foamy structure of clusters, superclusters, and voids that is observed today was not present early in the history of the universe.

The theory of gravitation allows astronomers to predict the overall motion of the universe in the future. It will depend on a balance between the motion of expansion and the attraction of gravity. If the expansion is fast enough, then the universe will coast on forever, always expanding. Stars will live their lives and burn out, and eventually the universe will become a cold, dark, lonely place. While this may seem good news for those with long-term high-interest investments, it will surely provide time for all forms of matter to decay to their simplest states. Since modern theories of particle physics predict that even the proton is unstable, this means that all matter as it is now known will eventually decay to electrons and photons.

On the other hand, if the density of matter is high enough, then the gravitational attraction will slow the expansion and eventually cause it to halt and reverse to become a universal contraction. The universe will become denser and hotter, eventually evaporating all the planets, exploding all the stars, and erasing all the interesting structures, from superclusters of galaxies down to the nuclei of atoms, that had developed in the tens of billions of years after the Big Bang.

Thus, the fate of the universe depends on the balance between expansion, which can be measured, and density, which can also be measured. Which fate is in store for us? Unfortunately, the measurements of both quantities are somewhat crude and depend on a clearer understanding of galaxy clusters and voids, as is discussed below. Therefore, both points of view are defensible. Robert Frost offered his opinion in the poem "Fire and Ice":

> Some say the world will end in fire
> Some say in ice.
> From what I've tasted of desire
> I hold with those who favor fire.

But the future of the universe is not just a matter for speculation and debate. The question will not be decided by eloquence, but by a concrete program of observation that yields a firmer value for the expansion rate and a more accurate estimate of the mass density in the universe.

Mass density and galactic distribution

To estimate the mass density in the universe one needs to know how many galaxies there are in a typical volume and the mass associated with each galaxy. This requires a detailed catalog for a volume of space large enough to be a fair sample of the universe. That volume must be larger than the largest structures; otherwise, if a dense patch of the universe is selected, there is the risk of badly overestimating the mass density. Conversely, if the sample is a void, the density would be badly underestimated. Therefore, to do this problem right, one needs to understand the three-dimensional distribution of galaxies, especially on large scales.

Determining the correct mass is also a difficult problem. The motions of stars in galaxies and of galaxies in orbit around each other reveal that

Horn-shaped antenna at the Bell Laboratories space communication station at Holmdel, N.J., was used by Arno Penzias and Robert Wilson to detect the background radiation that is considered to be a remnant of the Big Bang, the first event in the formation of the universe.

53

galaxies are much more massive than one might expect. The combined masses of all the visible stars in a galaxy falls short of the actual mass by a factor of ten or more. As with an iceberg, most of the matter in a galaxy is hidden from view and is in some unseen and unknown form. One possibility is that the hidden mass consists of subatomic particles such as neutrinos (which scarcely interact with other matter) or even more exotic (and as yet undetected) particles that can be imagined by particle theorists. There are some experimental hints that the neutrino might have mass. Although it would be extremely small, even by the standards of atomic physics, it is conceivable that these individually insignificant particles actually constitute most of the mass in the universe, and thus they could have a profound effect on its large-scale structure.

The most direct approach to determining the three-dimensional structure of galaxy distribution is to use Hubble's result. Since velocity is proportional to distance, the measurement of the velocity of a galaxy provides a measurement of its distance. The difficulty with this approach has been that velocity measurements have always taken considerable amounts of time at the telescope. When Hubble set out to see whether the galaxies were uniformly distributed in space, he resorted to a cruder method, since measuring a large sample of velocities was too difficult for the astronomy of the 1930s. Instead, he photographed 1,283 sample regions of the sky and counted a total of 44,000 galaxies as a function of apparent brightness. Hubble was well aware that galaxies are found variously in pairs, small groups of a few dozen, and great clusters of thousands, but he concluded from his counts that the variations that had been observed from place to place were about what would be expected from randomly distributed galaxies. He found no evidence from his

The distribution of galaxies in the universe was determined by Edwin Hubble as a result of photographing 1,283 sample regions of the sky with a 2.54-meter telescope. The size of each dot indicates the number of galaxies that were counted on one of those photographs. Dashes and open circles indicate few or no galaxies. The zone across the center of the map coincides with the visible Milky Way, where interstellar dust obscures other galaxies. The empty regions to the south could not be surveyed by the telescope. The numbers indicate galactic coordinates.

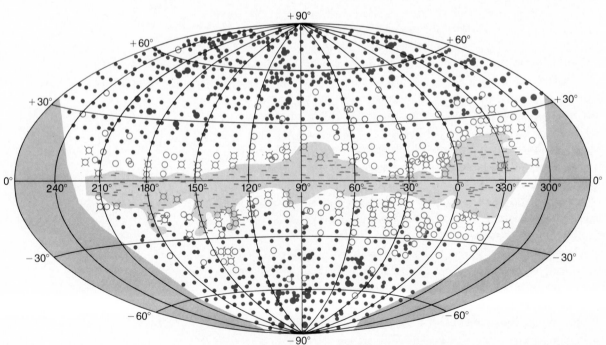

Galaxies in Corona Borealis, about 1,370,000,000 light-years away, are held together in a cluster by their mutual gravitational attraction.

investigation for the strings and superclusters revealed by later work. Hubble also compared the number of galaxies found at each apparent brightness and concluded that the number increased just as did the volume of the survey.

Galaxy counts are a crude way of surveying the three-dimensional structure of the universe because there is a large spread in the intrinsic brightness of galaxies. Thus, faint but nearby galaxies may appear as bright as luminous but remote systems. The only certain way to remove that ambiguity is to measure the velocity of each system so that its proper distance can be assigned and its intrinsic luminosity measured. Before recent breakthroughs in astronomical technique this task was too difficult to undertake for a large sample of distant galaxies.

The ultimate attempt to measure the structure of the Universe without velocity data was the monumental million-galaxy survey carried out in the 1950s by Donald Shane and Carl Wirtanen at Lick Observatory in California. The two men divided the sky into small bins and counted the number of galaxies in each one. In a map of the sky generated from the Shane and Wirtanen counts by J. E. Moody, E. L. Turner, and J. R. Gott III dense knots of galaxies appear to be woven into a mesh of filaments and voids. The question arises as to whether this is just an illusion caused by the propensity of human eyes to find patterns even in random data.

55

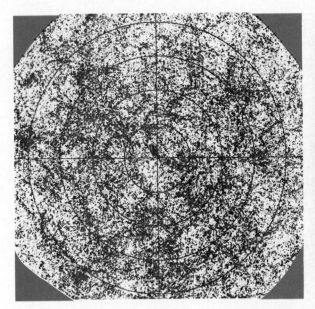 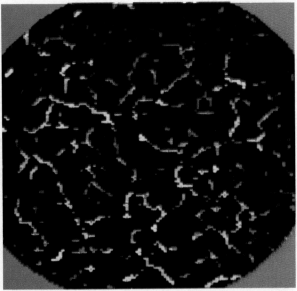

The Shane-Wirtanen survey of one million galaxies in the 1950s produced evidence of clustering (above). Other researchers generated from the Shane-Wirtanen counts a map in which dense knots of galaxies seem to be woven into a mesh of filaments and voids (above right). On the opposite page are a computer-generated model of galaxy clustering (left) and the model as applied to the filament structures (right). The filaments in the computer model are shorter and of lower contrast than are those from the actual survey, indicating that some aspect of galaxy clustering has not been accounted for correctly in the model.

Moody, Turner, and Gott tried to put the question of filamentary galaxy clusters on a firmer footing by defining a simple scheme for identifying filaments. They applied the scheme to the Shane-Wirtanen data from the sky and also to a model of galaxy clustering. Applying this filament finder to the real data and to a computer simulation of galaxy clustering shows that the real filaments are longer and of higher contrast to the background than are the filaments in the computer model. This indicates that there is some aspect of galaxy clustering that is not correctly accounted for in the model.

The development of new detectors for astronomical use has made practical the gathering of large redshift samples. As a result astronomers can now plot the location of substantial numbers of galaxies in their true three-dimensional locations. The change from Slipher's day is astonishing. While it took him many hours to record a faint smudge of a spectrum on a photographic plate for even a nearby and bright galaxy like M31, the efforts of present-day astronomers need not be so heroic. With a modern detector that counts individual photons and sends the results immediately to a computer for accumulation and analysis, a relatively small telescope such as the 1.3-meter (52-inch) instrument at the McGraw-Hill Observatory can do the same job in five minutes. Armed with these new tools, several groups have carried out surveys to try to determine how galaxies are distributed throughout the universe.

Some have concentrated on the known large clusters of galaxies to see how far across the sky they extend. These surveys show that filaments of galaxies extend over tens of degrees from the dense cluster core, corresponding to distances of roughly 100 million light-years. The volume in front of the cluster often shows large regions of low galaxy density.

A more comprehensive approach was taken by a group from the Harvard-Smithsonian Center for Astrophysics. Its survey covered the whole Northern sky, including 2,400 galaxies, with recession velocities

Photos, (opposite page left and this page left) reprinted courtesy of J. E. Moody, E. L. Turner, J. R. Gott, and *The Astrophysical Journal*, published by the University of Chicago Press; © 1983 The American Astronomical Society; (opposite page right and this page right) J. E. Moody, E. L. Turner, and J. R. Gott

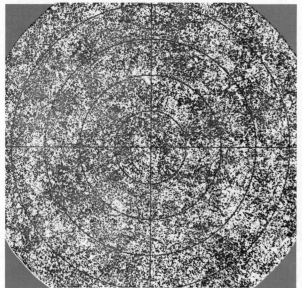 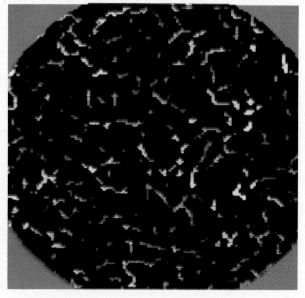

averaging 5,000 kilometers per second (3,000 miles per second, or about 10 million miles per hour). That recession velocity corresponds to a distance of about 300 million light-years. Within that relatively small volume their detailed survey showed a definite frothy structure, dominated by clusters, filaments, and voids.

Large-scale structure

To study the structure of the universe on larger scales requires a significantly fainter sample of galaxies. The typical galaxy in a faint sample is more distant than that in a bright sample, although the velocity measurement has to be made for each galaxy in order to pin down its position. While this makes the observations more difficult, it provides the data necessary to see the largest structures in the universe. Starting in 1976, Robert Kirshner of the University of Michigan has been engaged in carrying out redshift surveys of selected regions of the sky, together with Augustus Oemler, Jr., of Yale University, Paul Schechter of Kitt Peak National Observatory, and Stephen Shectman at the Mount Wilson and Las Campañas observatories.

The work of these astronomers did not start out with the intent of studying large-scale structure—in fact, they hoped to measure only the average properties of galaxies and sought to avoid extreme or unusual regions of the universe. They wanted to construct a fair sample of the universe so that they could measure the distribution of galaxy luminosities and thereby determine how many galaxies there are of each intrinsic brightness. Another aim was to measure the average density of galaxies in order to help decide the cosmological question of the future of the universe.

In their first efforts, carried out at the McGraw-Hill and the Kitt Peak National observatories, Kirshner and his colleagues found that their study of average properties was hampered by substantial fluctuations in the number of galaxies observed on very large scales. This result was unexpected because they were working on length scales of more than 150 million light-years, and expected that any fluctuations would be averaged out. It was also annoying since it made the analysis of the results more difficult. However, rather than resisting the nature of the universe (never a good idea), the research team decided to investigate the fluctuations of galaxies as well as trying to determine their average properties.

To study galaxy clustering on the scale of 100 million light-years or more required a significantly deeper and therefore fainter sample. The astronomers picked six fields, three in the North and three in the South, which they hoped would provide a fair sample of the universe. The fields were rather small, only two square degrees each. This resulted from the fact that redshifts for only a moderate number of galaxies could be measured because each velocity measured required roughly 20 minutes of observing time on a large telescope.

The observations were carried out at Kitt Peak, at the Palomar Observatory in California, at the Las Campañas Observatory in Chile, and at the Multiple Mirror Telescope Observatory in Arizona. These observatories have some of the largest and best-equipped telescopes in the world. The research team took advantage of their powerful spectrographs and detectors to make velocity measurements for 280 galaxies, at an average distance of roughly one billion light-years. Galaxies appear faint at those distances; the researchers' limit was about 50,000 times fainter than the faintest star one can see on a dark desert night.

If galaxies were uniformly distributed throughout the universe, one would expect that an investigation of them, selected by brightness, would reveal a few located nearby and then increasing numbers at higher redshifts. This would happen because the volume sampled increases as one looks farther and farther out into space. The increasing numbers at large distances would ordinarily extend to the point where distant galaxies become too faint to be included in a sample that is selected by apparent brightness. Then, at very large distances one would expect to see only a few galaxies because only those with the greatest intrinsic luminosities would appear bright enough to be selected. Therefore, the expected trend is to see increasing numbers of galaxies as one looks to greater distance and then decreasing numbers because of the dwindling fraction of highly luminous galaxies. Deviations from the expected distribution could come from galaxies that are not spread uniformly through space but instead are clumped in a pattern of clusters and voids.

The results of the research for the southern fields of the survey followed the expected trend for a roughly uniform density of galaxies spiced by a moderate amount of galaxy clustering, but the northern results looked peculiar indeed. The astronomers found a large excess of galaxies at a redshift of 10,000 kilometers per second and again at 22,000 kilometers per second with a vast region in between that contained only one galaxy where twenty would be expected if the galaxies were distributed uniformly. This same pattern appeared in each of the three northern fields, even though they were separated from one another by 35°.

58

Giant voids

Kirshner and his colleagues interpreted this result to mean that there was a vast region, extending from roughly 750 million light-years away out to 1,100,000,000 light-years, which was nearly empty—a giant void. Since the same blank appeared in all three fields, they reasoned that the void must cover much of a triangle that had the survey fields at the corners; this could be interpreted as covering a sphere with the astonishing diameter of more than 350 million light-years.

Since the fields were in the general direction of the constellation Böotes, the researchers called this huge gap the Böotes Void. Its size is truly remarkable: a billion galaxies the size of our Milky Way could be stuffed into it. Of course, galaxies are not packed like sardines, but one would still expect to have several thousand galaxies at the average spacing in a volume as large as the void.

The research team immediately considered whether there might be some other explanation for this result. One possibility that they envisioned was that even though the same pattern was present in each of the three fields, that result could just be an accident and the volume in between might be populated with galaxies distributed at the usual density. It is true that the sampling technique was a little like shooting three bullets into a box to find out what's inside. Thus, the researchers might have missed the real contents by sheer bad luck and falsely concluded that the box was empty.

In order to investigate this possibility, the astronomers conducted another survey of the Böotes Void. In this investigation they sampled 282 fields placed on a grid that covered the triangle formed by the original three fields. Again, they measured redshifts for a sample of galaxies selected by their apparent brightness. The low-velocity galaxies, which are the nearby ones, were found to be distributed over the sky in more or

Studies of galaxy clustering on a scale of 100 million light-years or more require powerful telescopes such as those at the Multiple Mirror Telescope Observatory (left) and the Kitt Peak National Observatory (right), both in Arizona.

59

less the same way as were the sample fields. This is the result that one would expect from a region where galaxies are spread fairly uniformly through space.

A similar distribution was discovered for the galaxies with high red-shifts, which are beyond the region of the proposed void. At the distance of the void, however, there was a conspicuous absence of galaxies in the center of the region, the place where the density of survey fields is highest. The void, therefore, is real, and its volume is immense, just as the earlier survey suggested.

The frothy nature of the galaxy distribution seems well established now, and the scale of structure extends at least as far as the 350 million-light-year diameter of the Böotes Void, which is the largest object (or non-object) known in the universe. This inhomogeneity does not really contradict the Cosmological Principle, since the scales of these structures account for only a few percent of the size of the whole universe. But the void provides important lessons about the history and future of the universe.

One simple lesson is that the measurement of average properties demands extensive samples. If astronomers hope to predict the future expansion of the universe by comparing the current expansion rate with the average mass density, they must make that average measurement over scales that are larger than the biggest voids and filaments. Otherwise, they might accidentally obtain a much lower-than-average region or a much higher-than-average region and get the wrong answer to one of the big questions.

With this caution in mind Kirshner, Oemler, Schechter, and Shectman carried out an analysis for their complete sample, including the extensive southern half of the survey that showed no void. Their best estimate, even including the mysterious matter that surrounds galaxies, is that the mass density in the universe is too low to stop the cosmic expansion, too low by a factor of four. Thus, it appears that the universe will expand forever, growing cooler and less dense and becoming a cold, empty place.

In a survey of the Böotes Void (the triangular region on the map below) a team of astronomers sampled 282 survey fields that occupy the region of the sky in which the void is located; this is seen in chart A below. On B are the galaxies in those fields detected at distances between 350 million and 750 million light-years; they are rather uniformly distributed at that distance range. On the opposite page chart C shows the galaxies detected at distances between 750 million and 1,100,000,000 light-years. The striking absence of galaxies in the central region implies a giant void at that distance. In chart D the galaxies at distances between 1,100,000,000 and 1,700,000,000 light-years are again more uniformly distributed.

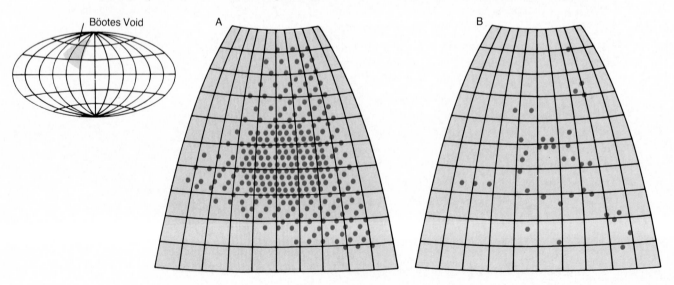

Böotes Void

A

B

As Frost concluded his poem:

> But if it had to perish twice,
> I think I know enough of hate
> To say that for destruction ice
> Is also great
> And would suffice.

Origin of cosmic structures

A more subtle lesson from the study of cosmic organization is that it must have some origin. Understanding that origin may reveal something about the conditions in the universe shortly after the Big Bang. The cosmic background radiation discovered by Penzias and Wilson is exceptionally smooth: there are no lumps or bumps in that glow at the level of one part in 10,000. Since the background radiation was emitted by the cooling gas of the universe some 100,000 years after the Big Bang, the current network of high-contrast galaxies and empty places must have formed since then. But how?

The force that draws matter together in the universe is gravitation, and gravitation plays the key role in every theory concerning the formation of structure. One theory, developed by Yakov B. Zel'dovich at the Institute of Applied Mathematics in Moscow, proposes that the largest structures formed first and that the likely shape for those structures would be flat sheets, dubbed "pancakes." Recent detailed calculations of the shapes generated by this model show a pattern of filaments and voids that bears considerable resemblance to the observed properties of the galaxy distribution, including the presence of giant voids. Recent calculations based on the physics of the Big Bang itself suggest that the starting conditions for the pancake picture may be generated naturally in the initial instants. All of these developments have cheered the adherents of the pancake theory.

There is even a neat connection to the possibility that neutrinos dominate the masses of galaxies. If neutrinos have mass (and the exper-

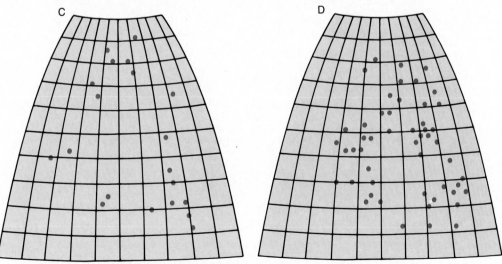

R. P. Kirshner, A. Oemler, P. L. Schechter, and S. A. Shectman

Joan Centrella and Adrian Melott; photos, courtesy, Lawrence Livermore National Laboratory

Three-dimensional simulations of the clustering of one million galaxies (top) and of voids (bottom) were generated by a Cray 1 supercomputer. At the top the clusters are formed into flat "pancakes" and filaments, while the voids, below, are more spherical in shape. Based on a theory by Soviet scientist Yakov B. Zel'dovich, these models resemble the observed properties of galactic distribution, including the presence of giant voids.

imental evidence is slim), then they could begin to cluster very early in the unfolding of the universe. Their lumpiness in the mass distribution would not be reflected in the cosmic background radiation, because the neutrinos do not interact with light. Thus, the enhancement of their density could develop without leaving a trace. Later, the ordinary matter that forms stars would fall into the deep gravitational wells created by the invisible neutrinos.

This theory draws particle physics—the study of matter on the smallest scale—into cosmology, the study on the largest scale. Of course, the properties of neutrinos are best determined in a physics laboratory, not by looking at galaxy clustering, but it is startling to think that the structure of superclusters and voids 350 million light-years across may be determined by the properties of a particle so elusive that its mass has not yet been securely measured.

Despite the successes of the pancake model there is one serious problem. In the pancake picture large-scale structures form first and then fragment further to form galaxies. Therefore, the galaxies would be younger than the clusters. Actually, however, the galaxies are ancient. The oldest stars in galaxies are nearly as old as the universe, and so the galaxies must have formed soon—probably within a billion years of the Big Bang. Conversely, the clusters of galaxies appear to be young; most galaxies, including the Milky Way, are just now falling into clusters.

These facts encourage the opposite school of thought. Instead of large structures being formed first, the galaxies might have come first; then, because the galaxies are unevenly distributed, the difference in density between various parts of the universe would have increased. The dense regions grow even denser by pulling galaxies in, and these areas eventually become the clusters. The low-density regions lose their galaxies to the dense areas. This picture of clusters growing from small scales up to large ones is the "hierarchical" model developed by P. J. E. Peebles at Princeton University. It agrees well with many statistical measures of galaxy clustering but is less satisfactory in accounting for the largest superclusters and voids.

Future prospects

Advances in observational techniques have brought the problem of large-scale structure in the universe to the point where interesting theoretical models can be compared with facts. While theoretical models are illuminating, observation, not argument, will ultimately reveal how the universe came to be arranged. More redshift surveys are needed to see the three-dimensional structure of the universe, but that will be slow work. To cover the whole sky at the distance of the void survey would require measuring 600,000 redshifts! Even 1/100 of that sample would take years of dedicated effort.

In addition, researchers need a direct way of seeing how clustering has evolved. Did it start with the giant superclusters and voids and then work down to galaxies, or did it start from galaxies and build up to the immense web that surrounds us? One can catch a dim glimpse of the past

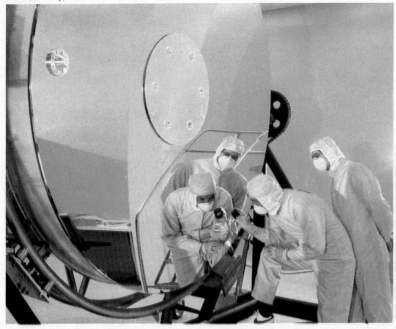

by looking at very faint and distant galaxies. Since they are at distances of several billion light-years, the galaxies are seen arranged as they were several billion years ago when the light was emitted. Thus, by studying very distant galaxies, scientists might be able to compare the clustering that was present before our solar system was formed and compare it with nearby and current samples.

Just as improved tools led to the present understanding of the universe, new tools will be needed for the next stage of the adventure. The Space Telescope now under construction and a giant telescope on Earth with a collecting area approximately 15 meters (50 feet) across, now under discussion, would help in this quest. While the facts are few, speculation is free, but as astronomers gain a more concrete notion of how the universe is arranged, they may see more clearly how it evolved from a featureless gas into our richly textured cosmos.

The 2.39-meter (94-inch) primary mirror for the U.S. National Aeronautics and Space Administration's Space Telescope is inspected by technicians at Perkin-Elmer Corp. (above left). The Space Telescope, shown above in a cutaway drawing, is scheduled to be launched in the mid-1980s and will be a powerful new tool for scientists.

FOR ADDITIONAL READING

Guido Chincarini and Herbert J. Rood, "The Cosmic Tapestry," *Sky and Telescope* (May 1980, pp. 364–372).

Timothy Ferris, *Red Limit: The Search for the Edge of the Universe*, rev. ed. (Quill, 1983).

Stephen A. Gregory and Laird A. Thompson, "Superclusters and Voids in the Distribution of Galaxies," *Scientific American* (March 1982, pp. 106–114).

Edwin P. Hubble, *The Realm of the Nebulae*, rev. ed. (Yale University Press, 1983).

Joseph A. Silk, Alexander S. Szalay, and Yakov B. Zel'dovich, "The Large-Scale Structure of the Universe," *Scientific American* (October 1983, pp. 72–80).

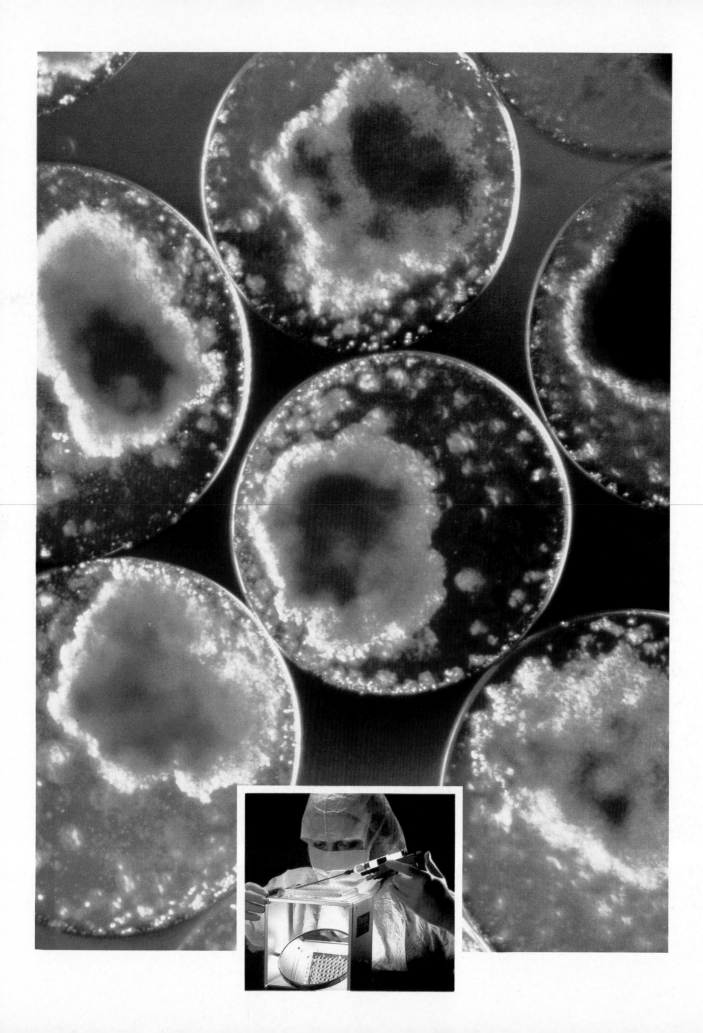

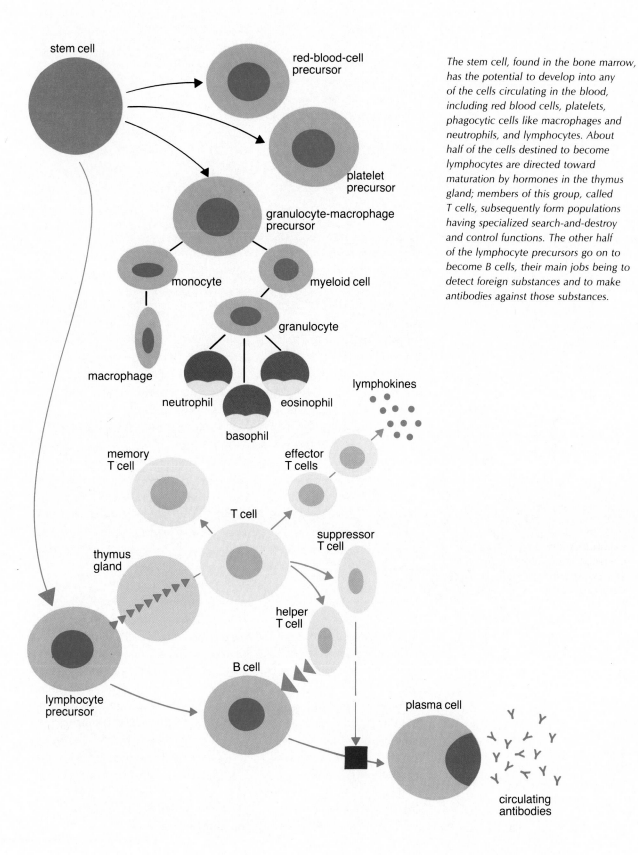

stem cell

red-blood-cell
precursor

platelet
precursor

granulocyte-macrophage
precursor

monocyte

myeloid cell

macrophage

granulocyte

neutrophil

eosinophil

basophil

lymphokines

memory
T cell

effector
T cells

T cell

suppressor
T cell

thymus
gland

helper
T cell

B cell

lymphocyte
precursor

plasma cell

circulating
antibodies

The stem cell, found in the bone marrow, has the potential to develop into any of the cells circulating in the blood, including red blood cells, platelets, phagocytic cells like macrophages and neutrophils, and lymphocytes. About half of the cells destined to become lymphocytes are directed toward maturation by hormones in the thymus gland; members of this group, called T cells, subsequently form populations having specialized search-and-destroy and control functions. The other half of the lymphocyte precursors go on to become B cells, their main jobs being to detect foreign substances and to make antibodies against those substances.

Courtesy, Abbott Laboratories

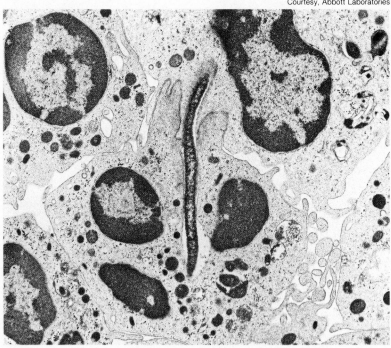

Microscopic thin section shows a neutrophil, one of the granulocytic white blood cells, in the process of engulfing a cell (dark elongated body) of the bacterium responsible for Legionnaires' disease. Neutrophils, which derive from stem cells, are the main phagocytic cells in the blood and defend against invasion by staph, strep, and pneumococcus bacteria.

of the cells circulating in the blood: the red blood cells, the platelets, and the several varieties of white blood cells. Which type of blood cell the stem cell will become is determined by regulatory factors in the body. Recently several of these factors, which are basically protein molecules, have been isolated in pure form. Collectively they are called colony-stimulating factors (CSF's) because in culture media they are capable of directing the stem cell to develop into colonies of blood cells. One pathway of development for the stem cell, for example, leads to the production of red blood cells, or erythrocytes. Other CSF's or combinations of them direct the stem cell to develop into megakaryocytes, the large multinucleated cells in the bone marrow that eventually bud into platelets, which play an important role in the clotting process.

The white blood cells, or leukocytes, that derive from the pluripotential stem cell include the monocytes and myeloid cells. Monocytes enter the tissues from the marrow and differentiate into macrophages, the large phagocytic (engulfing and consuming) cells that are responsible for ingesting invading bacteria that produce chronic tissue infections, such as the tubercle bacilli that cause tuberculosis. The myeloid cells develop into the several populations of granulocytes, the leukocytes containing granules in their cytoplasm. The most plentiful population of granulocytes, the neutrophils, are the main phagocytic cells in the blood and are responsible for defense in acute infections by staphylococcus, streptococcus, and pneumococcus bacteria. Other granular leukocytes are the eosinophils, which are important mediators of protection in parasitic infections, and basophils, which play a prominent role in allergic reactions. The development of each of these white cell populations from the stem cell is the responsibility of a particular mixture of CSF's.

68

The final offspring of the stem cell is the precursor of the lymphocytes. The lymphocyte is the keystone of the immunologic system because it is the cell charged with the special function of recognition. Before it can perform this function, however, the lymphocyte must undergo an orderly process of differentiation.

T cells

The maturation of lymphocyte precursors can take place along either of two pathways. About half of the approximately one trillion (10^{12}) lymphocytes in the human body at any given moment migrate to the thymus gland during their development, where their maturation is directed by thymic hormones. There seem to be several such hormones, all of them small, relatively simple proteins. The general term thymosin is applied to the mixture of thymic hormones. The goal of a great deal of contemporary research is to separate and define each of the thymic hormones in order to delineate their roles in lymphocyte differentiation and perhaps synthesize each of them in quantity. In infants whose thymus fails to develop properly, the immunologic system is unfit to function effectively. The future availability of thymic hormones may make it possible to remedy such an immunologic deficiency.

The lymphocytes that have been processed by the thymus are called T cells. In appearance they differ little from their lymphocyte precursors, but they have a special function and are distributed in a special way in the body. The vast majority of lymphocytes in the lymphatic fluids and about 70% of those in the bloodstream belong to the T-cell group, whereas only a minority of the lymphocytes in the organized lymphoid tissues, such as spleen and lymph nodes, are thymus derived. T cells are active migrators, circulating constantly through the tissues.

The most important event during the differentiation into T cells takes place when the lymphocyte acquires a recognition structure, or receptor, on its surface. This receptor, which consists of a large protein or protein-based molecule, enables the T cell to recognize one bit of molecular information called an antigenic determinant. An antigenic determinant is a structurally unique subunit of a larger molecule that has a shape complementary in its configuration to the T-cell receptor. The antigenic determinant combines with its T-cell receptor much as a key fits into a lock. Among the total population of T cells in the body there must be a few carrying receptors for any possible antigenic determinant in order to meet any challenge to the immunologic system. Since the number of T cells is so large, this requirement can easily be satisfied.

When the T cell encounters its complementary antigenic determinant, it is induced to undergo a striking series of changes. The small quiescent T cell enlarges and divides. Soon an entire colony, or clone, of identical T cells springs up, each carrying the same recognition structure as its forebear. This clone of T cells, now called effector T cells, is then ready and capable of carrying out some of the most important reactions of the immunologic system.

If the effector T cells find their complementary antigenic determinant

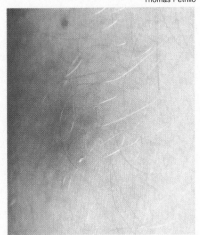

A localized inflammation appearing two or three days after a tuberculin test—a skin injection with protein derived from the tubercle bacillus—indicates that the person had previous contact with the organism and became sensitized to it. Such delayed hypersensitivity depends on the presence of T cells, which are stimulated by the foreign protein to release soluble products that initiate many of the signs of inflammation.

on the surface of some foreign cell, they are capable of killing that cell. T cells are therefore an important destructive force to be reckoned with when tissues are transplanted. Since virus-infected body cells often show changed molecular configurations on their surfaces, they also appear foreign and are subject to attack by T cells. For this reason T cells provide a measure of protection against repeated infections by viruses and other infectious agents that are present within the host's own cells. Fortunately some T cells, termed memory T cells, have an astonishingly long life. One attack of measles, for example, provides a person with permanent immunity.

On the other hand, if the effector T cell encounters its corresponding antigen in soluble form, for example, in solution in the blood, the T cell may be stimulated to release soluble products called lymphokines. These lymphokines, in their turn, are capable of activating other lymphocytes as well as macrophages and many other kinds of cells. They are responsible for many of the observable signs of inflammation (*e.g.*, fever, swelling, and redness), which is the body's general response to foreign invaders. In fact, the presence of T-cell immunity in an individual is usually demonstrated by means of an inflammatory skin reaction which follows the injection of a suspected antigen into the skin. The slowly evolving inflammation that ensues is called delayed hypersensitivity. An example of an inflammatory skin reaction is the well-known tuberculin test, in which a small amount of protein derived from the tubercle bacillus is injected into the skin. Inflammation at the injection site two or three days later shows that the person has had previous contact with

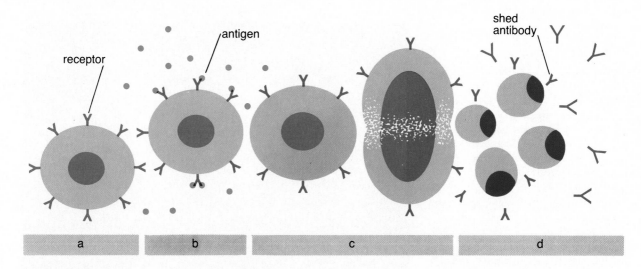

receptor · antigen · shed antibody

a b c d

the bacterium and has become sensitized to it. That person's immune system has been alerted to this organism at some earlier point in life and is ready for defense upon renewed encounters.

B cells

The second major population of lymphocytes develops even in infants whose thymus is defective and does not produce T cells. These lymphocytes derive directly from the pluripotential stem cell located in the bone marrow and are called B cells. Like the T cell, the B cell ensues from an orderly process of differentiation from a precursor lymphocyte. Although it resembles a T cell, it exhibits different functional properties. It is, for example, a major constituent of the lymphocyte population of the organized lymphoid tissues but is sparsely present (about 10 to 20%) in the lymphocytes circulating in the bloodstream, and it occurs in an even smaller proportion in the lymph fluid.

Like the T cell, the B cell develops a recognition structure on its surface. Although scientists have only begun to learn about the structure of the T-cell receptor, a great deal of information has already been obtained about the structure of the receptor on the B cell. Essentially it is an antibody molecule. It begins its career inserted into the membrane of a mature B cell. Like the T-cell receptor, it is specifically tailored to fit a particular antigenic determinant. When the B cell encounters its complementary antigenic determinant, it also enlarges and generates a clone of B cells bearing the same receptor. This clone of B cells continues differentiating until the cells become plasma cells. The latter cells produce the surface receptor in large amounts and secrete it into the body fluids. It is this secreted B-cell receptor that is present in the bloodstream as circulating antibody.

The production of antibodies by B cells is regulated by specialized populations of T cells. One type of T cell assists in the development of B cells into plasma cells; they are termed helper T cells. Another population of T cells, called suppressor T cells, inhibits B-cell differentiation into plasma cells. The balance between helper T cells and suppressor T

Antibody molecules begin their career as receptors inserted into the membrane of a mature B cell (a). All of the receptors on a given B cell are tailored to fit and bind to one particular antigenic determinant, part of a molecule of a foreign substance. When the B cell encounters that determinant (b), it enlarges and generates a clone of B cells all carrying the same receptor (c). Upon further differentiation the B cells become plasma cells, which produce the receptor in quantity and secrete it into the body fluids as circulating antibody (d).

Various degrees of B-cell immunity may develop in people whose thymus is defective and fails to produce T cells. There are also people who completely lack both T-cell and B-cell immunity, as in the much publicized case of David (facing page, bottom), the "bubble boy" who lived in a sterile environment from moments after birth to two weeks before his death at age 12. Although the cause of such severe combined immunodeficiency is not known, the success of bone-marrow transplants in curing some cases supports the view that the basic defect lies in the stem cell. In David's case marrow transplanted from his sister failed to take.

71

Graphic image by Richard J. Feldmann, Division of Computer Research & Technology, NIH, Bethesda, Md., based on structural determination by David R. Davies and co-workers, NIADDKD

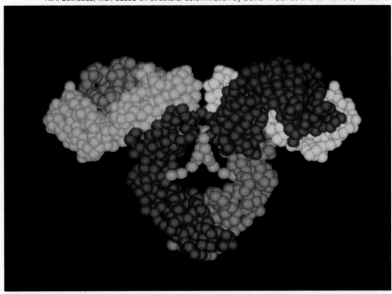

Structurally an antibody molecule comprises four protein chains—two identical light chains and two identical heavy chains—folded and bound together by disulfide bonds into a Y-shaped configuration (below). The variable region, which differs from one antibody to the next, recognizes and binds to a specific antigenic determinant. This interaction causes changes in the constant region, which depending on its makeup then carries out some immunologic task. In the computer-generated model of an IgG antibody molecule (right), spheres represent amino acid subunits. Red and blue designate heavy chains, green and yellow are light chains, and gray shows carbohydrate side chains.

heavy chain
light chain
variable region
constant region
disulfide bond

cells determines the quantity of antibodies produced by the B cells. To be able to assist the B cells in the production of antibodies and to regulate the amount of antibodies produced, the T cell must react either with the same antigenic determinant as the B cell or with another antigenic determinant borne on the same molecule.

Antibody structure

According to one system for classifying proteins, antibodies are members of a group called globulins, and since they are part of the immunologic system, they are known as immunoglobulins. Because of their special structure they are extraordinarily fit to carry out their immunological task. Like other proteins, antibody molecules are formed from molecular building blocks called amino acids linked together in a chainlike fashion. Each antibody molecule is made up of four such chains, two identical light chains and two identical heavy chains, all bound together and folded into a configuration resembling the letter Y. The light chains each comprise about 220 amino acid units, and the heavy chains about 440 units.

The most important part of the antibody molecule is its combining site, which is responsible for combining with the antigenic determinant. The amino acid sequences of a combining site on one molecule differ greatly from those of the combining site on another molecule. This portion of the antibody molecule, therefore, is called the variable region in order to distinguish it from the more constant portions. Each combining site forms a slightly different cavity or cleft, which fits closely around its respective antigenic determinant. It is precisely this close fit of the combining site on the antibody molecule with the antigenic determinant on the antigen that permits such selective interaction. This selectivity is what makes antibodies truly nature's "magic bullets" in the sense meant by the great medical scientist Paul Ehrlich, who envisioned molecular weapons that could seek out their specific targets, the microscopic causes of disease.

The antibody combining site consists of the variable end portions of both a heavy and a light chain. There are generally two such sites on each antibody molecule, one on each upward arm of the Y. Since these sites are identical, the antibody is termed monogamous and is able to bind two identical antigenic determinants. If an antibody in solution in blood or tissue fluids encounters molecules that carry its corresponding antigenic determinant, it can selectively aggregate these molecules, causing them to form an insoluble precipitate. The extraordinary feature of this precipitate is that it depends on the presence of a particular antigenic determinant on each of the precipitated molecules. In the same manner an antibody can cause the clumping of particles, such as bacteria, if they all bear the requisite antigenic determinant. Because of their ability to produce such effects, antibodies are widely used as highly selective reagents for diagnostic tests in medical and research laboratories. For example, an antibody that recognizes an antigenic determinant carried by a certain disease-producing virus is able to detect and eliminate that pathogen in cells or secretions of infected patients. It is also possible to use properly prepared antibodies to analyze important components of the blood such as hormones or enzymes.

Antibodies also provide protection against a number of infectious diseases. Some of these diseases are caused mainly by toxins, or poisons, secreted by particular bacteria. These toxin molecules are antigens because they elicit the production of antibodies, which combine with the toxins and neutralize their activity. Such antibodies, referred to as antitoxins, confer substantial immunity against diseases like tetanus or diphtheria. Other diseases are caused by tissue-invading organisms. In such cases the whole organism, not its soluble product, acts as the antigen and elicits antibody production. The antibodies will then combine with antigenic determinants on the surface of the invading organism itself.

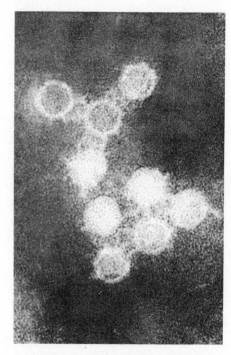

Microscopic cluster of hepatitis A virus particles (above) has been aggregated by a specific antibody. The ability of antibodies to selectively clump molecules and particles makes them valuable for analyzing chemical constituents of the body and identifying disease organisms. Antibodies elicited in the body by invading organisms can combine with antigenic determinants on the surfaces of the invaders, making them more easily recognized and engulfed by phagocytic cells. A macrophage from a mouse (left) binds and ingests "invading" sheep red blood cells that have become coated with IgG antibodies.

(Left) Work of Reiko Takemura and Zena Werb, University of California, San Francisco; (right) courtesy, Abbott Laboratories Electron Microscopy

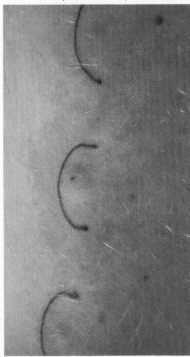

When a foreign substance injected under the skin during an allergy test evokes an immediate localized swelling, it is a sign that the person is allergic to that particular antigen. Allergic reactions are undesirable immunologic responses to environmental substances that usually are not intrinsically harmful. Antibodies generally play an important role in allergic reactions, and other components of the immunologic system such as basophils, neutrophils, and T cells may also be involved.

(Facing page) Schematic diagram summarizes details of the genetic mechanism, described in text on pp. 76–77, by which the maturing B cell becomes committed to producing a particular antibody molecule from among the millions of different kinds that must be available to confront every conceivable foreign substance. Generation of the heavy chain differs from that of the light chain in the involvement of an additional set of gene choices called diversity (D) genes.

Organisms coated with antibodies are more readily recognized, engulfed, and digested by phagocytic cells such as neutrophils.

Although antibodies combine with antigen at the variable ends of the molecule, this interaction also causes changes in the opposite end of the antibody molecule—the leg of the Y—that is, the part more constant in its amino acid sequence. The changes in the constant region activate a cascade of normally inactive enzymes that are present in the blood. These enzymes, referred to collectively as complement, have the ability to break down or dissolve certain kinds of invading microorganisms.

Depending upon the makeup of their constant regions antibodies have different biological functions. Antibodies of the IgM class, for example, are most active in triggering the activation of complement. IgG antibodies, which can activate the complement cascade as well, are able to cross the placenta from the mother to the developing fetus and are responsible for protecting against infection during the critical first months after birth when the newborn is not yet able to produce his or her own antibodies. Antibodies of the IgA class are present in colostrum and breast milk and offer additional protection to nursing infants; their primary stations are in tears, saliva, nasal mucus, and bronchial, gastrointestinal, and vaginal secretions where they defend the body against the numerous harmful bacteria that may invade these locations. Unlike other antibodies, members of a class called IgD antibodies do not circulate in the blood in large amounts but remain attached to the B-cell surface. Their function is still unknown, although some investigators suspect that they play a role in antibody production by the B cell.

Finally, a class called IgE antibodies has an unfortunate affinity for host cells, in particular the basophils and their related counterparts in tissue, the mast cells. IgE antibodies fix avidly to receptors on the surfaces of basophils and mast cells by means of their constant region sites. If the appropriate antigenic determinant subsequently encounters such antibody-coated cells, it stimulates the discharge of granules and the release of their contents—chemical mediators of the allergic reaction, including histamines. Allergy in a patient can sometimes be detected or predicted by injecting a small amount of the suspected antigen into the skin. If an immediate localized inflammation—called an immediate hypersensitivity reaction—occurs at the injected site, it is a sign that the patient is allergic to that specific antigen.

Generating antibody diversity

One of the striking characteristics of the immunologic system is its seemingly limitless capacity to respond to any foreign antigen. Upon entering the body an antigen will practically always find a lymphocyte with a complementary receptor on its surface. This statement holds true whether the antigen is among those occurring in nature or a novel molecule synthesized for the first time in the chemist's laboratory.

A great diversity of antibodies, something on the order of ten million, is required to enable the immunologic system to have a recognition structure on hand to confront any foreign antigen. To have a separate

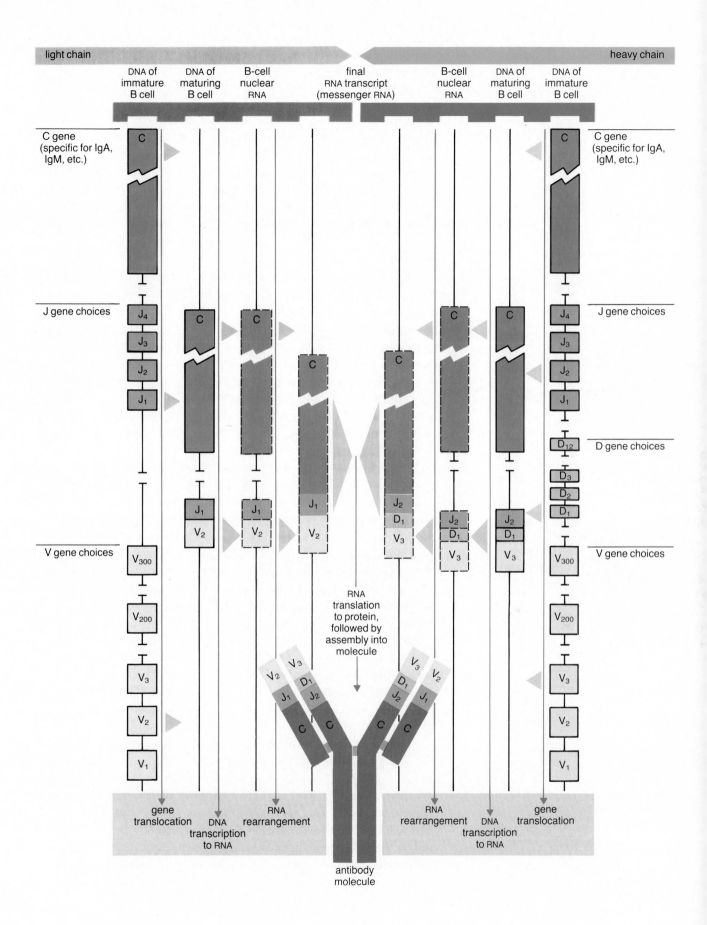

sequence of DNA, or gene, available to direct the synthesis of each of these ten million proteins would be wasteful on the part of nature, since the greater part of the antibody molecule is similar from one antibody to the next. Since the mid-1970s a great deal of painstaking research in several countries has gone into discovering the special genetic system of the lymphocyte that determines the sequence of the amino acids of which a particular antibody molecule is composed. This system involves at least two families of genes borne on two different chromosomes. One family carries the genetic code for making the heavy chains, while the other family carries the code for the light chains. Each family includes a few DNA stretches that code for the constant regions of the antibody molecule. These so-called C genes determine the biological class to which the antibody belongs; for example, whether it is in the IgG class of antibodies circulating in the bloodstream, in the IgA class present in secretions, or in the IgE class involved in allergic reactions. A much larger panel of genes, called V genes, codes for the variable portions of the amino acid chains. (See diagram on p. 75.)

It is now known that when an immature B cell commits itself to produce a particular antibody, it selects one from the few hundred V genes in its repertory. That stretch of DNA codes for the terminal— approximately 100—amino acids in the chain. The same gene is then somehow moved, or translocated, on the chromosome so that it resides next to one of a group of perhaps four genes, called J genes, that code for a short joining sequence of ten amino acids. Together these 110 amino acids make up the variable region of the antibody light chain. In the case of the heavy chain there is an additional short intermediate amino acid sequence, which is determined by one of a small group of 12 or more diversity, or D, genes. All of these genes are transcribed as a unit into RNA, the molecular form by which the genetic code is actually carried to the protein-synthesis machinery of the cell. Then they are joined with RNA transcribed from the C gene that codes for the constant portion of the antibody molecule. This final structure is the RNA transcript that will be used to direct the construction of the amino acid chain. In the light chain the constant portion consists of about 100 amino acid units, whereas in the heavy chain it consists of about 300. Finally the light chains and heavy chains are folded into their final configurations and connected by means of disulfide bridges (sulfur-to-sulfur bonds) to form the functional antibody molecule. A parallel genetic process probably takes place in the development of T-cell receptors, although the exact details are not yet known.

From the genetic point of view these novel mechanisms to bring about a reassortment of genes provide an economical way to generate the required number of different recognition structures on the T and B cells. With only about 200–300 V genes and 4 J genes available for the variable region of the light chain, about 1,000 different combinations are possible. The additional D genes involved in the synthesis of the heavy chain raise the number of different amino acid sequences to about 10,000. Since the combining site of the antibody molecule consists of the variable portions of the light chain and of the heavy chain, 10,000,000 (1,000 x 10,000) different specificities are possible based on these recombinations of genes alone. Moreover, there is some variation in the junctions of the V-D-J genes from one immature B cell to another. Finally, somatic mutation—random mutations of the genes during an individual's lifetime—adds to genetic diversity. An individual then can produce more than 100,000,000 different antibodies. The great degree of lymphocyte diversity is attributable to the many possibilities of gene reassortment.

Monoclonal antibodies

A naturally occurring antigen usually carries a large number of different antigenic determinants on its surface. Each of these antigenic determinants elicits a unique population of antibodies in the host. In fact, several different types of antibodies can be stimulated by the same antigenic determinant, each of which views the determinant in a slightly different manner. Hence, even a single foreign antigen can elicit an extremely diverse population of antibodies. For most purposes this diversity is of great advantage to the host. For example, it increases the ability of antibodies to coat invading bacteria in order to make them more palatable to phagocytes, since so many different antibody molecules are available to combine with a single organism. Similarly, when antibodies aggregate foreign molecules, the resulting precipitate is firmer if the molecules are linked by means of several different antigenic determinants.

This diversity of antibodies may be disadvantageous, however, if one wishes to use antibodies as analytical tools. If, for example, the goal is to develop a laboratory test to detect and measure the amount of growth hormone in the blood, it is essential that every antibody molecule recognize only growth hormone. Similarly, antibodies that might be used to detect the presence of rabies virus in the brains of infected animals would be more reliable if one were certain that every antibody molecule recognizes determinants that are unique for the rabies virus.

The only way to ensure that every antibody in a population is identical with every other antibody molecule is to derive all of the molecules from a single lymphocyte. As discussed above, when stimulated by its corresponding antigenic determinant, the B lymphocyte proliferates and produces a clone that, in turn, secretes its recognition structures as antibody molecules. This collection of antibody molecules, each identical with the other, can be referred to as monoclonal (i.e., coming from one clone), in contrast to the usual polyclonal mixtures of antibodies. A monoclonal antibody, then, comes from the descendants of a single lymphocyte ancestor.

Normally, after a B cell develops into a plasma cell, it can secrete antibody only for a limited period of time, perhaps a few weeks, before it dies. Some B cells, however, are considered immortal. These are cells that have undergone malignant, or cancerous, transformation. Such cells not only grow and divide uncontrollably in their original host but can be cultured indefinitely in the test tube. Sometimes such malignant B cells retain all of the machinery for secreting antibody molecules.

(Left) Courtesy, Abbott Laboratories; (right) Schering-Plough

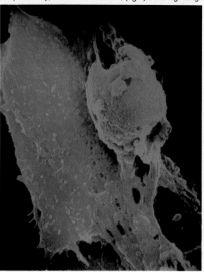

A standard laboratory method for producing monoclonal antibodies begins with the immunization of a mouse with the foreign substance against which the antibody is to be targeted (a). A few days later the animal's lymphocyte-rich spleen is removed and its population of B cells extracted; among these B cells are a few producing the desired antibody. Next, a compound called polyethylene glycol is used to fuse the spleen cells with cancer cells taken from a mouse B-cell tumor, or myeloma (b). The hybrid cells that result are grown in a special culture medium to form cell colonies called hybridomas (c). To single out those hybridoma cells that are secreting the desired antibody, the hybridomas are put through a multistage testing and reculturing process (d). The cells so selected are then propagated to produce clones of cells all making the same identical antibody molecule (e). Finally the cloned cells are either mass cultured to yield the antibody in useful amounts or injected into mice where they grow into tumors that secrete the antibody in high concentration (f).

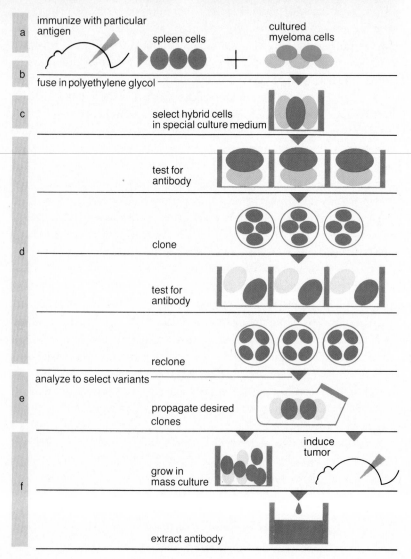

a immunize with particular antigen
spleen cells
cultured myeloma cells
+

b fuse in polyethylene glycol

c select hybrid cells in special culture medium

test for antibody

clone

d test for antibody

reclone

analyze to select variants

e propagate desired clones

induce tumor

f grow in mass culture

extract antibody

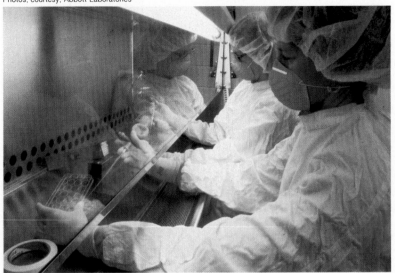

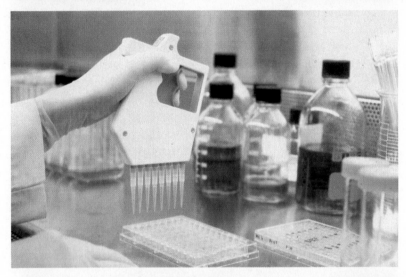

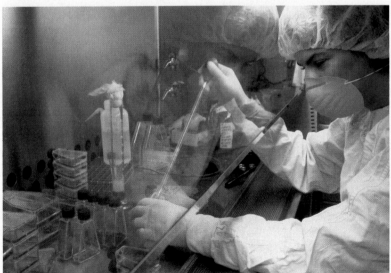

Laboratory technician (facing page, top left) counts mouse-spleen B cells prior to their hybridization with cancer cells, during an early stage of monoclonal antibody production. Color-enhanced scanning electron micrograph (facing page, top right) vividly captures the event of cell fusion central to hybridoma technology. (This page, top) Hybridoma cells maintained in the bottoms of small wells in a plastic tray are fed to encourage selective growth. Trays of hybridomas are screened for antibody production (center). Hybridoma cells producing identical antibody molecules are readied for large-scale production (bottom).

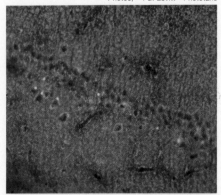

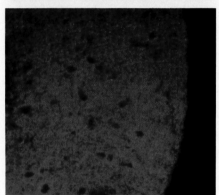

Monoclonal antibodies tagged with fluorescent dyes are becoming valuable tools for visualizing and distinguishing among cells and tissues of the body. Microscopic section of the hippocampus (top), a region of the brain, is delineated by a green-dye-tagged antibody that binds to a particular molecule on the surface of nerve cells. Individual nerve cells stand out as dark round or elongated silhouettes edged with green borders. (Above) An antibody tagged with a red dye differentiates a part of the cerebellum called the molecular layer from adjacent regions, to which the antibody does not bind. (Right) Two subpopulations of T cells, helper T cells (yellow) and suppressor T cells (green), are easily told apart with the aid of two kinds of monoclonal antibodies tagged with dyes of different colors. Knowledge of the relative sizes of lymphocyte populations in an individual can help determine how well the immunologic system is functioning.

In 1975 Georges Köhler and César Milstein at the Medical Research Council's molecular biology laboratories in Great Britain developed a method for fusing a B cell that is committed to producing a specific antibody with an immortal cell from a B-cell tumor, or myeloma. This fused cell, or hybrid, contains the genetic instructions to produce a particular antibody molecule as well as the machinery for indefinite proliferation and antibody secretion. In culture the hybrid cells grow into a small colony, or hybridoma, which continues to secrete antibodies indefinitely, each antibody being identical with the other. Furthermore, the hybridoma cells retain the malignant properties of their myeloma forebear, producing tumors when injected into mice. The blood serum and other body fluids of such tumor-bearing mice contain large amounts of the designated antibody. Thus, monoclonal antibodies can be extracted in quantity either from mass cultures of hybridomas or in even higher concentration from laboratory animals carrying induced tumors.

Equipped with the ability to recognize single antigenic determinants, monoclonal antibodies have already proved to be of enormous value in many areas of biology and medicine. For example, they are vastly superior to the usual immune sera used to detect and identify infectious microorganisms or as biochemical tools for analyzing constituents of the blood. Monoclonal antibody probes have been used to identify the surface proteins that are responsible for the particular behavior of different populations of cells and to sort out the soluble molecules that cells use in interacting with one another. They are even able to recognize the different subpopulations of T lymphocytes by distinguishing among different molecules on their surfaces.

In victims of lymphomas or leukemias, monoclonal antibodies are able to recognize whether the cancer originated from malignant changes in T cells or in B cells, thus providing information for better diagnosis and treatment. They are also able to distinguish the minute differences between cancerous and normal tissue cells. Monoclonal antibodies prepared

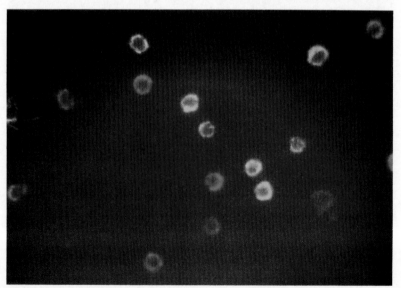

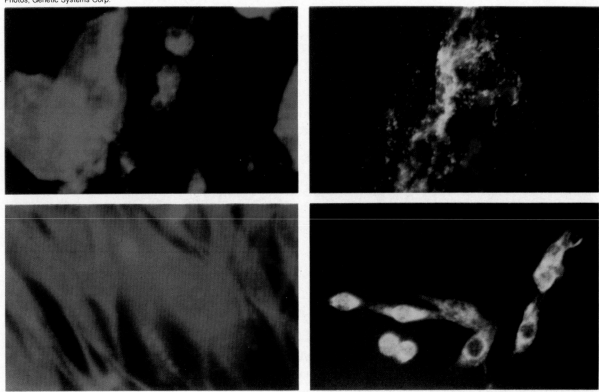

against certain cell-surface antigens have proved useful in detecting the presence of certain types of tumor cells in the body or in monitoring the growth of tumors. Soon it may be possible to attach radioactive isotopes, toxic drugs, or enzymes to tumor-directed monoclonal antibodies in order to carry death-dealing compounds to malignancies. These would be natural "magic bullets" armed with man-made warheads. Similarly, monoclonal antibodies may one day be targeted against elements of the body's own immune system to combat autoimmune diseases and other immunologic disorders or to suppress the immunologic rejection of organ transplants.

Because they are capable of extracting particular molecules in extraordinarily pure form from complex mixtures, monoclonal antibodies have even found applications in industrial processes, especially pharmaceutical manufacture. In a process called affinity purification, for example, an impure mixture containing the desired substance (perhaps a hormone extracted from genetically engineered bacteria or a viral antigen intended for vaccine production) is passed through a tube containing large numbers of an appropriate antibody molecule fixed to a solid support. The target molecules bind to their antibodies while the remainder of the material flows through. A chemical process then releases the target substance from the tube for collection in essentially pure form.

So many exciting prospects have already emerged from monoclonal antibody technology, a discovery barely a decade old, yet its vast future potential has only been glimpsed.

The ability of monoclonal antibodies to detect and identify infectious organisms is shown in the photomicrographs above. Cervical smear from a patient known to be infected with the organism Chlamydia trachomatis *(top right) fluoresces yellow-green after treatment with a dye-tagged antibody that binds to a membrane protein of the organism. By contrast, a smear taken from a patient free of chlamydia infection and treated with the same antibody (top left) shows no sign of binding, indicating that the organism is absent. Similarly, cells infected with herpes simplex virus type 1 (HSV 1) fluoresce when exposed to a tagged antibody specific for a molecule of the HSV 1 coat (bottom right). When the same antibody is used on cells infected with a related herpesvirus (HSV 2), no binding can be seen (bottom left).*

THE INCREDIBLE SHRINKING CHIP

MINIATURIZATION IN ELECTRONICS

by Dennis W. Hess

Scientists and engineers have steadily reduced the sizes and increased the operating speeds of electronic devices. Further miniaturization poses a formidable challenge.

Microelectronic devices and integrated circuits have contributed immensely to shaping the way in which we live. Applications of these circuits include consumer items such as handheld calculators, personal computers, digital watches, microwave ovens, and information processing units that have been used for communication, defense, space exploration, medicine, and education. The rapid development, miniaturization, and extensive use of solid-state circuits during the past 30 years has led to the term "microelectronics revolution."

The basis of this revolution is the ability to manufacture millions of electronic components or elements simultaneously. Thus, unlike the pre-1960 era, when elements such as transistors were made one at a time, hundreds of complete circuits utilizing these components can now be manufactured on a thin disk of silicon or, occasionally, of another semiconductor material. Silicon disks, or substrates, are 100 to 125 millimeters (4 to 5 inches) in diameter and 0.7 millimeter (0.028 inch) thick. At present individual circuits or "chips" range from a few millimeters to tens of millimeters on a side and may contain more than 200,000 components. This phenomenal progress has occurred because the size of solid-state elements has decreased steadily each year since 1960. Such miniaturization has permitted the design and production of integrated circuits with ever-increasing complexity and capability.

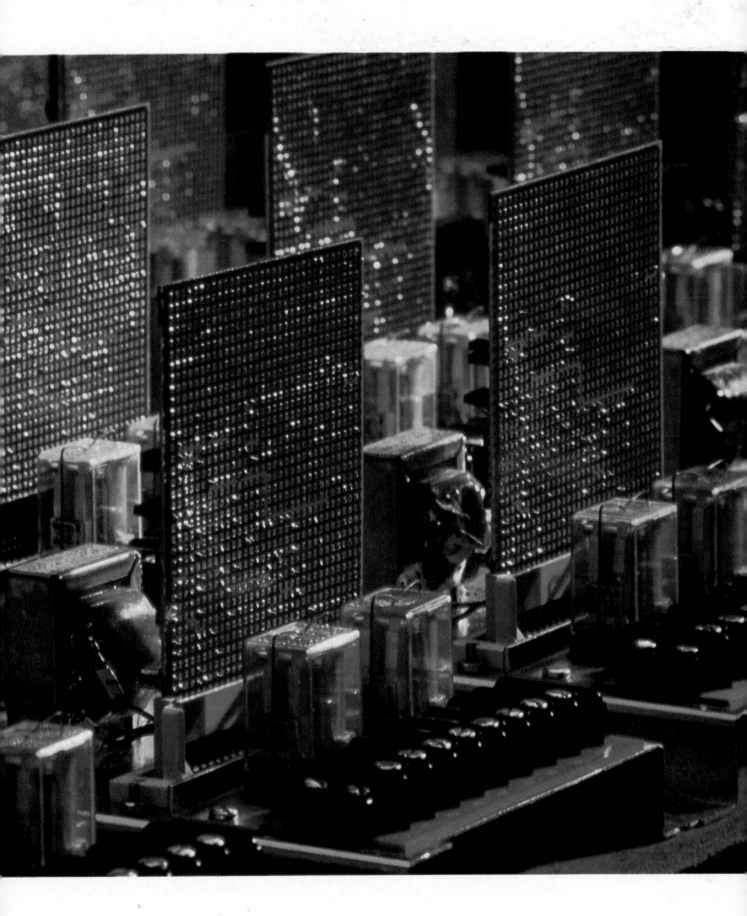

Burt Glinn—Magnum

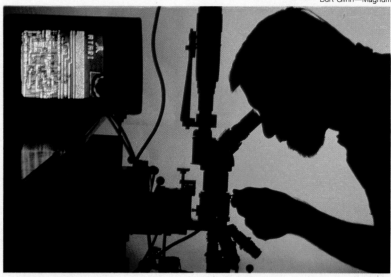

An inspector uses a computer display terminal to check a microchip for design accuracy.

(Overleaf) A circuit board for the IBM *3033 computer, when magnified greatly, resembles a city of the future.*

DENNIS W. HESS is Professor of Chemical Engineering at the University of California at Berkeley.

(Overleaf) Photograph by Erich Hartmann—Magnum

Why miniaturize?

Microelectronic devices are built of consecutive layers of insulating, semiconducting, and metallic thin films. Film thicknesses usually range from 10^{-7} (0.0000001) centimeter to 2×10^{-4} (0.0002) centimeter. For comparison, the diameter of a human hair is approximately 10^{-2} (0.01) centimeter, and that of the smallest bacteria is approximately 10^{-5} (0.00001) centimeter. Each film layer has a pattern or stencil formed in it, such that when these layers are properly aligned or registered one to another, electronic components result. Additional patterned films then connect many elements to form a circuit. This process is analogous to the wiring or connecting of individual components on a printed circuit board, except that the dimensions are much smaller.

Decreases in pattern sizes have in large part been responsible for the remarkable advances in these solid-state circuits. In 1960 the smallest pattern dimension on a circuit was approximately 3×10^{-3} (0.003) centimeter. Currently, elements with feature sizes of approximately 2×10^{-4} centimeter are routinely incorporated into microelectronic devices. When the size of each circuit component is decreased, the overall circuit dimension also drops, and more circuits can be contained in one silicon disk or wafer. Therefore, if the cost of producing a silicon disk or wafer remains the same, the price per circuit declines.

These factors allow the manufacture of circuits that have increasing numbers of components, and therefore are of greater complexity and capability. Indeed, such advances are responsible for the development of entire information processing units, or microprocessors, on small "chips" of silicon. The combination of decreased price and increased capability that has resulted from miniaturization has opened up a broad range of applications for solid-state circuits. In addition, because electrons travel shorter distances in smaller devices, circuit performance has increased, thus making possible increased computational capability and speed at reduced prices.

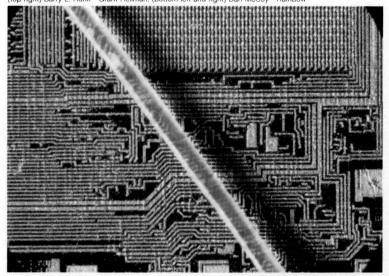

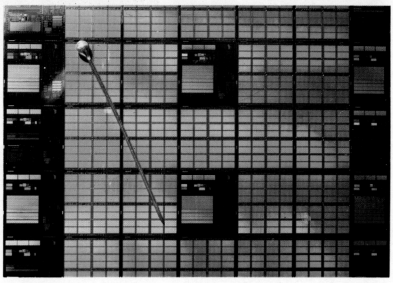

Semiconductors

To understand manufacturing processes for integrated circuits, it is necessary to have some knowledge of semiconductors, in particular, silicon. An insulator such as glass does not conduct electric current because all electrons present are tightly bound to individual ions or atoms. Therefore, the application of an electric field produces no charge carrier movement; *i.e.*, the electrons in the glass are not free to move within it and thus cannot carry an electrical charge through it. In an electrical conductor such as a metal, however, electrons are free to move throughout the solid, and electronic conduction occurs readily. Between these two extremes lie semiconductors, whose electrical conductivity can be systematically varied. This variation is accomplished by a process called doping, the controlled addition of specific impurity atoms to the pure silicon crystal. Thus, the conductivity of silicon is increased by substituting an atom with five valence electrons (phosphorus or arsenic) for some of the silicon

Top left, a human hair lies across part of a silicon-chip microcircuit; the picture is magnified 22 times. Top right, at a magnification of three, a microchip removed from the silicon wafer is held in tweezers. At the bottom left is a chip with a memory of 512 K (kilobits); the same chips in their silicon wafer are at the bottom right.

85

atoms, which, having four valence electrons, are tetravalent (figure 1). Because only four of the valence electrons of the phosphorus or arsenic atom are needed to bond to the four surrounding silicon atoms at a specific position in the solid matrix, one electron from each phosphorus or arsenic atom is free to conduct current. This material is called an n-type semiconductor, because conduction takes place primarily via negative charge carriers (electrons).

Silicon can also be doped with the trivalent boron atom (figure 1). In this case only three electrons are available to bond to four adjacent silicon atoms, thereby generating an electron "hole." Although a hole is simply an electron vacancy, it can be considered a charge carrier because it moves by virtue of an electron from a nearby atom jumping into the vacancy. In this way holes can diffuse throughout the crystalline lattice. Such semiconductors are called p-type because the dominant charge carrier (hole) has a positive charge. Although the principal charge carriers are holes, electrons are present in the p-type semiconductor, although at low concentrations, and contribute to the total conductivity.

Process technology

A multitude of individual steps is needed to produce an integrated circuit. Each one requires precise control and careful sequencing if the fabrication is to result in a properly functioning device. Even though the specific processes vary from one device to another, the overall steps are essentially the same. Every manufacturing operation draws heavily on the fundamental principles of materials science, chemistry, and chemical engineering. The design and testing of the devices fall within the domain of electrical engineering.

Although integrated circuits are made up of various combinations of resistors, transistors, capacitors, and diodes, the general configuration and operation of solid-state circuits can be appreciated by a consideration of just one of those elements, the transistor. An n-channel metal-oxide-

Figure 1. In a p-type semiconductor (below left) the silicon (Si) crystalline lattice is doped by adding a boron (B) atom. The boron atom has only three valence electrons to bind to the four electrons of an adjacent silicon atom, and so an electron "hole" is created at the fourth binding site. This electron vacancy can be considered a charge carrier because it moves by virtue of an electron from a nearby silicon atom jumping into it; in this way holes can diffuse throughout the lattice. The name p-type is given because the carrier (hole) has a positive charge. In the n-type semiconductor (below right) a phosphorus (P) atom with five valence electrons is added to the silicon lattice, and in this case the negatively charged extra electron is free to conduct current.

figure 1

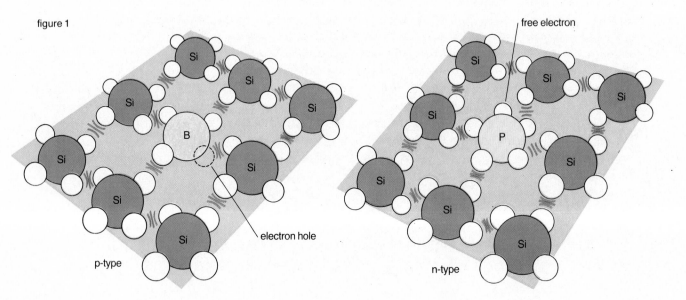

A technician inserts an ingot of silicon into a slicer, which will cut it into the wafers on which chips will be made.

semiconductor (MOS) transistor (figure 2) contains two n-type regions that are heavily doped (*i.e.*, have more than 10^{18} dopant atoms per cubic centimeter) and diffused into a p-type silicon substrate. Above this substrate and between the n-regions is a thin layer of silicon dioxide (typically 0.000003 to 0.00003 centimeter); and atop this insulator is an aluminum film. The term metal oxide semiconductor associated with such transistor configurations originated from this sandwich structure.

In brief, the n-channel MOS transistor operates in the following manner. A negative voltage is applied to one of the heavily doped n-regions and a positive voltage to the other. Electrical conduction between these regions can only occur if the surface of the p-type silicon becomes n-type, that is, if it accumulates electrons. This is accomplished by applying a positive voltage to the metal electrode on the silicon-dioxide film. The resulting electric field repels holes from and attracts electrons to the channel region. The applied voltage necessary to initiate conduction between the n-regions is called the threshold voltage, or "turn-on" voltage, which is one of the most important properties of the transistor. Specific electrical parameters of the MOS transistor, as well as other solid-state electronic devices, are determined by the applied voltages, the doping levels, and the physical dimensions of the device.

A relatively simple sequence for the construction of an n-channel MOS transistor can be envisioned that will illustrate the current status and limitations of miniaturization in electronic circuit manufacture. In figure 3 a clean p-type silicon wafer (a) is oxidized by exposing it to oxygen or water vapor at temperatures above 700° C (1300° F). This results in an amorphous layer of silicon dioxide (b) that serves as a mask against the introduction of dopants, because the usual dopants (boron, phosphorus, and arsenic in this kind of application) tend to diffuse much less rapidly in silicon dioxide than in silicon. In order to create the desired electronic

Figure 2. An n-channel metal oxide semiconductor is a sandwich structure consisting of a layer of aluminum film, a thin layer of silicon dioxide, and a p-type silicon substrate. Diffused into the substrate are two heavily doped n-type regions.

figure 2

n-channel MOS transistor

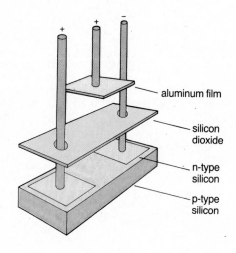

aluminum film

silicon dioxide

n-type silicon

p-type silicon

87

characteristics it is necessary to dope the p-type silicon selectively. This is accomplished by creating openings at desired points in the film of silicon dioxide by a lithographic procedure that is a sophisticated version of the process used in the graphic arts.

In this lithographic process the disk is coated with a radiation-sensitive film (often a polymer) called a resist (c). It is selectively exposed to ultraviolet light through a patterned chromium-on-glass mask on or in close proximity to the wafer (d). The light causes chemical changes in the resist so that exposed regions of it become soluble (for a positive resist material) and are dissolved away (e). What resist film remains serves as a protective layer so that the film beneath it (in this case silicon dioxide) can be etched or removed only where the resist has been removed. Now the wafer can be placed in a liquid bath, wherein the pattern in the resist layer will be etched into the underlying film (f). (With silicon dioxide a liquid mixture containing hydrofluoric acid may be used.) After rinsing away acid residues in high-purity de-ionized water, the remaining resist material is stripped away, leaving the patterned film (g).

The areas of the silicon exposed by the etching process are now doped to convert the p-type silicon in those regions to n-type (h). This can be

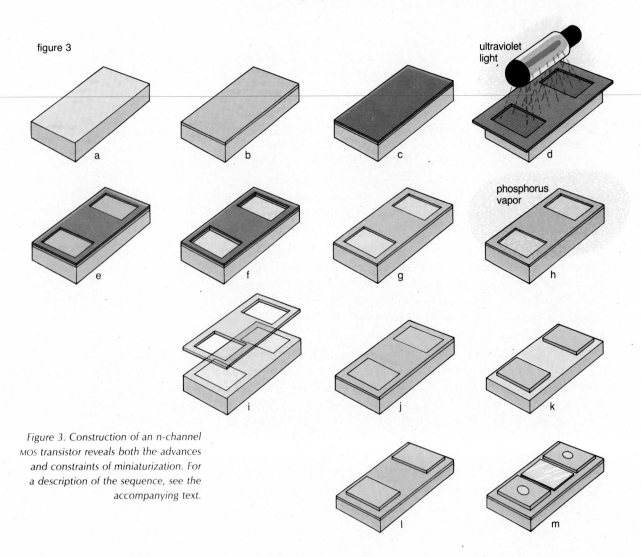

figure 3

ultraviolet light

phosphorus vapor

Figure 3. Construction of an n-channel MOS transistor reveals both the advances and constraints of miniaturization. For a description of the sequence, see the accompanying text.

Photos, Milton & Joan Mann

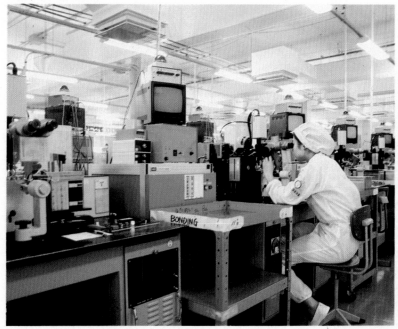

The manufacturing of integrated circuits has become an important industry in Japan. Two stages in the production process include bonding of wires onto the chip (left) and the doping of silicon substrates (right).

accomplished by bringing a vapor containing phosphorus or arsenic into contact with the silicon at temperatures above 900° C (1,650° F). Where the silicon dioxide remains, it prevents doping of the silicon beneath it. After doping the film is removed (i). A layer of silicon dioxide is formed over the n-type silicon regions by thermally oxidizing the entire silicon surface to form a fairly thick oxide (j). An opening is etched down to the p-type silicon using the lithography/etching process described above (k). Another oxidation cycle then grows a thin silicon dioxide film on the p-type region (l), and windows are etched over the n-type silicon areas in preparation for depositing the metal layer (m).

A thin conductor film, often aluminum, is deposited on the wafer surface. Subsequent patterning isolates the interconnections that this layer provides between the various circuit elements (transistors, resistors, etc.) created within the chip. At this point the transistor and, on a larger scale, the circuit, are electrically complete. Another layer of silicon dioxide is often deposited over the finished disk as an electrical and mechanical protective coating. Then a final lithographic/etching procedure opens windows in the protection coating so that leads from a package can be connected to the metallization pattern.

Limitations to miniaturization

Based on the developments of the last 30 years, the road to further miniaturization and, therefore, to more complex and cheaper electronic devices is clear: the widths of the patterns, or lines, should be reduced to still smaller dimensions. Unfortunately, as pattern sizes get smaller and smaller, approaching sizes of a micrometer (10^{-4} centimeter) or less, material and physical shortcomings become more severe, and new limitations arise.

In a yellow room, in which no ultraviolet light is allowed, workers inspect new microchips for defects. In such clean rooms it is possible to achieve air so clean that a cubic foot has fewer than 50 dust particles, none larger than 0.4 micrometers.

As described earlier, a chromium-on-glass mask plate is used to selectively expose light-sensitive resist materials to ultraviolet light. Pattern dimensions in the micrometer range are as small as dust particles, and a speck of dust on the mask or on the wafer surface interferes with light transmission, resulting in improper exposure and therefore in film imperfections. Thus, the room atmosphere and the chemicals used in circuit fabrication must be virtually free of such particles. In clean rooms it is possible to achieve, routinely, air with fewer than 50 particles per cubic foot that are smaller than 0.4 micrometers, albeit at considerable expense. However, it is difficult to attain similar cleanliness in the gases and liquids used in the process. In general, this difficulty is not inherent in the chemical manufacturing process but rather arises from the containers in which chemicals are stored and shipped. Another particulate problem results from physical contact between the mask and the wafer. In this case, resist material can be transferred to the mask, thereby creating additional particles and resulting in defects on wafers subsequently processed with that mask.

Because of the severe impact of particles on circuit yield and on miniaturization, efforts to reduce particle levels in processing operations and in source chemicals intensify as pattern sizes decrease. Contact between mask and wafer is being eliminated by the use of projection exposure tools. These systems use mirrors to project the mask pattern onto a wafer. In addition, robots are being considered as "workers" in ultraclean rooms having fewer than ten dust particles per cubic foot. By eliminating contamination-inducing traffic into and out of these clean areas, and by keeping humans, a significant source of particles, out of the clean rooms, still smaller dimensions with increased yields will be possible.

A fundamental limitation to further miniaturization involves the wavelengths of the ultraviolet light used for resist exposure (3.5–4.5×10^{-5} centimeter). When the spaces between the chromium patterns on a mask approach the wavelength of light used, diffraction occurs. Diffraction causes a loss of image fidelity as light passes through the transparent portions of the mask. As a result, the image exposed in the resist is not precisely that on the mask. In order to reduce this problem, light of shorter wavelength (deep ultraviolet) is used, but this procedure encounters another restriction: neither glass nor quartz transmits much light with a wavelength shorter than approximately 2×10^{-5} centimeter.

A more serious limitation to reducing the wavelength of light used for exposure is that of resist sensitivity. The resist materials employed with light waves longer than 3×10^{-5} centimeter are not particularly sensitive to shorter light waves. Long exposure times result in low throughput and ultimately high production costs; to avoid this, new resist materials have been developed. These are often polymer materials, although inorganic resists containing silver have been formulated. Considerable efforts are continuing in this important area of microfabrication. Ultimately, it is believed that large-scale production of pattern sizes of about 5×10^{-5} centimeter will be possible with ultraviolet exposure units.

Technician uses a microscope to put wires on a chip, an operation called bonding.

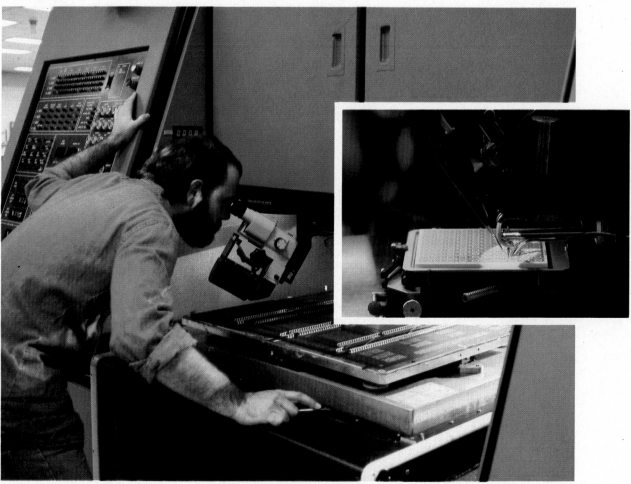

Photos, Erich Hartmann—Magnum

Ion gun trains beams of ions onto silicon chips to create pattern sizes as small as 4×10^{-6} centimeter. Ion beams produce better resolution in pattern definition than do electron beams because ion beams are not scattered as much by the resist and substrate.

A further reduction in feature size can be achieved by the use of X-rays at wavelengths of $5–50 \times 10^{-8}$ centimeter for resist exposure. Although most deep ultraviolet resists are sensitive to X-rays, chromium-on-glass or quartz cannot be used as masks. Since X-rays are absorbed to some extent by many materials, thin films composed of elements with low atomic weights (to minimize X-ray absorption) must be used for the transparent regions of the mask. Also, in order to absorb X-rays sufficiently, the mask pattern must consist of a relatively thick film of a material of high atomic number, such as gold or platinum. Therefore, masks at present are composed of gold patterns (gold is a good X-ray absorber) on a thin polymer film. Naturally, such composites are fragile and more difficult to manufacture than the standard masks. However, if good mask/wafer contact can be attained, pattern sizes in the 3×10^{-6} (0.000003) centimeter range can be achieved. Ultimately, however, X-rays will also suffer from diffraction limitations.

Current X-ray sources are capable of generating only fairly low photon fluxes; *i.e.,* source intensities are low. As a result, high-sensitivity resists must be used if short exposure times are desired. Alternatively, synchrotron radiation can be used as an X-ray source. (When high-energy charged particles that are moving at very high speeds are accelerated to speeds near that of light, they emit synchrotron radiation.) Due to the exorbitant cost of such an approach, routine implementation of synchrotron sources in manufacturing microelectronic devices seems unlikely within the next ten years.

Mask problems are a serious impediment to making features smaller than about one micrometer in width. Therefore, much interest has been generated in radiations that do not require a mask for selective exposure. Electrons, being charged particles, can be focused and scanned by the use of electrostatic and/or magnetic lenses. This approach eliminates the need for a mask, because the position of the electron beam can be controlled by a computer. Furthermore, because electron beams can be

92

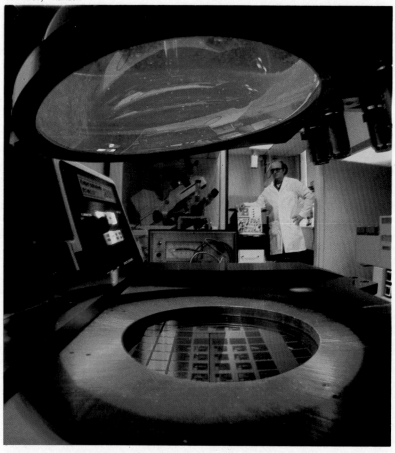

Electron beam processor is used in the production of silicon chips. Masking is not necessary when electrons are used to form patterns in the resist materials, because the position of the electron beam can be controlled precisely by a computer. This technique allows features smaller than one micrometer in width to be made on the chips.

focused to widths of less than 6×10^{-8} centimeter, extremely small pattern sizes, on the order of several atomic diameters, should be possible.

Although the potential exists for production of essentially atomic dimensions, material considerations make realization of such structures difficult at best. High-energy electrons (5–25 kiloelectron-volts) scatter as they pass through resist materials and generate secondary electrons. Also, when the beam of electrons strikes the substrate or film beneath the resist, some electrons are backscattered into the resist. These scattered and secondary electrons expose the resist in areas adjacent to the electron beam, thereby broadening the pattern.

Thus the prospect of using electron beams to form atomic-size patterns in resist materials poses difficulties. Nevertheless, pattern dimensions on the order of 2×10^{-7} centimeter have been reported, although these results are for isolated lines rather than the closely spaced features of various kinds necessary for manufacturing practical devices. In the latter case, 2×10^{-6}-centimeter patterns seem to be near the practical limit. However, an electron beam has been used without a resist to vaporize film material directly and form patterns as small as 1.5×10^{-7} centimeter.

Reduction of the secondary and scattered electrons inherent in electron-beam lithography can be achieved by using ion-beam exposure. Because their mass is higher than that of electrons, ions such as those of

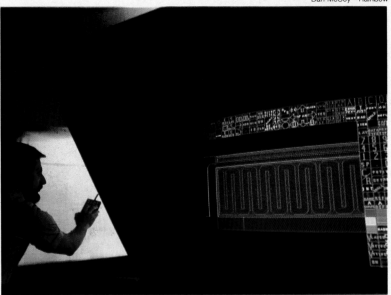

Computers are being used increasingly to aid in the design and production of integrated circuits.

hydrogen, oxygen, and gallium do not scatter significantly in resist materials or from substrates. In addition, resists display greater sensitivity to ions than to electrons. Finally, secondary electrons generated by ion exposure are of lower energy than those originating from electron beams. Therefore, the overall effect of using ion beams is improved resolution in pattern definition.

However, ion-ion interactions in the ion beam limit the size of the beam that can be produced. Nevertheless, pattern sizes of 4×10^{-6} centimeter have been achieved. Furthermore, ion current densities are typically low, thereby slowing production. Since this technique is in a rather embryonic stage, there is hope that improved sources capable of higher currents will be developed. Also, as scientific understanding of ion-beam processes is established, technological advances seem certain to occur.

But exposure of the resist is only half of the battle to generate smaller dimensions for the manufacture of microelectronic devices. The pattern must now be transferred into the underlying film. Because liquid etching agents dissolve the film at equal rates in all directions, the films etch laterally as well as vertically. This causes a loss of pattern size that cannot be tolerated when film thickness and width are roughly equal. Such limitations must be overcome by eliminating liquid etch processes in favor of techniques that etch faster vertically than they do laterally. Currently, methods that use glow discharges (plasmas), ion beams, or lasers to accelerate vertical etch rates in a reactive gas atmosphere are being intensively studied and will be for the foreseeable future. Because these processes are relatively new and poorly understood, the ultimate limits of pattern transfer are not known. However, ion beam methods have been used to define pattern sizes as small as 8×10^{-7} centimeter.

Despite the fact that dimensions of the order of 2×10^{-6} centimeter can be attained, the actual manufacture of devices on this scale is not yet possible. As lateral sizes decrease, vertical dimensions (film thicknesses)

94

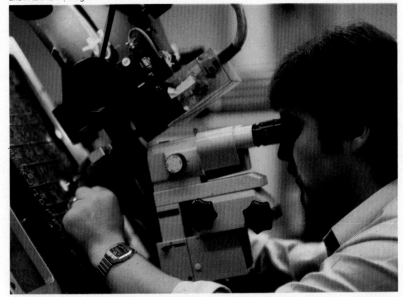

Inspector checks computer-controlled machine that routes wires through printed circuit boards. Chip holders are then placed on the boards, and the wires facilitate interconnections between the chips.

must also diminish. With thinner films the dielectric layer breaks down at lower voltages. Coupled with this phenomenon is the increased likelihood that a random material defect or a dust particle will destroy the film properties. In addition, as the thicknesses and widths of metal films decrease, the cross-sectional area declines rapidly, resulting in a substantial increase in current density for normal device operation. The densities become so high (more than 10^6 amperes per square centimeter) that conductor patterns are rapidly destroyed. For these reasons it is believed that if future devices operate electrically in the same mode as present ones, the smallest physical dimensions will be limited to approximately 3×10^{-5} centimeter. Also, the level of integration under consideration is such that more than ten million transistors could be built on a chip with an area of one square centimeter before the year 2000. Still more than this could be envisioned if layers of transistors were stacked on top of one another. Because the transport of electrons dissipates heat, the amount of heat transfer required to avoid harmful heating effects on the chip is significant. Therefore, for practical reasons either more efficient means of cooling must be devised or the component density must be reduced.

With tens of millions of elements on an integrated circuit, the design and testing functions for the circuit become prohibitively long. Such problems are being attacked by using the end product of this entire process, the computer. Computer-aided design of integrated circuits and computer-aided manufacturing processes are receiving considerable attention in an attempt to minimize the cost of future development.

Future directions

Current process technology and device structures appear to place a limit of approximately 3×10^{-5} centimeter on pattern dimensions for very-large-scale integration. This limitation will probably be attained by the end of the century. Still further miniaturization will, therefore, depend

95

upon the use of different materials and the development of alternate methods of storing, transferring, processing, and retrieving information.

One of the primary reasons for reducing pattern dimensions is that device speeds increase because of the smaller distances that electrons must travel. However, speed increases for electronic charge carriers can be achieved in other ways. For instance, a reduction in the operating temperature of the device significantly increases the conductivity of metal films. Furthermore, power dissipation is decreased at low temperatures. Thus, devices might be operated at the boiling point of liquid nitrogen (−196° C). Naturally, a substantial increase in the cost of electronic devices would be incurred with such refrigeration requirements. It is not yet known if the improvement in device performance will economically justify such expenses.

Further reduction in temperature to that of the boiling point of liquid helium (−269° C) opens the realm of superconductive devices. In this technology silicon structures and operating principles are replaced by materials such as niobium which operate by means of quantum mechanical tunneling phenomena when temperatures approach absolute zero (−273° C). Under such circumstances the zero electrical resistance permits high-speed devices to operate with virtually no power dissipation. However, the costs associated with application of this technology are extremely high.

From the standpoint of speed silicon is not the best semiconductor material for operating devices at room temperature. Materials such as gallium arsenide (GaAs) and indium antimonide (InSb) display electron mobilities greater than that of silicon by more than a factor of five. Indeed, microwave devices are presently fabricated in GaAs. Considerable effort is therefore being expended to develop the necessary technology for gallium arsenide integrated circuits. However, because of the low cost and extensive processing knowledge of silicon-based integrated circuits GaAs probably will not displace silicon for the manufacture of circuits on a large scale.

Although it seems astonishing that circuits smaller than a fingernail can store several hundred thousand bits of information, this storage capacity is not unusual in biological systems. To approach the level of integration present in biological units, information must be stored and processed in single molecules. This involves dimensions of less than 10^{-6} (0.000001) centimeter. Indeed, researchers in the field of molecular electronics have such "devices" as their goal. Recent results have demonstrated that certain ruthenium-imine complexes possess the ability to store electrons in specific sites within the molecule. If these molecules or their analogs can replace circuit elements such as transistors, electronic miniaturization will take on a whole new direction. Molecular computers would have tremendous computational capability combined with size scales considerably smaller than those envisioned for semiconductor devices. It is anticipated that at least a decade will pass before any practical devices result from this technology.

The exact road that electronic miniaturization will take from now until

the end of the century is not clear. Many paths are open, and surely more trails will be discovered in ensuing years. Consideration of the phenomenal progress of the past 30 years leaves one with a feeling of anticipation for what is yet to come. The only certainty in sight is that scientists, engineers, and consumers alike will continue to be amazed by the continuing "microelectronics revolution."

Motorola 68000 microprocessor is one of the new 16-bit integrated circuits that have allowed computers of small size and considerable power to be developed.

FOR ADDITIONAL READING

F. L. Carter, *Molecular Electronic Devices* (Marcel Dekker, Inc., 1982).

D. A. Doane, D. B. Fraser, and D. W. Hess (eds.), *Semiconductor Technology* (The Electrochemical Society, Inc., Pennington, 1982).

N. G. Einspruch (ed.), *VLSI Electronics: Microstructure Science*, vol. 1–7 (Academic Press, 1981–83).

T. Forester (ed.), *The Microelectronic Revolution* (The MIT Press, 1981).

R. E. Howard, P. F. Liao, W. J. Skocpol, L. D. Jackel, and H. G. Craighead, "Microfabrication as a Scientific Tool," *Science* (July 8, 1983, pp. 117–121).

E. L. Hu, "New Approaches to the Fabrication of Submicron Switches," *American Scientist* (September-October 1981, pp. 517–521).

S. M. Sze (ed.), *VLSI Technology* (McGraw-Hill, 1983).

ARTIFICIAL INTELLIGENCE
by Bruce G. Buchanan

*Computer scientists are striving to endow
their electronic creations with abilities
similar to human reasoning and learning.
"Expert" consultation systems that can
diagnose disease, analyze locomotive
problems, or do theoretical chemistry
are recent payoffs.*

Artificial intelligence (AI) is the branch of computer science that
deals with ways of representing knowledge using symbols rather
than numbers and with rules-of-thumb, or heuristic, methods for
processing information. The major goal of AI is to understand
intelligence—loosely, the processes that humans and other animals use to learn, solve problems, and understand language—by
constructing or programming machines that behave intelligently.
Artificial intelligence differs from other areas of computing in its
attention to both symbolic information and heuristic methods for
solving problems.

In general, the kinds of problems that AI methods address are
not well structured. That is, one does not already know in advance
from a description of the problem alone what is the best method
for solving it. In short, there are no algorithms; *i.e.*, no straight-
forward step-by-step procedures for solution. Broadly speaking, AI
substitutes exploratory search for precise, algorithmic methods.

Fundamental themes in AI
Although the intellectual roots of artificial intelligence research
stretch back to antiquity, its modern history began with work during the 1950s. Early, influential products that emerged from these
investigations were a computer program that proved theorems
of propositional logic, a program for the game of checkers that
learned from its mistakes, a theorem prover for plane geometry,
a program that recognized handwritten characters, and programming languages for general manipulation of symbols.
Alan Turing, Norbert Wiener, and other pioneers in computing
foresaw the use of electronic computers for intelligent problem
solving. In the 1940s and early 1950s chess and other games were
considered to be prototypical of many reasoning problems because
information about these games is not naturally represented math-
ematically, if at all, and because solving these problems requires
heuristics as it is far too time-consuming to look exhaustively at
all possible sequences of moves. Today games and game playing
remain a popular and convenient focus of much research in AI
because of the tidy, well-defined nature of the subject.

TOWARD
MACHINES
THAT
THINK

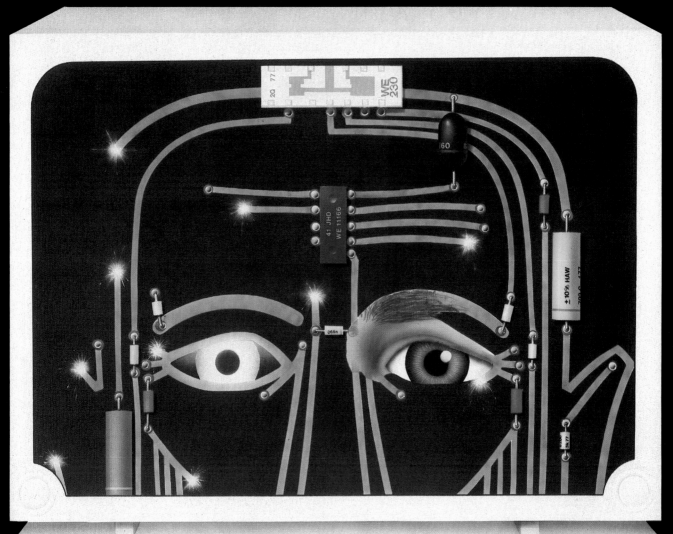

BRUCE G. BUCHANAN is Professor of Computer Science Research at Stanford University and has worked in the field of artificial intelligence since 1966.

(Overleaf) Illustration by Fred Nelson

In the late 1940s U.S. mathematician Norbert Wiener established the science of cybernetics, which is concerned with the common factors of control and communication in living organisms and automatically controlled machines. At a time when the electronic computer was still in its infancy, Wiener and other pioneers in computing foresaw its use for intelligent problem solving.

Massachusetts Institute of Technology

In addition to game playing early AI work focused on techniques for solving small symbolic reasoning problems, on robotics and associated vision and manipulation systems, and on understanding instructions given in natural human language. Researchers continue to ponder these problems as well. There was also considerable work on self-improving machines like the learning program for checkers, on pattern recognition like the character-recognition program, and machine translation of text from one language to another.

Another important dimension of work in AI was, and still is, psychological modeling. Not only have studies of the ways humans solve problems provided clues for how to program machines to behave intelligently but computer programs have helped test psychological models of human intelligence. Early work in AI gave rise to a branch of psychology known as information-processing psychology, and the intersection of AI and psychology (also overlapping philosophy, linguistics, and other related disciplines) is now known as cognitive science.

Two research themes, representation and search, dominated the first decade or so of AI work. How one represents descriptions of objects, processes, properties, and relations greatly influences the efficiency of the problem-solving system and the quality of the solutions. How one searches for plausible solutions and uses heuristics to guide the search also influences the efficiency and effectiveness of the system.

Search is the fundamental problem-solving paradigm for AI programs. Conceptually, if not practically, one can consider most problem-solving activity as the generation and selection of alternative solutions. Even random trial and error, which is not usually considered intelligent, can be viewed as generating a solution and then testing to see if the solution is correct. The section below on control discusses variations on the generate-and-test method that lead to more intelligent behavior.

Heuristic methods, rules that in the human sense could be said to be based on experience or judgment or even ''intuition,'' are central to research in artificial intelligence. They frequently lead to plausible solutions to problems or increase the efficiency of a problem-solving procedure. Whereas algorithms guarantee a correct solution (if there is one) in a finite time, heuristics only increase the likelihood of finding a plausible solution or increase the plausibility of the solutions. In safecracking, to use a classic example, a time-consuming but unfailing algorithm for opening a combination safe is to try all possible combinations of numbers on the dials. One heuristic that may work, and that will speed up the process if it does, is to listen for the tumblers in the dials to drop into place. In almost all human intellectual endeavors, there are numerous heuristics that guide our problem-solving activity. By contrast, algorithms are rare and tend to be specialized to tasks that are highly mathematical.

The fundamental difficulty with the search paradigm is that, for most interesting problems, the number of possible solutions grows exponentially with the size of the problem. Computer programs for generating solutions (or partial solutions) often are made to combine every element of the problem in all possible ways, as a legal-move generator for a chess-playing program combines all possible opening moves by White with all possible opening responses by Black—for several exchanges into the game. This exponential growth of possibilities is called the combinatorial explosion. It can be controlled by heuristics when sufficiently powerful judgmental knowledge can be found to constrain and focus the search.

Like other disciplines AI encompasses different approaches to research. These are broadly classed as theoretical and experimental. Theoreticians in AI prefer to look at problem solving and representation questions from a formal point of view, often using predicate logic as a lingua franca for discussing methods and results. Experimentalists, on the other hand, prefer to build programs that demonstrate the competence of an idea and then to investigate empirically the strengths and limits of the idea as implemented. Just as AI programs can reason "top down," from a model to concrete instances of it, or "bottom up," from data to generalizations, AI research itself follows these two approaches.

How AI systems represent knowledge

The problem of representation is one of finding an appropriate set of conventions for describing objects, relations, events, and other information. Different programming languages offer different features that make it easier or harder to represent and manipulate facts and relations about the world, and the choice is further complicated by the need to overlay higher level constructs on top of the programming language in order to form a complete AI system. The issue is finding or inventing constructs within a computer language that allow knowledge to be manipulated easily. List-processing languages, discussed below, were invented to facilitate the representation of facts and relations symbolically in linked lists.

It is widely accepted that people have difficulty solving problems when they represent the facts inappropriately. The "trick" for solving algebra word problems, for example, is to map the problem from English into a more suitable representation as a set of equations with correctly conceived variables, constants, and ways of linking them together. Similarly, computer programs must have appropriate constructs to work on.

Formal logic has been investigated as a way to represent knowledge for AI programs because it allows a program to maintain true and consistent beliefs about the world, provided that the starting axioms are true and consistent. Various logical formalisms are widely known and used; most are variations on a formal language known as first-order predicate calculus. For example, "All men are mortal" would be written in the form of a universally quantified statement whose main connective is implication: For all x, man(x) implies is-mortal(x), meaning "Whatever is man is mortal." Standard rules of inference allow an AI program to make deductively valid inferences from starting axioms and previously proved theorems in order to deduce new facts. A program cannot, however, keep all valid conclusions around, nor can it afford the time to make all valid inferences. (This is another instance of the combinatorial explosion.) Instead, once a program has a number of facts about the world represented as logical statements, one can ask about the truth of a new statement by posing the question "Is this statement a theorem?" For example, given the fact that all men are mortal, can one prove as a theorem "Socrates is mortal"? Considerable attention has thus been given to efficient means of proving theorems.

There are many extensions to first-order predicate calculus that make logic a more expressive language. For example, certain techniques allow a program to keep track of what it believes to be true, what might possibly be true, and so forth. These additions, however, substantially complicate the theorem-proving procedures. In recent years specialized programming languages such as PROLOG, which are based on logic, have been created to assist this approach to problem solving. MRS and FOL also use logic as the fundamental framework for representing knowledge.

Production rules, another way to describe facts and relations, were introduced into AI for use in psychological modeling of human problem solving. A production rule is a conditional sentence consisting of an "if" part and a "then" part, also called a condition and an action. The "if" part lists a set of conditions in some logical combination. If the "if" part of the rule is satisfied, the piece of knowledge represented by the production rule is relevant to the line of reasoning being developed. As a consequence, the "then" part can be added to the data base or acted upon.

MYCIN, an AI program developed to diagnose certain infections and select appropriate antibiotic treatment, is an example of a system based on production rules. During a diagnosis MYCIN will request information about a particular set of symptoms, findings, or test results—the "if" part of a rule. If these conditions are satisfied by the responses, the program presents a hypothesis—the "then" part. Further rules are applied until the program reaches the diagnosis that most plausibly explains the findings.

Semantic nets and frames are a third type of representational formalism. They are structures similar to each other that associate definitions of concepts by means of semantic links. A frame is a collection of associated symbolic knowledge about an entity. Typically a frame lists

An example of a production rule from MYCIN, an artificial intelligence program developed to diagnose and select antibiotic treatment for severe infections, is outlined below. If the "if" part of the rule can be satisfied from findings about the patient, the "then" part becomes a relevant piece of knowledge about the infectious agent and the appropriate treatment. The production rule is augmented with a certainty factor, (.7), that indicates the evidential strength of the premise and the importance of the conclusion. (Below right) Another medically oriented AI program, CADUCEUS, whose diagnoses range over the whole field of internal medicine, engages in a consultation session with one of its creators, physician Jack D. Myers of the University of Pittsburgh. CADUCEUS uses a frame-based system to represent knowledge and as of early 1984 contained the largest knowledge base of any expert system, encompassing definitions, symptoms, and diagnostic tests for more than 600 diseases.

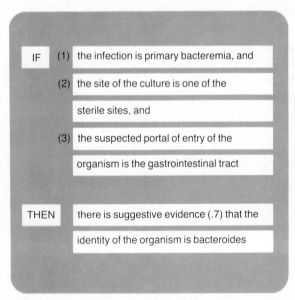

IF	(1)	the infection is primary bacteremia, and
	(2)	the site of the culture is one of the sterile sites, and
	(3)	the suspected portal of entry of the organism is the gastrointestinal tract
THEN		there is suggestive evidence (.7) that the identity of the organism is bacteroides

Photo, courtesy University of Pittsburgh

```
┌─────────────────────────────────────────────────┐
│  ┌──────────────┐                                 │
│  │ noun phrase: │                                 │
│  └──────────────┘                                 │
│  ┌───────────────────────────────────────────┐   │
│  │ necessary elements = N                     │   │
│  │ optional elements = (ART, ADJ, PP)         │   │
│  │ first-state = (ART) or (ADJ)               │   │
│  │ augmented first-state = first-state + ADJ* │   │
│  └───────────────────────────────────────────┘   │
│  ┌───────────────────────────────────────────┐   │
│  │ second-state = (augmented first-state + N) │   │
│  │              or (N)                        │   │
│  │ augmented second-state = second-state + PP*│   │
│  └───────────────────────────────────────────┘   │
│  ┌───────────────────────────────────────────┐   │
│  │ terminus = augmented second-state          │   │
│  └───────────────────────────────────────────┘   │
│  ┌───────────────────────────────────────────┐   │
│  │ default = ART + N                          │   │
│  │ examples = "the money," "the bungling      │   │
│  │             detective,"                    │   │
│  │             "the blind man with the monkey"│   │
│  └───────────────────────────────────────────┘   │
│  ┌───────────────────────────────────────────┐   │
│  │ part of = PP, S, VP                        │   │
│  └───────────────────────────────────────────┘   │
└─────────────────────────────────────────────────┘
```

key to codes:
N = noun
ART = article
ADJ = adjective
PP = prepositional phrase
S = sentence
VP = verb phrase
* = any number of; *e.g.,* ADJ* means "any number of adjectives"
( ) = alternative element; a parenthetically enclosed element is a member of a group of two or more alternatives

the properties of the entity, including necessary and optional defining properties and properties that indicate more general and more specific concepts. Because every problem-solving task involves many entities that stand in various relations to each other, the properties can be used to specify those relations. Furthermore, because the properties of an entity are entities themselves that are linked according to those same relations, one frame can give knowledge that is a "special case" of another frame, while some frames can be "part of" another frame. For example, CADU-CEUS is a medical diagnosis program that represents knowledge in frames. Each disease and each finding occupies a frame, with obvious two-way links between them and with links within families of diseases. The entire aggregation of frames and linking structure is sometimes called a node-link network, or semantic network, in which the frames are the nodes and the relations are the links.

Shown at left is a frame-based representation of a rule of grammar defining a noun phrase. The parts of speech mentioned in this frame are themselves frames, while the entity being represented exists as part of other frames than define a sentence, a prepositional phrase, and a verb phrase. In this kind of system any number of attributes may be attached to the concept being represented.

Controlling the problem-solving process

One way to think of problem-solving behavior is to envision a search through a treelike space of alternatives, called a search space. To explore this space, an artificial intelligence program might be given rules for legal (or sometimes only plausible) moves that tell it what element of the space to consider next. In chess, for example, it is simple to construct rules for legal moves according to the rules of the game. The space of all possible move sequences (complete games) is thus a tree of alternating moves by opposing players. In principle, it is possible to construct an algorithm that explores the consequences of each possible move, that is, all the paths to win, lose, or draw, because the tree is finite. The space is so large, however, that exhaustive searching would not finish in human lifetimes. Thus, ways must be found to control the search so that implausible branches of the tree will not be explored and the most promising branches will be explored first. By introducing heuristics that embody criteria of plausibility and implausibility, one transforms an exhaustive search algorithm into heuristic search.

One well-known heuristic-search program is DENDRAL, which searches a space of graphical descriptions of chemical structures to determine the molecular structure of an unknown chemical compound, given analytical data about it. The number of alternative molecular descriptions that can be constructed from a fixed number of chemical atoms of known types (*e.g.*, $C_8H_{16}O$) grows exponentially with the number of atoms, another example of the combinatorial explosion. DENDRAL successfully uses the same kinds of heuristics that chemists use to limit the number of alternative molecular structures actually considered and thus to avoid searching the space exhaustively. At the heart of the program is a "legal-move" generator that can, in principle, generate all possible alternatives. (This is very different from the ad hoc generation methods used by chemists.) But it can be constrained—using heuristic knowledge to infer the constraints—in order to focus on plausible molecular structures.

For many complex tasks there is no such legal-move generator that is a reasonable starting point for implementing a search program. In understanding speech—transforming acoustic patterns from a spoken English sentence to a sequence of words, for example—AI programs such as HEARSAY-II do not systematically generate successive legal sequences of English words. Instead, they use a variety of cues to trigger the generation of plausible additions to an emerging "best guess" at what the sentence is. While a legal-move generator will always be capable of generating the correct solution if the heuristics allow it to do so, a plausible-move generator may not have a rich enough set of generating principles to include the correct solution in every case. Thus it is a high-level assumption that plausible-move generators will eventually produce the correct solution.

The way a search space is explored depends on the choice of control strategy. The major strategies, all of which have variations, include depth-first search, which explores only the first branch at each level;

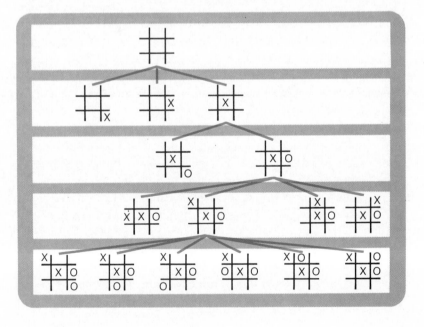

Diagram shows part of the treelike space of alternatives, or search space, for the game of ticktacktoe. Note that the other moves open to the players at each level are symmetric, and thus equivalent, to the ones shown. Only one move at each level is expanded to the next level; if these particular moves were being chosen by a heuristic that judged each of them best among the alternatives, this exploration would be an example of the strategy of best-first search.

breadth-first search, which explores all branches at each level (progressive deepening); and best-first search, which explores at each level only the branch most likely to lead to a solution.

Researchers in the field of AI are beginning to recognize the desirability of endowing their programs with the knowledge that would allow them to choose their own problem-solving strategy. Just as it deals with problem-solving knowledge itself, a program should be able to reason about strategy, change it, and explain it. Knowledge about how to use the contents of a knowledge base is one form of "meta-knowledge," a current topic of research.

A recent development in research on control is dependency-directed backtracking. The cost of backtracking through a search space from a path that no longer appears fruitful can be substantial because the program must redetermine its state of knowledge at a previous branch point in the search tree in order to continue the search along a different branch from that point. In dependency-directed backtracking the program keeps track of the origin of each piece of knowledge in its current state of belief. Then when backtracking is necessary, the program can look at the dependency links to deduce previous states of knowledge without having to regenerate them.

Learning as a problem-solving activity

Because a characteristic feature of intelligent living things is their ability to adapt their behavior to a changing environment, considerable work in AI has focused on methods for learning. Learning takes many different forms depending on the type and amount of data available, the nature of the feedback, the knowledge structures that are being learned, and the structure of the performance program that is being improved.

Out of early work on stimulus-response and statistical approaches to learning has come a strong competing concept founded in AI research— that learning is a knowledge-based problem-solving activity. The problem that the learning program is supposed to solve is to modify another program, called the performance program (e.g., a program that plays checkers) so that the performance program improves. With respect to games, improvement is generally measured in win/loss ratios. For other tasks improvement may mean increasing the correctness of predictions or advice, or it may mean decreasing the cost (in speed or memory space) of reaching conclusions.

Learning programs also take different forms depending on the extent to which a person is involved in selecting training instances, providing feedback, giving advice, and integrating new knowledge with old. New knowledge may come from any of several primary sources:

1. Experience: Rote learning is storing results of previously encountered situations (e.g., a board position in a game) without generalizing. Because it saves time whenever the same situation is encountered, a program using saved results can also search further to determine if a better response to the situation can be found.

2. Example: Learning by inductive reasoning can be thought of as

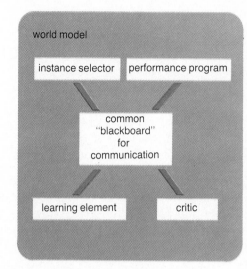

A conceptual view of learning that has emerged from AI research portrays the process as a knowledge-based problem-solving activity. In an AI system this activity can be assigned to a learning program whose task is to modify another program, the performance program, so that its performance improves. In such a system, diagrammed above, the problem-solving vocabulary, assumptions, and procedures are defined for all of the components of the system within a world model. One component, the instance selector, chooses training instances to present to the performance program. Performance is critiqued by the critic, whose advice is implemented by the learning element. These steps are not always separate or all automatic.

105

heuristic search through a space of possible knowledge structures (*e.g.,* predictive rules or concept definitions) to find new knowledge that "covers" positive examples presented in the training data and excludes counterexamples. As such, it requires a definition of the search space as well as heuristics that allow it to consider plausible elements in the space efficiently.

3. Discovery: Learning by discovery involves a program's considering many different knowledge structures and assessing heuristically their inherent value. Some heuristics, but not all, may examine how well the new concept applies to specific cases (as in induction) whereas others may examine how the concept or rule was derived in order to assess its value.

4. Advice: Learning by taking advice can range from a passive set of text-editing instructions that can accept and integrate new knowledge to an active program that assists in defining new knowledge and keeping the total knowledge base consistent.

5. Experts: Human experts may be the source of new knowledge, and the transfer of their expertise to a program generally is the duty of a programmer, in this context called a knowledge engineer, who helps structure new knowledge appropriately for a program. This activity has come to be known as knowledge engineering and is the primary method for building expert systems, discussed below.

6. Analogy: Learning by analogy has been successful in a few prototype programs. It requires rich knowledge structures for two or more areas and requires solving two difficult problems: finding relevant and useful analogies among all possible correspondences between areas of knowledge and using the correspondences in plausible ways (and only plausible ways) to discover new knowledge.

7. Watching: Learning may come from observing a person solve problems or perform a task correctly. Prototype programs exist that first examine the instructions that an expert gives to a computer in order to accomplish a task and then generalize those instructions to cover similar tasks.

8. Text: Learning by reading text requires broad, powerful programs that understand natural language.

Languages and AI systems

Because AI works more with symbolic information than numeric information, languages designed to support symbolic processing have been central. The two most influential languages have been IPL-V and LISP, and most AI work is presently done in various dialects of LISP. One of LISP's key advantages is the ease with which it can use programs as data in order to edit or explain parts of the program and can treat data structures as programs in order to execute newly created or edited parts of the program.

A recent development in AI has been the construction of personal computers specifically designed to use LISP efficiently. Many of these, often called LISP machines, are now commercially available. They have large main memories and disk storage capacities and come with high-

106

Photos, Milton and Joan Mann—Cameramann International

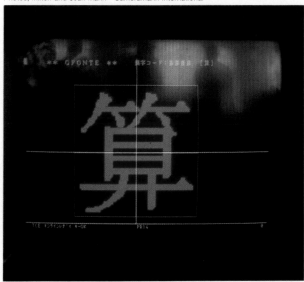 

resolution visual displays and some pointing device for identifying and manipulating displayed information. Local communications networks allow these personal workstations to be connected together and to communicate with large central computers and their facilities.

In the early 1980s the Japanese industrial and research communities announced their intention to design and build a new generation of computer specifically for symbolic reasoning, the fifth generation in the evolution of computers based on technological advances. In the Japanese design problem solving and inference will be the core of the processing functions. Power is measured in logical inferences per second (LIPS), where one LIPS is one such inference per second. Currently, one inference operation is estimated to require 100–1,000 steps; thus one LIPS is equivalent to 100–1,000 instructions per second. Machines of the present generation are said to work at 10,000–100,000 LIPS. The final target for fifth-generation machines is performance of about a billion LIPS, four or five orders of magnitude faster than current machines.

A natural-language understanding system, which will be an integral part of successful AI programs, will require large dictionaries of words and phrases. In the design for the Japanese fifth-generation computer, the design requirement for the natural-language system is a vocabulary of 100,000 words, each requiring hundreds to thousands of computer words of storage.

Applications

Two early AI systems, DENDRAL and MACSYMA, demonstrated that AI methods could be applied to practical problems; namely, identifying the molecular structure of chemical compounds and simplifying complex mathematical expressions. Other experimental researchers in AI selected similarly interesting problems as vehicles for investigating AI issues. Still others have recently begun commercial applications of AI methods to industrial problems.

Display of a kanji (character) conveying meanings of "number" and "calculation" (above left) is drawn from a massive computer dictionary, part of a natural-language system being developed for Japan's fifth-generation computer. At the Japanese government's Institute for New Generation Computer Technology (above) researchers conceive software for the advanced machine, in which AI approaches to problem solving and inference will form the core of the processing functions.

Photos, General Electric Research and Development Center, Schenectady, N.Y.

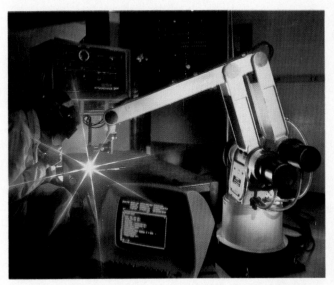

Robot welder (above) is basically a large computer-controlled reprogrammable mechanical arm. Whereas common industrial robots depend on numerical algorithms for their control, AI methods have begun to be used to program complex sequences of robotic movements. (Above right) Using a LISP machine, i.e., a computer designed to use the AI language LISP, a researcher develops programming for a robot-based factory workstation.

(Facing page, top) A major emphasis of AI work in robotics has been the development of programs that will allow computers to understand sensory data, particularly visual images. Recognition of an aerial view of a tank, for example (lower left), begins with the conversion of its video image to a digital form (upper left) made up of thousands of dots (pixels), representing light-intensity values, that are stored as arrays of numbers in the computer. "Intelligent" manipulation of these numbers can identify image areas containing sharp changes of intensity, which correspond to the edges of the object (upper right). Once the computer isolates the edge outline from the background (lower right), it then can apply a more refined degree of AI to find distinctive features, such as the gun barrel, that will help its recognition of the object as a tank.

Photos, Lockheed Electronics Company, Inc.

Industrial applications fall roughly into four classes: robotics, natural language, expert systems, and tools for developing software. One of the important developmental milestones for AI has been the commercialization of AI tools and methods in these four areas. Many industrial research laboratories have established groups to work on applications of AI, and new companies have been formed to provide AI tools and customized software to companies in nearly every segment of the economy.

Building intelligent robots has been an ambitious goal of researchers for centuries. Within AI this work has centered on computer-controlled mechanical manipulators and vehicles and on computer understanding of sensor data, mostly in the form of television signals. AI efforts in problem solving, speech recognition, and other general topics are also clearly relevant to building intelligent robots although not specialized to it.

Industrial computer-controlled manipulators are currently used in thousands of manufacturing operations, such as spray painting and welding. Most use little AI but are based on engineering control algorithms. AI-based languages for describing the movements of a manipulator have begun to be used for programming complex operations.

Without feedback from sensors, a manipulator must rely on precise alignment of parts, on correct positioning and orientation—in short, on everything being set up ahead of time in a foolproof, blind operation. In dynamically changing situations, this requirement is impossible. Therefore, an intelligent robot must be able to sense (see, feel, hear, or otherwise determine) what is in its environment. Apart from robots, understanding data from various sensors (*e.g.*, television, X-ray, sonar, infrared, or ultrasound) is also important in contexts ranging from medical diagnosis to military intelligence and surveillance activities.

Work on computer vision is carried out at several different levels. At the low end, closer to the data-collection process, are problems of digitizing, edge detection, line finding, region segmentation, and texture analysis. At the high end, closer to the interpretation process, are problems of recognizing meaningful shapes (*e.g.*, a house), and determining relationships among objects (*e.g.*, one object supporting another). Especially difficult problems include representing and recognizing three-dimensional objects and dealing with color, motion, and stereo images. (See *1983 Yearbook of Science and the Future* Feature Article: ROBOTS "MAN" THE ASSEMBLY LINE.)

Human-computer interactions have always presented interesting and difficult problems and are becoming increasingly important as software systems become more complex and powerful. From the early days of artificial intelligence, researchers have worked on programs that are intelligent enough to carry on dialogues with people in English or another natural language. One grand goal, the focus of much early attention, was computer translation of text from one language into another, a task that requires both understanding and generating natural language.

Purely syntactic approaches to understanding language were shown to result in too many ambiguities and not enough understanding. A syntactic grammar is a general grammar for the language; it deals with the way words are strung together into larger units and may embody such rules as "a noun phrase is either a determiner a word such as "his" in "his new idea"] followed by a noun or a determiner followed by an adjective followed by a noun." Semantic grammars specialize these rules to take account of specific meanings of words in particular contexts.

Augmented transition nets were a significant development as a convenient representation for grammars. They link different syntactic and semantic elements together in the form of labeled graphs to represent alternative ways of expressing meaningful sentences or parts of speech. Case frames are another important way to represent the information in sentences and groups of sentences. In this method framelike structures, each with predefined slots (some required, some optional, some forbidden in special cases) for various properties of the subject of the frame, define semantically meaningful cases.

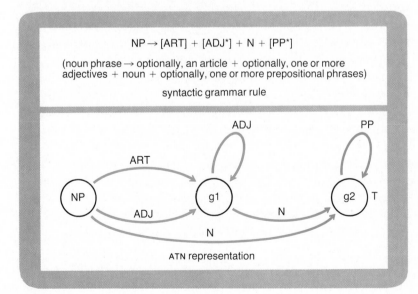

NP → [ART] + [ADJ*] + N + [PP*]

(noun phrase → optionally, an article + optionally, one or more adjectives + noun + optionally, one or more prepositional phrases)

syntactic grammar rule

ATN representation

A syntactic grammar rule for a noun phrase is compared with its augmented transition network (ATN) representation. In each case the noun phrase is defined as either (1) an article or an adjective, followed optionally by any number of adjectives, followed by a noun, followed optionally by any number of prepositional phrases, or (2) a simple noun. In the ATN representation, g1 and g2 are intermediate grammatical constructs, and T (terminus) indicates the point at which the representation is defined to be complete. ATN's, which link different syntactic and semantic elements in the form of labeled graphs, have proved to be a useful technique for representing grammar in AI research.

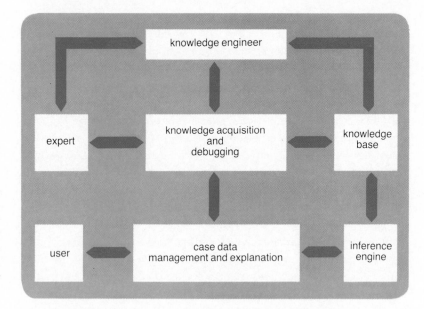

The conceptual structure of an expert system including the elements necessary to build it is illustrated at the right. Separation of the knowledge base and the inference engine (the interpreter of the knowledge base plus auxiliary procedures for keeping track of inferences) is a central idea.

DELTA, an expert system developed for locating faults in diesel-electric locomotives and advising on their repair, is demonstrated by computer scientist Frank Lynch of General Electric Co. (seated). Originally set up in LISP, the system is based on more than 500 "if-then" production rules derived from interviews with Dave Smith (standing), a GE field engineer with four decades of experience in locomotive repair. DELTA also displays charts, drawings, and training-film sequences on videodisc to assist the user in locating components and carrying out repairs.

General Electric Research and Development Center, Schenectady, N.Y.

Considerable progress has been made in understanding text within restricted contexts, such as a conversation with a restaurant waiter, a newspaper story about terrorist attacks, or specification of computer programs. Good results have been obtained with machine translation of technical information as well. Commercial applications include systems that understand queries about large, specialized computer data bases, and can thus translate an English request for information into a query phrased efficiently in a formal computer language. As with other AI problem-solving programs, programs for understanding natural language have difficulty representing and reasoning with common-sense knowledge. Dealing with metaphors and contextual cues is especially hard in understanding natural language.

Expert systems are AI programs that embody considerable human expertise to solve important problems. They are flexible in the sense that they can be changed and extended easily, and they are understandable in the sense that they can explain the contents of their own knowledge bases and their own lines of reasoning. In the early 1980s expert systems captured the interest of the commercial world. Both new and established companies have begun building expert systems for commercial purposes.

Applications of expert systems range from medicine to electronics and from machinery to computer software; their tasks range from diagnosis and troubleshooting (analysis) to planning and configuration (synthesis). Some examples include programs that diagnose disease (e.g., MYCIN), search for ore deposits, help solve oil-well drilling problems, troubleshoot locomotive breakdowns, and configure computer systems. Currently the major steps in building expert systems are selecting an appropriate problem (in terms of such attributes as size, difficulty, importance, and risk), selecting a representation and control structure (or framework system that supplies both), settling on an appropriate vocabulary and conceptualization for the problem, finding an available expert, transferring the expert's knowledge into the program (knowledge engineering), refining the knowledge base with feedback from test cases, packaging the system in a form that is acceptable to users, and validating the quality of the program's advice.

Probably the most successful commercial expert system so far is the XCON system developed at Digital Equipment Corp. Its task is to configure orders for the company's VAX computer systems to meet customers' specifications on such things as speed and memory size while keeping track of additional considerations such as cooling requirements and lengths of cables. After five years of development the system contains more than 3,000 rules and has been used to configure more than 80,000 orders.

Developing complex AI programs is becoming ever more dependent on programming-support tools; *i.e.,* other programs, particularly ones based on LISP. The dominant trend is for smarter tools that take over more and more of the routine programming chores. According to the manual for one of these support systems, the INTERLISP Programmers' Apprentice, it is designed to "cooperate with the user in the development of his programs, and free him or her to concentrate more fully on the conceptual difficulties and creative aspects of the problem he is trying to solve." Present capabilities at the apprentice level include spelling correction, remembering commands and contexts, and bookkeeping.

Automatic programming techniques are currently powerful enough to construct simple programs from abstract specifications. These techniques are a logical extension of the "Do what I mean" concept in programming, which attempts to reduce the amount of detail and precision necessary in framing commands for them to be accurately understood. Future designers and implementers of large AI systems will be able to turn over substantial coding jobs to automated apprentices, thus freeing them to work more on design and less on implementation. Current research projects such as the Programmers' Apprentice, PIE system, and SAFE are pointing the way toward tools for producing efficient programs from specifications, plans, or very high-level programming languages.

FOR ADDITIONAL READING

Avron Barr, Paul Cohen, and Edward Feigenbaum (eds.), *The Handbook of Artificial Intelligence,* 3 vol. (William Kaufmann, Inc., 1981 and 1982).

Bruce G. Buchanan and Edward H. Shortliffe, *Rule-Based Expert Systems* (Addison-Wesley, 1984).

Frederick Hayes-Roth, Donald Waterman, and Douglas Lenat (eds.), *Building Expert Systems* (Addison-Wesley, 1983).

Pamela McCorduck, *Machines Who Think* (W. H. Freeman and Co., 1979).

Patrick H. Winston, *Artificial Intelligence,* 2nd ed. (Addison-Wesley, 1984).

Periodicals focusing specifically on artificial intelligence include *The AI Magazine, Artificial Intelligence, Cognitive Science,* and the *Journal of Automated Reasoning.*

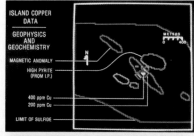

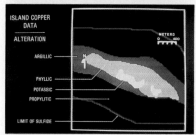

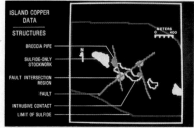

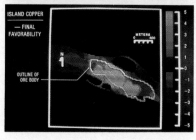

The expert system PROSPECTOR, largely a rule-based system, incorporates the expertise of several geologists in mineral exploitation and resource evaluation in order to predict ore deposit locations from existing geologic data. Of the PROSPECTOR-generated maps above, the top three portray the geology of a region of Vancouver Island, British Columbia, as synthesized from information that the system requested of the user in evaluating the likelihood of a copper deposit. The bottom map shows PROSPECTOR's prediction of the location of the deposit (red, high probability; blue, low probability) as well as an outline of the actual ore body.

THE NEW PROMISE OF COAL

by Charles B. Henderson

Because of recently developed methods of processing and transportation, coal is becoming a feasible low-cost alternative to oil as a fuel.

James Balog—Bruce Coleman, Inc.

The coal-fired Hunter Power Plant in Castle Dale, Utah, illustrates the environmental drawbacks of coal as it emits waste products of the combustion process into the atmosphere.

CHARLES B. HENDERSON is Senior Vice President and Director of the Research & Technology Division of Atlantic Research Corporation, Alexandria, Virginia.

(Overleaf) Gary Cralle—The Image Bank

Coal, an abundant fuel with a productive past and a problem-plagued present, faces an uncertain future. This fuel powered the industrial revolution, brought on the age of steam and the age of electricity, and provided the United States with more than two-thirds of its energy until 1945. It was not until the 1950s that petroleum and natural gas dethroned the "king of fuels" in the U.S., and more than two decades later than that in Western Europe. By the 1980s coal supplied only about one-fifth of the energy consumed each year in the United States.

Many factors influence the use of coal, including its production and transportation costs relative to the price of competing fuels, its ease of handling, and its impact on the environment. Except for mechanization of the mines new technology has not had much impact. The end of the era of inexpensive oil in 1973, however, provided the incentive to develop new technologies for coal. Since that time research and development have been directed toward producing coal-based fuels for use in industry and electric power generation. Because these fuels are cheaper than oil, there is an economic incentive for developing them. It is these industrial and utility markets that provide a new promise for coal.

Several problems impede the use of coal, particularly in industry. Oil and natural gas are fluids that can be utilized in totally enclosed systems until burned; they can be stored in tanks, pumped through pipelines,

114

shipped in barges or closed tank cars, and injected into boilers. Coal, on the other hand, is a dirty solid that requires considerable mechanical equipment to load and unload and to inject into furnaces. Coal piles lose some of their coal as the wind blows, always undesirable in residential and commercial neighborhoods and often in industry too. The burning of coal is an environmental problem of particular current concern. Natural gas is a clean fuel, any impurities being inexpensively removed prior to use. Fuel oil is also available in clean forms; its mineral matter content is always low, and it can be purchased with sulfur contents as low as 0.3%. The sulfur content of coal, however, is seldom less than 1%, and the mineral matter often comprises as much as 15% of the fuel. The mineral matter is expensive to transport, provides problems in the slagging and fouling of boilers, and results in the formation of ash that must be disposed of. Sulfur is oxidized in the combustion process to sulfur dioxide. Upon injection into the atmosphere sulfur dioxide is further oxidized to form sulfuric acid, polluting the environment as it comes back to earth in the form of acid rain.

Coal-water mixtures

One of the important problems inhibiting the use of coal is solved by converting it to liquid form. Of the several techniques under development to accomplish this, mixtures of coal and water called coal-water mixture (CWM) fuels appear ready to capture a significant fraction of the market for residual fuel oil. Typical CWM fuels contain 70–75% by weight of finely ground, moisture-free coal; 1% or less of additives (surfactants, stabilizers, biocides, pH modifiers); and the remainder water. The water allows the mixture to be pumped, stored, transported, and injected into the boiler or furnace as a liquid fuel. In the combustion process the water vaporizes, thereby using 3–4% of the energy value of the coal.

A ball mill is used to grind wet coal as part of the process of making a coal-water mixture fuel that can serve as a substitute for oil.

Two technologies are required in order for coal to achieve the fluid consistency needed to serve as an oil substitute and also the high concentrations necessary to serve as an efficient fuel. First, the distribution of the sizes of the coal particles must be just right. The smaller particles must fit within the interstices between the larger particles, thereby minimizing the volume occupied by the water. Second, the surface chemistry of the coal must be modified by a judicious selection of additives. When mixed with water, coal agglomerates and settles to the bottom by gravity. The additives change the surface chemistry of the coal and impart stability to the mixture by hindering the settling of the coal. Both the additives and the particle-size control contribute to the fluid nature achieved in CWM fuels, the viscosities of which are quite similar to those of motor oils.

Most CWM fuels use bituminous coals because of their high energy content, relative ease of grinding, and low concentration of chemically bound moisture. Lower rank coals (semi-bituminous and lignite) have been converted to useful CWM fuels, but their higher amounts of chemically bound moisture result in lower concentrations of coal in the resulting fuels. Petroleum-coke has also been employed as the fuel constituent for water-based fuels, but it is available in much smaller quantities than coal.

115

The principal market for CWM fuels is as a replacement for residual oil, between one and a half and two million barrels of which are used in the United States each day to generate electricity and process steam. In the near future the users will probably want to modify existing boilers to conserve their capital investment, but in the long term it is expected that boilers will be designed specifically for the new fuel or with a dual-fuel capability. To become a substitute fuel, CWM products must cost significantly less than oil, both to pay the conversion costs and to give the user an economic advantage. The present-day cost of CWM fuels is approximately two-thirds that of residual oil on an equivalent energy basis. This differential is expected to satisfy the economic requirements for a significant fraction of the residual oil market.

CWM fuels have other advantages. Because of vast coal reserves of the United States they offer that nation an independence from foreign sources of residual fuel oil. Unlike synthetic fuel plants, in which the coal is dissolved in a solvent and hydrogenated to form a liquid, plants designed for CWM are low in cost. A plant to process one million tons of coal per year will cost less than $25 million, compared with a cost of approximately $1 billion for a comparable synthetic fuel plant. Also, the processing of CWM fuels can be integrated into other important coal technologies, such as coal cleaning and the transportation of coal by pipeline using coal-water slurries.

Several semicommercial plants to produce CWM mixtures have been built in the last two years, one in Fredericksburg, Virginia, one in Nova Scotia, Canada, and three in Sweden. All five have a production capacity

This coal-water mixture plant in Fredericksburg, Virginia, can produce between five and eight tons of the fuel mixture per hour. The coal arrives by rail from the Appalachian Mountains; the liquid fuel is shipped to users by rail and tank truck.

Coal is transported by rail in Pennsylvania. Trains are used for shipping most coal from the mines to the users, but efforts are under way to reduce the cost of transportation by using pipelines more extensively.

of between five and eight tons of fuel per hour. Coal for the Virginia plant arrives by rail from the coalfields of the Appalachian Mountains in the eastern United States. After conversion to the liquid fuel, the product is shipped to the user by rail and tank truck. Eventually river and ocean barges will also be used and perhaps even oceangoing tankers.

A major demonstration of the fuel took place in August and September 1983. Several hundred thousand gallons of CWM fuel were successfully burned to provide industrial steam for a major chemical plant. Most of the fuel was manufactured in Virginia and shipped by railroad tank car to Memphis, Tennessee. Similar demonstrations are also planned in Canada and Sweden.

Transporting coal through pipelines

Coal-slurry pipelines are not products of a new technology, but new efforts, some based on new technology, are under way to increase the utilization of pipelines to transport coal. Most coal is transported by rail from the mine to the user. Rail transport rates typically represent between one-fourth and two-thirds of the delivered price of coal. Reductions in these transportation costs, perhaps made possible by the use of pipelines, can be translated into reduced electricity rates and lower fuel costs for industry.

As of 1983 only one coal-slurry pipeline was operating within the United States. The Black Mesa pipeline, built in 1970, transports four to five million tons per year of coal 440 kilometers (273 miles) from northeastern Arizona to southern Nevada. A slurry consisting of 54% coal

117

(11% moisture) and 46% added water is manufactured at the processing plant near the Kayenta, Arizona, strip mine. Water is supplied by wells almost a half mile deep. The coal is pulverized by rod mills after being mixed with water. Pumping stations are located along the pipeline itself.

The coal must be processed at the receiving end before being used to fuel two 790-megawatt boilers used to manufacture electricity. The slurry is first held in storage and agitated. It is then separated from the bulk of the water by 40 mechanical centrifuges. The coal cake contains approximately 20% moisture, and the excess water is discharged to evaporation ponds. The coal cake is fed into 20 pulverizers, which grind the coal to the proper size for the boiler and remove half of the remaining moisture. The dried, pulverized coal is then swept by a current of air into the boiler.

The success of the Black Mesa pipeline must be evaluated on the basis of economics. Preparation of the slurry requires 45 kilowatt-hours of energy per ton of coal. The pumping energy (including electrical line losses) required is 55 kilowatt-hours per ton. Removal of the water requires considerably more energy, approximately 200 kilowatt-hours of combined electrical and thermal energy per ton. These figures add up to an energy cost of one kilowatt-hour per ton-mile of transport. In comparison, a railroad would only use about 20% of the energy to transport the coal between the same two points. However, the cost to the user

In preparing the mixture for a coal-slurry pipeline the coal first is crushed into lumps two inches in diameter. A cage mill is then used to reduce it to smaller lumps of about ³/₈ inch in diameter, after which water is added. Further crushing takes place in a rod mill, and the mixture is passed through a mesh that screens out any large lumps that remain. The slurry is then kept suspended in tanks that are agitated (far right) until it is pumped into the pipeline.

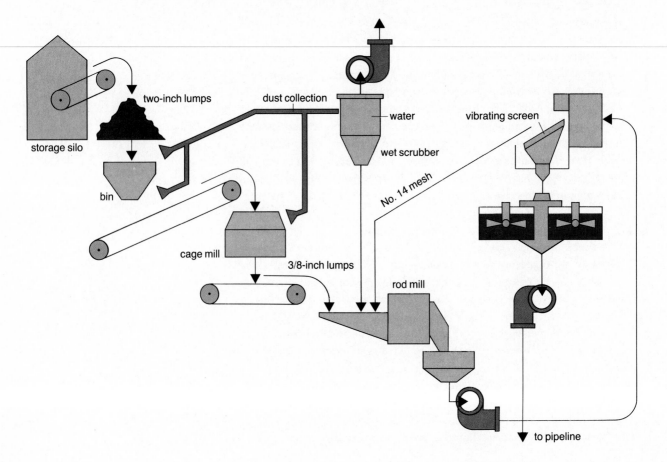

storage silo

two-inch lumps

dust collection

water

wet scrubber

vibrating screen

bin

cage mill

3/8-inch lumps

No. 14 mesh

rod mill

to pipeline

A supervisor checks coal entering bins at a coal-slurry processing plant near the Black Mesa pipeline in Arizona. The coal is ground to a fine consistency and then mixed with water to form the slurry that is transported through the pipeline.

depends on more than energy. The cost of transporting Black Mesa coal by pipeline (including dewatering) is four cents per ton-mile. The cost of shipping by rail over the same terrain would be considerably higher.

The Black Mesa pipeline employs technology developed in the 1960s. Newer technology has been developed for the proposed Energy Transportation Systems Inc. (ETSI) pipeline, which would transport coal from Wyoming to Arkansas and Louisiana. This pipeline has been designed to transport 25 million tons of coal per year for a distance of 1,600 kilometers (1,000 miles). Recently, competitive coal haulage bids were submitted to an Arkansas utility by both ETSI and two railroads. One of the railroads, Chicago and Northwestern, submitted the lowest bid and won the contract. As a consequence the pipeline may never be built, but it probably served a useful purpose, nevertheless, in increasing competition and reducing energy costs.

More than two-thirds of the energy consumed by the Black Mesa pipeline and one-third of the energy for the ETSI pipelines are used to separate the coal from the water at the receiving end. Most and perhaps all of this energy could be saved by combining the pipeline slurry and the CWM fuel technologies. Much higher coal concentrations in the pipeline could be employed by the use of CWM additives. It would also appear that additional development will enable the complete elimination of the dewatering process. Two processing plants would be required. At the sending end the coal would be mixed with water and additives, and then pulverized to pipeline consistency. At the receiving end the slurry would be mixed with more chemicals and ground to a fuel consistency. The finished fuel would then be shipped by rail, barge, or ocean tanker to the user.

A major impediment to the construction of slurry pipelines for coal

is the difficulty of obtaining the necessary right-of-way for the laying of the pipe. In 1983 the U.S. House of Representatives rejected a bill that would have given slurry pipelines the right of eminent domain.

Cleaning coal

The biggest drawback to the use of coal is its effect on the environment. A report by the U.S. National Academy of Sciences in mid-1983 directly linked acid rain to the sulfur dioxide and nitrogen dioxide generated by the combustion of fossil fuels. The majority of the sulfur comes from stationary units burning coal.

Removal of the oxides of sulfur from the flue gas is one method of coping with the pollution problem. Between 50 and 80% of the sulfur dioxide can be removed in this way, but the process is expensive and not totally reliable. Problems arise particularly as a result of impurities in the flue gas or in the reagents used in the process.

An alternative and perhaps a less expensive method of compliance is the removal of sulfur from the coal before it is burned. Not only can a large fraction of the sulfur be removed, but also significant reduction can be made in the mineral impurities in coal that lead to the formation of ash. Ash reductions can enlarge the market for coal by permitting the use of CWM fuels in boilers designed to burn oil.

Coal is a complex mixture of organic and mineral constituents. Its makeup varies widely with the geographic location of the coal bed and even within the coal bed itself. The mineral portion of the coal is composed of rock, clay, shale, and iron sulfide; the latter is commonly known as pyrite or fool's gold. Some of these impurities are mixed with the coal in finely divided form and are called inherent ash. Coal as mined also contains larger pieces of rock, particularly from very thin coal seams. The introduction of mechanized equipment into coal mining has led to increasing concentrations of such rock because of the machines' inability

120

Rod mills at the Kayenta slurry preparation plant in Arizona (opposite page) are huge machines that grind the coal to a fine consistency for the coal-slurry mixture. Pumps at Gray Mountain, Arizona (left), push the coal-slurry through the pipeline.

to distinguish the rock from the coal. The total mineral concentration in coal is typically between 9 and 30%.

The organic portion of the coal contains all of the useful part. But it also contains impurities. A substantial fraction of the sulfur in coal is called organic sulfur and consists of sulfur atoms chemically bound to the organic material. The total sulfur content of coal, both mineral and organic (and also small quantities of water-soluble sulfates), typically ranges from 1 to 7% by weight.

The diverse nature of coal impurities has led to a corresponding diversity in the methods for cleaning coal. The oldest and simplest method, employed now only in the smallest of mines, is to hand pick the rock from the coal. Cleaning processes currently in commercial use depend on the difference in density between the mineral and the organic matter. The organic portion of bituminous coal is 1.3 times the density of water, while the inorganic portion is 2–5 times denser than water. This density difference provides a relatively inexpensive means of reducing the concentrations of ash and pyritic sulfur. However, the organic impurities remain with the coal, and, as currently practiced, the finely divided "inherent ash" does also. To remove the latter would require grinding the coal prior to cleaning and would result in a wet coal, which is difficult to dewater and to transport in solid form. In the course of mining, conveying, and cleaning coal, as much as 25% is reduced to fine particles. Because of the difficulty of dewatering these particles and because, in dry form, they are a fire and explosion hazard, they are usually discarded. New technology currently practiced in some cleaning plants eliminates much of this loss (*see* below).

Coarse coal can be cleaned by a number of different methods, two of the most popular being jigs and heavy media washers. Jigs are simple devices consisting of a screen on which the coal is placed. Currents of water are forced upward in a pulsating flow. The denser impurities tend

121

Froth flotation, the most widely accepted method of cleaning fine particles of coal, is based on the difference in the surface chemistry of coal and the mineral matter in the particles. A small amount of an oil-based material is applied to the particles. It adheres to the coal but not to the mineral matter. The slurry of particles is then agitated in a froth flotation cell, where air is bubbled up through the mixture. The bubbles cling to the coal particles, which then rise to the surface while the denser mineral matter sinks to the bottom and is discarded.

to sink, while the less dense coal rises to the top. A much more efficient device is the heavy media washer. Instead of using water, which is less dense than either coal or rock, the liquid medium is a slurry of magnetite in water. The density of the medium is adjusted to be higher than that of coal but less than that of rock. The raw coal is mixed with the medium and is fed into a vessel. The dense fraction exits at a lower level and the lighter fraction at a higher one. The magnetite is then magnetically separated from both fractions and reused.

The fine-coal cleaning method that has gained greatest acceptance is froth flotation. Its use is growing rapidly to prevent the discard of the fine particles, which is an environmental problem as well as an economic loss. Froth flotation relies on the difference in the surface chemistry of coal and ash instead of the difference in specific gravity. Coal attracts oil and repels water, and the mineral matter does just the opposite. The fine particles are treated with a very small quantity of an oil-based surface agent that adheres to the coal particles rather than to the mineral matter. The resulting slurry of particles is then introduced into a froth flotation cell, where it is agitated. Air is bubbled up through the slurry. Air bubbles cling to the coal particles and rise to the surface, while the denser mineral matter sinks to the bottom where it exits and is discarded.

One disadvantage of froth flotation is that the finely divided iron-sulfide particles also repel water and remain with the coal fraction. To offset this problem, a process employing a second stage is under development using different additives (coal depressants, xanthate surfactants, frothers, and pH modifiers) that will selectively float the pyrites. A second disadvantage of froth flotation is the difficulty and expense of dewatering. In spite of these drawbacks the coupling of coarse-coal cleaning and fine-coal cleaning has made low-ash coal (2–5%) available in tonnage quantites.

The combination of fine-coal cleaning and coal-water fuel mixtures presents obvious advantages. First, the fine particles that normally occur

122

in coal handling do not require complete dewatering after the cleaning processes; they can be used directly in the manufacture of fuel. Second, the degree to which inherent ash can be liberated from the coal fraction depends on the degree of fineness to which the coal is ground: the finer the grind, the greater the separation. The fineness of the coal required for combustion of CWM fuels allows the coal to be cleaned more thoroughly.

New cleaning technologies are being developed. Of great interest are new microbial techniques to reduce the sulfur content, both the mineral and the organic. Different microorganisms are required for the two types of sulfur compounds, For mineral sulfur, microorganisms found in sulfur-containing natural springs have been found effective. The microorganisms used to remove organic sulfur were originally found in nature but have been genetically modified to be effective with a number of organic sulfur compounds, including those found in coal. These microorganisms liberate a complex enzyme that oxidizes the organic sulfur to form a water-soluble sulfate, which can then be separated from the coal by washing.

The cleaning of fine coal in a dry state is advantageous if the product is not to be used to manufacture CWM fuel, because it eliminates the dewatering step. The separation of mineral matter by high-gradient magnetic fields is under development. A magnetic field is set up in a matrix of stainless steel wool to produce high magnetic gradients. As raw coal is introduced into the matrix, the mineral matter adheres to the matrix and the coal passes through. The process at the present stage of development is expensive.

The future of coal as a fuel depends not only on the development of new technology but also on such considerations as the politics of foreign oil and the long-term outlook for nuclear power.

Future prospects

Coal in liquid form, coal flowing through long-distance pipelines, cleaner coal: will these developments bring on a resurgence in the use of this most plentiful fuel? The answer to this question will depend not only on new technology but on other factors too. How soon will the reserves of oil be depleted, what will be the price of oil, and what will be the politics of foreign oil? Will nuclear power regain the credibility it has lost, especially in the United States, or will it continue to decline there? And what will be the outcome of efforts to protect the environment? The road ahead for coal is difficult but is one of strategic importance not only for the United States but also for much of the rest of the world.

FOR ADDITIONAL READING

C. B. Henderson, R. S. Scheffee, and E. T. McHale, "Coal-Water Slurries—A Low-Cost Fuel for Boilers," *Energy Progress* (June 1983).

Proceedings of the Fourth and Fifth International Symposia on Coal Slurry Combustion and Technology, United States Department of Energy, Pittsburgh Energy Technology Center, Pittsburgh, Pa., May 1982 and April 1983.

E. J. Wasp, J. P. Kenny, and R. S. Gandi, *Slurry Pipeline Transportation* (TransTech Publications, 1977).

"More Coal Per Ton," *EPRI Journal* (June 1979, pp. 6–13).

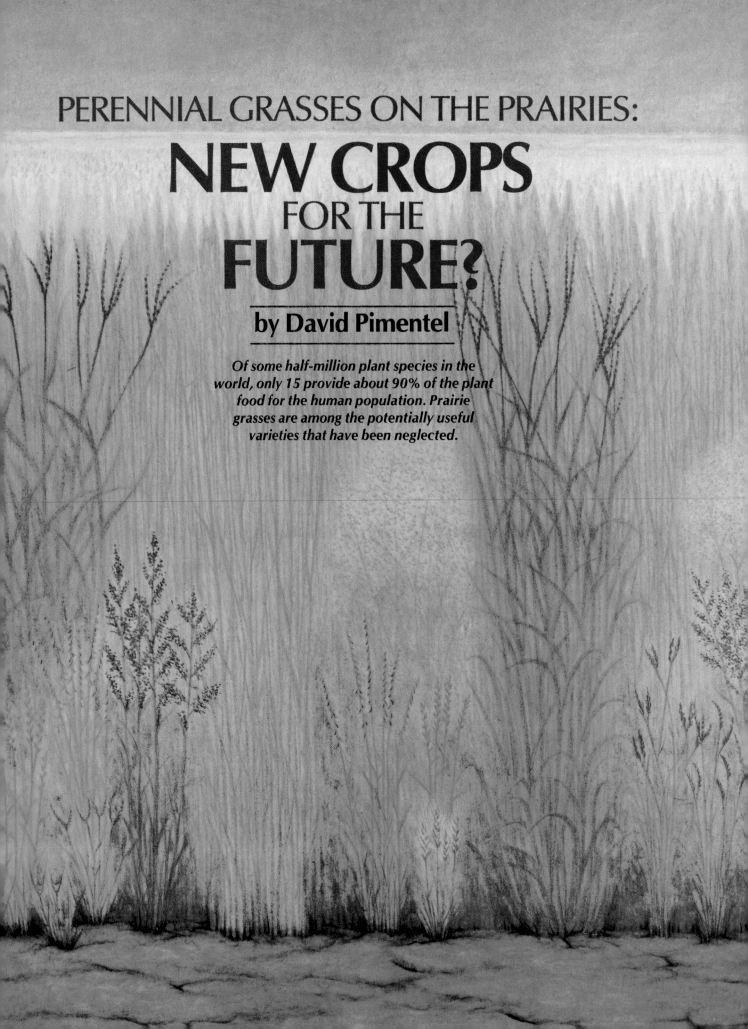

PERENNIAL GRASSES ON THE PRAIRIES:
NEW CROPS
FOR THE
FUTURE?

by David Pimentel

Of some half-million plant species in the world, only 15 provide about 90% of the plant food for the human population. Prairie grasses are among the potentially useful varieties that have been neglected.

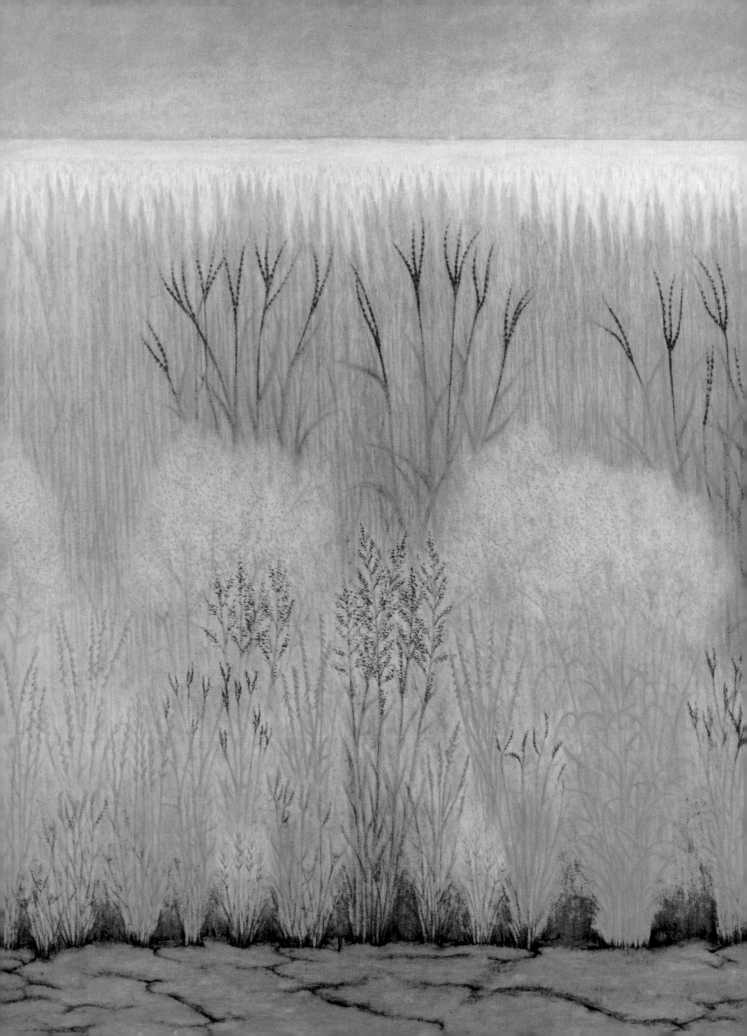

DAVID PIMENTEL is a Professor in the
Department of Entomology and
Section of Ecology and Systematics,
Cornell University, Ithaca, N.Y.

(Overleaf) Illustration by Leon Bishop

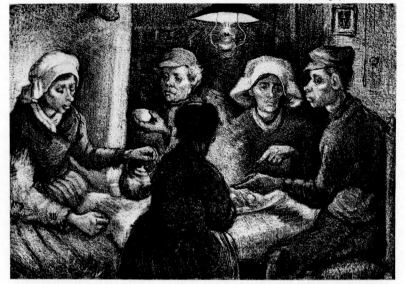

Collection, The Museum of Modern Art, New York.
Gift of Mr. & Mrs. A. A. Rosen; photograph, Art Resource

*Lesions on the leaf and rot on the ear
reveal the presence of southern corn-leaf
blight. In 1970 the disease destroyed
half the corn in some parts of the
United States.*

J. C. Allen & Sons

Considering that there are as many as ten million species of plants and animals, it is surprising that humans depend mainly on only 22 species for their food supply. Indeed, about 90% of the foods come from 15 major crops and 7 livestock types. The crops are rice, wheat, corn (maize), sorghum, millet, rye, barley, common bean, soybean, peanut, cassava, sweet potato, potato, coconut, and banana, and the livestock include cattle, buffalo, sheep, goats, swine, ducks, and chickens. When regional analyses are made, the variety of crops and livestock utilized becomes much smaller. For example, in some regions of Asia a single crop, rice, provides people with nearly 90% of their protein and calories.

Many hazards are associated with dependence on just a few crops for food. A classic example is the impact of the potato blight (*Phytophthora infestans*) in Ireland at a time when the human diet there was based mainly on potatoes. In the early 1800s adults in Ireland consumed each day about 4.5 kilograms (10 pounds) of potatoes and half a liter (one pint) of milk. In addition to supplying adequate amounts of calories, this diet also provided minimal requirements for protein, vitamins, and minerals. The food calories totaled 3,800 kilocalories per day; this compares with the 3,500 kilocalories consumed per person in the United States today. When the fungal potato blight spread through Ireland's potato fields, the crops were destroyed—and along with them the major food source of the Irish population. Other food crops were not available, and many people who could not leave Ireland starved.

More recently, in the United States during 1970, southern corn-leaf blight (*Helminthosporium maydis*) destroyed half of the corn in some regions of the nation. Corn is the prime feed grain of U.S. livestock, which in turn become a part of the food supply for humans. Genetic uniformity in the hybrid corn crop made it susceptible to the fungal pest outbreak; fortunately, within a year the problem was corrected and the disease outbreak curtailed.

126

When only a few crops are the source of food, pest outbreaks can greatly decrease the available food supply. Also, drastic changes in temperature and rainfall during the growing season may cause crop failures. For example, during the 1983 growing season in the U.S. corn belt states, unseasonably high temperatures and drought conditions reduced corn yields by as much as 50 to 80% in some areas. Although these losses are expected to increase food costs, especially of meat products, other crops can be substituted for the corn so that the human population in the United States will continue to have an adequate food supply. Crop diversity not only reduces the chances of crop failures but also helps ensure a dependable food supply.

"The Potato Eaters," by Vincent van Gogh, shows a family seated for their evening meal of potatoes and coffee. When a potato blight spread throughout Ireland in 1845, it destroyed the major food source of most of the Irish population.

Assets of grain crops

Information about the characteristics of the presently used grains is basic to evaluating the crop potential of other plants. Those crops now in use yield from 500 to 7,000 kilograms of grain per hectare (450 to 6,200 pounds per acre; 1 kilogram per hectare = 0.89 pound per acre) during a growing season of three to four months. A yield of 1,500 kilograms (3,300 pounds) is sufficient to feed five humans as vegetarians for a year. When cereal grains and legumes (such as soybeans) are combined in the correct proportions, human food energy needs as well as requirements of protein (amino acids), calcium, iron, vitamins, thiamin, and riboflavin are met.

Several characteristics of grains have enabled them to dominate world agriculture. Grains can be cultured under a wide variety of environmental conditions, including heavy and light soil types, annual rainfall levels that range from 25 to 200 centimeters (10 to 80 inches; 1 centimeter = 0.4 inch), and temperatures that range from 18° to 38° C (65° to 100° F).

All the grains now in use are considered tropical annuals. Because they are planted and harvested within three to four months, they can be grown during the short, favorable temperature and rainfall conditions in diverse environments throughout the world. For example, a tropical grain such as corn can be cultured in temperate regions such as the United States and Europe.

Weed and pest problems can be minimized by planting annual grain crops. Plowing and turning under the soil prior to planting buries most weeds, insect pests, and plant pathogens (disease agents) in the soil. The seeds are then planted in the generally pest-free soil, at an optimal depth, during a time that coincides with favorable temperature and moisture conditions for the particular crop. Under these favorable conditions the crop is provided a head start over competing weeds and attacking insects and plant pathogens.

Another major advantage of grains is their low moisture content at harvest. Only 10 to 15%, contrasted with the 80 to 95% moisture content of fruits and vegetables, this characteristic makes grains less susceptible to spoilage and destruction by insects and other pests. Low moisture content also decreases the costs associated with transportation and distribution of the harvested crop.

127

Grant Heilman

Tilling soil for annual crops can cause such problems as erosion, as seen above in an irrigated field of peanuts in Oklahoma. Contour planting of corn (light color) and wheat in Pennsylvania (below) uses the terrain to good advantage but can also lead to soil erosion.

Grant Heilman

(Top) Gary R. Zahn—Bruce Coleman, Inc.; (bottom) E. R. Degginger; (right) John Shaw—Tom Stack & Associates

Environmental problems with grain crop culture

Although tilling the soil for annual crops such as grains is advantageous for pest control, tillage causes many serious environmental problems, including soil erosion and rapid water runoff. Tilled soil is exposed to water and wind erosion. Water runs off barren soil 10 to 25 times faster than off soil with vegetation cover, and so tilled cropland rapidly loses both soil and nutrients. The sediments and nutrients subsequently carried to streams and lakes contribute to water pollution problems. Rapid water runoff increases the loss of soil moisture that is essential to crop production and also causes downstream flooding.

Erosion from land devoted to annual crops, especially row crops like grains, diminishes the nutrients needed for plant growth. Even under the best management soil formation is slow, averaging about 2.5 centimeters in depth in 200 to 300 years; in contrast, the average soil loss from U.S. croplands is estimated to be 2.5 centimeters in 15 to 20 years. Recent reports from the state of Iowa indicate that one-half of Iowa's topsoil has been lost since farming began there during the last century.

Perennial grain crops would save energy because the soil would not need to be tilled as often; they would also help prevent erosion. At the top left is a mid-grass prairie in South Dakota. A tall-grass prairie in Alberta, Canada, is shown at the bottom left, and a short-grass prairie surrounds an old church in South Dakota (above).

129

blue grama	western wheatgrass	buffalo grass	Eastern gamagrass
Bouteloua gracilus	*Agropyron smithii*	*Buchloe dactyloides*	*Tripsacum dactyloides*
short grass	mid-grass	short grass	tall grass

Sand dropseed, shown in midsummer in Texas, is a perennial grass that in one experiment yielded 1,008 kilograms of grain per hectare. Only small amounts of fertilizers and no pesticides were used.

Susan Gibler—Tom Stack & Associates

Topsoil loss adversely affects crop productivity by reducing organic matter and the fine clays that help hold plant nutrients, by diminishing the capacity of the soil to hold water, and by restricting rooting depth as the soil thins. In some regions of the southern United States soil losses during the past 100 to 200 years have resulted in yield reductions that range from 25 to 50% for such crops as corn, soybeans, cotton, oats, and wheat. Nonetheless, crop yields in most U.S. regions have been rising because of increased energy inputs (fertilizers and pesticides, for example) and the use of high-yielding crop varieties.

In addition to causing floods, water runoff carries sediments to reservoirs, rivers, and lakes. Each year in the United States more than two billion metric tons of sediments settle in the nation's aquatic ecosystems. As a result, about 375 million metric tons of sediments must be dredged from U.S. rivers and harbors in order to keep them navigable, at a cost of about $300 million each year. Also, sediments seriously harm freshwater fish and other aquatic life.

Energy use in crop production

Large quantities of energy are required to till the soil. About 60 liters of oil are required to plow and disk the soil of one hectare to ready it for planting (about 6½ gallons per acre). This is about 10% of the total of 600 liters of fuel equivalents that are required to produce one hectare of a crop like corn. If a hectare of land were tilled by hand to ready it for planting, about 400 labor hours could replace the fossil energy. Thus,

sand dropseed	split-beard bluestem	Indian grass	switchgrass
Sporobolus cryptandrus	*Andropogon ternarius*	*Sorghastrum nutans*	*Panicum virgatum*
short grass	mid-grass	tall grass	tall grass

tilling the soil for planting is energy-intensive whether carried out by tractor power or manpower.

Additional energy inputs into the system are required to offset both the loss of nutrients in the soil and loss of productivity of the land resulting from erosion. With a soil erosion rate of 20 metric tons per hectare, about 100 kilograms of nitrogen, 20 kilograms of phosphorus, 600 kilograms of potassium, and 160 kilograms of calcium are lost with the soil. Approximately 250 liters of fuel are required to replace the nutrients contained in those 20 tons of soil.

If, as reported, U.S. cropland has already lost more than one-third of its topsoil, then an additional 100 liters of fuel equivalents must be used to offset the lost productivity of the soil. Thus, it is evident that planting tropical annual crops is much more energy-intensive than the cultivation of perennial crops. Perennial grain crops would save energy because they would reduce the need to till the soil and would also help prevent soil erosion from rainfall and wind. Loss of nutrients would be decreased and the productivity of the land maintained.

Current agricultural practices based on the cultivation of annual crops are responsible for degrading arable land, depleting water reserves, and using substantial amounts of fossil energy. In fact, agricultural systems like that of the United States are "mining" these vital resources and, as a result, do not appear to be ecologically sustainable over the long run.

Some agriculturalists, aware of the growing environmental problems, are employing such techniques as no-till culture, crop rotation, contour

Buffalo grass produced about 2,000 kilograms of grain per hectare in a test conducted in 1964. By contrast, wheat yields in the United States average about 2,500 kilograms per hectare. The wheat, however, requires annual tilling.

Susan Gibler—Tom Stack & Associates

131

Among the perennial grasses that show particular promise as possible future crops are Eastern gamagrass (below), squirreltail barley (bottom left), blue grama (bottom center), and sideoats grama (bottom right).

planting, strip cropping, and terracing. Associated with all of these technologies are benefits and risks. For example, while no-till culture diminishes soil erosion, it leads to an increase in weeds, pest insects, and plant pathogens. To deal with the increased pest problems, much more pesticide has to be applied to no-till crops. Thus, the energy saved by not tilling is often expended in the increased use of pesticides. Considered overall, however, the benefits of no-till and other soil and water conservation practices outweigh the risks.

Perennial grains

Perennial grains provide continuous cover for the soil and protect it from water and wind erosion. The presence of a perennial crop prevents rapid water runoff and facilitates the percolation of water into the soil for later crop use. This in turn increases crop productivity and also reduces the need for irrigation. Irrigation is an energy-intensive operation, requiring about twice as much energy as do all other inputs to grow a grain crop. Thus, in areas where rainfall is low and partial irrigation is necessary, perennial grain culture could save substantial amounts of fuel each year.

Crops with a long growing season can collect large amounts of solar energy and convert it into grain. This is why some of the new hybrids, such as those of corn, have been highly productive. Perennial grains also have this advantage because they are established plants, ready to collect solar energy as soon as temperature and moisture conditions are favorable. All annual grains must be started each year from seed, and so most perennials have a longer, more productive growing season.

In the area of energy conservation estimates are that the perennial grains could save from one-third to one-half the fuel inputs now being used in annual grain production. Fuel is saved because there is no need

(Top) Russ Kinne—Photo Researchers; (bottom left) Steve Kraseman—DRK Photo; (bottom center) V. P. Weinland—Photo Researchers; (bottom right) Susan Gibler—Photo Researchers

Prairie grasses that are potentially valuable grain crops include western wheatgrass, June grass, Indian grass (above, left to right), and switchgrass (below left). Wild rice (below right) is a grass that grows near water in Minnesota and nearby regions and has long been harvested on a small scale.

Cordgrass, seen near Boston, Massachusetts (top), and on the coast of Georgia (bottom), is a perennial that could be cultivated as a crop in salt marsh habitats.

(Top) Townsend P. Dickinson—Photo Researchers; (bottom) Wendell Metzen—Bruce Coleman, Inc.

for tilling, reduced need for fertilizer to compensate for erosion loss, and less need for irrigation.

Prairie grasses are among several suitable perennial grasses that could be cultured crops. Ecologically, these grasses possess many assets that annual grains do not. Because they are native to North America, they have evolved beneficial ecological characteristics that enable them to survive. They are successfully adapted to the soil, temperature, and moisture conditions of the continent. They have evolved mechanisms that help them resist pests, and, in addition to being perennials, they also successfully reproduce. As with all perennials a minimum of cultivation is necessary. Overall, this natural grain system should be nearly self-sustaining.

As important as the ecological adaptations of perennial prairie grasses is their capacity to produce grain yields comparable to those of the major annual grains. In 1943 H. R. Brown reported grain yields of twelve native prairie grasses in Oklahoma. One of the grasses, sand dropseed (*Sporobolus cryptandrus*), yielded 1,008 kilograms per hectare with minimal inputs of fertilizers and no pesticides. It should be noted that the plants studied by Brown came directly out of the wild and had not been subjected to any selection and breeding program.

Since Brown's experiments, agricultural scientists have questioned whether perennial grasses can ever yield as well as do the annual varieties. Recent evidence suggests that they can. Experiments by R. M. Ahring in 1964 indicated that buffalo grass (*Buchloe dactyloides*) produced nearly 2,000 kilograms per hectare with only 67 kilograms of nitrogen and 67 kilograms of phosphorus used as fertilizer. Current U.S. wheat yields average nearly 2,500 kilograms per hectare and use about 70 kilograms of nitrogen and 30 kilograms of phosphorus. In contrast to wheat the buffalo grass has never been selected and bred for high-yielding characteristics. With such selection and breeding, scientists project that some of the prairie grasses eventually will produce yields equal to or greater than those of wheat.

Close-up of cordgrass growing near San Francisco Bay shows exuded salt crystals clinging to a leaf spear.

Jeff Foott—Photo Researchers

The research of Wes Jackson focused on the potential of another perennial prairie grass, Eastern gamagrass (*Tripsacum dactyloides*). A relative of corn, this plant is well adapted to most corn-growing regions of the United States. The plant produces rhizomes, enabling it to be propagated vegetatively. Similar to corn, the flower part that sets seed is separate from the part that produces pollen and, thus, is relatively easy to emasculate by plant breeders in the process of making crosses to improve yields. In addition, cattle like gamagrass as a forage.

Other prairie grasses also merit attention. Squirreltail barley (*Sitanion hystrix*) is a beautiful short-grass type that produces relatively large seeds. The long "whiskers" on the grain make it appear similar to barley and rye. Another well-established short-grass grain is blue grama (*Bouteloua gracilis*). Although its small seeds may limit its potential use, it could prove valuable as a forage grass for animals.

In the U.S. prairie region several mid-grass types also have potential for development. These include sideoats grama (*Bouteloua curtipendula*), western wheatgrass (*Agropyron smithii*), June grass (*Koeleria cristata*),

135

Photos, Noel D. Vietmeyer

The winged bean (top left), growing in pods on vines (above) and at a vegetable market in Thailand (top right), is a legume especially suited for cultivation in tropical regions. It is an annual and therefore requires yearly tillage.

and perhaps split-beard bluestem (*Andropogon ternarius*). To date no research has been carried out with these grasses as food crops.

Two tall-grass types in the prairie that should be given some consideration for a grain crop are Indian grass (*Sorghastrum nutans*) and switchgrass (*Panicum virgatum*). An increase in the use of fertilizer with tall-grass types may result in producing even taller grasses that could "lodge" (fall over) before harvest. Years ago lodging was a major problem with traditional rice varieties when large amounts of fertilizer nitrogen were first applied to the crop. Fortunately, selection and breeding using a short-stem rice type easily corrected this problem. This approach also may be desirable with any of the wild prairie grasses that respond to fertilizers by growing too tall for successful handling.

Legumes and other perennials

In addition to prairie grasses other unused plants deserve attention. Wild rice (*Zizania aquatica*) is a grass that is harvested in Minnesota and nearby regions and is a valuable grain. Although it is a profitable small-scale crop, no major effort has been made to select and breed wild rice for commercial agriculture.

Bulrush sedge species that thrive in moist habitats produce seeds that may be used as a food for either humans or animals. Several perennial grasses, such as smooth cordgrass (*Spartina alterniflora*, both "wet" and "dry" types), have the potential for cultivation in salt marsh habitats.

Other important food crops include leguminous grains such as the common bean, soybean, and peanut. These are also tropical annuals with many of the same environmental hazards for agriculture as the annual grains. A new popular legume in many parts of the world is the winged bean. It has many desirable characteristics, but unfortunately it is another tropical annual that would not be well suited to correct some of the ecological problems of temperate U.S. agriculture.

136

Little or no research has been devoted to investigating the potential of native perennial legumes for U.S. agriculture. There are some native wild pea, clover, and vetch species that may have some potential to produce grains for human consumption or forage for livestock use. A major advantage of the perennial legumes is their capacity for biological nitrogen fixation, the ability to utilize atmospheric nitrogen for nourishment. Commercial nitrogen fertilizers are extremely costly in terms of energy, and for some crops the energy input for nitrogen represents nearly one-third of the total energy for the crop system. Thus, native perennial leguminous grains have a significant ecological advantage as potential new crops and should be investigated.

Conclusion

The world food supply at present relies primarily on ten grain crops. In the United States these might be expanded to include grains from many underexploited species of prairie grasses and wild legumes. Increasing diversity in the human food supply helps protect against the catastrophes of pest outbreaks, droughts, and freezes that can destroy crops.

Culturing perennial grass crops could conserve water and fossil energy supplies and could also help maintain the quality of cropland by reducing erosion. In addition, the increased use of perennial legume grains would reduce agriculture's reliance on nitrogen fertilizers.

Perhaps not all the suggested new crops will be commercially successful or will produce foods acceptable to humans, but many might at least provide feed and forage for livestock. When one considers that 10 to 100 kilocalories of plant material must be fed to livestock to produce 1 kilocalorie of animal protein, the advantages of using new crops for livestock production are obvious.

These potential new crops are not new but are simply underutilized or ignored because the major tropical annual grains have thus far produced most of the needs of human society. The prairie grasses, in particular, deserve the attention of the plant breeders and agriculturalists who have been striving to make agriculture both more productive and ecologically sustainable.

FOR ADDITIONAL READING

R. M. Ahring, "The management of buffalo grass for seed production in Oklahoma," *Technical Bulletin T-109* (Oklahoma State Experimental Station, May 1964).

H. R. Brown, "Growth and seed yields of native prairie plants in various habitats of the mixed-prairie," *Transactions of the Kansas Academy of Science*, Vol. 46 (The World Company, 1943).

Wes Jackson, *New Roots for Agriculture* (Friends of the Earth, 1980).

National Academy of Sciences, Advisory Committee on Technological Innovation, *Underexploited Tropical Plants with Promising Economic Value* (National Academy of Sciences, 1975).

David Pimentel and Marcia Pimentel, *Food, Energy, and Society* (John Wiley & Sons, 1979).

OVERLOOKED ANIMALS:

NEW HOPE FOR THE TROPICS

by Noel Vietmeyer

In the world's tropical regions many animals are great potential sources of food, clothing, and labor.

In Europe and the United States a person consumes an average of about 9 kilograms (20 pounds) of meat each month, whereas in the less developed countries a person eats less than that in an entire year. One important cause of this difference is that most of the less developed countries are in tropical or subtropical regions and the livestock species the world depends on today are best adapted to temperate conditions. In turn this is because some 10,000 years ago Stone Age peoples in temperate areas of Europe, the Middle East, and central Asia captured and tamed aurochs, mouflon, wild boar, and wild horses, and the best-known breeds of their descendants—cattle, sheep, pigs, and horses—usually perform best in regions with moderate temperatures.

In the past it was thought that the best way to raise animal productivity outside the temperate zone was to introduce high-performing breeds from North America, Europe, or Australia and adapt them to the alien climate. As a result, since the 1950s in particular, less developed countries in Africa, Asia, and Latin America have at great expense imported many high-performance breeds from temperate areas. But all too often these imports failed to survive or reproduce, let alone maintain their high production of meat and milk amid the heat and diseases of the tropics.

139

Male banteng engage in combat in Indonesia. These animals flourish in hot, humid areas.

NOEL VIETMEYER was staff officer for a 1983 report on Asia's overlooked animals published for the benefit of less developed countries by the National Research Council in Washington, D.C.

(Page 138) Zebu cattle and water buffalo approach the Jalmahal (Water Palace) near Jaipur, India. (Overleaf) A domestic water buffalo peers out of its ground-level living quarters in its owner's house in Nepal.

(Overleaf) Photos, Gerald Cubitt

For example, in 1982 a herd of 98 pregnant Holstein heifers was imported to the lowlands of Venezuela from Virginia. Of their calves 23 aborted or were born dead and 62 died during their first year. Furthermore, within nine months of arrival 8 heifers died, 40 had foot or leg problems, 20 had severe mastitis, and the yield of milk declined until it was no greater than that of the local breed. Thus the enormous cost of airfreighting the animals from the United States to Venezuela could hardly be justified.

More recently some animal scientists have objected to the wholesale importation of temperate-zone livestock into tropical countries until a fair evaluation of the existing indigenous livestock has been made. Native animals may not compare with the imports in maximum productivity, but, being adapted to the tropical environment, they usually have qualities of survival that the imported "superior" livestock lack. Also, in many cases the local animal's poor growth and low yield of meat and milk are not due to any lack of genetic potential but to poor management. Given attention, some of these animals show remarkable gains in productivity.

There is a slow awakening to the potential value of these indigenous tropical animals, and Asia is one of the areas that is gaining recognition as a source of livestock species that could prove to be of great value. Some examples include banteng, kouprey, gaur, mithan, several varieties of pigs, and the babirusa. In 1983 the U.S. National Academy of Sciences published a report drawing world attention to Asia's wealth of native animal resources. Today these species are overlooked, none of them well known to the rest of the world. Nevertheless, they offer promise as new and important alternatives for animal husbandry in the tropics.

Banteng

Banteng resemble small cows and are often called "Bali cattle." However, they are not a breed of cattle but a distinct bovine species, *Bos javanicus*. To the casual glance the golden-brown females and calves look like

140

Jersey cattle, but a closer look reveals some unusual features. Banteng have white rumps—as if they'd backed into a freshly painted barn—and their legs have white "stockings." Banteng males are distinct from the females. They are larger and black, though they also have white rumps and white stockings. The males reach heights of 1½ meters (5 feet) and may weigh as much as 550 kilograms (1,200 pounds).

Wild banteng are found throughout Southeast Asia from Burma to Indonesia. However, in prehistoric times they were domesticated only in what is now Indonesia. Today, these domesticated banteng number more than 1.5 million head and represent some 20% of the total "cattle" population in Indonesia. Gourmets consider the meat to be the finest of beef, and Indonesia cannot export enough to satisfy demand just in Hong Kong and Singapore without seriously depleting the breeding herds.

Only a few scientists outside of Asia have ever worked with these animals, but it is clear that banteng thrive under hot, humid conditions. In studying a small herd in northern Australia that has fended for itself and survived since the 1820s, Australian government researchers noted that when pasture quality is poor banteng maintain weight and body condition better than cattle. Also, these hardy little bovines seem to resist many tropical parasites and diseases—ticks and tick-borne diseases, for example.

David Butcher, assistant director of the Western Plains Zoo at Dubbo, New South Wales, is excited by this animal's promise. He has found that the banteng in his collection are docile, breed well, and have good rates of feed conversion. Butcher feeds them no concentrated rations—in fact, he finds that they will eat only natural grasses supplemented by some hay during winter. This basic diet keeps them in good (even overweight) condition. It is Butcher's view that the banteng's potential, especially for tropical and subtropical areas, has been overlooked.

Although banteng are promising in their own right, they may also benefit tropical regions by passing on their genetic traits to cattle. This is

A herd of domestic banteng cows grazes on a hillside on the Bila River Ranch in Celebes, Indonesia.

Allen D. Tillman

A team of banteng (right) is used for rice planting on Java in Indonesia. A Madura bull (below) wears a dress harness before a race. Madura hybrids, a combination of banteng and zebu, thrive in extreme heat and have been bred to race.

because banteng will crossbreed with domestic cattle to produce hybrids that are notable for vigor and heat tolerance; mating them with either European-type cattle (*Bos taurus*) or the hump-backed zebu cattle (*Bos indicus*) of India normally gives progeny in which the males are sterile owing to chromosomal incompatibility. But virtually all of the 575,000 "cattle" on Madura and nearby Indonesian islands are fertile hybrids that are the result of mating banteng with zebu. This probably occurred about 1,500 years ago when Indian invaders settled on Java with their cattle.

The Madura hybrids have lost the banteng's white rump and most of the zebu's hump. They reportedly show better growth rates than the pure banteng species itself. They are robust animals, able to grow and work well under extremes of heat and poor nutrition; indeed they have been bred to race.

Today, at least one cattle breeder in the United States is following the lead of the Madurese in studying banteng-cattle hybrids. Bert Wheeler, owner of the Camp Cooley Ranch near Easterly, Texas, has a herd of banteng, and researchers from nearby Texas A & M University have produced more than 200 hybrids by crossing them with Wheeler's Charolais and Aberdeen Angus cattle. Their goal is to produce a hybrid that is one-eighth banteng, which, they believe, will result in a high-yielding beef animal able to thrive in the Texas heat.

Kouprey

The kouprey is another overlooked Asian species with promise for upgrading tropical cattle. Among the rarest animals in the world, the kouprey (*Bos sauveli*) is a native of Kampuchea and Laos. The last large mammal to enter the biology books, it was discovered accidentally in 1937 when a collection of Indochinese animals was sent to Paris and the staff at the Vincennes Zoo could find nothing like it listed in the literature.

The kouprey is perhaps the most primitive of all wild bovines, a "living relic" that has features typical of some cattle that existed in the

142

Pleistocene Epoch approximately 600,000 years ago. It is probably the last of a genetic line descended from the prehistoric wild animal that also gave rise to zebu cattle.

This large, muscular wild ox is a candidate for domestication. Carvings on the temples at Angkor Wat in Kampuchea suggest that it may have been domesticated temporarily during the Khmer culture, 400 to 800 years ago. In the 1950s Prince Sihanouk of Cambodia (now Kampuchea) kept a tame kouprey in his palace in Phnom Penh.

Kouprey bulls stand about two meters (six feet) tall and may weigh almost 900 kilograms (2,000 pounds). They are generally gray in color with widespread horns and huge dewlaps that in some specimens almost touch the ground. This large pendulous surface sways as the animal walks and helps it to shed heat. This is probably one reason for the kouprey's exceptional tolerance for heat and humidity.

Koupreys survive on coarse forage in monsoon forests that are wet and humid for eight or nine months of the year and dry and parched for

Among the many varieties of animals that have been bred at Camp Cooley Ranch near Easterly, Texas, are (left) a hybrid that is one-half banteng, one-quarter Charolais, and one-quarter Brahman and (right) one that is one-half Aberdeen Angus, one-quarter banteng, one-eighth Charolais, and one-eighth Brahman. The goal is to produce a high-yielding beef animal that can thrive in the Texas heat.

Bert Wheeler's Camp Cooley Ranch; photo, Sandra Greaves

the remainder. Under such conditions many diseases are endemic, and koupreys are thought to resist rinderpest, a widespread and devastating cattle disease, as well as other tropical scourges that are prevalent in their habitat. These traits are economically appealing, and as it seems likely that koupreys are interfertile with cattle the animal's potential for improving tropical livestock production is great. Indeed, it has been called potentially the most valuable wildlife species in the world.

Today, however, the kouprey is perilously close to extinction. Only a handful of animals has ever been seen by scientists, and for years it has been feared extinct. In 1982, however, five koupreys were sighted in Thailand, near the Kampuchean border. A team of Thai foresters and conservationists immediately set out to capture them, but the animals apparently retreated across the border, and the attempt was abandoned when a guide stepped on a land mine. This experience exemplified the most tragic aspect of the kouprey: its native habitat has become a battleground. Nevertheless, researchers are hopeful that koupreys can be captured, and several museums and universities are holding funds in reserve for sending teams of scientists to Southeast Asia to capture these animals when they are sighted again.

Harold Coolidge Foundation/New York Zoological Society

Koupreys, among the rarest animals in the world, were photographed in Indochina in 1951. This single frame is from the only film footage of this animal known to exist.

Gaur and mithan

Sharing the kouprey's habitat is another wild bovine, the gaur (*Bos gaurus*), a shy ruminant found in hill forests from India and Nepal to Indochina and Malaysia. Like the kouprey, it developed in an environment that suffers flooding rains and searing droughts, as well as swarming pests and parasites.

It is a majestic animal, massive, muscular, somewhat resembling the bison in profile. Bulls can stand more than two meters (six feet) tall and weigh well over 900 kilograms. Females and young bulls are coffee-colored or red-brown; bulls are jet black, their horns large and gently curving. With its large size and massive muscles the gaur would seem to be a potentially valuable meat-producing animal for the tropics.

Despite their reputation for being fierce and untamable, gaur adjust well to human presence. In Malaysia, for instance, they feed in farm fields, along roadsides, and near villages and towns. In captivity they in fact become tame and manageable and are promising as a domesticated species—perhaps as an exploited captive like the bison now found on several hundred farms in North America.

A gaur family of cow, calves, and bull (left to right) is observed in Kanha National Park in central India. A large animal that can withstand heat and drought, the gaur has adapted well to the presence of humans.

G. B. Schaller—Bruce Coleman, Inc.

Mithan bull in the East Berlin zoo allows the zoo's assistant director to give it a friendly pat, while a mithan calf looks on. These unusually gentle animals have been domesticated to pull plows and other implements in India, Burma, Bhutan, and Bangladesh.

Gaur can interbreed with cattle, thereby introducing into cattle genes for muscular development, tolerance of heat and humidity, and resistance to parasites. If the cross retains the mild temperament of domestic cattle, a powerful and productive beast of burden could result.

Once gaur were common throughout South and Southeast Asia from India to Vietnam, but by the 1980s the total world population had been reduced to only a few thousand animals found mainly in scattered reserves in India, Thailand, and Malaysia. Agricultural development, war, hunting, hydroelectric dams, human settlements, logging, and disease transmitted by feral cattle threaten to wipe out even those few.

The possibility that gaur could become domestic animals or that they could be bred with cattle is exemplified by the existence and uses of the mithan (*Bos frontalis*). This animal is considered to be a domesticated form of gaur, although this has not been firmly settled. It is a large bovine used by the hill peoples of Bhutan, northeastern India, Bangladesh, and western Burma and is the main domestic animal of the Nagas of Assam.

The mithan is large and handsome. Bulls are usually black and occasionally exceed 1⅔ meters (5½ feet) in height and 900 kilograms in weight. Most females and calves are brown, but piebald animals of both sexes are also common. The Indian state of Arunachal Pradesh has some 50,000 mithan, and nearby Bhutan has a national herd of approximately 60,000 head of mithan-cattle hybrids.

The mithan includes more tree leaves and shrubs in its diet than grazing animals such as cattle, and herds are often allowed to range freely and feed themselves in the woods. They have an insatiable craving for salt, and people keep the animals from wandering too far by placing salt licks near their villages.

Mithans are unusually tame and gentle. They are easily raised, and normally even a stranger is safe in approaching one. Villagers use mithan and mithan-cattle hybrids as draft animals to pull plows and other implements. The government of Bhutan is developing a dairy breed by mating mithans, which produce rich milk with a high butterfat content, with local cattle.

145

Bearded Pig
Height: 100 cm
Weight: 150 kg

 Javan Warty Pig (female)
Height: 45 cm
Weight: 40–60 kg

 **Javan Warty Pig (male)**
Height: 90 cm
Weight: 80–120 kg

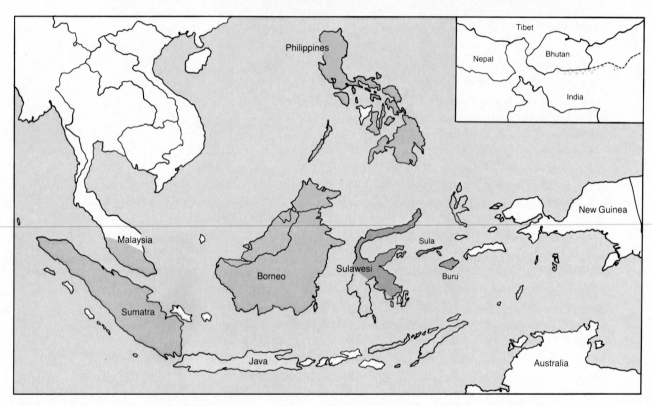

Babirusa (female)
Height: 40 cm
Weight: 50 kg

Babirusa (male)
Height: 80 cm
Weight: 100 kg

Sulawesi Warty Pig
Height: 60 cm
Weight: 40–70 kg

Pygmy Hog
Height: 25 cm
Weight: 10 kg

(Left) Zoological Society of San Diego; (right) Tom McHugh—Photo Researchers; (bottom) James J. Fox

Pygmy hogs, seen in their natural habitats in northeastern India (left and below), are small pigs that are well adapted to tropical conditions. Sulawesi warty pigs (bottom) forage in a field in Timor, Indonesia.

Tropical pigs

As noted earlier the introduction of high-yielding cattle from the temperate zones to the tropics has often met with failure. The experience with pigs has been even worse. The common pig *Sus scrofa* is notably affected by heat. Researchers have shown that at temperatures above 32° C (90° F) respiration commonly increases to rates of 150 to 200 per minute; at such rates the pigs stop eating and lose weight and, if forced into activity, may even die of heat exhaustion. This is particularly true with heavy, highly inbred varieties. In the tropics the common pig also succumbs to certain prevalent parasites, such as the kidney worm (*Stephanurus dentatus*), for which no satisfactory treatment has been developed.

However, tropical Asia has a mix of wild and domesticated pigs that seem tolerant of tropical conditions and that have seldom been investigated by livestock scientists. In parts of Southeast Asia, for instance, pigs are the most abundant source of meat. Most of them are various subspecies of the common domestic pig that represent a genetic treasure trove for tropical swine improvement, but there are, in addition, four species that have been grossly overlooked.

The pygmy hog (*Sus salvanius*) is native to northeastern India and is one of the world's most endangered animals. This tiny animal stands only ⅓ meter (one foot) high and ⅔ meter long when fully grown. Its curly tail is about 2½ centimeters (one inch) long. Although once found widely along the southern foothills of the Himalayas, the pygmy hog is now apparently restricted to one reserve in Assam, where its numbers are fast dwindling because each year people burn the grasses that cover its habitat to make it easier to hunt game.

Indonesia has two species of "warty" pigs. The Javan warty pig (*Sus verrucosus*) is found on Java and nearby islands. The Sulawesi warty pig (*Sus celebensis*) inhabits eastern Indonesia. The Sulawesi warty pig is domesticated on the island of Roti, near Timor, and the pigs of New Guinea seem, at least in the main, to derive from hybridization between it and the common pig. These unusual species are roughly the size of ordinary pigs, but both have long snouts from which hang eruptions of

147

(Top and center) Raleigh Blouch

Javan warty pigs (right and below), roughly the size of common hogs, are native to Java and nearby islands in Indonesia. Once believed to be extinct in the wild, they were found again in 1981 in a small herd on a remote mountainside in eastern Java.

flesh several inches long. The Javan warty pig was thought to be extinct in the wild, but in 1981 Raleigh Blouch of the U.S. found a herd of them on a remote mountainside in eastern Java.

The bearded pig (*Sus barbatus*) has not been domesticated, but it is one of the most eagerly sought sources of wild meat. This is a large hog of the Philippines, Malaysia, and Indonesia (Kalimantan and Sumatra); boars may weigh more than 135 kilograms (300 pounds). It has a long history as one of man's important resources in parts of Indonesia and the Philippines and is a progenitor of some presently domesticated forms. However, it too has become rare as the lowland forests are logged.

These wild pigs are potential sources of genes for improving the domestic hog for the tropics. They apparently do not put on as much fat as do common pigs, which could be of particular nutritional and economic benefit. In many areas where wild pigs occur, strict religious taboos prohibit the eating of their meat. As a consequence the animals are considered vermin, and their populations are being wiped out.

A bearded pig, a large hog of the Philippines, Malaysia, and Indonesia, is a prized source of meat but has never been domesticated.

J. M. Dolan

Babirusa

The babirusa (*Babirousa babyrussa*) is one of the strangest animals of the world. This piglike beast is native to Celebes (Sulawesi) and the Molucca islands of Indonesia and is a retiring animal of the dense jungle. Its feed includes roots, berries, and grubs, and it browses for leaves, more like a deer than a pig. Its closest relative appears to be a wild pig known to have lived in Europe 35 million years ago.

The babirusa is gray-brown and about the size and shape of a large hog. It may weigh more than 90 kilograms (200 pounds). Males have upper tusks that grow upward, piercing through the flesh of the muzzle before curving backward toward the eyes.

The babirusa is a possible species for domestication. It is frequently captured young, tamed, and even bred by the villagers. It is so little known to science that its physiology and capabilities are only slightly understood. Its stomach has an extra sac, which may enable it to digest vegetation high in cellulose, and it has been called a possible "ruminant pig." If this proves true, then the babirusa could be a very important animal for areas of the world where grain and other high-energy feeds are too scarce to feed to pigs.

Human disturbance by hunting, logging, and land clearing for cultivation threaten the babirusa's survival. However, in northern, central, and eastern Celebes the animal remains abundant despite hunting and the widespread burning of the forest to convert it to agriculture.

The babirusa, wild pigs, mithan, gaur, kouprey, madura, and banteng are just some examples of the overlooked livestock on the continent of Asia. Others include the yak, yak-cattle hybrids, tamarau, anoas, goat-antelopes such as the takin and goral, and various species of wild sheep, wild goat, and deer. That it is not idle to speculate on the potential global utility of such animals is demonstrated by the growing worldwide enthusiasm for the water buffalo.

The babirusa, a piglike animal native to dense jungles in the Celebes and Molucca islands of Indonesia, has been easily tamed when captured young and may become an important food source for that region. At the left, a sow and her pig; above, a large old boar, whose tusks have been sawed off to prevent their growing back through its skull.

149

Gaur
Height: 1.8 m
Weight: 940 kg

Kouprey
Height: 1.7 m
Weight: 900 kg

Water Buffalo
Height: 1.6 m
Weight: 900 kg

Wild Banteng
Height: 1.6 m
Weight: 635 kg

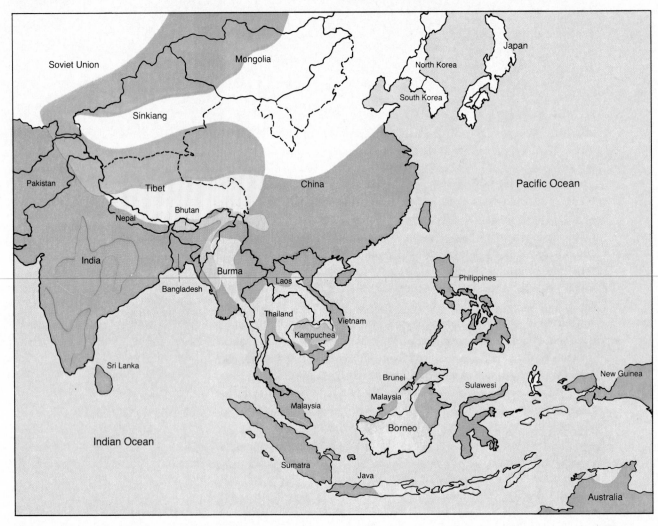

Soviet Union

Mongolia

Japan

North Korea

South Korea

Sinkiang

Pakistan

Tibet

China

Pacific Ocean

Nepal

Bhutan

India

Burma

Bangladesh

Laos

Philippines

Thailand

Vietnam

Kampuchea

Sri Lanka

Brunei

Sulawesi

New Guinea

Malaysia

Malaysia

Borneo

Indian Ocean

Sumatra

Java

Australia

Mithan
Height: 1.5 m
Weight: 540 kg

Domestic Banteng
Height: 1.4 m
Weight: 450–500 kg

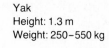

Yak
Height: 1.3 m
Weight: 250–550 kg

Anoa
Height: 80 cm
Weight: 200–300 kg

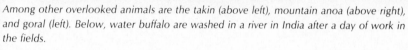

Among other overlooked animals are the takin (above left), mountain anoa (above right), and goral (left). Below, water buffalo are washed in a river in India after a day of work in the fields.

(Top) Ralph W. Phillips; (center) Robert M. Kloepper—ANIMALS, ANIMALS; (bottom) W. Ross Cockrill

Water buffalo dairy cows (right) are raised at an experimental farm in Italy. Mozzarella cheese is made from their milk. Five teams of water buffalo plow in tandem in India (below), and a rare albino swamp buffalo drinks from a puddle in Vietnam (bottom).

Water buffalo

Water buffalo are quite different from bison, which are often mistakenly called buffalo. They are roughly the shape of cattle and are gray-black in color with either swept-back or curly horns, wide muzzles, and a sagging stance. They can grow very large, weighing in at well over 900 kilograms.

The water buffalo has received little but neglect from cattle ranchers and animal scientists alike, yet it is now gaining recognition and appreciation in many parts of the world. Indeed, a book published by the United Nations says, "Of all domestic animals, the buffalo has the greatest unexplored potential for development in meat production, milk yield, and work output."

To most Westerners the water buffalo is an alien animal, and myths about it abound. It is said, for instance, that it is a vicious breed, whereas it is actually probably the gentlest farm animal in the world: sociable,

152

(Top) New York Zoological Society; (bottom) G. B. Schaller—Bruce Coleman, Inc.

genial, and fond of humans. And despite what is widely reported, water buffalo do not need water in which to wallow; they grow and reproduce normally without it, as long as shade is available. Also, they are not exclusively tropical animals. Half a million water buffalo are scattered throughout Eastern Europe, Greece, Italy, and the Soviet Union. Genuine mozzarella cheese is made from the milk of Italian water buffalo raised near Naples. Bulgarian farmers routinely use buffalo to pull snowplows.

The first commercial U.S. herd of water buffalo (53 head) landed in Florida in February 1978. The University of Florida has since become familiar with the animals, and Hugh Popenoe, head of the school's international agriculture programs, reports that water buffalo have potential for the United States, especially Florida with its subtropical climate. Under conditions of poor feed they seem to have a competitive advantage; they grow more quickly and produce more calves than cattle raised in the same area.

Among other advantages observed by the scientists were the breed's tolerance of heat and humidity, its liking for aquatic weeds that blanket many of Florida's waterways, and its meat. Indeed, 12 students and faculty at the University of Florida recently took part in a blind taste test. They were served prime rib of beef and the corresponding cut from a water buffalo. In their summaries some of the tasters noted that one of the meats had an off-flavor. It turned out to be the beef!

Embryo transplants

Although the animals described above seem remote and unusual, it is likely that modern technology will substantially enhance human exploitation of them variously for milk, meat, and draft service. One of the most promising of the new biotechnology techniques is embryo transplantation. In this process multiple eggs (produced by hormonally stimulating female animals) are fertilized and transplanted to other female animals. The hormonal cycles of the donor and receiving animals are synchronized so that a pregnancy results. This technique is already widely used to transfer embryos between cattle.

Because embryos are thought to be free of many diseases, their shipment between nations may soon be permitted without elaborate quarantine precautions. Methods for freezing them have been worked out so that the tiny bundles of cells can be airfreighted inexpensively in small, insulated containers and then implanted in compatible female animals in the receiving nations. This may make scores of exotic species available to animal breeders everywhere. Under such circumstances banteng, madura, kouprey, gaur, mithan, tropical pigs, babirusa, and water buffalo may become widespread livestock species and contribute significantly toward improving the diet and health of people in the tropics.

Young gaur (top) nurses from the Holstein cow into which it was transplanted as an embryo. Such transplantation can increase the numbers of rare and potentially useful animals. The yak, another animal not now used to its full potential, forages at 4,250 meters (14,000 feet) in the Himalayas (above).

153

The Soviet Union in Space

by James E. Oberg

Despite many frustrating setbacks, the Soviet Union continues its determined movement toward a permanent manned space station, a shuttle-style transport system, a space warfare capability, and other long-term goals.

Painting by Andrei Sokolov; courtesy, Space Art International

The orbiting of Sputnik 1 (above) on Oct. 4, 1957, is depicted by Soviet space artist Andrei Sokolov. Within four years another Soviet satellite would carry the first human being into orbit. A-class booster topped with a Soyuz spacecraft (facing page, top) moves toward a launch pad at the Tyuratam space center. At the aft end can be seen two of its "strap-on" boosters; the cluster of nozzles at the forward end, above the encased Soyuz, belongs to the abort rocket used to blast the cosmonauts to safety in the event of a launch emergency. Soyuz T-6 (facing page, bottom) awaits launch at Tyuratam in June 1982. (Overleaf) In another painting by Sokolov, a Salyut station and two docked Soyuz craft pass over nighttime Paris.

JAMES E. OBERG, a mission control center specialist at NASA's Johnson Space Center in Houston, Texas, is a keen and continuing observer of Soviet space activities. His publications include Red Star in Orbit and more than 200 magazine and newspaper articles.

(Overleaf) Painting by Andrei Sokolov; courtesy, Space Art International

The Soviet Union inaugurated the "space age" in October 1957 when it orbited Earth's first artificial satellite, an 84-kilogram (185-pound) instrument package called Sputnik 1. Today, as that nation's space program enters its second quarter century, its space traffic rate runs at 100 satellite launchings per year, three-quarters of the world's total. In recent years Soviet space engineers have been moving methodically toward attaining several important long-term space goals, including the establishment of a permanent manned space platform, the deployment of a large array of satellites for particular applications (primarily communications and meteorology), and the setting up of a significant war-fighting capability from space and in space itself. Lesser goals include the continuation of a modest but persistent interplanetary program aimed almost exclusively at the planet Venus, the steady improvement in lifetime of military reconnaissance satellites, and a small, specialized series of unmanned scientific research satellites. Finally, significant groundwork is being laid for an impressive array of new space transportation systems including two different types of "space shuttles" that could be introduced by the end of the 1980s.

The massive volume of Soviet space traffic is counterbalanced by a continuing limitation in the lifetime of its payloads compared with those of Western nations. Many missions have lasted only weeks, while other long-term satellites characteristically have suffered electronic breakdowns after a year or two. Of the 100 launchings in 1982, almost half were no longer operating by the end of the year; most of the others were replacements for failed satellites launched in previous years. At any given time the U.S.S.R. has about 80 active satellites in orbit, arranged in specialized groups called constellations whose orbits are coordinated. In any given year, therefore, only a few launchings are really new or different from the routine maintenance of existing space-based functions.

Sites and launchers

Soviet space operations are conducted from three space centers and involve four basic types of launch vehicles. The center north of Tyuratam in Kazakhstan, just east of the Aral Sea, is the site of all manned and deep-space launches as well as of most test flights of new space vehicles. It is officially called the Baikonur Cosmodrome in a deliberate geographical deception, for the town of Baikonyr, or Baikonur, is hundreds of kilometers from the actual launch site. Near Plesetsk, north of Moscow, is the main Soviet satellite launch center, accounting for the majority of all operational space shots. Because of the predominantly military nature of this activity, Soviet officials did not publicly acknowledge the existence of this space center until mid-1983. At that time public anxiety over "flying saucers" had become widespread. Actually, the "saucers" were twilight rocket launchings from Plesetsk that were seen from Moscow, Leningrad, and other major cities in northwestern Russia. To allay this concern it was deemed necessary to provide at least a partial accounting of the widely witnessed apparitions. There is also a small rocket center at Kapustin Yar on the lower Volga River, where the Soviets conducted

(Top) Novosti Press Agency; (bottom) Tass/Sovfoto

rocket tests in the late 1940s and from which a handful of small satellites are still launched every year.

The mainstay of the Soviet launching stable is a booster designated the A-class (or simply "A") by Western observers and *semyorka* by unofficial Soviet accounts. Carrying various configurations of upper stages, it has been launched more than 1,000 times since 1957. Originally developed as an intercontinental ballistic missile (ICBM), the SS-6 in NATO terminology, this booster has a central core and four long conical "strap-on" boosters that are used in the first two minutes of flight. A third and sometimes fourth stage may be mounted atop the core vehicle, allowing the delivery of about eight tons into orbit. A smaller vehicle, based on an intermediate-range ballistic missile (IRBM) and capable of orbiting a one-ton payload, is called the C-class. In addition, the SS-9 ICBM plus an upper stage is capable of carrying about four tons into orbit; it is designated the F-class. The most powerful Soviet launch vehicle currently available is the Proton, or D-class, which can carry 20 tons into orbit. Only eight to ten Proton vehicles are launched every year, and they are devoted almost exclusively to manned space station activities, geosynchronous communications satellites, and interplanetary probes.

157

Photos, Tass/Sovfoto

Non-Soviet "guest cosmonauts" who have visited a Salyut space station include Vladimir Remek of Czechoslovakia (photo above; figure on left), aboard Salyut 6 in March 1978; Dumitru Prunariu of Romania (top left photo; center figure), pictured on Salyut 6 in May 1981; and Jean-Loup Chrétien of France (top right photo; figure on right), following a stay in Salyut 7 in July 1982. In the top left photo, with a view toward the aft end of Salyut 6, several pieces of equipment are visible: part of an Earth-viewing multispectral camera at the bottom center, exercise equipment in use on the left, an airlock for small instruments and garbage jettison just behind Prunariu's head, and a shower apparatus at the upper right.

Salyut space stations

The feature of Soviet space activities most visible to the Western public is the man-in-space program, involving the frequent launchings of teams of cosmonauts aboard 7-ton spacecraft in the Soyuz T series for linkups with a 20-ton Salyut space station. Some of the crews remain in orbit aboard the Salyut for extended duration, the longest being 211 days in 1982. Others only visit the station for about a week, on support missions for the long-term crews.

Occasionally non-Soviet "guest cosmonauts" from other countries have been included in the crews of these visiting Soyuz missions. The first, in 1978, was from Czechoslovakia followed by one each from Poland, East Germany, Bulgaria (whose vehicle failed to rendezvous with the Salyut), Hungary, Vietnam, Cuba, Mongolia, and Romania. In 1982 Salyut visitors included a French pilot and a Russian woman (the latter took part in an eight-day mission as another guest cosmonaut, but not as a functioning member of the actual flight crew). In April 1984 an Indian cosmonaut flew, and others are expected, possibly from Finland, Greece, Afghanistan, the Palestinians, Nicaragua, and Austria. The political and propaganda value of such activities is significant, and the cost is low because the brief visiting missions must be flown in any case in order to support the long-term missions of the all-Soviet crews.

The Salyut space station (Salyut is Russian for "salute") is roughly cylindrical in shape, about 14 meters long with a diameter ranging from 4 meters at the aft end to about 2½ meters at the forward end (1 meter is about 3.3 feet). The middle section, 3 meters in diameter, has three long solar panel wings extending from swivel fixtures upon which they can turn to face the Sun. At each end of the station is a docking port where spacecraft from Earth can attach to pressurized tunnels that give access to the main station. The forward end contains an airlock chamber and side hatch for spacewalks; this section also contains most of the windows for external observations. The aft section, which carries a small airlock

158

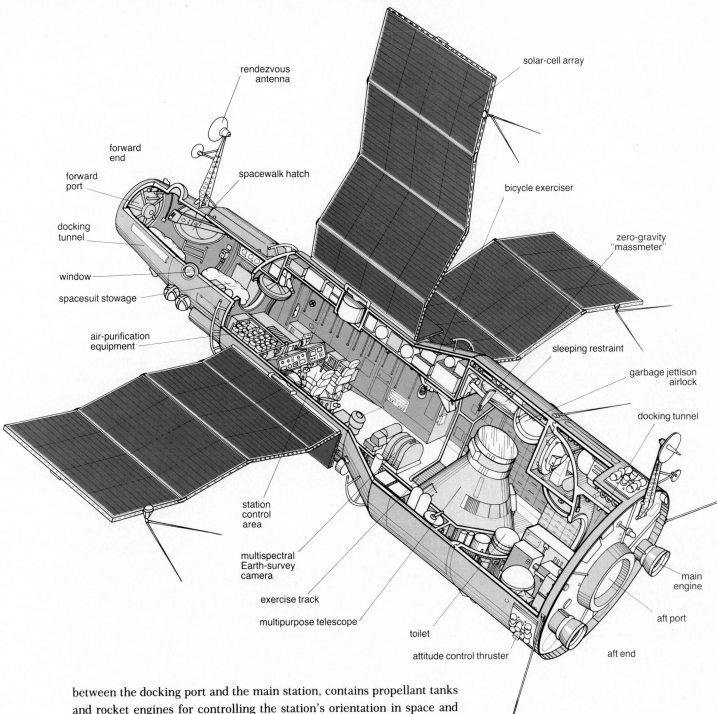

rendezvous antenna

forward end

forward port

docking tunnel

window

spacesuit stowage

air-purification equipment

spacewalk hatch

solar-cell array

bicycle exerciser

zero-gravity "massmeter"

sleeping restraint

garbage jettison airlock

docking tunnel

station control area

multispectral Earth-survey camera

exercise track

multipurpose telescope

toilet

attitude control thruster

main engine

aft port

aft end

between the docking port and the main station, contains propellant tanks and rocket engines for controlling the station's orientation in space and for raising or lowering its orbit as required.

The single main room of the Salyut is generally crammed with research and life-support equipment. A large telescope housing occupies the middle of the widest section. On the ceiling above it are two small airlocks, one for trash disposal and the other for exposing scientific apparatus to space conditions. The crewmen's sleeping bags are also strapped to the "ceiling" at this point. Near them is found such health equipment as a bicycle exerciser, a treadmill-style running track, and a "massmeter" that measures the mass, and therefore the equivalent weight on Earth, of a human body by swinging it back and forth and displaying the period

Cutaway diagram depicts many of the details common to the Salyut 6 and Salyut 7 stations. Salyut 6, launched in September 1977, spent almost five years in orbit. Months before its final fiery plunge into the Earth's atmosphere in July 1982, Salyut 7 was already in space and occupied by cosmonauts.

Adapted from information obtained from *Aviation and Cosmonautics* magazine

Aboard Salyut 7 visiting cosmonaut
Svetlana Y. Savitskaya (below; on right),
the second woman to fly in space,
enjoys a free moment with primary crew
member Valentin V. Lebedev. (Bottom)
Salyut 7 is readied for stowage inside a
payload shroud before mating with its
Proton booster. The station was launched
in April 1982 from Tyuratam.

oscillation (a true measure of mass even in weightlessness). A sophisticated six-band Earth-viewing camera assembly is also mounted here for taking multispectral photographs, similar to Landsat satellite imagery, that reveal natural resources on the Earth's surface. Many different kinds of apparatus for manufacturing drugs, crystals, and metal alloys under weightless conditions are installed at various points in the station.

The first Salyut, launched in 1971, housed a three-man crew for 24 days; they perished on return to Earth when the air leaked out of their Soyuz 11 spacecraft. In July 1972 a Salyut launch attempt failed and was never announced, and two other Salyuts, placed in orbit in the spring of 1973, went out of control before crews could be launched to occupy them. In mid-1974 a space station of a different design, intended primarily for manned military reconnaissance, was launched under the code-name Salyut 3 although it bore little relationship to the first Salyut or to today's vehicles. One crew managed to reach it and live aboard for 15 days. The Salyut 4 mission in 1975 was markedly more successful: two research visits of 30 and 63 days duration were conducted. Orbited in 1976, the so-called Salyut 5 was a repeat of the Salyut 3 military space station; a number of crews occupied it but serious problems reportedly existed in its life-support system, and no further launches of this type of station were attempted.

The Salyut 6 station, launched in September 1977, was the first with docking ports at both ends. This station remained in orbit for almost five years and was repeatedly occupied by long-duration expeditions and short-term visiting missions. The first Soviet spacewalks in a decade

were conducted from this station, both for routine engineering tests and on several occasions for emergency repairs to the station. In 1982 the station was officially "retired" and replaced in orbit by the extremely similar Salyut 7.

Soyuz spacecraft

The manned spacecraft that actually carries cosmonauts into orbit and back to Earth is called Soyuz (Russian for "union"). As many as three cosmonauts can sit in its conical command module, which is mounted atop a cylindrical service module containing power and propulsion systems. Forward of the command module is a spherical orbital module that contains additional equipment as well as living and storage space. The equipment for docking with the Salyut is attached to the forward end of this orbital module.

When the Soyuz returns to Earth, it pulls away from the Salyut station, jettisons the orbital module to reduce weight, fires its rocket engine to knock itself out of orbit, and then separates the command module from the service module for the fiery plunge back into the atmosphere. At an altitude of about 6½ kilometers (4 miles) parachutes open in series to slow the descent, and immediately before impact with the ground a small solid-fuel rocket at the base of the command module fires to slow the fall to what cosmonauts have described as "an elevator-like landing."

Between 1967 and 1981 the Soviets launched Soyuz 1 through Soyuz 40, which included 38 manned missions; three Soyuz ships were launched unmanned, and one manned launch attempt in 1975 failed and was never numbered. Two crews perished in flight. About one-third of the rendezvous attempts ended in failure, but the success rate climbed steadily with accumulating experience.

In 1980, after several years of unmanned developmental test flights, the Soyuz T variant was introduced. Although based on the standard Soyuz exterior outline, the interior of the new ship was totally redesigned, carrying new propulsion, life-support, navigation, recovery, and power systems. Two short manned test flights took place that year, and a 75-day space station visit was made in 1981. In 1982 the Soyuz T took over all manned space activity, and three flights were made to the new Salyut 7 station. In 1983 the Soviets initiated attempts to set up a permanently manned modular station based on the Salyut 7 but were frustrated by another rendezvous failure and another launch failure, this time an extremely hazardous on-pad explosion that was never officially acknowledged by Moscow. Another lengthy mission, which included a doctor, the first scientist ever aboard a Salyut, was conducted in 1984.

Resupply and support vehicles

With the introduction of the two-port Salyut 6 in 1977, the Soviets also unveiled a special unmanned supply ship called Progress, which operated either on automatic pilot or via ground control. Based on the Soyuz design, the Progress could carry as much as 2½ tons of cargo, either dry goods in the hold (which consisted of a modified orbital module) or

Spacesuited cosmonaut Lebedev (above) exits from the side hatch of Salyut 7's forward docking tunnel to replace some external equipment during a spacewalk in July 1982. Illustration (below) shows the three-part construction of a Soyuz spacecraft: the cosmonauts' command module (center); the orbital module (top), which carries docking apparatus, supplies, and living space; and the service module (bottom), containing power and propulsion systems. The command module separates from the other components for the return to Earth.

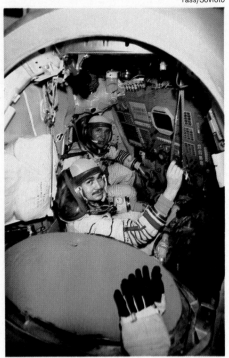

Cosmonauts Lebedev (at rear) and Anatoly N. Berezovoy rehearse in a Soyuz command module trainer at the Gagarin Cosmonaut Training Center near Moscow. Launched aboard Soyuz T-5 in May 1982, the two men functioned as the primary crew for Salyut 7 until December for a record 211 days in space.

rocket propellant in a set of tanks where the command module would be on the Soyuz. The Progress service module at the aft end was a basic Soyuz service module with an extra set of control equipment.

The use of Progress freighter-tankers to refuel Salyut stations in orbit is a notable engineering accomplishment, since the propellants, nitrogen tetroxide and hydrazine, are particularly dangerous chemicals. The chemicals are pumped from one set of tanks to the other through couplings built into the collar of the Salyut's aft docking port. The hazardous nature of this operation can be judged by the fact that in 1979 Salyut 6 lost one of its three sets of tanks when a leak developed in a pressure diaphragm, and in 1983 Salyut 7 reportedly lost two of its three sets of tanks when a line ruptured during refueling operations. In both cases redundant backup systems aboard the Salyuts permitted subsequent refueling operations and allowed the completion of planned missions.

In 1983, for the first time, Salyut 7 cosmonauts occupied a new type of module designed for major resupply operations and for service as an "extra room" of the Salyut. Cosmos 1443 was the code name of this vehicle, and it was launched unmanned in March. Its configuration in some ways resembled that of the abortive "military Salyut" vehicles of the early 1970s and might well be an outgrowth of that program, downrated to auxiliary status. It consists of a single cylinder containing a working room and a storage room, together with a large capsule for returning to Earth substantial quantities of manufactured materials, films, samples, and other items too bulky or too numerous for transport inside the cramped Soyuz command modules. This new module has two large solar panels whose power output can augment that of the Salyut; it also contains a propulsion system with a substantial reserve of propellant.

The appearance of this vehicle culminated a long development program dating back about ten years. In 1977 the first known flight of this vehicle took place as Cosmos 929, which made major orbital maneuvers during a 200-day unmanned mission. A subsequent gap of almost four years baffled Western observers, but in April 1981 Cosmos 1267 was launched and immediately identified itself as a related vehicle because of similar telemetry signals picked up by amateur radio listeners. This vehicle subsequently docked to the unmanned Salyut 6 and remained attached for more than a year until both plunged back into the atmosphere together and burned up.

Military and civil applications satellites

Cosmos, the designation under which many vehicles destined for the Salyut and Soyuz programs were first tested, is not a unique satellite program at all but merely a cover name for at least 20 different types of space vehicles. More than three-quarters of all Soviet satellite launchings are made under this designation. It is also used for satellites that fail in their missions, go off course, or go dead right after launching. Through the end of 1983, after 22 years of activity, more than 1,500 satellites in the Cosmos series have been placed into orbit, and analysts believe that as many as 100 others have been destroyed during launching mishaps.

Since spacecraft with different missions go into standardized orbits with different characteristics—such as altitude and inclination to the Equator—it is possible in most cases to determine the actual missions of the vast majority of Cosmos satellites merely by examining the published data about the shape of the orbits (*see* table on p. 164). Soviet space engineers generally follow preset patterns; hence, satellites with similar missions tend to be launched into similar orbits.

By far the largest portion of Cosmos satellites are military photoreconnaissance vehicles. In 1983 there were 37 such launchings, accounting for more than a third of all Soviet satellite launchings and almost half of all Cosmos vehicles. These satellites consist of unmanned variants of modified Soyuz and the earlier Vostok manned space vehicles, which circle the Earth for two to six weeks before returning with film that

Artist's conception depicts Cosmos-1443 module docked to Salyut 7 as a Soyuz T spacecraft approaches. Designed for major resupply missions and as an extra workroom for Salyut cosmonauts, in March 1983 Cosmos 1443 linked up with the Salyut via remote control while both craft were unmanned.

Painting by Andrei Sokolov; courtesy, Space Art International

Soviet specialists man the main control room of the Kaliningrad mission control center north of Moscow during the 1978 docking of Progress 1 with Salyut 6, the first resupply mission to a Soviet station by a Progress freighter-tanker. The central map dominating the room displays spacecraft orbits and tracking station ranges, while the side screens carry operational data and television images from space.

Tass/Sovfoto

Cosmos satellite identification				
characteristics		**conclusions**		
inclination (degrees)	altitude (kilometers)	site[1]	launch vehicle	mission[2]
0	40,000	TT	D	communications
50.7	200–230	KY	C	spaceplane tests (short flight)
50.7	340–550	KY	C	"minor military"
50.8	200–400	TT	A?	new reconnaissance
51.6	185–450	TT	A/D	man-related test (or failure)
62.8	160–400	PL	A	reconnaissance
62.8	400–40,000	PL	A	early warning
63.0	20,000	TT	D	navigation (three at once)
64.9	160–400	TT	A	reconnaissance
65.0	250–265	TT	F	RORSAT (nuclear-powered)
65.0	425–445	TT	F	EORSAT (solar-powered)
65.8	380–520	PL	C	"minor military"
65.8	145–2,100	PL	C	ASAT target
65.8	145–2,100	TT	F	ASAT warhead
67.1	160–400	PL	A	reconnaissance
70.4	160–420	TT	A	reconnaissance
71.4	160–400	TT	A	reconnaissance
72.9	160–420	PL	A	reconnaissance
74.0	465–520	PL	C	"minor military"
74.0	500–550	PL	C	ELINT
74.0	780–810	PL	C	communications
74.0	1,200–1,400	PL	C	geodetic
74.0	1,400–1,700	PL	C	communications
81.2	630–660	PL	A	ELINT
81.2	855–895	PL	A	failed METSAT
81.3	160–400	PL	A	reconnaissance
82.3	160–400	PL	A	reconnaissance
82.5	635–670	PL	F	oceanographic
82.6	1,500–1,700	PL	F	communications
82.9	965–1,020	PL	C	navigation
82.9	1,100–1,200	PL	C	geodetic
83.0	465–520	PL	C	"minor military"
83.0	300–2,000	PL	C	"minor military"
98.0	600–660	TT	A	failed METSAT

[1] TT—Tyuratam, KY—Kapustin Yar, PL—Plesetsk
[2] "minor military"—small satellites on unknown military missions, usually associated with radar calibration
RORSAT—radar ocean reconnaissance satellite
EORSAT—electronic ocean reconnaissance satellite
ELINT—electronics intelligence ("ferret") satellites
ASAT—antisatellite vehicle
METSAT—meteorological satellite

has been exposed over Western military-industrial targets. Usually two or three are in orbit at any one time; occasionally as many as five or six have been up simultaneously. Newer vehicles with longer lifetimes and a telemetry image-transmission system are being developed and tested.

A particularly notorious class of Cosmos satellite is the one used for military observation of Western naval movements. Called RORSAT by Western analysts (for radar ocean reconnaissance satellite), this type is equipped with a radar system powered by a nuclear reactor that is fueled with uranium-235. To enchance the strength of radar echoes from target

164

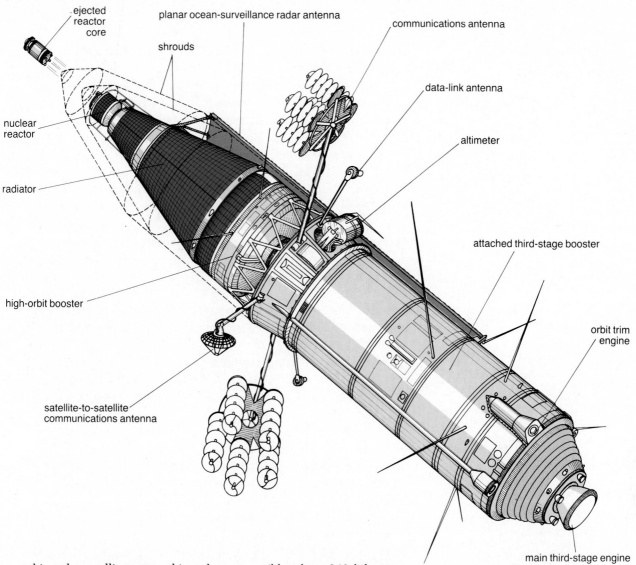

ejected reactor core

planar ocean-surveillance radar antenna

communications antenna

shrouds

data-link antenna

nuclear reactor

altimeter

radiator

attached third-stage booster

high-orbit booster

orbit trim engine

satellite-to-satellite communications antenna

main third-stage engine

ships, the satellite must orbit as low as possible, about 240 kilometers (150 miles) above the surface. Following several weeks or months of operation, the satellite is supposed to jettison its nuclear reactor, which then is pushed into a much higher, long-lived orbit where its radioactive material can safely decay. On two occasions—Cosmos 954 in January 1978 and Cosmos 1402 in January 1983—satellites in this series failed to accomplish this safety measure and entered the atmosphere instead, contaminating regions on Earth—northwestern Canada in 1978 and the far southern Indian Ocean in 1983. A third accident occurred during a launch failure in April 1973 when a satellite of this type disintegrated north of the Hawaiian Islands.

Because of its capability to track surface ships and possibly submerged submarines, RORSAT is viewed by U.S. defense planners with particular alarm. It has been explicitly identified as the prime potential target for American antisatellite weapons now under development.

RORSAT is complemented by another, related series of Cosmos satellites called EORSAT's in the West. These electronic ocean reconnaissance satellites passively listen in on radio and radar transmissions from Western

Built to track Western naval movements with a scanning radar system, the Soviet Union's military RORSAT satellite is powered by a uranium-fueled nuclear reactor. After its reconnaissance mission in low Earth orbit is completed, a high-orbit booster lifts its reactor into an orbit intended to last 600 years; thereafter, the reactor core is ejected into an orbit having an additional 50-year lifetime. On two occasions RORSAT's failed in this safety measure and entered the atmosphere, contaminating regions on Earth. The artist's conception above is based upon available information; many of the actual details of design are not known.

naval vessels. They orbit at a somewhat higher altitude than do RORSAT's and have an operational lifetime of a year or more.

A series of satellites called Molniya (Russian for "lightning") provide both military and civilian communications services for Soviet ground sites. The Molniyas are characterized by an extremely elongated orbit, ranging between 450 and 40,000 kilometers (250 and 25,000 miles), with an orbital inclination of 63° to the Equator and an orbital period of 12 hours. In such an orbit the satellite dwells for many hours near its high point, which is placed over the Northern Hemisphere. During this time it serves as a radio or television relay between ground sites both within the U.S.S.R. and elsewhere (such as space-tracking ships in the North Atlantic). As one Molniya gradually passes out of joint viewing, another approaches its high point and can be used in turn. Such a system is better for far northern locations than is the more well-known, 24-hour equatorial geosynchronous mode used by many Western countries, since the latter satellites, from their stationary positions over the Equator, would appear very low on the southern horizon for locations in the far northern U.S.S.R.

There are two Molniya constellations. One, designated Molniya 1, consists of eight satellites; the other, Molniya 3, consists of four. As old satellites break down, replacements must be launched at a rate of four to six per year.

In recent years the Soviets have also been placing communications satellites into 24-hour geosynchronous orbits, where they hang over the Indian Ocean to provide relay services. There are usually about half a dozen of these satellites—with such names as Gorizont ("horizon"), Statsionar ("stationary"), Ekran ("screen," a television relay), and Raduga ("rainbow")—active at any one time.

Another set of satellites uses the Molniya's 12-hour "semisynchronous" orbital path. These are missile warning satellites, which keep watch for the launching of rockets anywhere in the world, particularly from North America. Because of the military nature of this program, it has not been officially acknowledged by Moscow; the satellites merely become "Cosmos scientific research space vehicles" when new ones are launched. This constellation consists of nine satellites following one another in orbit. The fourth-stage rocket burn that places these satellites into their special orbit occurs over South America, and when the overflights occur at dawn or dusk, the propellant clouds occasionally have sparked massive UFO panics in Argentina, Chile, and Uruguay.

A handful of long-lived Soviet Earth-observation satellites are placed into what is called a Sun-synchronous orbit, a retrograde (east-to-west) polar orbit with an inclination of about 108° (72° to the Equator, but retrograde). Such an orbit provides year-round flyovers of ground targets at a constant local time, a great advantage to observation satellites whose images of ground subjects are to be compared at many dates during the year. A special constellation of weather satellites called the Meteor 2 uses such an orbit. Other Meteor weather satellites operate in more conventional west-to-east (posigrade) orbits.

166

Warhead of a Soviet ASAT spacecraft detonates, sending a shower of fragments toward a nearby target satellite in orbit above the Earth. Soviet tests of killer satellites, under way since the late 1960s, have spurred the U.S. to develop a comparable system based on an air-launched missile.

Painting by William K. Hartmann; courtesy, Donald J. Kessler

Numerous other types of Cosmos satellites exist, some very poorly understood by Western observers. Navigation beacons are placed in one of three predetermined constellations. The two oldest comprise six and four satellites each and operate at about 970 kilometers (600 miles) altitude; a third constellation (initiated in 1983) consists of six satellites in 12-hour circular orbits 19,300 kilometers (12,000 miles) high. There are a six-satellite constellation of electronic eavesdroppers ("ferrets") and two constellations of specialized low-altitude military communications satellites, one consisting of three satellites spaced 120° apart and the other consisting of about two dozen small relays, spread out in the same orbital plane and launched eight at a time by a single booster rocket. A few Cosmos satellites perform geodetic research, and others are used for calibration of Soviet antimissile and antisatellite radar systems. Lastly there are launchings for which there simply is no available explanation in the public literature.

Antisatellite spacecraft

The Soviet "killer satellite" program has attracted considerable attention in recent years, especially in light of the U.S. decision to develop a corresponding system based upon an aircraft-launched antisatellite (ASAT) missile. The Soviet system, which involves orbiting a three-ton spacecraft armed with an explosive charge, has been evolving at least since the late 1960s. Soviet engineers conducted their first orbital tests of the satellite in 1968 and achieved operational status in 1971 following introduction of an on-board radar guidance system. In the late 1970s, tests involving shorter flight times and a less jammable guidance sensor (presumably some sort of infrared detector) took place, with apparently unimpressive results. The older radar-guided system, still operational as of 1984, showed a reliability better than 85%.

In a typical test of the system a target satellite (called just another Cosmos vehicle) is launched from the military space center at Plesetsk.

167

Soviet technicians prepare to unload rats, fish, and two monkeys from Cosmos 1514, a spacecraft of the Biosatellite series, following a five-day stay in space in December 1983. Satellites in this scientific program have carried "guest experiments" from non-Soviet countries including the U.S. and France.

The actual killer satellite (again, officially called a routine Cosmos scientific satellite) is launched several days later from the Tyuratam test center. The killer satellite is launched directly into the orbital plane of the target satellite, and after two orbits of the Earth (about three hours) the killer satellite makes a close pass at the target, within 1½ kilometers (about a mile). To actually achieve a "kill," the weapon's warhead would be detonated at this point, but in tests the target satellite is left undamaged to relay tracking data back to Earth. The killer satellite later detonates its warhead and then dives back into the atmosphere where it burns up. Such tests have been occurring at intervals of one to two years, sometimes coordinated with other military space activities such as launchings of ICBM's and spy satellites; the most recent was in June 1982. In August 1983 Moscow announced a moratorium in an attempt to freeze development of the U.S. system.

Maximum altitude demonstrated by the current system, which is based on the modified SS-9 ICBM (F-class) launcher, is about 1,900 kilometers (1,200 miles). Reaching target satellites in higher orbits (such as geosynchronous) would require either that the payload weight be cut in half or that a substantially larger booster (such as the Proton) be used.

Orbital and interplanetary research craft

The Soviet Union maintains a small but significant series of purely scientific research satellites. One group, called Prognoz ("forecast"), puts payloads into highly elongated orbits to monitor solar activity. Another satellite, the Astron, follows a similar high orbit (maximum altitude is more than 193,000 kilometers, or 120,000 miles, half the distance to the Moon) and functions as a platform for astronomical observations. The Biosatellite series, flown under the Cosmos label, uses a modified Vostok space vehicle to carry biological specimens on flights of one to three weeks. This program, which conducts a flight every two or three years, involves significant international cooperation including "guest experiments" from Eastern Europe, France, the United States, and other countries. The most recent mission was in December 1983 and, for the first time in the Soviet program, involved monkeys as test subjects.

The Soviet interplanetary program for the past decade has remained restricted to flights to Venus, the nearest planet to Earth and the most accessible in terms of distance, required velocity, and travel time. Launch windows, or favorable time intervals for launches, open up approximately every 18 months due to the combined motions of Earth and Venus in their solar orbits, and since 1975 the Soviets have launched a pair of five-ton vehicles every second launch window. These vehicles each drop off a heavily insulated lander probe as they near the target planet; the remaining "bus" spacecraft then either enter orbit around Venus or fly on past. The landers enter the planet's atmosphere, plunge as rapidly as possible to the surface, and then relay television images and geochemical data during the hour or two in which they resist the incredibly inhospitable surface conditions, including temperatures of more than 480° C (900° F) and an atmospheric pressure more than 100 times as great as Earth's.

In 1983, during a normally unused window, the U.S.S.R. launched Venera 15 and Venera 16. These probes are of an essentially new design, intended for making radar surveys of the cloud-shrouded surface from orbit. The probes were very successful, mapping the north polar region with a resolution of one to two kilometers.

The next Venus window will occur late in December 1984, and Soviet scientists have announced the intention of equipping their next missions with a pair of floating atmospheric balloon probes in addition to the regular landers. They also intend to direct the "bus" vehicles of the planned landing attempts to fly past the planet, make an additional two circuits of the Sun, and then intersect Halley's Comet in March 1986 as it makes its close approach through the inner solar system. This project has been designated Venera-Galley (after the Russian spelling of Venus-Halley) or, for short, Vega. Instruments for observing the comet will be provided by scientific groups in several European countries including France and Austria.

Early in the 1970s the Soviets launched a series of unmanned lunar probes that included orbiters, robot sample-return missions (three of six attempts worked), and a pair of Lunokhod remote-controlled "Moon buggies" which spent several months rolling across the lunar landscape. However, the last Soviet unmanned lunar probe flew in 1976, and although Soviet scientists speak wistfully about new probes to retrieve rock samples from the hidden far side of the Moon or to map the Moon from orbit, no new probes are expected in the near future. Additionally, the Soviet unmanned Mars program between 1969 and 1973 was a frustrating series of debacles. Nine Mars probes including seven landing attempts were launched to upstage the U.S. Viking program, and all failed either to land on Mars or to return satisfactory data to Earth once they did land. Recently revealed Soviet plans call for a Mars orbiter and a rendezvous mission with the Martian moon Phobos in the late 1980s.

Some important consequences

The effect of Soviet space activities both within the U.S.S.R. and on other countries has been varied. Scientific progress frequently has been disappointing, but commercial applications—particularly in communications and navigation—have probably made significant economic contributions. The manned program has been exploited as a keystone of Soviet domestic propaganda illustrating the Soviet Union's "pioneering role" in world history, and in the 1960s it was crucial in setting off a massive American response, which resulted in the Apollo and Skylab programs. Practical benefits have been slower in coming but are now highly promising, particularly in space manufacturing and space-based Earth resources surveying.

Although military implications of the Soviet manned program are nebulous at best, the long-term military benefits are profound—in that any activity that enhances Soviet technological virtuosity must enhance Soviet military capabilities, the goal toward which the best of Soviet research and development efforts are traditionally directed. Outside the

(Top) Tass/Sovfoto; (bottom) Novosti Press Agency

In the years immediately following the first manned Moon landings by the U.S., the Soviet Union excelled in the use of robot probes for unmanned exploration of the lunar surface. In 1970 Luna 16 (above) soft-landed on the Moon, collected lunar soil with a mechanical drill rig, and launched a container with the soil sample back to Earth. Lunokhod 1 (top), a remotely controlled, self-propelled rover about the size of a small car, spent more than ten months in 1970 and 1971 traveling across the lunar landscape, taking television pictures and analyzing the soil. A second Lunokhod trekked over the Moon in 1973.

A modular station resembling the configuration illustrated on the facing page will likely be the next step toward a permanently manned Soviet outpost in space. The core module, similar to Salyut 7 in design, will be capable of docking with as many as six spacecraft including Soyuz and Progress vehicles and "workroom" modules similar to Cosmos 1443 for scientific experiments and materials processing. Eventually such linkups could provide enough space for an 8–12-man crew.

Adapted from information obtained from Peter Smolders

Diagram (below right) compares the U.S. space shuttle with three new Soviet space launch vehicles believed to be under development: two expendable boosters and a shuttle-style orbiter/ booster configuration. In 1982 and 1983 the U.S.S.R. also conducted orbital tests of another kind of winged shuttle in subscale model form, which was photographed by Australian patrol planes during Soviet retrieval operations in the Indian Ocean (below).

(Left) RAAF/Australian Department of Defense; (right) adapted from *Soviet Military Power*, second edition, March 1983, U.S. Department of Defense

country Soviet-instigated space weapons programs, carefully camouflaged by highly skilled propagandists, have been eliciting American responses in a number of volatile areas including antisatellite weapons systems.

The future

Future Soviet space activities seem to involve the development of at least two different types of "space shuttle" vehicles. The West learned that a small "space plane" was being tested in subscale model form on orbital missions in 1982 and 1983 when the models splashed down in the Indian Ocean within sight of Australian patrol planes. A larger version of this design could carry several cosmonauts and a small amount of cargo, and it might become operational later in the 1980s. A mockup of a larger vehicle, dubbed the "shuttleski" by Western analysts, reportedly has been photographed atop its carrier aircraft by U.S. reconnaissance satellites. It is supposed to closely resemble the American shuttle design, with similar capabilities in terms of crew and cargo. Official U.S. government estimates place this vehicle's initial operation in the early 1990s.

Also under development, according to these same official Department of Defense reports, are two new expendable boosters. One intermediate-class vehicle, believed to be a replacement for the Proton launcher, would carry payloads as heavy as 14 tons into Earth orbit. The other is supposed to be a giant carrier rocket more powerful than the U.S. Saturn V moon-ship launchers of the Apollo program and capable of orbiting 150 tons or more. Neither operational dates nor expected missions are known.

Future modular construction of large space stations has been a consistent theme in Soviet predictions about their manned program. With a manned core module similar to Salyut 7, specialized modules similar to the new Cosmos 1443 design could remain attached for months at a time to support research and applications programs before being replaced by a new special section. Eventually several such modules could be welded together to form an 8–12-man permanent Soviet space outpost. Such a development appears likely before the end of the 1980s.

Manned expeditions beyond Earth orbit are an exciting option for the 1990s, and Soviet spokesmen frequently make very general and speculative comments on sending humans to the Moon and Mars. While it may

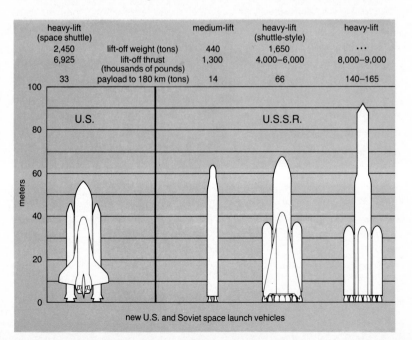

		heavy-lift (space shuttle)		medium-lift	heavy-lift (shuttle-style)	heavy-lift
		2,450	lift-off weight (tons)	440	1,650	•••
		6,925	lift-off thrust (thousands of pounds)	1,300	4,000–6,000	8,000–9,000
		33	payload to 180 km (tons)	14	66	140–165

U.S.

U.S.S.R.

new U.S. and Soviet space launch vehicles

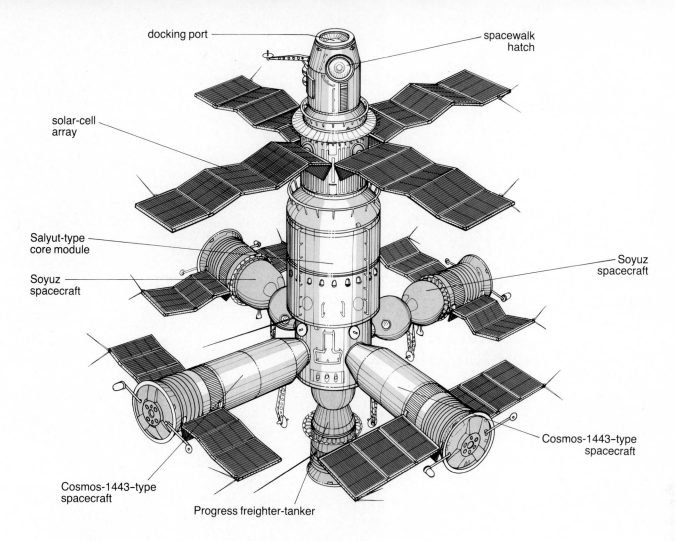

docking port

spacewalk hatch

solar-cell array

Salyut-type core module

Soyuz spacecraft

Soyuz spacecraft

Cosmos-1443–type spacecraft

Cosmos-1443–type spacecraft

Progress freighter-tanker

be premature to suppose that formal, funded programs currently exist, it is a fact that current Soviet space activities are assembling the "building blocks" for such missions. At a future time, for example, should Moscow decide on a manned flyby of Mars in the post-1990 era, it will have spacecraft, boosters, and life-support equipment already built (and paid for) from earlier projects that can readily be converted to Mars-mission activity. Such a situation provides far-reaching capabilities at relatively low cost. Analysts have estimated that even a full-blown Mars landing project would cost the U.S.S.R. much less than the American Apollo program. And closer goals, such as a permanently manned scientific station in lunar orbit, would be correspondingly easier and cheaper.

The variety, scope, and ambition of the Soviet space program are truly impressive. The U.S.S.R. has shown remarkable persistence in achieving long-range space goals even in the face of frustrating setbacks. For Soviet space planners, space operations offer an opportunity to overtake Western science, technology, and military might. The scale of the commitment, estimated to be three times as high as U.S. expenditures in terms of the percentage of gross national product, testify to the secure political status of these programs within the Soviet government. With such continuity and dedication, the U.S.S.R. will continue to achieve spectacular results while maintaining valuable routine services.

Captioned "Awake at last?", this Sputnik-era editorial cartoon heralds the massive American response during the 1960s to the Soviet Union's first achievements in unmanned and manned spaceflight.

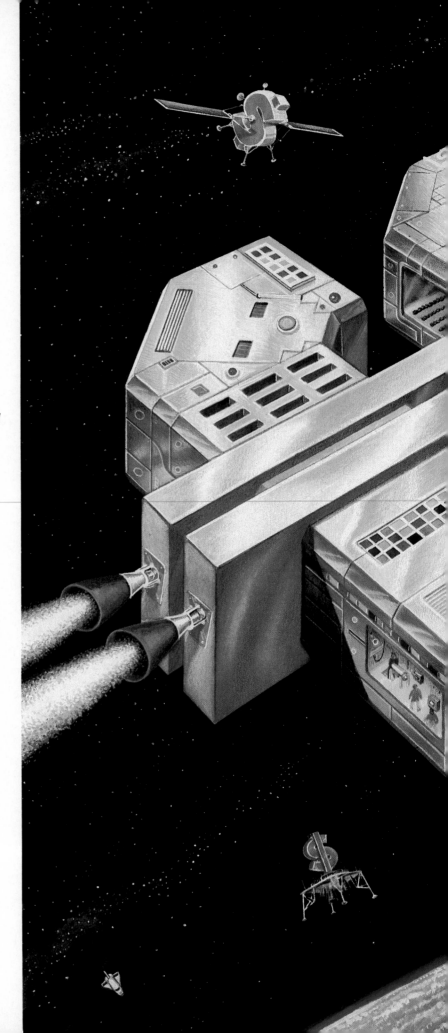

SPACE:
A NEW FRONTIER FOR INDUSTRY

by E. Brian Pritchard

Conditions in space are particularly beneficial for many kinds of technical and manufacturing operations.

In 1959 the world stood on the threshold of space exploration. During the following years man walked on the Moon. Unmanned spacecraft explored the solar system, and one even passed beyond the limits of the solar system into galactic space. Today, after 25 years, there are new thresholds to cross.

A number of analogies can be drawn between events in space and events of the past. For example, one can consider the discovery and development of the Americas. First there was exploration, defining the limits and the resources of the new world. This was followed by exploitation, the plundering of the treasures of the Indians. Finally, there were colonization, commercial development, and eventually industrialization. In space there has already been extensive exploration. Many nations also have exploited space, using it to observe the Earth for both civil and military purposes. Colonization, in the sense of establishing permanently manned space stations, will be accomplished soon. The U.S.S.R. has the capability of establishing a permanent base in orbit during the next year or two. In the United States the National Aeronautics and Space Administration (NASA) is actively studying a permanently manned space station that could be placed in low-Earth orbit by the early 1990s.

In today's technological society it is not necessary to colonize space before industrializing it. In fact, space industrialization began in 1975 with

E. BRIAN PRITCHARD is Special Assistant to the Director for Space of the U.S. National Aeronautics and Space Administration at the Langley Research Center, Hampton, Virginia.

(Overleaf) Illustration by Dan Clyne

174

the launch by RCA Corp. of Satcom 1, the first commercially developed communications satellite. Since that time the communications satellite industry has grown steadily. Prospects for the continued development of space industries are good, but further growth will not be achieved easily. The cost of getting to and from space remains high, even with the advent of the U.S. space shuttle. Nevertheless, industry is beginning to consider actively the use of space for new potential products and services.

The space environment

It is necessary first to consider what it is about the space environment that is especially conducive to industrialization. First, a spacecraft placed in orbit above the effects of the Earth's atmosphere remains in a highly predictable orbit ideally suited for observing the Earth or for relaying communications between any two points on the Earth's surface within its view. This characteristic, along with the absence of atmosphere and clouds, also makes space ideally suited for astronomical observations.

Weightlessness is caused by the exact balance between the centrifugal force produced by the spacecraft's motion and the Earth's gravitational attraction. This condition, which can only be attained on Earth for periods of a minute or two by aircraft flying parabolic trajectories, has great advantages for the production of certain materials.

The extremely high vacuum of space may also be conducive to the development of new materials, but the commercial utility of this phenomenon has not yet been demonstrated. Two other features of space, its electromagnetic environment and its fields of energetic particles, also appear to have limited commercial utility.

RCA technicians perform a final inspection of a communications satellite (Satcom) before it is shipped to the launch site (opposite page, left). At the right is an artist's rendition of RCA's Satcom 1 in orbit around the Earth.

(Opposite) Photos courtesy, RCA

NASA/JSC

Carrying a bag of tools, U.S. astronaut F. Story Musgrave walks in space along the edge of the payload bay of the space shuttle "Challenger" in April 1983. The purpose of the extravehicular activity was to evaluate the techniques required to make such a walk while holding tools.

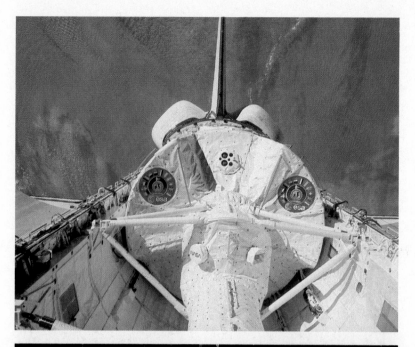

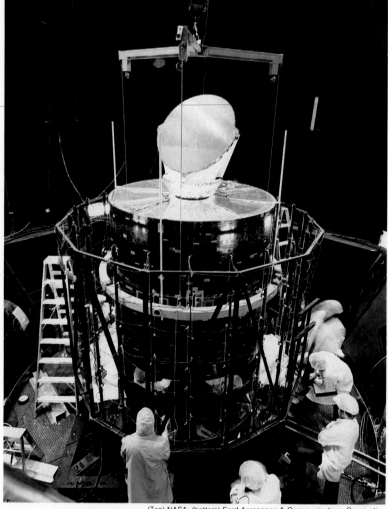

Spacelab, built by the European Space Agency (ESA) as a facility for performing scientific experiments in space, sits in the cargo bay of the space shuttle "Columbia" (top). The tunnel in the foreground connects Spacelab with the cabin of "Columbia." A Japanese communications satellite (bottom) is tested in a chamber in which pressure and thermal conditions simulate those that would be encountered in orbit.

(Top) NASA; (bottom) Ford Aerospace & Communications Corporation

Communications industry

The commercial communications satellite industry has matured since its beginning in 1975. By 1984 there were some 120 communications satellites in orbit. The industry can be divided into three categories: international communications, U.S. domestic communications, and domestic and regional communications of other countries. Recent studies by members of the satellite communications industry, notably Satcom General, led to the conclusion that the industry would continue to grow substantially over the next two decades. In international communications user demand was expected to grow at an average annual rate of 15%. As many as 60 new Intelsat and Inmarsat satellites may be launched during the period from 1984 to 2000, with a total mass placed in geostationary orbit of more than 100,000 kilograms (220,000 pounds). (A satellite in a geostationary orbit remains above the same place on the Earth's surface at all times.) The total capacity of all Intelsat satellites in orbit may increase by a factor of five by the year 2000. The capacity of a single Intelsat 7 may be as high as 250,000 one-way voice channels.

The U.S. domestic communications market during the next several decades is expected to enjoy its greatest growth in the area of data services (an annual growth rate of almost 20%). About 150 new and replacement U.S. spacecraft are expected to be launched between 1984 and 2000 to meet U.S. market demands. Spacecraft trends will be toward heavier, higher-capacity satellites that provide increased numbers of high-speed video and data channels at comparatively low costs. New or enhanced services provided by these satellites will include direct broadcasting (satellite to home or office), electronic banking, electronic mail, teleconferencing, and land mobile vehicle communications. The total mass placed in geostationary orbit to meet U.S. needs is expected to be about 200,000 kilograms (440,000 pounds). In addition, one or two large geostationary platforms accommodating a number of communications payloads may be built by the end of the century. Such platforms have the potential to provide operational flexibility and cost savings in comparison with single-mission spacecraft.

A third major category of communications satellites includes those serving either single countries or regional groups of countries. Approximately 175 new or replacement satellites of this type are expected to be launched by the year 2000. About 60% of them will provide conventional services, including voice, video, and data transmission. The remaining 40% will be used primarily for direct broadcast service. The total mass of such satellites placed in orbit is expected to be about 200,000 kilograms.

Technological improvements and developments projected for the next decade are expected to facilitate the growth in the communications satellite industry described above. These include the development of lightweight gallium arsenide solar cells that are more efficient than silicon cells and also less susceptible to radiation damage, more efficient and more durable microwave power amplifiers, and batteries with a high amount of energy per unit volume. These innovations are expected to increase the lifetimes of spacecraft and also make them more reliable.

177

With the exception of large geostationary platforms all the communications satellites projected to be in operation at the end of the century can be placed in orbit by using currently available launch vehicles and upper stages. Several potential U.S. space systems of the 1990s could have substantial impacts on the communications satellite industry, however. The two most significant are a space station and a reusable, space-based orbital transfer vehicle. A U.S. space station in an orbit that is inclined 28.5° to the Equator (equivalent to the latitude of the Kennedy Space Center launch site) permits launches to be made due east from the space center and thus permits the maximum size of payload to be sent to the space station orbit. The space station could then serve as a way station for the transportation of communications satellites to geostationary orbits via a reusable orbital transfer vehicle. One potential benefit is the ability to check out the satellite from the space station prior to transferring it to its operational position in space. Any necessary repairs could then be made at the space station, thereby preventing the loss of a valuable satellite. A second benefit is a substantial saving in transportation costs because the transfer stage is not thrown away upon completion of its mission. It returns to the space station for refueling in preparation for its next mission.

The space station can also serve as a research and development facility where advanced technology to meet future communications needs will be developed. For example, construction and testing of large antennae could be conducted there. Large geostationary platforms could be assembled at the space station and communications payloads attached. The total system would then be checked out before being transferred to its geostationary orbit. A final capability that may be available by the end of the century is the repair or replacement of communications satellite components in geostationary orbit by coupling an automated or robotic repair system with the reusable orbital transfer vehicle.

Materials processing

Materials processing in space has perhaps the greatest untapped potential of all the space industrialization activities that have been considered. The single most important characteristic of the space environment for this area of endeavor is weightlessness, or zero gravity. One gravity [g] is the unit of force equal to the force exerted by gravity on a body at rest; the term is often used to indicate the force to which a body is subjected when accelerated.

Research studies into materials processing began in the 1960s. They were focused on crystal growth, purification and solidification of materials, separation of biological materials, and mixing and homogenization in metals and composite materials. Significant results of such studies were obtained during the Skylab and Apollo-Soyuz projects in 1973–75. For example, the uniformity of electrical resistivity in silicon ribbon was improved by a factor of five to six; almost perfect crystal surfaces of silicon and of iridium antimonide were grown; and the length of germanium selenium crystals was increased by a factor of two to three.

Scientific payloads destined for the cargo bay of the space shuttle "Challenger" on the STS 7 mission in June 1983 include (top to bottom) West Germany's Shuttle Pallet Satellite; OSTA 2, an experiment sponsored by the Office of Space and Terrestrial Applications of the U.S. National Aeronautics and Space Administration; Palapa B, an Indonesian communications satellite; and Anik C-3, a Canadian communications satellite.

NASA

178

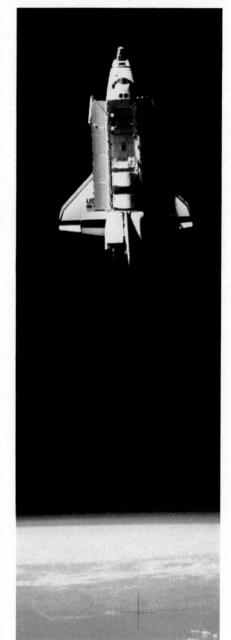

Aft end of the space shuttle "Challenger" (top left) contains several scientific payloads in the foreground. One of them, West Germany's Shuttle Pallet Satellite, is grasped by "Challenger's" remote manipulator arm (center left) and then released (bottom left). After the separation the satellite photographed "Challenger" (above).

Guion Bluford prepares to insert a sample syringe containing live cells into a continuous-flow electrophoresis device in the space shuttle "Challenger" in August 1983 (above). The device, as shown below, separates into columns biological materials that have different electric potentials.

The first dramatic example of the commercial potential for the production of materials in space was the use of electrophoresis to separate biological substances. In 1978 Ortho Pharmaceutical Corp. (a division of Johnson & Johnson) joined with McDonnell Douglas Corp., a major aerospace firm, to investigate the feasibility of the commercial production of pharmaceuticals in space using electrophoresis. This technique is an electrochemical process in which macromolecules with a net electric charge migrate in a solution under the influence of an electric current. It allows biological materials having different electric potentials to be separated into columns according to their potential. The desired materials can then be drawn out from the appropriate column. On the Earth only very small quantitites of a given material can be obtained by electrophoresis because gravity causes the material to become diffused throughout the solution. The elimination of gravity thus becomes desirable.

The experimental equipment developed by the above companies has been flown in space aboard the space shuttle several times. The results from these tests have been impressive. In comparison to Earth-based efforts, yields of desired materials have been increased by a factor of 500 and purities by a factor of 5. Additionally, and very importantly from a production viewpoint, the tests demonstrated that the process can be repeated with consistent results and validated the design concept for the equipment. The two firms planned to fly a production prototype unit on the shuttle in 1985, and they expected to have the first production unit in Earth orbit by 1987.

Even though a new product can be made more efficiently in space, it still may not be commercially feasible to do so. As already noted, transportation costs and automated production unit costs are very high. Thus, a product must have a very high market value per unit of mass

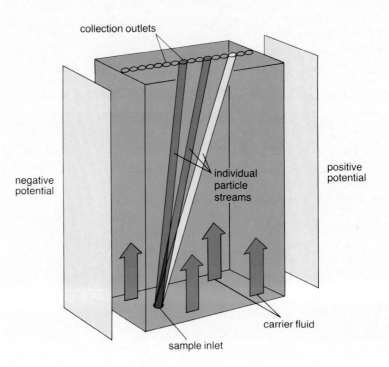

Potential products for production by electrophoresis		
Typical products	Beneficial medical applications	Annual patients (U.S.)
α_1 Antitrypsin	Emphysema	100,000
Antihemophilic factors VIII and IX	Hemophilia	20,000
Beta cells	Diabetes	600,000
Epidermal growth factors	Burns	150,000
Erythropoietin	Anemia	1,600,000
Immune serum	Viral infections	185,000
Interferon	Viral infections	10,000,000
Granulocyte stimulating factor	Wounds	2,000,000
Lymphocytes	Antibody production	600,000
Pituitary cells	Dwarfism	850,000
Transfer factor	Leprosy/Multiple Sclerosis	550,000
Urokinase	Blood clots	1,000,000

to make it commercially viable for production in space. Pharmaceuticals fit this requirement ideally. The social and economic benefits resulting from the commercial production of pharmaceuticals in space are truly astounding. For example, Ortho and McDonnell Douglas identified 12 candidate products that potentially can be produced in space by using electrophoresis. They are listed in the accompanying table along with their medical applications and the annual number of patients in the U.S. who suffer from the ailments that are listed.

With present-day space systems capabilities as advanced as they seem to be, it is a slow and difficult process to bring a pharmaceutical product to the marketplace. A total of nine years will have elapsed (1978

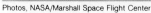
Photos, NASA/Marshall Space Flight Center

Vapor Crystal Growth System furnace (far left) is to be used to grow crystals in the low-gravity environment of space. A mercuric iodide crystal (left) was grown in the furnace during a ground test. Above and to the left of the crystal is the source material from which it was grown.

to 1987) before the first product from the Ortho/McDonnell Douglas venture can possibly reach the market. Flights of the space shuttle have been short and until recently have been widely separated. Thus the development process has been slow. Production units will have to be placed on unmanned, automated spacecraft serviced by the space shuttle at regularly scheduled intervals. A one-product industry could require six shuttle flights a year to transport raw materials to and finished products from one or two small production facilities in orbit. Furthermore, if a breakdown occurs, it cannot be repaired until the next scheduled visit, and in the intervening period there will be no production. Future U.S. space systems such as the space station will eliminate these problems.

While the pharmaceutical industry appears to be closest to bringing a product made in space to the marketplace, there are a number of other industries that can benefit from the space environment. All make products having a high value per unit mass. They include electronic materials (large, high-quality crystals of silicon, gallium arsenide, and iridium antimonide); ultrapure glasses; and ultrapure metal alloys and composites. The relatively short time in orbit provided by the space shuttle, coupled with the requirement for manned participation in the experiment process, will make it difficult to develop some of these products. For example, growing high-purity gallium arsenide crystals to a diameter of five centimeters may take 20 to 30 days. Clearly, what is needed is a permanently manned orbiting research facility dedicated to scientific research.

One of the most important uses for a U.S. space station during the 1990s will be to support such a facility. Recent studies by NASA demonstrated the need for an orbiting research and development facility that would provide about 60 cubic meters (2,100 cubic feet) of volume and 10 to 15 kilowatts of power. There, a research staff of government, university, and industry scientists could conduct a broad range of studies in a gravity-free environment. It has been estimated that the use of such a facility could bring new products to the marketplace five times as fast as could be obtained by using the space shuttle and automated spacecraft.

Earth and ocean observations

Earth-viewing satellites have revolutionized our understanding of the planet on which we live. Sensors developed for observing global weather patterns were among the first such instruments flown on U.S. satellites. Today the U.S. depends on satellite observations for weather prediction. Within the past year the U.S. Congress assessed the desirability of turning the meteorological satellite program over to private industry. Although Congress concluded that such a transition was inappropriate at that time, increasing movement into this field by the private sector seemed likely in the near future.

The ability to predict crop yields on a worldwide basis received a major boost with the advent of the Landsat series of satellites. Mapping of the world's forested regions was also accomplished by the use of Landsat data. Routine observations of cropland and forest can provide early warnings

182

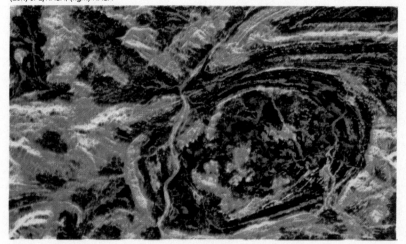

Image of a part of the Hammersley Mountains in Western Australia (left) was obtained by the shuttle imaging radar aboard the space shuttle Columbia in 1981. Red areas are rough mountain terrain; pink is less rugged; and yellow, green, and blue are areas of lower elevation. Below, the ocean color experiment on the same mission reveals areas of high chlorophyll concentrations (dark gray tones). Land areas are shown in white.

of disease and insect infestation, and there appeared to be a substantial commercial market for such information. In fact, as of 1984 more than 50 private companies were analyzing and distributing U.S. Landsat data. But it was not clear whether the market was sufficiently strong to justify the private development of satellite systems to supply such information.

Observations of the Earth's oceans and polar regions have historically been limited simply because of the relative inaccessibility of those regions. Satellites, however, have made those areas routinely accessible. Seasat and Nimbus 7 have demonstrated that sea-surface temperature, wave heights, sea-surface directional wind velocities, ocean topography, and ocean-color structure can be measured from space. Observation of ice, particularly its extent, thickness, and age, is becoming increasingly important as extensive petroleum exploration and production take place in the Arctic regions. Among the commercial users of oceanographic and ice data are offshore drilling rigs, ship operators, and commercial fishermen. (See Feature Article: OCEANOGRAPHY IN ORBIT.)

Offshore drilling rigs can cost as much as $100 million. In order to optimize the design of the rigs, the industry needs detailed environmental data for the local region, particularly in regard to wind and waves. Costs associated with rigs that have been "overdesigned" in order to account for uncertainties in environmental data can be as high as $5 million per rig. Elimination of such overdesign can thus save the industry millions of dollars per year.

Routing ships so as to minimize transit time and, therefore, fuel costs requires real-time data on sea states, winds, currents, and such navigational hazards as fog and ice. Such information can optimize ship routing at a saving to a single typical large commercial vessel in excess of $1 million per year.

Commercial fishermen are concerned about catching the most fish possible at the minimum cost. Thus they need reliable and accurate information on those oceanographic phenomena that affect fish feeding, such as water temperature and ocean color (from which the presence of phytoplankton and zooplankton—fundamental links in the food chain—

183

Possible space stations of the future, as revealed by artists' renditions, include (above) a shuttle orbiter visiting a space operations center in low-Earth orbit. Below are two designs for manned space stations. Solar cells could be installed on the beam structures to provide electrical energy.

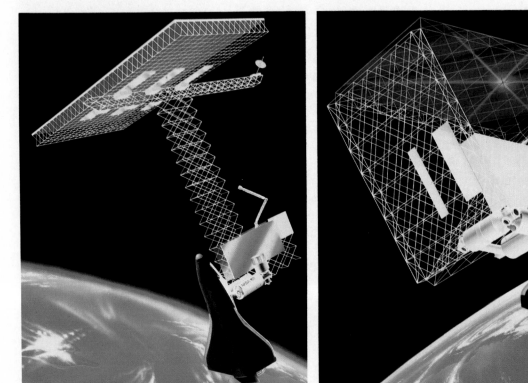

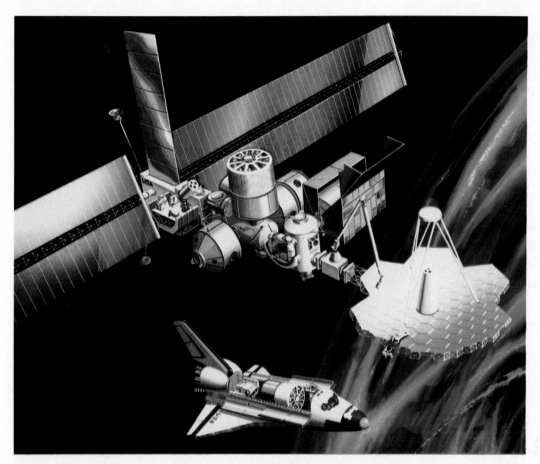

Manned space station concepts include the Science and Applications Manned Space Platform (above), in which four or more crew members would live on 90-day assignments, and (below) a structure in which modules for living and working are clustered between large, winglike solar panels.

Photos, NASA/JSC

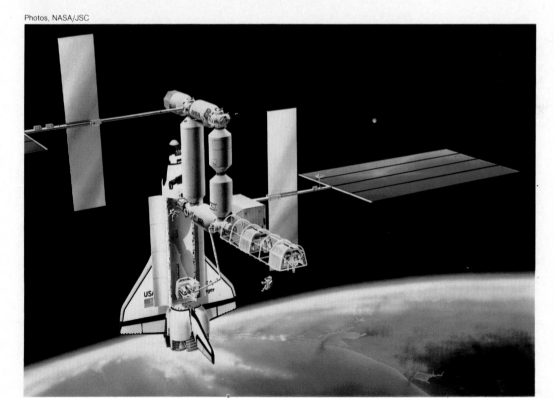

The Insat 1-B weather and communications satellite of India, at the top of the photograph, is launched from the space shuttle "Challenger" in August 1983. The Payload Assist Module developed by McDonnell Douglas Corporation carries the satellite into orbit.

can be inferred). They also need accurate weather data in order to evaluate the safety of their vessel and crew.

The potential value of ocean and ice data obtained via satellite sensors to the three user communities discussed above is uncertain at this time. However, a conservative estimate of the value of these data by the end of the century is certainly in excess of $1 billion per year.

Because it is difficult to predict future markets for remotely sensed data and also because of the likelihood of unforeseen technological breakthroughs, one cannot easily determine which sensor systems will be commercially feasible in the near future. Recent NASA studies indicate, however, that the most promising are stereoscopic imaging, stereoscopic synthetic-aperture radar, and a multispectral ocean-color sensor. (Synthetic-aperture radar is a system in which an aircraft or spacecraft

NASA; photo, courtesy, McDonnell Douglas Corporation

moving along a straight path emits microwave pulses continuously at a frequency constant enough to be coherent for a period during which the craft travels about one kilometer; all echoes returned during this period can then be processed as if a single antenna as long as the flight path had been used.) The primary users of stereoscopic imaging data are the mineral and energy resource industries. The availability of high-resolution three-dimensional images of the Earth will substantially enhance precise identification of those geological features associated with mineral and energy resources. Stereoscopic synthetic-aperture radar data will be of major value to the minerals and energy resource industry (increased geological information) and to Arctic ship routing and offshore platforms (precise data on ice dynamics). The ocean-color sensor data provide the commercial fisheries industry with precise information on the location of feeding fish. The combination of these sensors on a single platform in near-polar orbit may be an exciting commercial opportunity by the 1990s.

Services

The provision of services, whether to government or to the private sector, has become a major enterprise in the U.S. The same phenomenon is likely to occur in the commercial development of space. In fact, it has already begun. Privately developed, built, and marketed space transportation systems are in existence today, and more are being developed. The McDonnell Douglas Delta Model 3914 has been in use for nine years as an Earth-to-orbit transportation system. Other launch systems, such as the highly publicized Space Services Inc. Conestoga, are being developed. McDonnell Douglas has also developed the successful upper stage vehicle, Payload Assist Module (PAM). Market projections indicate that 15 to 20 PAM's will be in use per year by the last half of the 1980s.

Most satellites in orbit today are single-purpose spacecraft, tailored for a specific mission. By 1987, however, commercially provided space platforms will be circling the Earth. They will provide all utilities, environmental protection, and communications for a single sensor, collection of sensors, or other payload. Thus someone who wants to fly a particular sensor can rent space and services from the platform company.

As space assets become more expensive and technologically mature (i.e., do not become obsolete in a few years), their maintenance and servicing by private industry should become a significantly large endeavor. By the end of the century a host of other service industries may well come into being. They may include logistics services for resupplying a large manned space station; commercially supplied research laboratories attached to a space station; a commercially provided and operated transportation and service station in low-Earth orbit as a way station to geostationary orbit and beyond; reusable and space-based orbital transfer vehicles; and the construction and assembly of large antennae for the communications satellite industry.

The use of space for commerce and industry is not a future hope. It is already under way. Private firms will continue to move forward in this field, offering a wide range of products and services.

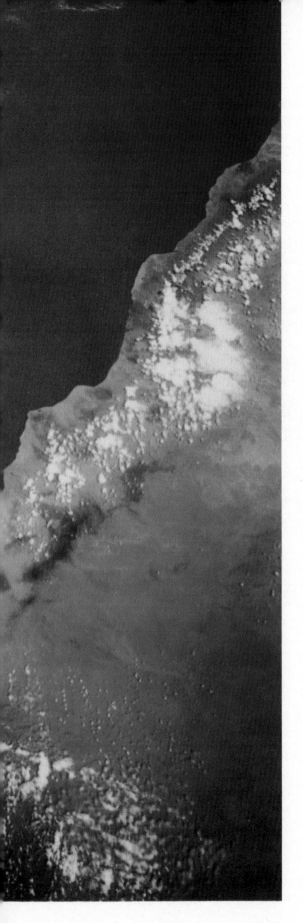

OCEANOGRAPHY in ORBIT

by Robert E. Stevenson

Satellites orbiting the Earth are providing scientists with new and valuable vantage points for studying the world's oceans.

Space oceanography is the scientific effort that describes, evaluates, and models the physical, chemical, and biological dynamics of the ocean based on data gathered remotely from orbiting spacecraft. In contrast, remote sensing of the ocean is the technology of measuring physical emissions from the sea surface that are manifested in the visible, infrared, or microwave portions of the electromagnetic spectrum. The practice of space oceanography is in its infancy, little more than ten years old. Remote sensing, on the other hand, has been practiced for at least a century. There are few space oceanographers, therefore, and literally hundreds of people who are expert in the many aspects of remote sensing.

The story of space oceanography is one of discovery. From the time Yury Gagarin and John Glenn returned from Earth orbits with reports of unsuspected subtle colors in the ocean to the report by Richard Truly, commander of the space shuttle "Challenger" in August 1983, of 100,000 square kilometers of "the most complex ocean imaginable," the manner in which oceanographers study the ocean has undergone a revolution. This great change in scientific research has been made possible only by the technology that has resulted over the past two decades from the increasing sophistication of space systems.

Space and oceanography would seem to be unrelated to one another. Yet it is the case that the most fundamental dynamics of the ocean, turbulent eddies of 100–150 kilometers (60–90 miles) in diameter, can be examined most readily from Earth-orbiting spacecraft. Indeed the existence of such features as orderly, organized, and ubiquitous structures in

Ocean Data Station is a buoy 14 meters (46 feet) in diameter that measures continuously all pertinent oceanic and atmospheric conditions and transmits the data to a shore-based weather computer.

ROBERT E. STEVENSON *is Scientific Liaison Officer at the Office of Naval Research of the U.S. Navy.*

(Overleaf) A huge eddy 400 kilometers (250 miles) in diameter was photographed in the Gulf of Aden, between the Arabian peninsula (top) and Africa, from a Gemini spacecraft at an altitude of 1,000 kilometers. Photograph, NASA/JSC

the ocean was completely unsuspected until the electronic developments from space systems gave oceanographers the capability of measuring the ocean at the appropriate scales and frequencies.

As one looks back over the past 20 years at the events that have resulted in new oceanographic knowledge, a history of a seemingly orderly progression can be put together. As the events actually took place, however, they were anything but orderly. There were many twists and turns into scientific blind alleys. In 1963, when oceanographers convened at Woods Hole Oceanographic Institution in Massachusetts to consider what might be accomplished from space, the emphasis was on such characteristics of the ocean as water color and temperature. Such data would produce charts with which every oceanographer was familiar and had been for more than 100 years.

The suggestion that electronic images of the ocean were possible was hardly considered. Had anyone offered the idea that such images would completely change the concepts of the dynamics of the ocean that had been developed since 1875, he would have been granted scant time in any forum. Yet, through a seemingly illogical sequence of events, that is exactly what has happened. Furthermore, the visual observations from manned spacecraft have played a greater role in this scientific revolution than all of the electronic sensors yet placed in orbit.

Early studies

After being placed in orbit in 1960, the U.S. Navy's Satellite Navigation System became available to oceanographic research vessels in the latter part of that decade. It permitted ships to return to a precise location and repeatedly examine the conditions of the ocean there. Soon it became apparent that the ocean was never the same from one time to the next, no matter how often the same location at sea was revisited. This was not exactly a big surprise, but the real question was, "What are the frequencies and the ranges of the ocean's variability?" That could be answered only by constantly occupying a position for many months. There were a few weather ships in the North Atlantic and North Pacific oceans from which some data came. Their positions were not easily maintained, however, and there was concern about the influence of a large ship on the surrounding ocean and atmosphere. The answer seemed to be automated ocean buoys.

In the early 1970s oceanographers began a series of test deployments of buoys equipped with up-to-date electronic measuring devices. The data that were obtained produced a major surprise. The ocean was variable at all frequencies that could be measured—from microseconds to months. The long-term variations seemed to be more cyclic than those with small frequencies, but there appeared to be no easily defined coherence in the variations from one location to another. It was necessary to learn whether or not the variations were structured, in both time and space. Measurements at discrete points had shown little coherence with one another, and so, although a network of sampling locations could be established, not much sense was made of the data from the computer models.

190

The solution came from two totally unassociated sources, manned space observations and laboratory facilities designed to study turbulent mixing layers. In each case, the benefactor was serendipity, perhaps the most usual component of scientific advances.

From spacecraft astronauts were able to view and photograph the ocean from altitudes of a few hundred kilometers. Their early photographs, at first taken at random, revealed strikingly organized structures in the oceans at scales never before imagined. Problems in understanding the origin of the ocean features then became apparent. There had been no simultaneous measurements of the oceans (the one attempt in 1965 being wiped out by Hurricane Betsy), and so there was much skepticism at the significance of the features seen from space.

In the case of research taking place near Taiwan, historic data were helpful. An ancient fishery existed in the Formosa Straits in the waters outlined by the island's wake as observed by the flight of the U.S. spacecraft Gemini 10. The view from the spacecraft also indicated that a fishery should exist along the Pacific coast of the island. A research cruise by the Taiwanese eventually confirmed the existence of a Pacific fishery. That alone was enough to lend some confidence to the view from space, especially when added to similar discoveries from such well-

Ocean currents flowing around two of the Cape Verde islands in the Atlantic Ocean (above left) were photographed by astronauts in the Apollo 9. A huge bow wave spreading away from the southern shore of Taiwan (above) was viewed from the spacecraft Gemini 10. The smooth near-shore blue water supports fisheries.

191

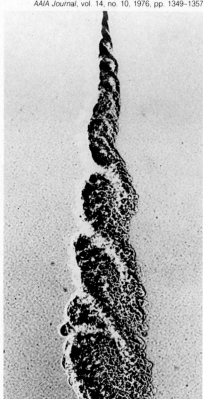

From "Structure of Turbulent Shear Flows: A New Look," Anatol Roshko, *AAIA Journal*, vol. 14, no. 10, 1976, pp. 1349–1357

Eddies form along the boundary of two fluids moving at different velocities, as revealed in the shadowgraph above.

(Opposite page) Rounded features on the sea surface (top), as photographed from Skylab (center), are vortices about 150 kilometers (95 miles) in diameter caused by the presence of a cold eddy stream. The map shows surface currents in the Caribbean Sea and Gulf of Mexico and the flight paths of a U.S. Navy patrol plane that gathered water temperature data to a depth of 500 meters (1,640 feet) and confirmed the existence of the cold eddy stream. The profiles of water temperatures from flight paths A (upper) and B (lower) are shown at the right.

known ocean areas as the waters around the Florida Keys. In a sense it was these "diamonds" from a mound of "common pebbles" that permitted oceanographers to consider the reality of space oceanography.

It seemed that the question of the scale of much of the ocean's variability could probably be answered from space. As yet, however, there were no substantial measurements; indeed, there was little beyond subjective interpretations. Nor were any repetitive observations available. One could argue convincingly, therefore, that a single photograph of a condition in the ocean probably did not represent an organized, orderly pattern of repetition.

Meanwhile, at two university laboratories in southern California (California Institute of Technology and the University of Southern California) scientists were conducting experiments which showed that the turbulence in the mixing layer between two streams of fluid was dominated by coherent structures. The structures, which were vortices (also called eddies) increased their size downstream by entraining and amalgamating adjacent vortices. It seemed astonishing that so many years of previous research, using sophisticated measuring techniques, had failed to define these coherent distinctive features. Both groups of scientists had used visualization techniques, however, and concluded that there is no substitute for the intelligent, knowledgeable eye. (Interestingly, astronauts were coming to the same conclusion.) These experiments, as elemental as they seemed at the time, were fundamental for understanding the ocean dynamics that were soon to be observed and sensed remotely from space.

The Skylab data

The first significant discoveries from space were made by the U.S. space station Skylab, which was occupied by three crews from May 1973 to February 1974. It was, and remains today, the most ambitious and the most productive scientific and technological effort conducted from low-Earth orbit.

On Skylab a group of specially designed sensors obtained data in all but the thermal infrared spectral bands. Interestingly, it was from the camera, the simplest of all the systems on board, that the image came that initiated the solution to the question of scales of the ocean's variability. A photograph of the northwest Caribbean Sea taken from the space station in July 1973 showed on the surface what appeared to be a series of vortices. A U.S. Navy patrol plane flew to the area at a time when Skylab was again orbiting overhead. From the aircraft water temperature data were gathered to depths of 500 meters. This information confirmed the suspected existence of a cold eddy stream. What seemed to have been discovered was that the coherent structures seen in laboratory experiments did indeed exist in the ocean, in the form of vortices along the boundaries of major current systems. The implications were enormous. If such vortex-eddy streams were the normal consequence of current boundaries, then tremendously more kinetic energy was bound up in such ocean structures than had ever been considered. All previous models of the ocean would be completely inadequate.

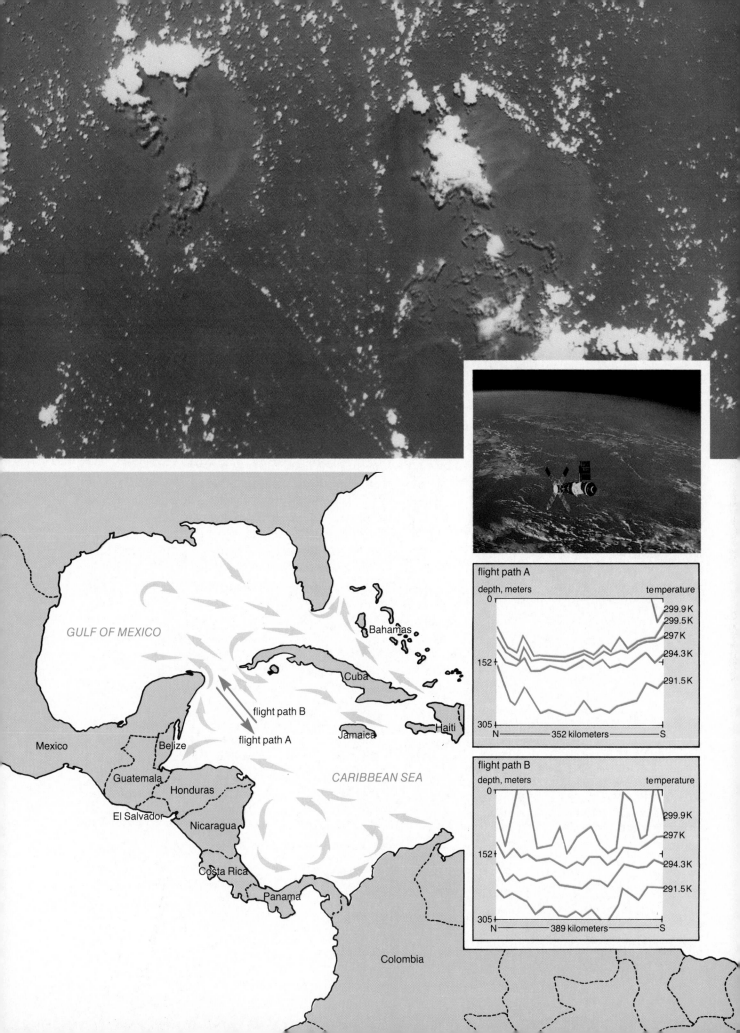

GULF OF MEXICO

Bahamas

Cuba

flight path B

flight path A

Jamaica

Haiti

Mexico

Belize

Guatemala

Honduras

El Salvador

Nicaragua

Costa Rica

Panama

CARIBBEAN SEA

Colombia

flight path A

depth, meters

0

temperature

299.9 K
299.5 K
297 K

152

294.3 K

291.5 K

305

N ⊢———— 352 kilometers ————⊣ S

flight path B

depth, meters

0

temperature

299.9 K

297 K

152

294.3 K

291.5 K

305

N ⊢———— 389 kilometers ————⊣ S

(Left) Scripps Institution of Oceanography, University of California at San Diego; (right) NASA/JSC

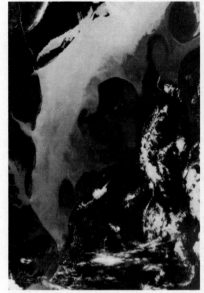

Infrared images of the western Atlantic Ocean (right) were obtained from the NOAA 5 satellite. The light gray area off the coast of the United States is cold water, while the dark gray regions indicate warm water. At the bottom is the Gulf Stream, and the rounded areas at its northern edge are warm-water eddies. Bright blue-green bands (far right) are plankton blooms in the Falkland Current off the coast of Argentina, as observed by Skylab.

Thus, the search was on. Was the ocean awash in these mesoscale eddies measuring about 150 kilometers in width, or were such structures isolated anomalies? Not that rotating vortices in the ocean were unknown: they had been seen in such places as the Gulf of California and the Gulf of Aden. Also, Gulf Stream rings, huge, long-lived eddies that dominate the northwest Atlantic Ocean, had been studied for some time. However, those features seemed to be unique to particular parts of the seas. For example, it is the tremendous range of the tide that creates daily the huge vortex in the Gulf of California, and the flow of dense saline water from the Red Sea produces the large continuous eddy in the western Gulf of Aden. Gulf Stream rings and their counterparts in the north Pacific Ocean next to the Kuroshio Current are formed when meanders in the currents pinch off, leaving circular masses of waters flowing past each other.

Visual images from Skylab provided no further evidence on organized

The radar altimeter aboard Skylab measured the time difference between the transmission and return of a radar pulse so precisely that altitude variations as small as one meter could be determined. At the right are the measured altimeter returns compared with a calculated reference geoid (mean sea level). A cross section of the Puerto Rico submarine trench at the far right reveals that the 15-meter (48-foot) sea-surface depression measured from Skylab lay over the trench.

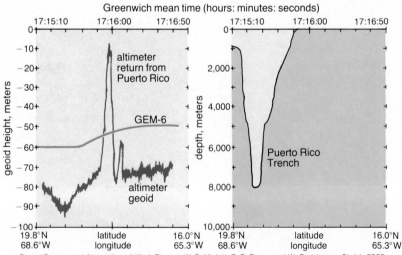

From "Oceans and Atmosphere," W. J. Pierson, W. E. Marlatt, Z. B. Bryns, and W. R. Johnson, *Skylab EREP Investigations Summary*, NASA SP-399, 1978

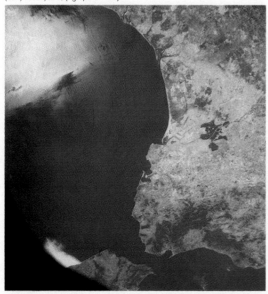 

coherent eddies, but they did reveal many other oceanographic conditions for the first time. One of the most exciting was the vast plankton blooms in the Falkland Current east of Argentina. The first sightings of these by astronauts in Skylab in November 1973—springtime in the Southern Hemisphere—caught everyone by surprise. The astronauts reported a brilliantly iridescent ocean extending for nearly 2,000 kilometers (1,250 miles). The multicolored, oily appearance was so unexpected that the Skylab crew told Mission Control of an "oil spill so vast it's hard to believe." Indeed, it was hard to believe—to create a spill of such scope would require more oil than was being transported in a year. Moreover, the "spill" lay along a route known mainly for fishing rather than commerce. The reality of plankton bloom continuing throughout the three months of November, December, and January and covering so vast an expanse of ocean was just as difficult to believe. But the data proved otherwise.

A breakthrough

Skylab provided a major step in remotely sensing the oceans, not only by means of photography but also through the successful testing of microwave sensors that acquired data from the open ocean from which wind direction and velocity and sea level could be measured. To receive such measurements routinely would permit calculations of energy variability and dynamic ocean height changes to a precision never before possible. A major breakthrough occurred in 1975 in a way that was unplanned—serendipity again. It began with a modest project, sponsored by the U.S. Office of Naval Research, to analyze ocean observations by the astronauts during the Apollo-Soyuz Test Project. Scientists from New Zealand, Australia, Great Britain, and the U.S. were involved and data concerning the ocean were gathered by the naval forces of those nations. The prime area of study by the U.S. was west of Spain, where a sus-

Dark vertical lines in the Atlantic Ocean off the coast of Spain indicate two cold-water fronts (above left). The photograph was taken by astronauts in an Apollo spacecraft. Above, cold water (light gray) off the coast of Portugal (black area in the upper left center) was detected by satellite. The cold water is seen to spread south and east into the Gulf of Cadiz and around a large warm eddy near Gibraltar. The African coast is shown in the lower half of the picture.

(Left) Scripps Institution of Oceanography, University of California at San Diego; (right) JPL/NASA

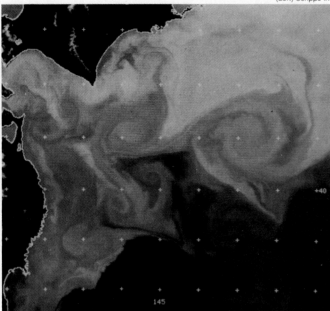

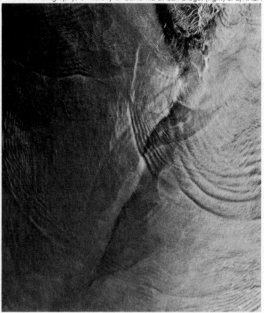

Above, large eddies interact and rotate together in a complicated pattern off the east coast of Hokkaido (dark area at the top left) and Honshu (dark area at the bottom left) in Japan. The very cold (light gray) water flowing south past Hokkaido is the Ogashio Current, while the darker area to the south is the warmer Kuroshio Current. The image was based on data transmitted by the NOAA 7 satellite. Image from Seasat (above right) shows a series of complex internal waves in the Gulf of California and also a straight-line shear (extending from the center toward the bottom left). The shear lies over a fault scarp on the seafloor, about 800 meters (2,625 feet) below the surface.

pected cold-water front in the ocean was to be studied—if it existed. It did. From the Apollo spacecraft it was observed and photographed, while U.S. Navy ships and aircraft collected ocean temperatures that showed a sharp thermal boundary. This effort was the first successful coordinated space/surface study.

At the same time, aboard the aircraft carrier USS "Kennedy" a meteorologist, using his satellite receiver, taped all of the data collected and transmitted by the U.S. Air Force's Defense Meteorological Satellite throughout the nine days of the Apollo-Soyuz mission. The tapes included data from both the visible and thermal infrared channels on the satellite. The visible-channel data revealed the familiar land masses, clouds, and gray water, but the information obtained from the infrared held some surprises. Until that time satellite infrared data had been used to determine cloud-top temperatures; in 1975, however, U.S. Navy technicians used the data to obtain sea-surface temperatures. The resulting images were startling. Huge vortices, never suspected, were detailed in the Mediterranean Sea.

One could not imagine that those waters were unique; the question therefore arose as to whether such features could exist throughout the entire ocean. If so, the old concept of oceans moving only in huge, majestic currents must be abandoned.

Further analyses were then made. The results confirmed the first observations. No matter where in the oceans the studies were made, fronts, eddies, and sharp thermal gradients seemed ubiquitous. Areas throughout the world were studied, and oceanographic data confirmed the satellite-image interpretations. Great eddies—turbulence with diameters of 100–150 kilometers (60–90 miles)—were moving through the ocean at frequencies ranging from weeks to months. These were the dominant dynamic features of the upper ocean.

196

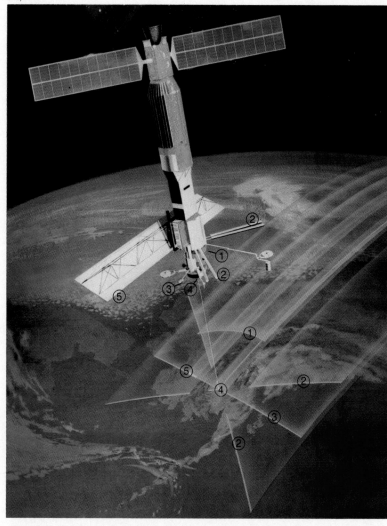

1. **Scanning Multifrequency Microwave Radiometer**

   all-weather sea-surface temperature

   water in atmosphere

   wind speed

2. **Fan-Beam Scatterometer**

   surface wind speed and direction

3. **Visible and Infrared Radiometer**

   wide-swath images for object recognition

   clear-air sea-surface temperature

4. **Radar Altimeter**

   satellite altitude

   ocean surface wave height

5. **Synthetic Aperture Radar**

   all-weather images

   ocean wave frequency and direction

Seasat

When obtaining data from thermal infrared channels on a satellite, scientists confront a major problem. Atmospheric moisture absorbs the emissivity from the sea surface, preventing useful images from being obtained when clouds are present. Radar-microwave-electromagnetic wavelengths penetrate cloud cover, however, and mitigate that problem; they permit all-weather, day-night coverage of the world ocean. This could be accomplished from Seasat, a satellite equipped with technologically sophisticated microwave sensors.

Oceanography was ready for Seasat, but most oceanographers were not. When the satellite was launched into a polar orbit in June 1978, it was scheduled to operate for at least a year and probably for two or three. As a consequence only a small handful of coordinated experiments at sea had been conducted when Seasat failed in September after operating for just 100 days. Therefore, the great impact that the space-derived data could have had was lost.

From the few oceanographic evaluations that were made, it was

Artist's depiction of Seasat shows the satellite's sensors fully deployed and the swaths that each made across the Earth's surface. The sensors provided for all-weather data acquisition during the day and night.

197

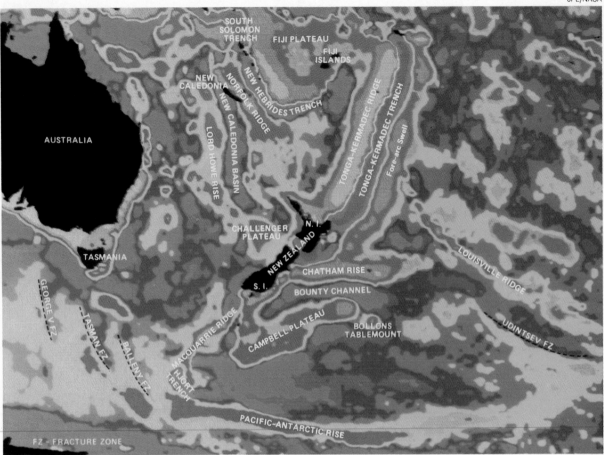

Labels on image: SOUTH SOLOMON TRENCH, FIJI PLATEAU, FIJI ISLANDS, NEW CALEDONIA, NORFOLK RIDGE, NEW HEBRIDES TRENCH, NEW CALEDONIA BASIN, TONGA-KERMADEC RIDGE, TONGA-KERMADEC TRENCH, Fore-arc Swell, AUSTRALIA, LORD HOWE RISE, CHALLENGER PLATEAU, N. I., NEW ZEALAND, LOUISVILLE RIDGE, TASMANIA, CHATHAM RISE, S. I., BOUNTY CHANNEL, GEORGE V FZ, TASMAN FZ, BALLENY FZ, MACQUARRIE RIDGE, HJORT TRENCH, CAMPBELL PLATEAU, BOLLONS TABLEMOUNT, UDINTSEV FZ, PACIFIC-ANTARCTIC RISE, FZ = FRACTURE ZONE

Seafloor topography in the southwest Pacific is portrayed on the basis of a computer analysis of data gathered by the radar altimeter of Seasat. After the influences of gravity, ocean tides, and sea-surface heights were taken into account and removed from the measured altitudes, charts of the seafloor to within a precision of one meter were drawn.

learned that the microwave sensors on Seasat worked perfectly. Data from the scatterometer and the scanning radiometer permitted the winds over the ocean and the sea-surface temperatures to be calculated with precisions never before possible, 20–25% better than had been expected from the specifications. This was not surprising because those sensors had been tested for a decade, both in aircraft and in Skylab. But two big and exciting surprises did come from the data gathered by the active sensors, the radar altimeter and the synthetic aperture radar.

The radar altimeter, modified from one that was flown on Skylab, was designed to provide readings precise within ten centimeters from the Seasat altitude of 790 kilometers. That meant that when all of the factors affecting the satellite and the measurement were taken into account— the shape of the geoid, the Earth's topography, the precise altitude of the satellite, and the sea-surface texture—a difference in sea-surface height of ten centimeters could be detected over the width of the microwave pulse. Such a precision would easily permit the determination of ocean current boundaries and large eddies, each of which typically have height differences of one or two meters over a distance of 100 kilometers. Where the satellite's altitude could be measured by laser ranging, as over Bermuda, it was learned that the altimeter was actually providing a precision within seven centimeters. That remarkable achievement stimulated more oceanographic plans than any instrument development since the Nansen bottle in the early years of the 20th century.

But the images from the synthetic aperture radar (SAR) created the greatest excitement; they stimulated the imagination of oceanographers around the world. The SAR was designed to be deployed to image waves on the sea surface and it did just that, returning patterns previously unknown and features that were never expected. For example, a series of three repeated satellite passes off the east coast of the United States caught the development of a warm-core eddy. No further images of the eddy appeared, nor were there measurements at the sea surface. Consequently, the structure, rotation, and variability of the eddy remain unverified, but its warm water temperatures were detected by a meteorological satellite.

The imaging of these intriguing eddies by the all-weather SAR roused enthusiasm throughout the oceanographic community. All of the scientists hoped for a second Seasat to be launched as soon as possible. However, such enthusiasm and the potential scientific payoff were not enough to offset the cost of at least $100 million to build another. As of 1984, therefore, oceanographers were still awaiting another polar-orbiting SAR and would have to be satisfied through the mid-1980s with occasional short-term orbits of an imaging radar on the space shuttle.

In spite of its short lifetime Seasat obtained oceanographic data that were greatly satisfying to remote sensing experts, satellite technicians, and oceanographers alike. It proved that the concept of such an oceanographic satellite system was logical and useful, not only to physical oceanographers but also to many other scientists. In this regard the fields of geodesy and hydrography may reap the greatest benefits. Particularly intriguing is the opportunity to chart the seafloor to a precision of one meter without a massive deployment of survey ships.

After Seasat

To the satellite remote sensing community the early and sudden loss of Seasat was a stunning blow. Many planned systems tests, orbital changes, and data analyses could not be attempted. Oceanographers and the experts in ocean remote sensing were not so disturbed, however. Although they certainly mourned the data they would never receive, they realized that Seasat had already provided extraordinary information which confirmed that eddies are widespread throughout the oceans.

Oceanographers began increasingly to take advantage of whatever data they could get from space about the ocean. Satellite receivers and processing capabilities were taken seriously, and receiving facilities blossomed at marine institutions. The first was built at Scripps Institution of Oceanography in California as a joint program of the U.S. Office of Naval Research, U.S. National Aeronautics and Space Administration (NASA), and the U.S. National Science Foundation. Other similar facilities soon followed, and from these research centers, coupled with national satellite receivers in France, West Germany, and Great Britain, oceanographers were able to "cover the world ocean" by analyzing thermal

Photos, Scripps Institution of Oceanography, University of California at San Diego

 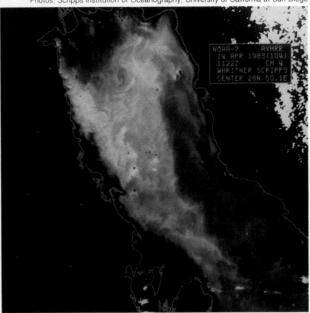

Above, a computerized color enhancement of an image produced from data obtained by the Nimbus 7 satellite shows the waters of the Persian Gulf, Strait of Hormuz, and Gulf of Oman. Clouds are yellow-green, mountains are purple, and valleys are shades of dark and light blue. In the gulfs and strait, forming an arc from lower left to bottom right, the brightest blue shades indicate large amounts of chlorophyll; the thin streaks of green in the coastal waters reveal chlorophyll more than four days old. Thermal infrared image from data obtained by NOAA 7 (above right) reveals the extent of a large oil spill (light gray region) in the Persian Gulf.

infrared images from meteorological satellites and data from NASA's new Nimbus 7 spacecraft.

Nimbus 7 was designed to measure the variations in the color of the ocean. Because the greatest variety of water color is near coasts, resulting from river muds and strong biological activity, the primary sensor was designed to scan the visible emissions from the sea surface in five bands of the spectrum from the blue (0.443 micrometers) through the far red (centered at 0.750 micrometers). A thermal infrared band was also incorporated into the sensor to permit comparisons between both temperature and color of the water.

By such a division of the visible spectrum, scientists were able electronically to add, subtract, or divide the data acquired from the various channels to determine the origin of the colors. As a result the sediment discharge from a river, or a local rain or dust storm, could be readily distinguished from active, or inactive, biological growth in the coastal waters. The amount and relative age of chlorophyll could be determined with considerable precision, nearly as well as from a ship at sea. By simultaneously equating the chlorophyll levels with the water temperature and following daily changes in both, marine biologists were able for the first time to define biological productivity volumes.

The combination of Nimbus 7 and meteorological satellites provided data that have permitted oceanographers to study problems they otherwise would not have considered. A good example is the study of the disastrous oil contamination of the Persian Gulf that began in February 1983 as a result of the conflict between Iraq and Iran. The oil, still flowing a year later, has had calamitous effects on the gulf as a marine habitat, causing the elimination of entire populations of some species and total removal of viable fisheries. New and old cities alike on the western shore of the gulf were severely threatened by the contamination of

200

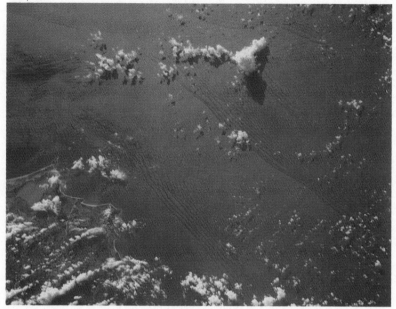

Several series of waves in the South China Sea are seen from the space shuttle "Challenger" approaching the southeast coast of Hainan (bottom left). They were not formed by surface winds but by the pulsing of the daily tide.

the coastal water used for desalination. Marine scientists throughout the world were keenly interested in this situation, but political circumstances made difficult the collection of data at the site. Thus, the circumstances were perfect for remote sensing from space.

In April 1983 thermal infrared images from NOAA 7 sensors were processed to determine the extent of the oil pollution. Normally the Persian Gulf waters exhibit little, if any, temperature variations in the spring, and so the extent and amount of apparent cold water seen in the images was surprising indeed. It was known that oil in small amounts does lower the emissivity of water in the thermal infrared band, thus giving the appearance of cold water when such temperatures do not really exist. The amount of such water that seemed to be depicted by the NOAA satellite data was so great, and the area covered so extensive, however, that without good corollary data the experts hesitated to make conclusions. Oddly, perhaps, it was the newest space system in the inventory of the United States, the space shuttle "Challenger," that provided the confirming information.

The sixth space-shuttle mission was already orbiting when it became clear that observations by the crew might be the best way of answering the Persian Gulf oil question. The crew could easily see the oil, especially in the southeastern gulf near the coast of Qatar. Large masses of black, tarry oil, some three to five kilometers in diameter, were observed floating beneath the surface and stranded on shallow sandbars, reefs, and shorelines. Surface oil slicks up to 15 kilometers long were seen and photographed south of the Strait of Hormuz.

The crews on the space shuttle thus proved their ability to acquire useful information for space oceanography. Because the shuttles orbit at altitudes of almost 200 kilometers (120 miles), they are perfectly suited to observe, photograph, and remotely sense those most significant ocean

201

features, the 150-kilometer eddies and the associated internal waves, wakes, and ocean boundaries.

During the seventh shuttle flight the following June, the crew observed interesting sets of waves in the South China Sea. Spreading across their field of view southeast of Hainan were packets of waves, two to four kilometers apart, with crests extending 60 kilometers across the sea. Clearly not surface wind waves, these features had been formed hundreds of kilometers away beneath the surface as the daily tide pulsed into the South China Sea. Rarely visible in deep water, such "internal" waves reach the surface as they approach a shore. Although internal-wave packets are not unknown in the ocean, they had not been observed previously in that part of the world.

The most exciting, and perhaps significant, oceanographic phenomenon encountered in recent years began with data gathered from the Shuttle Imaging Radar (SIR) aboard a flight of the space shuttle "Columbia" late in 1981. Oceanographers had been intrigued by the images of the ocean from Seasat's SAR that had shown them an ocean so different from their expectations, and so they eagerly awaited a further look at the sea surface. They were not disappointed by the shuttle and its SIR. Some 250,000 square kilometers of the ocean were imaged, from 40° north to 40° south latitude, in a swath 50 kilometers wide. Among the many sea-surface features that emerged on the images one phenomenon in particular stood out—an eddy with spiral nebula-like streamlines some 15–25 kilometers in diameter that seemed to defy accepted hydrodynamic theory. Such features are known well in the atmosphere, and in the ocean where they are caused by an island interfering with the air and water flow. But in open sea no such obstructions were known to exist, and the only stress may be from shears along boundaries of ocean currents. However, shearing stresses were not known to create other than circular eddies, and there was no theory to explain spiraling rotations. The search for an explanation was on, therefore, and there seemed no better way to do it than by observations from space by knowledgeable astronauts.

Counterclockwise spiraling eddy in the Caribbean Sea is revealed by the shuttle imaging radar aboard the space shuttle "Columbia."

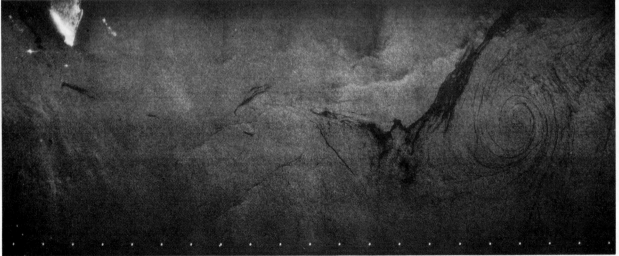

During the summer of 1983 considerable progress on understanding the spiral rotations was made. First, infrared satellite imagery processed over the preceding three years was reexamined. It became clear that the spiraling ocean features had thermal "signatures" that were readily imaged in the infrared spectrum. Sequential images taken daily of eddies off Japan not only permitted the rate of rotation to be determined but also showed that the spiral structure remained basically the same for the seven-day period of study.

In June 1983 observations and photographs from the space shuttle were made of spiral eddies south of the Equator, in this case in the southeastern Indian Ocean. The rotational direction was clockwise, opposite to that previously observed in the Northern Hemisphere. That in itself was not particularly surprising. The observations suggested, however, that the eddies are in balance with the prevailing ocean density and Coriolis force (which deflects moving objects to the right in the Northern Hemisphere and to the left in the Southern) even though they are small compared to most circular eddies. If indeed such is the case, the spiraling features are fundamental to upper ocean motion. Futhermore, if they are fundamental to the ocean and if what appear to be streamlines are actually embedded ocean spirals, then a new theory must be forthcoming to fit

STS 8, the space shuttle "Challenger," lifts off at the Kennedy Space Center in Florida on August 30, 1983 (above left). The "Columbia" (above) was rotated during its mission so that its imaging radar pointed to the Earth at an angle of 45°. This allowed an image 50 kilometers (30 miles) in width to be obtained.

203

A "complex, tortured ocean" is observed by astronauts aboard the space shuttle "Challenger" in June 1983. This view of the southwestern Indian Ocean, along with other accompanying photography, provided the data that allowed oceanographers to determine the fundamental properties of spiral ocean eddies.

such observations. Also, it must be determined whether or not the spiral formations are as widespread as circular eddies appear to be.

A series of observations in August 1983 from the space shuttle answered part of the question, but also startled oceanographers even further. The nighttime launch of the space shuttle "Challenger" permitted repeated views and photographs of the ocean in the Southern Hemisphere. On the second day a report came from the spacecraft to Mission Control in Houston: "Tell the oceanographers there that the ocean from Africa to Australia past New Zealand appears flat; no features at all." The scientists on the ground had hoped for more than that, yet it was interesting that even with clear skies and excellent viewing conditions the ocean would appear so motionless. That condition, however, did not last long. Two days later, as the "Challenger" orbited south of the Mozambique Channel over the southwest Indian Ocean, the astronauts reported an interesting observation. "We are looking at the most complex ocean you can imagine—as far as we can see—for at least 2,000 kilometers—the sea surface is one continuous mass of eddies." Similar observations were repeated throughout the remaining five days of the mission across the Indian Ocean, along with other views of increasing movements in the Tasman Sea and the South Pacific Ocean.

Future prospects

It was truly amazing information. For the first time oceanographers had learned the apparent "spin-up time" of an ocean. More than four million square kilometers had changed from seeming quiescence to tortuously turbulent in a 48-hour period. Of course, the observations raised additional questions. Could a major part of an ocean become turbulent in such a short time? What forces could energize such systems? Are eddies moving through the ocean continuously and only occasionally reaching the surface where they can be "seen" from space? If the ocean did become turbulent—spin up—in such a short time, how long does such an event last?

204

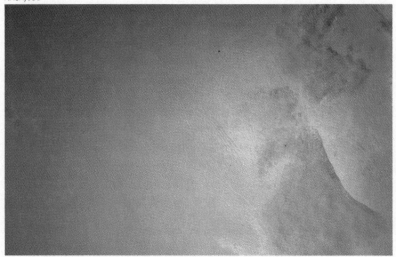

Packets of interacting internal waves off the coast of Peru were photographed from the space shuttle "Challenger" in 1984.

It is clear to all oceanographers that the recognition of mesoscale eddy formation has revolutionized the study of their subject. One can also comprehend and appreciate the role of space observations and measurements in this new appreciation of the ocean. Indeed, every flight provides new knowledge.

In the Dark Ages the monasteries were the bastions of knowledge and they were the origins of the resurgence of science in the Renaissance. To the modern scientist the space shuttle together with the space stations it will build and service may become the Renaissance abbeys of scientific discovery and progress in the twenty-first century. It is obvious that space scientists and oceanographers have banded together into a powerful team, one that already has brought entirely new understandings of oceanic and atmospheric interactions of profound significance to mankind's well-being on Earth.

FOR ADDITIONAL READING

T. D. Allan (ed.), *Satellite Microwave Remote Sensing* (John Wiley and Sons, 1983).

J. R. Ford, J. B. Cimino, and C. Elachi, *Space Shuttle Columbia Views the Earth with Imaging Radar: the SIR-A Experiment* (Jet Propulsion Laboratory, California Institute of Technology, 1983).

V. M. Kamenkovich, M. N. Koshlyakov, and A. S. Monin, *Synoptic Eddies in the Ocean* (Gidrometeoizdat, 1982).

P. Scully-Power, "Mesoscale Inhomogeneities and Turbulence in Ocean Acoustics," in W. Lauterbom (ed.), *Cavitation and Inhomogeneities in Underwater Acoustics* (Springer-Verlag, 1980).

R. E. Stevenson, "Antipodal Seas," in *Apollo-Soyuz Test Project, Summary Science Report, NASA SP-412* (NASA, 1979).

R. E. Stevenson, L. D. Carter, S. P. Vonder Haar, and R. O. Stone, *Visual Observations of the Ocean, Skylab Explores the Earth,* (NASA, 1977).

R. H. Stewart, *Methods of Satellite Oceanography* (University of California Press, 1984).

PURPLE SKIES AND COOLING SEAS:
VOLCANISM
AND
CLIMATE

by Reginald E. Newell

Volcanic eruptions spew forth great quantities of ash and dust into the atmosphere. This material affects climate and other conditions on Earth, sometimes for many months afterward.

From *The Eruption of Krakatoa and Subsequent Phenomena; Report of the Krakatoa Committee of the Royal Society*, edited by G. J. Symons, London, 1888

(Overleaf) Mt. St. Helens erupts on May 18, 1980. Colorful skies result from the interaction of sunlight and volcanic aerosols.

REGINALD E. NEWELL is Professor of Meteorology in the Department of Earth, Atmospheric, and Planetary Sciences at the Massachusetts Institute of Technology, Cambridge.

Admirers of sunsets, particularly observers situated with a clear view of the western horizon, witnessed many spectacular, colorful displays in 1982–83. After the Sun dipped below the horizon, a bright yellow band appeared above it; this then became a red glow, often so intense that it looked as if there were a fire just beyond the horizon. Meanwhile, at angles of 15° or 20° above the horizon the sky appeared purple. Each day the panorama was different. Sometimes one had the impression that a faint yellow sheet extended almost to the zenith, and frequently ripples appeared in the sheet lined up parallel to the horizon. Occasionally the effects persisted for almost an hour after sunset, by which time the Sun was 15° below the horizon. Early risers reported equally brilliant displays in the hour before sunrise.

Why were these phenomena so frequent and widespread in 1982 and 1983, while only a few were noticed in the period from 1965 to 1979? It seems that the displays are associated with large volcanic eruptions, and there were several of these in 1982: El Chichón in Mexico had three substantial eruptions, on March 28, April 3, and April 4; and on April 5 Galunggung Volcano in Indonesia began a series of explosions that continued on and off for much of the summer. These were quite massive in May, June, and July, causing the evacuation of 40,000 people in Indonesia. After the explosion of June 24–27 a British Airways jumbo jet flying 150 kilometers (95 miles) away from Galunggung at an altitude of 11 kilometers (1 kilometer = 0.62 mile) ran into an ash cloud that stalled all four of its engines and abraded the windshield and wings. After a fall of 7.5 kilometers the pilot managed to restart the engines, and the plane landed safely. A Singapore Airlines jumbo jet went through a similar experience in July, after which air traffic was rerouted away from the volcano. Thus, while many air travelers have been delighted by the beautiful sunsets caused by the volcanoes, others have had nerve-racking experiences on account of the same events.

When Mt. St. Helens in the state of Washington erupted on May 18, 1980, areas immediately to the east experienced an unusual darkness, and the following day a heavy overcast spread southeastward. A few days later on the east coast of the United States the blue color of the sky was washed out even at noontime.

The golden sunsets, the jet-engine problems, and the unusual daytime skies were caused by particles associated with the volcanic eruptions. Much of the ash and small rocks thrust into the atmosphere fall out fairly quickly because of their mass, but smaller particles can remain airborne for days, months, or years after an eruption. Sometimes they can be seen on satellite photographs, trailing away from the volcano like a plume from a giant smokestack. It is not unusual for hot tephra, as the larger particles are often called, to shower down on towns 50 kilometers away and cause injuries. When Katmai Volcano in the Aleutian Range of Alaska erupted on June 6, 1912, ash fell to a depth of approximately 25 centimeters (10 inches) at Kodiak, Alaska, 100 kilometers to the east, and up to 140 centimeters (55 inches) were deposited at Amalik Bay only 24 kilometers away.

Crayon sketches of the sky at 4:10, 4:20, and 4:40 PM (opposite page, top to bottom) were made near London in November 1883, three months after the eruption of Krakatoa in Indonesia. Particles emitted by the volcano caused the glowing sunset.

El Chichón in southern Mexico had three major eruptions in March and April 1982, during which large quantities of ash were emitted into the atmosphere. In the nearby town of San Cristóbal de las Casas people line up to stockpile food during the sunless day after the April 4 eruption. The flash of the camera makes spots of the ash that was falling on the town.

Photos, M. Ackerman, Institut d'Aéronomie Spatiale de Belgique

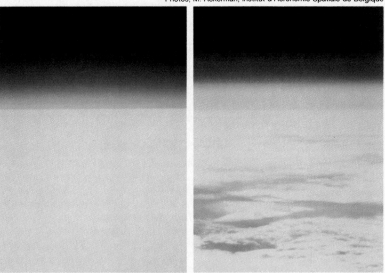

Photographs of the Earth's limb were taken with identical exposure settings from high-altitude balloons over France on June 5, 1980, eighteen days after the eruption of Mt. St. Helens (left), and on Oct. 15, 1980 (right). In the June photograph material ejected by the volcano has spread over a large area of the lower stratosphere, causing a brightness that obscures the cloud cover; in the October picture the volcanic material has been dissipated, and the clouds can be seen clearly.

For a long time it has been thought that these eruptions may influence climate. Benjamin Franklin has been widely quoted for his comments about the volcanic dust clouds of 1783 (W. J. Humphreys drew attention to Franklin's ideas in his classic book *Physics of the Air* in 1920). The clouds came from Icelandic eruptions in May and June and from large eruptions in August in Japan. Because of the constant fog that covered Europe and a great part of North America that summer, Franklin suggested, "Hence, perhaps the winter of 1783–84 was more severe than any that happened for many years." There were very few stations reporting air temperature at that time, but in the northeastern United States that winter was colder than average—although, as Humphreys points out, the summer of 1783 was apparently warmer than average.

Influence of the atmosphere on volcanic clouds

Atmospheric temperature decreases with altitude up to about 16 kilometers in the tropics and to about 10–12 kilometers in middle latitudes, this low region being termed the troposphere. Above those heights temperature generally increases up to about 50 kilometers; however, in winter at high latitudes the decrease continues at a slower rate to a height of about 25 kilometers before the increase appears. These higher levels, above the troposphere and up to 50 kilometers, are called the stratosphere, and the boundary where the rate of temperature change alters is called the tropopause. During an explosive eruption a cloud of hot gases and particles rises into the atmosphere, and when the momentum from the explosion has been lost, the material stops rising and the larger particles fall back to the surface. The gas may continue to rise if it is still warmer than the surrounding air and therefore buoyant, but as it rises atmospheric pressure diminishes and it expands and cools. In the stratosphere, where ambient temperature is often increasing with height, the gas eventually reaches a level where its temperature is equal to that of the surrounding air. At that point buoyancy is lost, and the ascent is

210

halted. Winds then move the cloud horizontally, and it can be tracked for two or three circuits of the Earth before its concentration becomes too low to be seen from satellites observing at visible wavelengths.

The direction in which the cloud travels depends upon its height, the season, and its latitude of injection into the stratosphere. Parts of the El Chichón cloud reached altitudes of 20–25 kilometers and moved off to the west, extending around the Earth and returning to Mexico three weeks later. Some of the cloud was caught in westerly winds at about 12 kilometers and moved toward the east-northeast. Likewise, the Mt. St. Helens debris went off in several directions depending on the height, with the material at 16 kilometers moving to the southeast and that at 21 kilometers drifting first to the northwest.

The residence time in the stratosphere for small particles, which are typically less than one micrometer (one ten-thousandth of a centimeter) in diameter, is about two years. After that they either fall by gravitational settling into the troposphere or are carried into the troposphere during the normal processes of stratospheric-tropospheric interchange. Particles remain in the troposphere only 10–15 days on the average before they are washed out by rainfall. Gases injected into the stratosphere may form additional small particles, and, because these gases are not removed from the stratosphere by gravitational settling, new particles may be formed many months or a year or more after the initial explosion.

The volcanic aerosol

A characteristic yellow deposit of sulfur is often seen on the ground in the vicinity of a volcanic explosion, and observers frequently comment on the smell of sulfur. Many volcanic particles caught in filters mounted on aircraft or on wires exposed to the airstream in the stratosphere have been identified as sulfuric acid droplets or ammonium sulfate. Three separate programs collected this material, called the volcanic aerosol.

M. Ackerman, Institut d'Aéronomie Spatiale de Belgique

Layers of volcanic ash and dust in the stratosphere were photographed from a balloon floating at an altitude of 36.6 kilometers (22.7 miles) over southern France. The photograph was taken on May 3, 1982, about one month after the major eruptions of El Chichón in Mexico.

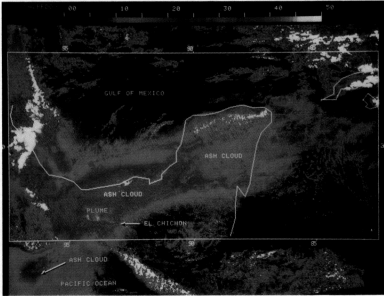

NOAA/NESDIS

Visible-wavelength images gathered by satellite reveal the spread of the plume and ash cloud from El Chichón 15 hours after its first substantial eruption on March 28, 1982. Reflectivity differences in the plume and cloud are shown by the colors; the most reflective debris, directly above the volcano, is red, while the less reflective material is blue and green. The figures on the superimposed grid indicate latitude and longitude, and a reflectivity scale is shown above.

Adapted from "Circumglobal Transport of the El Chichón Volcanic Dust Cloud," Alan Robock and Michael Matson, *Science*, vol. 221, pp. 195–197, July 8, 1983, © 1983 AAAS.

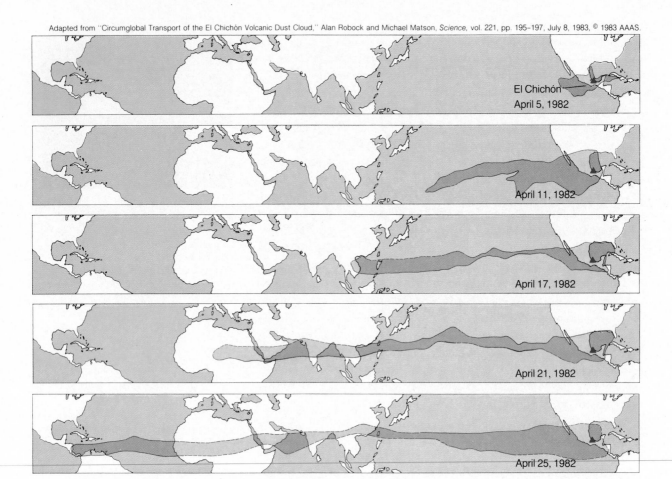

El Chichón
April 5, 1982

April 11, 1982

April 17, 1982

April 21, 1982

April 25, 1982

Maps of the spread of the volcanic cloud during the first three weeks after the April 4 eruption of El Chichón were made by combining data from three satellites. The boundary of the cloud is a broken line where its edge could not be determined exactly.

The High Altitude Sampling Program of the U.S. Department of Energy (DOE) used a WB-57 aircraft that could reach about 21 kilometers; the samples that it collected were sulfuric acid droplets generally smaller than a micrometer in diameter. The U.S. National Aeronautics and Space Administration (NASA) at Ames Research Center in California used a U-2 aircraft; in the samples that it collected the growth in size of the sulfuric acid droplets was quite clear until diameters of four micrometers were reached in December 1982 compared with less than half a micrometer before El Chichón. The NASA group at Johnson Space Center in Houston, Texas, used the DOE's WB-57 aircraft and was looking for cosmic dust; their experiments were marred by the El Chichón products. However, they photographed the dust collected in their filters and measured its composition with X-ray fluorescence; in so doing they found a variety of elements, including silicates, iron, sulfur, and calcium.

Some particles of up to 27 micrometers in diameter were also collected months after the eruption. Presumably they consisted of low-density ash because such material must have had low fall velocities, rather like fluffy snowflakes. Both the types of particles and their sizes depended strongly on the source regions of the air masses; sometimes while collecting over California the NASA U-2 intercepted larger particles falling out of a volcanic cloud well above the aircraft.

Ames Research Center/NASA

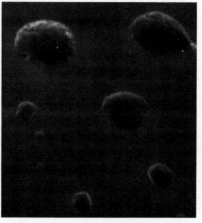
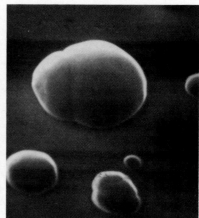

Airborne and ground-based measurements of the absorption of solar ultraviolet radiation by sulfur dioxide gas showed a substantial cloud south of latitude 35° N in early May 1982, and on the basis of these W. F. J. Evans and J. B. Kerr of Canada's Atmospheric Environment Service estimated that about 13.4 megatons of sulfur dioxide were injected into the stratosphere by El Chichón. In addition, sulfur dioxide was detected by a NASA satellite. Janet P. Kotra of the Department of Chemistry at the University of Maryland and her colleagues made measurements in the plume of El Chichón close to the volcano in November 1982 and found that hydrogen sulfide was the primary gaseous sulfur species, with sulfur in the particulate form only accounting for 4% of the total sulfur. It seems, therefore, that the conversion of sulfur component gases to sulfur-containing particles is a major process occurring in the stratosphere.

Aircraft sampling of the lower stratosphere was carried out by the U.S. Department of Energy between Panama and Alaska at least three times a year up to the spring of 1983. These flights were started in 1958 to check the stratosphere for the by-products of nuclear explosions. From 1970 onward the filters have been examined for sulfates, and it is worth

Sulfate aerosols were collected at altitudes of about 20 kilometers (12 miles) on Oct. 16, 1981, before the eruptions of El Chichón (left); on July 20, 1982, four months after the eruptions (center); and on Dec. 13, 1982, about 8½ months afterward (right). The samples were taken over California and Baja California and were photographed at a magnification of 10,000 times.

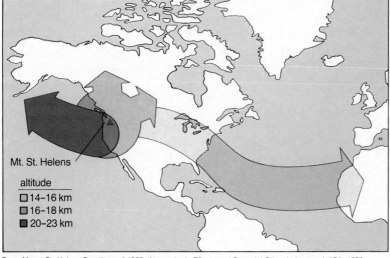

Mt. St. Helens

altitude
□ 14–16 km
□ 16–18 km
■ 20–23 km

From *Mount St. Helens Eruptions of 1980: Atmospheric Effects and Potential Climatic Impact*, NASA, 1982

Distribution in the stratosphere of volcanic aerosol from Mt. St. Helens shows that the material moves in different directions at different altitudes. The measurements were taken several days after the volcano erupted in May 1980.

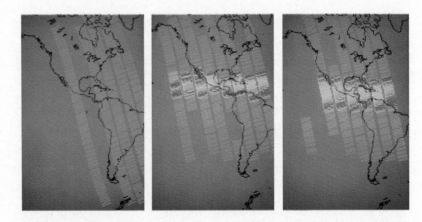

noting that the highest values ever recorded, over 150 micrograms of sulfate per kilogram of air, were found in filters collected immediately after the eruption of El Chichón in April 1982. By contrast, after Mt. St. Helens in 1980 the maximum concentration was only nine micrograms, while before this eruption in 1979 maximum values were close to one.

Three techniques were used to examine the cloud above the 21-kilometer limit set by the aircraft's ceiling. They included satellite measurements of the Earth's limb, in which the satellite scans up and down just above the Earth's horizon, thereby seeing a vertical profile of the atmosphere; direct balloon sampling; and lasers that measure the back-scattered light. Remote sensing techniques cannot, of course, distinguish the nature of the particles.

Charles Barth and his collaborators at the University of Colorado used the Solar Mesosphere Explorer satellite to track the vertical and horizontal extent of the particles. This satellite carries several spectrometers that scan the Earth's limb and measure the visible radiation scattered by the aerosol as well as the infrared radiation emitted by it. Looking at the Earth's limb produces a much stronger signal than looking straight down—a typical advantage is about sixty to one—and also avoids

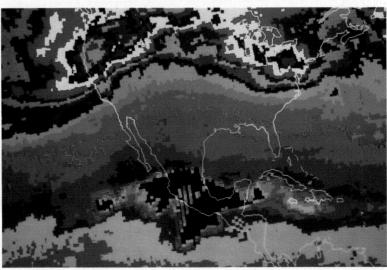

Goddard Space Flight Center/NASA

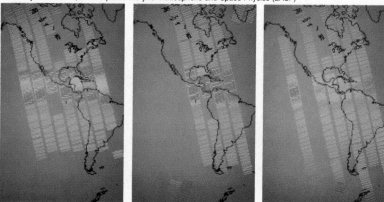

problems with light reflected from the Earth's surface. Data from these instruments show that the aerosol reached above 30 kilometers at 20° N and in June 1982 showed a maximum concentration at about 26 kilometers. Balloon measurements over the U.S. in August 1982 revealed a maximum of 78 micrograms of sulfate per kilogram of air at about 23.5 kilometers, while only about 10 micrograms were being recorded at aircraft altitudes. In early November maximum values were 56 at 22.5 kilometers.

Laser measurements from a number of places around the world showed initially a number of discrete aerosol layers, in particular at about 17 kilometers and 25 kilometers, but by November 1982 a more uniform layer seemed to fill the region between 20 and 30 kilometers with a maximum concentration at about 23 kilometers. Even at this long time after the eruption, lasers were measuring seven times more backscattered light than is normally received from these altitudes from molecular scattering. Thus the clouds from these 1982 eruptions were extensive and persistent and occupied a large fraction of the stratosphere below 30 kilometers. The total amount of sulfate in October 1982 was estimated to be close to six megatons, while only about half of a megaton was present below the maximum aircraft altitude after Mt. St. Helens.

Considerable information about the particle size distribution was obtained by David J. Hofmann and James M. Rosen at the University of Wyoming using balloon-borne particle counters. Because their program had been in operation for several years, they were able to study conditions before and after El Chichón. After the eruption the size distribution showed the presence of two main types: small particles with a mean radius of 0.02 micrometers at concentrations of up to 150 particles per cubic centimeter and larger particles with a mean radius of 0.7 micrometers at concentrations of about 4 per cubic centimeter; the latter contain most of the total mass. These small particles coagulate rather rapidly and are thus lost in a few days. Therefore, they must be continually produced, presumably in the process of conversion of sulfur-component gases to sulfate aerosol, a process that is quite complex chemically and seems to involve reactions with hydroxyl and water vapor. Prior to the eruption there were only about five small particles per cubic centimeter

Altitude distributions of the aerosol cloud from El Chichón were measured by instruments aboard the Solar Mesosphere Explorer satellite on May 21, 1982 (below), and June 5, 1982 (bottom). On the left in each illustration are the distributions as measured by the infrared radiometer at a wavelength of 6.8 micrometers; on the right are measurements by the infrared spectrometer at 1.9 micrometers. Orange and red indicate increasing density, while black means no data and white reveals that the detector was saturated with data.

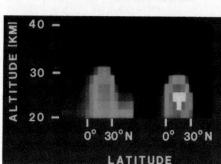

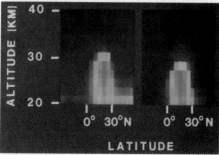

215

with a mean radius of 0.08 micrometers. By October 1982 most of the small particles had disappeared, and the larger particles were considerably reduced in concentration by gravitational settling.

Particles much smaller than the wavelength of light (about 0.5 micrometers at the peak response of the eye) scatter light following Rayleigh's law, which states that scattering depends inversely on the fourth power of the wavelength; these small particles therefore scatter blue light more than red light. Also, the light is scattered almost equally in all directions. Larger particles follow the more complicated Mie theory. In this case the scattering that depends on the particle size distribution either varies little with wavelength or depends inversely on it, though not to the fourth power; the directional dependence is such that much of the scattering occurs in the forward direction. This is the light, depleted in the short wavelengths, that is seen near the horizon after sunset. The red light from the particles and the blue light scattered from the background sky blend together to produce the purple glow so typical of volcanic sunsets.

Volcanic aerosol and climate

Does the presence of these stratospheric aerosols influence climate? A clear-cut "yes" to this question can only be given for stratospheric temperature. For average tropospheric temperature, surface air temperature, and sea-surface temperature the answer can only be "possibly yes," the qualification being necessary because of the number of other variables that influence these parameters.

The large effect on stratospheric temperature was found quite clearly in the case of the eruption of Mt. Agung in Bali during March 1963. Air temperature at about 20 kilometers increased by about 6° C (10.8° F) in a few weeks. This sudden increase and the maintenance of a high level could not be accounted for by any other natural phenomenon. R. E. Newell suggested that it was due to the absorption of sunlight by the particles, although this was questioned by many at the time.

Diran Diermendjian of the RAND Corporation in 1969 computed the scattering from dispersions of various types and sizes of particles, including water, iron, and silicates, and his results showed that iron and certain silicates absorbed substantial amounts of visible radiation. A few years later J. Neumann of the Hebrew University of Jerusalem showed that droplets of sulfuric acid could absorb solar radiation in the near-infrared regions of the spectrum (at wavelengths of about 2 micrometers), while ammonium sulfate absorbed infrared radiation near 9 micrometers and so could be important for absorption of upwelling radiation from the Earth. His general conclusion was that part of the Agung heating could be due to the absorption of solar radiation by the sulfuric acid droplets.

This conclusion was carried further by John DeLuisi of the U.S. National Oceanic and Atmospheric Administration (NOAA) Environmental Research Laboratories at Boulder, Colorado. Working with B. M. Herman of the University of Arizona, he studied that part of the refractive index controlling absorption of the Agung aerosol. They based their research on measurements made at the ground of the direct and diffuse solar flux.

The equivalent heating rates that they deduced for the air that contained particles were within a factor of two of those observed for the stratosphere. In 1976 James Pollack and his colleagues at NASA Ames Research Center showed that the silicate material present in the early stages of the cloud could also absorb the upwelling infrared radiation from the Earth, which has maximum intensity at a wavelength of about 10 micrometers. Indeed, although the first reaction to the observed temperature increase was that it could not be due to the eruption, within a few years several potential volcanic mechanisms for heating came to be accepted.

After the explosion of Mt. St. Helens in May 1980, some of the stratospheric aerosol was collected from an aircraft by Robert Charlson and his colleagues at the University of Washington and found to exhibit significant absorption of solar energy that would produce heating rates very close to those observed for the Mt. Agung eruption. The fact that stratospheric temperature did not change after Mt. St. Helens was due to the relatively small total amount of material ejected by the volcano. These researchers found similar absorption of solar energy after El Chichón.

As a result of the debate about the effect of the Mt. Agung eruption on stratospheric temperature, several groups of investigators followed stratospheric temperature closely after El Chichón erupted. Karin Labitzke and B. Naujokat of the Free University of Berlin, D. E. Parker and J. L. Brownscombe of the British Meteorological Office, R. S. Quiroz of NOAA, and Rennie Selkirk and R. E. Newell at Massachusetts Institute of Technology (MIT) all noted that by August 1982 the temperature at about 24 kilometers over the tropics had risen to 4–5° C (7.2–9° F) above normal. Furthermore, the increase was reported later at an altitude of about 21 kilometers; this time delay (of three months) corresponded to a particle-settling velocity of about 30 meters (99 feet) per day, which is the terminal velocity for particles 1.4 micrometers in diameter. The changes in temperature corresponded to heating rates of about 1° C (1.8° F) per month, somewhat lower than was observed initially for Agung. Scientists speculated as to whether it was iron, silicate, sulfate, or sulfuric acid droplets that produced the observed temperature change. Whatever the cause, the volcanic effect on climate, a temperature increase of 4–6° C in the tropical stratosphere, was real and indisputable.

If solar energy is absorbed in the stratosphere, there will be less radiant energy reaching the troposphere, and one might, therefore, anticipate cooling there. This is difficult to measure, however, because a number of other factors act on the troposphere apart from radiation. During the Agung period solar radiation was regularly measured at the ground at Mauna Loa, Hawaii; Tucson, Arizona; Aspendale, Australia; and the South Pole. At Mauna Loa the direct beam was measured with a pyrheliometer equipped with a quartz window that could transmit radiation with wavelengths between 0.2 and 3.0 micrometers. On a clear day about 93.5% of the radiation in the direct solar beam at the top of the atmosphere reaches the ground.

In 1963, after the eruption of Mt. Agung, the transmission of radiation dropped to 90% and in 1982 after El Chichón to 80%. By December

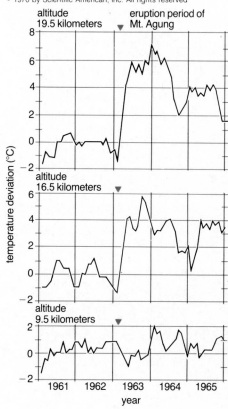

Agung volcano on the island of Bali in Indonesia, inactive for a century, erupts in March 1963 (opposite page). More than 1,500 people were killed. As indicated on the graphs above, the temperature at various levels in the Earth's stratosphere rose sharply after the Agung explosion. The increase was less at lower altitudes.

Courtesy, Bernard G. Mendonca, U.S. Department of Commerce, National Oceanic and Atmospheric Administration, Geophysical Monitoring for Climatic Change Division, Boulder, Colorado 80303

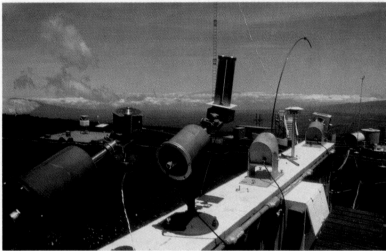

Instruments used to measure incoming solar radiation are arrayed at Mauna Loa, Hawaii. In the foreground the pyrheliometer measures the direct beam of radiation from the Sun's disk. Next to it is an infrared radiometer, which measures the infrared energy from the Sun. In the background the pyranometer, with a shade ring, measures all the solar radiation except the direct beam.

1983 the transmission had still not recovered, reaching about 91%. The difference between 93.5% and these numbers represents the additional energy lost from the direct solar beam, but because much of this energy is scattered by the particles in the forward direction most of the energy lost out of the direct beam still reaches the surface. For example, after Mt. Agung the direct beam at Aspendale, Australia, was reduced by 24%, but the diffuse radiation received at the ground from the sky increased by 100% and the total radiation was apparently depleted by only about 7% according to A. J. Dyer and B. B. Hicks. Likewise, work at the South Pole by H. J. Viebrock and E. C. Flowers showed that the total radiation was depleted by about 7% in February 1964 relative to February 1962. John DeLuisi and his colleagues recently reported that the total radiation at Mauna Loa was reduced by 7.7% in June 1982 after the eruptions of El Chichón in March and April of that year.

Many years ago Herbert Kimball, professor of meteorology at Mount Weather Observatory in Virginia, constructed curves describing solar radiation received at the surface, based on data obtained from a number of stations in the Northern Hemisphere during the period 1883 to 1923. The curves show significant depletion of the direct solar beam after Krakatoa in 1883, after a series of eruptions at different places in 1886–90, after eruptions of Pelée and Soufriere in the West Indies and Santa María in Guatemala in 1902, after Shtyubelya Sopka in the Kamchatka Peninsula, U.S.S.R., in 1907, and after Katmai in Alaska in 1912—the latter being the largest instrumentally recorded depletion in the period. After this event there were no eruptions that injected significant material into the stratosphere until Agung in 1963. Hekla in Iceland (1947) and Bezymyannaya in Kamchatka (1956) had explosive phases that injected clouds up to 27 and 45 kilometers, respectively, but the amount of material involved was apparently small for the former, while that for the latter was so coarse that it fell out quickly.

What sort of temperature changes occur in the troposphere and near the surface as a result of these depletions of solar radiation? To make

218

this assessment properly it is necessary to know the wavelength of the radiation in which the maximum depletion occurs. For example, if near-infrared solar radiation (wavelength ranging from 0.6 to 4 micrometers) is depleted, this results in less heating in the upper troposphere where those wavelengths are normally absorbed. If visible radiation suffers the main depletion, then it is sea-surface and land-surface temperatures that will be lowered, as well as the adjacent air temperatures that depend on these surface readings. In addition, if lowered sea-surface temperatures result in decreased evaporation, then less latent heat will be liberated in the troposphere, particularly in the tropics.

The maximum sea-surface temperatures are limited to about 30° C (86° F) in the tropics, this limit being set by the balance between incoming solar radiation and evaporation. Near this maximum the sensitivity of temperature to radiation changes is about 1° C (1.8° F) for a change in radiation of 30 watts per square meter. Therefore, based on radiation changes observed in the El Chichón eruption, a drop of about 1° C in maximum sea-surface temperature might be anticipated if all other factors remain constant in the areas covered by the dense aerosol cloud. However, the satellite data reveal that the El Chichón cloud reached its greatest density at about latitude 20° N; because this is a little farther north than the warm (30° C) pool of water in the tropical Pacific, a much smaller surface temperature change is expected.

A major complication affecting the weather in much of the world occurred in 1982. A few months after El Chichón erupted in April of that year the tropical Pacific Ocean began to warm up as a result of an oceanic phenomen known as El Niño. El Niño is the occurrence of warm water off the coast of Peru and along the Equatorial region of the eastern Pacific. It takes place when the normal easterly winds along the Equator weaken and sometimes turn to westerly. By the end of 1982 scientists were witnessing the largest El Niño on record. Instead of the normal

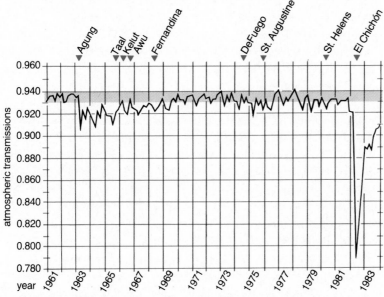

Atmospheric transmission of incoming solar radiation has been measured at Mauna Loa in Hawaii. On a clear day about 93.5% of the radiation in the direct solar beam reaches the ground. The graph reveals the effect of volcanic eruptions on such transmissions. The shaded area is considered to be the range of average atmospheric transmission values over Mauna Loa during times when there are no significant amounts of volcanic debris in the stratosphere.

Courtesy, Bernard G. Mendonca, U.S. Department of Commerce, National Oceanic and Atmospheric Administration, Geophysical Monitoring for Climatic Change Division, Boulder, Colorado 80303

upwelling of cold water from below, El Niño promotes downwelling and a rise of surface temperatures.

Scientists wondered whether El Chichón was somehow responsible for the tendency toward westerly winds in the tropical Pacific. To explore this question one needs to examine the pressure patterns characteristic of El Niño and their possible relationships to volcanic activity. The average temperature for the strip of the eastern tropical Pacific just to the south of the Equator gives a good measure of El Niño. Prior to 1982 there were large Niños in 1976, 1972, 1965, and 1957. There is no obvious relationship between these warm periods and volcanic activity. There is a relationship, however, between the equatorial sea temperatures and air temperature in the layer of troposphere between the altitudes of three and seven kilometers in the tropics, and studies have revealed that eastern equatorial Pacific sea-surface temperature changes a few months ahead of the air temperature; therefore, the surface changes may be regarded as a kind of control on the air temperature. If these two variables are related statistically, then it is easy to show that a significant fraction of the variability of the air temperature can be accounted for on the basis of previous variations in the sea temperature. If this "explained" variability in air temperature is subtracted from the real air temperature changes, a procedure carried out by Newell and B. C. Weare, what remains is a curve that parallels the atmospheric transmission that is due to volcanic activity. In other words both sea-surface temperature and volcanic activity appear to influence the air temperature in the tropics. The residual temperature change associated with the Agung eruption was about 0.5° C (0.9° F) for this layer of three to seven kilometers in the tropics, but, interestingly enough, the maximum change did not occur until 1964. This suggests that the particles which caused the stratospheric heating in the early stages, probably silicates and iron, are different from those which produced the later tropospheric cooling.

In 1982 the volcanic activity and sea temperature effects tended to act in opposite directions. Increasing sea temperature warmed the air, via evaporation and liberation of latent heat, while the increasing amount of volcanic aerosols tended to shield the Earth from solar radiation. Because both these phenomena were very extensive in 1982, the net effect was difficult to determine.

The effects of volcanic aerosol on sea-surface temperatures and air temperatures just above the sea in middle and high latitudes have recently been analyzed. In two studies using different data sets Newell and Jane Hsiung found that the North Atlantic and North Pacific both became colder after the eruption of Agung in 1963 and in fact for several years were 0.3–0.4° C (0.5–0.7° F) colder that they had been before the eruption. (There is a certain complication in identifying 1963 as a real temperature discontinuity because the data sets showed a substantial increase in the number of ships' reports at that time.) Surface air temperature above the sea also dropped in phase with this change. In late 1982 and 1983 North Pacific sea-surface temperatures showed a drop of close to 2° C (3.6° F). At first thought this could be partly attributed to

220

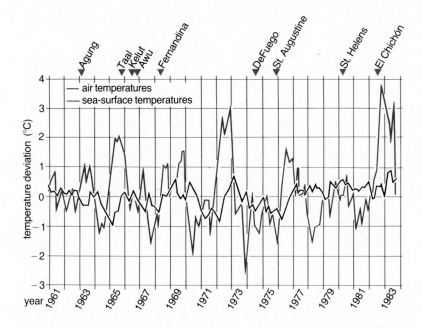

Average sea-surface temperatures in a region of the Pacific Ocean ranging from the Equator to latitude 5° south and from the coast of South America to longitude 140° west reveal the occurrences of the warm current El Niño. The especially large El Niño of 1982–83 can be seen. Mean air temperatures in the tropical atmosphere at altitudes ranging from three to seven kilometers generally declined during times of volcanic eruptions and rose during the El Niño periods.

El Chichón, but that interpretation is complicated by the fact that the temperature of the North Pacific generally drops as a result of additional cloudiness in an El Niño period. Thus, again it is difficult if not impossible to unscramble the influences of the two phenomena.

In regard to the possible effects of volcanoes on surface air temperature there have been an extremely large number of studies. In April 1815 Mt. Tambora on Sumbawa Island in Indonesia underwent an eruption so immense that it produced darkness for three days as far as 500 kilometers from the volcano. This event is generally blamed for the fact that 1816 was "the year without a summer" in much of the United States and many other parts of the world. A global network of meteorological stations was organized in the 1850s, and so for more recent eruptions it has been possible to obtain at least continental coverage of air temperature changes in the Northern Hemisphere. Many studies have been made of the deviation of the air temperature from the long-term monthly mean values. An example by Herbert Kimball suggests that Northern Hemisphere surface temperature dropped by about 0.8° C (1.4° F) in the few months after the eruption of Katmai in June 1912 but then recovered to be warmer than average by December, an effect he suggested may have been due to the dust trapping outgoing long-wave radiation. But, as has already been mentioned, it is difficult to sort out the volcanic effect from other factors controlling air temperature.

One conclusion upon which scientists are agreed is that at higher latitudes the effect of the aerosol is amplified because the solar beam, operating at lower elevations there, passes through the aerosol layer obliquely and therefore intercepts more mass. Ryozaburo Yamamoto and his colleagues at Kyoto University, Japan, demonstrated that at high latitudes in 1951–72 surface air temperature seemed to respond to the 1963 eruption of Mt. Agung by cooling, and may have done so in some of the

221

other recent eruptions. Because these studies also did not take account of the possible changes due to sea-surface temperature, perhaps the main point to note is that the greatest changes were found at high latitudes.

B. L. Taylor, Tzvi Gal-Chen, and S. H. Schneider showed that the largest temperature drop after major eruptions occurred in the summer season at high latitudes and in winter at low latitudes. They focused attention on eight years that included one or more large eruptions (1815, 1822, 1831, 1835, 1845–46, 1883, 1902, and 1963) and found a surface temperature drop of about 0.5° C (0.9° F) two years after the eruption year, a finding quite similar to that of Newell and Weare for Mt. Agung in 1963. Again, however, no account was taken of sea-surface temperature changes. While their finding about changes at high latitudes supports the idea that in summer the solar beam is of major importance in controlling temperature (whereas in winter high latitudes depend for their energy supply on energy transport from low latitudes), the finding about the winter low-latitude changes is difficult to explain. Even the summer conclusion is at variance with 1783 (colder winter, warmer summer)— suggesting that it is a little dangerous to group volcanic events together in this type of study.

Michael R. Rampino and Stephen Self looked at the effects on surface temperature of the eruptions of Tambora in 1815, Krakatoa in 1883, and Agung in 1963 and found declines of a few tenths of a degree Celsius in subsequent years. None of these cases was materially affected by the explosive power of the eruption. Rampino and Self suggested that the delayed response was due to the sulfate particles and that there was much less variation in sulfate between these three eruptions than in other measures of volcanic effects.

Annual layers of an ice core from central Greenland reveal rises in their levels of acidity during periods of volcanic eruptions and also occasionally at times when no eruptions were reported. These increases were caused by the fallout of volcanic acids ejected into the atmosphere from eruptions north of latitude 20° south.

In a recent analysis J. K. Angell and J. Korshover examined temperature trends between 1958 and 1982 and found evidence for a 0.3° C (0.5° F) decrease in Northern Hemisphere temperature following Agung in 1963, with no evidence for changes following subsequent eruptions (their analysis stopped in the spring of 1982). They also found the relationship discussed above between sea temperature and subsequent air temperature, although they have not yet tried to separate the volcanic

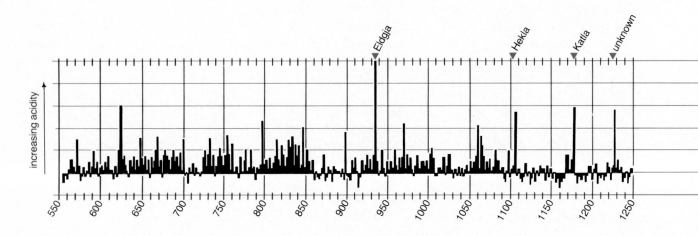

and oceanic effects on air temperature. In the next few years there will be more detailed information becoming available on El Chichón. First results by C. B. Sear and P. M. Kelly of the University of East Anglia at Norwich, England, suggested that in June 1982 the Northern Hemisphere surface air temperature was about 0.2° C (0.4° F) below normal, although the situation was complicated because it had already been below normal a few months before the eruption of El Chichón that April.

Volcanic aerosol in ice cores

Eventually the volcanic sulfate aerosol descends from the stratosphere into the troposphere, and its presence has been noted as "acid snow" in ice cores collected in Greenland and Antarctica. In the case of Greenland the transfer from the stratosphere appears to take place in conjunction with active low-pressure systems that suck the stratospheric air down to an altitude of about five kilometers or even lower, according to aircraft measurements made over Canada in 1977 by Edwin F. Danielsen and R. Stephen Hipskind, who were then at Oregon State Unviersity, and recent aircraft soundings made near Greenland by Melvin Shapiro of the NOAA's Environmental Research Laboratories at Boulder, Colorado. Because the ice cap is about three kilometers high, the sulfate rather easily falls out on the snow or is washed out by falling snow, and a permanent record of past fallout is available in the ice cores.

C. U. Hammer and Willi Dansgaard of the University of Copenhagen analyzed the Greenland cores for sulfate and showed that most of the major recorded eruptions left their mark in the record of acidity, at least back to AD 550. In fact, there were several acidity peaks for which there was no reported volcanic eruption, which is not surprising; there was a mystery cloud found in the stratosphere in January 1982 whose volcanic origin was unknown. Another interesting aspect of the situation is that acidity levels in general were very low in the periods 1100–1250, 1850–70, and 1920–60 and were very high in 1400–1700. This latter time span was cold and is often called the Little Ice Age, while the 1100–1250 and 1920–60 periods were relatively warm. In view of this apparent association the question arises as to whether enhanced volcanic activity

Ice core from Antarctica is examined for dust bands (top). A volcanic ash band deposited about 13,000 BC is revealed in the core (bottom).

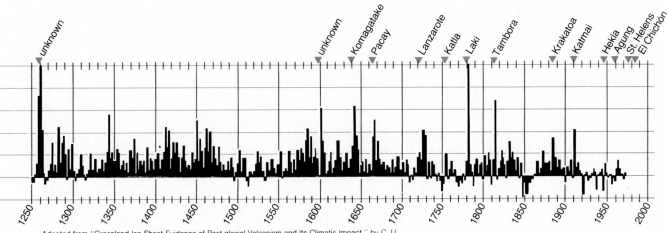

Adapted from "Greenland Ice Sheet Evidence of Post-glacial Volcanism and Its Climatic Impact," by C. U. Hammer, H. B. Clausen, and W. Dansgaard, reprinted by permission from *Nature*, vol. 228, no. 5788, pp. 230–235, November 20, 1980. Copyright © 1980 Macmillan Journals Limited.

Large volcanic eruptions cause a significant rise in the temperature of the stratosphere in the tropics and subtropics, but their influence on air temperature closer to the Earth's surface is difficult to evaluate because many other factors are also involved.

causes ice ages. J. H. Cragin and his colleagues at the Cold Regions Research and Engineering Laboratory in Hanover, New Hampshire, found evidence for enhanced sulfate in the Greenland ice cores in the period 28,000 to 12,000 years before the present, and volcanic activity presumably associated with this could be considered to be the cause of the ice ages of that time. However, it is equally likely that the enhanced cyclonic activity that may have accompanied the steeper Pole-to-Equator temperature gradients sucked more sulfate out of the stratosphere.

A similar explanation is a possibility for the background changes described above; if some other climatic factor caused the warmth of the 1200s, then the generally weaker high-latitude storm systems could have deposited less sulfate in the ice cores. For the Little Ice Age steeper temperature gradients and stronger high-latitude storms could have brought down more sulfate. If less aerosol came out of the stratosphere at high latitudes, then more would presumably come out at middle latitudes. It is difficult, however, to find evidence of any extra mid-latitude fallout. Perhaps the Swiss glaciers are the only place to look for the records of the past several hundred years.

Future prospects

What then is really known about the influence of volcanoes on climate? One established conclusion is that large eruptions such as Agung and El Chichón cause the stratospheric temperature to increase by 4–6° C (7.2–10.8° F) in the tropics and subtropics, provided the volcanic cloud reaches those regions. How much of this change is due to absorption of solar radiation by silicates, iron, ash, and so forth, and how much is due to the absorption of outgoing long-wave radiation from the Earth is not known. But the great volume of data acquired from El Chichón should enable this point to be examined in depth, if not settled.

Air temperature changes at the surface and in the region ranging from one to ten kilometers in altitude are much more difficult to relate to volcanic activity because they can be influenced by many other factors. It is possible that the air cools by a few tenths of a degree Celsius on average for the year or two after a large eruption, this effect stemming from the reflection of solar energy back to space by the long-lived sulfate aerosol in the stratosphere. Most of these studies need to be looked at again now that scientists know that sea-surface temperature strongly influences subsequent air temperature.

By October 1982, according to an airborne laser survey carried out between latitudes 46° N and 46° S by M. P. McCormick of NASA Langley Research Center and his colleagues, there were about 12 megatons of aerosol if all altitudes were included. The 13 megatons of sulfur dioxide from El Chichón that were originally measured by the Canadians would convert to about 20 megatons of sulfate; in addition, there may have been substantial hydrogen sulfide. Therefore, it seems possible that conversion to additional aerosol continued for some time after October 1982. Meanwhile, beautiful sunsets were still being seen throughout 1983.

The reason that there was no marked cooling in the 1982–83 winter, an effect widely predicted, was probably the occurrence of the exceptionally strong El Niño. By early 1984 El Niño had disappeared, and the airborne debris from El Chichón might be expected to exert its influence. Indeed, many areas in the United States experienced their coldest December on record in 1983. It must be remembered, however, that the average change after an eruption is only a few tenths of a degree Celsius, and nearly two years after the eruption the cloud density is much decreased. In addition, sea temperature patterns in the middle latitudes are altering, and these also help to govern middle-latitude air temperature. El Niño is as unpredictable as volcanic eruptions and has been known to recur in January of the year after its maximum. For these reasons, therefore, long-range forecasting of climate must remain, for the present, an enigma.

FOR ADDITIONAL READING

H. H. Lamb, "Volcanic dust in the atmosphere; with a chronology and assessment of its meteorological significance," *Philosophical Transactions of the Royal Society of London* (Vol. 266, pp. 425–533, July 1970).

W. J. Humphreys, *Physics of the Air* (Dover, 1940).

Geophysical Research Letters, November 1983 issue, Volume 10, Number 11, pp. 989–1060 are devoted to papers on the El Chichón eruption. American Geophysical Union.

Reginald E. Newell and Adarsh Deepak (eds.), "Mount St. Helens Eruption of 1980: Atmospheric Effects and Potential Climatic Impact" (NASA publication SP–458, 118 pp., NASA, Washington, D.C., 1980).

Tom Simkin and Richard S. Fiske, *Krakatoa: The Volcanic Eruption and Its Effects* (Smithsonian, 1983).

Aden and Majorie Meinel, *Sunsets, Twilight and Evening Skies* (Cambridge University Press, 1983).

Henry and Elizabeth Stommel, *Volcano Weather: The Story of 1816; The Year Without a Summer* (Seven Seas, 1983).

Deep-Sea Hydrothermal Vents

by Richard A. Lutz

OASES on the OCEAN FLOOR

Among the most remarkable discoveries in recent years are hydrothermal vents, fissures in the seafloor through which hot water flows. Dense populations of unusual marine animals surround these openings.

Galápagos—the name evokes memories of Charles Darwin and a marvelous group of East Pacific islands with astonishingly varied life forms. Approximately 150 years after Darwin and the HMS "Beagle" first set anchor at the archipelago and discovered its remarkable animal life, a considerably more sophisticated research vessel, "Alvin," arrived at a site only a few hundred kilometers to the east. There, in mid-February 1977, the small submersible descended through 2,500 meters of water to uncover another, perhaps even more incredible, assemblage of organisms thriving in the permanent darkness of the deep sea. The pilot and two geologists on board were the first to behold the biological and geological wonders of a hydrothermal system along an active seafloor spreading center known as the Galápagos Rift. Temperatures as high as 23° C (73° F); thin encrustations of ferromanganese oxides on top of fresh basalt; high concentrations of hydrogen sulfide; and an abundance of new families, genera, and species of organisms sustained by sulfur-oxidizing bacteria were but a few of the striking discoveries that would send shock waves through the oceanographic community.

(Left) Richard A. Lutz; (right) John M. Edmond, Massachusetts Institute of Technology

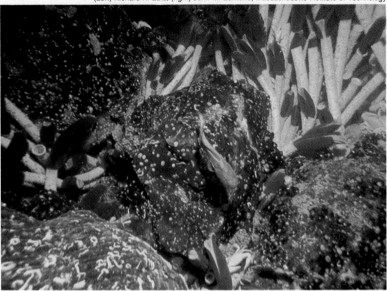

*Above, research submersible ''Alvin''
prepares to dive. In 1977 ''Alvin''
discovered a hydrothermal vent
system along the Galápagos Rift, a
seafloor spreading center, near the
Galápagos Islands. A wide variety of
marine life, including giant tube worms
(pogonophorans), vent fish (bythitids),
crabs, clams, limpets, and annelid worms
(polychaetes), was found clustered near
the vents (above right).*

***RICHARD A. LUTZ** is an Associate
Professor in the New Jersey Agricultural
Experiment Station, Cook College,
Rutgers University, New Brunswick,
New Jersey.*

*(Overleaf) Photograph,
J. Frederick Grassle,
Woods Hole Oceanographic Institution*

Regions explored

The Galápagos Rift represents one small segment of a 74,000-kilometer (46,000-mile)-long system of oceanic ridges and rifts that extends through all the major ocean basins as seafloor spreading centers. The existence of hot (thermal) springs along active mid-ocean ridge systems was hypothesized as early as 1965 (more than a decade prior to their discovery), based on observations of anomalous heat flows, altered oceanic basalt (an aluminum silicate that comprises the oceanic crust), and the occurrence of metalliferous deep-sea sediments. The detection of hydrothermal plumes and the presence of large white clams in photographs taken using a deep-tow, sledlike vehicle known as ANGUS (acoustically navigated geophysical underwater system) added final pieces of evidence for the existence of such submarine hydrothermal systems prior to their actual discovery in 1977.

Extensive exploration since 1977 has uncovered numerous additional sites of hydrothermal activity at the boundaries of the huge plates that form the Earth's crust. Efforts to date have focused on moderate- to fast-spreading centers in the eastern Pacific, where active thermal springs and associated assemblages of marine animals have been found as far north as latitude 48° N along the Juan de Fuca Ridge (spreading rate ≅ 6 centimeters per year) and as far south as latitude 22° S along the East Pacific Rise (spreading rate ≅ 18 centimeters per year). The most active of these areas are characterized by massive sulfide deposits associated with chimneylike structures known as ''smokers'' that spew mineral-laden water at temperatures of approximately 350° C (660° F). These temperatures are in marked contrast to the 2° C (35° F) seawater surrounding the sites.

Extensive populations of ''vent'' organisms are commonly associated with the relatively low-temperature ''Galápagos-type'' vents that are frequently encountered over extensive areas in the general vicinity of the smokers. Along the relatively slow-spreading (2–5 centimeters per year) Mid-Atlantic Ridge only a few temperature anomalies have been identified to date, although the presence of extensive sulfide deposits and reports of "large white clams" along various sections of the ridge suggest the presence at some time of both low- and high-temperature vent systems. Finally, recent studies of deep-sea plumes of methane, a common constituent of vent water, have provided evidence for the first known off-ridge vents, located in the Mariana Trench in the western Pacific.

Observations and studies of the many active and inactive hydrothermal vents found during the past few years have radically altered many views of biological, geological, and geochemical processes in the deep sea. Three of the most significant discoveries may be summarized as follows: (1) The vents and associated chemical constituents provide the energy source for chemosynthetic bacteria, which, in turn, are the primary producers sustaining the lush biological communities at the hydrothermal sites. (Chemosynthetic bacteria are those that use energy obtained from the chemical oxidation of inorganic compounds, such as hydrogen sulfide, for the fixation of carbon dioxide into organic matter.) (2) The vents appear to be the main source of the metal-rich sediments and nodules that carpet the ocean floor and may be the ultimate source of many of the valuable ore deposits that have been emplaced on continents by the motions of crustal plates. (3) The chemical content of hydrothermal vent waters is an important determinant of the chemical composition of the oceans themselves. In order to gain an appreciation of the factors responsible for the vent water characteristics that have such profound effects, one must understand the processes that drive the circulation of hydrothermal fluids through mid-ocean ridge systems.

The source of vent waters

The mid-ocean ridges represent portions of the ocean floor where new oceanic crust is formed by intrusions of hot magma from the Earth's

Cross section of hydrothermal ore-forming system shows a seafloor spreading center. Hot magma from the Earth's interior forms new crust on the seafloor. As this crust cools, cracks and fissures develop in it. Cold seawater seeps into the fissures and is heated to 350° C (660° F) or more, dissolving basaltic rock from the crust. The dissolved ions combine with circulating seawater to form mineral precipitates and an acidic metalliferous hydrothermal solution. The hot, mineral-bearing water then rises and bursts through the seafloor at vents along the spreading center. As the exiting water rapidly cools and reacts with surrounding bottom waters, solid metallic sulfides precipitate out of solution and form huge chimneylike structures.

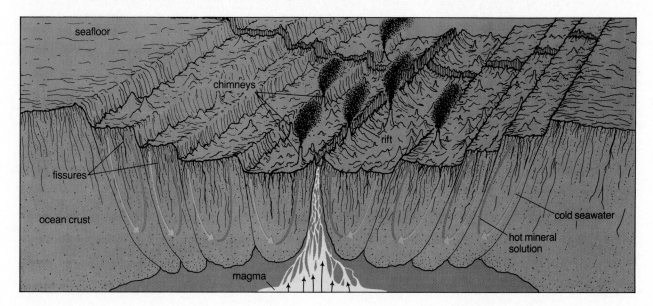

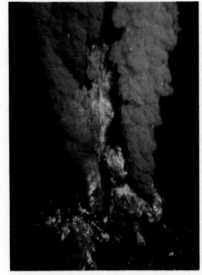

Black "smoker" (right) at a hydrothermal site spews forth fine particles of iron sulfide that precipitate out of solution as the hot vent water meets the much colder seawater. Glistening on a sample of black-smoker chimney wall are deposits of zinc sulfide and chalcopyrite (far right).

In a black smoker calcium sulfate precipitates out of a hydrothermal solution as the mineral anhydrite. When the leading edge of the anhydrite becomes exposed to more of the hot solution, it redissolves and acts as a template for metal sulfides. Where the sulfides engulf it rapidly, the anhydrite is preserved.

black smoke (FeS)

seawater

leading edge of anhydrite

SO_4^{2-}

Ca

350° C hydrothermal solution

anhydrite stringers

sulfides of iron, zinc, and copper

metalliferous sediment

partially molten interior. As the newly formed crust cools, extensive cracks and fissures develop throughout the basaltic rock. Cold seawater penetrates downward to depths of several kilometers through these openings and is heated by contact with rock at temperatures in excess of 400° C (750° F). A curious observation made from recent deep-sea drilling operations along a ridge crest not far from the Galápagos Rift suggested that the pressure at the bottom of the deepest hole drilled to date along ridge systems (Hole 504-B, 1,076 meters) is less than that at the ocean floor. While the mechanisms that are responsible for such a reverse pressure gradient are poorly understood, the observed relatively low pressures in lower layers of the crust may play a significant role in hydrothermal circulation by pulling seawater from the ocean floor down into the crustal fissures. After being significantly heated at depth in the fissures, the hot, relatively light water rises to the surface to escape through vent openings along the ridge crest.

As seawater passes through the system, some of its ions such as calcium, magnesium, and sulfate precipitate out of the solution, while others react with hot basaltic rock in the lower layers of the crust to produce mineral precipitates and an acidic (pH ≈ 3) metalliferous hydrothermal solution. One reaction of major importance to biological systems, as will become obvious later in this discussion, is that of sulfate from circulating seawater with iron in the rock to produce large quantities of hydrogen sulfide (H_2S) in the exiting 350° C water and iron oxides. The leached elements and compounds are carried upward, and the heated solution is cooled by dilution with the colder surrounding seawater. This process of cooling and mixing results in the precipitation of metal sulfides (through reactions of the metal positively charged ions with hydrogen sulfide) and of calcium sulfate (vent calcium and ambient seawater sulfate). This can take place either at the surface of the seafloor or in subsurface layers where considerable mixing with surrounding waters occurs prior to arrival at the ocean floor.

J. Frederick Grassle, Woods Hole Oceanographic Institution

Metallic oxides and sulfides carpeting the seafloor along various sections of oceanic ridge systems were produced from active hydrothermal vents and from the deterioration of extinct chimneys.

The black "smoke" emanating from the top of vent chimneys is composed of fine particles of iron sulfide that precipitate out of solution as the exiting 350° C water is rapidly diluted with the cold (2° C) seawater. The iron and manganese, which are in particularly high concentrations within exiting thermal plumes, are eventually oxidized and fall as a metalliferous sediment over extensive areas of the ocean floor. It has been estimated that sufficient manganese is released from hydrothermal vents to account for all the accumulation of that element in the metalliferous sediments and nodules carpeting the seafloor.

In addition, undiluted, high-temperature vent waters are particularly rich (relative to seawater) in zinc, copper, nickel, cobalt, cadmium, and europium. Calculations suggest that active vent processes release between five and ten times more lithium and rubidium, and between one-third and one-half as much potassium, calcium, barium, and silica as rivers introduce into the sea. Conversely, hydrothermal circulation along ridge axes "consumes" most of the magnesium and sulfate entering the ocean from the continents and converts most of the bicarbonate produced by continental weathering back into carbon dioxide. From global measurements of conductive loss of heat from the ocean floor, it has been estimated that a volume of seawater equal to the volume of all the oceans (1.37×10^{21} liters) circulates through ocean ridge systems approximately every eight million years.

Geologic manifestations

Signs of ancient submarine hydrothermal activity may be found at numerous sites throughout the world, including, surprisingly enough, extensive areas on top of continental crust. The island of Cyprus, mountains of Tibet, and regions in Oman on the Arabian Sea represent a few of the areas where great slabs of oceanic crust, known as ophiolites, have been thrust onto the continents by collisions of crustal plates. Detailed studies of many of these areas, such as the great ophiolite of Oman, have provided

A stalked crinoid (sea lily) and various other attached deep-sea organisms live on a lava pillar on the East Pacific Rise. Such pillars form when hot magma surges up through fissures in the seafloor and traps water in rock crevices. The superheated water then expands and blasts through the molten magma, which hardens in a tube around the jet.

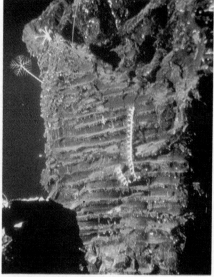

J. Frederick Grassle, Woods Hole Oceanographic Institution

evidence that seawater once penetrated the basaltic rocks that comprise the formations to depths in excess of five kilometers (three miles). This water was heated to extremely high temperatures and rose again to the surface to form massive deposits of quartz and metallic sulfides (consisting largely of pyrite, or "fool's gold"), as well as extensive regions of metalliferous sediment, known as umber, that are several meters thick. Perhaps one of the most striking geologic realizations resulting from recent studies of heat loss and sulfide precipitation at the 350° C vents is that massive sulfide deposits originally interpreted as forming over periods in excess of 10,000 years may, in fact, have been formed during periods of decades or less.

Other continental deposits of massive sulfide-ore bodies, known as Besshi deposits, have also been attributed to hydrothermal activity at oceanic ridges. In such deposits, which derive their name from one of particular economic importance in Japan, the ore lies in the midst of rock (shale) comprised of fine-grained sedimentary clay. The current hypothesis regarding the origin of these structures suggests that the ridge axis responsible for the formation of the deposits was close to a land mass (either a continent or island arc) that provided a source of large amounts of erosional debris. Basaltic dikes and sills are frequently found within the shale several hundred meters below the Besshi deposit and reflect, respectively, vertical and horizontal intrusions of magma that provided the heat source to drive hydrothermal circulation through original sedimentary layers.

A recently discovered hydrothermal vent field in the Gulf of California's Guaymas Basin appears to represent a Besshi deposit in the process of formation. There, at a location where the East Pacific Rise penetrates the North American continent, massive sediment from Mexican rivers has buried the active ridge axis to a depth of several hundred meters. Temperatures as high as 315° C (600° F) have been recorded from venting waters that exit from edifices shaped like Japanese pagodas atop

Pagoda-shaped structure (below left) sits on top of a huge sediment mound at the Guaymas Basin hydrothermal vent field in the Gulf of California. Vent waters exit from such pagodas at temperatures as high as 315° C (600° F). Tube worms and sulfide chimneys (below right) emerge from sediment at the Guaymas Basin field.

(Left) J. Frederick Grassle, Woods Hole Oceanographic Institution; (right) Alvin External Camera, WHOI

J. Frederick Grassle,
Woods Hole Oceanographic Institution

huge sediment mounds several hundred meters long and tens of meters high. In contrast to the hydrothermal circulation patterns described above for ridge systems of open oceanic environments, circulating seawater at the Guaymas Basin site must percolate through the thick layers of silt containing countless calcium carbonate tests (firm shell-like structures) of buried organisms. The dissolution of these tests through reaction with the ascending acidic fluids causes a marked increase in alkalinity, which, when coupled with the cooling effects of penetrating seawater, results in the subsurface precipitation of sulfide minerals. As might be expected, the composition of the hydrothermal fluids exiting at the Guaymas Basin floor is markedly different from that of the fluids expelled along ridge systems of the open ocean. An alkalinity four times that of the surrounding seawater and extremely small concentrations of the characteristic vent metals are a few of the unusual properties identified to date from analyses of thermal fluids sampled at the Guaymas Basin site.

One final characteristic of the Guaymas Basin hydrothermal fields that has received considerable attention is the presence of relatively large quantities of petroleum hydrocarbons within the sedimentary layers. Sediment cores and dredged samples from the region have a strong odor similar to that of diesel fuel, and retrieved water samples frequently contain "globules of wax." The petroleum appears to arise from the "cracking" of organic molecules into hydrocarbons by the intense heat of the hydrothermal fields.

Oily rock containing high concentrations of petroleum hydrocarbons is found at the Guaymas Basin hydrothermal site. The petroleum is believed to be produced by the "cracking" of organic molecules into hydrocarbons by the intense heat of the hydrothermal fields.

Deep-sea oases of life: geothermally-driven ecosystems

Until the 1977 discovery of the Galápagos Rift communities, understanding of deep-sea biology and ecology was based primarily on studies of life in the vast soft-bottom habitats of the seafloor. Although there are large numbers of species in that "typical" deep-sea environment, population densities and biomass are low. Furthermore, biological processes, such as metabolism, growth, and colonization, are slow compared with their rates in shallow-water ecosystems. These reduced rates have been attributed to the low food supply, high pressure, and low temperature on the deep-sea floor. In marked contrast to these vast and relatively stable deep-sea environments, active deep-sea hydrothermal vents are relatively restricted and unstable environments that are characterized by lush communities of biological organisms. Research to date suggests that these "oases" of life have high densities and biomass, low species diversity, rapid growth rates, and high metabolic rates.

Food is generally considered to be the primary limiting resource for organisms of the deep sea. Only a small percentage of the available food energy produced through photosynthesis in the surface waters of the ocean is transferred down through the water column to the deep-sea floor. The lavish biological communities at the hydrothermal vents, therefore, are a fascinating enigma.

At first, two alternative hypotheses were proposed to explain the sources of food necessary to support these dense assemblages of animals: (1) Thermal plumes rising from the vents create local inflowing bottom

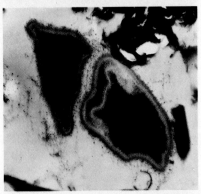

Chemosynthetic bacteria, whose metabolic energy source is obtained from the oxidation of inorganic compounds such as hydrogen sulfide, flourish at hydrothermal vent sites and, in turn, sustain the lush biological communities there. Electron micrographs reveal microbial cells on the surface of a mussel shell (top), thermophilic bacteria from water emanating from a black smoker (center), and symbiotic bacteria in a tube worm (bottom).

currents that concentrate food from surrounding waters. (2) The ultimate source of food is provided by chemosynthetic bacteria that oxidize sulfur compounds, especially H_2S, which, as mentioned above, is present in high concentrations in the hot waters discharged from the vents. With regard to the first of these hypotheses it is conceivable that a few of the organisms found at the periphery of the vent areas may obtain significant quantities of food from particles swept toward the vents by convection currents. It has been suggested, in fact, that the concentrations of large numbers of black corals near the base of sediment mounds at the Guaymas Basin hydrothermal site may be an example of such food-concentrating effects of rising thermal plumes. However, results obtained from the vast majority of studies conducted to date strongly suggest that bacterial chemosynthesis supplies most of the food energy necessary to maintain the vent communities. These bacteria can oxidize H_2S to elemental sulfur and sulfates; the energy released in this reaction is used to reduce carbon dioxide to organic carbon, just as in the dark reactions of photosynthesis.

Although chemosynthetic bacteria live in other habitats, such as sulfur springs, swamps, and estuaries, none is known to sustain major communities such as those encountered at deep-sea vents. To date, more than 250 strains of bacteria have been isolated from deep-sea thermal vent environments. Preliminary studies suggest that some of them may be capable of oxidizing nitrite, iron, ammonia, manganese, or thiosulfate instead of, or in addition to, H_2S. In the case of most or all of the chemosynthetic bacteria isolated to date, it appears that oxygen contained in the surrounding water or in the circulating hydrothermal seawater serves as the electron acceptor for oxidation of the energy-rich, geothermally-derived compounds (such as H_2S). It should be emphasized that the majority, if not all, of this oxygen is derived from photosynthesis. Therefore, while the energy source driving this system is geothermal (the Earth's internal heat resulting from processes associated with core formation, planetesimal accretion, and the radioactive breakdown of long-lived radioisotopes of uranium, thorium, and potassium) and not solar, the chemosynthetic-based food chains at the vents may, in fact, be dependent ultimately upon photosynthesis, a Sun-driven, food-manufacturing process. A possible exception may be found in recent reports of isolated thermophilic (*thermo* = "heat"; *philos* = "loving") bacteria from high-temperature black smokers. Based on a series of laboratory experiments, it appears that certain chemosynthetic bacteria may be capable of survival and growth at temperatures in excess of 300° C (575° F). Furthermore, it has been suggested that certain non-biologically synthesized compounds, such as manganese dioxide or nitrous oxide, might serve as electron acceptors for oxidative microbial activity in anaerobic hydrothermal waters (those that lack free oxygen). If certain chemosynthetic microbes are indeed capable of metabolizing under such anaerobic, high-temperature conditions, the spectrum of environmental conditions under which life could have originated on Earth would be significantly increased, as would the number of extraterrestrial environments capable of supporting life as we know it.

A further exciting discovery arising from microbiological and physiological studies of several of the larger vent organisms added a new dimension to the understanding of food-chain dynamics in these hydrothermal systems, as well as in other sulfide-rich marine environments. Evidence from a wide variety of sources indicates that certain chemosynthetic bacteria have symbiotic relationships with several of the dominant invertebrates at the vents, including the vestimentiferan tube worm *Riftia pachyptila* and the large white vesicomyid clam *Calyptogena magnifica*. (In a symbiotic relationship two dissimilar organisms live together intimately in a mutually beneficial relationship.) The tube worm, which can achieve a body length of up to 1.5 meters (tube length of 2.5 meters with a diameter as great as 4 centimeters), lacks a mouth, a digestive system, and an anus. This organism may represent the first example of a major taxon (the new subphylum Obturata in the relatively obscure phylum Pogonophora) that is totally dependent on symbiotic microbes for nutrition.

One of the intriguing questions concerning these and other vent organisms asks how they are capable of survival and growth in an environment that is extremely enriched in sulfide, a substance which, even in relatively low concentrations, is poisonous to many organisms. The deep-sea waters surrounding the vents generally contain no detectable quantities of sulfide. In marked contrast, high concentrations of H_2S have been measured in waters surrounding many of the organisms at the vents. Recent studies of the blood of tube worms collected from hydrothermal fields at latitude 21° N along the East Pacific Rise appear to have unlocked at least one of the secrets of success for survival in this seemingly toxic environment. Their blood contains a sulfide-binding protein that prevents appreciable amounts of free sulfide from accumulating in it and from entering the intracellular compartment. In addition, the blood, with its affinity for both sulfide and oxygen, may serve the function of transportation of these necessary metabolites to the symbiotic bacteria that reside in a special tissue called the trophosome.

An abundance of new species

Extensive populations of vent organisms have been found associated with all six of the major active ridge sites visited or extensively photographed to date in the eastern Pacific. From north to south, these areas may be summarized as follows: the Juan de Fuca Ridge (44°–48° N); Guaymas Basin (Gulf of California); 21° N along the East Pacific Rise (EPR); 11°–13° N along the EPR; the Galápagos Rift; and 17°–22° S along the EPR. The biological communities at the five studied sites south of the Juan de Fuca Ridge are remarkably similar, with many of the same species apparently present, despite separation by relatively large geographic distances. The lack of a connecting oceanic ridge system between the Juan de Fuca Ridge and the East Pacific Rise may account for observed differences in the species composition of biological assemblages along those two ridge systems.

Perhaps the most spectacular organism encountered to date at various hydrothermal sites is the tube worm *Riftia pachyptila*. Many of the

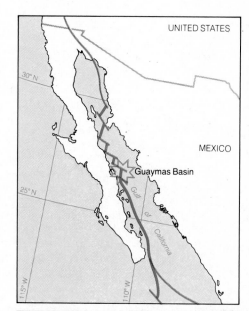

Hydrothermal vent sites explored to date lie along seafloor ridge systems in the eastern Pacific Ocean.

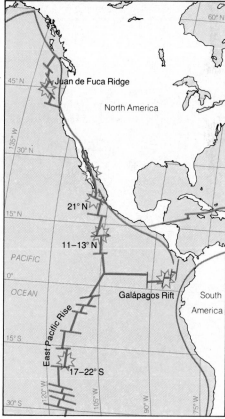

235

(Top left) Woods Hole Oceanographic Institution;
(top right) Dudley B. Foster, Woods Hole Oceanographic Institution;
(bottom left) James J. Childress, University of California at Santa Barbara; (bottom right) Richard A. Lutz

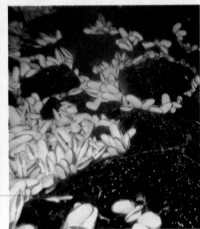

Tube worms are perhaps the most spectacular inhabitants of hydrothermal vent sites. At the Galápagos Rift a container for sample collection lies in front of a cluster of tube worms (top left). A close-up view of the worms (top right) reveals their bright red coloration, which is caused by the presence of extracellular hemoglobin. Large white clams occur in extensive beds in an area known as "Clam Acres" at the 21° N hydrothermal site (bottom right). The large rough foot of this species (bottom left) is usually extended deep within the cracks of the basaltic substrate where temperatures as high as 16° C (60° F) have been recorded.

Red coloration of the soft tissues of a clam from the Galápagos Rift hydrothermal site results from intracellular hemoglobin, which may help transport oxygen to the symbiotic bacteria in the gills of the clam.

Richard A. Lutz

unusual characteristics of this organism have been described above. The bright red appearance of the animal's soft tissues is due to the presence of extracellular hemoglobin, which is at least one of the proteins present that may account for many of the remarkable blood functions outlined above. A second, smaller tube worm species, which may represent a new genus within the family Riftiidae, has been found in large mucous-bound clumps at sites along the Juan de Fuca Ridge and adjacent seamounts. Several additional species of small pogonophorans (marine worms) within the other family of vestimentiferans (Lamellibrachiidae) have been collected from the Galápagos Rift and from the sites at 11°–13° N and 21° N along the East Pacific Rise.

Large white clams (family Vesicomyidae) up to 26 centimeters (10 inches) long have been sampled from both the 21° N and Galápagos sites (the same species, *Calyptogena magnifica*, at both sites) and photographed at vent sites along the Juan de Fuca Ridge between 44° N and 45° N and along the East Pacific Rise as far south as 17° S. The shells of the photographed specimens from these northern and southernmost sites appear morphologically similar to those of *C. magnifica*, but specific identification of the organisms awaits the collection of samples from those areas. These huge organisms have a large, extendable foot

236

which they extend deep within the cracks of the basaltic substrate where temperatures as high as 16° C (60° F) have been recorded. As in the case of the tube worm, chemosynthetic bacteria appear to play a role in the nutrition of these organisms. Intracellular hemoglobin, which gives their soft tissues a pinkish-red color, may help transport oxygen to the microbial symbionts concentrated in their gills.

Living clams have not been found to date at vents between 11° N and 13° N along the East Pacific Rise despite extensive expeditions to numerous sites of hydrothermal activity in that area. While *Calyptogena magnifica* is not present at the Guaymas Basin site, a second, closely related species, *Calyptogena pacifica,* lives within the heated sediments there. This latter species has also been collected around fault vents (depth ≅ 1,750 meters) off San Diego, California.

Mussels are extremely abundant at the Galápagos Rift site and have been found in small numbers at the base of black smokers at the 11°–13° N hydrothermal fields. Photographs suggest that they may also occur in large numbers as far south as 22° S along the East Pacific Rise. The presence of certain enzymes in the soft tissues of this organism suggests that it may be yet another vent species housing symbiotic bacteria.

Numerous gastropod mollusks, including at least 14 new species of limpets and 13 species of undescribed coiled gastropods, have been collected from the vent sites. Perhaps the most noteworthy of these is *Neomphalus fretterae,* a relatively large limpet common at 11°–13° N, 21° N, and the Galápagos Rift. This organism has no living relatives or known fossil record and represents a new superfamily.

Strange yellow-orange spherical organisms, about five centimeters (two inches) in diameter, are anchored to peripheral rocks by threadlike structures at a number of the hydrothermal sites visited to date. Geol-

Mussels are found in great profusion at the Galápagos Rift site. Certain enzymes found in the soft tissues of these mollusks indicate that these organisms may house symbiotic bacteria.

(Top) Robert R. Hessler, Scripps Institution of Oceanography, University of California at San Diego; (center) Al Giddings, Ocean Images, Inc.; National Geographic Society; (bottom) James J. Childress, University of California at Santa Barbara

"Dandelions" (right and below), colonial siphonophores found at many of the hydrothermal vent fields, are related to the Portuguese man-of-war. Enteropneusts, commonly known as acorn worms, form large mats in peripheral areas at the Galápagos Rift site (bottom).

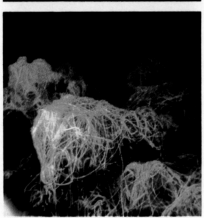

ogists who first viewed them called them "dandelions." Subsequently identified as a siphonophore during the first biological expedition to the Galápagos Rift, this organism is related to the Portuguese man-of-war. Only one intact specimen, which subsequently "fell apart" despite careful handling, has been collected to date. A second somewhat smaller siphonophore species appears to live at the 21° N site.

Organisms originally called "spaghetti" form large mats in peripheral areas of the Galápagos Rift site. These enteropneusts, more commonly known as acorn worms, have not been encountered at any of the other vent sites visited to date, although photographs taken at 20° S along the East Pacific Rise have suggested the presence of a different enteropneust-like organism near active vent sites in that area.

Brachyuran crabs (*Bythograea thermydron*) are common at a number of the sites, including 21° N and the Galápagos Rift, where they are frequently observed on the sides of active sulfide chimneys or nestled among clusters of tube worms. These porcelain-white crabs are totally blind and, like their shallow-water cousins, are largely scavengers.

Unlike the animals mentioned so far, galatheid crabs, or "squat lobsters," are common in many deep-sea habitats. One species, which is sparsely distributed elsewhere, is extremely common at both the Galápagos Rift and 21° N sites, taking advantage of the concentrated food supply. A second species was also collected from the 21° N site.

Several new species of polychaetes (marine annelid worms) also inhabit the hydrothermal sites. Serpulid polychaetes (as yet unclassified) with coiled calcareous tubes are extremely abundant on rock surfaces at a number of the deep-sea vent areas. In addition, researchers have collected a new species of a densely aggregated tubiculous polychaete (the Pompeii worm, *Alvinella pomejana*) from the sides of smokers in 50° C (120° F) water at both 11°–13° N and 21° N. A second polychaete

238

(Left and center) Kenneth L. Smith, Scripps Institution of Oceanography, University of California at San Diego;
(right) Robert R. Hessler, Scripps Institution of Oceanography, University of California at San Diego

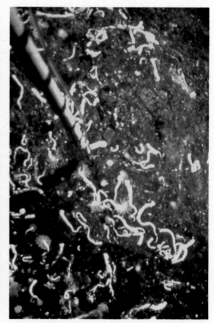

species (*Paralvinella grasslei*) has been collected from all of the vent sites sampled to date except 21° N; it may be one of the few species that the Juan de Fuca Ridge system shares with the more southern hydrothermal regions.

While numerous species of deep-sea fish have been seen in the vicinity of hydrothermal vent sites, only two appear to be "characteristic" of these environments. An undescribed pink bythitid (possibly in the genus *Diplacanthopoma*) is common only at the warmest vent areas of the Galápagos Rift. There, it points its head directly into the vents, where it may feed upon bacteria. A second species, an eelpout (family Zoarcidae), is abundant at the 21° N site, where it is most commonly observed swimming near the sides of smoker chimneys or nestling among clams and tube worms in the warm water. Stomach content analyses indicate that this vertebrate, which is also found at the 11°–13° N site, is a general scavenger and carnivore, commonly feeding upon amphipod crustaceans, gastropods, and bits of tube worms.

Although several species are shared between the East Pacific Rise vent sites and the Guaymas Basin hydrothermal site, the community structure of the latter area is quite distinct due to the thick covering of sediments through which the hydrothermal fluids percolate. High densities of bivalves and polychaetes thrive within the hydrocarbon-rich sediment, while dense mats of filamentous bacteria (*Beggiatoa*) cover extensive areas of the sediment surface. Many of the filaments of these bacteria have diameters in excess of 110 micrometers (millionths of a meter), larger than any other known bacteria. As mentioned earlier, thickets of black corals are found at the base of the large sediment mounds at the site and may provide an example of a "vent" organism whose nutrition is dependent upon the food-concentrating effects of convective currents generated by rising thermal plumes.

Other marine animals found at hydrothermal vent areas include galatheid crabs (left), Pompeii worms (attached to the sides of smoker chimneys) and brachywan crabs (center), and serpulid polychaetes (marine annelid worms) (right).

239

Biological rates and organism dispersal

A biological picture of the vents cannot be considered complete without at least a brief consideration of two of the fundamental questions concerning these environments: (1) Are biological processes in these systems relatively fast or slow? (2) How do the relatively sedentary organisms encountered at the vents locate and colonize these restricted, geographically isolated environments?

The first of these questions has been partially addressed earlier. Measurements of invertebrate (primarily molluscan) growth and metabolism indicate that these processes are occurring at rates comparable to those of closely related organisms in shallow-water environments. By comparison with the "typical" deep-sea habitat, these rates must be considered extremely fast. The most striking comparison comes from a consideration of results obtained from analyses of naturally occurring radionuclides (such as radium-226, radium-228, thorium-228, polonium-210, lead-210, uranium-234, and uranium-238) within the shells of mollusks from both "normal" and hydrothermal vent deep-sea environments. These studies revealed extremely slow growth rates (0.0084 centimeter per year) for specimens of a small (less than 8.4 millimeters long), deposit-feeding bivalve (*Tindaria callistiformis*) that inhabits soft sediments in nonhydrothermal areas at depths of more than 3,000 meters in the North Atlantic. In contrast, similar analyses conducted on specimens of *Calyptogena magnifica* from several hydrothermal vent areas along the Galápagos Rift suggested that the growth of this species may be extremely rapid (approximately 4 centimeters per year).

Additional evidence for accelerated growth in deep-sea vent environments has been obtained from a series of "mark-recapture" studies conducted directly on the bottom at the Galápagos Rift site. In these studies the growing shell margin of numerous mussels was "marked" using a small triangular file held in the manipulator arm of "Alvin." All file-marked specimens were located within a single "clump" of mussels that was identified with a cube-shaped wire marker and recovered by "Alvin" 294 days later. Subsequent laboratory analyses of the retrieved

Dense mats of the filamentous bacteria Beggiatoa *cover large areas of the surface of the hydrocarbon-rich sediments at the Guaymas Basin site.*

specimens revealed growth rates of approximately one centimeter per year for mature mussels. These rates, when combined with those determined from the radiometric analyses, are by far the highest documented for deep-sea bivalves and, as mentioned above, are comparable to growth rates encountered in shallow-water populations of closely related species. On a more practical note the realization that growth and other biological processes are occurring at relatively fast rates in vent environments has stimulated studies that may have commercial applications. Researchers at Woods Hole Oceanographic Institution in Massachusetts recently designed an artificial vent system in which common blue mussels (*Mytilus edulis*) are fed large quantities of sulfur-oxidizing bacteria that have been cultured in water enriched with hydrogen sulfide. If this pilot system proves successful in promoting rapid growth, the developed technology may add a new dimension to the rapidly expanding field of aquaculture.

The second fundamental question, which focuses on the problem of dispersal of the relatively sedentary organisms from one vent site to another, is one that has proved to be quite complex. As mentioned above, recent geologic studies have estimated that the "lifespan" of individual vents is on the order of decades or less. Furthermore, measurements of molluscan shell dissolution in vent and nonvent deep-sea environments have provided evidence for the recent (less than 15 years) cessation of hydrothermal activity at frequently observed "dead" vent sites characterized by the empty shell valves of *Calyptogena*. Much of the present state of knowledge concerning the dispersal of organisms to and from these ephemeral environments has been derived from mollusks, which are the only organisms at the vents that preserve (within their shells) a record of early development. First, larval stages are calcified and retained as the organisms grow. Second, the presence or absence of a yolky food supply during development, which is one of the most significant factors controlling the amount of time a free-swimming larval stage is capable of remaining in the water column, affects egg size, which in turn is reflected in the structure of the larval shell. Consequently, study of both larval and well-preserved juvenile molluscan shells from the vents permits inferences to be made concerning not only modes of larval development but also the dispersal capability of early stages in the life of the organisms. Initial studies focused on examination of the shells of juvenile Galápagos Rift mussels and revealed the existence of a planktonic larval stage capable of long-range dispersal. Researchers estimated that these larvae may be able to drift in the water column for periods ranging from several weeks to several months. Current speeds as high as 18 centimeters per second have been recorded approximately 50 meters above the East Pacific Rise, while other measurements at comparable depths in the Pacific have been as high as 33 centimeters per second. If larvae have a planktonic existence lasting several weeks or months, such currents could easily disperse them over hundreds or even thousands of kilometers. Another possibility, suggested by French scientists, is that the larvae of these organisms may rise to the surface waters, where more rapid currents could disperse them over even greater

Horst Felbeck, Scripps Institution of Oceanography, University of California at San Diego

A small zoarcid (eelpout), found at the 21° N hydrothermal site, is one of only two species of fish that are "characteristic" of the vent regions.

(transoceanic?) distances. Individual mussels are capable of producing millions of larvae during their lifespan. What percentage of these larvae ever find a suitable vent at which to settle is an intriguing question.

Analyses of an increasing number of vent mollusks over the past few years have revealed that the array of reproductive strategies in hydrothermal vent communities is more complex than was previously believed. While a few species of vent mollusks do appear to undergo a high-dispersal mode of development similar to that described above for the vent mussel, the vast majority (15 out of 18) appear to have an extremely brief free-swimming existence. It has been suggested that the dispersal of such organisms may proceed via a stepwise process somewhat analogous to "island-hopping." Such a mode of dispersal may be sufficient to maintain far-flung populations, but it is insufficient to overcome the isolation that would result from extinction of intervening populations as their vents became extinct. The dissimilarities in animals between communities found along the Juan de Fuca Ridge system and those present along the East Pacific Rise and contiguous Galápagos Rift system may well be a reflection of the limited dispersal capability of the majority of organisms present at the vent sites.

Future expeditions

While numerous deep-sea hydrothermal vents have been studied over the past few years, it is important to realize that man has only visited or photographed a few hundred kilometers of the 74,000-kilometer (46,000-mile) oceanic ridge system. Many sections of this system are completely isolated from those regions explored thus far. The array of possibilities for geological and biological wonders yet to be discovered staggers the imagination. What valuable minerals lie waiting along unexplored ridge crests, and what social, political, and moral questions will arise concerning their commercial exploitation? How different will the animals and evolutionary history of undiscovered vent communities be from those that are now known, and will they perhaps further change the traditional views of life and its origin? With each new dive we hold our breath with the anticipation of unlocking yet another well-kept secret hidden for so long beyond our grasp in the dark waters of the deep sea.

FOR ADDITIONAL READING

Robert D. Ballard, *Exploring Our Living Planet* (National Geographic Society, 1983).

Robert D. Ballard and J. Frederick Grassle, "Return to Oases of the Deep," *National Geographic* (November 1979, pp. 689–705).

John M. Edmond and Karen Von Damm, "Hot Springs on the Ocean Floor," *Scientific American* (April 1983, pp. 78–93).

Holger W. Jannasch and Carl O. Wirsen, "Chemosynthetic Primary Production at East Pacific Sea Floor Spreading Centers," *BioScience* (October 1979, pp. 592–598).

Peter A. Rona and others (eds.), *Hydrothermal Processes at Seafloor Spreading Centers* (Plenum, 1984).

Science
Year in Review

Science
Year in Review
Contents

Anthropology

Human evolution. Important advances in understanding human evolution have taken place in recent years. New fossil discoveries coupled with a greater integration of knowledge between physical anthropologists and molecular biologists contributed greatly to this progress.

It was generally accepted in 1984 that humans and present-day African apes are genetically similar, while Asian apes are considerably less similar to humans. This fact is consistent with a consensus within the profession that the common ancestor of humans and the African apes existed considerably more recently than did the common ancestor for all hominoids (the great apes—gorillas, orangutans, chimpanzees, and gibbons—and the ancestors of man). This consensus received support from both morphological (form and structure) and molecular research. Furthermore, evidence now strongly suggests that hominids (ancestors of man) split from the African ape lineage about 7 million or 8 million years ago and not 10 million to 16 million years ago, as paleontologists had previously thought. This new estimate was based on three factors: a greater reliance on molecular evidence; a significantly improved fossil record data base, which prior to recent years only included fragmentary pieces of little use to taxonomic reconstruction; and a greater understanding of the diversity of hominoid species in the middle and late Miocene Epoch (from 15 million to 7 million years ago).

The separation of the great apes from their relatives, the Old World monkeys, was established to have occurred approximately 30 million years ago, while the split between the large Asian and African apes probably took place about 16 million years ago. Important information about hominoid evolution was contributed by analyses of *Proconsul africanus*, a primitive tree-dwelling ape from the early Miocene for which a nearly complete skeleton now exists.

A review by anthropologist David Pilbeam of new data on *Sivapithecus* led him to infer that this primate enjoyed a close association in Asia with *Ramapithecus*, considered an early forerunner of man, and may even have belonged to the same genus. New *Sivapithecus* fossils, including a portion of the skull and various limbs, resembled the orangutan and not, as presumed, *Australopithecus*, an African species. Either parallel evolution or the sharing of features from a common ancestor is now thought to be a likely explanation for certain resemblances between *Ramapithecus* and the *Australopithecus* jaws and teeth. The correctness of this assertion has implications for establishing the date of the split between African and Asian hominoids.

Some issues surrounding early hominids recently were resolved, while others remained controversial. Bipedal hominids were known to have inhabited eastern Africa at least 3.5 million years ago. Key evidence included footprint remains uncovered by Mary Leakey's team in Tanzania, demonstrating the capacity for two-legged walking by a hominid perhaps 3,750,000 years ago.

The 40% complete skeleton of "Lucy" uncovered in Hadar, Ethiopia, promised to add to the store of knowledge on early hominids. At issue were two unresolved questions. Given that bipedality was within the locomotive repertoire of these animals, was it accomplished with a bent-hip, bent-knee posture? Were these individuals also inhabitants of trees for portions of their daily routine?

Portion of the skull of the early primate Sivapithecus *(below center) is flanked by skulls of a chimpanzee (left) and an orangutan (right). David Pilbeam (right) concluded that* Sivapithecus *was closely associated in Asia with* Ramapithecus, *an early forerunner of man.*

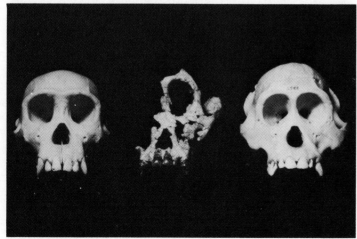

Photos, courtesy, David Pilbeam, Harvard University

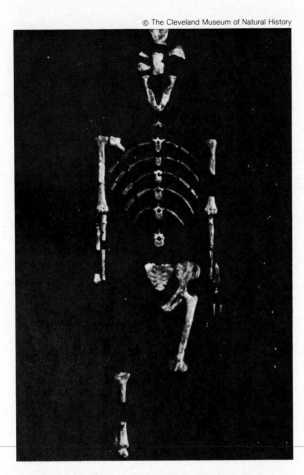

Partial skeleton of "Lucy," a hominid more than three million years old, was studied in an effort to determine whether she was able to walk erect.

How and where *Australopithecus afarensis*, as "Lucy" was termed by her discoverers, moved from place to place was the focus of an important but inconclusive conference held in Berkeley, Calif., in April 1983. Arguments ranged from "full and complete bipedality" (Owen Lovejoy) to an arboreal mode of locomotion (Jack Stern and Randall Susman). Stern and Susman marshaled new evidence to support their position that *A. afarensis* spent much of its time in the trees.

At the conference anatomical evidence was presented in an effort to show that the hip and knee did not fully extend during walking. Analyses of the toe bones, fingers, limbs, and pelvis convinced Stern and Susman that the larger primates were better suited for bipedality than were the smaller Hadar individuals (Lucy included).

The argument for arboreality was countered by Lovejoy, who brought the biomechanics of bipedality to bear on the question. The relatively small forelimb of *A. afarensis* was promoted by Lovejoy as evidence of terrestrial bipedalism.

According to anthropologist H. M. McHenry's report on the conference, none of the principals appeared to have altered their views after all was said. McHenry explained that both sides can point to seemingly convincing anatomical evidence. *A afarensis* and *Homo sapiens* (contemporary man) share a long list of derived anatomical features, but so do *A. afarensis* and the hypothesized common ancestor of pongids and hominids. The question of bipedality hinged on whether or not its unmistakably primitive traits were actually employed by *A. afarensis* or rather were nonfunctional survivals of its ancestry. While one side argued that these features were no more than primitive retentions, the other side insisted that they were part of the functional morphology of arboreality. McHenry's own position was that the skeletal similarities between *A. afarensis* and *A. africanus* represented "a relatively stable adaptation," leading to the conclusion that grasping fingers and curved toes were important functional structures for the Hadar individuals and, therefore, supporting the arboreal hypothesis.

Structure in history. "The idea is that history is culturally constructed from the bottom up." So said anthropologist Marshall Sahlins during his Distinguished Lecture presented to the American Anthropological Association in December 1982. He pointed out that history which deals with all classes of society and that which focuses on the actions of the elite tend to alternate through time and anticipate one another.

Anthropologists in 1983 came to share Sahlins's fascination with history as a cultural construction, but not all agreed with him that "different cultural orders have their own modes of historical action. . . ." Sahlins supplied a case study of "heroic history" from Fiji in the 1850s. The Fijian conception of history at that time was a history of kings and their battles, but only because, Sahlins argued, of a cultural order that gave disproportionate weight to the lives (and deaths) of kings. Sahlins made the structuralist point that the anthropological distinction between "ritual" and "battle," in which only the latter qualifies as "history," serves to preserve our own Western conception of history while it obscures the underlying structural principle of order.

—Lawrence E. Fisher

Archaeology

Advances during the past year in archaeology were concerned with research methods, new perspectives on old evidence, and discoveries in the field. Ingenious new laboratory analyses promised greater understanding of the eating habits of early humans. Use of the carbon-14 dating method (measurement

246

Photos, Thomas H. Loy, British Columbia Provincial Museum, Victoria, British Columbia

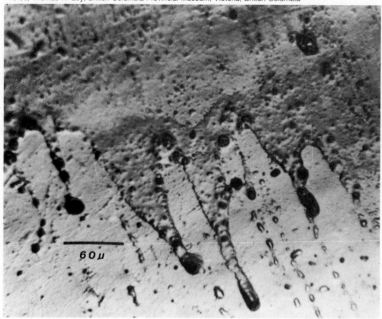

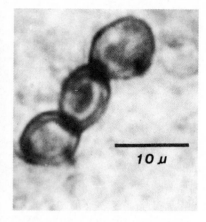

Residual blood film (left) on an obsidian flake knife from British Columbia and red blood cells (above) from another knife can be analyzed to reveal how the tools were used and which animals were hunted and butchered.

of the amount of carbon-14 present in a specimen) corrected a previous error in the evidence for early agriculture. Understanding of Paleolithic cultures and of the agricultural decline in Peruvian civilizations was advanced both by new discoveries and new theories.

Prehistoric blood residues. A new approach to identifying the uses of prehistoric stone tools was reported by Thomas Loy of the British Columbia Provincial Museum. In a microscopic and chemical study of approximately 100 chipped stone projectile points, knives, and microblades ranging between

Bifacial stone hand axes that were fashioned during the Lower Paleolithic Period (400,000–100,000 BC) were found at Chon-gok-ni in Korea. Their discovery disproved the widely held theory that such tools had not been made in any area east of the subcontinent of India.

Photos, Seonbok Yi and G. A. Clark, Arizona State University, Tempe

A team from Allahabad University and the University of California, Berkeley, under the direction of G. R. Sharma and J. Desmond Clark, assisted by Jonathan Mark Kenoyer of Berkeley and J. N. Pal of Allahabad University

Circular platform of small blocks of sandstone rubble (right) was made about 11,000 years ago in northeastern India. A triangular slab from the center of that platform (below, far right) closely resembles a stone from a present-day religious shrine in the same area (below right).

1,000 and 6,000 years in age, Loy identified amino acids, hemoglobin, and red blood cells in the residues left on 90 items. Species identified through chemical analysis of the hemoglobins included human, caribou, deer, mountain sheep, moose, grizzly bear, snowshoe rabbit, sea lion, and squirrel.

The promise of this new method, said to be both inexpensive and reliable, is great. Whether certain stone tools were used in hunting and butchering can now be determined directly. Animals exploited by an ancient group of humans may be identified even in places where acid soils cause rapid decay of bones. The study of blood residues can provide evidence on the blood types of ancient populations. And the zoological study of blood protein evolution may profit from a vastly increased data base.

Lower Paleolithic cultural diversity in Eurasia. In the late 1940s Hallam Movius of Harvard University first brought together the sparse evidence then available on the Lower Paleolithic Period in eastern Asia (400,000–100,000 BC). He concluded that the earliest cultures there were quite different technically from those of Europe and Africa. From India eastward stone tool industries featuring choppers and chopping tools prevailed, while from India westward the stone tool industries were marked by bifacially flaked Acheulean hand axes. This concept of a "Movius line" between east and west, drawn through the Indian subcontinent, has reigned for more than 30 years.

Among Asian Paleolithic specialists the inadequacy of this view has gradually become apparent, and a new synthesis by Seonbok Yi and G. A. Clark of Arizona State University brought it up for reevaluation. Yi and Clark showed first that bifacial hand axes of the Acheulean type are in fact found throughout the area east of the Movius line. In particular, the Korean site of Chon-gok-ni produced some 50

bifacial hand axes and cleavers that resemble Acheulean specimens from Europe and Africa. Comparable finds were unearthed in northern China and Southeast Asia. It is thus clear that the simplistic division made by the Movius line must be abandoned.

The Yi and Clark review revealed that Lower Paleolithic cultures varied much more than had previously been thought. Kubet Luchterhand of Roosevelt University suggested that artifacts of the Acheulean time range represent the first spreading of mid-Pleistocene *Homo erectus* people into the temperate zones of the Old World. Others pointed out that Lower Paleolithic assemblages in both the Eurafrican and Eurasian zones differ significantly among themselves in the artifact types they contain. Future research will no doubt define a complex mosaic of differing early cultural patterns throughout the Old World. Adaptation to different environments and so-

248

cietal differences fostered by environmental necessities must be studied as causes of Lower Paleolithic cultural variations.

Early grain culture in Egypt. During recent years several grains of carbonized barley have been found in the Late Paleolithic, Upper Egyptian site of Wadi Kubbaniya, dated between 17,000 and 18,300 years ago. This evidence suggested that the process of domestication leading to early agriculture began thousands of years earlier than was previously believed. However, these conclusions have now been revised, as reported by Fred Wendorf of Southern Methodist University. His study of some of the grains in order to determine how much they might have been heated led to suspicions about their age. The tests showed that the grains had never been subjected to high temperature. Since it was believed that at least some degree of charring would have been necessary to preserve the seeds over the millennia, the finding that they had never been greatly heated raised doubts about their true age.

Carbon-14 dating of two of the cereal grains in the special small-sample linear accelerator dating facility at the University of Arizona yielded ages for them of only 820 and 1,090 years before the present. This suggested that the grains were quite recently intruded into the Paleolithic site. The results of carbon-14 dating of four other grains previously obtained were inconclusive. Those cereal grains had apparently been contaminated by other kinds of laboratory analysis to which they had been subjected. Thus the view that cereals were exploited in Late Paleolithic times at Wadi Kubbaniya can no longer be supported.

Late Paleolithic religious shrine. At the Late Paleolithic site of Baghor I in northeastern India archaeologists found a small stone platform that closely resembles ceremonial shrines still made by the natives of the region. The site was dated by geological and comparative evidence to about 10,000 to 11,000 years before the present. The platform was well buried beneath a layer of flaked stone tools of Late Paleolithic age. There is no question of its antiquity despite its uncanny resemblance to modern local shrines.

Excavations were conducted at the site by J. M. Kenoyer and J. D. Clark of the University of California, Berkeley, and J. N. Pal and G. R. Sharma of Allahabad University in India. They revealed a circular platform, somewhat less than one meter across, formed by small blocks of sandstone rubble. At or near the center of the platform were several fragments from a natural sandstone concretion. These fitted together to form a thick triangular slab about the size of a small human hand. The slab had apparently been whole when originally put on the platform but became cracked and broken by natural weathering processes over the millennia. A striking quality of the stone was the clear pattern of alternating light and dark concentric triangles displayed on it; they were formed by natural laminations within the rock itself. The unique sandstone of which the triangular slab was formed came from a known geological bed on top of the nearby Kaimur Escarpment, about two to three kilometers (1.2 to 1.8 miles) distant.

The significance of the find was made clear by a visit to a modern shrine of the goddess of Kerai, about one kilometer (0.6 mile) from the site. There excavators saw a circular platform of stone rubble on which had been placed several stones virtually identical in color and markings to that from Baghor I. Further searching turned up a number of similar shrines in the vicinity, made by local tribesmen. To these people the distinctive colored stone, with its natural geometric laminations, serves as a symbol of the mother goddess, or *Mai*. Indeed they search out suitable specimens for use in shrines to her. The finding of such a remarkable congruence between ceremonial motif, practice, and belief, spanning the 10,000 years between Late Paleolithic times and the present day, elicits wonderment at the incredible continuity of Indian religious tradition.

Plate tectonics and agrarian collapse. At many places in coastal Peru the remnants of old field systems and irrigation works reveal that lands now abandoned to the desert were once farmed. The extent of such evidence is great, and its shows that much more land was under cultivation in the past than is farmed today. Prehistorians have sought to explain this decline, as well as declines in the political fortunes of ancient Peruvian states, by proposing such causes as overpopulation, soil depletion, engineering failures, stagnation of leadership, bureaucratic mismanagement, social revolt, and conquest.

After years of work in coastal Peru Michael Moseley of the Field Museum of Natural History in Chicago developed a new theory to explain the decline in agriculture. Based on plate tectonics, it promises to unify previous socially oriented hypotheses around an underlying geophysical event. Aerial photography and on-the-ground surveys in northern coastal Peru seem to show that some segments of ancient canal systems either do not slope at all or slope the wrong way, against the direction of intended water flow. Nearer the coast researchers found that sunken gardens, which rely on natural groundwater to supply their crops, have moved steadily seaward over time. The earliest such gardens, about four kilometers (2½ miles) inland, now lie abandoned some ten meters (35 feet) above the present-day water table. By the early 1940s sunken gardens were in use only within approximately one kilometer of the ocean. These anomalies suggested to Moseley that geophysical forces were at work.

The Andean cordillera is geologically young and tectonically active. This tectonism results from an underthrusting of the South American continental plate by the eastward-moving Nazca oceanic plate. The rate of underthrusting is believed to be about ten centimeters (four inches) per year. A geological study carried out between 1960 and 1970 in coastal Peru showed that the land rose a maximum of 12 centimeters (4.8 inches) during that period, with an overall rate of rise of one to two centimeters per year. North of the Río Santa the shoreline has risen more than ten meters since the time of an uplifted beach surface dated to about 5,200 years ago. Other geological evidence also indicates significant rising of the land during the time of human presence.

Moseley concluded that this gradual rising of the land had powerful effects on irrigation and ground-water agriculture in Peru. Most important is the fact that, as the land rose, rivers bringing water out of the Andes Mountains automatically downcut their channels to maintain a proper gradient with the sea. As a result canal intakes that drew water from the rivers for farming have again and again over the centuries been left high and dry as the rivers eroded below the intakes' base levels. The ancient cultivators responded by digging new intake channels that intersected with the rivers farther upstream. But each time the canals were lengthened the cost of watering a given area became greater, and eventually bedrock outcrops higher up in the canyons prevented any further upstream migration of the intakes.

As a result of these processes the amount of arable land decreased over time. River downcutting had the further effect of lowering the groundwater table, so that over time only lands nearer and nearer the sea could be farmed by the sunken garden method. Moseley also contended that the slow rising of the land is responsible for the fact that some ancient canal segments now run uphill, while some scholars believe that these observed gradients simply reflect colossal engineering failures, Moseley thinks that the Peruvians were far too experienced and sophisticated at building canals to make such errors.

It is of interest too that even while this process was gradually constricting the agricultural base in north coastal Peru, the kingdom of Chimor, which controlled the area, was aggressively expanding its political control. This political-military expansion may well be seen as one kind of response to increasing pressure on the local resources, brought about at least in part by the tectonic factors just outlined. Thus, as Moseley noted, his hypothesis of agrarian collapse based on plate tectonics theory does not replace sociologically based theories about the rise and fall of agrarian developments and related cultural phenomena but instead powerfully underpins them.

—C. Melvin Aikens

Architecture and civil engineering

Architecture. The glass box that dominated architecture for the last 50 years was beginning to yield ground to new designs. Under the umbrella of postmodernism, architects were beginning to use the past, the existing built or natural environment, and the restoration of existing buildings to develop new forms and styles.

"All of us architects are at the biggest turning point of our careers because we're pulling out of the modern movement," said New York City architect John Burgee. And Henrick Bull of Bull, Field, Volkmann & Stockwell in San Francisco commented that "the reaction against modern architecture will not fade away. People simply want more humanity and individuality in their surroundings."

Among the notable structures that have cracked the modernist mold is the Public Services Building in Portland, Ore. Designed by architect Michael Graves of Princeton, N.J., it incorporates all the aspects of postmodernism. Unsympathetic architects called it "an enlarged jukebox," while supporters described it as "an unquestioned triumph of architectural humanism and symbolism."

Much of the building's design impact is a result of Graves's use of color. The reinforced-concrete exterior walls are covered with glazed terra-cotta at the base and top. Sharply contrasting hues of rose, cream, and black dominate the surface and give the building the appearance of a huge art object.

The building was intended as the cornerstone of a governmental center. On two sides are the existing historic city hall and county courthouse, and on the other two are a recently developed transit mall and public park. The building blends with its neighbors because of its scale and simple box shape, but the colors and symbols on its face cause it to stand out from the taller structures nearby. For example, bas-relief Art Deco garlands of reinforced concrete painted pastel blue span most of the width of one facade. The exterior of the base is painted dark green to emphasize its relationship to the ground and to the neighboring park.

The building received a 1983 American Institute of Architects Honor Award. According to the jury of the Institute its "distinctive overall style offers an alternative to the design and construction of modern office buildings."

In stark contrast to the mass, color, and Art Deco symbolism of the Portland Building is a pair of small but airy wood-shingled houses that fit perfectly into their environment. Built on an open, windy site overlooking a saltwater pond on Block Island, R.I., The Coxe/Hayden house and studio by Robert Ven-

Public Services Building in Portland, Ore., designed by Michael Graves, is an example of postmodernism in architecture. It won a 1983 American Institute of Architects Honor Award.

turi, Rauch & Scott Brown of Philadelphia typifies the country style of many 19th-century buildings on Block Island. It is an important example of the freedom that architects are feeling to use the heritage of the past with boldness.

The larger of the two buildings has living, dining, and kitchen areas on the ground floor, a bedroom and bath on the second floor, and a writing studio in the gable above. The smaller building has a garage-workshop below, with two guest rooms and a bath above. Windows of different sizes and shapes provide distinctive views. Inside, the rooms and walls are arranged and angled in unexpected ways to prevent a boxy look.

The Philadelphia Stock Exchange on Market Street in downtown Philadelphia is another project that proclaims the new architectural diversity. Architect Cope Linder Associates and developer William Rouse decided to create a half-acre park with terraced pools and hanging gardens and then wrap an office building around it. The structure features a tree-filled atrium under a skylight measuring 1,400 sq m (15,000 sq ft). Containing terraced pools and 2,900 trees and plants, the atrium resembles a lush tropical forest.

The color scheme of the interior of the atrium is achieved with white walls, red brick tile paving on the floor and garden, and green trim in several shades. A series of greenhouse-like window boxes project from the south wall of the atrium. They are 1.2 by 3.6 m (4 by 12 ft) in size, and each has a pitched roof made of glass. Their design is echoed by the twin elevators on the south wall, which look like mini-greenhouses floating up and down the facade. The building has been a success financially for the developer as well as aesthetically for its users.

A well-publicized example of the expanding interest and skill in the preservation of individual buildings is the Old Post Office building on Pennsylvania Avenue in Washington, D.C. Completed in 1899, it twice cheated the wrecker's ball and after renovation reopened in September 1983. Local architect Arthur Cotton Moore won a competition to renew the building for commercial use on its lower floors with government offices on the floors above.

The building's most interesting space is its multi-storied cortile, a courtyard enclosed by the building's walls. Moore altered the dungeonlike space of the cortile by replacing its black aluminum roof with a glazed roof that reveals the sky and tower. The old interior low glass roof, which hid the original mail-sorting room, was removed, leaving the trusses ex-

251

Venturi, Rauch and Scott Brown; photo, Thomas Bernard

The Coxe/Hayden house and studio on Block Island, R.I., (above) and the Philadelphia Stock Exchange (left) reveal the diversity in design of recent architectural projects. The former exemplifies the freedom with which architects are using the heritage of the past.

posed. Moore opened the cortile floor with a curved cutout area and a sweeping staircase to the basement level. Shops and restaurants line the pavilion at the base of the cortile. The overall result is a bright and lively blend of glass, brass, wood, lights, and color, where new details blend together pleasingly with restoration work.

A project that combines both sensitive renewal and a sleek, new high-tech aura is Vienna's new subway system designed by Viennese architect Wilhelm Holzbauer. Winner of the 1983 Reynolds Award, the subway was begun as Otto Wagner's "Stadbahn" system in 1893. World War I, the Great Depression, and World War II canceled completion of the system and all but destroyed Wagner's original stations. The green line, one of two that have recently been completed, consists of a combination of restored stations and new ones. The other, the red line, is entirely new. Two of the green-line stations were completely reconstructed by Holzbauer from original Wagner drawings, while others were partially restored. One of the green line's delights is that it repeatedly surfaces at street level to capture views of the historic Ringstrasse and the Danube canal.

Holzbauer's intent was to give the system a distinct identity and visual unity. To do this he used a variety of interchangeable, white, plastic-coated aluminum and curved clear glass panels framed in either green or red metal ribs to create street-level pavilions. By adding or deleting panels he gave each station an individual appearance. Red and green panels are used in the subway stations along with curved overhangs.

Civil engineering. In 1976 engineers from the Parsons Corp., based in Pasadena, Calif., landed at Yanbu', a small fishing village on the Red Sea in Saudi Arabia. Their assignment was to start building an ultramodern industrial city in the desert that eventually would be the size of Cleveland, Ohio. Within a year after breaking ground there was housing for 20,000 and a floating desalination plant. By 1984 the Saudi Arabian component of Parsons Corp. had supervised site development and construction valued at about $10 billion. The population of workers at the site was approaching 50,000.

The goal of the project, according to the Saudi Arabian Royal Commission for Jubail and Yanbu', is to spur the economy of Saudi Arabia's less developed western region and place the nation's export production closer to European markets. The project's crude-oil terminal was expected eventually to export 3.7 million bbl per day.

Another remarkable project, this one in Orlando, Fla., is Walt Disney World's Experimental Prototype Community of Tomorrow (EPCOT). More than 600 designers and engineers, 1,200 consultants, and 500 construction workers participated in EPCOT, reportedly the largest privately financed construction project ever built. Walt Disney conceived EPCOT as a "showcase to the world for the ingenuity and imagination of the American people." In many ways no other project provides a greater opportunity for the public to appreciate the work of engineers. In addition to the highly computerized rides and flashy electronic displays EPCOT is packed with structural, geotechnical, and agricultural engineering achievements.

Much of EPCOT's 104-ha (260-ac) site in Orlando consisted of swampland. An omnipresent muck, peatlike organic material with a 95% water content, presented the biggest geotechnical challenge to site development. Before the land was ready for building and road construction, 1.9 million cu m (2.5 million cu yd) of the muck had to be removed and replaced by 3.8 million cu m (5 million cu yd) of clean material from on-site pits. On-site drilling revealed two deposits of muck with a depth of 48 m (160 ft). After extensive consultation engineers decided that the muck could be consolidated by surcharging it, squeezing it like a sponge. The surcharge was carefully engineered to prevent breaking through the root mat on the surface. Breaking the root mat after loading would have resulted in pushing the muck to the surface and an almost impossible task of sealing it off.

Structural engineers designed and built the 18-story Spaceship Earth, the only large-scale geodesic dome that is totally spherical. Built to withstand winds of 320 km/h (200 mph), the dome is elevated 4.5 m (15 ft) off the ground on steel supports that are 9 m (30 ft) wide. Inside the dome a transportation system shuttles passengers along a spiral track past dioramas that depict the history of human communication.

Even the agriculture at EPCOT is engineered. The close tie between agriculture, aquaculture, and engineering is dramatized in the center's 2-ha (5-ac) greenhouse. Exhibits include lettuce growing in a rotating cylinder, vegetable plants on a conveyor receiving spray irrigation, subterranean irrigation systems that provide both water and nutrients, and water filtering systems that promote maximum fish production. The primary civil and structural engineer for EPCOT was Greiner Engineering Sciences of Tampa, Fla.

The Civil and Mineral Engineering Building at the

The Old Post Office building in Washington, D.C., built in 1899, reopened as an office building after renovation in 1983. An outstanding feature is its cortile, a multistoried enclosed courtyard.

Arthur Cotton Moore/Associates; photo, © Maxwell Mackenzie

Spaceship Earth at Walt Disney World's EPCOT center in Florida is the only large-scale geodesic dome that is totally spherical. It was built to withstand winds of 320 kilometers per hour (200 miles per hour).

University of Minnesota in Minneapolis broke new frontiers in the use of underground space. Winner of the American Society of Civil Engineers' 1983 Outstanding Civil Engineering Achievement Award, the building made use of three earth stratas to construct efficient and comfortable facilities from 7.5 m (25 ft) to 33 m (110 ft) below ground level.

The building contains two types of underground space: conventional cut-and-cover space near the surface, and deep-mined space 24–33 m (80–110 ft) below the ground in the sandstone strata. Space was constructed in the deep sandstone strata rather than in the limestone strata near the surface because sandstone is soft and can be mined economically. The cost of constructing space in the sandstone strata was $215 per sq m ($20 per sq ft), the same as it would be to construct a pre-engineered building above the ground.

Vienna, Austria, subway system won the 1983 R. S. Reynolds Memorial Award for architecture using aluminum. The perforated aluminum panels absorb noise and diffuse light in the underground stations.

The sandstone walls of the deep-mined area were stabilized by using a sodium silicate spray grouting technique and were then overlaid with reinforcing mesh. The walls have a slightly concave shape to take advantage of arch action. The problem of groundwater was solved by installing horizontal drains beneath leaking fissures. A metal "rainroof" was installed just below the limestone stratum over the mined space area. Collected water is directed to the perimeter of the space, where it is collected and drained to an underground storm sewer.

The building makes maximum use of renewable energy, both the Earth's and the Sun's. The temperature of the underground space remains at 10° C (50° F) throughout the year, thereby reducing both heating and cooling loads. Solar optical systems direct collected sunlight into the building by means of an assembly of lenses and mirrors. The building was designed and developed primarily by the Department of Civil and Mineral Engineering at the University of Minnesota.

—John Davis

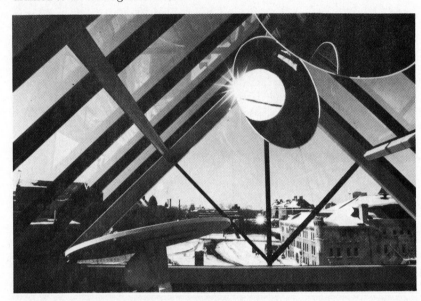

Civil and Mineral Engineering Building at the University of Minnesota (below) extends to 33 meters (110 feet) below ground level and won the American Society of Civil Engineers' 1983 Outstanding Civil Engineering Achievement Award. Mirrors in the diamond-shaped tower (left) direct sunlight to the below-ground areas.

Photos, courtesy, Bennett, Ringrose, Wolfsfeld, Jarvis, Gardner, Inc., Minneapolis, Minn.

Astronomy

Among the interesting developments in astronomy in 1983 were the discovery of new pulsars, the detection of previously unknown objects, and the evidence of large amounts of undetected mass in the universe.

Instrumentation. The Infrared Astronomical Satellite (IRAS), a joint project of the United States, the United Kingdom, and The Netherlands, was launched Jan. 25, 1983, and functioned until November 21. It was placed in a nearly polar orbit at an altitude of 900 km (560 mi); this location was selected because it permitted IRAS to orbit above the dividing line between the day and night sides of the Earth. Consequently, it could observe the sky in a direction always perpendicular to the direction of the Sun.

The satellite carried a telescope with an aperture of 57 cm (22.2 in). Four sets of detectors that operated in the far infrared portion of the spectrum were arranged in rows, or bands, at the focal plane of the telescope. Each band had 15 or 16 detectors and measured radiation at different wavelengths, which peaked at 12, 25, 60, and 100 micrometers (μm; a micrometer is one one-millionth of a meter or about $\frac{1}{25,000}$ inch). The shorter wavelengths were chosen to measure relatively warm material in the solar system, while the longer ones were selected for studying colder interstellar sources. The entire telescope was cooled by liquid helium to 2.7 K ($-270.5°$ C) in order to suppress radiation from the telescope itself and thereby allow extremely faint objects to be detected. It was the eventual evaporation of this coolant that ended the useful life of IRAS.

The data-gathering rate of IRAS was enormous, roughly 700 million bits per day. The satellite relayed its data twice daily to the Rutherford Appleton Laboratory in the U.K. and also received commands at those times to control its operations for each succeeding 12-hour interval. Complete analysis of the data was not expected until about 1986, but by early 1984 scientists had concluded that IRAS had measured more than 200,000 far-infrared point sources. The various observations of the satellite, incompletely analyzed as they are, will be discussed in the sections that follow.

Solar system. On average, four or five comets are discovered each year. IRAS by itself discovered five. The first of these, now named IRAS-Araki-Alcott, after the satellite and the two Earthbound observers credited with its independent discovery, turned out to be particularly interesting. It made the second closest known cometary approach to the Earth, coming within 4.8 million km (2,976,000 mi). The only known closer approach was Comet Lexell in 1770. Comet IRAS-Araki-Alcott developed a coma (head) that measured 3° across at its closest approach. It is the first comet in which diatomic sulfur (having two atoms in a molecule) was identified, from observations made by another satellite, the International Ultraviolet Explorer (IUE). The comet was also detected by radar at Arecibo in Puerto Rico, and Goldstone, Calif.

The other comets found by IRAS were extremely faint in visible light and, therefore, had little chance of discovery by Earth-based observers. IRAS detected them because the instrumentation aboard the satellite was particularly suited to measuring the dust clouds that are associated with comets. The discoveries by IRAS suggest that the number of comets in the solar system may be much larger than previously suspected.

Early in October IRAS detected another rapidly moving faint object, but this one, on being photographed by Earth-based astronomers, had the sharp trail that is characteristic of an asteroid. The object, designated 1983 TB, was tentatively identified as a minor planet. It has an unusual orbit, with its shortest distance from the Sun at 19.5 million km, smaller than that of any other known asteroid. Two weeks after its discovery, however, Fred Whipple noted that the orbital elements of 1983 TB were

Technician prepares the Infrared Astronomical Satellite (IRAS) for launch. IRAS was placed in a nearly polar orbit on Jan. 25, 1983, and functioned until Nov. 21, 1983. During that time it made many noteworthy discoveries.

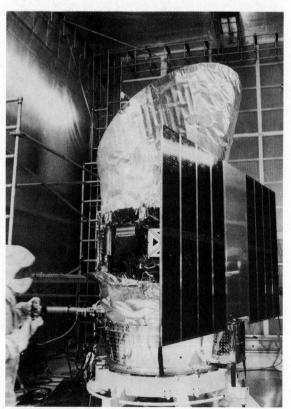

IRAS-Araki-Alcott, one of five comets discovered by IRAS, in 1983 made the second closest known cometary approach to the Earth.

almost the same as the average of the orbital elements previously calculated for 19 meteors observed in the Geminid meteor showers. This, coupled with the fact that its very eccentric orbit is highly inclined to the Earth's orbit, implies that 1983 TB is not an asteroid but probably is a burned-out comet, the original source of the debris that causes the December Geminid showers.

IRAS also found a previously unknown torus (doughnut-shaped ring) of dust particles orbiting the Sun between Mars and Jupiter in the asteroid belt region. The radiation received from the dust corresponds to a temperature of 165 to 200 K (−108° to −73° C), appropriate for small particles heated by the Sun at a distance of 300 million to 500 million km. When a small particle absorbs solar energy and subsequently reradiates energy into space, it loses orbital angular momentum and very slowly spirals in toward the Sun. Thus, like the dust particles in the inner regions of the solar system which cause the zodiacal light, these particles must also be continuously replenished if the torus is to last longer than a few tens of thousands of years.

Frank Low, of the University of Arizona, proposed two possible causes for the dust particles. They could have arisen from a collision of a comet with an asteroid, in which case the torus would be a relatively transitory phenomenon. Also, however, they could arise from collisions between asteroids, in which case the torus would be capable of continued replenishment from random crashes and would be a long-lived phenomenon. Detailed analysis of the dust distribution may permit a choice to be made between these two possibilities.

Stars. Pulsars, rapidly rotating neutron stars with intense magnetic fields, are believed to be the remnants of supernova events. A recent addition to the more than 300 pulsars known in our Galaxy was designated PSR 1937 + 214 and became the object with the shortest known rotation period. This pulsar rotates 20 times faster than the previous record holder, the pulsar in the Crab Nebula. It spins once on its axis every 1.558 milliseconds, or 642 times a second, during which time it radiates two unequal pulses of radio energy toward the Earth as the two poles of its magnetic field alternately cross the line of sight to the pulsar. It has been called the "millisecond" pulsar. It is spinning so fast that matter on its surface is moving at 13% of the speed of light.

Pulsars slow down in their spin rate as they lose rotational energy when charged particles are ejected along their magnetic poles and when their magnetic fields interact with surrounding matter. Very young, newly formed pulsars lose energy most quickly, and thus their rate of spin declines rapidly at first. Consequently, the usual interpretation is that the more rapidly a pulsar spins, the younger it is. But the millisecond pulsar, while having the fastest spin rate known, also has the slowest spin-down rate; less than one millionth the spin-down rate of the Crab pulsar. Based on this slow spin-down, the lower limit of its age has been estimated at 100 million to one billion years.

Several theories have been proposed to explain how a pulsar so old could be spinning so rapidly and losing energy so slowly. These involve an increase in the rate of spin of the pulsar by acquisition of mass from a binary companion star. Or, in a more extreme proposal, a very close binary system could actually have coalesced because of orbital energy loss due to gravitational radiation, resulting in a single object (the pulsar) having the total angular momentum (rotational motion) of the initial system. If proposals such as these prove to be correct, the millisecond pulsar would indeed be a rare object. On the other hand there is the argument that the millisecond pulsar simply is an object with a magnetic field that is weaker than those of other known pulsars. If this is the case, the usual braking mechanisms would be so weak that the spin-down rate would be small, and the phenomenon of the millisecond pulsar might be quite common. The only reason that astronomers would not have found more such pulsars is that most pulsar surveys have been designed to search for periods measured in tens of milliseconds.

Observations of this pulsar have shown it to be the most accurate timekeeper known. Its spin-down rate of 1×10^{-19} second per second is better than the 10^{-14} parts per second accuracy of the atomic clock network currently used to keep precise time. If it continues its present behavior, PSR 1937 + 214 could become the time reference of the future.

The first pulsar external to our Galaxy was discovered at the radio observatory in Parkes, New South Wales, Australia. P. M. McCulloch and P. A. Hamilton of the University of Tasmania and J. G. Ables and A. J. Hunt of the Commonwealth Scientific and Industrial Research Organization announced the discovery of the first pulsar to be found in the Large Magellanic Cloud. The new pulsar is designated PSR 0529-66. It has a period of 0.9757 second, more typical of the pulsars in our Galaxy than is the rapid pulsar just discussed.

Among observed novae there are seven known as slow novae because they take decades to return to normal brightness after a nova outbreak. All have spectra that simultaneously display the characteristics of a hot and a cool star. One of these objects, RR Telescopii, visible in the Southern Hemisphere skies, was observed in the infrared from 1.2 to 3.5 μm by M. W. Feast and colleagues at the South African Astronomical Observatory over a ten-year span.

Before its last nova outbreak in 1944, RR Telescopii showed small brightness changes with a cyclic variation of about 387 days. Since that outburst, however, these variations have been observed only in the infrared. The spectrum of RR Telescopii now shows at long wavelengths the features of a cool M-type star and a heated dust shell, while the blue and visual part of its spectrum has a continuum corresponding to a hot star with the presence of many emission lines. (An M-type star is one having a spectrum characterized by the presence of titanium oxide bands.)

Feast and his collaborators argued that their observations indicate that RR Telescopii consists of a cool long-period variable star and a hot companion, either a main-sequence or a white-dwarf star. (A main-sequence star is one whose energy is derived from core burning of hydrogen into helium. In a white-dwarf star the thermonuclear energy sources are exhausted.) The cool star maintained the same average brightness and period of fluctuation throughout the nova outburst and decline. The huge brightening of the system occurred when the cool variable expanded enough to transfer mass to the hot star, causing a runaway nuclear reaction on the surface of the latter.

Feast and his colleagues believe that all of the slow novae are binary systems containing a cool giant or supergiant component. The two components of such novae have separations that are much larger, however, than those usually associated with the phenomenon of mass transfer between stars. It is only the tremendous sizes of the cool stars that allow their outer regions, upon additional expansion, to approach close enough to their hot companions to lose material to the smaller stars. In the case of such large component separations the mass transfer can occur at a rather leisurely pace, prolonging the abnormal energy output that is described as the nova phenomenon. With this evidence that even in the extreme case of a slow nova a binary system is required, the theory that all novae are binary systems becomes more firmly supported.

Red supergiant stars, even when single, are known to throw off material at large rates. They literally expand to the point where they lose gravitational control over their outer extremities. IRAS returned data showing that Betelgeuse, the ruby-red star in the shoulder of Orion, has a series of dust shells extending as far as 4.5 light-years from the star. The measurements suggest that Betelgeuse had at least three major eruptions that cast off the shells between 50,000 and 100,000 years ago. The observed shells, however, are not symmetrical around the star. They are believed to have been emitted as spheres about Betelgeuse, but, as the star moved through the dense interstellar matter in the Orion region, they were left behind due to the retarding influence of the surrounding matter.

Possibly the most exciting discovery made by IRAS concerns the bright star Vega. The satellite's data on Vega show the presence of a ring of solid particles orbiting the star, presumably material left over after Vega was formed a billion years ago. The material in the rings appears to resemble the meteoritic matter and zodiacal dust found in our solar system. Vega therefore becomes the first star for which direct evidence has been found for the possibility of the formation of another solar system beyond that of our Sun.

Galactic astronomy. A search for faint variable stars by M. R. S. Hawkins of the Royal Observatory, Edinburgh, using the 1.2-m United Kingdom Schmidt telescope, led to an unexpected clue to the mass of our Galaxy. Hawkins discovered a faint RR Lyrae variable in the constellation of Grus. Since RR Lyrae variables all have about the same intrinsic brightness, the apparent brightness of one of them can be used to estimate its distance. (Intrinsic brightness is the total amount of radiation emitted by a star over a specified range of wavelengths.) The faintness of this star indicates that it lies approximately 200,000 light-years from the galactic center and 150,000 light-years from the galactic plane.

The spectrum of the star shows a Doppler shift corresponding to a velocity of approach equal to 465 km per second. Assuming the star to be gravitation-ally bound to the Galaxy, it is possible to calculate the mass of the Galaxy needed to impart the measured velocity. The calculated mass is at least 1.4 trillion solar masses, about seven times the mass estimated from the Sun's motion about the Galaxy. Furthermore, this is a lower limit because if the star has any motion perpendicular to the line of sight, a property that cannot be measured at the present, the mass of the Galaxy must be even greater.

Over the last decade evidence has been accumulating that the original estimates of the galactic mass are too low. There appears to be a large amount of matter that has not been directly detected except by its gravitational influence. Much of this matter is believed to be in a huge halo surrounding the Galaxy, but its composition remains unknown. The gravitational influence on the Sun by such matter, which is more distant from the galactic center than is the Sun, would not contribute to the solar motion. Consequently, the mass of the Galaxy estimated from the Sun's motion is too small.

One of the revelations made by IRAS was the presence of faint patchy dust clouds over the whole sky. Their appearance is not unlike that of high cirrus clouds in the Earth's atmosphere, and the newly observed matter has been referred to as the "infrared cirrus." The radiation temperature of the clouds is roughly 30 K ($-243°$ C), which suggests that the particulate matter in the clouds is composed of graphite (carbon) dust. A comparison with radio data shows that some of the cloud patches appear to be associated with previously discovered clouds of neutral hydrogen. This suggests that the infrared cirrus is galactic in character. But much of the cirrus does not correspond to such clouds. This implies that the cirrus is not galactic in character but instead could be associated with the Oort comet cloud, a huge spherical shell, 50,000 to 100,000 astronomical units away, surrounding and bound to the Sun. (One astronomical unit = 150 million km.) This cloud is believed to be the source of comets that make their way close enough to the Sun to become visible. So far the most that can be said from measurements of the infrared cirrus is that it is at least 1,000 astronomical units distant.

In addition to the infrared cirrus, IRAS has returned data from investigations at wavelengths of 100 μm which suggest that there is a large component of very cold dust pervading the Galaxy, extending even to its poles. The measurements indicate that at least as much mass is present in this material as there is in the interstellar dust that has previously been analyzed by scattered starlight in the visible portion of the spectrum. Depending upon its ultimate mass, this dust component could turn out to supply a significant part of the "missing mass" of the Galaxy.

Besides the diffusely spread dust, IRAS also found dust concentrations along the plane of the Milky Way. A large number of small dust and gas globules glow strongly enough in the infrared that they must contain solar-mass stars (those with masses approximately equal to that of the Sun) in the process of formation. Much of what astronomers know about star formation has come from the study of huge cloud complexes such as Orion, where stars of large mass and large luminosities tend to form. These huge clouds are all so distant that the formation there of stars of smaller mass cannot be seen because of the relative faintness of these objects. But a large number of the globules detected by IRAS lie within a distance of 650 light-years. The number of possible star formations seen within this volume implies that solar-mass star formation, if the same rate holds throughout the Galaxy, is quite high, possibly as large as one per year.

Extragalactic astronomy. When IRAS scanned the sky away from the plane of the Milky Way, the long-wavelength detectors (at 60 and 100 μm) found many galaxies. Most of them could be identified with spiral galaxies already seen at visible wavelengths. This is not surprising since spiral galaxies usually contain copious dust that radiates strongly in the long infrared. But some of the infrared galaxies seen by IRAS, including some of the very brightest ones, are very faint in visible light. Normal spirals tend to have about the same relative brightness in both the visible and the infrared portions of the spectrum. The odd galaxies seen by IRAS, however, are about 50 times as bright in the infrared as they are in the visible. It could be that these objects are so shrouded in dust that their visible radiation is abnormally obscured, or it could be that some as yet unknown process is taking place within them.

In addition to those sources found by IRAS that could be associated with visible objects, there were a significant number, roughly 10%, for which there was no known visible counterpart. Some appear to be related to sources measured at infrared wavelengths by ground-based observers, but the bulk of them are not. Since these first-seen objects are rather uniformly distributed over the sky, the odds are that they are extragalactic objects. They could be extreme examples of infrared galaxies, but this would require that their infrared brightness exceed their visible brightness by a factor of more than 100. The IRAS data were being processed to refine the positions of these objects so that they may be searched for in the visible part of the spectrum by ground-based telescopes.

At least one other invisible extragalactic object was announced in 1983. Yervant Terzian, Stephen Schneider, George Helou, and Edwin Salpeter, all at Cornell University, were using the Arecibo radio telescope to measure neutral hydrogen clouds

Image of the center of the Milky Way Galaxy was produced from observations made by IRAS. The infrared telescope carried by the satellite saw through the gas and dust that obscures the stars; this material cannot be penetrated by optical telescopes.

in other galaxies. In calibrating their system, they observed a region of the sky between two groups of galaxies that lie in the constellation of Leo. But instead of a small signal, essentially an indication of the noise in their measuring system, they received a significant one. They had observed a huge cloud of hydrogen in what is a blank field in visible light. The cloud does not appear to be part of our Galaxy because the 21-cm radiation received from it is highly

NGC 4151 is a Seyfert galaxy, one of a relatively rare group of spiral galaxies with very bright nuclei. Observations of NGC 4151 by the International Ultraviolet Explorer satellite have revealed it to be variable in brightness and to have strong emission lines of doubly and triply ionized carbon.

Mount Wilson and Las Campanas Observatories,
© Carnegie Institution of Washington

red-shifted. Thus, if the cloud is taking part in the expansion of the universe, it must be at a distance of approximately 30 million light-years and have a diameter ten times that of our Galaxy. Based on the radio energy from the cloud, it contains between 8 billion and 30 billion solar masses of hydrogen. But even this large amount of matter when spread over the expanse of the cloud results in a very low density, 10^{-3} to 10^{-4} atoms per cubic centimeter, much too small for spontaneous gravitational collapse into stars to take place. The cloud thus appears to be a proto-galaxy that did not quite make it to the stage where star formation could begin.

The cloud has a puzzling feature, its western edge showing a velocity of recession that is 80 km per second greater than that of the eastern edge. This implies that the cloud is rotating, but to keep such a spinning cloud from dispersing would require a mass within it of 100 billion solar masses, considerably more than there appears to be in the form of neutral hydrogen. No clues have yet been found as to the nature of the invisible mass.

—W. M. Protheroe

See also Feature Articles: GIANT VOIDS IN THE UNIVERSE; SECRETS FROM THE FALLEN STARS.

Chemistry

The image of chemistry has sunk to an unprecedented low among the general public, largely because of overdramatization by the news media. Reports of harmful chemicals abound, yet little attention is given the fact that virtually all manufactured chemicals are useful, helping to prolong life and make it more enjoyable. In truth, our human bodies, the foods we eat, and all of the matter that surrounds us are chemical in nature. It is simply wrong to create the impression that all chemicals are toxic or cause cancer.

Nevertheless, it was another good year for research developments in chemistry. In the U.S. the National Academy of Sciences requested preparation of a report on opportunities in the chemical sciences. Already known informally as the Pimentel report after its committee head, George Pimentel of the University of California, Berkeley, it would identify research areas in chemistry that were likely to yield the highest scientific dividends in the years to come.

Inorganic chemistry

Worldwide recognition was afforded inorganic chemistry during the past year when Henry Taube of Stanford University received the 1983 Nobel Prize for Chemistry. Taube's fundamental discoveries on electron transfer reactions provide the cornerstone for understanding all such reactions in chemistry and biology. Inorganic chemistry also continued to make significant strides in solid-state chemistry and in the chemistry of the main-group elements as well as in organometallic chemistry, homogeneous catalysis, bioinorganic chemistry, photochemistry, and syntheses of new materials.

Electron transfer reactions. Chemical reactions are mostly of two general types, acid-base reactions and oxidation-reduction, or redox, reactions. The generalized concept of acid-base reactions was elegantly provided in 1916 by the late Gilbert N. Lewis. He defined an acid as a substance that, when forming chemical bonds, accepts a share of a pair of electrons. A base is a substance that donates a share of a pair of its electrons. In the examples in (1) it should be noted that the electron pair (represented by a pair of dots) is shared, not given up by one substance and taken on by another.

Unlike acid-base reactions, oxidation-reduction

reactions do involve giving up and taking on electrons. In the examples in (2) the sodium atom gives its electron to the chlorine atom to form sodium chloride. Likewise, in water solution zinc metal gives copper ion two electrons and copper metal separates from solution. A similar process is true for the formation of sulfur dioxide. A common process in all of these redox reactions is the transfer of electrons from reductant to oxidant.

The fundamental question of the way in which this electron transfer takes place was answered very intellectually in the 1950s by Taube, then at the

$$[Co(NH_3)_5Cl]^{2+} \; + \; [Cr(H_2O)_6]^{2+} \; + \; 5H_3O^+$$

$$\xrightarrow{\cdot Cl^-} \; [Co(H_2O)_6]^{2+} \; + \; 5NH_4^+ \; + \; [Cr(H_2O)_5Cl]^{2+}$$

3

University of Chicago. After making a thorough study of the rates of substitution reactions of metal complexes, he was prepared to design the appropriate experiments to address the problem. His research was also greatly assisted by the use of radioactive isotopes, which had become available from work on the atomic bomb during World War II. His classic experiment was the reduction of an appropriate complex of cobalt(III) (a cobalt atom deficient three electrons, Co^{3+}) by chromium(II) (Cr^{2+}) in the presence of radioactive chloride ion ($*Cl^-$) (3).

The key to this extremely well designed experiment is that the chlorine in the original cobalt(III) complex is transferred completely to the chromium(III) product. It is also significant that none of the added radioactive chloride ion in solution appears in the chromium(III) product. Had the physical process involved just movement of an electron from $[Cr(H_2O)_6]^{2+}$ to $[Co(NH_3)_5Cl]^{2+}$, then the resulting Co(II) would have rapidly given up all its groups, or ligands, to solution, forming a mixture of free Cl^- and $*Cl^-$; the $[Cr(H_2O)_5Cl]^{2+}$ product thus would have contained some $*Cl^-$. Because no $*Cl^-$ appeared in the product, Taube concluded that the electron does not just jump from reductant to oxidant but must move by means of a process he called an "inner-sphere electron transfer." Such a mechanism requires the intermediate formation of an inner-sphere

acid		base		
H^+	+	$:OH^-$	$\longrightarrow$	$H:OH$ (or H_2O)
Cu^{2+}	+	$:NH_3$	$\longrightarrow$	$[Cu:NH_3]^{2+}$
BF_3	+	$:O(C_2H_5)_2$	$\longrightarrow$	$F_3B:O(C_2H_5)_2$

1

reductant		oxidant		
$Na\cdot$	+	$\cdot\ddot{C}l\!:$	$\longrightarrow$	$Na^+, :\ddot{C}l\!:^-$ (or NaCl)
$Zn:$	+	Cu^{2+}	$\longrightarrow$	Zn^{2+} + $Cu:$
S^0	+	O_2^0	$\longrightarrow$	$S^{IV}O_2{}^{2-}$ (or SO_2)

2

$$[(NH_3)_5Co \cdot \cdot \cdot Cl \cdot \cdot \cdot Cr(H_2O)_5]^{4+}$$

4

$[Co(NH_3)_5Cl]^{2+} + [Cr(bipy)_3]^{2+} + 5H_3O^+ + H_2O \longrightarrow [Co(H_2O)_6]^{2+} + 5NH_4^+ + Cl^- + [Cr(bipy)_3]^{3+}$

5

bridged complex (4). The chlorine bridge between cobalt and chromium allows the ready flow of electrons, as a copper wire conducts electricity.

Taube went on to show that systems having metals that are devoid of ligands suitable for forming such a bridge react by means of an "outer-sphere electron transfer." For example, if in reaction (3) $[Cr(H_2O)_6]^{2+}$, which quickly loses H_2O to allow inner bridge formation, is replaced by the less reactive $[Cr(bipy)_3]^{2+}$, then bridge formation during the time of electron transfer is not possible (5).

Details of exactly how electrons go from reductant to oxidant in outer-sphere processes is less well understood than it is in inner-sphere processes. Yet knowledge of both kinds has been exploited extensively by chemists and biologists in the design of their experiments in various fields of research.

Solid-state chemistry. Much of chemistry has involved studying the properties and reactions of substances in solution, but in recent years interest has increased in solid-state chemistry and in the new materials that it produces. High-technology industry is primarily concerned with solid-state electronics and improved integrated circuits for computers, a focus that has opened up important domains for inorganic chemistry. For example, in the past year research flourished on the syntheses and properties of materials that act like one-dimensional metals; i.e., materials that have the electrical and optical properties of metals in one spatial direction. The ultimate goal in such investigations is to discover a material with superconductive properties at room temperature.

Ground was broken for a new area of solid-state inorganic chemistry thanks largely to the research of John Corbett and co-workers at Iowa State University and of A. Simon and co-workers at Stuttgart University in West Germany. They discovered new compounds with extended metal–metal bonding in metal halides of some early transition metals— scandium (Sc), zirconium (Zr), yttrium (Y), and niobium (Nb)—and lanthanides—lanthanum (La), gadolinium (Gd), and terbium (Tb). These highly reduced metal halides have very strong metal–metal bonds in the form of clusters, chains, and sheets of metal atoms. New compounds with such metal–halide proportions as Sc_7Cl_{10}, Sc_5Cl_8, and ZrCl were prepared and investigated in some detail.

To solution-oriented inorganic chemists these compounds represent some most unconventional chemistry. For example, both $ZrCl_4$ and $ZrCl_3$ are well known, but inorganic chemists have always felt it impossible to reduce zirconium to an oxidation state lower than 3 (as in $ZrCl_3$). Hence, it was quite a surprise to learn that extended layered sheets of ZrCl are extremely stable. This frontier of inorganic chemistry will require revision of textbooks on the subject.

Such research is being made possible because of the availability of containers of tantalum metal. An unconventional material is needed because under the necessary reaction conditions most of the elements of interest combine with traditional container materials such as silica and other ceramics, gold, and platinum to form highly stable compounds. An example of the general method of syntheses of these new materials is given in (6). The Sc_2Cl_3 product occurs as a dense furlike material covering the surface of the scandium metal sheet. Another novel scandium compound, Sc_7Cl_{10}, has the formulation $\frac{1}{\infty}[(ScCl_2^+)(Sc_6Cl_8^-)]$; because of its structure (7) it is affectionately termed "star wars II." (The "one" and "infinity" in the formula signify that the formula represents one base unit of a structure that can be extended indefinitely.) It is too early to know what important uses might be made of these new materials, but the investigators are optimistic that some will have valuable electrical or magnetic properties.

Main-group chemistry. The main-group elements, which include both metals and nonmetals, are those elements in the periodic table other than the transition metals and the inner transition metals (lan-

$ScCl_3$ (gas) + Sc (excess, in sheet form) $\xrightarrow{800°\text{–}850°\ C}$

Sc_2Cl_3 (solid)

6

thanides and actinides). Whereas much of main-group chemistry in the past was largely done outside the U.S., in recent years a deliberate effort has been mounted to encourage such research in American laboratories. Early indications of success include some significant breakthroughs; an example is the production of polysilastyrene, the silicon analogue of the important commercial polymer polystyrene (see *1982 Yearbook of Science and the Future* Year in Review: CHEMISTRY: *Inorganic chemistry*).

The presence of double bonds between atoms of carbon in olefin compounds ($R_2C{=}CR_2$, in which R is a generalized atom or group) has long been recognized to be an important characteristic of organic chemistry. For this reason chemists have felt strongly that it should be possible to make similar compounds with double bonds between two atoms of

other main-group elements. After many years of unsuccessful attempts chemists were finally rewarded in 1981 with the syntheses of disilene compounds ($R_2Si{=}SiR_2$), prepared independently in the laboratories of Robert West of the University of Wisconsin and Satoru Masamune of the Massachusetts Institute of Technology.

Concomitantly attempts were under way to obtain diphosphenes (R—P=P—R) and diarsenes (R—As=As—R). During the past year these accomplishments were reported from the laboratories of Alan Cowley at the University of Texas and of Masaki Yoshifuji at the University of Tokyo. The Tokyo researchers used the large *tert*-butyl group [t-Bu, or —C(CH$_3$)$_3$] to stabilize the diphosphene, which they prepared according to the procedure in (8). X-ray crystallographic analysis of this com-

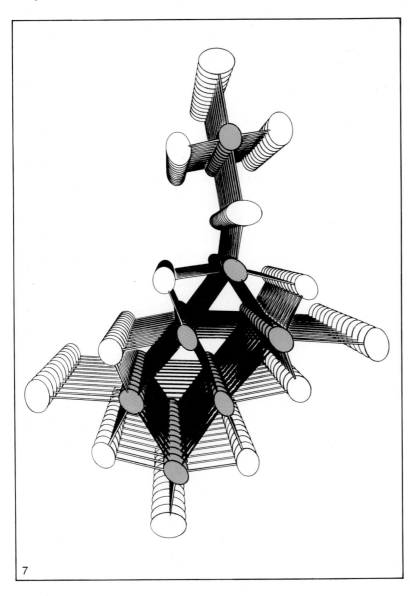

Illustration of the structure of the metal halide $\frac{1}{\infty}[(ScCl_2{}^+)\,(Sc_6Cl_8{}^-)]$, dubbed star wars II, shows a chain of Sc(III) Cl_6 octahedrons at the top and a double chain of distorted scandium octahedrons at the bottom. Both chains are formed by sharing edges. Scandium atoms are represented by dark ellipses; chlorine atoms, as light ellipses.

7

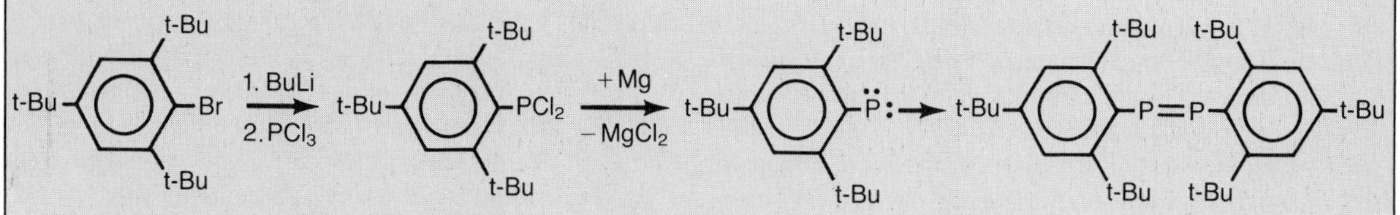

8

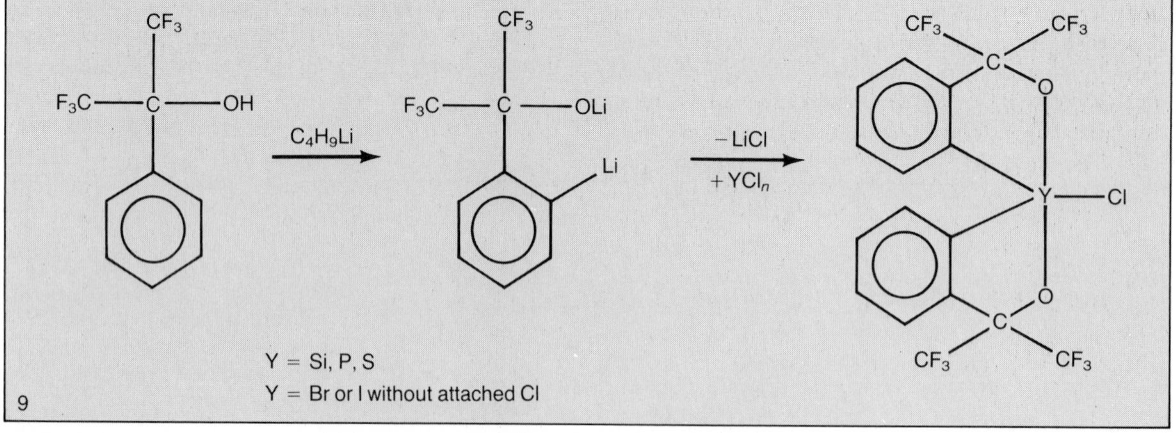

Y = Si, P, S
Y = Br or I without attached Cl

9

pound showed the P=P bond distance to be 2.03 angstroms compared with 2.24 angstroms for P—P, just as expected from the fact that a double bond between carbon atoms is shorter than a corresponding single bond (an angstrom is a hundred-millionth of a centimeter). Cowley's team used the large —C(Si(CH₃)₃)₃ group to stabilize the diphosphene ((CH₃)₃Si)₃CP=PC(Si(CH₃)₃)₃.

These noncarbon olefin analogues are very reactive toward electrophiles (electron-seeking reagents) such as hydrogen chloride, sulfur, and sulfur dioxide. When their ligands are not too bulky, the compounds do react with metal carbonyls to give organometallic complexes. Exactly what this proliferation of double-bonded compounds means for chemistry is still too early for speculation. One certainty is its new challenges for talented experimental and theoretical research chemists in the years ahead.

Organometallic chemistry has been an important field for many years and in particular during the past two decades. Currently on the horizon is organo-nonmetallic chemistry, which deals with compounds of the organometallic type in which the metal is replaced by a nonmetal. The term organo-nonmetallic was coined by J. C. Martin of the University of Illinois, whose research group has been making major contributions to the field. The investigators designed organic ligands capable of stabilizing specific bonding modes and geometries of compounds of nonme-

tallic elements. The most versatile of the ligands prepared and some of its organo-nonmetallic compounds are shown in (9).

Some of these compounds can be viewed as frozen transition states. For example, tetravalent silicon compounds (those in which the silicon atom participates in four bonds) react by associative mechanisms through pentavalent (five-bond) transition states or active intermediates. This new organic ligand makes it possible to isolate stable compounds of the type presumed to be involved in reactions that proceed by nucleophilic (nucleus-seeking) attack on the central nonmetal in the compound. These compounds are examples of hypervalent compounds, in which the central element exhibits a higher valency than its normal stable valence. Again it is uncertain where this research will lead, but the ability to fine-tune the reactivity of such compounds offers considerable promise for the development of new reagents and catalysts of potential utility in synthetic chemistry.

—Fred Basolo

Organic chemistry

During the past year substantial gains were made in characterizing and synthesizing unusual molecules of natural origin as well as in preparing exotic, previously unknown structures. Considerable effort also was devoted to unraveling the processes by which

264

living organisms manufacture naturally occurring substances. Aiding in these pursuits were new, remarkably powerful instrumental methods.

Instrumentation. Research in organic chemistry has been greatly aided by such instrumental techniques as natural-abundance carbon-13 (^{13}C) nuclear magnetic resonance (NMR) spectroscopy. This procedure was popularized by John D. Roberts of the California Institute of Technology, who received the American Chemical Society's 1983 Willard Gibbs Medal for this achievement and others. In the NMR procedure a sample of a carbon-containing molecule is spun between the poles of a powerful magnet and simultaneously irradiated with pulses of radio-frequency energy, which induces atoms such as ^{13}C to produce characteristic electrical signals, or resonances. After computer-assisted analysis of the resulting signals the distribution (spectrum) of resonances for the different carbon atoms in the molecule is plotted. The position, or chemical shift, of each carbon resonance in the spectrum is related to the local environment of the carbon atom in the molecule.

The predominant carbon-12 isotope is not detected by this method, and computer enhancement is necessary to magnify the signal of the rarer ^{13}C isotope (1% natural abundance). Assigning these spectra unambiguously to carbon positions can sometimes be difficult. A technique developed by Ray Freeman of the University of Oxford and Richard Ernst of the Swiss Federal Institute of Technology in Zürich, termed two-dimensional Fourier transform NMR (2D FT-NMR), is of great value in analyzing both carbon and proton (hydrogen-nuclei) NMR spectra by providing direct information on connectivity; e.g., by identifying those carbons or carbon-hydrogen pairs that are directly connected and those protons that are coupled. The data are often presented as contour diagrams. Several examples of recent applications of this method are given below.

Natural product chemistry. The oceans provide a rich source of plants and animals possessing unusual chemicals, some of which perhaps serve as defensive agents. Species of the Pacific sponge *Amphimedon* were found to make the cytotoxic fused pentacyclic (five-ring) alkaloid amphimedine (1); the marine sponge *Xestospongia exigua* yielded the antibiotic pentacyclic polyketide halenaquinone; and the marine red alga *Laurencia poitei* afforded the chlorine- and bromine-bearing 12-membered cyclic ether poitediene (2). The structure of amphimedine was determined by Francis J. Schmitz and colleagues at the University of Oklahoma by 2D FT-NMR methods; of halenaquinone by Paul J. Scheuer of the University of Hawaii and Jon Clardy of Cornell University, Ithaca, N.Y.; and of poitediene by Amy E. Wright, Richard M. Wing, and James J. Sims of the University of California, Riverside, by X-ray crystallography. From the roots of the South African plant *Aloe pluridens* Du Pont Co. scientists Pat N. Confalone, Edward Huie, and Narayan G. Patel isolated the natural insecticide pluridone, $C_6H_5C(O)CH_2OCH{=}CHC(O)SCH_3$.

Organic chemists reported a number of notable syntheses of natural products during the past year. Philip Magnus and Timothy Gallagher of Indiana University built the complex heptacyclic (seven-ring) cage alkaloid kopsanone (3) by a nicely efficient 14-step procedure. Chaenorhine (4), a bicyclic polyamine alkaloid, was prepared by Harry H. Wasserman, Ralph P. Robinson, and Charles G. Carter of Yale University; isochorismic acid, a molecule with a key role in the biosynthesis of aromatic substances in plants, was synthesized by Glenn A. Berchtold and Frank R. Busch of the Massachusetts Institute of Technology; and tabtoxin, the toxin from the microorganism responsible for wildfire disease of tobacco plants, was synthesized by Oxford chemist Jack Baldwin and co-workers.

Investigation of traditional folk medicines can sometimes lead to discovery and synthesis of useful

amphimedine 1

poitediene 2

new drugs. For example, since ancient times the plant *Artemisia annua* has been used as a traditional Chinese herbal medicine known as Qinghao for treating fever. Chemists G. Schmid and W. Hofheinz of Hoffmann-La Roche in Basel, Switz., succeeded in synthesizing the highly oxygenated sesquiterpene lactone qinghaosu (5), which was found to be the effective agent of the plant and was shown to be a potent agent of promise for destroying drug-resistant malaria parasites.

Biosynthesis. Organic chemists and biochemists have long been interested in understanding the ways in which molecules are synthesized in plants and animals. Once obtained, this information is frequently used to design laboratory syntheses and to develop new drugs, pesticides, and other valuable substances. Recently David Cane of Brown University, Providence, R.I., Walter D. Celmer of Pfizer Inc., John W. Wesley of Hoffmann-La Roche, and John C. Vederas of the University of Alberta, Canada, proposed mechanisms for the biosynthesis of such natural products as the tricyclopentanoid pentalenene, the fungal metabolite mevinolin, the macrolide metabolite avermectin, and erythromycin and other polyether antibiotics; they did this after they had supplied appropriate isotopically labeled precursor molecules to the organism or enzyme isolate responsible for biosynthesis and then assessed the labeling patterns that appeared in the final products. When ^{13}C-labeled precursors were used, 2D FT-NMR methods became a convenient means of determining the locations of the label in the natural product.

Nonnatural product synthesis. In 1982 a number of propeller-shaped molecules called propellanes were synthesized (see *1984 Yearbook of Science and the Future* Year in Review: CHEMISTRY: *Organic chemistry*). During the past year another curious class of related molecules, termed paddlanes, was report-

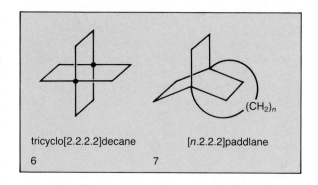

tricyclo[2.2.2]decane

6

[n.2.2.2]paddlane

7

ed by University of Chicago chemists Philip Eaton and Bernard D. Leipzig. Having as the ultimate goal the generation of the extraordinarily strained tricyclo[2.2.2]decane (6), the investigators prepared derivatives of a series of [n.2.2.2]paddlanes in which $n = 10$–14 (7). (The numbers in brackets refer to the numbers of unshared ring atoms in each of the four rings.) Given a large enough bridging group (for example, $n = 11$–14) the rigid three-lobed ring system is able to rotate freely, much like the paddle arrangement on a paddle-wheel steamboat. When $n = 10$, however, free rotation is impeded due to molecular congestion between the "paddle wheel" and the ten-atom bridge.

Other unusual unnatural organic molecules include tricarbon monoxide, C_3O, prepared by high-temperature methods by Ronald D. Brown and colleagues at Monash University in Australia; sexipyridine (8) containing an electron-rich cavity due to the presence of the six nitrogens, synthesized by George R. Newkome and H.-W. Lee of Louisiana State University; 8-carboxy[6]paracyclophane (9), possessing a benzene ring bent 20° from planarity, as indicated by X-ray crystallography, by Yoshito Tobe and coworkers at Osaka University in Japan; and a relat-

3   kopsanone

4   chaenorhine

5   qinghaosu

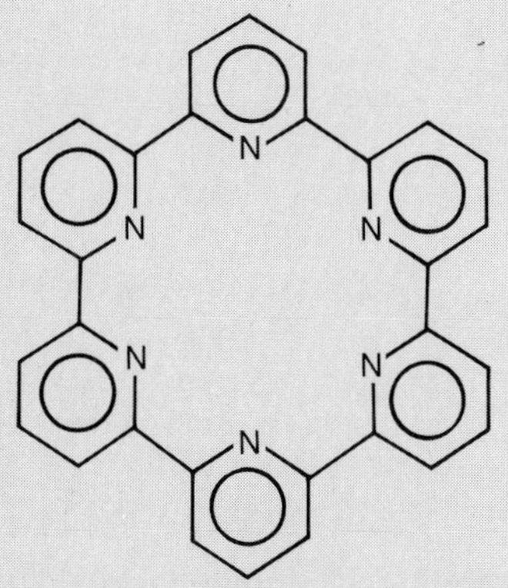

sexipyridine
8

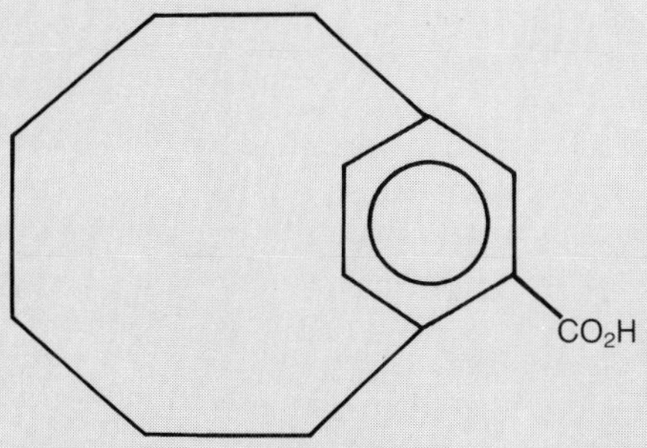

8-carboxy[6]paracyclophane
9

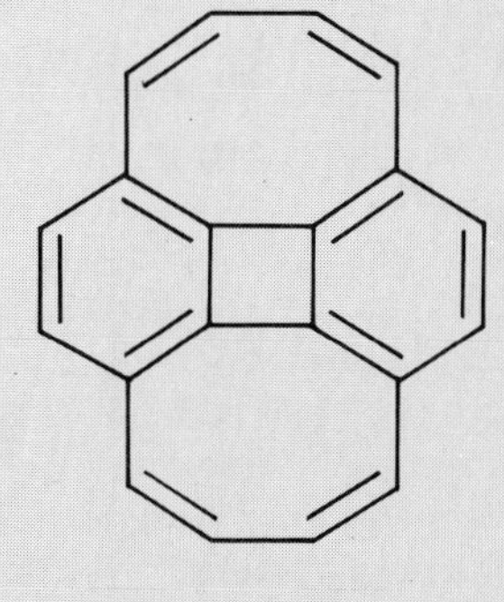

dicycloocta[1,2,3,4-*def*:1',2',3',4'-*jkl*]–
biphenylene
10

methyl trimethylsilyl
dimethylketene acetal

methyl methacrylate

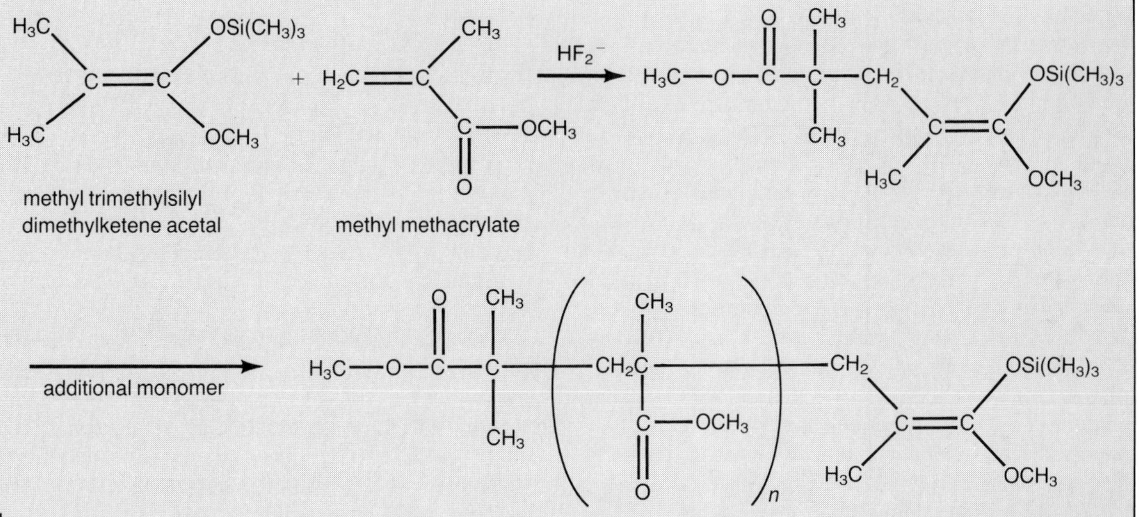

11

ed molecule severely distorted from planarity by a nine-atom bridge, synthesized by David Dolphin of the University of British Columbia, Frederich W. B. Einstein of Simon Fraser University, Burnaby, B.C., and co-workers.

Also of note is the preparation by Joseph B. Lambert and William J. Schulz, Jr., of Northwestern University, Evanston, Ill., of the first isolable silicon counterpart of a carbon-based positive ion (a carbocation), *i.e.*, a silicon-based positive ion, $(i\text{-PrS})_3Si^+ClO_4^-$. Charles F. Wilcox, Jr., and Erik Farley of Cornell University, Ithaca, N.Y., constructed a molecule with the sonorous name dicycloocta-[1,2,3,4-*def*:1',2',3',4'-*jkl*]biphenylene (10), notable for the presence of fully conjugated (having alternating double and single carbon–carbon bonds throughout) four-, six-, and eight-membered rings and showing by NMR abnormal circulation of electrons in the benzene rings.

In the field of polymer chemistry Du Pont chemist Owen W. Webster and co-workers devised a new polymerization procedure for building up large molecules (polymers) from small molecular units (monomers), termed group transfer polymerization, that may give greater control of size and size distribution of the polymers formed, copolymer composition, and functional end groups than was available by previous methods. For example, in the case of the polymerization of methyl methacrylate to polymethyl methacrylate (11), the reaction proceeds by continuous transfer of an activating trimethylsilyl [—$Si(CH_3)_3$] group from an appropriate compound to the carbonyl oxygen (═O) of each methyl methacrylate unit as it is added to the front of the chain. The trimethylsiloxy [—$OSi(CH_3)_3$] end group is said to be a "living" end, which continues to grow as long as the monomer is available.

—Eric Block

Physical chemistry

For several years the physics and chemistry of solid surfaces have been of intense interest to a wide spectrum of scientists. Of utmost importance to the chemical industry, for example, is heterogeneous catalysis. In most instances a heterogeneous catalyst is a solid material that helps steer a chemical reaction toward the desired product but is not consumed in the process. Surfaces are the site of the action in heterogeneous catalysis as well as in other economically important phenomena such as the corrosion of structural materials. Furthermore, the chemical and physical processes that engineers use to build microelectronic circuits for computers, video games, and a host of other electronic marvels mostly take place at surfaces. In recent months scientists reported on two techniques, one new and one old, that should help considerably in solving the elusive problem of surface geometry; *i.e.,* where the atoms are.

Surface imaging. The new technique, called scanning tunneling microscopy, is the brainchild of Gerd Binnig, Heinrich Rohrer, Christoph Gerber, and Edmund Weibel of the IBM Zürich Research Laboratory in Switzerland. In essence this technique scans the surface of a sample substance, tracing out the hills and valleys that correspond to the surface atoms and the spaces between them with a resolution of a few angstroms. (For details of its operation see *1984 Yearbook of Science and the Future* Year in Review: PHYSICS: *Solid-state physics.*) Binnig's group reported results that made significant contributions to settling current controversies concerning the surfaces of silicon, the semiconductor from which microelectronic circuits are built, and of gold. In the case of gold, for example, they found that some of its surfaces consist of ribbonlike facets with two different atomic structures rather than a smooth plane with a single arrangement of atoms.

Transmission electron microscopy is the older, established technique, but L. D. Marks and David J. Smith of the University of Cambridge pushed it in a new direction to obtain atomic-scale imaging of metal surfaces. The British scientists examined small particles of gold that had been evaporated onto heated insulating substrates. Working with the Cambridge high-resolution electron microscope, they positioned their sample such that the electron beam was almost parallel to the surface. In contrast to previous investigators who had tried similar experimental geometries, Marks and Smith used so-called bright-field imaging.

Bright-field imaging uses all the electrons in the microscope beam to generate the image, whereas dark-field imaging uses only the electrons scattered or diffracted from the beam as it passes through the sample. The virtue of bright-field imaging in the

From "Direct Surface Imaging in Small Metal Particles," L. D. Marks and David J. Smith, reprinted by permission from *Nature*, vol. 303, no. 5915, pp. 316–317, May 26, 1983. Copyright © 1983 Macmillan Journals Limited.

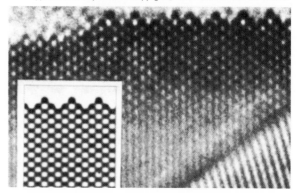

Atomic-scale image of part of a tiny particle of gold, in which the black dots directly correspond to columns of gold atoms in the crystal lattice, was obtained with the Cambridge high-resolution electron microscope in the U.K. Image in the inset, a computer simulation based on calculations, agrees well with the experimental image.

present case is that the image is directly interpretable in terms of atom locations, as the investigators verified by calculating the image expected for the gold surface, which matched the one they obtained experimentally. Although gold is not a catalyst of note, commercial catalysts often do come in the form of small particles, thus lending hope that the new electron microscopy technique will aid in studying real catalyst materials.

Chemical bonding. Physical chemists are interested not only in locations of atoms in molecules and solids but in the chemical bonding between the atoms. Another well-established experimental technique, nuclear magnetic resonance (NMR), figured strongly in a long-standing controversy concerning bonding involving carbon atoms. The dispute involves a molecule called norbornyl chloride, which contains seven carbon atoms and a chlorine atom,

Two competing models for the bonding structure of the positively charged norbornyl ion are compared.

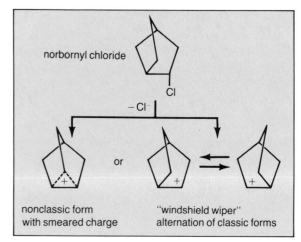

as well as several hydrogen atoms that do not figure in the issue. There are two models for the bonding structure of the positively charged norbornyl ion that remains of the molecule upon the loss of a negatively charged chloride ion. The most widely accepted model has the positive charge shared between three carbons in such a way that one of the carbons appears to participate in five bonds. The more recent but nonetheless classic view is that the positive charge jumps back and forth between two carbons, in this way maintaining the traditional convention of organic chemistry that carbon participates in four bonds.

NMR provides a way to differentiate between the two alternatives if the measurements are done at a sufficiently low temperature. Because it takes energy to jump from one configuration to the other in the classic picture, at low temperature everything should be frozen in place, and the NMR spectrum should reflect the existence of populations of norbornyl ions in each configuration. What Costantino Yannoni and Volker Macho of the IBM Research Laboratory in San Jose, Calif., and Philip Myhre of Harvey Mudd College, Claremont, Calif., saw was just the opposite. As they lowered the temperature from 77 degrees Kelvin (K) to 5 K, the spectrum remained unchanged, suggesting a single structure of the nonclassic type.

In a related experiment at Yale University, Martin Saunders and Mandes Kates carried out NMR measurements on norbornyl ions in which deuterium (a heavy hydrogen isotope) was substituted for the hydrogen atoms. In other molecules that are known to obey the classic picture, this substitution has the effect of adding an extra peak to the resonance spectrum. When it was tried with norbornyl ions, however, a different effect occurred, again suggesting a single structure of the nonclassic type.

New NMR technique. Most atomic nuclei have an angular momentum, or nuclear spin. In the presence of an applied magnetic field these nuclei tend to align their spin axes with the field like tiny magnets. The angle between the spin axis and the applied field—called the precession angle—takes on several characteristic values that reflect the environment of the nucleus (identity, number, and location of nearby nuclei, for example) and the strength of the field. Resonance occurs when an applied pulse of radiowave energy of the correct frequency is absorbed and thereby changes the precession angle. The frequencies, appearing as peaks in the NMR spectrum, provide structural information about crystalline materials. However, Daniel Weitekamp of the University of Groningen in The Netherlands and Anthony Bielecki, David Zax, Kurt Zilm, and Alexander Pines of the University of California, Berkeley, discovered a way to create NMR spectra with no applied field that provide detailed structural information about disordered materials.

The nuclei in disordered materials are oriented randomly, so there is also a random angle between any applied magnetic field and the nuclear spins. Whereas this randomness ordinarily smears out the NMR spectrum, the zero-field technique resolves the problem. Actually to obtain a resonance spectrum there must be a field at some time, but Weitekamp, Pines, and their co-workers devised a sequential process in which the sample is first immersed in a high magnetic field, removed, then reimmersed. The effect is that frequencies in the resonance spectrum are determined during the zero-field period so that all nuclei contribute equally as if they were in a crystal lattice, but the measurement occurs while the field is on, after reimmersion.

Laser chemistry. Lasers remain one of the paramount tools of the physical chemist. Part of their popularity derives from the view, no longer widely held, that lasers can drive chemical reactions to produce very specific products, in contrast to the distribution of different products frequently obtained when reactants are heated in a reaction vessel. The idea was that the frequency of the laser light could be tuned to excite vibrations in specific chemical bonds of the reactants. Although this is indeed possible, the energy of the vibrations redistributes itself throughout all the bonds of the molecule before the target bond can break. The laser then acts like an elegant furnace. Nourished by a few counterexamples, however, the hope of selective laser-induced chemistry remained alive during the past year.

For example, James Shirk, Paul McDonald, William F. Hoffman III, and Amy Shirk of the Illinois Institute of Technology in Chicago irradiated 2-fluoroethanol (ethyl alcohol with a fluorine atom replacing one hydrogen atom) with an infrared laser to selectively change the conformation of the molecule. Selectivity was achieved by fixing the frequency of the laser to excite different vibrations within the molecule, and the key to success lay in immobilizing the molecule in a matrix of solid argon. The matrix hindered the redistribution of energy within the molecule.

Subsequently George Pimentel, Heinz Frei, and Leif Fredin of the University of California, Berkeley, took this procedure a step further. They studied the reaction of ethylene and fluorine to produce vinyl fluoride and hydrogen fluoride. They found that the reaction was promoted increasingly effectively as the frequency of the infrared laser was increased. At one particular frequency, however, which corresponded to exciting a specific vibrational mode of ethylene, they found a peak in the otherwise smooth curve of increasing reaction efficiency, this peak being the desired selectivity. Once again, immobilizing the reactants, this time in solid nitrogen at 12 K, was a key ingredient. For the present the finding

Photos, Los Alamos National Laboratory

Laser beam directed vertically through a small flow tube (left) causes about 1,000 molecules of a fluorescent dye in liquid solution to produce a tiny spot of light. Scientists at the Los Alamos National Laboratory in the U.S. (right) are developing the technique, a form of laser-induced fluorescence, to detect small numbers of molecules in liquid samples.

is more applicable to research than to any commercial process.

One of the difficulties in investigating the redistribution of laser-excited vibrational energy in molecules is that it occurs so rapidly. The recent development of ultrahigh-speed pulsed lasers may help. Generally, to study the dynamics of molecular processes optically requires pulsed lasers or other light sources with pulse durations not much longer, and preferably shorter, than the lifetime of the phenomenon under investigation. At Bell Laboratories in New Jersey Jay Wiesenfeld and Benjamin Greene demonstrated the potential of lasers capable of generating pulses less than one picosecond (a millionth of a millionth of a second) long.

They studied the Rydberg states of benzene and toluene molecules. A Rydberg state is one in which electrons have very large orbits about their atoms; it is often very short-lived. Wiesenfeld and Greene measured the lifetimes of such states to be 70 femtoseconds in benzene and 170 femtoseconds in toluene (a femtosecond is a thousandth of a picosecond). They obtained these values by means of a pulsed visible laser with pulse length of 190 femtoseconds. The laser beam was split into two components in such a way that each component arrived at the sample at a slightly different time. Two photons from one beam excited the sample molecule into the Rydberg state. One photon from the second beam ionized the molecule in the Rydberg state provided that the photon arrived before the Rydberg state decayed. By varying the arrival time of the second beam and measuring the number of ionized molecules, the investigators could determine the lifetime of the Rydberg state.

—Arthur L. Robinson

Applied chemistry

Much of research in applied chemistry during the past year was devoted to the search for alternative sources of energy, one of which, solar energy, showed a number of new developments. Progress was also made in cosmochemistry and the origin of life, insecticides and rodenticides, bonding diamonds, stringed instruments, and degradable plastic.

Solar energy. A new type of chemical solar cell having high efficiency, long lifetime, and the ability to store energy was developed by Arthur T. Howe, a chemist at Standard Oil Company of Indiana's Amoco Research Center in Naperville, Ill. In the past, inexpensive and rugged silicon had been used as the electrode in such devices, but short lifetimes (measured in minutes) resulted from corrosion, and light-to-electricity conversion efficiencies hovered around 1%. Although the new cell also employs silicon, corrosion is minimized by coating the electrode surface with an extremely thin, integral layer of platinum, which increases the lifetime to weeks. Howe expects eventually to achieve lifetimes of more than a year.

The cell's high efficiency, 12%, stems from the use of alumina or magnesia to dope the oxide on the silicon surface just beneath the platinum coating. These impurities generate a fixed negative charge in the oxide layer in contrast to the usual fixed positive charge in silicon dioxide layers of earlier devices. The cell's ability to store the collected sunlight in the form of chemical energy for later use makes it promising for remote power sources in stand-alone installations or as a possible photoelectrochemical generator of hydrogen or oxygen.

Solar cells made of semiconductor-liquid junctions

Courtesy, Arthur T. Howe, Amoco Research Center. Naperville, Ill.

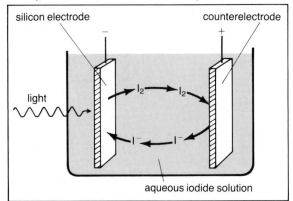

silicon electrode   counterelectrode

light

I_2 → I_2

I^- ← I^-

aqueous iodide solution

Chemical solar cell from Standard Oil of Indiana uses special coatings on its silicon electrodes to increase efficiency and lifetime. Its light-driven energy-conversion process depends on a circuit of iodine molecules and iodide ions in solution to transfer electrons from one electrode to the other.

offer possible alternatives to conventional solid-state photovoltaic conversion devices, but unfortunately they have not been stable or efficient. In recent months a new cell of this type showing excellent stability in an atmospheric environment and an energy conversion efficiency of 9.5% was announced by Shalini Menezes and Hans-Joachim Lewerenz of the Hahn-Meitner Institute for Nuclear Research in West Berlin and Klaus J. Bachmann of North Caro-

lina State University, Raleigh. The cell's n-CuInSe$_2$ anode (negatively doped single crystals of copper, indium, and selenium) immersed in an aqueous iodide solution uses relatively inexpensive, nontoxic components and requires less stringent sealing, making the cell a more feasible candidate for practical applications than its predecessors. The on-site formation at the anode-electrolyte interface of a film induced by addition of copper ions to the electrolyte solution yields anodes that are stable for more than five months, comparable to the best stability observed for any semiconductor-liquid junction.

Cosmochemistry and life. During the past year research continued on cosmochemistry, the study of the chemical composition of the universe. Since 1953, when U.S. chemists Stanley Miller and Harold C. Urey subjected a mixture of methane, ammonia, water, and hydrogen to an electric discharge and obtained α-amino acids, the building blocks of proteins, researchers have made similar attempts to duplicate the origin of organic matter on the primitive Earth from various primordial conditions (see *1980* and *1981 Yearbook of Science and the Future* Year in Review: CHEMISTRY: *Applied chemistry*). Most recently Cyril Ponnamperuma and co-workers at the Laboratory of Chemical Evolution at the University of Maryland in College Park subjected a model primitive atmosphere (a mixture of methane, nitrogen, and water) to an electric discharge (to simulate

Unusual chemical reactions that produce three-dimensional waves in solution are being studied as models for nerve transmission, the excitation of heart muscle, and other biological wave phenomena. Photo (left) of a three-dimensional wave propagating (in the direction of the arrow) in a solution-filled test tube appears as a three-dimensional spiral, or scroll, curling counterclockwise on the left and clockwise on the right. Computer-generated idealization of the scroll wave with a section removed (right) shows its internal organization. This kind of wave may underlie potentially fatal heartbeat irregularities, and scientists are attempting to discover the conditions that start it as well as those that can stop it promptly.

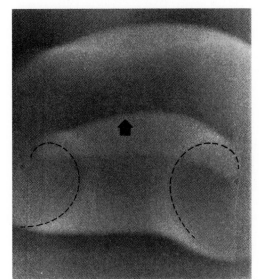

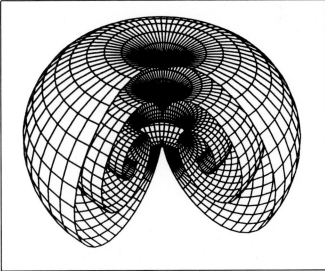

(Left) B. Welch, A. Burgess, and U. Gomatam, Glasgow Institute of Technology; (right) A. T. Winfree, Purdue University; S. H. Strogatz, Harvard University; and Melvin L. Prueitt, Los Alamos National Laboratory

Los Alamos National Laboratory

Los Alamos chemist Gene W. Taylor holds a diamond-grit grinding wheel created by his new process, in which the diamond is bonded by means of a fluorocarbon resin.

lightning) and for the first time obtained all five of the chemical compounds, called nucleotide bases, that encode the genetic information for life on Earth (previous experiments had produced one or more of these prebiotic bases). Four of the bases (adenine, guanine, cytosine, and thymine) comprise the "letters" of the genetic code structured into the double helix of DNA, while the fifth (uracil), along with adenine, guanine, and cytosine, is part of the protein-making instructions coded in RNA. According to Ponnamperuma, the experiment's success "makes the creation of life chemicals appear to be simple, almost inevitable" and suggests that "life elsewhere in the universe is likely."

Ponnamperuma also reported finding all five bases in samples of the Murchison meteorite that fell in Australia in 1969, but some scientists suspected that his results were due to contamination with terrestrial matter. The Murchison meteorite is a member of a class of rare meteorites, called carbonaceous chondrites, that are believed to represent closely the primitive material from which the solar system formed more than 4.5 billion years ago.

For the first time interstellar carbon dust has been found on Earth, according to chemists Edward Anders and Roy R. Lewis of the University of Chicago. The carbon grains, carrying material from a time before the solar system existed, were preserved within the Murchison meteorite where they remained protected from contamination and chemical alteration. The meteorite contained the gaseous element xenon having an isotopic ratio consistent with formation in a red giant star. Mass spectrometrists at the University of Cambridge confirmed that the carbon contained twice the normal amount of carbon-13 and was therefore of "exotic" origin. Further studies of isotopic abundances in the Murchison meteorite and other carbonaceous chondrites were under way to learn more about the stars in which such dust originated. (For additional information on cosmochemistry and the origins of life *see* Feature Article: SECRETS FROM THE FALLEN STARS and *1984 Yearbook of Science and the Future* Feature Article: PROBING THE ORIGIN OF LIFE.)

Scientists at the Australian National University in Canberra reported finding the Earth's oldest known rocks in a sedimentary formation in the Mount Narryer region of Australia. Chemical analysis of radioactive isotopes in a number of grains of the mineral zircon that were isolated from the rocks showed ages of 4.1 billion to 4.2 billion years, only about 300 million years younger than the estimated age of the Earth itself. The oldest previously dated rocks, from Greenland, were estimated to be 3.8 billion years old.

Insecticides and rodenticides. Many organic compounds not considered to be insecticides show strong ability to kill insect eggs and larvae when sensitized by ultraviolet light. This effect, a recently discovered type of phototoxicity, may lead to effective, ecologically acceptable insecticides. Although it has been known for almost a century that many organic dyes can kill microorganisms in the presence of visible light, this "photodynamic effect" has been seriously studied as a means of insect control only since the mid-1970s. Because the shorter the wavelength, the more energetic the light, chemist Jacques Kagan of the University of Illinois, Chicago, and co-workers tested for insecticidally active molecules that absorb mostly in the ultraviolet, or UV (especially in the 300–400-nanometer range; a nanometer is a billionth of a meter), rather than in the visible region of the spectrum. Unlike infrared or visible light, UV radiation is not significantly filtered by clouds, and UV-sensitized compounds should maintain their activity during cloudy days.

Kagan discovered more than 50 compounds that, when photosensitized, killed eggs or larvae of the common fruit fly and the yellow fever mosquito. These chemicals killed the mosquito larvae at concentrations of one to ten parts per million with less than two hours' exposure to sunlight—and in some cases instantaneously. A dose of two nanograms (two billionths of a gram) per egg killed all the fruit fly ova. For compounds showing egg-killing activity in the dark, exposure to UV light increased their toxicity as much as 10,000 times or more.

The tested compounds ranged from simple hydrocarbons to complex multi-ringed molecules; polyacetylenic compounds and thiophenes were most effective. None contained the polyfunctional groups (halogens, phosphorus, or carbamates) characterizing many commercial insecticides. Several are noncarcinogenic, and one is even on the list of chemicals approved in the U.S. for use in foods, drugs, and cosmetics.

The World Health Organization has urged development of new insecticides because many insects have become resistant to older compounds. Kagan's photoactive compounds kill DDT- and dieldrin-resistant mosquitoes and fruit flies as effectively as nonresistant ones. Some of the photoactive molecules, e.g., phenylheptatriyne, α-terthienyl, and 8-methoxypsoralen occur naturally in plants, and Kagan speculates that the plants themselves or crude extracts might be used directly. The phototoxic mechanism may involve the reaction of free single atoms of oxygen with cell components to cause the damage.

Warfarin, a safe but effective rodenticide that suppresses the blood-clotting factor vitamin K, was discovered in 1945, but by 1960 rodents (first Norwegian rats, then mice, and then populations of "super rats") became resistant to anticoagulant poisons. In a recent example of serendipity Barry A. Dreikorn and George O. P. O'Doherty of Lilly Research Laboratories, Greenfield, Ind., developed a potent rodenticide that kills both ordinary and "super" rats. The researchers were investigating chemicals to control fungus, using a routine rat toxicity test, and found a compound too toxic to be used as a fungicide but showing promise as an excellent rat poison. Since the rats did not like its taste, the scientists changed its structure slightly, making it more appetizing without reducing its toxicity. The compound, bromethalin, acts by slowing the transmission of nerve impulses, causing paralysis and death. It was more than 90% effective in killing resistant rats and mice after one feeding. Since the rodents do not die until two or three days after eating the poison, they should not learn to avoid it as they have learned to avoid arsenic and strychnine. According to the investigators, bromethalin-treated rodents should also pose no threat to animals eating the poisoned carcasses.

Bonding diamonds. A new method for bonding diamonds to metal far more strongly than hitherto possible was invented by Gene W. Taylor of the explosives technology group at Los Alamos National Laboratory in New Mexico. The process has led to extremely long-wearing diamond-encrusted wheels that can cut and grind the hardest new ceramic materials developed at the laboratory and that may one day revolutionize the art of making jewelry. The basis of the bond is a fluorocarbon resin similar to the non-

stick Teflon coating used for cookware. All previous efforts to bond such fluorocarbons to diamonds had been unsuccessful. In the method developed by Taylor and technician Herman Roybal, radio-frequency energy is pumped into a mixture of argon and sulfur hexafluoride gases, some of the molecules of which are broken down into their constituent atoms. The highly reactive free fluorine atoms combine with the carbon atoms on the diamond's surface, creating a microscopic film of fluorocarbon. This film is then easily bonded to Teflon, which in turn bonds strongly to the aluminum grinding wheel and to other metals, including gold.

Stringed instruments. Since the 18th century, violin makers have unsuccessfully tried to duplicate the rich, even tones produced by the instruments of the

Microscopic views compare the open cells in wood from a Guarneri cello (top) with a pectin-plugged cell in spruce used to make modern stringed instruments (center). A new treatment extracts the plugs (bottom), resulting in instruments of greatly improved quality.

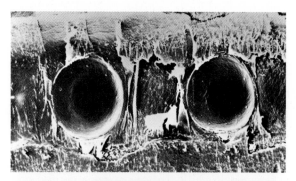
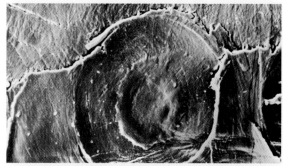

Photos, Joseph Nagyvary, Texas A&M University, College Station

ancient craftsmen of Cremona, Italy. After studying the historical literature on the masters and after examining wood samples of their instruments, biochemist and violinist Joseph Nagyvary of Texas A&M University, College Station, developed a method for treating wood that, in the opinion of music critics and professional violinists, gives his custom-made stringed instruments very nearly the same sound as the products of Stradivari, Amati, and Guarneri. Using elemental analysis Nagyvary discovered that the wood of the best Cremonese instruments was partly mineralized and hardened, apparently from soaks in a variety of mineral solutions, a common preservation treatment employed by furniture makers of the time. By contrast, modern instrument-making wisdom calls for untreated wood.

Under the electron microscope the old wood revealed another surprise: most of the tubular, air-filled cellular units making up the wood were open on their ends. Normally when wood is cut and dried, a component of tree sap called pectin seals the cell ends and solidifies. According to Nagyvary, these microscopic closed chambers are responsible for much of the harshness of modern instruments. The mineral soaks of the Cremonese masters must have dissolved the pectin from the cells, an effect Nagyvary duplicated in treating wood for his own instruments. Furthermore, after analyzing the tough, non-oily varnish that he found on the old instruments, Nagyvary developed a varnish based on the natural chitin armor of insects and crustaceans, which he felt had less vibration-dampening effect than modern instrument coatings.

Degradable plastic. To bring marginal desert lands into agricultural use Israeli farmers lay plastic sheeting on their fields. The sheets retain scarce soil moisture and keep young plants warm during cold desert nights; in this way some summer crops can be planted as much as six weeks earlier than usual. Nevertheless, picking up the sheets before harvesting is time-consuming, and missed pieces interfere with harvesting machinery. While working at Kibbutz Hazorea, a communal farm in northern Israel, Israeli polymer engineer Dan Gilead and British chemist Gerald Scott modified plastic by adding ferric dialkyldithiocarbonate to produce a sheeting called Plastor that is stable on shelves but slowly decomposes under the Sun's ultraviolet rays. The additive protects the plastic from these rays but only for one to seven months, depending on the farmer's needs, whereupon it becomes brittle and cracks. The pieces do not interfere with harvesting and can be plowed under the soil, where they disintegrate into simple carbon compounds and water. The new plastic is currently being tested on American, Australian, and Puerto Rican farms.

—George B. Kauffman

Defense research

When Ronald Reagan took office as president of the United States in January 1981, his administration began an analysis of U.S. strategic forces that broadened considerably the overall program of the predecessor administration of Pres. Jimmy Carter and dismissed a fragile, hard-won plan for the deployment of a major Carter weapon, the MX intercontinental ballistic missile (ICBM). Within a year the Reagan Pentagon had replaced the Carter plan for basing the MX with a phased but indefinite plan of its own. A year later the U.S. Congress rejected that approach, and the administration began the search for a successor. That search, by a presidential Commission on Strategic Forces, produced in 1983 a basing plan found acceptable only after the virtual abandonment of the principal goal of all earlier plans—elimination of the vulnerability of U.S. ICBM's to an attack by ICBM's of the Soviet Union.

This vulnerability was a major reason for the full-scale engineering development of the MX, which began in 1979. The Minuteman ICBM, then as now the most modern U.S. ICBM in operation, was deployed during the 1960s. In the 1970s some 550 of the 1,000 missiles were converted into Minuteman IIIs, each with three nuclear warheads instead of one. These multiple, independently targetable reentry vehicles, or MIRV's, were made possible by technological advances in the inertial navigation systems that determine how accurately warheads can be delivered to their targets over intercontinental distances. Increased accuracy made it possible to use a smaller, lighter, less powerful warhead with no loss in destructiveness to the target.

Two achievements by the Soviet Union during the 1970s led the Carter administration to develop the MX. The Soviets fortified (hardened) many of their most important military installations, particularly the launch silos of their most effective ICBM's, to the extent that the Minuteman III's combination of accuracy and explosive power could not be counted on to destroy them. In addition, the Soviets surprised the U.S. with missile accuracy improvements of their own. During the mid-1970s they introduced into service three new ICBM's, designated the SS-17, SS-18, and SS-19, having up to four, ten, and six MIRVed warheads per missile, respectively. U.S. intelligence concluded that the most accurate versions of the SS-18 and SS-19 could destroy U.S. ICBM silos and that the Soviets could "kill" most of the 1,000 Minuteman ICBM's in their silos while keeping ICBM's of their own in reserve. By the time of the MX basing debates of 1980–83 the Pentagon had counted 308 SS-18s and 330 SS-19s.

To be sure, these advances did not threaten U.S. submarine-launched ballistic missiles (SLBM's). The

MX Peacekeeper missile is thrust out of its canister by steam. During its first flight, in June 1983, the missile traveled 4,100 nautical miles to its target.

Poseidon missile, introduced in 1970, and the longer-range Trident I, introduced in 1979, remained a secure retaliatory force and would continue to do so unless and until the Soviets discover how to find the nuclear submarines that carry them. Long-range bomber aircraft, taking off on warning of an attack, could fly bombing missions, and in 1982 the U.S. Air Force began equipping them with cruise missiles, small missiles armed with a nuclear warhead and powered by a jet engine instead of a rocket. The bombers could launch cruise missiles outside the range of the increasingly formidable Soviet air defenses.

What the ICBM's offered that the other weapons did not was, in Pentagon parlance, prompt, hard-target kill capability. Aircraft dropping bombs can destroy hard targets and so, in some cases, can cruise missiles, but neither can do so "promptly"; each takes hours rather than minutes to reach its targets. SLBM's travel as fast as ICBM's, but their moving launch platforms and other factors prevent them from being accurate enough to destroy hard targets. And Minuteman III itself, even if it were not vulnerable to an attack by Soviet ICBM's, was increasingly unable to challenge Soviet targets as they were hardened more and more effectively.

The Pentagon's MX planners relied on increased accuracy to make the new ICBM effective against hard targets and on increased size to enable it to deliver ten MIRVed warheads instead of three. To deal with vulnerability, they chose what was termed Multiple Protective Shelters (MPS) basing. In a strategic nuclear variation on the carnival shell game—a connotation that was derided during later debates—200 MX missiles were to be moved about and concealed among 4,600 aboveground shelters in Nevada and Utah. The shelters, fortified only minimally, would be separated enough so that the Soviets could not destroy two of them with a single warhead. If the location of the missiles could be concealed, the Soviets would have to attack all of the shelters to be sure of destroying those with missiles in them. Sending two warheads against each MX shelter to allow for misses, the Soviets would have to use 9,200 warheads to destroy the 200 MX missiles and the 2,000 MX warheads. If the Soviets responded by deploying additional missiles and warheads, then the U.S. could deploy more MX's and shelters and/or try to develop a ballistic missile defense system to protect the MX.

The greatest technical challenge of MPS was concealing the missiles from on-the-ground and space surveillance by the Soviets. Failure to accomplish this would enable the Soviets to ignore empty shelters and wipe out the MX's with 400 warheads instead of 9,200. For concealment to be effective empty shelters would have to be given the same "signature" as full ones—they would have to be kept at the same temperature, emit the same radiation, and be the same in all other characteristics that could be sensed remotely. The signature of each transporter vehicle used to move missiles from one shelter to another would have to be the same regardless of whether or not it contained a missile. Even if it was empty, the vehicle would have to cause the same ground vibrations while moving as it did when it was full. Alternatively, shelters and transporters might be made to vary unpredictably in their signatures, whether empty or full, so that the Soviets could draw no conclusions about observed differences.

MPS survived action by the U.S. Congress on the defense budget in 1980 but remained controversial, especially in Nevada and Utah, because of the large area of land it would consume. Ronald Reagan opposed MPS when he was a candidate for the presidency and scrapped it after he was elected. The new secretary of defense, Caspar Weinberger, commented that the Soviets could add warheads at no greater expense than the U.S. could expand MPS or defend it and that MPS might be delayed greatly or defeated altogether by threatened lawsuits in the deployment areas. The Pentagon launched a study of all strategic forces.

The resulting program, announced in October 1981, went far beyond MX. The Reagan administration decided to produce an updated version of the B-1 bomber, developed during the mid-1970s but kept out of production by President Carter, to replace the B-52 and preserve the ability to penetrate Soviet air defenses. An Advanced Technology Bomber, based on supersecret "Stealth" technology to minimize the ability of radar and other sensors to detect it, would be developed for the 1990s. The Trident II

SLBM, for the first time having accuracy sufficiently improved to destroy hardened targets from under the sea, would be developed for availability starting in 1989. Command, control, and communications systems serving strategic nuclear forces would be upgraded and, in particular, made more robust and survivable. Systems to detect a bomber attack on the U.S., and interceptor aircraft to defend against it, were to be modernized.

Decisively advocating all of these programs, the administration asked for more time to deal with the issue of basing the MX. It said that MX development should proceed without delay in order to permit deployment beginning in 1986, and it decided that these missiles should be placed on an interim basis in existing ICBM silos, modified as needed for MX. The administration and Congress would decide in 1984 either on a long-term, survivable basing mode for the missile or on a defense system for it. Basing systems under consideration included an aircraft that would be almost continuously airborne, flying for long periods and launching the missile while in flight; and facilities buried so deeply underground that missiles could survive any attack and be tunneled out through the debris. Both of these concepts would require technical advances never before demonstrated, and research was scheduled to begin at once to find out whether they were feasible.

Acting on the defense budget in 1982, Congress accepted all of the strategic program except MX basing. With Congress edging toward the position that the MX should be kept out of production until a long-term, survivable basing mode was chosen and approved, the administration offered to accelerate its long-term decisions and, late that year, put forward a

A U.S. Navy/General Dynamics Tomahawk surface-to-surface cruise missile is launched on a simulated land attack mission from the battleship USS "New Jersey" in May 1983.

A mock-up of the U.S. Air Force F-16 is tested for vulnerability to lightning. Simulated lightning is applied to the skin of the aircraft through wires from a generator.

concept that seemed to be wholly unrelated to what had gone before—Closely Spaced Basing, which came to be known as Dense Pack. The administration also gave the MX missile a name, Peacekeeper.

A product of studies of ballistic missile defense and of research on the superhardening that Soviet accomplishments had suggested was possible, Dense Pack relied on a concept of "fratricide," by which the first Soviet warhead to explode in an attack on the MX field would disable or render ineffective Soviet warheads that followed it. MX missiles would be contained in silos superhardened to withstand pressures of several thousand pounds per square inch. Silos that strong could be located within 600 m (2,000 ft) of one another without permitting the Soviets to destroy more than one MX per warhead. The explosion of a warhead attacking one silo would have a devastating effect on an unexploded warhead attacking an adjacent silo, however. The nuclear effects of such an explosion, which would occur virtually instantly, and the blast effects, including a cloud of dust and debris, which would develop within seconds and last for minutes, would disable nearby incoming warheads or deflect them from their targets. Most MX's would survive and could be launched soon after the attack; although a dust cloud would persist, missiles being launched through it would be traveling so slowly that they would not be affected by it. With MX missiles located in such a small area Soviet reentry vehicles trying to attack them would have to approach the MX field along so narrow a path that

they would be particularly vulnerable to interceptor missiles defending the site.

Congress was skeptical about this approach. The technical basis for it defied common sense; one did not protect one's eggs by putting them in a single, densely packed basket. The Pentagon conceded that its fratricide and superhardening assumptions remained to be demonstrated. As MX opponents in Congress pressed the attack on MX production funds, thereby threatening delay in deployment of the missile, the administration abandoned the Dense Pack concept and reverted to a time-honored device for resolving unsolvable problems: creation of an above-the-battle commission with credentials so respected and views so broad that its conclusions would outweigh any opposition opinion.

The resulting Commission on Strategic Forces represented one of the Reagan administration's few attempts to emphasize continuity in defense policy. For example, William Perry, undersecretary of defense for research and engineering in the Carter administration, was a member and Weinberger's predecessor, Harold Brown, was a consultant. The chairman was Brent Scowcroft, a former national security adviser. In what came to be regarded as a wise political decision the commission consulted congressional leaders as well as military and technical experts as it went about its work, thereby making its eventual conclusions less surprising and, perhaps, more palatable to those who carried the greatest weight in judging them.

In April 1983, only three months after it was formed, the commission recommended what Scowcroft termed "a fundamentally new departure." It said that 100 MX's should be deployed in existing Minuteman III silos near Francis E. Warren Air Force Base in Wyoming and Nebraska as a short-term measure to demonstrate "national will and cohesion," reduce the imbalance in the superpowers' capabilities against hardened targets, and induce the Soviets to accept attempts to increase stability through arms control. Arms control, it said, should be based on the number of warheads and perhaps on the destructive yield of the weapons, as well as on the number of launchers, because emphasis on launchers alone had promoted MIRVing. As the most fundamental of its departures the commission recommended development of a small, single-warhead ICBM for availability in 1993. Its size would maximize the options for basing the missile and minimize the value to the Soviets of destroying any single missile in an attack.

The Air Force and the Department of Defense accepted the commission's recommendations without exception or reservation and sent them to Congress. MX opponents and silo-basing skeptics noted immediately that the search for survivable MX basing had ended in failure—MX ICBM's in Minuteman silos would be just as vulnerable as Minuteman ICBM's in Minuteman silos—and the administration conceded the point readily. Weinberger acknowledged that the belief for most of a decade that a survivable basing mode could be devised was unfounded: "By now it is clear that this was an illusion."

The commission took the position, however, that this did not really matter and would not matter until the Soviets could make their SLBM's accurate enough to destroy hardened targets. The U.S. would be able to do this with Trident II no sooner than 1989, and Scowcroft estimated that the Soviets would need a few years more than that. Current Soviet SLBM's could be effective against bomber bases, and their flight times from launch points off the U.S. coast would be much shorter than those of ICBM's launched from the Soviet Union. However, only ICBM accuracy would be effective against Minuteman or MX silos.

The dilemma for the Soviets, as seen by the commission, was their inability either to attack U.S. ICBM's effectively with their own ICBM's without giving the U.S. bombers enough warning to escape or to attack the bombers effectively without giving the U.S. time to launch its ICBM's. If Soviet SLBM's and ICBM's were launched simultaneously against bombers and ICBM silos, respectively, the SLBM's would arrive at the bomber bases first and U.S. ICBM's could be launched following this physical evidence of an attack without fear of a mistaken response to a false alarm. If Soviet SLBM's were launched later than the ICBM's in order to strike bomber bases and ICBM silos simultaneously, the bombers could be scrambled on the first warning of the ICBM launches. In this case the U.S. ICBM's would be lost, but the bombers would survive because of the delayed SLBM launch. Only when all U.S. land targets can be attacked by SLBM's, with no disparity of flight times, will the Soviets be able to challenge U.S. hardened silos and soft bomber bases equally and simultaneously. By then, under the commission's recommendations, U.S. deployment of the small, proliferated, single-warhead ICBM would have begun.

Congress debated ICBM issues throughout 1983 and at the end of the year approved production of the MX and its deployment as recommended by the Scowcroft commission. It adopted measures intended to prevent the administration from abandoning devel-

Electric-powered Sikorsky S-52 helicopter undergoes ground testing. Lead acid batteries drive four motors that are connected to a single shaft and provide 245 hp.

Courtesy, Orlando Helicopter Airways and Kaylor Energy Products, Menlo Park, Calif.

opment of the small ICBM. Thus the years of search for an MX basing mode ended only after what had been considered its essential characteristic, survivability, was abandoned.

—David F. Bond

Earth sciences

The effects of the eruption of the Mexican volcano El Chichón and of the unusually strong El Niño in the Pacific Ocean occupied the attention of Earth scientists in many disciplines during the past year. Other subjects of research included the remote sensing of phenomena by satellites, the long-range prediction of earthquakes, and the extinction of species.

Atmospheric sciences

During 1983 four areas of atmospheric science achieved particular advances. These were the monitoring of the atmosphere, the modeling and simulation of the atmosphere, the investigation of inadvertent climate change, and the distribution of weather information to the public.

Monitoring the weather. The Wave Propagation Laboratory of the National Oceanographic and Atmospheric Administration (NOAA) in Boulder, Colo., continued the development and testing of an atmospheric remote profiler system that provides almost continuous measurements of wind and, somewhat less accurately, of moisture and temperature throughout the lowest 10 km (6 mi) of the atmosphere. The winds are estimated by using an upward-looking Doppler radar, while temperature and moisture profiles are evaluated by using a vertically pointing radiometer. Used in conjunction with temperature soundings from satellites, the profilers may make upper-air balloon soundings obsolete.

Also under development was a Doppler radar system referred to as NEXRAD (Next Generation Radar). In contrast to current weather radar systems NEXRAD will monitor the wind flow within the atmospheric boundary layer in addition to estimating the intensity of rain and snowfall. (The atmospheric boundary layer is the thin layer of air near the Earth's surface within which the wind distribution is directly influenced by friction due to the ground.) The prototype NEXRAD system was proposed to be installed at the National Severe Storms Laboratory in Norman, Okla., where much of the U.S. research on severe convective storms has taken place.

During the summer of 1983 an experimental program utilized Doppler radar, profilers, and other meteorological measurement systems in order to determine if improved prediction of severe convective storms could be achieved. Part of an effort called the Program for Regional Observing and Forecast-

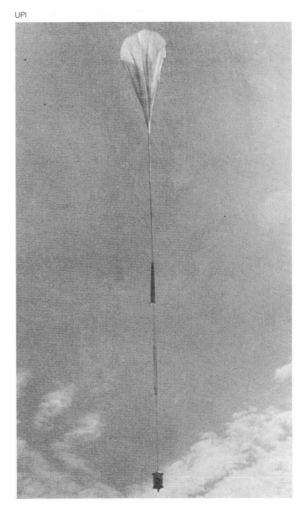

A balloon 135 m (450 ft) in height lifts a gondola containing scientific instruments that will study the ozone layer in the Earth's upper atmosphere.

ing Services, the investigation was organized by the Environmental Research Laboratories in Boulder. Probability forecasts for severe thunderstorms and tornadoes were made for several sectors of eastern Colorado, with chase teams using vans and automobiles sent out to verify forecasts. Initial evidence suggested that the new monitoring tools did help meteorologists improve their forecasts of severe storms.

Imagery from the Geostationary Earth Satellite (GOES) located 35,800 km (22,245 mi) above the Equator showed that during the summer thunderstorms preferentially develop over mountainous terrain in Montana and Colorado and then move out over the Great Plains during the afternoon as a result of the westerly winds which typically blow at that latitude. The composite imagery shows great promise for providing improved weather forecasts.

Modeling and simulation of the atmosphere. The application of computer models to simulate atmo-

279

spheric flow began in the early 1950s. The current high-speed supercomputers such as the Cray 1 and Cyber 205 permit large and comprehensive model simulations to be made. During the past year a series of comparisons were made using such models at several national centers and research institutes in the U.S., Canada, Europe, and Japan. Forecast accuracy for as many as seven days in the future was achieved with the models, although even after the first day certain aspects of the atmospheric circulation pattern were incorrectly predicted. The source of these errors appeared to be related to the inability of scientists to monitor adequately the initial state of the atmosphere.

On a smaller scale, simulation models of the Earth's planetary boundary layer received heightened attention during 1983. Referred to as large-eddy simulation models, they were designed to resolve the dominant energy-containing turbulent eddies in the lower kilometers of the atmosphere. The understanding of turbulent processes is essential in order to achieve better weather and climate predictions. A working group organized in 1983 by John Wyngaard of the Mesoscale Research Section of the U.S. National Center for Atmospheric Research was leading the effort to expand the use of large-eddy simulation models.

Intermediate between the scales discussed above is a range of atmospheric motions called the mesoscale, which have horizontal scales on the order of ten to several hundred kilometers. In 1983 a U.S. initiative referred to as STORM (for Stormscale Operational and Research Meteorology), organized by George Benton, Rick Anthes, and others working with the University Corporation for Atmospheric Research in Boulder completed reports and meetings designed to focus attention on the nation's mesoscale program. The first major STORM research project, referred to as STORM-Central, was designed to investigate large mesoscale clusters of thunderstorms and rain that frequently develop over the Great Plains of the U.S. during the summer. These features, referred to as mesoscale convective systems, contribute substantially to the total number of severe thunderstorms that occur over that part of the U.S.

Inadvertent climate change. The sensitivity of the Earth's climate to natural and man-made effects continued to receive considerable attention in 1983. As reported by the Climate Analysis Center of NOAA, the major Pacific Ocean anomaly called the El Niño/ Southern Oscillation decreased dramatically in both magnitude and extent during the Northern Hemispheric summer of 1983, after being dominant in influencing the unusual atmospheric circulation pattern during the preceding winter and spring. The term El Niño refers to a major warming of the surface water along the South American Pacific coast associated with the reduction or elimination of the large-scale wind flow parallel to the coast. This wind change occurs because of a substantial change in the atmospheric pressure pattern across the tropical Pacific Ocean (hence the name Southern Oscillation).

The effects of the El Niño/Southern Oscillation are worldwide. Bill Gray of Colorado State University, for example, correctly predicted that there would be fewer tropical storms than normal in the Atlantic Ocean in 1983, based on climatological data from previous seasons in which an El Niño preceded the fall Atlantic hurricane season.

The influence on climate of the eruption of the El Chichón volcano in Mexico in 1982 appeared to continue throughout 1983 and into 1984. This volcano ejected into the stratosphere large volumes of the gas sulfur dioxide, which was then converted to sulfuric-acid droplets a few tenths of a micrometer (millionth of a meter) in diameter. These particles act to reduce the solar radiation that reaches the Earth's surface and to warm the stratosphere. Alan Robock of the University of Maryland suggested that an average surface cooling of as much as about 0.4° C could occur over the Northern Hemisphere in 1983 and from 0.4° to 0.5° C in 1984 and 1985. Robock suggested that even after ten years cooling as a result of the volcanic eruption would persist,

Rows of air samplers are inspected. They are to be used to study how the pollutants that may contribute to acid rain are dispersed by winds.

although it would be of a smaller magnitude. (For another view and an extended discussion of the effect of volcanic eruptions on climate, *see* Feature Article: PURPLE SKIES AND COOLING SEAS: VOLCANISM AND CLIMATE.)

During 1983 a number of both Soviet and U.S. scientists suggested that a major nuclear exchange between the superpowers would cause even greater climatic change. They postulated that the enormous volumes of dirt and smoke that would be ejected into the upper atmosphere and stratosphere by surface thermonuclear releases and the conflagrations following such an exchange would darken the sky for an extended period, reducing the sunlight reaching the ground and thereby resulting in subfreezing temperatures at the surface throughout much of the world, even in the summer. The protagonists of this view claimed that the massive "human volcano" effect could cause the extinction of human life. This scenario became the subject of considerable debate, with a number of scientists suggesting that the model used to estimate the meteorological impact of a thermonuclear war was much too simplistic.

The subject of acid rain continued to receive widespread attention during the past year. In the U.S. federal legislation to limit sulfur emissions from power plants was urged. Sulfur dioxide from power plants is considered to be one of the major precursors of and contributors to acid rain. A major controversy concerning acid rain, however, focused on the relationship between the sources of the acid material and the eventual receptors. The question that arose was whether all the material is transported over long distances or is some of it recirculated locally. A limited attempt to answer this question was the Cross Appalachian Transport Experiment conducted during the fall of 1983. The tracer material perfluorocarbon was released into the atmosphere in Dayton, Ohio, on five occasions and in Sudbury, Ont., twice. By sampling the atmosphere downwind of the release areas, scientists hoped to determine the trajectories of the acid material.

Concern regarding the impact of the steady increases of carbon dioxide on the Earth's atmosphere continued in 1983. The U.S. Environmental Protection Agency released reports in the fall which suggested that by 2100 the average global temperature could increase by 5° C (9° F) with an associated rise in global sea level of between 144 cm (4.8 ft) and 217 cm (7 ft) as a result of the increased levels of carbon dioxide and other trace gases put into the atmosphere primarily through the burning of fossil fuels. These gases act to reduce the emission of longwave radiation out into space yet still permit solar radiation to reach the Earth's surface. This mechanism of heat increase is referred to as the "greenhouse effect." At about the same time the U.S. National Research Council (NRC) issued a somewhat more conservative report on the same subject, which emphasized the remaining uncertainties in estimating the effect of carbon dioxide and other trace gases on climate. The report concluded, for instance, that if deforestation has contributed significantly to the increase in carbon dioxide during recent decades, then existing models that project future atmospheric concentrations based on man-made sources may overpredict the fraction of carbon dioxide remaining airborne. The NRC report concluded that existing evidence does not support a change away from fossil fuels but did suggest that some priority be given to the enhancement of long-term energy options that do not involve the combustion of such fuels.

Increased levels of aerosols in the upper atmosphere and lower stratosphere that are associated with high levels of industrial activity could counter the greenhouse effect of high levels of carbon dioxide. This possibility was not adequately examined in either of the studies. These aerosols appear to be ejected into the upper atmosphere and stratosphere via deep cumulus clouds, a process that is referred to as cloud venting.

Weather information. Two major changes in the ways in which weather information is distributed to the public received recognition in 1983. *The Weather Channel,* distributed via cable television, provided continuous 24-hour weather analyses and forecasting to about 11,200,000 subscribers in the U.S. as of December 1983. National Weather Service warnings and watches were relayed routinely as part of the broadcasts. Also, a full one-page discussion of past weather, a national forecast, and specific city forecasts were prepared during the week by *USA Today,* a national daily newspaper. Color graphics were used to make the treatment more effective.

These two mechanisms to distribute weather information represented major deviations from past efforts at public communication. They may herald a new era in the dissemination of meteorological analyses and forecasts.

—Roger A. Pielke

Geological sciences

No major theoretical breakthrough occurred in geology during the past year, which is to say that it was like almost every other year. It has become fashionable since the publication of Thomas Kuhn's *Structure of Scientific Revolutions* in 1962 to call almost any scientific change a revolution. An examination of the history of science will plainly reveal, however, that fundamental conceptual changes of the kind that occupied Kuhn's attention are much rarer than anything likely to be reflected in an annual report. On the other hand, 1983 was a year in which there

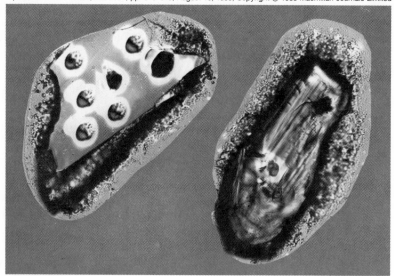

From "Ion Microprobe Identification of 4,100–4,200 Myr-old Terrestrial Zircons," D. O. Froude, T. R. Ireland, P. D. Kinny, I. S. Williams, W. Compston, I. R. Williams, and J. S. Myers, reprinted by permission from *Nature*, vol. 5927, pp. 616–618, August 18, 1983, Copyright © 1983 Macmillan Journals Limited

Photomicrographs reveal two zircons with ages estimated at 4.1 billion (left) and 3.5 billion (right) years. The older of the two is one of several rocks, discovered near Mount Narryer in Australia, that are by far the most ancient yet found on Earth.

was a great deal of exciting and significant geological activity. It involved the use of highly sophisticated techniques drawn from various scientific disciplines, both within and without geology, that were brought to bear upon the solution of complex problems.

Geology and geochemistry. The decline in petroleum exploration in the U.S., which began after a peak of activity in 1981, continued in 1983 with consequent effects upon those parts of the geological community most closely associated with the petroleum industry. The director of a school of geology that had trained many petroleum geologists through the years reported a decline of 60% in freshmen enrollment in geology programs in 1983. Several petroleum geologists offered the opinion that the search for oil would quicken during the next two years but that exploration activity would not equal the peak achieved in 1981.

Mass extinctions. Some of the most dramatic developments in geology during 1983 were not associated with immediate economic factors but rather with long-standing conceptual issues whose relevance to practical affairs was, at best, remote. For example, the problem of mass extinctions in the history of life and their relationship to catastrophic geological events has been of almost perennial interest during the past 200 years. Current concern with the issue began with the introduction of the hypothesis in 1980 by Luis Alvarez, Walter Alvarez, Frank Asaro, and Helen Michel that an asteroid had struck the Earth with dramatic consequences for plants and animals about 65 million years ago.

The asteroid-impact hypothesis has been a controversial one since it was first proposed. Attempts have been made to explain the high concentrations of iridium, osmium, and other platinum-group metals in sediments deposited about 65 million years ago

in terms of other events. It is now generally conceded that an event of great magnitude is necessary to account for the unique concentrations of metals in these 65-million-year-old rocks which mark the boundary between the Cretaceous and Tertiary periods. Recent isotope studies indicate that the asteroid impact provides a better explanation than some other cataclysmic event such as an explosive volcanic eruption. (For additional information see *1982 Yearbook of Science and the Future* Feature Article: OF DINOSAURS AND ASTEROIDS.)

A conference on the dynamics of extinction at Northern Arizona University in Flagstaff in August 1983 reflected the fact that interest in mass extinction had broadened since the introduction of the asteroid-impact hypothesis. Although the possible role of such an impact at the end of the Cretaceous Period continued to be considered, interest in the causal factors in mass extinction had widened to include other mechanisms during other times in the Earth's history.

The hypothesis that some species had become extinct was an especially significant one in the history of geological science, because, unlike many hypotheses concerning the history of life, it could be plausibly tested by paleontology. The recognition by naturalists in the late 18th and early 19th centuries that certain fossils represented the remains of animals that were not known to live anywhere on Earth at that time provided compelling evidence for the extinction of species. The recognition of such extinctions was an important factor in the change from an older steady-state view of the history of animals and plants to the modern progressivist belief. The link between extinction and catastrophes was established at the outset, because the early 19th-century naturalists assumed that an effect so profound as the extinction of a species required a cause of commensurate magnitude.

With the publication of Charles Darwin's book on the origin of species in 1859, theories of extinction began to take on something like their present form. Acceptance of the evolutionary hypothesis entailed, in the first place, that many species would cease to exist not by being obliterated in some cataclysm but by being transformed into another species. The theory of evolution by means of natural selection did not, moreover, require some catastrophic event to explain extinction. Darwin contended that a species might become extinct simply because it did not produce the heritable variation needed to meet changing environmental conditions. He noted that what appeared to be evidence of mass extinction might result from long intervals of time between the deposition of fossil-bearing sediments. Although Darwin did not reject the possibility that events such as volcanic eruptions might contribute to the extinction of a species, his view of extinction was, because of his theoretical commitments, remarkably free of catastrophic events as causal agents.

Difficulties have always plagued attempts to employ fossils in the testing of historical hypotheses. The notorious problems presented by the incompleteness of the fossil record have recently been alleviated by the recovery, in the course of deep-sea drilling, of increasing numbers of fossils from marine sediments. The sediments of the ocean basins represent a record of nearly uninterrupted sedimentation in contrast to the record of separated episodes in continental sediments. Paleontologists have begun to exploit this recently available record. John Sepkoski and David Raup, both of the University of Chicago, reported on their efforts to identify episodes of extinction among families of marine organisms throughout the Phanerozoic Eon, roughly the last 500 million years. Their elaborate statistical analysis led them to recognize a "normal" rate of extinction of from three to five families of plants and animals per million years. In addition to this background extinction there have been five mass extinctions with rates as high as almost 20 families per million years and five mass extinctions of lesser magnitude. Sepkoski began a long-term study of the extinction of genera by means of which he expected to increase the precision of his analysis.

A dramatic result of the investigation by Sepkoski and Raup was their recognition of an apparent periodicity of mass extinctions during part of the time span they were studying. Their data seem to indicate that during the past 240 million years there has been a 26-million-year cycle of mass extinctions. Many geologists and paleontologists have expressed serious doubts about this suggestion. Sepkoski and Raup were aware that this rather astonishing periodicity may reflect a statistical condition rather than the actual course of events. Even if the periodicity holds up under continued statistical and taxonomic scrutiny, ultimate support for the hypothesis would have to await the formulation of a satisfactory explanation of the extinctions and their periodicity in terms of some internal or external causal factors.

A case of the extinction of land animals that is well documented involves the disappearance of many species of large mammals at the end of the ice age, about 10,000 years ago. A number of attempts to explain this dramatic event were presented at the conference. Russell Graham of the Illinois State Museum at Springfield suggested that the fragmentation of plant communities at the end of the ice age, rather than simply their geographic displacement, may have been a significant factor in the extinction of animals that were adapted to the ecological integrity of the plant communities. Paul Martin of the University of Arizona defended the view that hunting by man contributed significantly to the extinction of large mammals. More work remains to be done before this most recent episode of mass extinction can be fully understood.

Uniformity of nature. Another venerable geological issue was raised in connection with the current interest in mass extinction. Since the late 18th century the uniformity of nature has been a matter of vigorous debate among geologists. Although James Hutton (1726–97) of Scotland was by no means the first to introduce the assumption of the uniformity of nature into geological inferences, he was able to see the methodological issues attending the problem of uniformity with great clarity. He said in 1795, for example, "we are not to make nature act in violation of that order which we actually observe."

A number of writers who have considered the status of the uniformitarian principle in 20th-century geology have concluded, following Hutton, that geologists do, or if they do not, should, assume that no event may occur in the history of the Earth which violates the principles of contemporary physical theory. Stated in this way, the principle of uniformity appears not to be a special assumption of geology but simply a rather conventional view about the nature of science.

In an account of a meeting on the dynamics of extinction Erle Kauffman of the University of Colorado stated that "It is a great philosophical breakthrough for geologists to accept catastrophe as a normal part of Earth history." At the same meeting Jerre Lipps of the University of California at Davis is reported to have said, "We have to accept asteroid impacts as part of the uniformitarian process."

There is no reason to think that there is a philosophical breakthrough involved in supposing that there have been such catastrophes as asteroid im-

The volcanoes Kilauea (above) and Mauna Loa (below) erupt on the island of Hawaii in March 1984. The two had not erupted simultaneously for more than 100 years.

pacts in the past, if by philosophical breakthrough is meant the abandonment of some widely held fundamental principle. Although the change in attitude among geologists about the role of events of great magnitude in the history of the Earth should not be regarded as conceptually revolutionary, its significance should not be overlooked. There is no question that geologists and paleontologists are much more inclined to invoke "catastrophic" events in their historical explanations than they were even as recently as a decade ago. Changes in climates of opinion can be as significant in shaping the character of a science as can be fundamental conceptual changes.

Volcanoes. The volcanic activity that has continued at Mt. St. Helens in Washington since the initial explosive eruption of May 18, 1980, has provided an unusual opportunity for devising and testing methods for the prediction of explosive volcanic episodes. The large eruption of May 18, 1980, was followed by a smaller one a week later that had not been predicted. D. A. Swanson, J. T. Casadevall, D. Dzurisin, C. G. Newhall, and C. S. Weaver of the United States Geological Survey and S. D. Malone of the University of Washington reported that each of the other 13 eruptions occurring between June 1980 and the end of 1982 were predicted anywhere from a few tens of minutes to a few hours before the event. More significant from a social and economic point of view is the fact that seven eruptions starting in 1981 were predicted at least three days and as much as three weeks before the event. There were no incorrect predictions during the period in question. The predictions were based largely upon local seismic activity and upon deformation of the lava dome and crater floor.

A U.S. Geological Survey report by R. A. Bailey, P. R. Beauchemin, F. P. Kapinos, and D. W. Klick entitled *The Volcano Hazards Program: Objectives and Long-Range Plans* represented an attempt to identify volcanoes that are likely to erupt in the future. The assessment of the likelihood of future eruptions at particular sites is based largely on the frequency of eruptive behavior as judged from volcanic rocks, and on the monitoring of seismic activity. The report identified a group of volcanoes that have erupted on an average of every 200 years or less or have erupted during the past 300 years, or both. This high-risk group includes Mt. St. Helens, Mono-Inyo Craters and Mt. Shasta in California, Mt. Rainier and Mt. Baker in Washington, and Mt. Hood in Oregon. In the case of Mt. Baker steaming from holes known as fumaroles has increased in the last few years.

Mineral exploration. At a time when highly sophisticated technology dominates the search for minerals, it was refreshing to learn that methods which rely upon the unaided senses of living beings, though not human beings, may still prove to be useful. R. R. Brooks of Massey University in New Zealand reported that animals have been found to be useful in mineral prospecting. In 1964 Aarno Kahma of the Geological Survey of Finland trained an Alsatian (German shepherd) dog to locate sulfide-rich minerals by scent. Since then the technique has been exported to Sweden and Canada with some success. Studies have also been undertaken to test the possibility that the mineral content of an area might be assessed from an analysis of the chemical composition of the internal organs of insects and fish.

—David B. Kitts

Geophysics. Earthquakes and volcanoes caused widespread devastation and loss of life during the past year. Earth scientists continued their efforts to better understand the workings of the Earth and mitigate the hazards posed by these destructive events.

Volcanoes. Eruptions of more than 30 volcanoes in 18 countries were reported during the past year. Unlike earthquakes, which send out waves that can be recorded at distant stations, the detection of volcanic activity rests primarily on visual observation. Because of this a number of eruptions are undoubtedly not detected, particularly those occurring beneath the surface of the oceans.

That such submarine volcanic activity does take place is unquestioned. During the past year several ships reported encountering rafts of pumice (a frothy, light rock sometimes formed during eruptions) floating on the sea; people on New Britain Island reported a glow in the ocean and a roar resembling that of a jet airplane coming from the sea; and pressure sensors in the ocean near Polynesia in the southwest Pacific recorded acoustic waves that had their origin in the MacDonald seamount. This seamount has undergone eight eruptions since its discovery in 1967 (the discovery was based on acoustic waves from an eruption). One of the most damaging eruptions during the year took place on the island of Una Una in Indonesia. An explosive eruption in July subjected 80% of the island to temperatures greater than 200° C (390° F), burning all of the 700,000 coconut trees, all the livestock, and all the homes. Fortunately, a series of smaller eruptions and earthquakes had prompted an evacuation of the island before the devastating explosion, and so no human lives were lost.

Most of the volcanoes that erupted during the past year were distributed around the rim of the Pacific Ocean basin. A notable exception was Mt. Etna in Sicily. Periodically active for many hundreds of years, it had an eruption in 1983 that lasted for 131 days and resulted in the extrusion of about 75 million cu cm (4.5 million cu in) of lava. No lives were lost. Various partially successful attempts were made to block and divert the lava flow. These included the construction of embankments to stop the flow and artificial explosions to help divert the flow into specially built runoff channels.

Another volcanic area in Italy has the potential for causing significant damage in the near future. The Campi Flegrei near Naples consist of a number of vents within an ancient caldera. Volcanic eruptions have occurred there a number of times. Tide-gauge records and leveling surveys in this now densely populated area showed that a general trend of ground subsidence was reversed in 1970, when an uplift of as much as 5 mm per day occurred near the town of Pozzuoli. This initial high rate then decreased until late 1982, when an uplift of several millimeters per day began and continued into 1984. Accompanying the uplift was a dramatic increase in shallow, small earthquakes. The best explanation for these phenomena is that they are caused by the swelling of a chamber of magma (molten rock) some 3 km (1.8 mi) below the Earth's surface; the swelling, in turn, is a result of continued injection into the chamber of magma from a deeper reservoir. Especially disturbing in connection with the uplift is an eruption that took place in this area in 1538. A reliable record of surface deformation at that time is available from holes produced by marine organisms in three marble columns of the ruins of a Roman marketplace, as well as from historical records. These data indicate that the 1538 eruption was preceded by several meters of uplift.

The Long Valley region of California bears many similarities to the Campi Flegrei, including renewed activity in an ancient caldera, swelling of the ground surface, and the occurrence of earthquake swarms. During the past year the seismicity and ground uplift in the Long Valley region decreased in comparison

A woman mourns her dead children in the town of Erzurum in northeastern Turkey. The town and many nearby villages were devastated in October 1983 by an earthquake that measured 7.1 on the Richter scale.

with previous years. The significance of this in terms of potential eruptive activity was not clear, and the area continued to be intensively monitored by many geophysical measurements.

Earthquakes. In 1983 there were fewer large earthquakes and fewer deaths from earthquakes than usual. The number of deaths and the number of large earthquakes is not necessarily correlated, for many deaths are caused by moderate earthquakes in regions where construction of poor quality exists. During the past year more than 2,000 people died in earthquakes, but only about 124 of these perished in the nine earthquakes having surface-wave magnitudes greater than or equal to 7.0. More than half of the deaths resulted from an earthquake on October 30 in eastern Turkey. This event destroyed nearly 50 villages and left 25,000 people homeless. Rescue efforts were hampered by road closings and bad weather.

In the United States two people died in an earthquake that occurred in central Idaho. The most significant U.S. earthquake, however, took place near the town of Coalinga, Calif., and destroyed or damaged beyond repair 90% of the town's business section and 20% of the houses. Amazingly, there were no deaths. The damage was largely due to unreinforced masonry construction of poor quality and to inadequate connections between the buildings and their foundations. These inadequacies had long been known, and the damage came as no surprise. What was a surprise was that an earthquake of that size (magnitude 6.5 on the Richter scale) should occur

in a region away from a recognized large fault. The earthquake took place about 35 km (22 mi) northeast of the San Andreas Fault. The fault on which it occurred did not rupture the ground surface, as usually happens in California earthquakes of that size. Therefore, studies of the fault mechanism had to be done from remote observations, using seismic waves recorded on seismographs and distortions of the Earth's surface revealed by precise geodetic surveys. In 1984 these studies were underway. Probably the most important lesson is that even in California, with its well-defined major faults, moderate earthquakes can occur in places where they would not be predicted.

Ironically, although there were few seismological instruments in the vicinity of the Coalinga earthquake, it occurred only about 40 km (25 mi) from the most densely instrumented part of any fault in the world—the region of the San Andreas Fault near the small town of Parkfield, Calif. Moderate earthquakes with similar characteristics have occurred there with surprising regularity: 1857, 1881, 1901, 1922, 1934, and 1966. On this basis, and by studying the amount of slip released in the previous earthquakes and assuming a constant strain rate, the next in the series is expected in 1988 (with a margin of uncertainty of several years).

The previous Parkfield earthquakes occurred along a section of the San Andreas Fault that is in transition from being locked to the southeast and creeping to the northwest. The size of the earthquakes seems to be controlled by some small but distinct geometrical irregularities in the fault trace. These features, along with the sparse habitation of the region and ease of access to it, made it a natural laboratory in which to study both the mechanisms that produce earthquakes and earthquake prediction. To this end many sensitive instruments were installed in the area and were being continuously or periodically monitored. They included creepmeters along the fault, more than 20 seismometers to pinpoint the locations of earthquakes (including the very small events occurring every few days), laser devices to measure the deformation of the crust in the vicinity, and about 50 rugged accelerographs to record the strong shaking associated with large earthquakes.

Tectonics. Scientists' understanding of how continents were formed is undergoing a revolution that many believe ranks with the increased understanding of ocean basins that followed from the development of plate tectonics. The basic idea is that mountainous areas along the edges of continents have grown by the progressive addition of crustal fragments. This model owes much to geophysical measurements and helps explain the previously bewildering geological observation that adjacent mountain blocks are often geologically distinct, being bounded by faults.

Termed accretionary tectonics, the model reached its fullest development in studies of the mountain ranges stretching along western North America from Mexico to Alaska. Paleobiologic studies of fossils within rocks in these ranges and paleomagnetic studies of the orientation of the Earth's magnetic field, imprinted in the rocks at the time of their formation, imply that the rocks in these geologically distinct mountain ranges—now called "terranes"—traveled from hundreds to thousands of kilometers to their present locations and rotated with respect to one another as a result of jostling en route. For example, rocks now in large areas of Alaska came from near the Equator.

The geophysical measurements that have aided in the development of accretionary tectonics include the previously mentioned paleomagnetic studies (which also played a key role in the formation of plate tectonics) and the study of crustal structure in which scientists use the travel times of seismic waves that echo from contrasting varieties of rocks. The sources of the seismic waves include conventional explosions and vibrations that are set up by the vertical oscillations of specially built vehicles. These techniques were used to map out variations in

Sheriff's deputy and his bloodhound leave the ruins of a building in Coalinga, California, that was destroyed by an earthquake in May 1983. The dog searched for persons trapped in the wreckage.

the thickness of the Earth's crust, and they revealed the unsuspected presence of low-angle thrust faults in the crust that extend for hundreds of kilometers. In effect, these thrust faults form boundaries along which separation of the layers (delamination) of the crust can occur; their presence helps make the highly mobile character of the "terranes" easier to understand.

The new conceptual framework embodied by accretionary tectonics has resulted from interdisciplinary and multinational studies. The recent joint Sino-French field studies of the tectonics of Tibet stand as a good example of what can be accomplished by cooperative research. It has been recognized for some time that Tibet holds important clues to understanding the collision between India and Asia that formed the Himalayas. The crustal thickness of 70 km (44 mi) under Tibet is twice that of normal crust, and it was thought that this was caused by the underplating of Asian crust by the crust of the Indian subcontinent as a result of the collision. Recent seismic and geologic work, however, revealed that a more complex situation existed. It appears that several "terranes" are involved and that the thickness of the Tibetan plateau may be caused by the squeezing of Tibet between northern Asia and India along with delamination and subsequent underthrusting of Indian crust. The squeezing of Tibet also produced extensive horizontal deformation, which is similar in effect to that of toothpaste being squeezed out of a tube.

Multinational and interdisciplinary studies, of which the Tibet experiment is just one example, are in their infancy. In the years to come they should provide an increasingly clear view of the geologic history of the Earth's surface.

—David M. Boore

Hydrological sciences

The powerful El Niño of 1982–83, a current of warm water that spread westward in the Pacific Ocean from the coast of South America, provided hydrological scientists with a major focus for research during the past year. Among other significant developments were the increasingly effective use of satellites to provide data and new studies of marine biology.

Hydrology. Like many other geophysical research fields, hydrology benefited in 1983 from the focus provided by the XVIII General Assembly of the International Union of Geodesy and Geophysics (IUGG) in Hamburg, West Germany. Many countries took the opportunity to present to the IUGG summaries of research carried out during the period 1979–82. In addition there were major symposia on hydrological applications of remote sensing; the relation of groundwater quantity and quality; the hydrology of humid tropical regions; planning, design, and man-

Map reveals the upper mantle of the Earth at a depth of 100 kilometers (60 miles). Shaded areas indicate where seismic wave velocities are high and, therefore, where the mantle is cooler than average.

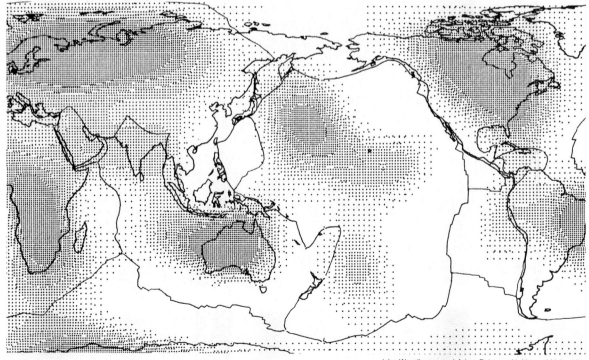

John Woodhouse and Adam Dziewonski, Harvard University

Jack F. Hannaford; courtesy, Al Rango, USDA

Imagery from the LANDSAT satellite reveals unusually heavy snow cover (white area) in the Sierra Nevada in California during late May 1983. This information was used to help predict the volume of water runoff from the melting snow.

agement of water resources systems; the dissolved loads of rivers; and the relationships between the quality and quantity of surface water. The titles reflected the concern of hydrologists both with the pragmatic aspects of the subject, related to water management, and with the research aspects, which involve understanding hydrological processes. The symposia also reflected an increasing concern with water quality as well as water quantity.

All these facets of the subject were to be found together in the first of the symposia at Hamburg on remote sensing. The symposium lasted six days and featured presentations of papers from 22 countries. It provided a convenient forum both for summarizing the experience of researchers and for looking forward to the future developments likely to result from the launch of new satellite systems.

Remote sensing has the potential to revolutionize the study of hydrology. This will not happen because remotely sensed measurements are likely to prove more accurate, reliable, or economically attractive than conventional measurement techniques. Indeed, that is unlikely to be the case. However, the limitations of conventional techniques lie in their restricted spatial extent; for management purposes hydrologists are generally interested in the integrated effects of water movement over large areas. Remote sensing, whether of snow cover, vegetation canopy surface temperatures, surface soil moisture, precipitation,

land use categories, or other conditions, focuses attention on spatial patterns. This type of information does not fit easily into traditional methods of hydrological analysis and prediction, which, because they lacked spatial information, often were based upon one-dimensional representations of the complexities of hydrological systems. The application of remote sensing to hydrological problems will force a reconsideration of such methods, and research into spatially distributed models of hydrological processes can be expected.

Some examples of the use of remotely sensed data in spatially distributed models were presented at the Hamburg symposium. The types of information used varied from LANDSAT data for the determination of land use categories to ground-based radar data to obtain precipitation fluxes in real time for flood forecasting purposes.

Some interesting applications of remote-sensing techniques for measuring hydrological variables were also presented at the IUGG conference. LANDSAT imagery has been used in many countries for water resources purposes. One particular application, a cooperative project between the U.S. and Egypt, used LANDSAT images to monitor the advance of the annual Nile River flood into the Aswan Dam and, consequently, to determine the spatial and temporal distribution of sedimentation in the dam's reservoir over a period of eight years.

Earth sciences

In the field of soil moisture estimation some promising work concerning the use of passive microwave sensors to measure soil moisture near the surface of the ground was reported from the U.S. To date the sensors have been mounted on trucks and aircraft, but hydrologists hoped that the technique could be extended to satellite platforms.

One application in which remote-sensing techniques appeared to have only limited success was the estimation of precipitation. At Hamburg there were reports of attempts to use thermal infrared data from geostationary satellites and multichannel microwave data from Nimbus 7. In France there is a radar system that allows mapping of precipitation over the whole country every half hour. However, the accuracy has been limited, and hydrologists there are likely to continue to rely heavily on point measurements of precipitation.

One area of research that may benefit particularly from the widespread availability of remotely sensed data is the assessment of the water equivalent of snow cover and the prediction of runoff from snowmelt. Al Rango of the U.S. Department of Agriculture's Hydrology Laboratory at Beltsville, Md., provided a useful review of the application of remote sensing to snow hydrology. He concluded that scientists were ready to begin assessing snow cover from

Hoover Dam in Nevada is overtopped for the first time (above), and residents of Salt Lake City, Utah, battle extensive flooding in the spring of 1983 (below)—results of heavy snows that melted rapidly.

satellite transmissions of data and that hydrological models to which such data could be applied were also available. The possible utility of such methods to operational snowmelt forecasts was highlighted during the exceptional snowmelt runoff experienced in the Colorado River basin and elsewhere in the western United States during 1983, when the Hoover Dam was overtopped for the first time since its construction.

Many countries had become interested in improving their assessment of snow water volumes accumulating in mountain areas during the winter. Such areas are usually poorly instrumented; conditions for ground-based measurements are harsh; and snow cover accumulation may vary markedly over short distances. The spatial information provided by remote sensing may consequently prove invaluable in achieving accurate assessments. Studies of this kind were reported from the Soviet Union, India, Canada, the U.S., Greenland, Austria, Switzerland, and Japan. There were also promising reports of airborne gamma-ray spectrometry from Sweden, the Soviet Union, and the U.S. This technique is based on the attenuation of natural gamma radiation by a snow cover.

The use of remote sensing data was also a topic of discussion at the World Meteorological Organization technical conference on the intercomparison of snowmelt runoff models at Norrköping, Sweden. There it was generally agreed that the remote sensing of snowpack extent and properties could greatly improve forecasts of snowmelt if the data could be made available quickly and with good enough resolution. The spatial resolution of LANDSAT imagery produced extremely good estimates of snow-covered areas, but with images taken only at 9- or 18-day intervals, forecasting models must be used to predict melt rates at intermediate times.

In regard to future prospects a number of new satellite systems that will be of interest for hydrological uses are expected to be available soon. France is cooperating with Belgium and Sweden on SPOT, a program involving four satellites over the period 1985–95; they were to be equipped with sensors having a resolution of 10 m (33 ft) and sensitive to light in all colors of the visible spectrum. The Soviet Union is already making use of the microwave sensors in its new Meteor-Priroda satellite. India plans a satellite that would allow high-resolution radiometer measurements. The U.S. plans to continue to use both geostationary (remaining over the same place on the Earth's surface) and polar-orbiting satellites with developments expected in the use of microwave measurements for hydrological purposes.

In time, remotely sensed data may be producing on a routine basis maps of the spatial patterns of such variables as surface soil moisture or precipitation. A topic that has so far been the subject of little research is the use that hydrologists make of this data. Among the specific questions that arise in this connection are: What sort of forecasting models can make best use of this data, with its detail of patterns and possibility of updating, and which differences in space are hydrologically significant and which can be safely ignored? These are questions that seem likely to stimulate hydrological research in a radical way and lead to work that could change the nature of the subject.

—Keith Beven

Oceanography. One of the major themes in oceanography during the past year was an emphasis on the large-scale, long-term aspects of all of the disciplines represented in this diverse field. The major El Niño that occurred in the Pacific Ocean, its global climatic effects, and new warnings about the environmental effects of increasing atmospheric carbon dioxide (CO_2) all served to enhance the perceptions of experts and the public alike on the need to understand climatic variability and on the crucial role of the ocean in producing that variability.

El Niño. The term El Niño ("The Child") refers to the appearance of large masses of warm water about Christmas time off the coasts of Peru and Ecuador, where the water normally is cold. Such warm water appears every year but usually not in amounts large enough to endanger the important fisheries there. Large El Niños, such as the one in 1982–83, have been documented as far back as 1726; they appear to be linked to atmospheric changes around the world, leading to major climatic anomalies such as severe winters, flooding, and droughts.

The 1982–83 El Niño was perhaps the strongest such event in the 20th century, and it was the best documented. Thanks to the foresight of planners in the U.S. National Oceanic and Atmospheric Administration (NOAA) and in the National Science Foundation (NSF), significant field measurement programs were in place in the tropical Pacific Ocean well before the event started, and documentation of oceanographical, meteorological, and biological events was provided during its course.

The El Niño arises from unusually weak trade winds that lead to unusually high sea-surface temperatures in the tropical Pacific Ocean. The westward-blowing trade winds are accompanied by ocean currents that free masses of deep, cold, and nutrient-laden ocean water to well upward off the coast of South America. The nutrients provide a plentiful supply of food for plankton and the fish that feed on them.

The El Niño occurs when the trade winds slow or die out. As a result the warm tropical water in the eastern Pacific blocks the normal upwelling of colder, deeper waters off the South American coast.

These warm waters are poor in nutrients, and thus disastrously affect the populations of the fisheries of Peru and Ecuador, resulting in drastically reduced yields for those countries.

The 1982–83 El Niño differed from this scenario in two respects. First, it started about six months earlier than other El Niños, and lasted well into the summer of the following year, much later than its predecessors did. Second, the warm water was of warmer temperature, and there was more of it than had been seen before during this century. The detailed study of the meteorology of El Niño revealed the major influence of tropical Pacific sea-surface temperature on the atmospheric circulation. It appears that relatively small variations of sea-surface temperature can cause changes in surface wind, which, in turn, cause further changes in sea-surface temperature until the full El Niño cycle is played out.

Many questions remained unanswered, such as the "chicken and egg" problem of whether the atmosphere drives the ocean or vice versa. It appears, however, that the 10,000-km (6,200-mi) width of the tropical Pacific Ocean allows a coupling of the atmosphere to ocean processes there that could not happen in any other ocean. The analysis of the 1982–83 El Niño should prove valuable in developing a sufficient understanding of the interaction of the tropical ocean and the global atmosphere so that a basis for predicting those events can be developed.

The severe El Niño also had significant effects on local biology. In October 1982 the upwelling marine ecosystems (those dependent on deeper, nutrient-rich waters) in the coastal regions of Peru and Ecua-dor began a series of transitions from their normally highly productive conditions to greatly reduced productivity. By July 1983, the highly productive condition had returned. It seems clear that nutrients in the water are considerably reduced by El Niño, with consequent adverse effects on fish, sea birds, and marine mammals. However, several more years of observation of the slowly changing biological populations are required in order to determine accurately the magnitude of these consequences.

Ocean circulation. Interest continued in the study of the large-scale circulation of the ocean. Observations reported during the past year from a systematic survey of the North Atlantic Ocean showed a significant and widespread decrease in the salinity in the deep waters there. These measurements, when compared with similar measurements made in the early 1960s and 1970s, revealed that the change had occurred over the past two decades. An even stronger freshening was found in the shallower waters. Why and how such a freshening could occur is not yet understood, but relationships between the fresher water and atmospheric changes and shifts in ocean circulation patterns were thought to be involved.

New techniques designed for the observation of large-scale circulation of the ocean were tested successfully during the year. A good example was the deep drifter. This instrument is a buoyant float that carries a satellite transmitter. It is placed at a given depth, floats with the currents for a period of several weeks or months, and then surfaces and radios its position to the satellite. The data that it collects during this process allow oceanographers to determine average currents at a given depth and were suc-

Fishing boats are beached on the coast of South America because of the unusually strong El Niño of 1982–83. El Niño, the appearance of large masses of warm water off the coasts of Peru and Ecuador at about Christmas time, blocks the normal upwelling of cold, nutrient-rich water and thus causes many fish to lose their food supply and die.

Photograph from the space shuttle "Challenger" in 1983 reveals strong wakes (light shaded areas) in the ocean around the Hawaiian Islands, probably a result of the strong El Niño of 1982–83.

cessfully used in the Gulf Stream. Clusters of such instruments are expected to be of great importance for future large-scale studies of the circulation.

Biological oceanography. The study of large-scale processes was also of interest to biological oceanographers, whose work on the transport of biologically important substances from the surface of the ocean to the sediments on the bottom achieved important successes during the year. The use of sediment traps, which capture material at various depths, showed the speed with which material such as radiolarian skeletons dissolve during their trip to the bottom. (Radiolaria is a large order of marine protozoans.) This information coupled with accurate measurements of the rate of deposition of material on the bottom helps scientists explain the relative abundance of different species in the sediment record. This work is important both for biological research and for paleoclimate studies, which depend on a knowledge of the particular species being deposited during any given climatic era.

Strong interest continued in the study of the dynamics of submarine rift vent hydrothermal systems, including their biology, geology, and chemistry. New species of bacteria that live comfortably at 300° C were the object of much interest. Biogeographical differentiation was also being studied. How and why the various species grow where they do, and how the biological systems match their lifetimes with

the growth and decay of the geological structure were subjects of much study. (*See* Feature Article: DEEP-SEA HYDROTHERMAL VENTS: OASES ON THE OCEAN FLOOR.)

The interrelation of optical and biological properties in the ocean was under study with a series of experiments that began in 1982. Some initial results of the simultaneous measurements of the optical properties of the water and of phytoplankton dynamics suggest that the variations in optical properties are caused by the variation in the adaptation of cells with depth.

Satellite studies and new research programs. Work continued on the global data collected by the Seasat satellite mission that operated for three months in 1978. New results on the global ocean circulation, on the global wind stress, and on the global distribution of wave heights were published during the past year. These observations were being used to design a new program of satellite measurements that could for the first time give oceanographers a global view of the ocean and its variability. Large-scale biological information from satellites was also exciting. The Nimbus 7 satellite, launched in 1978, continued to operate during the past year; its data on ocean color revealed a biological variability in the oceans that few had expected.

The new research techniques were among the major driving forces behind a workshop held in the

293

summer of 1983 to plan a world ocean circulation experiment. The goal of the experiment is to understand the general circulation of the global oceans well enough to be able to predict ocean response and feedback in relation to long-term changes in the atmosphere. Central to the experiment was to be an expanded program of measurements in the ocean and satellite measurements of currents and wind at the ocean surface.

The world ocean circulation experiment and the continuation and expansion of measurements of the interaction of the tropical ocean and the global atmosphere are both key parts of the World Climate Research Program, the goal of which is to understand and to lay the basis for the prediction of climate variation. A third part of the program is long-term measurements of the ocean by means of a global ocean observing network. In 1984 the pieces of such a network were being put into place; they included sea-level measurements at islands and coastal stations throughout the world and measurements from ships of air temperatures near the ocean surface.

A good example of how such data from satellite and expendable instruments have been used to forecast currents came from work on warm core rings in support of drilling operations on the Atlantic continental margin. In that case forecasts involve tracking the rings by means of drifting buoys placed within them and by satellite infrared images. Probes are used to map the temperature structure in the upper layers of the ocean and to determine the water velocity. To date there has been good agreement between the satellite-tracked images and the measurements in the ocean, suggesting that the images could be used for operational forecasting.

Studies of sea ice also used satellite measurements to good advantage. A program was carried out in the eastern Arctic to measure changes in the vicinity of the ice edge, an area important to climate. Microwaves transmitted by satellites were useful in estimating ice extent and thickness. Synthetic-aperture radar, designed to provide high-resolution data on the shape of the ice surface, was also used. From these data it was possible to determine how far ocean waves penetrate into the ice pack.

During the year a major report was issued by the U.S. National Academy of Sciences on the topic "Changing Climate." This report pointed to the serious consequences of a predicted general warming from the increased quantities of carbon dioxide in the atmosphere. The potential rise in sea level as a result of melting of the ice caps was noted as a special problem. The role of the oceans in absorbing excess carbon dioxide and therefore delaying a warming was also noted, but the research models were too crude to account for this effect correctly.

Satellite data also proved invaluable for devising global geological maps. Combining oceanic and continental data sets obtained by satellite, marine geologists were able to resolve features important for tectonic studies of the Earth's crust and lithosphere in ocean and continental areas. This combined use of data is a new step; the total impact is more than just the sum of the parts because each set enhances the other.

Deep-sea drilling. The year began with uncertainty about the continuation of the Deep Sea Drilling Project, which had operated successfully for 15 years aboard the "Glomar Challenger." With much effort by the marine geological and geophysical community, however, the uncertainty was resolved, and a new Ocean Drilling Program was scheduled to begin its first expedition in early 1985. The "Glomar Challenger" was retired in November 1983; it will be replaced by a larger ship jointly owned by Sedco and British Petroleum.

Four expeditions were completed by the "Glomar Challenger" during 1983. On them oceanographers studied the nature and history of basalt-sea water and the hydrogeological interactions on the East Pacific Rise. Of special interest was the discovery of cycles in sediment transport, the discovery of a Lower Cretaceous sandy turbite fan complex in the lower continental rise, and the recovery of a complete upper core section from the seafloor that included the period of the Cretaceous/Tertiary boundary, about 65 million years ago.

The continued use of techniques to yield a two-dimensional picture of the seafloor, rather than the simple one-dimensional data available from echo sounding by radar, revealed some remarkable new features of the ocean. These new techniques include sonar that can scan from side to side and multibeam echo-sounding techniques. With these instruments swaths of seafloor as wide as 5 km (3 mi) can be observed, and seafloor structure as small as a few meters in diameter can be seen with great accuracy. The resulting images identified evolutionary patterns in the tectonics of ridge crests, including seamounts along the East Pacific Rise axis.

In March 1983 U.S. Pres. Ronald Reagan proclaimed an Exclusive Economic Zone of the United States. The zone extends to a distance of 200 mi from the shore, and within it the U.S. claimed sovereign rights for exploring, conserving, and managing natural resources, both living and nonliving. The recent discovery of a potential mineral resource at the ridge crests, some of which lie within the zone, will require a variety of new activities to be initiated. The U.S. Departments of the Interior and Commerce will both be involved as manganese nodules, polymetallic sulfides, and other minerals are assessed.

See also Feature Article: OCEANOGRAPHY IN ORBIT.

—D. James Baker

Electronics and information sciences

Progress continued in many areas of electronics and information sciences during the past year. Supercomputers capable of 10 billion calculations per second were a major focus of development, and gallium arsenide was under investigation as a possible replacement for silicon as the material from which high-speed integrated circuits could be manufactured. Semiconductor production methods stressed increased miniaturization of components so that as many as 250,000 electronic circuit elements could be packed on a single chip that measured 0.5 cm on each side.

Communications systems

The speed, capacity, and efficiency of communications systems continued to increase during the past year in large part because of the applications of electronics and fiber optics technology. The ability to do new and different things is largely the result of onrushing technology; the opportunity to do them is largely the result of the deregulation policies pursued by the U.S. Federal Communications Commission (FCC) and the court-approved breakup of American Telephone and Telegraph Co. (AT&T).

Telephone switching systems. Central office switching equipment (used to connect one telephone to another) has always been the mainstay of the telecommunications business, but since its first use in 1892 this equipment has been electromechanical and analog in nature. (Analog mechanisms transmit continuous electrical signals that vary in amplitude or frequency in response to changes in sound, light, heat, position, or pressure; an example is a thermometer recording temperature.) It was not until 1960 that the first switching system to be controlled by a program of instructions stored in bulk electronic memory (stored-program control) went into service, in Morris, Ill. The first "digital" office became operational in 1974, and by 1984 there was a headlong dash to make the nation's switching equipment digital.

With digital equipment a voice is sampled a large number of times per second, and the result of each sample is converted to a coded character. (Usually this sampling is done at the switching equipment to which the telephone is connected, but recent technology has allowed the conversion process to take place at the telephone itself.) Digital switching equipment is less expensive, smaller, and more flexible than analog switching equipment.

In terms of applications there are, essentially, two categories of switching equipment: the central office

Courtesy, IBM

Researchers at an IBM laboratory in Zürich, Switzerland, insert a communications station into a Zürich ring, a prototype local area network developed at the laboratory.

equipment mentioned above and Private Branch Exchanges (PBX's). Central office equipment is owned by telephone operating companies and thus is part of a country's vast telecommunications infrastructure. The size of the market for such equipment is more than $3.5 billion per year. But the price for participation in this market is high; Western Electric and ITT each spent $750 million to develop their digital switching products.

The private branch exchange, on the other hand, forms the hub of many business telephone systems. Often as small as a file cabinet (and getting smaller), it is loaded with microprocessors and other sophisticated electronic equipment. Many dozens of manufacturers are participating in this market. The PBX's have more features than the average user will ever need.

It is interesting to note that more and more switching systems (particularly central offices) are being configured so that electronic equipment is located close to the actual subscribers. This approach (called distributed processing) further increases capabilities and reduces costs.

Data transmission. A significant development during the past year was the transmission of data as well as voice through a PBX. More and more companies were transmitting huge amounts of data over their telecommunications networks. New PBX's were being

295

designed with this in mind, and old PBX's were being enhanced to provide the capability.

This demand for data capability was becoming evident in at least two other ways. First was the concept called Local Area Networks (LAN's). Office buildings, industrial parks, and other such installations require their own local communications network for intra-company transmission. Configurations of these networks included trunk circuits, loops, and stars. The second concept is packet switching, a scheme whereby powerful computers store data supplied by individual subscribers and then transmit this information at high speeds in bundles, or packets. The packets received at a distant city are slowed down for delivery to the intended recipient. Packet switching permits economical use of the transmission channel.

Several technologies have been developed for the transmission of high-speed data and voice signals. One of these is "photonics," a system using fiber optics. The intelligence to be transmitted is modulated by an extremely-high-frequency carrier—so high, in fact, that it is in the infrared range. For this reason the transmission medium is not electricity-carrying copper but light-carrying glass. Ultra-pure glass is drawn into a thread no thicker than a human hair, and a pulsating light source at one end causes a pulse to be transmitted to the distant end—often several miles away. Such glass fibers are called "light guides." Technical advances during the past year have resulted in improved light sources (lasers and light-emitting diodes), better photo detectors, and, most important, better glass.

Early light guides permitted several "rays" to traverse their lengths. But because one particular ray might be moving at a different angle from the next, its total length as it passed through the light guide would be different, and the signal being transmitted consequently would become garbled. This made it necessary to intercept and regenerate the signal at regular intervals. With the ultrathin fiber, called the "single mode" fiber, only one ray is allowed to traverse the length, and regeneration need not take place so often.

Splicing techniques for fibers are also improving. For example, two strands can be spliced together with epoxy and also joined with specially designed connectors.

Perhaps mention of a single application for glass fibers is appropriate. Southern New England Telephone Co. recently completed an agreement with CSX Corp., one of the nation's largest transportation companies. The agreement calls for laying an 8,000-km (5,000-mi) network of fiber along railroad rights-of-way, linking cities in 20 states east of the Mississippi River and capable of reaching 60% of the population of the U.S.

A second transmission scheme that gained prominence was Digital Termination System (DTS). A microwave signal is broadcast from a transmitter in a broad fan-shaped pattern (90° or more). In order to restrict a particular burst of intelligence to a particular receiver, a "header" is placed in front of this burst. Only one station recognizes this header, thereby activating its receiver. Thus special coding techniques, high-speed data, and microwave signals are combined to permit a communications system to be implemented in places where more conventional techniques could not be used.

Another aspect of data transmission of concern during the past year involved transborder data flow (TBDF). Restrictions on such flow by some countries were creating compliance problems for several mul-

Cellular radio systems combine high-quality radio and the telephone and can be applied to mobile radio in metropolitan areas without overloading the system. Calls from mobile telephones are picked up by the nearest antenna (far right), and relayed to a computerized central switching office (right), which patches them into the phone system. As the mobile user moves on, the switch passes the call from one antenna to the next.

Photos, © Mark Godfrey—Archive

tinational firms. TBDF regulations had been adopted by 24 nations since Sweden enacted the first such law to protect data privacy.

TBDF legislation generally defines practices for collecting, storing, using, and communicating personal data held in public- and private-sector automated records. Among specific actions by nations, Mexico was replacing all private-line leasing with the state-run network. Brazil controlled and taxed certain classes of data entering and leaving the country. France considered assessing import levies on the intrinsic value of software data.

Cellular radio. Perhaps the most exciting application of technology during the past year has been cellular radio. Although the concept was developed by a Bell Laboratories engineer more than 30 years ago, it was not until the recent development of microprocessors and stored-program controlled switching equipment that the theory became a reality.

A cellular radio system can be applied to mobile radio in metropolitan areas without fear of overloading the system. The area is divided into "cells" of no more than a few miles in diameter, with each cell operating on a particular set of frequencies. An important aspect of the system is that each cell site transmitter operates only at a strength necessary to cover its particular cell. Therefore, that same set of frequencies can be reused several cells away. Thus coverage can be attained with a relatively few number of frequency sets.

Among the technological challenges of cellular radio are how to deal with a vehicle that moves from one cell to another without losing the signal (called hand-off) and how to direct a call to a vehicle when its location is unknown (called locating). Both challenges have been met by the extreme power of stored program systems and the power and small size of microprocessors. In the hand-off process, for instance, the signal strength from a particular mobile radio operating on a particular frequency set is constantly monitored by receivers in adjacent cells as well as by receivers in the cell in which the mobile unit is located. As the vehicle approaches a cell boundary, this signal strength gradually becomes lower in one cell and stronger in the adjacent cell. At some point the two sets of cell-site equipment decide that the hand-off should take place. Over a separate channel the vehicle is signaled to switch from frequency set A to frequency set B, and, without the user even being aware of it, the transfer is made.

By 1984 a number of cellular systems in the U.S. and Europe were in operation. An initial delay in the approval of cellular systems in the U.S. was caused more by politics than by technology. As finally established, one wire line carrier (such as a telephone company) and one radio common carrier are each permitted to operate one cellular radio system in each of the nation's Standard Metropolitan Statistical Areas.

Interactive videotex. A communication system that is just starting to receive serious attention is called interactive videotex. In this system large data banks are connected, by means of the conventional telephone system, to a subscriber's telephone and television set. By using the touch calling pad on their telephones subscribers can "call up" particular sets of data and have them displayed on their television sets. Examples include airline schedules, restaurant menus, stock prices, and weather forecasts. Since the system is interactive, subscribers can place orders, make reservations, and buy products. In short, they can conduct business without leaving their homes. Such systems are in operation in New Jersey and Florida, as well as in several other countries.

Regulations. The telecommunications industry in the U.S. has, for the most part, been controlled by AT&T and its Bell operating companies and the independent telephone firms. But two FCC decisions changed this. In the first it was decided that long-distance telephone service could be provided by companies other than the long-lines subsidiary of AT&T. In the second it was decided that end-to-end connections of telephone calls were not the sole prerogative of the telephone companies. Thus, other manufacturers and providers of service were allowed to enter the field and to make maximum use of developing technology.

The breakup of the Bell System, a result of U.S. Department of Justice action against AT&T, created seven holding companies, each of which was permitted—even encouraged—to purchase the billions of dollars of needed telecommunications equipment from manufacturers other than AT&T's Western Electric (now called AT&T Technologies). Thus, even more companies entered the field, each drawing upon the most advanced technology available to secure a footing in the industry.

This activity in the communications arena is an excellent example of synergy in action: Each new technology is exciting and impressive by itself, but when combined with other technologies, horizons are expanded well beyond what was ever imagined. Sophisticated radio equipment, plus stored program control, plus microprocessors and other subminiature electronics components, all have been combined to provide extremely powerful new communications systems.

The government of China announced plans to update that country's telecommunications system. A major feature of the policy was the granting of low-interest loans to cities in order to upgrade local facilities. Total cost of the program was estimated at more than $2 billion.

—Robert E. Stoffels

Computers and computer science

Technological and scientific developments in the computer industry during the past year included proposed new supercomputers and discussion of gallium arsenide as a replacement for silicon. An issue that attracted attention was computer security.

Supercomputers. During 1983 Control Data Corp. announced its intention to build a powerful successor to its Cyber 205 supercomputer. In August 1983 at a conference on supercomputers at Los Alamos, N.M., Control Data announced that its next-generation supercomputer would not be developed by the company itself but would instead be designed by a new corporation, ETA Systems Inc., in which Control Data would hold no more than a 40% interest. Control Data made a major investment in the new company and committed itself to purchase and market a number of the new supercomputers. According to announcements made at Los Alamos and in subsequent statements, Control Data executives concluded that a crash project to build a next-generation supercomputer system would have a greater chance of success in a small company in which the key members of the development project had a significant financial interest than in the large and conservative firm that Control Data had become.

ETA Systems announced that it planned to build a supercomputer system with up to eight processors, each of which would be three to five times as fast as the Cyber 205. When it processes a single problem, the new system is expected to be 12 to 30 times as fast as the Cyber 205, with peak speeds in excess of 10 billion calculations per second. ETA Systems hoped to be able to deliver its first such system before the end of 1986.

The emitter coupled logic (ECL) technology used in the Cyber 205 provides about 250 gates per chip. (A gate is the basic unit of computer logic and corresponds to several interconnected transistors.) For the new system, however, ETA expected to be able to place more than 20,000 gates on a single silicon chip. Packing densities of this magnitude for very high speed circuits can be achieved by using complementary metallic oxide semiconductor (CMOS) technology (see Electronics, below) because it uses less power and generates less heat per gate than other methods. To further enhance the performance of these CMOS circuits, ETA planned to use liquid nitrogen to cool the circuits to the very low temperature of 77 K ($-196°$ C).

Cray Research Inc. announced in 1983 the delivery of the Cray X-MP, the first supercomputer having two central processing units. Seymour Cray, the founder of the corporation and designer of the Cray 1, had left Cray Research in 1981 to set up an independent consulting activity in which he would be able to design future generations of Cray supercomputers under contract to the corporation. During 1983 he announced that the Cray 3, his supercomputer for the late 1980s, would not use integrated circuits formed on chips made of silicon. Instead he planned to pioneer the use of gallium arsenide (see below) in a large-scale production computer in an effort to achieve supercomputer speeds beyond any now planned for silicon-based machines.

Japan continued its efforts to remain competitive with the U.S. in the area of computer technology. Supercomputers developed by Hitachi and Fujitsu were reported to be achieving speeds of close to one billion computations per second. Japanese firms were also marketing 256-kilobit memory chips. (A kilobit equals 1,024 bits, a bit being the smallest increment of usable data for a computer.)

The Cray X-MP, developed by Cray Research Inc., is the first supercomputer to have two central processing units.

"It must be you. The computer, it so happens, is user-friendly."

Gallium arsenide. The first transistors were made of germanium, but silicon soon came into general use as the material from which wafers and chips are produced for the integrated-circuit industry. Germanium and silicon are both in column IVa (the carbon group) of the Periodic Table of Elements. Scientists predicted that some compounds of elements from columns IIIa and Va would have properties similar to those of the semiconductors in column IVa. A number of such compounds have been studied. The most interesting and most promising from the point of view of the computer industry is a compound of the elements gallium and arsenic, gallium arsenide.

Some of the characteristics of gallium arsenide suggest that it should be superior to silicon as a material out of which very-high-speed, very-large-scale integrated circuits can be manufactured. For example, electrons move more rapidly within gallium arsenide than they do in silicon. These are technical considerations that should, at least theoretically, make it possible to achieve switching speeds five to ten times as fast as can be achieved in silicon circuits using the same amount of power. Among other advantages of gallium arsenide is that it is less sensitive to temperature changes and to radiation than is silicon.

Gallium arsenide is used commercially in communications, but as of 1984 it had not been used except experimentally in the computer industry. It has been difficult and expensive to produce the pure, uniform gallium arsenide crystals out of which relatively large wafers can be cut. The wafers that have been cut are brittle and must be handled carefully. Experimental integrated circuits that perform switching in tens of picoseconds (a picosecond is 10^{-12} seconds) have been produced but only at a relatively low level of integration (a relatively small number of circuits within a given area). The com-

bination of large-scale integration and picosecond speeds has not yet been achieved but seems to be almost within reach. It is expected that commercial production of gallium arsenide chips at a medium level of integration will begin in 1984 or 1985.

As mentioned above, supercomputer designer Seymour Cray planned to use gallium arsenide as the basis for the Cray 3, and possible delivery dates for the machine as early as 1986 or 1987 were predicted. It seemed reasonable to predict that a multibillion-dollar gallium arsenide integrated-circuit industry would help accomplish several orders of magnitude of improvement in computer performance by the mid-1990s.

Josephson junction technology. One of the areas of great interest in research laboratories in the computer industry during the past few years has been Josephson junction technology. Part of its interest arises from the fact that it makes use of properties of matter and principles of physics that have only relatively recently been discovered and understood. One of these properties is superconductivity, the fact that at or near a temperature of absolute zero ($-273.15°$ C) the electrical resistance of a metal disappears. By utilizing this property with alloys of lead and gold and niobium, researchers have fabricated superconductor logic and memory components that contain very large numbers of circuits within a very small area and that switch at picosecond speeds. There is, of course, a refrigeration problem, since Josephson junction circuits must be kept at a temperature close to absolute zero. But semiconductor circuits have a corresponding problem, since an attempt to obtain equivalent speed and density with semiconductors may create very large amounts of heat that must be removed.

In the summer and fall of 1983 research laboratories at Sperry Corp., IBM Corp., and Bell Laboratories

299

The motion picture WarGames raised the issue of computer security, particularly in regard to the many young people who are becoming increasingly sophisticated about computers. The movie starred Matthew Broderick and Ally Sheedy (right).

announced major cutbacks in Josephson junction research. At IBM most of the 115 researchers in this area were reassigned, and an experimental Josephson junction manufacturing project was shut down. Research in this area will continue, but the expectations of a few years ago that Josephson junction computers would be in widespread use before the end of the 20th century will probably not be realized. There was no great difficulty in achieving the very low temperatures needed, but there were problems in building up larger structures from modules that had to operate at those temperatures. Perhaps another reason why Josephson junction technology does not seem as attractive now as it did several years ago is the fact that it now appears possible to achieve comparable performance in other ways, possibly through developments in CMOS technology or through the successful development of gallium arsenide technologies mentioned above.

Computer security. The word "hacker" came into popular use during 1983 as the result of the release of a movie called *WarGames*. In earlier computer usage the designation "hacker" usually referred to a college student who became fascinated with the world of computers to such an extent that he would neglect conventional academic pursuits and instead try to become expert in the intricacies of the most sophisticated computer system available to him. The goal of the hacker often was to break into the system, to find a way to gain for himself privileges reserved for the chief system programmer, and to put himself in a position to take over control of the whole computing system. In many cases the student hacker had no malicious intent. Most university computing centers have had experiences in which students who had broken into the system would volunteer the informa-

tion that they had done so and would also volunteer suggestions about how to improve the security of the system to avoid future break-ins.

The recently developed personal computers have made it possible for even younger people to become intimately involved with computer technology, and the movie *WarGames* tells about a high-school student who has a fairly elaborate home computer installation with automatic dial-out equipment that makes it possible for him to communicate with other computers by telephone. It is easy for this enterprising teenager to discover the poorly concealed password that is supposed to protect the high-school data processing system from unauthorized users, and he proudly shows a classmate how he can change one of his grades and then one of hers by dialing into the school computer system from his home computer.

The young hero of the movie knows that many computers are accessible by telephone and that some of them have files of games for recreational use. He sets up his computer to dial all of the phone numbers in a particular area, and he just happens on the phone number of a computer system that controls a huge defense complex and that does, indeed, have all kinds of interesting war games available. Here the movie becomes farfetched. This average teenage student somehow manages to almost start and then miraculously stop an all-out nuclear war. But, farfetched or not, the movie raised many questions about the security of computer systems. Also, almost inevitably, it inspired hosts of imitators, teenagers and others, who tried to break into all kinds of computer systems. The press picked up the word hacker to describe these imitators, and "hacker" now seems to have become a generic term for anyone who tries to obtain unauthorized access to a computer system.

There are serious questions as to whether computer systems are protected adequately. Students probably do sometimes break into school computer systems and alter their records, but it is probably not possible for an amateur to break into a major defense system. The press reported that some teenagers did indeed manage to get into a computer at a major weapons laboratory at Los Alamos, but that incident apparently involved no security breach at all; they had merely gained access to unclassified bulletin-board information.

Computer security and computer crime are important areas of study at many levels. One case reported in 1983 illustrated some interesting aspects of these areas. During the summer of 1983 someone managed to insert a program of a type referred to as a "Trojan horse" into a computer system at Stanford University. An intruder installed his own program in place of one of the operating system routines. As a result users who subsequently logged on to the system would execute the intruder's program, thereby giving the intruder access to all of the private files and privileges of those users. Later the intruder could log on to the system and use their files and privileges as if they were his own.

The system programmers in charge of the invaded system soon realized that something unusual was happening, and they discovered that a substitution had been made. They then tried to find the intruder,

Introduced in 1984 by Apple Computer Inc., the Macintosh personal computer contains a 32-bit microprocessor and a built-in disk drive.

Apple Computer Inc.

but that turned out to be difficult. The computer involved was connected to one of the major national computer networks, Arpanet, that was set up by DARPA, the U.S. Defense Department Advanced Research Projects Agency. It was thus possible to log on to the Stanford computer from other computers quite remote from Stanford, and the intruder apparently had access to a number of such computers. Most computer accounts are protected by passwords, and access to an account is denied to anyone who does not know the appropriate password. However, many authorized users set passwords for their accounts that are relatively easy to guess, such as a first name, the name of a spouse, or, as in the case of *WarGames*, the name of one's child.

The intruder had managed to gain access to a computer in the Arpanet network and then through the network had obtained a list of the authorized users of the Stanford system. He had then been able to guess the password of a system programmer at Stanford who was authorized to make the kind of system changes that permitted the intruder to insert his Trojan-horse program. Because of the Arpanet involvement those in charge of the computer at Stanford called in the FBI, and ultimately the perpetrator was apprehended—a 19-year-old college sophomore at UCLA. As in the case of the teenager in *WarGames* he was almost certainly just a hacker, someone trying to see how far he could go in breaking into the most sophisticated computer system available.

Although it has no direct connection with the previously described event, it is interesting to note that during 1983 Arpanet was split into two separate networks. One of these, EXPNET (Experimental Network), retains the original network research orientation of Arpanet. The other, MILNET (Military Network), was designed to concentrate on providing a reliable high-speed data communications service for government agencies that had come to rely on Arpanet for such services. Even though MILNET is not meant to be a secure communications system in the sense of providing full military security, it will be much less likely than the former Arpanet to be subject to misuse by the community of hackers.

—Saul Rosen

Electronics

Rapid growth continued in the field of electronics during the past year. While some new fabrication methods were developed and tested, previous methods continued to be the mainstay of production. The U.S. semiconductor industry produced in excess of $10 billion in semiconductor components, of which about $1.3 billion were for discrete components (such as diodes and transistors) and in excess of $8.4 billion were for integrated circuits (ICs; includ-

Erich Hartmann—Magnum

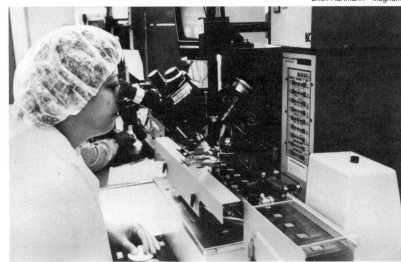

Technician performs a step in the manufacturing of the Motorola 68000 16-bit microprocessor. Such small and powerful units are used in many personal computers.

ing computer chips, memory chips, and calculator chips).

Semiconductor production techniques continued to stress increasing the yield (number of good chips per wafer) and the density factor (number of components per chip). Along with this increased density was the continued reduction of line widths (lines used to define the device areas and separations) to 1.5 μm (1.5-millionths of a meter). New chip designs permitted packing up to 250,000 electronic circuit elements in a single chip measuring 0.5 cm (0.2 in) on each side.

Quite naturally, as the density increases and line widths become smaller, the quality of the materials must also improve. The current industry goal of 1-μm lines requires improving the Czochralski crystal growth technique (the process by means of which pure silicon is manufactured) and quality control techniques.

Computers. While the early microcomputers were constructed using four-bit architecture (a bit is a binary digit—1 or 0) and most units from 1977 to 1982 used eight bits, computers in 1984 are designed to use 16-bit microprocessors to perform the required operations in reduced periods of time. (The microprocessor is the IC containing the control and arithmetic parts of a computer—the heart of a computer system.) By packaging a greater amount of circuitry in a single IC or in fewer ICs, manufacturers developed smaller and more powerful portable units that could be placed in a standard-sized briefcase.

All computers utilize two forms of memory, ROM and RAM. The ROM (read-only memory) ICs contain program and data information that is permanently stored in the IC. ROM memory is not erased when power is turned off and is always available for use. However, it cannot be changed by the user. In contrast, RAM (random-access memory) can be read or written into and is used to enter and operate different programs and data. It is erased when the power is turned off.

The amount of computer memory in personal computers continued to increase. For example, the IBM PC/XT has an upper limit of 640 KB (kilobytes, or thousands of eight-bit words) of RAM and 48 KB of ROM. The capability of the RAM ICs increased from the 16K bits (16,000 bits) of previous years to 64K bits at present with 256K bits on the horizon.

AT&T's Dynamic Random Access Memory chip was the first commercially produced memory chip to have a capacity of more than 250,000 bits.

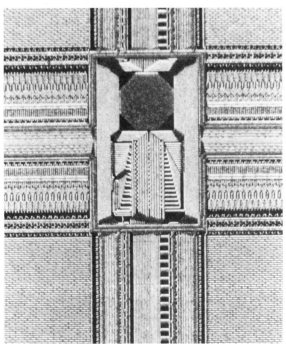

Courtesy, AT&T/Bell Laboratories

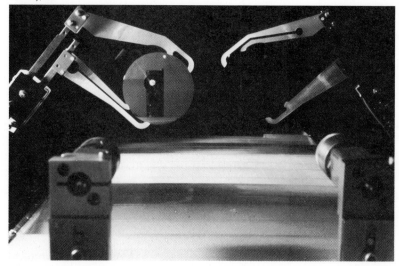

Robot arm dips a silicon wafer into a solution of chemicals. Improvements in design have resulted in robots that can control their movements to within 0.0025 centimeter (0.001 inch).

In addition to the internal memory described above, there is external memory in the form of magnetic storage that can be used to save programs and data. The magnetic storage for personal computer systems is usually provided by floppy (flexible) diskettes having diameters of 13.34 cm (5.25 in). A diskette can be either single- or double-sided with single- or double-density storage. A double-sided, double-density diskette has a capacity of 360 KB, equivalent to about 180 pages of double-spaced type-written material. IBM PC/XT uses 5.25-in diskettes, but the Apple Macintosh provides about the same storage capacity on 8.9-cm (3.5-in) diskettes.

For those users requiring greater storage capacity, a hard magnetic disk provides millions of bytes of information. Hard-disk units operate at higher speeds than floppies, with the magnetic heads held off the disk surface by an air cushion that is created by the rapidly spinning disk. (A magnetic head is an electromagnet used for reading, recording, or erasing signals on a magnetic disk, drum, or tape.) The heads remain within one-millionth of an inch from the disk's surface, close enough so that a particle of dust could damage both the head and the disk surface. The Winchester disk and drive unit are, therefore, enclosed in an airtight container. The Winchester unit that is provided with the IBM PC/XT can store 10 million bytes, and data can be accessed in milliseconds. (One millisecond equals 0.001 sec.)

Robotics. The field of robotics continued to attract considerable interest and development. Improvements in microprocessors, programming languages, and sensors (both visual and tactile) contributed to the increasing use and popularity of robot units in industrial applications. The Robot Institute of America defines a robot as "a reprogrammable multifunctional manipulator designed to move material, parts, tools, or specialized devices through variable pro-grammed motions for the performance of a variety of tasks." The uses of robots range from those which simply move within a single axis and repetitively perform the same operation to the sophisticated units that can function in four, six, or more axes and that have some ability to recognize patterns.

A typical misconception about robots is that they perform independently instead of as part of an integrated system. A great deal of planning by the manufacturing engineer is required if a robot is to be used effectively in the production cycle. During recent years robots have been effectively used for such purposes as spot welding, spray painting, and the installation of minor parts. Improved designs have resulted in robots that can control their movements to within 0.0025 cm (0.001 in) and therefore are useful in the production and testing of circuit boards and the manufacturing and assembly of computer components. These robots are sufficiently versatile to detect and compensate for production problems.

At present robot units are expensive, but their cost is expected to drop as more units are used and produced. In fact, robot units were available in 1984 that cost less than half as much as did similar units a year earlier.

Automotive applications. For the layman the automotive industry is probably the most obvious application of the recent advances in electronic devices. Dashboards now provide digital readouts that include everything from the time of day to the average miles per hour for a given trip. Electronically controlled fuel-injected engines have resulted in increased fuel economy, performance, and reliability. Recent developments include voice communication and onboard diagnostic systems that monitor a wide variety of functions and localize malfunctions for the automotive technician. In 1984 Daimler-Benz of West Germany offered an electronically controlled antiskid

303

system, and the Ford Motor Co. developed a 22.9-cm (9-in) video display that provides regional maps and uses satellite interactive navigational systems to show the driver's location.

The heart of all the advances listed above is a microprocessor designed not only to perform the desired functions but also to withstand its sometimes hostile environment (heat, vibration, and moisture). Automobile manufacturers have placed the development of automotive semiconductors high on their list of priorities and have, in fact, established their own microelectronic design centers. As of 1984 most of the automotive IC units were of the eight-bit variety; however, research efforts on 16-bit units suggested that they would provide more flexibility in design and be easier to program.

Synthesized voice and music. As the cost of ICs decreased and their complexity and sophistication continued to grow, synthesized voice was being included in more and more products. Speech synthesis can be accomplished by using circuitry and programs to produce sound that is based on the approximately 40 phonemes that represent all the sounds of the English language. Text is converted into phonemic form using a lexicon, a dictionary of specific sequences to represent that word. The quality of voice obtained with this scheme is better than that obtained by using voice coding, in which speech output is converted into digital form for transmission and then converted back to speech at the receiver.

Recognition of voice was also undergoing considerable development. Texas Instruments Inc. was working on a speech analyzer that would be based on a model of human speech. Speech recognition usually is limited to a small selection of words and is generally restricted by the ways in which the words are phrased or pronounced.

CMOS technology. The recent trend in semiconductor manufacturing has been an increased use of CMOS (complementary symmetry MOS; metal-oxide semiconductor) transistors. While CMOS circuits have been used since the early 1960s, the recent interest in CMOS technology is due to two main factors: the cost of producing CMOS has declined, and CMOS is better able to meet the needs of producing densely packed semiconductor circuits. Because CMOS circuitry uses less power than other circuit types, it permits a greater number of circuits in a single package.

A CMOS circuit contains both an n-channel and p-channel MOSFET (metal-oxide semiconductor field-effect) transistor connected to a common input as the active element. The result is that turning the n-channel device on also turns the p-channel device off (or vice-versa). Therefore, one of the two is always off, resulting in zero current through the CMOS circuit. Because there is no current, no power is drawn from the power supply and no power

is dissipated by the circuit. While this is true during direct-current and low-frequency operations, the CMOS circuit does draw current as the signal frequency increases because during the time that the off/on conditions change both n-channel and p-channel devices may momentarily be on, with a correspondingly small current. Even so, the total power dissipated by a CMOS circuit is generally less than that of other circuit types.

Flat screens. The development of flat-screen displays maintained a high level of priority during the past year. As of 1984 the size of the majority of video displays was limited primarily by the required depth of the standard cathode-ray tube. Although a variety of techniques was being investigated, the use of LCD's (liquid crystal displays) remained at the forefront of the technology because of their low power requirements and low operating temperatures. The former characteristic lends itself well to portable battery-operated systems. A liquid crystal is a material that will flow like a liquid but has some molecular structure characteristics usually associated with solids. In the simplest of terms an LCD has a liquid crystal between two parallel transparent plates that will display a character when particular regions are energized. Unlike LED's (light-emitting diodes), which emit their own light when energized, LCD's require an internal or external light source. Many modern watches utilize some form of LCD crystal.

Manufacturers have developed flat screens that are more than 4½ m (15 ft) across and that employ a large number of liquid crystal modules. Television receivers manufactured by Seiko have a screen measuring 5.4 cm (2.13 in) diagonally that provides a mosaic of 240 pixels across and 240 down. A pixel is the smallest element on a screen the intensity, shading, and color of which can be controlled by an external microprocessor.

See also Feature Articles: THE INCREDIBLE SHRINKING CHIP: MINIATURIZATION IN ELECTRONICS; ARTIFICIAL INTELLIGENCE: TOWARD MACHINES THAT THINK.

—Robert Boylestad; Louis Nashelsky

Information systems and services

The world is in the midst of an information revolution in which new modes of communication are being developed and traditional modes are being expanded. It is a world in which information systems and services are the new growth industries, providing unprecedented opportunities for social and economic progress. The expanding uses of cable television, satellite communication facilities, and local area networks enable professionals, managers, clerks, teachers, students, and others to have fast and efficient access to one another and to a myriad of electronic information-processing resources.

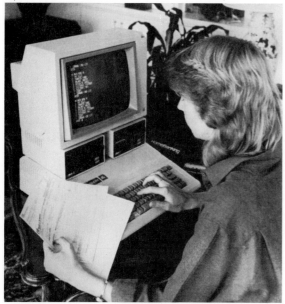

HomeBanking system developed by the Bank of America enables owners of personal computers to perform bank transactions at their home terminals.

Paradoxically, one of the strongest incentives stimulating the growth of these information services has been the rising costs of energy, for to achieve energy conservation it is necessary to replace transportation with communication and to replace materials with information. In an information-based society many workers will choose to telecommute instead of driving to work. People will use home information systems so as to eliminate the need to use their automobiles for such errands as banking and shopping. Industry, making use of specialized data bases, will be able to use goods more efficiently.

The merging of communication and computer technologies is leading toward the creation of new home information and entertainment systems based upon telephones, television receivers, personal computers, electronic games, and videotex systems. However, the most important ingredient in these new products and uses is not the technology itself but the information received through these devices, for it is the information that will create consumer acceptance of the new technologies.

High-technology industries need highly educated and trained employees, yet the U.S. Bureau of Labor Statistics estimated that during the 1980s there would be a shortage of 2.5 million skilled workers in all technical fields. Such a shortage of trained personnel could inhibit the future technical growth of the U.S. and might present a threat to national security. To deal with this situation the U.S. Senate Subcommittee on Science and Technology proposed the establishment of a Commission on High Technology that would study various means of implementing a comprehensive national policy on training skilled workers to meet the expected labor demands of high-technology industries. A companion bill, introduced in the U.S. House of Representatives, sought federal support to promote science and mathematics education in the U.S. at all levels.

Without waiting for government action, academic institutions were taking steps on their own to provide the needed training. Most colleges and universities offered courses in computer literacy and encouraged students in all disciplines to become familiar with computers and their many applications. Some schools were requiring all entering freshmen to own and use computers in their college studies.

By 1984 most colleges and universities were offering courses in the operation and applications of computers.

U.S. information systems. The number of information data bases continued to increase rapidly as did the number of organizations providing access to them. Although the U.S. remained ahead of the rest of the world in both the number and the size of information data bases being produced, European countries were progressing rapidly.

Questions were raised as to whether the policy in the U.S. of allowing most scientific and technological material to be published openly was causing damage to the U.S. economically and also jeopardizing national security by aiding Soviet military development. A special Panel on Scientific Communication and National Security was convened by the U.S. National Academy of Sciences to study this question. While conceding that there has been a substantial transfer of U.S. technology, the panel found little evidence that universities and open scientific communication were the sources of this transfer. Furthermore, the panel's report pointed out that scientific communication flows in both directions; scientific contacts at open meetings have yielded useful insights into Soviet science and technology. The report concluded that except for information directly related to military product development, national security might be better served through a policy of open scientific communication rather than through one of secrecy that would have "limited and uncertain benefits."

The U.S. government continued to be a major producer of information data bases. For example, the U.S. Department of Commerce maintained an industrial output data base containing information about shipments, inventories, and products for 450 manufacturing industries as defined by the 1972 Standard Industry Classification system. Annual data were available beginning in 1958 and could be used for analyzing productivity, growth rates, and, in combination with trade data, competitive performances. An energy data base available from the same department contained U.S. energy use information organized by 122 sectors of the economy, by 64 energy products, and by 28 functional use categories for 1947–77. The information, available in machine-readable form, was useful for analyzing the changes in both industry-specific consumption and cost of energy in a particular end product.

Another U.S. government-sponsored service was the National Library Service for the Blind and Physically Handicapped (NLS/BPH). This organization developed a recorded and voice-indexed dictionary of 55,000 entries taken from the *Concise Heritage Dictionary*. The work was contained on 219 tracks of 55 cassettes plus an additional cassette that contained detailed instructions on the use of the system. To find a word, a user listened to spoken index terms audible when the cassette was played in fast-forward speed. After the desired word was heard, the user

put the player on normal playing speed in order to hear the full dictionary entry. The voice dictionary was distributed nationwide to cooperating libraries servicing NLS/BPH readers and could also be purchased at cost from the American Printing House for the Blind.

Although the 1990 U.S. census was still a few years away, planning for it began. Large amounts of data had to be collected, and the organizational tasks were complex. The Census Bureau created a network of 44 state data centers based upon a voluntary agreement between the bureau and the cooperating state governments. Each data center received free copies of the census publications, microfiches, maps, and summary computer tapes specially produced for that state. These materials included population, housing, and survey census reports as well as economic data concerning retail and wholesale trade, manufacturing, construction, agriculture, services, and transportation.

International information systems. Euronet DIANE is a direct information access network for Europe. Sponsored by the Commission of the European Communities, it began operation in 1980. By 1984 it had grown to include more than 350 data bases, more than 2,500 users spread among 14 countries, and an average of more than 30,000 calls per month. Among the recently added data bases were Credoc-Coralie, produced in Belgium and containing technical and juridical information on the use of additives in foodstuffs; Economic Abstracts International, a bibliographic data base compiled by the Dutch Ministry of Economic Affairs that provides access to worldwide information on exports, market trends, economic developments, and management science; EMIS, a data bank developed in the U.K. of research results providing information on the properties of substances used in physical electronics; Ergodata, a data bank created in France that lists the physical measurements of several hundred thousand people and thereby provides information that benefits manufacturers of items designed to fit in or around the human body; Transinove, a French-produced data base of patents, processes, and other transferable techniques; and Newsline, a daily headline service that covers all British daily newspapers and a few others and which includes references to the original newspaper stories.

Aslib, the British Association of Special Libraries and Information Bureaux, announced an expanded and redirected program to better meet the current needs of its clients and to promote the more effective use of information resources by providing its members and associates with a range of products and services designed to improve the efficiency and effectiveness of information management activities. Aslib planned to continue to provide data base

```
 .-------1.--------2--------3---------4 .-------5---------6-------.]--- -- *.
 *AWLN     *EXPLANATORY LINE-FORMULA      *NAME (see list's FOOTNOTES)]       **:

 .-------0--------0--------0-------.0 ,-------0--------0-------.]--- -- *.
20Y1&02   C2H5-0-CH(CH3)0-C2H5           acetal= 1,1-diethoxyethane   1230?15 *7
OD1       0:CH-CH3    [L] below 21C      acetaldehyde ='AAD'=etha.[g.g]242  2 *3
ZYQ1  $   NH2-CH(OH)CH3                  acetaldehyde ammonia          ]        #*4
QN=D1     HO-N=CH-CH3                    acetaldoxime          [c/t]            #*5
ZV1       NH2-C0.CH3                     acetamide =ethanamide.      ]---?20 *3
QV1       HO-C0.CH3                      acetic acid ='AAC'=ethanoic .]221 24a*3
1VOV1     CH3-C0.0-C0.CH3                acetic anhydride ='ACA'      ]221w24a*5
QX1&1&CN  HO-C(CH3)2.CN                  acetone cyanhydrin='ACY'     1412 14 *8
1V1       CH3-C0.CH3                     acetone='ACT'=dimethyl ketone]130 18 *3
NC1       N!C-CH3                        acetonitrile ='ATN'=meth.[g.g]230?14 *3
1VR       CH3-C0.C6H5                    acetophenone='ACP'=methyl ph.]120    *3
1VOOVR    CH3-C0.0-0-C0.C6H5             acetyl benzoyl peroxide      ]        #*6
EV1       Br-C0.CH3                      acetyl bromide ='ABM'        ]332w?1a*3
GV1       Cl-C0.CH3                      acetyl chloride ='ACC'       ]332w 1a*3
IV1       I-C0.CH3                       acetyl iodide =ethanoyl iodi.]        *3
1VOOV1    CH3-C0.0-0-C0.CH3             (di)acetyl peroxide           ]124P22b*6
```

Displayed on a computer screen is a line notation system devised by chemist William Wiswesser for identifying and cataloging the thousands of new chemical compounds developed each year.

searching services and to publish reports, sponsor technical meetings, and assist less developed countries that requested information services.

France embarked upon Minitel, a national program to replace both white- and yellow-page telephone directories with home videotex terminals. The first phase of the program began in the Brittany region with a local data base containing more than one million names, addresses, and phone numbers. Searches in this new directory could be made by using either a complete or partial name or by profession and could be further facilitated by adding a location such as the local department (equivalent to a U.S. county) or home address. The electronic directory also will offer direct access to emergency numbers, public utilities, and local community services. Subscribers will not be charged for accessing the directory data within their own department, but they will pay regular phone charges when searching for telephone numbers in another area. The service was expected to reach the homes and offices of three million telephone customers by the late 1980s.

With the support of the Luxembourg government a European Institute for Information Management, said to be the first of its kind in the world, began offering postgraduate training in modern information management techniques. The curriculum provided for four main areas of concentration: (1) the information environment, communication policies, and regulatory aspects; (2) organizational structures and objectives, and internal and external information flow; (3) marketing and economics, including market research; and (4) information systems analysis and design, the management of document collections, and the development of online data bases stored in large, remotely located computers and accessed directly through local terminals. The institute's teaching staff was international.

Also located in Luxembourg was the European Center for Automatic Translation (ECAT). Using the Systran English-French and French-English machine translation systems developed by the Commission of the European Communities, ECAT provided either raw or post-edited computer-translated texts to meet the large volume of translations required by members of the Commission.

Information science research. An important focus of current information science research was knowledge-based systems. In order to develop sophisticated information systems that display human-like intelligence, it is necessary first to détermine how humans organize events in memory. A research project at Emory University near Atlanta, Ga., studied two levels of event organization: a global level, at which experiences are organized into broad categories, and a detailed level, at which experiences are organized within a given category. Also, investigators at St. Joseph's University in Philadelphia were studying the role of formal logic in unifying different concepts and procedures for achieving efficient storage and retrieval of information relating to a specific subject area. Conclusions from those studies could lead to the construction of data bases that can be more efficiently manipulated by humans.

A knowledge of existing regularities of meaning patterns associated with words both in a single language and across several languages could contribute to progress in the design of intelligent information systems. Research at Lehigh University (Bethlehem, Pa.) was focused on the development of procedures for the selection of words used in querying textual retrieval systems. In addition to the development of selection procedures, this effort was to encompass measures of performance and analysis of failures. Results should lead to improvements in text searching and computer-aided indexing.

Electronics and information sciences

At Harvard University researchers were seeking to develop a set of theoretical constructs to test the economic and social consequences of such information technologies as computers, microprocessors, and digital communications. The goal was to be able to analyze and guide changes resulting from scientific advances in information technology. At the Massachusetts Institute of Technology researchers were attempting to understand the relationship between the demand for information at national, industry, and individual firm levels and subsequent structural changes in the economy so as to increase the understanding of factors affecting productivity. At the Free University of Berlin a project was under way to try to determine the relationship between human and technical factors in information system design.
—Harold Borko

Satellite systems

Earth-orbiting satellites that utilize their vantage points in space for economic benefit and military purposes are termed applications satellites. There are three basic classes of such satellite systems: communications, Earth observation, and navigation. Satellite systems are developed and operated by individual nations, groups of nations, and by private industrial concerns.

The U.S. and the Soviet Union continued to dominate such activities because of their large booster rockets. Both nations launched satellites for other countries.

The European Space Agency (ESA), a consortium of 11 Western European countries, achieved two launches during the year. The ESA Ariane booster is in direct competition with the U.S. for commercial satellite launch business.

Communications satellites. Rapid growth and expansion continued in the area of communications satellites. An example is long-distance telephone service via satellite to businesses and private homes. Costs of such telephone calls are substantially lower than those through the lines of American Telephone and Telegraph Co. (AT&T). AT&T rates are tightly controlled by the U.S. Federal Communications Commission (FCC). Among the leading competitors of AT&T were MCI Communications Corp. and General Telephone and Electronics Corp. (GTE). Another independent firm was Satellite Business System (SBS), which was owned jointly by IBM Corp., Communications Satellite Corp. (Comsat), and Aetna Life and Casualty. Three SBS satellites were in orbit as of 1984, and the firm planned to provide high-speed data communications. In 1983 SBS launched the Skyline telephone service in the 20 largest U.S. cities, thereby acquiring 85,000 new customers.

Direct Broadcast Satellite (DBS) service of tele-

vision programs to homes and hotels was another highly competitive field. Satellite Television Corp. (STC), a division of Comsat and the originator of this concept, announced the advancement of the date when it would begin providing commercial DBS television service from 1986 to 1984. United Satellite Communications Inc., a year-old company backed by Prudential Insurance Co., offered immediate five-channel service in Indiana and in the Washington, D.C., area.

In 1983 the flood of applications submitted to the FCC evidenced the rush to capture a financial foothold in the increasing demand for satellite communications. Nineteen U.S. companies requested FCC approval to launch domestic communications satellites. Among their purposes would be to establish or replace existing systems or make additions to present satellite networks.

In the international arena the 108-nation consortium International Telecommunications Satellite Organization (Intelsat) was being challenged. Several U.S. firms requested FCC approval to capture a portion of the lucrative North Atlantic satellite communications market. Strong unanimous opposition by Intelsat members resulted. It was argued that approval of such a precedent would weaken the global

Tracking and Data Relay Satellite System communications satellite is launched from the cargo bay of the space shuttle "Challenger" in April 1983.

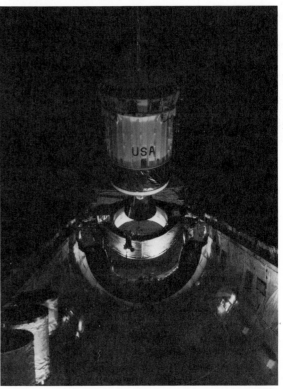

NASA

308

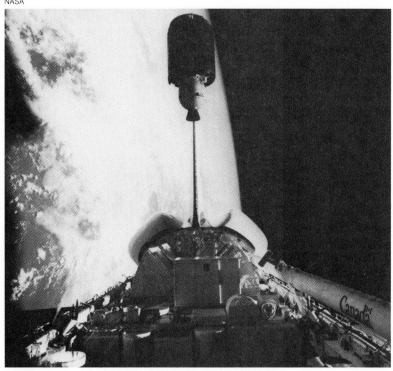

Indonesia's Palapa B communications satellite is sent into Earth orbit from the space shuttle "Challenger" in June 1983. In the foreground are experiment packages, and the Earth can be seen in the background. The shuttle's Canadian-built remote manipulator arm is at the right.

service at the expense of the less developed nations, which represent 75% of the members of Intelsat.

In April the U.S. National Aeronautics and Space Administration (NASA) launched the first of three planned Tracking and Data Relay Satellite System (TDRSS) satellites from the "Challenger" space shuttle orbiter. A malfunctioning orbital transfer booster failed to place the TDRSS in the desired orbit. Skillful use of onboard thrusters stopped the craft's wild tumbling. By means of dozens of subsequent firings over the next several weeks the 2,270-kg (5,000-lb) spacecraft was propelled to its assigned location, 35,900 km (22,300 mi) above the Equator.

On its next flight, two months later, "Challenger" launched two communications satellites, the Anik C-2 for Canada and Palapa B-1 for Indonesia. Anik C-2 was designed to provide direct-to-home pay television service in the continental U.S. High-quality pictures would be received via a 1.2-m (4-ft) dish antenna. Palapa B-1 serves Indonesia and the Association of Southeast Asian Nations (ASEAN) by providing improved telephone, telegraph, television, and high-speed data transmissions. Its capacity allowed 12,000 two-way voice circuits and 24 color television channels or combinations thereof.

On its third flight (August 30–September 5) "Challenger" orbited the Indian Insat 1-B satellite. A multipurpose communications (8,000 two-way telephone circuits) and meteorological satellite, Insat 1-B broadcast nationwide television to tens of thousands of rural villages in India.

Two 2,000-kg (4,400-lb) Intelsat 5 satellites were launched during 1983, one by NASA in May aboard an Atlas-Centaur and the second in October by the ESA Ariane booster. This was the first of five Intelsat satellites to be launched by a non-U.S. booster. Four more were scheduled using the ESA Ariane.

In June NASA launched the Hughes Communications, Inc., Galaxy A satellite. Stationed in geostationary orbit (remaining over the same place on the Earth at all times) at a point roughly due south of Juneau, Alaska, Galaxy A relayed TV programming to cable networks in the 50 U.S. states.

Using expendable boosters, NASA launched three other domestic satellites during the year. Telstar 3-A, owned by AT&T, was the first of a new series of domestic satellites providing television, telephone, and other services for the 50 U.S. states and Puerto Rico. Two RCA Corp. communications satellites, RCA-F and RCA-G, were launched in March and August.

Early in 1984 Japan placed in orbit the national broadcast satellite BS-2. Designated Yuri, it transmitted two TV channels throughout the main Japanese islands and also, for the first time, provided high-quality service to the dozens of smaller islands.

Earth observation satellites. This category of applications satellites includes those used for meteorological (weather), Earth resources, and military reconnaissance purposes.

Weather satellites. The U.S. National Oceanic and Atmospheric Administration (NOAA) throughout the year maintained operational geostationary and polar-orbiting weather satellites providing continuous monitoring of global weather. NOAA satellites provided atmospheric profiles of temperature and moisture as well as detailed information on cloud cover, snow cover, sea-surface temperature, solar activity, and magnetic fields. These data were provided to the U.S. National Weather Service and other users. The polar-orbiting satellites monitored ice pack and iceberg hazards for the U.S. Navy and commercial shipping. Among the special uses of the Geostationary Operational Environmental Satellites (GOES) was the relay of data transmitted from hundreds of unattended rain gauges, river-level tide gauges, and tilt gauges near faults in the Earth's crust. GOES 6 was launched into orbit by NASA in June.

Launched in March from Vandenberg Air Force Base in California, a NOAA 8 environmental spacecraft represented the U.S. contribution to an international search-and-rescue satellite program. The satellite was part of an international project in cooperation with Canada, France, Norway, the United Kingdom, and the Soviet Union.

Both U.S. and Soviet satellites carried systems that are able to detect distress signals, even in remote areas of the world, and swiftly relay positional data to ground stations. In the U.S. alone more than 200,000 aircraft and 6,000 ships carry transmitters

Three-stage N-2 rocket carries into orbit Japan's first practical-applications satellite, the Sakura-2a. It was designed to provide telecommunications services.

Galaxy A communications satellite is placed in its protective container before being attached to a Delta rocket for a launch on June 28, 1983.

able to be picked up by the satellite systems. With this technique an emergency site can be pinpointed within an accuracy of 21 km (13 mi). By the end of 1983 the systems, which were established in October 1982, were credited with the saving of 90 lives.

Earth-observation satellites. On Jan. 31, 1983, NASA turned over the operation of the Earth-resources Landsat 4 satellite to NOAA. Failure of one of the spacecraft's components prevented the transmittal of information gained by the thematic mapper, which collected seven narrow bands of spectral data. Other Landsat transmitters, however, sent detailed photographs of various cities via the TDRSS 1 satellite. Because of failure of Landsat 4's power-producing solar panels, NOAA planned to launch a backup Landsat.

Military reconnaissance satellites. Reconnaissance satellites of the U.S. and the Soviet Union continued to observe and remotely sense military targets and activities on a global scale. The Soviet Union, while relying primarily on unmanned satellites for intelligence-gathering, reportedly used cosmonauts and equipment aboard their Salyut 7 orbiting laboratory for military purposes.

The Soviets relied on a relatively large number of unmanned vehicles circling the Earth to carry out reconnaissance functions (including early warning, ocean surveillance, and electronic intelligence gathering). By comparison, the U.S. has sent fewer photographic reconnaissance satellites into orbit, due to the greater durability of U.S. spacecraft—several months or years as compared with two to six weeks for the Soviet vehicles. The U.S.S.R. was believed to have launched 26 reconnaissance satellites in 1983.

On August 19 China launched a reconnaissance satellite, its thirteenth. China's satellite booster, known as the FB-1, was undergoing constant revision at the "East Wind" space center located near the Gobi Desert.

Navigation satellites. The U.S. Global Positioning System (GPS), known as NavStar, continued evaluation of Block I developmental satellites, scheduled for their first launch in 1986. Testing of military and civilian applications of these spacecraft demonstrated the system's ability to calculate by onboard computer the user's location in three dimensions. An improved version, with ten times greater accuracy, was anticipated.

—F. C. Durant III

See also Feature Article: SPACE: A NEW FRONTIER FOR INDUSTRY.

Energy

Continuing with trends that first emerged in 1981, energy developments during the past year took place largely in the marketplace instead of the political arena. A growing U.S. general political stalemate continued to prevent significant action on energy legislation (or on environmental laws that might have significant impacts on energy). Such U.S. political developments as occurred were either administrative or involved the reduction of appropriations to various programs. Also, no major initiatives appeared to have been taken in other countries.

Petroleum. The members of the Organization of Petroleum Exporting Countries (OPEC) managed to continue limiting the erosion of their market positions. The decline in world oil production that began in 1980 persisted into 1983. The tendency of OPEC output to contract as nonmembers expanded their output also prevailed. Such expansion as did occur was mainly scattered among countries that up to now have been minor oil producers. None of the leading non-OPEC producers significantly altered their output in 1983. In particular, Mexico and Great Britain showed no growth in 1983.

Another development of the 1980s that persisted was the pressure on Saudi Arabia to contribute significantly to restriction in OPEC output. Through the 1970s and on into August 1981, when output peaked, the Saudis benefited from production drops

Table I. World Crude Oil Production
(000 bbl per day)

Country	1973	1979	1982	July 1983
United States	9,208	8,552	8,649	8,647
U.S.S.R.	8,465	11,460	12,053	11,900
Total OPEC	30,989	30,928	18,780	18,475
Saudi Arabia	7,596	9,532	6,470	5,435
Iran	5,861	3,168	2,214	2,600
Iraq	2,018	3,477	972	1,000
Kuwait	3,020	2,500	827	1,085
Libya	2,175	2,092	1,158	1,100
Nigeria	2,054	2,302	1,295	1,715
Venezuela	3,366	2,356	1,891	1,695
OPEC less Saudi Arabia	23,393	21,396	12,310	13,040
Mexico	465	1,461	2,749	2,685
Non-OPEC Total	24,685	31,607	33,352	35,254
World	55,674	62,535	52,132	53,730

Source: U.S. Department of Energy, *Monthly Energy Review.*

elsewhere and could expand their own. This occurred both during the period of essentially stable OPEC output from 1973 to 1979 and through the initial declines of 1980 and 1981.

Beginning in September 1981, however, the Saudis started an output reduction program that persisted into 1983. From the peak of 10.3 million bbl per day in August 1981, Saudi production declined to 8.6 million bbl per day by December 1981 and to 5.3 million a year later; it reached a low of 3.6 million in March 1983 and then rose later in the year.

The onset of the Saudi decline coincided with Nigerian price cutting in mid-1981 that allowed the latter country to recover from a sharp drop in production. Through the end of 1981 Saudi declines were largely offset by Nigerian increases, and total OPEC output remained level at approximately 21 million bbl per day. From February 1982 to February 1983, total OPEC output declined to a low of 14.4 million bbl per day. By July 1983 OPEC production had recovered to 18.5 million bbl per day.

Saudi Arabia thus endured about three-fourths of the February 1982 to February 1983 declines, but the subsequent rise in Saudi output only amounted to a bit more than 40% of the total rise. Thus, Saudi leadership of OPEC appeared to involve accepting a lower share of the organization's total production.

Crude oil prices continued their downward drift during the past year. One indicator, the U.S. Department of Energy figures on the average cost of imported crude oil, reached its peak of $39 per bbl in early 1981. By late 1981 the cost had declined to about $36 per bbl; by December 1982 it was down to $33 and by mid-1983 to $29.

This average was affected by the differences in price trends among the various countries and also by the levels of imports from those nations. For example, U.S. oil imports reached their peak of 8.8 million bbl per day in 1977. In the first nine months of 1983 they were averaging below 5 million bbl per day. The OPEC portion of those imports declined from more than 6 million bbl in 1977 to 4.3 million in 1980 and then to an average of 1.7 million bbl per day during the first eight months of 1983. Non-OPEC supplies gradually rose from 2.6 million in 1977 to more than 3 million during the first months of 1983.

The decline in dependence on OPEC reversed a pattern that had emerged in the 1970s. As late as 1970 approximately 1.3 million of the 3.4 million bbl per day imported by the U.S. came from OPEC countries, with Venezuela accounting for almost 1 million bbl of the OPEC total. During the rise in dependence on OPEC, Saudi Arabia, Nigeria, and Libya were the largest sources of increased imports. During the subsequent decline, U.S. purchases from Libya stopped; those from Saudi Arabia dropped from a peak of 1.4 million bbl per day to little more than 200,000; and those from Nigeria declined from slightly more than 1 million to less than 300,000.

Natural gas and coal. While the decline in oil use was abating somewhat, the tendency for accelerating declines in natural gas consumption appeared to persist into 1983. In 1983 oil consumption in the U.S. was about 3% below that of 1982, while consumption of natural gas was down about 10%.

Coal consumption and production in 1983 declined from their 1982 levels. The consumption decline began in late 1981 and was predominantly due to sharp drops in steel production, which caused, in turn, equally sharp drops in the use of coal to make coke for iron manufacture. The decline was aggravated by modest decreases in coal use by electric utilities and other industries.

The desire to rebuild inventories depleted by the 1981 coal miners' strike and the absence of a strike allowed coal production to rise in 1982. However, the continued weakness of domestic demand and the collapse of the export boom that emerged in 1980 caused a sharp drop of coal output in early 1983. (For additional information on coal, *see* Feature Article: THE NEW PROMISE OF COAL.)

Energy policies. Major decisions affecting energy policy in the U.S in 1983 were largely negative—not to reform natural gas regulation, not to pass major new environmental regulations, not to alter the laws covering nuclear power or administratively reform the implementation of those laws, to cease funding a breeder reactor demonstration plant, to phase out a program to subsidize synthetic fuel production, and to impose a moratorium on federal coal leasing until a study commission completed its report.

In the first two cases deep political divisions have precluded action for the last several years. As of 1984 natural gas policy was still guided by 1978 legislation that was intended gradually to eliminate most price controls on natural gas. The law established numerous categories of natural gas, each one

Experiment station near Rifle, Colorado, is the site of tests to determine whether it is technically and economically feasible to recover natural gas from deeply buried sandstone deposits.

subject to different rules about both when or even whether deregulation would occur and about the allowable prices while regulation persisted.

Concerns arose about the wisdom of the legislation, particularly because it failed to provide a means to respond to the impacts of another oil price rise such as the one that occurred in 1980–81. Opponents of regulation suggested that higher oil prices implied the need to speed up gas deregulation.

It was recognized that decontrol would allow the production of gas that is cheaper to extract than it is to import oil. This was supposed to have the offsetting disadvantage of raising average energy prices because domestic suppliers, released from controls, could charge more for their products. This would cause economic hardships for consumers. However, declining OPEC prices prevented any such development because imported oil became cheaper than the domestic supplies. Deregulation may have had an influence on this price decline, and political proponents of decontrol were quick to claim so. While this probably was a dubious claim, it could be validly argued that weakness in world oil prices makes it desirable to accelerate and extend gas price decontrol because the oil weakness would cause any price rises of gas resulting from decontrol to be relatively small,

Others argued that gas prices would rise more than expected when the deregulation provisions are fully implemented and that decontrol should, therefore,

Coal combuster developed by TRW Inc., is part of a system that allows converted oil- and gas-fired units to burn coal cleanly.

TRW Inc., Electronics & Defense Sector

be slowed. The divisions between the two factions were so great and the priorities for resolving the issue so low in a period of international crises and concern over overall budgetary policy that no action was possible.

Similar divisions occurred over air pollution regulation. The Reagan administration made suggestions for loosening some of the widely criticized provisions of the Clean Air Act Amendments of 1977, including those imposing restrictions on allowable increases of pollution. The administration feared that these restrictions could severely hinder economic expansion. Instead of acting on these, the U.S. Congress began to consider policies to reduce greatly the discharge of sulfur and nitrogen oxides that were believed to cause harmful deposits of acid in rainfall.

The critical problem was that the cleanup effort would have to concentrate on electric power plants that emitted significant amounts of sulfur dioxides. Several areas of discord arose. First, a distinction was made between nationwide controls and controls directed at mitigating the impact on the northeastern United States, the area most severely affected. Even nationwide controls would have uneven effects because the total sources of discharges were unequally distributed among different regions.

Efforts to assuage fears of the regions most likely to be affected by controls included spreading the financial responsibility for the controls throughout the United States by means of a nationwide tax on electricity generation. However, representatives of such regions as most of the western U.S., which would have to bear some of the cost but reap no benefits, opposed such efforts. Northeastern states and Canada, whose eastern provinces suffer materially from acid rain, maintained their pressures for corrective action.

The demise of the breeder reactor demonstration project resolved many years of controversy. The project had generated debate over both the basic idea and the specific program adopted. A breeder reactor involves reactions of higher speeds than those in other reactors. The result is that the reactions transform more of the nonreactive uranium-238 isotopes in the reactor fuel to a reactive fuel such as plutonium or uranium-235 than do the other reactors. In fact, more reactive material is created than is used up, giving rise to the description "breeder."

The breeder reactor, therefore, was envisioned as a means to extend uranium supplies by producing more fissionable fuel from it. The plans were developed in the late 1960s and early 1970s when fears of rapid increases in uranium use and of shrinkages of available supplies existed. Even then, critics argued that the program was based on overly pessimistic views of the prospects of uranium supply. Some of those who believed that some attention should be

Rotor about to be installed in the rest of the assembly is the heart of an experimental superconducting electric generator that in recent tests produced 20,600 kilovolt-amperes of electricity, about twice as much as could be produced by a conventional generator of comparable size. The rotor operates at a temperature of −269° C (−452° F).

devoted to the breeder argued that it was better to work slowly and evaluate several technologies on a small scale than to build as rapidly as possible a fairly large demonstration plant using one technology. The latter alternative was the one actually adopted.

The reduction of nuclear expansion plans and widespread success in uranium exploration alleviated pressures on uranium availability and made use of the breeder less urgent. However, the demonstration plant program attracted enough political support that it was allowed until 1983 to limp along rather than being killed or replaced by an alternative program. Much of the political opposition to the project was residual antagonism generated by campaigns against nuclear weapons and, although less intensely, this also affected conventional nuclear plants under planning or construction.

In Western Europe, meanwhile, a six-nation consortium set about negotiating to build a fast breeder reactor. Belgium, Finland, France, Sweden, and Switzerland all generated more than 25% of their electricity by nuclear energy—a significantly greater proportion than in the U.S.

In the United States and Canada there were 90 reactors operating, and another 70 were under construction or planned. However, in the Soviet Union and Eastern Europe (excluding Yugoslavia and Albania) there were 52 reactors operating and 119 building or planned. In the United Kingdom 32 were operating and 11 building or planned.

Elsewhere on the U.S. nuclear front, prospects continued to be depressing. Streamlining of the Nuclear Regulatory Commission was nowhere in sight. The commission found it had made itself the captive of local officials opposed to nuclear power by requiring those officials to join with it in drawing up plans that would evaluate the advantages and disadvantages of locating nuclear plants in a particular area. Officials, particularly in New York State, prevented the development of such plans by refusing to participate.

Several nuclear plants became enmeshed in controversies over the quality of their construction and operation. In one particularly severe case a utility in Ohio was accused of inadequate quality control in the construction of a plant supposedly almost completed. In another, the Nuclear Regulatory Commission told Chicago-based Commonwealth Edison, the leading U.S. producer of nuclear-generated electricity, that defects in construction procedures prevented the licensing of a nearly complete two-unit plant.

Among other disputes concerning nuclear power, a reactor on Long Island was nearing completion after years of procedural delays, but some questioned the wisdom of allowing it to become operational. Efforts to secure certification of the correction of design errors in a two-unit California plant were going slowly.

In addition, reduced expectations about the growth of electricity generation continued to affect adversely plans to build coal-fired plants. Previous plans were delayed, and no new units were announced for the first time in many decades.

The fossil-fuel counterpart of the breeder reactor was an ambitious program aimed at extracting oil and gas from coal and oil shales. This was proposed and enacted, despite severe criticism by energy specialists, during the last half of the administration of Pres. Jimmy Carter. It fell into disfavor with the administration of Pres. Ronald Reagan even more rapidly than did the breeder. The synthetic fuels program suffered from a series of decisions by major oil companies not to proceed with their extraction projects even with government aid.

An initially quiet debate arose in regard to how well the U.S. Department of the Interior was managing its coal-leasing program. In the wake of rumors of premature disclosure of critical information and two investigative reports claiming that the department had sold coal too cheaply, Congress voted in mid-1983 to establish a Commission on Fair Market Value Policy for Federal Coal Leasing to determine whether the administration of coal-leasing policy was satisfactory.

The commission began work in late August. At first little notice was taken, but on September 21 Secretary of the Interior James Watt made an off-hand comment at a public meeting about the gender, ethnicity, religion, physical attributes, and, as a seeming afterthought, talent of the commission. The result was a storm of publicity in which critics of Watt's policies gained the support of those offended by the tone of the secretary's statement. When the furor persisted, Watt resigned and was replaced by William Clark.

The commission continued its work during and after this publicity. It discovered that Watt and his associates had been conducting coal leasing in a fashion that needlessly created suspicion of the program. The procedures and their inadequate explanation could be and were used as ammunition by the many critics of coal leasing.

Those critics were a coalition of many groups. They included environmental organizations whose general opposition to energy supply development particularly involved severe criticism of surface mining in the western United States. That type of mining generally occurred after a federal coal lease was granted. Western landowners, especially those owning the surface over coal-bearing lands in which the federal government held mineral rights, wanted protection to ensure either their right to prevent undesired intrusions or substantial compensation for tolerating such disturbance. Others, suspicious of private enterprise, worried that the federal government would be inadequately paid for the leases. Still others, such as coal industries in states without federal coal, feared competition.

Much of the criticism was based on claimed defects in the methods for ensuring adequate payment to the government for the leases. The controversy centered on decisions made during the Carter administration. One was that small tracts that are most valuable when leased to the operator of a nearby mine could be sold for half their estimated value. Coupled with this were decisions made by civil servants that tracts be valued on the assumption that the winning bidders might not make enough profits immediately to write off against their income taxes what they paid to secure their lease and that a formula based on studies by a staff mining engineer be

Table II. Consumption of Major Fuels in the United States (000,000,000 BTU's)

Year	Coal	Natural gas	Petro-leum	Water	Nuclear	Total
1947	15,824	4,518	11,367	1,326	0	33,035
1960	10,110	12,390	19,920	1,650	10	44,080
1970	12,600	21,790	29,520	2,650	240	66,830
1973	13,292	22,512	34,840	3,010	910	74,609
1974	12,935	21,732	33,455	3,309	1,272	72,759
1975	12,837	19,948	32,731	3,219	1,900	70,707
1976	13,733	20,345	35,175	3,066	2,111	74,510
1977	13,979	19,931	37,122	2,515	2,702	76,332
1978	13,977	20,000	37,965	3,141	3,024	78,175
1979	15,175	20,666	37,123	3,141	2,715	78,910
1980	15,424	20,391	34,202	3,118	2,739	75,988
1981	15,956	19,930	31,931	3,066	2,974	73,984
1982	15,389	18,319	30,416	3,571	3,084	70,887
1983	15,785	16,588	29,749	3,917	3,140	69,272

Source: U.S. Department of Energy, *Monthly Energy Review.*

used to evaluate the effect of production rates on lease values.

Critics dismissed the contentions of the government economists that values could not be validly based on a single sale in 1980, at the height of optimism about the prospects for coal. Such dependence on a single data point is always questionable. It was made more so by the radical changes in expectations about coal markets that occurred between 1980 and the criticized coal sale in 1982. During that time the recognition emerged that the only solid market for coal was electricity generation, and that it would grow more slowly than had been previously predicted; also, the flurry of steam coal exports in 1979 and 1980 would not presage massive further increases. In addition federal coal was poorly located to serve the export market.

Thus, the prospects for federal coal and, therefore, the value of coal leases had been reduced. This reduction, however, was not considered in the value estimation process. In this connection it is interesting to note that, after the lease sale, the property whose 1980 price was used as the basis for setting the values of the 1982 leases was resold for a much lower price.

Energy consumption. The United States and many of the other industrialized nations seemed headed for another year of declining energy consumption. The decreases were expected to be sharper in the area of household, commercial, and industrial use than for electric utilities and transportation.

Generally, energy problems were of less pressing concern than they had been in the recent past. Nevertheless, a wide variety of interest groups remained active. Their main accomplishments in the future seemed likely to be in the marketplace rather than in the political realm.

—Richard L. Gordon

Environment

By far the most important event related to the environment in 1983 occurred at the end of the year. On December 23 two articles appeared in *Science* magazine concerning the global environmental consequences of a thermonuclear war. The conventional wisdom has held that while very large numbers of people would be killed in a nuclear war, a significant proportion of the population would survive, even in the United States and the Soviet Union. There is, however, an important reason to be suspicious of this contention. Scientists suspect that during the history of the planet there were times when large numbers of plant and animal species became extinct in a brief period. These mass extinctions are believed to have been caused by an extremely large volcanic eruption, the simultaneous occurrence of several major volcanic eruptions, or the impact on the Earth of a large object from outer space. In all these cases, there would be so much dust, gas, and aerosol material ejected into the upper atmosphere that only three-quarters or less of the usual solar energy would reach the surface of the Earth, and the extinctions would occur because of chilling.

Nuclear war and the environment. Reconsideration of the implications of a nuclear war received new impetus in 1982 and 1983. Several scientific reports were published pointing out that dense clouds of soil particles may have played a major role in past mass extinctions of life on Earth. It is certainly a fact that large groups of species that were formerly dominant, such as the reptiles (including dinosaurs) of the Mesozoic Era (225 million to 65 million years ago), have become extinct.

An individual hydrogen bomb only has one two-thousandth the explosive force of a volcanic eruption such as that of Tambora in 1815 (which produced the "year without a summer" in all countries for which weather or agricultural records exist). However, in a nuclear war there would be at least several hundred such weapons exploding simultaneously. Furthermore, many of them would start major fires that would quickly overwhelm any surviving fire-fighting capability.

Richard Turco, Owen Toon, Thomas Ackerman, James Pollack, and Carl Sagan used models from the rapidly developing science of geophysics to ascertain the effects on the atmosphere of various plausible nuclear wars. Their specific objective was to determine the effect of dust and smoke particles on the optical properties of air, so as to calculate the likely penetration of the planetary air shield by solar radiation and the resulting air temperatures. They explored the implications of imaginary nuclear wars ranging from 300 to 28,300 explosions. All the scenarios were highly realistic: there are now 17,000

As Richard Turco and other scientists project the effects of a nuclear war that begins in the Northern Hemisphere (top photo; America at left, Europe at bottom), a dense pall of smoke and dust would cover most of the globe (center), leaving a frozen and defoliated world (bottom).

warheads in the world's nuclear arsenal, counting only primary strategic and theater weapons.

Total smoke emission in their base case (5,000 megatons of TNT equivalent) is only 225 million tons, released over several days. At first, this does not seem extraordinary, because the current global annual smoke emission is about 200 million tons. The problem is the very small size of many of the particles. It is the smallest particles ejected into the atmosphere from volcanic eruptions that take the longest time to drift down to the Earth. Therefore, they have a long time aloft in which to increase the planetary reflectance (albedo) to incoming solar energy. The authors postulated several mechanisms, all known to be realistic, by which nuclear explosions could generate fine particles; they include ejection of soil particles into the atmosphere, vaporization of rock, and blowoff and sweepup of surface dust and smoke. They pointed out that analysis of particles in dust samples from previous nuclear explosions shows that a significant proportion of the particles are extremely small.

The most important conclusion reached by the authors is that three to four weeks after a nuclear war, the average minimum land temperature in the Northern Hemisphere would be −23° C (−9.4° F). Subfreezing temperatures would last for several months. If the war should occur during the summer, it would become winter. Because fine dust would linger in the stratosphere, prolonged cooling would last for a year. Disturbances in atmospheric circulation and hence in weather patterns would be likely. There is a prevalent notion that a limited nuclear war need not have calamitous consequences. The authors point out that even a limited nuclear exchange could have relatively large climatic effects if urban areas were heavily targeted. Burning of several hundred of the world's major population centers would involve the chemical transformation of massive amounts of combustible material. This would generate vast quantities of smoke, thus reducing the optical transparency of the air surrounding the planet. Intense fire storms would pump smoke into the stratosphere.

Previous planning for disaster management after a nuclear exchange may have overlooked the consequences of interactions among the various effects of such an exchange. Low light levels, subfreezing temperatures, exposure to radioactivity, heavy air pollution from combustion, and the destruction of medical facilities and all energy sources would occur in combination. All the "solutions" that people may subconsciously assume would be available would be destroyed or grossly inadequate. While the authors did not mention the point, retrospective analysis of hurricane disasters shows that any thought of mass evacuation from urban areas is simply foolish; there would be inadequate warning beforehand, and after the blast roads would be covered by trees and utility poles knocked down by high winds (as after Hurricane Iwa on the island of Kauai, Hawaii, in November 1982). Since most heavy equipment would have been destroyed, it would not be possible to clear away the debris.

The biological consequences of nuclear war were discussed in a paper by Paul Ehrlich and 19 distinguished environmental scientists. The paper was an outgrowth of a workshop involving 40 scientists and was said to represent a consensus of all 40. They conclude that, as the result of a nuclear exchange, 30% of the mid-latitude land area of the Northern Hemisphere would receive a radiation dose comparable to or more than the acute mean lethal dose for healthy adult human beings. A major problem would be the effect on plant life. Plants can withstand cold temperatures if they have the time to adjust gradually, but an extremely fast temperature drop, with no preparation time, would be lethal. The intensity of near-ultraviolet radiation would be increased by a factor of about 50, and this would suppress the immune systems of humans and other mammals, destroy plant leaves, and suppress the normal process of genetic repair (of DNA). Seeds stocks for most North American, European, and Soviet crops, stored predominantly in or near target areas, would be depleted.

Thus survivors in the Northern Hemisphere would face extreme cold and darkness, water shortages, lack of food and fuel, heavy burdens of radiation and pollutants, disease, and severe psychological stress. The authors conclude that because of these and many other effects, civilization would be destroyed, at least in the Northern Hemisphere.

Volcanoes and cold. Coincidentally, just as these discussions of nuclear winter were appearing, many parts of the United States were suffering through the coldest December in the history of weather records. In an article published early in 1984, Michael Rampino and Stephen Self offered an explanation. Although presumably prepared long before the December cold wave, the article suggests that such occurrences might result from two eruptions of El Chichón volcano in southeastern Mexico, which took place on March 28 and April 4, 1982. Since the effects on weather of pollutants from a nuclear exchange would be similar to those of volcanic debris, their hypothesis is of more than passing interest.

Only about 0.6 cu km (0.24 cu mi) of ash and pumice was discharged by El Chichón. Compared with other historic eruptions, this is very little; Krakatoa discharged 20 cu km (8 cu mi) in 1883 and Tambora discharged more than 175 cu km (70 cu mi) in 1815. However, there are large sulfur deposits under El Chichón, and the eruption was unusually rich in sulfur gases, which have a disproportionate effect on mean temperature. Satellite tracking of the plume showed that by April 25 it had girdled the Northern Hemisphere at the latitude of the volcano. Using computer models of climate cause-effect mechanisms, Rampino and Self projected that the gaseous clouds from El Chichón would depress Northern Hemisphere temperatures by 0.4° C (0.7° F) by late 1983, and 0.5° C (0.9° F) by the winter of 1984–85.

According to Rampino and Self, El Chichón also

altered the vertical profile of atmospheric temperatures and, therefore, atmospheric circulation patterns. Temperature gradients constitute one of the driving forces behind the planetary wind circulation patterns, as heat flows from hot to cold locations. The aerosol cloud from El Chichón might have warmed the upper stratosphere in the tropics, thus reducing the temperature difference between it and the surface of the Earth. This would lead to a weakening of the atmospheric circulation and of the ocean circulation it drives. An atypical atmospheric circulation pattern of this sort occurred in 1963, associated with the eruption of Mt. Agung on Bali. Living organisms would see the evidence of such a pattern in the form of a nonvigorous, "meandering" jet stream, so that, for example, much of the United States might be affected by weather coming from subarctic or even arctic latitudes (in the vicinity of Alaska or eastern Siberia) rather than by weather coming from the west at the latitude of the central Pacific Ocean.

There is no doubt that December 1983 was phenomenally cold in the United States, while weather in Europe was mild (suggestive of a meandering wind circulation). In at least 26 U.S. cities, from the Rockies to the northern plains and south to Texas, new record low average temperatures for December were set: 24.7° F (−4.1° C) for Amarillo, Texas (previous record 27.5° F [−2.5° C] in 1898); 2.1° F (−16.6° C) for Sioux Falls, S.D. (8° F [−13.3° C] in 1917); 13.2° F (−10.4° C) for Kansas City, Mo. (22.2° F [−5.4° C] in 1909). The proximate cause is clear: a change in the global wind circulation pattern that brought arctic winds very far south into the United States. Almost certainly, this was caused, in turn, by a reduction in energy driving the global wind system, and Rampino and Self's analysis suggests that the ultimate cause was reduced temperature gradients attributable to the atmospheric haze produced by El Chichón. (For a full discussion of this subject, see Feature Article: PURPLE SKIES AND COOLING SEAS: VOLCANISM AND CLIMATE.)

The "growth" issue. When the U.S. environmental movement was at its height, between 1968 and 1973, a widely voiced concern was the likelihood of excessive "growth" and its attendant ills, such as overpopulation, pollution, resource depletion, and landscape degradation. By 1984, however, there was growing evidence that self-regulatory mechanisms were at work, slowing growth or even bringing it to an end. In the United States, for example, there were 4,308,000 live births in 1957, but at the beginning and end of the peak period of concern about the environment, in 1968 and 1973, there were 3,502,000 and 3,137,000 live births, respectively. This number crept up steadily after 1973, reaching 3,646,000 by 1981. However, the increase masked an important phenomenon: birthrates per woman had fallen. Thus

there were 261 births for every 1,000 women 20–24 years of age in 1957, but only 116 in 1979. Actual births had remained high because of the large number of women in the prime childbearing age group, the result of the postwar baby boom. However, the number of women in this category would fall drastically in the next few years, possibly bringing about a spectacular drop in the rate of population increase.

Energy statistics, another major indicator of growth, also showed decline. Total energy consumption in the United States in 1981 was only 93.5% as great as in 1979. Similar trends appeared in international statistics. The average annual rate of world population growth was 2.1% from 1965 to 1970, 2% from 1970 to 1975, 1.8% from 1975 to 1980, and only 1.7% from 1980 to 1982. World production of crude petroleum fell from 22.9 billion bbl in 1979 to 20.5 billion bbl in 1981.

One plausible explanation for this braking mechanism lies in the ratio of real wages to consumer prices. The world's supplies of raw commodities are becoming genuinely depleted, and the cost of obtaining them is, therefore, rising. One example makes the point. In 1970 the cost of discovering one new barrel of crude oil in the United States averaged 18 cents in constant 1967 dollars. That cost, still in 1967 dollars, had risen to $2.02 by 1976 and to $4.68 by 1979. During the last several years the news has been full of stories about extremely expensive oil-exploration efforts, such as that in the Baltimore Canyon off the east coast of the U.S., that failed to find any commercially useful deposits. As such costs are passed along through the economic system, the cost of living is driven up, and people respond by having fewer children and consuming less. If these trends continue, concern about excessive growth may be only a distant memory by the year 2000.

Energy analysis overview. Two important new publications on systems analysis of entire nations appeared in 1983, the first by Howard Odum, the second by Odum, his wife, Elisabeth, and an international team of nine collaborators. Both publications were based on a powerful new concept developed by Odum, which he calls embodied energy. This idea is most simply explained as follows. Throughout a complex modern society energy is constantly being transformed from one type to another, as when water falling over the blades of a turbine generates electricity. Because of the qualitative differences among the various energy types, the energy of each type must be converted to some common measure—such as solar or coal equivalents—if they are to be compared in a meaningful way. Odum uses the term energy transformation ratio to express the energy of one type required to generate a unit of energy of another type. All energy flows and storages in a society expressed in energy equivalents of one type constitute the embodied energy of that type.

Odum and his colleagues have used this new perspective to conduct a comparative analysis of 12 nations, ranging from the most advanced to the least developed. One measure is the fraction of national embodied energy that is of indigenous origin. That fraction ranges from a low of 0.104 in West Germany to a high of 0.97 in the Soviet Union; the statistic for the United States is 0.77. Another interesting index is the ratio of imports to exports expressed in embodied energy, which ranges from a low of 0.151 for Liberia to a high of 4.3 for The Netherlands. This means that Liberia, in energy terms, has extremely unfavorable terms of trade, whereas The Netherlands has favorable terms of trade. The corresponding values for the United States and the Soviet Union are 2.2 and 0.23, respectively, indicating that the United States, in energy terms, is underpaying for imports and overcharging for exports, while the reverse is true for the Soviet Union.

Another revealing statistic is the ratio of embodied energy to dollar flow in a nation. That ratio ranges from 0.9 for Brazil to 34.5 for Liberia. This means that Brazil gets tremendous economic leverage out of its energy, but Liberia gets very little. The corresponding data for the United States and the Soviet Union are 2.6 and 3.4. Thus, the United States gets somewhat more leverage out of its energy than does the Soviet Union. Put as simply as possible, a nation where this ratio has a very high value is an exploited third world nation, while the ratio for an exploiting nation has a very low value. It is extraordinary to discover that, by this measure, Australia is a grossly exploited third world nation and Spain is an exploiter. In short, when the yardstick is energy rather than money, the appearance of the world is altered.

Basic research in ecology. As long as people have paid careful attention to nature, there has been curiosity and speculation about the causes of the cyclical fluctuations that occur in the populations of many animal species, particularly furbearers in the northern latitudes and insects. Scientists have discovered various reasons for these cycles, one firmly established cause being interaction with pathogens. However, an increasing body of research, notably that by Lloyd B. Keith and his students at the University of Wisconsin, has implicated the impact of herbivores on their vegetation resources and the consequent impact of the quality and quantity of the vegetation on the herbivores as a key cycle-producing mechanism.

In 1983 important support for Keith's findings appeared in a doctoral dissertation by Andreas Fischlin at the Swiss Federal Institute of Technology in Zürich. He used systems analysis and computer modeling to expose the driving mechanism underlying the nine-year cycle of the larch bud moth of the Swiss Alps. Previous research had shown that abundance of the larvae, as well as other characteristics, was deleteriously affected by a decline in the nutritional quality of the larch needles. Furthermore, chemical analyses had demonstrated that the raw fiber content of larch needles served as an index of the nutritional quality of the needles for the bud moth larvae: the greater the raw fiber content of the larch needles, the lower the survival rate of the larvae. Field research had shown that there was an astonishingly high statistical association between the raw fiber content and survival of the larvae; it accounted for 97% of the variation in survival of small larvae and 99% of the variation in survival in large larvae. Statistical associations that high are rare in this type of research.

Fischlin invented an elaborate mathematical model to mimic the reciprocal relationships between the larch trees and the larch bud moth populations. Two key ideas were incorporated into the model. The first was that excessive grazing of the needles by the larvae, resulting from abnormally high larval populations, weakens the plants, causing the fiber content of the needles to increase and lowering their nutritional value, and that this in turn raises the mortality rate of the larvae. The second idea was that lowered nutritional value of the needles results in lowered fecundity of the adult female bud moth. The model was used to generate population cycles for the bud moth, and the results matched the fluctuations observed in nature with respect to both size and duration. Supporting these findings, it has been discovered that the size and duration of fluctuations in the snowshoe hare population in Alberta can also be duplicated, using a computer model based on the assumption of a delayed response of hare survival and fecundity to depleted vegetation caused by prior excessive hare populations.

These studies raise a deeper issue: the significance of computers in research on ecology and the environment. As cheaper and more powerful computers become widely available to scientists, important questions arise as to how they should be used. Fischlin addresses these questions head on. There is a temptation to build models that attempt to mimic reality in detail, but experience in many fields has demonstrated that very large, complex computer models do not necessarily bring new, deeper insights. Fischlin concludes that the aims of the modeler should be to optimize realism, holism, simplicity, and generality, and that this leads the investigator to a certain strategy of modeling. Rather than constructing models that are basically linear in structure and involve very large numbers of equations and variables, he will choose those with a basically nonlinear structure and very small numbers of equations and variables.

Technicians from the U.S. Environmental Protection Agency drill to obtain soil samples at Times Beach, Missouri. Because of extensive soil contamination by the toxic chemical dioxin, Times Beach was declared unfit for human habitation.

The philosophical implications are far-reaching. Is nature linear or nonlinear in its operation? Simple logic indicates that it must be nonlinear. For example, if the growth of any population (including human) is constrained by any limits (and all populations studied are so constrained), then the growth rate must decline as the limit is approached. Similarly, the effectiveness of a parasite or predator declines as the number of previously unattacked hosts or prey declines or the number of attackers increases. Wherever one looks in nature, nonlinear mechanisms are at work. Linear models, therefore, can never "capture" the real character of nature, whereas relatively simple nonlinear models may mimic it much more faithfully. Fischlin's dissertation, simply by demonstrating the vastly greater effectiveness of the nonlinear route in accounting for the observed data, suggests that it will be the one chosen more and more frequently in the future.

Environmental pollutants. Another possible carcinogen entered the public vocabulary early in 1984, when the U.S. Environmental Protection Agency (EPA) ordered an end to the use of the pesticide ethylene dibromide (EDB) on grain in the U.S. and announced guidelines for permissible levels of EDB in grain products. Several states removed bake mixes and other products found to be contaminated from grocers' shelves, and in some areas sales of such products plummeted. However, EDB had been used as a fumigant on grain and citrus since the 1940s, and evidence that it caused cancer in laboratory animals had been noted in the early 1970s. Bureaucratic delays and the complicated requirements embodied in the federal pesticide laws had prevented action, but in early 1983 traces of EDB were found in groundwater and wells, mostly in citrus-growing areas, and late in the year a number of states began moving against EDB-tainted products on their own. Under pressure to set federal standards, the EPA promulgated guidelines for grain, although these did not have the force of law. Yet to be announced were guidelines for citrus. While consumer groups criticized the EPA actions as insufficient, EPA spokesmen insisted that, although EDB might represent a long-term health risk, there was no immediate public health emergency.

Controversy over other environmental pollutants continued. Soil contamination with dioxin, a highly potent carcinogen, was discovered in Newark, N.J., in June on the site of a factory that had manufactured the herbicide Agent Orange (2,4,5-T) during the Vietnam war. However, the affected area appeared to be small, and the contamination was less severe than at Times Beach, Mo., where the federal government had bought the entire town and declared it unfit for human habitation. In Europe it was announced that the last two factories producing 2,4,5-T, in West Germany and Austria, would be closed.

West German authorities announced that the sale of leaded gasoline would be prohibited as of Jan. 1, 1986, and that all cars would have to be fitted with catalytic converters by that date. Britain also planned to ban leaded gasoline, beginning in 1990, although there was disagreement between the oil industry and automobile manufacturers as to how this would be implemented. Research at Cornell University, Ithaca, N.Y., indicated that ozone, mainly from vehicle exhausts, might be reducing crop yields in the United States by as much as 25%. Exposure to high levels of ozone caused the plants to mature rapidly, shortening the period during which photosynthesis could take place. Ozone was also implicated in the extensive damage to trees in the Black Forest of West Germany, generally attributed to acid rain. Lichens, which are sensitive to sulfur dioxide (a main component of acid rain), were found to be growing abundantly on dying trees. Nevertheless, new laws designed to reduce sulfur dioxide emissions from West German power plants came into force in July. Damage from acid rain was reported from countries as widely separated as Czechoslovakia and China. The Czechoslovak Communist Party newspaper estimated that some 600,000 to 800,000 sq m (700,000 to 950,000 sq yd) of timber in that nation were being lost each year as a result of pollution.

Britain's Health and Safety Commission issued new regulations, believed to be the strictest in the world, governing exposure of workers to asbestos, and recommended a ban on the importation of blue (crocidolite) and brown (amosite) asbestos. Demolition of an old power station in London was halted in July until the contractor could prove that the asbestos insulation in the building could be removed safely. In the United States evidence continued to mount that children in old school buildings where asbestos insulation had been used were being exposed to unacceptably high levels, but in many cases financially squeezed school districts were unable to make the necessary repairs.

While authorities attempted to cope with pollution problems stemming from old industries and industrial practices, it was widely believed that the new "high tech" industries were clean and that, as these industries became dominant, pollution would decrease or even vanish. That this might not be the case was indicated in 1983, when it was discovered that wells in the "Silicon Valley" area of California, site of a large concentration of electronics plants, had been contaminated by toxic wastes.

—Kenneth E. F. Watt

Food and agriculture

Drought significantly reduced overall 1983 production of feed grains, but bumper crops elsewhere tended to offset these declines, and some countries reported record harvests. Drought combined with political and economic upheaval to cause feed shortages in at least 20 countries. At the same time, advances in biotechnology brought numerous benefits to the livestock industry and new promise to horticulture. World meat production rose, but so did feed prices.

Agriculture

The agricultural picture was mixed in 1983. In France grain exports were near record levels, but drought in Eastern Europe, notably in Bulgaria, Hungary, and Romania, was the worst in decades, and world production dropped some 6%. Wheat hit an all-time world high, with India achieving a record

Severe drought destroyed crops in many parts of the world during the past year. One of the hardest hit areas was southern Africa, where a cornfield in the Transvaal, South Africa, lies parched and ruined.

Mark Peters—Black Star

Food and agriculture

harvest of 42.5 million metric tons, Australia's production greatly improved, and the U.S. produced a major surplus. The Soviet Union's output of coarse grains was up sharply, and the Soviets were substituting some of that harvest for wheat. The world rice harvest was up generally.

Oilseed production declined in the world at large but improved substantially in China, which attained virtual self-sufficiency thanks especially to the rapeseed harvest. China's bumper cotton crop, in excess of 3.6 million metric tons, established that country as the world's largest producer.

The world's major meat-producing countries increased their total output, with enough pork to offset a decrease in cattle, except for the Soviet Union, where beef production increased; there and also in the U.S. pork increases were noteworthy. Poultry continued a moderately paced increase everywhere. Global production of milk rose except in the U.S., where continuing support programs limited cutbacks.

Drought affected cassava crops, while coffee and cocoa were improving generally after the impaired crops of 1982–83. Sugar production was up around the world, especially in India and Western Europe.

Consumption of agricultural products in the major industrial nations rose less than 2% in real terms during 1983, and a similar trend was expected in 1984. Agricultural experts predicted that U.S. consumption would grow at a rate of 3% per year over the next ten years, a lower rate than during the 1970s boom.

Biotechnology research. The U.S. led the way in biotechnological advances during 1983. The Alexander von Humboldt Award, the most significant agricultural research prize in the world, was given to Howard L. Bachrach of the U.S. Department of Agriculture (USDA) Plum Island (N.Y.) Animal Disease Center and George E. Seidel, Jr., of Colorado State University. Bachrach was honored for work leading to the first vaccine produced through gene splicing, Seidel for work in animal reproduction using the techniques of biotechnology to clone calves.

The use of living organisms or their components is not new to agriculture. In a rudimentary way biotechnology has been practiced for several millennia, and it has been the basis of improvements in plants and animals made during the last century. Modern biotechnology developed as a result of new research techniques involving cell and tissue culture, cell hybridization, embryo transfer, and gene splicing. As currently used the term refers to the improvement or modification of organisms employing contemporary tools available to the scientist.

To date, most biotechnology research has focused on eradicating diseases of humans and animals, developing plant tolerance to adverse environmental conditions, and elucidating cellular structure, especially that of single-cell organisms. Several agri-

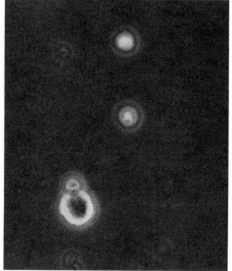
Antibodies to coccidiosis, a disease of chickens that costs U.S. poultry producers about $250 million annually, are injected into chickens (left). The antibodies are secreted by hybridomas, created when the spleen cells of a mouse immunized against coccidiosis are fused with larger myeloma cells from another mouse (below).

Agricultural Research Service—USDA

cultural applications already have emerged. Commercially produced bovine growth hormone is now available. Tissue culture is being used to produce new varieties of plants, such as potatoes, clones of superior specimens of other vegetables, and disease-resistant, drought-resistant, or salt-resistant grains.

A safe vaccine for foot-and-mouth disease emerged as the result of 25 years of work at the USDA laboratory at Plum Island using gene-splicing techniques. A research team, led by Bachrach, developed basic information about foot-and-mouth disease virus that paved the way for the first genetically engineered vaccine. Research demonstrated that an effective vaccine for swine could be made from a portion of the virus called VP_3 or viral protein number 3. At this stage a collaborative effort was established with scientists from Genentech, a San Francisco research firm. This led to expressing the VP_3 in a bacterium—the first production of an effective vaccine against any disease of animals or humans through gene splicing.

One of the principal advantages of biotechnology is that it tends to reduce significantly the number of years between basic discovery and practical application of research results. For example, insulin, interferon, and growth hormone were being produced commercially just eight years after the discovery of the gene-splicing technologies developed by Stanley Cohen and Herbert Boyer. The major constraint on accelerated application of biotechnology to agriculture and food production is the lack of fundamental knowledge about which specific genes must be manipulated to achieve specific results. However, a storehouse of fundamental knowledge is being built up. New techniques for studying deoxyribonucleic acid (DNA) and DNA sequencing now permit plant genes to be isolated and subjected to molecular analysis, enabling scientists to obtain a better understanding of their structure, regulation, and expression. New methodologies in cellular and molecular biology are unlocking the mysteries of developmental processes in plants. Such efforts include identification of genes and regulatory elements affecting development of the molecular mechanisms responsible for the expression of genes. With this knowledge genetic manipulations and modifications can be undertaken and their effects on development and growth monitored.

An understanding of plant growth at the molecular level will provide information that can be used to improve crop production. Regeneration of old plants from individual cells and the manipulation of plant embryos offer great promise in isolating unique genetic materials and selecting those that exhibit resistance to environmental and biological stresses. Currently, scientists have only an elementary understanding of the mechanisms involved in plant resis-

Agricultural Research Service—USDA

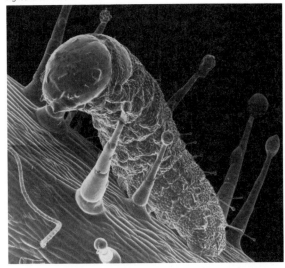

Photomicrograph reveals larva of an alfalfa weevil that has become fatally trapped in the sticky hairs of a newly developed variety of alfalfa.

tance and susceptibility to viruses, bacteria, fungi, and insects and to environmental stresses such as heat and cold, soil salinity, flooding, drought, and mineral deficiency and toxicity. Of paramount importance is the identification and isolation of genes for transfer into crop species that lack resistance to these stresses.

Techniques for inducing superovulation (production of a larger than normal number of eggs) in female animals that have exceptionally desirable features, in vitro fertilization of the eggs, and non-surgical implantation of the embryos into host animals of lower quality are practices now routinely used in the U.S. livestock industry. More recently, the ability to freeze partially developed cow embryos has made it possible to take embryos through several stages of development under controlled conditions in the laboratory. The original work was done in mice in the early 1970s by a group at the Oak Ridge (Tenn.) National Laboratories, and later work with cattle was performed by a group at the University of Cambridge in England. Such studies provide information on environmental conditions affecting embryonic development that is directly applicable to food-producing animals, and the findings are already being used by the agricultural industry.

More familiar methodologies are being improved as a result of biotechnology research. Vaccines are powerful tools in the prevention of disease, but vaccines produced by traditional methods often cause undesirable or even injurious side effects. Recent discoveries make it possible to produce large amounts of vaccines in a highly purified form at relatively low cost, through the cloning of genes and the use

323

Rangeland Improvement Machine (left) was developed to increase crop yields on semiarid land. It includes a unique packing wheel system (above) in which a gap in each wheel leaves a small dam at intervals to collect and retain water.

of bacteria as "microfactories" to produce protein. Microorganisms have traditionally been used in the production of many foods and beverages; examples include yeasts in baking and brewing and bacteria in making such dairy products as yogurt. Gene transfer techniques, coupled with a better understanding of gene regulation in the cellular environment, will make it possible to enhance the existing capabilities of such microorganisms and endow them with desirable new properties. This will have a major effect on the development of food products and also in the beverage and spirits industry.

Other research. More effective, environmentally acceptable use of fertilizers should result from basic research at the Iowa Agriculture and Home Economics Experiment Station on nitrogen and sulfur transformations in soils and their effects on air and water pollution. The principal research accomplishments were discovery of a bacterial pathway by which nitrous oxide is produced in the soil and emitted into the atmosphere, and determination of a way to inhibit production of nitrous oxide. This work earned the Alexander von Humboldt Award for the research leader, soil biochemist J. M. Bremner.

Oregon State University scientists showed that when a lodgepole pine is freed from competition by proper thinning, its crown becomes more efficient photosynthetically. This allows the tree to reach its full growth rapidly. At the same time, the vigorous growth causes the tree to become resistant to attack by the mountain pine beetle. An important byproduct of this research was the development of an easily applied method of assessing tree vigor by measuring tree-ring cores. The research represents a significant breakthrough in controlling mountain pine beetle damage to lodgepole pine, which regularly causes losses amounting to millions of dollars in the western U.S. Increased tree growth after thinning would also provide a large addition to the nation's softwood timber supply. These findings have led to the development of an easily applied "stand improvement" model for lodgepole pine. The new information was being taught to professional foresters.

A new vaccine to prevent pasteurellosis or shipping fever in cattle was announced. This disease, which generally attacks animals when they are under stress, as during shipping, has been the animal health problem of greatest concern to beef-cattle producers. It was estimated that shipping fever cost the U.S. beef industry at least $20 per head annually. Ohio scientists spent more than six years developing the vaccine, which involves a novel approach in which the bacterium causing the fever is injected between layers of skin. It was tested in an estimated 10,000 animals with no adverse effects and was considered to be the first really effective preventative for the disease.

Food processors now have available a natural soybean oil that contains less than 3% linolenic acid, thanks to the research efforts of Iowa State University food scientists and agronomists. Linolenic acid can cause oil to develop "off" flavors. The level of linolenic acid in soybean oil in the U.S. generally ranges between 7 and 10%, but U.S. oil processors use hydrogenation to prevent the development of off flavors. However, in countries where hydrogenation is not used and where cooking techniques differ from those in the U.S., the flavor problem has impeded the expansion of soybean oil markets. Soybean breeders and food technologists cooperated in the successful research effort.

—John Patrick Jordan

Nutrition

As the American public placed increasing emphasis on nutrition, exercise, and environmental health, matters of nutrition inevitably became political issues. One such issue before Congress was the lack of a comprehensive human nutrition research program. Nutrition scientists from the public and private sectors testified unanimously that health and nutrition monitoring is a proper role for the federal government and should be part of a clearly defined health plan. Also in the headlines was the question of whether "hunger," in the sense of serious malnutrition, existed in the U.S. and, if so, whether it was due to cuts in the level of federal spending on such programs as food stamps.

Prenatal nutrition. The Committee on Nutrition of the Mother and Child of the Food and Nutrition Board (National Research Council) concluded that behavior associated with food selection and consumption is difficult to change, since it is deeply rooted in cultural and religious convictions and taboos. Thus physicians and dietitians must pay special attention to the backgrounds of pregnant women who avoid eating foods generally thought to be needed during pregnancy. Food patterns differ among various groups; for example, many black, Asian, Hispanic, and native American peoples are not accustomed to drinking milk or to eating different cheeses or meats cooked in an unfamiliar manner. Considerable variation in food acceptance also occurs among white

middle-class Americans. After evaluating a pregnant woman's total diet and attitudes toward food, practitioners should establish an "empathetic nonjudgmental dialogue" with her to encourage the use of foods that will serve her nutritional needs.

The committee report included an analysis of practices that affect the success of pregnancy, namely, use of tobacco, alcohol, caffeine, over-the-counter drugs (salicylates and others), megadoses of vitamins (especially A and D), and strictly vegetarian diets. Any one or a combination of these practices can result in low birth weight at full term, an impaired central nervous system, mental deficiency, and overall delayed development. Excessive use of tobacco, alcohol, and other drugs may pose a double health hazard by interfering directly with fetal development while at the same time reducing the mother's food intake and her ability to utilize certain nutrients effectively. The report, "Alternate Dietary Practices and Nutritional Abuses in Pregnancy," was available without cost from the Food and Nutrition Board in Washington, D.C.

Trace elements in nutrition. Sensitive analytical methods show that at least some traces of all naturally occurring elements can be found in human and animal tissues. What is not clear is which of these are contaminants and which are truly essential. The ultimate test of an essential element is that "reduction of [its] concentration in a specific body tissue from optimal to suboptimal must result consistently and reproducibly in a reduction of an element-specific function from optimal to suboptimal." On the basis of present knowledge an organism is capable of maintaining physiological tissue concentrations of such trace elements with intakes that range from those just meeting the requirement to approximately ten times that amount. Thus there is a relatively wide zone of acceptable and adequate

Lionel Delevingne—Stock, Boston

Nutrition of pregnant women was the subject of a study by the Food and Nutrition Board of the U.S. National Research Council. The study revealed that it is difficult to change habits of food selection and consumption.

Food and agriculture

intake between deficient and excessive amounts.

Only 27 naturally occurring elements on Earth had been confirmed as essential by 1984. For purposes of nutrition, the elements are classified into three categories. In the first group are those for which need has been established and the amount required has been quantified. Those in the second group have a known connection with nutritional problems, but the amount needed has not been defined. The third category consists of elements having no known connection with nutritional problems in humans. The first category includes iodine, iron, zinc, lead, and fluorine, and the second includes chromium, cobalt, copper, selenium, and molybdenum. Some elements that are essential in small amounts are toxic in larger concentrations. Iron and lead are well-known examples. Another is selenium. Schoolchildren in the mountains of China require weekly doses of selenium to maintain health. In the U.S., on the other hand, selenium occurs in a variety of foods, and the amount ingested may reach toxic levels.

Salt and sweeteners. The U.S. Food and Drug Administration (FDA) noted that educational programs urging people to reduce their salt intake were receiving outstanding support from industry, professional groups, and other government agencies. Over 100 food manufacturers had introduced new lines of food products that were salt free or had reduced salt content. Among the items already available were snacks, canned vegetables, soups, sauces, cheeses, canned tuna, baked goods, peanut butter, luncheon meats, and cereals. In 1982, 19% of processed foods had labels giving the salt content, and four out of ten adults said they were trying to reduce salt consumption.

From the newborn to the centenarian, sweet tastes are preferred over all others. Average per capita sugar consumption in the U.S. is 100 to 150 g per day, or 1½ lb per week. This is equivalent to 400 to 600 kilocalories per day. Two noncaloric sweeteners, saccharin and cyclamate, have been implicated as possible carcinogens, while various forms of carbohydrate used as sugar substitutes, such as corn syrup and honey, have as many calories as sugar (sucrose) itself. A new entrant in the search for a safe, noncaloric sweetener was aspartame, a protein derivative peptide said to have 200 times the sweetness of sucrose. A white, soluble powder stable in acid solutions, aspartame separates during the digestive process into two amino acids; these join amino acids derived from protein foods and are used up in the body's metabolic processes. It was approved as safe by the FDA and by early 1984 was being widely used, especially in soft drinks. However, some consumer groups expressed doubts about its safety and were urging that it be withdrawn until further research could be done.

Appetite. Increased knowledge of appetite control

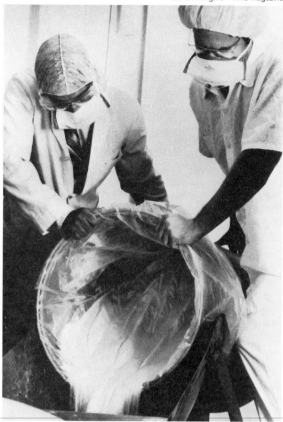

The search for a safe noncaloric sweetener resulted in the development of aspartame (NutraSweet), a protein derivative peptide.

by the section of the brain called the hypothalamus may soon help man to understand and control his desire to eat. The hypothalamus controls a number of bodily processes, including appetite, but the mechanism is not completely understood. It had been thought that the signals of hunger and satiety were transmitted via the nervous system, but the discovery of 20 to 30 gastrointestinal peptides with hormone-like and neurotransmitter-like effects influencing appetite has confused what once seemed to be a simple answer. It has been suggested that the function of these peptides is regulatory and that they are analogous to radio knobs for changing volume and frequency, supporting and moderating nerve function by raising or lowering the sensitivity of target cells. This raises the possibility that these key appetite-control components might be translated into pharmaceutical products that could be used to regulate appetite. Allen S. Levine and John E. Morley of the U.S. Veterans Administration and the University of Minnesota have emphasized that elucidation of ways to control the signals sent out by the hypothalamus is of special interest today. The discovery by pharmacologists at the National Institutes of Health of what seems to be an appetite receptor in the brain may lead to a coherent theory of appetite regulation.

Dietary treatment of anorexia nervosa (self-starvation) offers a challenge to dietitians and doctors alike. Since the disease has a large psychological component, each case must be treated individually with concern for the total person and with support systems designed to meet more than dietary needs. In fact, one approach, effective mainly with young children who have not developed a severe aversion to food, is to shift the focus of concern away from eating and allow normal hunger to take over. Anorexia patients who have lost 25% or more of their normal weight still may be treated as outpatients if some response to treatment is apparent. Those with a more advanced and severe form of the illness, who exhibit poor motivation and strong resistance to treatment and who have lost an inordinate amount of weight, frequently require hospital care. Therapy must begin with stopping weight loss and improving the nutritional status.

The anorexic patient should not be encouraged to gain weight until he or she has achieved success in eating some food voluntarily. To confront an anorexic person with a 3,000-calorie diet is irrational, since the refusal to eat often stems from a fear of gaining fat tissue and body weight. An initial step in the feeding program used at the Mayo Clinic and Foundation is to establish regular consumption of some food while acquiring a detailed history of the patient and attempting to change his or her attitudes to life problems.

Health foods and supplements. While some people try to solve personal problems by developing an aversion to food, others fortify their diets without plan or analysis. In a sample of 150 adults, 19 to 87 years old, living in Colorado, 53% used some form of diet supplement. Vitamin C and a multivitamin were the most common supplements chosen, supplying more vitamin C, vitamin E, riboflavin, and vitamin B-12 than the U.S. government's Recommended Daily Allowance (RDA). Dietary consumption of protein, vitamin A, riboflavin, niacin, and vitamin C also averaged above the RDA.

In the area of diet supplements the belief continued that if some is good, more is better. Though only 15 mg a day of vitamin C is needed to prevent scurvy and the recommended dietary intake is 60 mg, some self-styled therapists believed that several hundred times that amount promotes health, prevents colds, and assures well-being. Research showed that large doses are retained in the body for only a few hours before being excreted and are of questionable value. Nevertheless, sales of over-the-counter vitamins had become a highly profitable business.

A survey of health food stores in the New York City area conducted by the New York City Department of Consumer Affairs found that foods sold in such stores were generally more expensive than those sold in conventional food markets. No data supported the concept that products in these stores

Shelves in a health food store are filled with high-fiber foods and vitamin products. Recent research indicates the food sold in such markets is not demonstrably superior in quality to comparable products sold in conventional supermarkets.

Sybil Shelton—Peter Arnold, Inc.

were demonstrably superior to those in supermarkets or neighborhood groceries. The lack of pesticide or chemical fertilizer residues claimed for "health foods" did not affect the products in terms of nutritive composition, appearance, or taste. No residues were found on foods from either type of store, and the foods appeared to be of equal quality.

The health food stores also sold pseudovitamins, diet aids, and other nonfood items, including kelp, dolomite, and "starch blockers," products that allegedly prevent dietary starch from being metabolized and thus inhibit weight gain. (The FDA later ordered the "starch blockers" off the market for testing of their safety and effectiveness.) The report of the survey concluded that consumers will do little to aid their health by shopping for overpriced food at health food stores.

—Mina W. Lamb

See also Feature Articles: PERENNIAL GRASSES ON THE PRAIRIES: NEW CROPS FOR THE FUTURE?; OVERLOOKED ANIMALS: NEW HOPE FOR THE TROPICS.

Life sciences

Much of the research in the life sciences during the past year focused on the study of genes and the effects that they have on the growth and development of organisms. The recently developed techniques of genetic engineering helped scientists in many fields pursue these studies.

Botany

Plant genetics, nitrogen fixation by marine algae, alternatives to traditional fertilization, and new discoveries concerning interactions between plants and animals were among the major subjects of attention by botanists during the past year.

Plant genetics. Some of the most exciting developments in botany result from research at the genetic level. One example is the discovery of the ways in which resistance may be imparted to crop plants. The widespread use of herbicides is important to farmers because chemicals can be used to kill weeds. One problem with using this technique, however, lies in the necessity for the crop to be resistant to the chemicals at the same time that the weeds are susceptible to them. It has been found that a single mutant gene can bring about resistance to atrazine, a herbicide for corn crops that has been used widely for 25 years. During that time at least 30 types of weeds developed resistance to the chemical; studies on some of these revealed information on how resistance can be controlled.

Charles Arntzen of Michigan State University reported that atrazine resistance can be produced by mutation of a gene in the chloroplasts of green-plant cells rather than in the genetic material of the nuclei of these cells. (Chloroplasts are structures in a cell, located outside the nucleus, in which photosynthesis and starch formation take place.) Studies of the way in which atrazine actually affects plants have shown that a derivative of atrazine binds to one of the substances involved in photosynthesis, thus interrupting that process. Cloning of the gene made it possible to study how the atrazine binding site was affected in the mutant so that photosynthesis was not interrupted. Arntzen and Lawrence Bogorad of Harvard University worked out the function of the gene, called photogene 32. Lee McIntosh cloned the gene while at Harvard, and worked out the actual changes in the mutant form with Joseph Hershberg after moving to Michigan State. They found that a single base substitution of a guanine for an adenine was responsible for the single amino-acid change in the atrazine binding site of the resultant protein that confers the herbicide resistance.

On another front plant geneticists were becoming concerned about the loss of genetic diversity among crop plants. Problems may arise when successful strains are raised repeatedly and exclusively for long periods of time because genetic variability is no longer bred into these strains. When adverse conditions are imposed by a new disease or physical environmental change, the crops may not possess the genetic variability to cope with the change. The late-blight fungus, *Phytophthora infestans*, produced disaster in Ireland's potato crop in 1845–46, and the fungus *Helminthosporium maydis* did the same in large areas of hybrid corn in 1970 for reasons related to genetic vulnerability. To counteract such vulnerability gene banks were established in developed nations and were becoming more common in less developed countries.

In recent times seed has been stored in three

Marine algae Rhizosolenia castracanei *and* Rhizosolenia imbricata *var* shrubsolei *are mat-forming diatoms that contain high densities of nitrogen-fixing bacteria.*

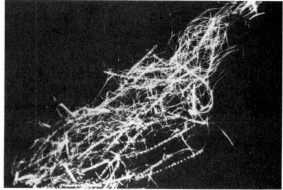

From "Nitrogen Fixation by Floating Diatom Mats: A Source of New Nitrogen to Oligotrophic Ocean Waters," L. Martinez, M. Silver, J. King, and A. Alldredge, vol. 221, no. 4606, pp. 152–154, July 8, 1983. Copyright © 1983 Macmillan Journals Limited.

Burt Leidmann—*Time* Magazine

Evergreen trees in the Black Forest of West Germany reveal damage that has been attributed to acid rain. New needles on the trees, smaller than usual, turn yellow or brown and fall to the ground, while some trees stop bearing needles altogether.

ways: long-term base collections, where samples are kept at temperatures of −10° to −20° C (14° to −4° F) for several decades or more; medium-term collections, with seeds kept at 0° to 5° C (32° to 41° F) for up to 20 years; and short-term collections, with seeds kept above 5° C for a few years. Seeds are used from the latter two collections for evaluation and breeding purposes. Thus strains of various crop plants may be made available for crossing to enhance genetic variability.

If crops are not of the kind reproduced by seeds, vegetative reproduction is employed and gene banking becomes more difficult. Plants must be grown continuously to provide cuttings or other vegetative means of reproduction. Such reserves are difficult to maintain, and certain types of crop plants—such as bananas—are poorly represented in the gene-banking system because of this.

As of 1984 cereals formed the main collections in gene banks, although some effort was being made to store germ plasm for important lumber trees. In 1974 the International Board for Plant Genetic Resources (IBPGR) was established in Rome to stimulate the development of germ-plasm storage facilities. By 1984 more than 30 of these had been established.

Operational procedures of gene banks insure the protection and survival of stored strains and make them available when a strain is acquired for a gene bank, when a sample is left in the country of origin for its use, when germ plasm (usually seeds) is made available to researchers, and when long-term collections are duplicated for maintenance in more than one location. Preserved germ plasm may be screened for resistance to insect and disease attack as well as for tolerance to poor soils and climate extremes.

Marine algae. LeeAnne Martínez and associates of the University of California reported that certain mat-forming diatoms (minute planktonic algae) are responsible for nitrogen fixation in some oceanic areas traditionally considered biological deserts. Gradually it is being shown that these areas may be highly productive.

Martínez and colleagues demonstrated that two mat-forming diatoms, *Rhizosolenia castracanei* and *R. imbricata* var *shrubsolei*, were able to fix 1.17 micrograms (μg) of nitrogen per mat per hour during studies in the eastern Pacific. Such mats average 7 cm (2.7 in) in length and have an average density of 2.3 per cu m in the upper five meters of water where they are found. Microscopic examination of the diatoms revealed that they contain high densities of nitrogen-fixing bacteria. This source of nitrogen fixation had previously been totally undetected by standard shipboard techniques because the mats break up and the diatoms escape.

Other researchers reported that large proportions of the primary production in tropical oceans is carried out by algae that measure no larger than one micrometer. (Primary production is the total amount of new organic matter produced by photosynthesis.) Cells of this size are called picoplankton. A group of researchers from the Bedford Institute of Oceanography in Nova Scotia studied areas of the Pacific Ocean off Costa Rica and the Atlantic Ocean west of the Azores. W. K. W. Li and associates reported on the Pacific studies. They collected plankton from a site of upwelling of water from deeper to shallower levels, which is, therefore, a nutrient-rich area, and also from a site typical of the larger part of the tropical ocean. By using a technique that involves the measurement of chlorophyll a ($C_{55}H_{72}O_5N_4Mg$) by the amount of radioactive carbon dioxide taken up by the sample, they calculated that 25 to 70% of chlorophyll a is found in the picoplankton of the upwelling site and 55 to 90% in the non-upwelling site. Thus they concluded that picoplankton are responsible for a large proportion of the photosynthesis and, therefore, of the biomass in those areas.

Trevor Platt and associates reported on the Atlantic research. Samples from 11 sites were examined in a number of ways to conclude that picoplankton may contribute up to 60% of the total primary productivity. They were also able to show that the picoplankton consisted mostly of blue-green algae (cyanobacteria).

Plant development. Attempts to increase plant growth and crop yield have traditionally employed the application of fertilizers to the soil. Modern applications of synthetic fertilizers are responsible for high productivity of field crops, such as corn, but there are some undesirable side effects such as cost, wastefulness, and pollution. Efforts to develop alternatives to traditional fertilization include the use of foliar (leaf) spray. One promising report during the year recorded the experimental growth of corn and rice seedlings under foliar application of 1-triacontanol (TRIA). R. G. Laughlin and R. L. Munyon of Procter & Gamble and S. K. Ries and V. R. Vert of Michigan State University found that colloidal TRIA concentrations of 100 nanograms per cu dm (decimeter), sprayed on the seedlings just until the liquid began to drip off the leaves, produced maximum growth in corn. Plants that were six or seven days old were sprayed and, upon harvest seven days later, demonstrated nearly 20–30% more growth than plants that were not sprayed. The investigators thus concluded that colloidal TRIA may be one of the most active plant growth regulators reported.

A familiar method of plant propagation is vegetative sprouting of stems or leaves. Usually a cutting is made, though sometimes just a leaf is used. When placed in an appropriate rooting medium, the cutting produces roots and a new shoot. These are described as adventitious because they are produced in a somewhat abnormal way. African violets are propagated both commercially and in many homes in this manner. Three researchers showed that adventitious bud formation involves all layers of leaf tissue in African violets, contrary to previous reports.

R. Norris, R. H. Smith of Texas A & M University, and K. C. Vaughn of the U.S. Department of Agriculture studied the way in which adventitious shoots developed from African violet chimeras. A chimera is a plant composed of tissues, two or more of which are genetically different. Observations of the plant leaves are particularly useful in studies of this kind because their tissue layers can be traced back to distinct layers in the buds from which they developed. These layers are LI, which gives rise to leaf epidermis; LII, which gives rise to the subepidermal layer of leaf cells; and LIII, which gives rise to the remaining internal leaf cells. Leaf chimeras that are variegated—that have both white and green tissue—may have developed in that way because any one of the layers is genetically unable to produce green cells. Different chimera strains have this deficiency in different layers—some in LI, some in

LII, and some in LIII. A study of all three kinds of chimeras would reveal that adventitious buds from the leaves were derived from all three layers if the variegated pattern persisted in offspring shoots. By contrast, if buds arose from single cells or single layers, the offspring shoots would be either all green or all white. The investigators found that all chimeras were uniformly replicated by adventitious budding, confirming the contribution of all three layers.

Seed plants and ferns differ in many ways; for example, the fern leaf is usually the only part of the plant that extends above ground, whereas the whole shoot system of the seed plant usually does so. The development of the fern leaf is a process that may match that of the whole seed-plant shoot system in some ways. Richard Mueller of Utah State University recently reported on his studies of a fern with climbing leaves reminiscent of seed-plant climbing stems.

Mueller worked with the tropical fern *Lygodium japonicum*, in which the embryonic tissue (meristem) at the leaf tip is enclosed in a curve of the leaf axis called a crozier. Protection is afforded the growing tip in this way, and the leaf gets longer by an uncoiling of the crozier as new cells are added to its inner tip. In this respect *Lygodium* is like other ferns, but its leaves continue to lengthen far more than most other ferns and may become as much as 30 meters (98 feet) in length. For this reason it is said to have indeterminate growth, while the more limited growth of other fern leaves is described as determinate. In addition, the lengthening end of the *Lygodium* leaf circumnutates, or twines, around any support, just as do certain seed-plant stems.

Plants and animals. Each year brings new findings on interactions between plants and animals. R. W. Gibson and J. A. Pickett of the Rothamsted Experimental Station in the U.K. showed that the wild potato *Solanum berthaultii* produces a chemical, probably from hairs on its leaves, that repels the aphid *Myzus persicae* at a distance of 1–3 mm. This chemical is (E)-β-farnesene, the main component of the pheromone used by most aphid species to communicate alarm through short distances.

L. Anders Nilsson of the Institute of Systematic Botany in Sweden demonstrated that the flowers of a certain orchid mimic the flower color of bellflowers to attract a pollinator. The orchid *Cephalanthera rubra* lacks nectar but deceives male solitary bees of the species *Chelostoma fuliginosum* and *C. campanulorum* by producing colors nearly identical to those of several bellflower species. The orchids bloom about two weeks before the bellflowers and thus attract the male bees, which emerge from the nest burrow earlier than the females.

Nickolas Waser and Mary Price of the University of California at Riverside suggested that they have observed a case of natural selection in the larkspur

Delphinium nelsonii. When they found that white-flowered plants produced fewer seeds and were rarer than blue-flowered plants, they decided to study the bumblebee and hummingbird pollinators of the plants. They found that the white flowers had less contrast among the flower parts, particularly in regard to the nectar guides of contrasting color, than did the blue flowers. The resulting reduction in the rate of locating and processing the white flowers causes pollinator discrimination against them.

See also Feature Article: PERENNIAL GRASSES ON THE PRAIRIES: NEW CROPS FOR THE FUTURE?

—Albert J. Smith

Microbiology

Some of the most important topics in microbiology during the past year included the use of fermentations for the development of products of commercial and medical importance; ice-nucleating bacteria associated with cold injury to plants; and recombinant DNA studies. The latter includes such subjects as the application of genetics to clinical microbiology and to the production of indigo.

Ice-nucleating bacteria. Within the past decade it has been recognized that frost damage to plants is often caused by the ice-nucleating activity of certain bacteria on the plant surface. The presence of these bacteria has been shown to induce ice nuclei at about $-1.7°$ C ($29°$ F), just below the freezing point. However, in the absence of ice-nucleating bacteria ice does not form on a plant's surface even at temperatures of $-10°$ to $-13°$ C ($14°$ to $9°$ F).

Ice nucleation has been identified as a bacterial gene product. In California scientists genetically engineered ice-nucleating bacteria in such a way that the nucleus was identical with that of the naturally occurring bacteria except that the ice-nucleating gene was deleted. They proposed the first outdoor test of any genetically altered organism, spraying plants with the altered bacteria, expecting the new forms to diminish and then replace the naturally occurring ice-nucleating bacteria. The National Institutes of Health (NIH) approved, but a suit by six environmental activists and groups won a Federal District Court order delaying the test, probably for a year or more, pending detailed assessment by the NIH of damage that might result from releasing the recombinant DNA mutants into the environment.

Scientists at the University of Georgia proposed spraying plants with the antibiotic streptomycin in order to kill the ice-nucleating bacteria. This procedure, however, seems not to be a good idea for a number of reasons. First, the time involved must be considered. For example, about two days are required to spray an 80-ha (200-ac) peach orchard—too long a time when a severe frost warning is received. Second, the dead bacteria possessing the ice-nucleating gene product would also have to be removed from the plant surfaces by such natural phenomena as rain or wind—another time factor. Third, many of the ice-nucleating bacteria identified to date have high levels of intrinsic resistance to streptomycin. Fourth, extensive spraying of antibiotics would select for an increased population of antibiotic-resistant bacteria in nature, an effect to be avoided if possible.

Fermentation. In the area of biotechnology, fermentations continued to receive worldwide attention. Microbial fermentations have long been used in industry to produce such substances as antibiotics, vitamins, amino acids, enzymes, various organic acids, alcohols, and other products, and the list has increased with the introduction of genetic engineering. A problem for genetic engineers, however, is that even though a cloned organism can be made to produce a product, a great deal of technological innovation must be developed before the process is practical.

Production of alcohol from cellulosic waste products was an important subject of fermentation research during the past year. Efforts were being made to clone thermophilic cellulase genes (those exist-

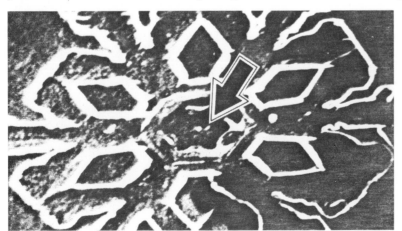

Photomicrograph shows an ice crystal that has formed around three bacteria. The arrow points to a single bacterium, and two others lie to the left of it. Frost damage to plants often is caused by such ice-nucleating bacteria.

Robert G. McDonald; photo, courtesy, Russell C. Schnell, University of Colorado, Boulder

ing at high temperatures) that encode for the heat-tolerant enzyme cellulase; this enzyme can break down cellulose to simple sugars in common bacteria such as *Escherichia coli*. If successful, the next step would be to further modify *E. coli* so that it would produce larger amounts of the enzyme. The enzyme thus produced could then be used with other microbial systems to break down the simple sugars to alcohol or to feedstock chemicals (the latter are chemicals that can be used as starting materials for the manufacture of plastics and other synthetic substances).

One problem encountered with the use of *E. coli* as a cloning vehicle is that frequently this organism does not secrete or transport outside of the cell the gene product that it was cloned to produce, resulting in low yields of the product. A second problem is that *E. coli* produces certain toxic substances which contaminate the end product during the isolation and purification procedures. In an effort to eliminate these problems increasing attention was being directed to yeast as a cloning vehicle. In this regard recent work has shown that yeast and mammalian hormones share common features. Thus, there is hope that yeast may be useful in producing a variety of mammalian proteins to include hormones that can be efficiently secreted by the yeast cells without the toxic products produced by *E. coli* cells.

Generally speaking, yeast has been used in the temperate zone to convert sugar-containing substances to alcohol. In the tropics, however, a bacterium, *Zymomonas mobilis*, has been used to form alcohol as an end product. *Z. mobilis* produces alcohol at about twice the rate of yeast. Unfortunately, unlike yeast *Z. mobilis* can utilize relatively few sugars for growth. In order to extend the nutritional capability of *Z. mobilis* scientists at Rutgers University attempted to clone genes into *Z. mobilis* to develop strains that can utilize for alcohol production such biomass materials as wood, starch, waste milk whey, and municipal wastes.

Most countries are interested in converting cellulosic waste materials into fuels such as alcohol, into feedstock chemicals, or into single-cell proteins. An important agricultural product of the state of Yucatán in Mexico is henequen, a plant whose fibers are used for sisal or hemp. Mexican microbiologists were studying ways to convert henequen pulp, which is a waste obtained during the process of removing the fibers from the leaves of the plant, to useful products.

Japan's fermentation activity exceeded 7% of its gross national product. This was the highest percentage of any country in the world.

Bacteria and biodegradation. There were two reports during the year on bacteria that by means of biodegradation can destroy polychlorinated biphenyls (PCB's), man-made cancer-inducing products that have become pollutants of major concern. One report appeared to be without major foundation, but the second, by scientists from the University of Tennessee, appeared to have greater validity. In the case of the latter, microorganisms were shown to have the ability to degrade some of the simpler PCB's. However, when given a choice, bacteria will normally utilize energy sources that are more readily broken down than PCB's. Thus, microbial degradation of PCB's in nature, if it ever happens naturally, will be a slow, long-range prospect.

The other side of the coin, unexpectedly, is that microorganisms are breaking down pesticides (insecticides and herbicides) in soil at an alarming rate, thus diminishing their effectiveness. Biodegradability of pesticides has generally been regarded as a good thing because of the recent unhappy experiences with persistent pesticides. Now, however, biodegradable pesticides appear to be broken down so rapidly by soil microorganisms that their effectiveness has been greatly lessened.

It is thought that some of the genetic information for pesticide degradation may be encoded in plasmid DNA (deoxyribonucleic acid). In bacteria, plasmids are circular particles of DNA found in the cytoplasm (the cell protoplasm external to the nucleus) and not in the chromosome. Plasmids that encode for en-

Heliobacterium chlorum, discovered by accident in a classroom experiment, grows only in the absence of oxygen and contains a previously unknown form of chlorophyll that lacks an oxygen atom where one would be expected. This suggests that the organism has preserved a form of photosynthesis that developed before the Earth's atmosphere contained oxygen.

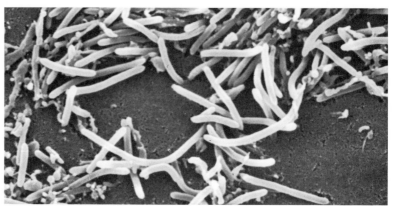

F. R. Turner; Photo, courtesy, Howard Gest

Health hazards to young children in day-care centers include the transmission of communicable diseases, particularly diarrheal disorders. Such transmission is facilitated by the tendency of the children to handle the same objects.

zymes that break down antibiotics or that degrade a variety of chemical compounds have been extensively studied. University of Georgia scientists recently found evidence that bacterial plasmids may also encode for resistance to certain industrial biocides that are used to kill or inhibit microorganisms in products of industrial importance. Thus, it may not be too surprising that plasmid DNA molecules may also be involved in both pesticide degradation and industrial biocide resistance.

Since the most common type of bacterial resistance to antibiotics is due to plasmid-mediated genes, the question is raised as to whether such plasmids existed prior to the age of antibiotics, that is, before 1945. By studying a bacterial collection made by an eminent Canadian microbiologist, British researchers confirmed that such plasmids were indeed widespread in those bacterial species. However, genes encoding for antibiotic resistance were uncommon, which is not surprising. Thus the general genetic mechanisms for inheritable bacterial antibiotic resistance were present before the age of antibiotics. However, because the culture collection used in these studies was made before the age of antibiotics, the question as to how the microorganisms acquired the genetic information for antibiotic resistance could not be answered.

Other developments. Although nitrite has been used since pre-Christian times to preserve foods, its mechanism of action has remained elusive. Recently University of Georgia scientists showed that nitrite attacks the respiratory system of bacteria. Scientists at Utah State University confirmed this evidence by showing that nitrite attacks bacterial proteins containing iron and sulfur that are involved in the generation of energy for the organism. Thus nitrite seems to prevent bacterial cells from generating the energy that they need for their preservation and multiplication.

Lignin is the most abundant "renewable" organic material after cellulose. It surrounds cellulose and, unless degraded itself, protects the cellulose from degradative enzymes secreted by microorganisms. Much work is being done on fungi that decompose wood by secreting enzymes that degrade lignin. Within the near future scientists hope that the technology will be developed to isolate these lignin-degrading enzymes and to employ them in a practical manner.

There are certain health hazards in confining young children to day-care centers, particularly in the transmission of communicable diseases from child to child. Of particular importance is the transmission of diarrheal diseases. A team of scientists from Texas demonstrated that diarrhea may be spread in day-care centers by commonly used objects such as door handles, countertops, other inanimate objects, contaminated food, and person-to-person contact.

Scientists succeeded in cloning genes into *E. coli* to produce indigo. One of the oldest dyes known to man, indigo can be extracted from certain plants. Although synthetic indigo has been available for some time, it is interesting that recombinant DNA techniques allow a bacterium to produce it.

Although bioaccumulation of heavy metals by microorganisms has been known for several years, scientists from Israel and Japan recently reported that a common fungus, whether living or dead, could absorb uranium. Although the absorption mechanism is not understood, this property is significant since it may serve as a means to decontaminate waste water and to recover heavy metals.

See also Feature Article: ANTIBODIES—NATURE'S "MAGIC BULLETS."

—Robert G. Eagon

Molecular biology

The most interesting problems in biology, such as how a single fertilized egg develops into a differentiated individual with brain, muscles, bones, and other body parts, can be reduced to questions at the cellular level: How does a cell "decide" which of its thousands of genes to express, and when should it express them? By applying molecular biological techniques to study the structure of genes, scientists obtained considerable insight into critical cellular phenomena during the past year.

Retrovirus research. Work on the molecular basis of cancer received the most attention. In order to understand the newest work it is useful to describe the viruses, now called retroviruses, that at the beginning of this century were found to cause tumors in chickens and, later, in other animals. Retroviruses, like all viruses, are parasites at the molecular level. They consist of small particles, each of which contains a protein shell protecting one or more molecules of nucleic acid, the viral chromosomes. When a virus infects a cell, the genes contained in the viral chromosome are released from the protective protein coat of the virus and begin to function inside the infected cell. The detailed molecular mechanism differs for each virus, but all have the ability to subvert the cell's machinery for making RNA (ribonucleic acid) and protein and to use that machinery for the production of viral RNA, viral proteins, and, in some cases, viral DNA (deoxyribonucleic acid). These substances are packaged into hundreds of new virus particles, which are then released from the infected cell and are capable of repeating the cycle of infection whenever a new susceptible cell is encountered.

A number of variations of this scenario are known in nature. Some viruses, upon entering a susceptible cell, do not complete the infectious cycle just described but instead enter into a more lengthy relationship with the cell, at first remaining latent within it and entering the full infectious cycle at a later date. Other viruses, during the course of a normal infection, exchange some genetic material (DNA) with the cell, in the process giving up genes essential for the complete viral infectious cycle and themselves acquiring cellular genes. In most cases the acquired cellular genes confer no new properties on cells that are subsequently infected by these now defective virus particles. However, in the case of retroviruses, occasionally a host cell gene is acquired that has a drastic consequence for the infected cell: it is transformed into a tumor cell.

When a population of virus particles is purified from tumors, for example, Rous sarcoma virus from infected chickens, the particles all have similar protein coats but there are two families of particles in terms of the viral nucleic acid. One family contains all the viral genes necessary for infection. The other family is missing all or part of a viral gene and carries instead a new gene called v-src. This gene is responsible for the formation of malignant growths known as sarcomas; how it causes them is not completely understood, but some information on the process is described below. The gene is called v-src to identify it as the viral version of src and to distinguish it from c-src, the cellular version. Normal cells contain a related gene—not surprising in view of the origin of v-src described above.

If the retrovirus merely returns to the chicken a gene that originated with the chicken, why does it cause tumors? That question cannot be answered completely, but it is known that the protein product coded by the src gene is an enzyme that modifies other proteins by the addition of phosphate groups to the amino acid tyrosine at particular positions in the protein chain. This modification is believed to change the catalytic properties of the target protein. One can imagine regulatory circuits of proteins involved in the control of DNA replication, for example, in which modification of one protein or an increase in its amount disrupts the normal controls of cell division. Introduction of a modified src gene, or extra copies of the src gene, might induce proliferation of cells in that way, even though cells normally contain an src gene.

Direct identification of genes. An entirely independent line of investigation of the molecular mechanism of tumor induction led during the past year to information converging with the results obtained from retrovirus research. The new work arose from attempts to identify modified or reorganized or amplified genes in cancer cells directly. This work was rather heroic in conception, because cancer cells differ from the normal cells from which they were derived in dozens or even hundreds of ways. To believe that the multitude of changes could be triggered by one or a small number of gene modifications took a great act of faith. Nevertheless, experiments done by Robert Weinberg of Massachusetts Institute of Technology (MIT) showed that DNA taken from several different tumors, when introduced into mouse cells, transformed some of them into cells capable of inducing tumors in mice. The cells used were the 3T3 skin cells, which already differ from normal mouse skin cells in being able to grow indefinitely in the laboratory. DNA from the transformed cells could be isolated, and it too was capable of transforming a new batch of 3T3 cells to tumor cells.

The DNA preparation containing the "transforming principle" consisted of hundreds of thousands of genes. In order to isolate the single gene or group of genes responsible, DNA from transformed 3T3 cells was used to prepare a library of recombinant DNA fragments by means of molecular cloning techniques.

Photos, Erika Hartwieg and Jonathan A. King, Electron Microscope Facility, Department of Biology, Massachusetts Institute of Technology

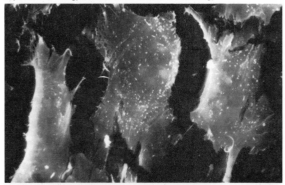

Electron micrographs reveal transformation of normal cells by an oncogene. Normal mouse cells (top) were treated with DNA extracted from human tumor cells, which then transformed the mouse cells (bottom).

Three different procedures were used: by Weinberg at MIT, by Geoffrey Cooper at the Dana-Farber Cancer Institute at Harvard University Medical School, and by Michael Wigler at Cold Spring Harbor (N.Y.) Laboratory. Each of these procedures resulted in the isolation of a single fragment of human DNA capable of transforming mouse 3T3 cells into tumor cells. With that DNA fragment it was possible, using molecular cloning techniques, to isolate the corresponding DNA from normal human tissue.

Comparison of the nucleotide sequences of the tumor-inducing and normal DNA fragments indicated that there was a single nucleotide difference between the two. In each case the change was from a guanine (G) residue in the normal DNA to a thymine (T) residue in the tumor-inducing DNA. This single change in the genetic code would result in a change in the amino acid sequence of the protein that is encoded by the gene in question. In this case the change is from the amino acid glycine present in the normal protein to the amino acid valine found in the tumor-inducing protein.

The results just described indicate that the gene in certain human tumors (bladder carcinoma, in particular) which is responsible for the transformation of mouse 3T3 cells to tumor cells differs from the corresponding gene in normal human cells as a result of mutation—that is, a change in the nucleotide sequence of DNA. The question arose as to whether that mutation could be demonstrated directly during the production of the initial tumor. The researchers found that it could, although the experiment was done necessarily in animals. Workers in the laboratory of Mariano Barbacid at the National Cancer Institute used the chemical nitrosomethylurea, a powerful carcinogen, to induce mammary carcinomas in female rats. DNA from those tumors transformed 3T3 cells, and so the gene responsible for the transformation could be isolated and used to find the corresponding gene in the original tumor tissue. In each of nine independent tumors the gene was found to be mutated at the same glycine residue. Thus, in this case chemical carcinogenesis was shown to produce a tumor-inducing gene (oncogene) by mutation.

The oncogenes isolated from human bladder carcinoma by Weinberg, Cooper, and Wigler and from rat mammary carcinoma by Barbacid turned out to be the same gene. When the nucleotide sequence of that gene was compared with the sequences of genes from known retroviruses, it was found that two viruses of rats, the Kirsten sarcoma virus and the Harvey sarcoma virus, contained genes named *ras* that were identical to the oncogenes.

At this time molecular biologists have established that normal cells contain a gene which has been named proto-*ras*. The oncogene can be isolated either from naturally occurring tumors (c-*ras*) or from certain retroviruses (v-*ras*). In either case it will transform 3T3 mouse cells into tumor cells. But 3T3 cells are not quite normal themselves; they already can grow in culture indefinitely. The oncogene will not transform normal skin cells in culture. Two new lines of evidence point to the multistep nature of cancer at the molecular level. First, if normal skin cells are first treated with chemical carcinogens or are X-rayed, some will give rise to progeny capable of growth in culture indefinitely (like 3T3 cells). These cells can be transformed by DNA containing the *ras* oncogene so that they become tumor producers. Second, the normal skin cells can be treated another way to make them targets for *ras* DNA transformation. They can be treated with DNA from a different class of retrovirus, the avian myeloblastosis virus. This virus of chickens contains an oncogene called *myc* which appears to be capable of the immortalization step needed for *ras* to transform the cell fully into a tumor cell.

In other work at both MIT and Cold Spring Harbor, genes from DNA-containing viruses called polyoma virus or adenovirus were found to substitute for either *myc* or *ras*. Although the polyoma or adenovirus genes do not share nucleotide sequences with *myc* or *ras*, they seem to be able to carry out the same functions. Thus, in order to transform a normal skin cell into a tumor-producing cell, one needs an oncogene from group I (adeno EIA, polyoma large T, or *myc*) and an oncogene from group II (adeno EIB, polyoma middle T, or *ras*).

In describing the conversion for *ras* from proto-oncogene to oncogene, evidence was cited to indicate that this event is a mutation. For *myc* the situation is more complicated. In human cells the normal proto-*myc* gene is located on chromosome 8. In Burkitt's lymphoma cells the *myc* gene is found translocated to chromosome 14, into a region that codes for heavy chains of antibody molecules called immunoglobulin G. Work in the laboratories of Michael Cole at Saint Louis University School of Medicine, Philip Leder at the Harvard University Medical School, and Carlo Croce at the Wistar Institute in Philadelphia demonstrated that *myc* gene translocation results in oncogene activation. The precise mechanism of activation is unknown; Croce's results suggest that the translocated *myc* gene makes more of its product than normal cells, while Leder and Cole believe that the product differs in quality rather than abundance.

Proteins and cell proliferation. Having dwelled at length on the gene alterations resulting in the transformation from normal cells to tumor cells, one can next consider the proteins produced by those genes. How do they cause cells to proliferate without control? Earlier in this article it was mentioned that the product of the *src* gene of Rous sarcoma virus is a protein kinase; this enzyme adds phosphate groups to the side chains of proteins, a process known as phosphorylation. Most normal cellular protein kinases add phosphate groups to the amino acids serine or threonine; the *src* gene product phosphorylates the amino acid tyrosine instead. Other cellular protein kinases also phosphorylate tyrosine. They are the receptors for polypeptide hormones, the best known of which is insulin. When insulin binds to a cell, that binding is mediated by a protein on the surface of the cell called the insulin receptor protein. The insulin receptor is a latent tyrosine phosphokinase that is triggered into activity by insulin binding. Thus, the action of the insulin hormone is mediated by a cascade of intracellular events initiated by phosphorylation of a tyrosine residue by the hormone receptor.

A number of other polypeptide hormones have been described on the basis of their ability to stimulate proliferation of cells in culture. Because their real physiological role in animals is not known, they are simply called "factors." One, liberated by the blood cells called platelets during the blood clotting process, is called platelet-derived growth factor, or PDGF. This protein causes cells to divide in culture. In an animal it might promote cell division in connection with wound healing. During the past year Michael Waterfield and his colleagues at the Imperial Cancer Research Fund Laboratories in London determined the amino-acid sequence of PDGF. When they compared this sequence with all the amino-acid sequences of proteins already known (this was done by computer, using one of several existing databanks), a striking similarity was observed with a retroviral oncogene called *sis* in simian sarcoma virus. Indeed, the protein product of the *sis* gene mimics the cell-proliferating activity of PDGF.

Thus, if a cell produced a growth factor continually, it might, by means of a regulatory cascade that begins with protein phosphorylation, stimulate itself to divide continually. If this possibility is admitted, then one might wonder whether the receptor might be so modified as not to need activation by the factor in order to trigger cell division. Again Waterfield and his associates obliged with a spectacular discovery. Epidermal growth factor (EGF) is a peptide that also stimulates cell proliferation in culture. The receptor for EGF was purified from human placenta, and the protein was partially sequenced. Sure enough, the sequence is homologous to a retroviral oncogene called v-*erb*B, found in avian erythroblastosis virus. Detailed comparison of the two genes is not complete, but it appears that v-*erb*B is shorter than the native EGF receptor protein. It may be that the oncogene retains both the membrane-spanning part of the receptor and the part that stimulates cell proliferation but lacks the part that is controlled by EGF.

It should be made clear that cancer is not the only field to be revolutionized by recombinant DNA methods, which made possible all of the results described above. Equally exciting developments took place in the ability to analyze transposable elements in plants and to introduce genes into plants; the analysis of transposable genetic elements in the fruit fly *Drosophila* that permit detailed study of differentiation at the molecular level; and the discovery of multiple regulatory elements of bacterial genes that permit fine control of gene expression during development and in response to changing environments. Space does not permit their inclusion in this review.

—Robert Haselkorn

Zoology

Significant developments in zoology during the past year included a description of changes in nerve cells associated with learning in a sea slug, the discovery of a new phylum of animals, and the application of genetic engineering techniques to the understanding of how malaria parasites change their antigenic coats. Marine biologists found that shipworms harbor a bacterium that can digest cellulose and fix atmospheric nitrogen into organic compounds. Climatic changes associated with the El Niño phenomenon

Photos, from "Nocturnal Aerial Predation of Fireflies by Light-Seeking Fireflies,"
James E. Lloyd and Steven R. Wing, *Science*, vol. 222, pp. 634–635, November 11, 1983, © 1983 AAAS

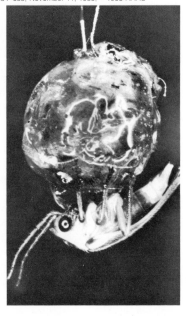

Light-emitting diodes, one glowing, one flashing, one unlit, and all covered with paste, were rotated at the ends of fishing poles in the motor-driven apparatus at the far left. More than 30 predatory female fireflies of the Photuris species attacked the glowing diode in a 34.7-hour period; one is shown at the left.

wreaked havoc with the marine iguana populations in the Galápagos Islands. Evolutionary biologists using computers identified a 26-million-year periodicity to extinction patterns in the fossil record and developed a computer model that identifies the important factors in the evolution of flight in the vertebrates.

Neurobiology. Analyzing the way in which the nervous system functions in learning in animals as complex as mammals is an overwhelming task. Consequently, many researchers have turned their attention to the simpler nervous systems of invertebrate animals. Two theories suggest how learning occurs. One postulates that learning involves the development of new connections between nerve cells. The other is based on the belief that all contacts between nerve cells already exist in the nervous system and that learning occurs by the interactions becoming stronger or weaker. Evidence is accumulating that supports both theories.

Daniel Alkon of the Marine Biological Laboratory at Woods Hole, Mass., worked out the neuronal changes involved in learning in the sea slug, *Hermissenda*. Unconditioned sea slugs usually move toward illuminated areas. If these animals are trained by simultaneously exposing them to light and spinning them on a turntable, they learn to associate the light with spinning and do not move. When later exposed to light only, the animals hesitate as if bracing for the effects of rotation. Alkon found that this learning involved changes in six cells in the eyes. Rotation stimulated the balancing organs, which then sent impulses to the eye cells. The impulses activated an enzyme, protein kinase, which altered the eye cells' membranes in such a way that they became more sensitive to light. Terry Crow of the University of

Pittsburgh found that these six cells then sent inhibitory impulses to locomotor muscles. Thus, learning was localized in a small group of cells that integrated the inputs from two sensory systems and produced an inhibitory effect on muscles. This is the first evidence that membrane changes in specific nerve cells lead to memory of a behavioral act.

Other scientists searching for cellular mechanisms underlying memory were concentrating their efforts on neuronal structure. Most neurons have mushroomlike projections called spines that contact other nerve cells. In the cerebral cortex 80–90% of the excitatory synapses (the points at which the nervous impulses pass from one neuron to another) involve spines, and the transmission between cells changes when the shape or number of these spines changes. Alfredo Caceres and others at the University of Virginia School of Medicine found actin, the muscle contractile protein, in these spines. The spines are also rich in MAP II, a protein found in microtubules. Actin and MAP II can interact to form gels in laboratory experiments. The investigators suggest that learning could occur by modification of the contact between neurons caused by the fluid-gel transition.

Behavior. Insect sex pheromones are substances, usually aliphatic alcohols, acetates, and aldehydes, released by the female to attract males and stimulate male mating behavior. Previous studies have emphasized the attractant nature of pheromones. Little work has been done on how pheromones trigger other courtship behaviors in males. J. W. S. Bradshaw and co-workers at the University of Southampton in the U.K. showed that female pine beauty moths release a blend of chemicals as a pheromone package. Each released chemical elicited a separate be-

337

Reinhardt M. Kristensen, Smithsonian Institution

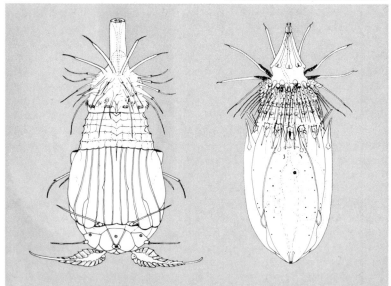

Loricifera ("girdle wearer"), a new zoological phylum, was proposed by Reinhardt Kristensen of the University of Copenhagen on the basis of his discovery in 1982 of the adult form of the microscopic marine animal (far right). Kristensen had discovered the larval form of the animal (right) in 1975.

havior in males, including searching, landing, and copulation.

Male fireflies seek mates by emitting flashes of light. James Lloyd and Steven Wing of the University of Florida at Gainesville, discovered that females of several species of fireflies attack males by homing in on this light. The scientists discovered this behavior by using light-emitting diodes attached to slowly rotating long poles to simulate males in flight. Females of several species in the genus *Photuris* attacked the dimly glowing diodes. Attacks were most frequent on continuously glowing diodes and less so on flashing ones. To test for predation, Lloyd and Wing attached living males to the diodes. These were promptly eaten by the attacking females. The intermittent flashing seen in North American male fireflies may be a defense mechanism to this predatory behavior. Male fireflies of Asian species, where predatory females are unknown, emit a steady glow rather than intermittently flashing as do North American species. Flashing targets are harder for the females to hit than ones that glow steadily. Some American species have taken this defense one step further. The males have lost the ability to glow entirely and depend on chemical sex attractants instead. For an extended discussion of firefly behavior, see *1984 Yearbook of Science and the Future* Feature Article: LIGHTS IN THE SUMMER DARKNESS.

Many fish (eels, wrasses, porgies, sea basses, and others) can change their sex. Some start life as males and then change to females, but the reverse pattern is more common. Biologists have been intrigued by these changes and have sought to determine what causes them. Milton Diamond of the University of Hawaii, Honolulu, found that in the saddleback wrasse the sex of an individual is determined by social influences, particularly the relative size of neighboring fish. If two females of different sizes are placed in a tank, the larger one becomes a functional male after two or three months and the smaller one remains a female. The gender of a neighbor does not influence the process. If a large female is placed with a small male, she still undergoes a sex change. Large females raised in isolation or with smaller fish of a different species do not change sex. Janice Aldenhoven of the University of Monash, Australia, reached similar conclusions in her study of the pygmy angelfish found on the Great Barrier Reef. These fish live in harems where one male services five to ten females that live in his territory. If the male dies or is removed from the harem, the largest female changes sex and takes over the harem. Interestingly, if the harem increases in size so that there are more than ten females, the largest female undergoes a sex change and starts a new harem by kidnapping females from the original group.

Organismal zoology. A tiny creature dredged from the ocean floor off the coast of France was new to science and so different from all other living animals that it was placed in a new phylum, the Loricifera. The name combines the Latin words for girdle and wearer and describes a distinguishing characteristic, a ring of plates that encircles the midsection of the organism. The animals are less than 0.01 in long, and have a flexible retractable tube for a mouth and a crown of club-shaped spines about the head.

Reinhardt Kristensen of the University of Copenhagen, Denmark, discovered the animal, named *Nanoloricus mysticus*, through a bit of serendipity. Pressed for time while on a field expedition, he did not follow his normal procedure of using a salt solution for washing gravel from dredge samples.

Instead, he washed the gravel with fresh water, loosening clinging organisms by means of a rapid change in the osmotic pressure. When the sands settled, a complete set of the life stages of the animal was collected. Since that time Kristensen has found

Larva (bottom) of the horsefly Tabanus punctifer *lies in mud and uses its large mandibles (center) to grasp a small young spadefoot toad (top). The larva pulls a captured toad down into the mud and then kills it by feeding on its blood and other body fluids.*

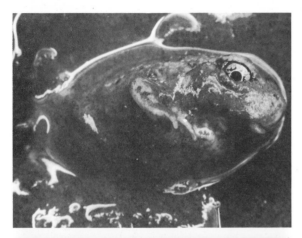

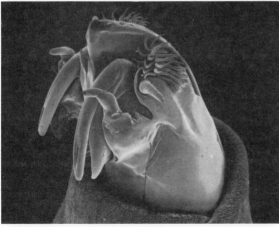

the animal in samples taken off the coasts of western Greenland, the Coral Sea in the South Pacific, and Florida. He was able to do this, however, but only when using the osmotic shock technique. This surprising abundance emphasizes the importance of sampling techniques in science. Only one other specimen, a larval form, had ever been collected. Robert Higgins of the National Museum of Natural History in Washington, D.C., found it but did not have enough specimens to describe it adequately.

Marine biologists studying shipworms, clamlike mollusks, discovered something that genetic engineers have tried for years to develop, a bacterium that digests cellulose for energy and uses atmospheric nitrogen to make amino acids and other biochemicals that contain nitrogen. John Waterbury of the Woods Hole Oceanographic Institution in Massachusetts and C. Bradford Calloway and Ruth Turner of Harvard University isolated the still-unnamed bacterium from the gland of DeShays, a brownish irregular mass of tissue associated with the gills of shipworms. They were able to grow the bacterium in pure culture in a medium containing only cellulose and salts with no source of organically bound nitrogen. The bacterium was isolated from six different species collected from coastal waters off Massachusetts, Bermuda, and Venezuela. The practical interest in this bacterium is obvious: It could possibly be commercially developed to convert industrial wastes such as sawdust or paper into proteins that could be used for animal feed or fertilizers.

In Queensland, Australia, a rare species of frog broods its young in the stomach. Females swallow the eggs, which develop for eight weeks; then juvenile frogs emerge from the females' mouths. Biologists have speculated that the developing young must release a substance which inhibits the secretion of acid in the stomach to prevent them from being digested. Michael Tyler and David Shearman of the University of Adelaide in Australia have found that the young release a substance identified as prostaglandin E_2. It inhibits the production of acid by the stomach, thereby protecting the young during the incubation period. After the young leave, the stomach lining again functions normally.

Parasitology. In Africa and Asia malaria is more of a problem today than it was 50 years ago because the parasite that causes it, the protozoan *Plasmodium falciparum*, has become resistant to drugs. *P. falciparum* invades and destroys the host's red blood cells and can eventually cause anemia and death. Mosquitoes transmit the disease from one host to another. Recent work has been directed at developing vaccines to prevent infection. However, there have been difficulties because once the protozoan enters the blood, it goes through several life-cycle stages, each immunologically distinct.

Life sciences

Sporozoites, the first stage, have only one major antigen on their surfaces. (Antigens usually are proteins that cause the formation of antibodies in the host.) Joan Ellis and colleagues at the New York University Medical Center isolated the gene for this protein and cloned it in the bacteria *Escherichia coli*, thereby making large amounts of the protein available for use in experiments. Jurg Gysin and colleagues, also at the New York University Medical Center, analyzed the protein and found that it is a large polypeptide consisting of 12 amino acids repeated 12 times. A synthetic peptide containing only one of the 12 amino acid repeating units was made; it has similar antigenic properties to the large polypeptide and raises the possibility of producing a vaccine in large quantities. However, because the sporozoite stage is short-lived, the effectiveness of such a vaccine would be limited.

Researchers were also looking at the next life-cycle stage in the red blood cells. David Kemp and colleagues at the Royal Melbourne Hospital, Australia, cloned the genes for the antigens that occur on the surfaces of these stages by growing the parasites in culture and chemically isolating their RNA (ribonucleic acid). These RNA molecules represent copies of individual active genes. Using genetic engineering techniques, the scientists made DNA (deoxyribonucleic acid) from the RNA and inserted it into bacteria. The bacteria then were used to make proteins that the parasites would normally make at this stage. The bacteria-synthesized proteins were screened for antigenicity by mixing them with sera from people who had recently had malaria. If the proteins were antigenic, the antibodies in the sera combined with them. The researchers thus identified several hundred proteins with antigenic properties.

This research was a breakthrough because it showed that it is possible to isolate the surface determinants of blood stages of the parasite and may lead to the development of vaccines. Much work remains to be done, however. The most reactive antigens must be isolated, and parasites from different geographical areas will have to be investigated to determine if one vaccine will be effective for all. Also, because the parasites go through a sequence in which they invade red cells, multiply, and then invade new cells, the time sequence of antigen appearance will have to be determined.

D. J. Weatherall and colleagues at the University of Oxford, England, addressed the problem of preventing infection from a different perspective. They isolated proteins from the parasites that are involved in recognizing the host's red blood cells. This recognition is a key process in the infection. If it could be blocked, then the disease could be controlled by preventing the entry of the parasites into the blood cell and interrupting their life cycles.

Environmental zoology. The warm currents and weather pattern shifts accompanying the El Niño phenomenon in the Pacific Ocean in 1982–83 had devastating effects on the marine iguana populations of the Galápagos Islands. Surface seawater temperatures around the islands have been 4.3° C (7.74° F) warmer, and the islands, which normally receive only 374 mm (15 in) of rainfall per year, have had about ten times as much. Erosion has been greatly increased by storm runoff and increased wave action on the beaches. Andrew Laurie from the University of Cambridge, England, observed iguanas during these changes and reported that they were suffering. Algae on which the iguanas normally feed disappeared, and the animals were eating less desirable species and carrion. Most of the iguanas were underweight, and about half had died. Though El Niño dealt a severe blow to the ecology of these islands, conditions seemed to be returning to normal in 1984. There appeared to be no danger of extinction of the iguanas, and this quirk of nature offered a unique opportunity for biologists such as Laurie to study how animal populations recover from natural disasters.

By 1984 the California condor population was only about 20 birds in the wild and three males in captivity. Only four mating couples were observed during the past year. The San Diego (Calif.) Wild Animal Park was participating in a program to boost the reproductive success of the population. Zoo personnel observed nesting couples and removed the single egg that was laid, taking it back to the zoo and incubating it there. The parents then would remate and produce a second egg, thus doubling the reproductive rate of the population. During the past year two chicks were hatched at the zoo. When large enough, they will be released into the wild.

Once considered on the verge of extinction, the black-footed ferret is making a comeback in Wyoming. Its near demise is attributed to the decline in its primary food source, the prairie dog, as a result of elimination programs aimed at the latter. In 1981 biologists captured one of the first ferrets seen in ten years and fitted it with a radio transmitter. By tracking this individual, the biologists located nine more black-footed ferrets and defined a study territory. Tim Clark from Idaho State University sighted at least 60 of the animals. The Wyoming Game and Fish Department began coordinating the efforts of several agencies to preserve the population.

At the Love Canal toxic-waste site in Niagara Falls, N.Y., a four-year study showed that meadow voles were dying prematurely. Tissues from these mouse-like rodents showed elevated levels of halogenated hydrocarbons, including the pesticide lindane, according to John Christian of the State University of New York at Binghamton. Liver abnormalities and other organ changes were found in the contaminated

340

animals, but the cause of death was not definitely identified. Of great concern was the fact that some of the animals with the highest levels of pesticide were captured in an area surrounding the toxic-waste site where people still live.

Massive oyster mortalities were observed on the reefs of Mississippi Sound by Bill Demoran of the Gulf Coast Research Laboratory in Ocean Springs, Miss. More than 2,800 ha (7,000 ac) of oyster beds were lost when water salinity dropped to almost zero. In April and May huge quantities of fresh water poured into the sound from the Mississippi River through the Bonnet Carré Spillway flood control diversion and from the Pearl River. Oysters seem to thrive in water that has a salinity of 15–28 ppm (parts per million) compared to seawater, which has 32–34 ppm. They can tolerate brief exposure to 2.5 ppm primarily by closing their shells, preventing fresh water from leaching salts from their tissues. However, after several weeks or shorter times at elevated temperatures, they must open their shells to obtain oxygen. Prolonged passage of fresh water overhead therefore leads to problems for these non-mobile animals. The Bonnet Carré Spillway was built in 1932. The flood control gates have been opened six times since then, and each time massive oyster mortalities resulted. Though in the short term the biological effects of these openings are disastrous, there is a long-term benefit. The floodwaters bring additional nutrients into the sound, thereby increasing oyster production about two years later.

Evolution. The dynamics of the extinction of species were discussed at a conference held at Northern Arizona University. Scientists attempted to determine the causes of the mass extinctions observed in the fossil record. Most scientists now accept that asteroid impacts on the Earth are recurring events and that they may explain several of the past episodes in which large groups of animals disappeared. The late Cretaceous extinction in which the dinosaurs disappeared is considered one such event. Asteroid impact is now viewed as part of the theory of uniformitarianism, in which both earthbound and extraterrestrial natural processes influence the biological environment. When an impact occurs, sunlight would be blocked by dust for periods up to several months, causing reduction in temperatures and widespread deaths in populations of plants and animals.

John Sepkoski and David Raup of the University of Chicago reported a quantitative study that they performed on the fossil record. Using data on extinctions at the taxonomic family level, they plotted extinctions as a function of time. They found a background extinction rate per million years of three to five families, equivalent to 180 to 300 species. At intervals of about 26 million years there were periods of rapid extinctions in which the rate jumped to 20 families or about 1,200 species per million years. The study did not offer an explanation as to why extinctions occurred. The greatest extinction took place 240 million years ago in the Permian Period and correlates with the formation of the supercontinent Pangea. More than 95% of the marine species disappeared at that time because of the reduction in the continental shelf areas. The University of Chicago study opened a new way of looking at the past quantitatively, and much new work along this line was expected.

Contemporary events were also discussed at the conference. Paul Ehrlich of Stanford University suggested that current extinction rates were producing a record that would equal past geologic extinctions. This concept is difficult to grasp since extinction normally is considered on a time scale of millions rather than hundreds of years. Urban growth, chemical pollution, and agricultural development in tropical countries have tremendous impact on species diversity, but no one is sure what the effects are.

Black-footed ferret stands before its prey and chief food source, a prairie dog. The ferret, native to North America, was believed to be nearly extinct until one was seen in the wild in 1981, the first such sighting in almost ten years. Zoologists tracked this ferret and soon found others.

Tim Clark, Idaho State University, Pocatello

Indeed, scientists do not know exactly how many species currently exist. Some estimates are as low as 2 million, and others are higher than 30 million. There are no good figures on the current rate of extinction, because monitoring of ecosystems is not uniform.

Daniel Simberloff, an ecologist at Florida State University, shared Ehrlich's views and attempted to assemble a computer model to forecast future events. Simberloff predicted that within 100 years 66% of the existing plant species and 69% of the existing bird species will have disappeared.

How flight originated among the vertebrates has been a subject of debate among evolutionary zoologists. Two theories predominate. The arboreal theory suggests that the first fliers climbed trees and glided to a landing place. The cursorial theory suggests that flight developed from running animals. Several years ago John Ostrom of Yale University suggested that bird flight might have originated from small, insectivorous dinosaurs that used their primitive forelimbs as nets to sweep insects into the mouth while running, thus increasing their efficiency as predators. Flight developed from this preadaptation, perhaps from jumping movements.

In recent months scientists from Northern Arizona University entered the debate, using aerodynamic computer models to support their arguments. Gerald Caple, a chemist and leader of the group, was intrigued by Ostrom's ideas and enlisted the help of Russell Balda, an ornithologist, and William Willis, a physicist and former fighter pilot. Their conceptualization of the problem focused on a factor that others had overlooked: If an animal is to be successful in flight, it is not just lift that is important. The animal must also have control of its body position in three dimensions. Pitch, roll, and yaw must be controlled whether the animal is a glider or is jumping. To model this, the scientists started with a hypothetical animal that was a cylinder with two projecting arms forward of the center of mass. By modeling simple movements of the arms, they were able to investigate the amount of control possible. By changing arm dimensions to make airfoils, they could explore lift possibilities and could add other control surfaces such as a tail or legs while exploring the effects of head and body movements. From their study came a complete list of the problems that animals would have to overcome before they could become airborne. A major advantage of flight was found to be a saving on the expenditure of energy. It takes more calories for an animal to run a distance than it does for it to run, jump, and glide over the same distance.

The models developed by Caple, Balda, and Willis struck down the arboreal theory on two grounds. First, if the wings are moved during gliding, lift and the glide path are reduced. Second, animals that are gliding must first have control, especially bipedal animals that might land in trees. The arboreal theory does not address this. The researchers thus concluded that their model argues strongly for the cursorial theory of flight development. Short jumps do not need as much control at first but do provide a starting point to try out various adaptations. Ostrom's insectivorous idea was viewed as one that has outlived its usefulness but was important because it instigated the interdisciplinary research. The models that have been developed by the Arizona scientists will no doubt stimulate new analytical approaches to the problem.

See also Feature Article: OVERLOOKED ANIMALS: NEW HOPE FOR THE TROPICS.

—Warren D. Dolphin

Materials sciences

The development of advanced ceramics for such electromagnetic applications as fiber optics continued to be a major focus of research in the materials sciences. Considerable attention also was given to improving the processes involved in making steel.

Ceramics

In a recent survey 100 executives of major Japanese companies were asked to name the ten most important technical innovations of the past decade. Advanced ceramics ranked fifth in their view, only slightly lower than industrial robots and above office automation and supercomputers. In 1981 Japan's Ministry of International Trade and Industry initiated a ten-year program aimed at the development of basic technologies for the next generation of Japanese industries. Advanced ceramics was one of the core programs within that initiative.

Japan's current annual production of advanced ceramics, including primarily ceramics for electromagnetic applications, cutting tools, seals, and pump components, totals about $1.4 billion. Authorities estimated that Japanese sales of advanced ceramics would reach $9 billion–13 billion by 1990, with most of the growth concentrated in electro-ceramics; in ceramics for high-temperature, high-strength, and wear-resistance applications; and in ceramics for biological applications. Estimates by Kim Clark of the Harvard University Business School and by H. Kent Bowen of the Massachusetts Institute of Technology (MIT) indicated similar growth rates, not only for Japan but also for the U.S. These growth projections represent attractive opportunities for companies interested in expanding into new markets, and many of them began focusing their research and development activities on advanced ceramics.

During the last year electro-ceramics accounted for a large fraction of sales in advanced ceramics, and recent advances suggest that it will continue to play a major role. The installation and operation of fiber-optic communication links as demonstration projects in the U.S., France, West Germany, Canada, and Japan were extremely successful, and communications companies in the U.S. began to purchase access to railway and power company rights-of-way for future fiber-optic cable installations. Industry projections forecast that optical fiber sales would rise from the level of several hundred million dollars per year in the early 1980s to between $2 billion and $6 billion by the 1990s. Two factors that seem likely to influence the rate and extent of that growth are the cost of the fibers and the availability of advanced light sources.

A new semiconductor laser announced by Bell Laboratories appeared to be exceptionally well suited to solving many fiber-optic communication problems. Developed by Won-Tien Tsang and his colleagues, this cleaved coupled-cavity laser uses a resonance technique to eliminate all but one of the many optical modes that lead to the spectral width of a normal single-cavity diode laser. This should solve a major problem that has hampered long-distance fiber-optic communications. At the infrared wavelength where single-mode silica glass optical fibers are most transparent, 1.55 µm (micrometers), the velocity of light in silica glass is very dependent on its frequency. If a light pulse from a conventional diode laser with a wavelength spread of 50 to 100 Å (angstroms) is used, the different frequency components of the pulse travel through the fiber at different speeds. (One angstrom equals one ten-billionth of a meter.) This limits the distance and the rate at which one can transmit information without serious distortion. The new cleaved coupled-mode laser emits pulses with a spectral width of less than one angstrom at rates of amplitude modulation of approximately one billion cycles per second. With this new capability Bell Laboratories recently demonstrated digital transmission rates of 10^9 bits per second through 104 km of optical fiber without the need for any intermediate amplification. As pointed out by Tsang, at that rate the entire text of the *Encyclopædia Britannica* can be transmitted in less than half a second.

Work also continued on the fabrication of the optical fibers themselves, with particular emphasis on further improvements in quality and reductions in cost. To achieve the purity required for low-loss communications fibers, silica glass rods several centimeters in diameter are produced first by chemical vapor deposition (CVD) processes. Silicon tetrachloride gas is reacted, generally by flame hydrolysis or oxidation, to form very fine silica glass soot particles that are deposited on a mandrel or on the inside walls of a silica glass tube. The soot is then fused into a solid glass rod that can be drawn out, in a furnace at temperatures above 2,000° C, into the very-fine-diameter fibers required for optical cable use. Automation of the processes involved has helped to improve consistency and reduce cost, but the CVD and the fiber-drawing processes are both tediously slow. Direct melting techniques in which the fibers are pulled directly from molten glasses contained in crucibles have been investigated as a means of circumventing the CVD step, but the difficulty of maintaining the purity required for communication applications has been a problem.

Sol-gel processing is considered by many researchers to have the greatest long-range potential for reducing the cost of high-purity fibers. In this process organic chemical derivatives of the key elements of the final ceramic are mixed with a water-ethanol solvent. The ingredients and the solvent are reacted

Cleaved coupled-cavity laser, seen on a U.S. penny, emits pulses having very narrow spectral widths and thereby improves fiber-optic communications.

General Electric Research and Development Center, Schenectady, N.Y.

Thin glass fiber (loop in foreground) can carry an intense beam of light from a stationary laser to an industrial robot about 25 meters away. An optical assembly reduces the 0.75-inch-diameter laser beam to the 0.04-inch size of the glass fiber.

to form a uniform colloidal "sol," which can then be heated to drive off most of the solvent and the unnecessary organics to form a semisolid gel. The gel can then be fired to consolidate it into the desired end product.

While still in a very early stage of development, the sol-gel process has many advantages and is likely to play a major role in future ceramic technology. It would be useful not only in the production of optical fibers but also for such other products as ceramic coatings and ceramic matrix composites.

Sungchul Ji and his colleagues at Rutgers University showed that rather than using fiber optics just to illuminate tissues within the body, as physicians do with endoscopes, the fibers can be used to study reactions between cells and enzymes as they take place within the body. The researchers used two fibers bonded together to form a light guide photometer. One fiber transmits light at a suitable wavelength to the target area, where it excites the cells and generates fluorescence characteristic of the reactions that are occurring. The other fiber transmits the fluorescence back out to a photodetector for analysis. The technique has already been used to study the effects of alcohol on liver cells. Another obviously important use would be in cancer drug therapy. If the fibers could be used to monitor the effects of a drug on both malignant and normal tissue, it might be possible to control the administration of the drug so as to enhance its effect on the cancer and minimize its adverse effects elsewhere in the body.

Japanese researchers were especially effective in exploring another electro-ceramic area, the use of the grain boundaries (surfaces between individual grains) and pores present in polycrystalline ceramics to produce materials with new properties. High-technology electro-ceramics are normally produced by compacting fine ceramic powders to a desired shape and then heating them until they sinter together to form a strong, dense component. In making these materials in the past, producers emphasized minimizing the influence of the grain boundaries and pores that remain in the final body. High-purity starting materials were used to minimize the presence of impurities or undesirable phases at the interfaces between grains, and components were normally densified to eliminate as many of the pores as possible. Researchers at the Matsushita Electric Industrial Co., however, showed that by carefully controlling the structure and composition of the grain boundaries in polycrystalline strontium titanate they could achieve both a voltage-dependent electrical resistance (varistor behavior) and a high effective capacitance. The varistor behavior is useful for current-control applications. These multifunctional devices are already in use as electrical noise filters.

Shigeru Hayakawa and his co-workers also used the effects of the adsorption of water vapor and various gases on the surfaces of open pores to make humidity and gas sensors. For example, they showed that a solid solution of magnesium chromate and titanium dioxide with about 35% porosity, carefully controlled to fall within a size range of 0.1 to 0.3 μm in diameter, changes resistance by more than a factor of 10,000 over a relative humidity range of 0 to 100%. These sensors are now used as cooking controls in microwave ovens and other related applications.

Many observers believe that the growth in advanced ceramics for high-temperature structural and wear applications will dwarf even the rapid growth anticipated for electro-ceramics. The most promising high-volume, near-term structural application appears to be in vehicular engines. While ceramic turbine parts for large-scale vehicular equipment appear to be at least a decade away, small ceramic components for diesel engines seem likely to be available commercially within the next few years. Key engine parts will be insulated with ceramics, thereby retaining that part of the engine's heat output normally lost to the water cooling system and increasing the amount of heat available for useful work. Many Japanese and U.S. firms were developing ceramic pistons or piston caps, cylinder liners and heads, valve seats, and valve guides.

—Norman M. Tallan

Metallurgy

During the past year there was considerable interest in the development of innovative steelmaking processes. In the iron- and steelmaking sequence, iron ore is chemically treated in a blast furnace to produce hot metal, which is liquid iron that contains small amounts of carbon, silicon, manganese, sulfur, and phosphorus. In the subsequent steelmaking process the silicon, manganese, and phosphorus are selectively oxidized from the metal to form their oxides, which are then dissolved in a slag, and the concentration of carbon is decreased to the desired level by its removal as carbon monoxide gas. Maximum removal of the silicon, manganese, sulfur, and phosphorus is required before the desired concentration of carbon is reached. After separation of the slag, the metal is deoxidized and solidified to form raw steel.

Steelmaking was revolutionized in 1949 with the introduction in Austria of the LD (Linz-Donawitz) process, which over the years was developed into the modern BOF (Basic Oxygen Furnace) process. In the BOF process the heat-resistant steelmaking vessel is charged with lime (the slag-making ingredient), after which the hot metal is poured in and scrap steel is added. Pure oxygen gas is then blown through a vertical water-cooled tube onto the surface of the melt. In the 1970s experiments were conducted in which gaseous oxygen and powdered lime were introduced to the metal through tuyeres, openings located in the bottom of the steelmaking vessel. This led to a distinction between "top-blowing" and "bottom-blowing," and the current interest centers on the extent to which the two processes can be combined to produce a "mixed-blowing" practice.

The major difference between the two processes is that the top-blown BOF produces an emulsion of metal droplets suspended in the slag, while the bottom-blown process produces in the metal an extensive dispersion of lime-rich slag particles which rise, with the bottom-blown gas, through the metal. In the bottom-blown process slag formation begins in the melt near the tuyeres, where the oxides of iron, manganese, silicon, and phosphorus, formed by the oxidation of those elements in the metal, react rapidly with the injected lime powder. Simultaneously, the oxygen reacts with carbon dissolved in the melt to produce carbon monoxide in the rising bubbles. As the slag particles rise through the molten bath, they undergo secondary reactions with the carbon in the melt so that the concentrations of iron oxide and manganese oxide in the slag at the upper surface of the bath are less than those in the slag formed at the tuyere level. In the bottom-blown process the injected oxygen is the source of turbulence in the metal bath.

On the other hand in the top-blown BOF process

General Electric Research and Development Center, Schenectady, N.Y.

In a vacuum chamber a white-hot stream of molten metal is sprayed onto a form, where it quickly solidifies and is built up, layer by layer, to make a jet-engine turbine blade. Parts fabricated in this way have high tensile strength and thermal-fatigue resistance.

the turbulence of the decarbonization reaction produces an emulsion of metal droplets in the slag. Also, pure oxygen is transferred directly to the slag with the result that the iron-oxide content of the slag is higher than it is in the slag produced during the bottom-blown process. Oxygen transfer via the slag is essential in top-blowing because a large part of the decarbonization and most of the oxidation of manganese and phosphorus occurs at the slag-metal interface in the emulsion. Toward the end of the top-blown BOF process the rate of decarbonization decreases, and therefore the turbulence caused by the evolution of carbon monoxide also decreases. The consequent decline in the degree of intermixing of the slag and metal and the continued oxidation of the slag cause the slag to become significantly hotter than the metal at the end of the process. In bottom-blowing in which the slag rises upward through the metal, the slag is usually cooler than the metal at the end of the process.

The intensive stirring action that is maintained throughout the bottom-blowing process causes the concentrations of oxygen, sulfur, phosphorus, and manganese in the slag to be almost in equilibrium with those in the metal. In top-blowing, however, the disequilibrium between the slag and metal, caused by the overoxidation and overheating of the slag near the end of the blow, cannot be eliminated by the weak stirring at the end of the blow. Consequently,

A sheet of titanium in a die is heated by infrared quartz lamps so that it becomes pliable and can be formed by gas pressure into a strong but lightweight aircraft part. This new method of fabricating parts is expected to save manufacturers millions of dollars in production costs.

the advantages of bottom-blowing include a lower iron oxide content of the slag, allowing less iron to be lost to the slag; better removal of phosphorus and sulfur from the steel; and a lower oxygen concentration in the steel for any given carbon content. The disadvantages include a lower capacity to use recycled steel scrap; difficulties that arise in making "catch-carbon" heats (a process that involves adding deoxidants such as ferrosilicon or ferromanganese to stop the decarbonization reaction once the required carbon content has been attained); and a higher rate of erosion of the heat-resistant lining of the bottom of the furnace.

Attempts at combining top- and bottom-blowing in a single vessel were thus aimed at improving the scrap-melting ability of the bottom-blowing process and improving the metallurgical features of the top-blown process. Initially, it was found that, if 1–5% of the total oxygen used is bottom-blown, the amount of the slag-metal emulsion that is formed is decreased. This allows better control of the disequilibrium between the slag and metal. However, bottom-blown gas in such small amounts as 1–5% was found to be insufficient to ensure a strong enough mixing action at the end of the blow; that action is necessary to eliminate the disequilibrium between the slag and metal when low-carbon steels are being made. In order to eliminate the disequilibrium the melt had to be stirred by bottom-blowing for several minutes after the cessation of top-blowing. The researchers found that 20–30% of the total oxygen must be bottom-blown to produce a stirring action equal to that obtained in pure bottom-blowing. In these processes the bottom-blown oxygen was shrouded by hydrocarbon gases; that is, oxygen was injected through a central pipe, and hydrocarbons, acting as coolants, were injected through an annular pipe that surrounded the central pipe.

Attempts to produce combined-blowing processes included bottom-blowing with inert gases such as argon or nitrogen, with oxygen-nitrogen mixtures shrouded with nitrogen, and with carbon dioxide-oxygen mixtures shrouded with carbon dioxide. With the use of small amounts of bottom-blown inert gas it was found that the formation of the emulsion can be controlled by varying the flow rate of the inert gas; the role of the top-blown gas then becomes only one of supplying oxygen to the system and partitioning the oxygen between the gas phase and the metal bath.

Variation of the flow rate of the inert gas during the process facilitates instantaneous balancing of the oxygen between the slag and the metal, and thus the formation of the slag-metal emulsion can be controlled or even prevented. This permits the production of high-carbon steels by the catch-carbon process. However, the amount of inert gas that can be blown in the bottom is limited by the excessive cooling that occurs at the tuyeres under conditions of high flow rate. Excessive cooling causes partial clogging of the tuyeres, which, in turn, leads to an unstable gas flow. Researchers found that when small amounts of inert stirring gas are used, an improvement of the metallurgical features can only be achieved when the final carbon content of the steel is less than 0.06% by weight.

In trials with carbon dioxide-oxygen mixtures the best metallurgical results were obtained with relatively large bottom-blowing rates. However, ejection of metal from the vessel limited the flow rates to considerably less than those giving the best metallurgical results. Generally, the results obtained with carbon dioxide-oxygen mixtures were almost identical with those obtained using inert gases. High bottom-blown flow rates of oxygen-nitrogen mixtures at the beginning and end of the process decreased the extent of the disequilibrium between the slag and metal at the end of the blow, and this disequilibrium was eliminated by continuing bottom-blowing for three to five minutes after the end of top-blowing.

In all of the processes described above, when the state of the slag-metal disequilibrium is being controlled by the bottom-blown gas, top-blowing can be adjusted to increase the extent of oxidation of carbon monoxide to carbon dioxide inside the vessel. The transmittal of the heat generated by this combustion to the metal increases the scrap-melting capacity of the process.

Optimization of the combined blowing process has been hindered by a lack of knowledge of the various mechanisms of slag formation and of the slag-metal reactions that occur. Improvements are being sought by means of experimentation with the mode of bottom injection, such as the use of porous plugs, pipes, and annular tuyeres, and also with the nature of the bottom-blown gases. Although it is likely that the ultimate choice of equipment and procedures will depend on the grade of steel being produced, it is already apparent that the performances obtained in combined blowing are significantly superior to those achieved when the top-blown BOF process is used.

—David R. Gaskell

Mathematics

As has often happened recently, problems that have had a long history contributed significantly to contemporary research in mathematics during the past year. Two of the most active areas of mathematical research in 1983 and 1984 built directly on some very old ideas.

Factoring large numbers. For several years mathematicians have been working with computer scientists to develop codes that would enable computers to communicate with one another with guaranteed security. Their work has depended on "trapdoor" functions in mathematics that are easy (for computers) to compute in one direction but essentially impossible to compute in the other direction. Thus, they are like trapdoors—easy to fall through and hard to climb out of. Many of the codes depend on large prime numbers, and so research into factoring such numbers has increased enormously in recent years. (A number is a prime if its only divisors are ± 1 and its own absolute value.)

The latest strategy is a modern form of divide and conquer: all equations involved in the problem of factoring a large number are divided by a large number of small known primes, and the remainders are used to form several sets of new equations. This method, using the arithmetic of "residue classes," is exactly like the old parlor trick in which one person can unfailingly determine another's age after being told only the remainders upon division by 2, 3, 5, and 7. This trick, like the current prime number research, uses the arithmetic of residue classes; at its heart is Euclid's algorithm, a method for determining common factors that was developed in ancient Greece.

In the research on factoring large numbers the residue arithmetic produces several sets of equations, each similar to the original single set but involving smaller numbers. These several sets can be handled simultaneously on some of the new computers that employ parallel processing, thus making it possible for the first time to factor 60-digit numbers.

Mordell's conjecture. The highlight of mathematics research in 1983 was the proof by Gerd Faltings

Mathematician Gustavus Simmons shows a chart that reveals recent progress in factoring large numbers. Simmons headed a research team that factored the largest number yet, a quantity most economically expressed as $2^{251} - 1$.

(Left) Courant Institute of Mathematical Sciences, New York University; (center and right) University of California at Berkeley

Major prizewinners in mathematics in 1983 included, left to right, Paul Garabedian, Shiing-Shen Chern, and Gerard Debreu. Garabedian solved complex problems of aerodynamics, while Chern made important breakthroughs in global differential geometry. Debreu developed mathematical models of economic systems.

of Wuppertal University in West Germany of an important unresolved conjecture about solutions to algebraic equations. This conjecture, which was first proposed in 1922 by the British number theorist Louis Mordell, suggests a relationship between the number of solutions that equations may have and the geometry of certain surfaces determined by those equations. After 18 months of intense work the 29-year-old Faltings verified Mordell's conjecture in a 40-page proof that builds on and completes half a century of work by mathematicians from the Soviet Union and the United States.

Faltings's proof of the Mordell conjecture is important not just for its own sake but also because it is the first major step in over a century in the struggle to verify Fermat's last theorem. In 1637 the French mathematician Pierre de Fermat claimed in a note scribbled in the margin of a book to have discovered a "truly remarkable" proof that there were no non-trivial solutions to the Pythagorean-like equation $x^n + y^n = z^n$, in which x, y, z, and n are integers, for values of n greater than 2. (The trivial solutions are $0^3 + 0^3 = 0^3$ and $0^3 + 1^3 = 1^3$.) For $n = 2$, the 3-4-5 "carpenter's triangle" is a well-known solution: $3^2 + 4^2 = 9 + 16 = 25 = 5^2$. Other "Pythagorean triplets" such as 5-12-13 also satisfy this equation, but no similar solutions have ever been found if n is greater than 2.

Mordell's conjecture arose from his study of integer solutions to algebraic equations, the type of equation studied in high-school algebra. The interest in integer solutions to equations dates back to the 3rd century AD when Diophantus of Alexandria wrote a book posing problems of this type. Since then, equations that must be solved with integers are called Diophantine equations.

One way to classify such equations—indeed, the way it is done in high-school algebra classes—is by degree: linear equations such as $2x + 3y = 5$, in which the exponents of the terms x and y are understood to be 1, are of degree 1; quadratic equations such as $x^2 + 3y = 7$ are of degree 2; cubic equations such as $y = (x - 3)^3$ are of degree 3.

Another means of classification is by what geometers call "genus"; this involves a counting of the holes in the surface created when one graphs the equation using complex numbers in place of the variables x and y. (Complex numbers are of the form $a + bi$, in which a and b are real numbers and i is the imaginary unit such that $i^2 = -1$.) Since complex numbers are themselves two-dimensional, and since each equation expresses a relationship between two or more complex numbers, the "surface" determined in this way will not exist properly in three-dimensional space. Nevertheless, by employing sufficiently powerful imagination, mathematicians can visualize these higher-dimensional surfaces and analyze their properties.

The key property of a surface, it turns out, is the number of holes it has. A sphere, for example, has no holes, while the surface of a torus, or doughnut shape, has one hole. The number of holes in the surface is its genus. Equations of degrees 1 and 2 produce surfaces of genus 0; that is, they have no holes. Equations of degree 3 usually correspond to surfaces with one hole (like the surface of a torus).

348

Some cubic equations, however, produce no holes; others produce two holes. Generally, equations of degree higher than 3 yield surfaces with more than one hole.

The connecting link between the genus of a surface and Diophantine equations is formed by whole numbers (integers) or fractions (called rational numbers, for "ratio"). Finding integer solutions to equations was discovered to be the same as finding rational solutions, since if one has a rational, *i.e.*, fractional, solution to an equation, then one can always multiply both sides of the equation by a common denominator to find a solution in integers.

An equation whose associated complex surface has no holes has either no rational solution or infinitely many rational solutions. Mordell showed that the rational solutions to an equation whose complex surface had precisely one hole can be generated from a finite set of basic solutions. He then conjectured, in an enormous leap of faith for the state of mathematical knowledge in 1922, that any equation whose corresponding complex surface had two or more holes could have at most a finite number of rational solutions.

This is what Faltings proved in very general terms, not just for ordinary algebraic equations but for a whole class of generalizations of algebraic equations. Fermat's equation, it turns out, is in this class whenever n is greater than 2. Thus, Faltings's proof implies that there can be at most finitely many rational solutions to such an equation. The step from there to Fermat's theorem—that there is no rational solution—is still enormous, but seems more within grasp than ever before.

Prizes. Progress in mathematics is measured in two ways: by exciting breakthroughs such as Faltings's work on the Mordell conjecture and by the steady growth of major theories, one small step at a time. Prizes often signal the progress of these slower growing though fundamentally important parts of mathematics.

The 1983 Birkhoff Prize of the American Mathematical Society and the Society for Industrial and Applied Mathematics was awarded to Paul R. Garabedian of the Courant Institute of Mathematical Sciences of New York University. Garabedian was cited for his innovative methods for solving problems of aerodynamics. In the 1950s he discovered how to solve equations for the design of blunt bodies in hypersonic flow; in the 1960s he applied these methods to the design of transonic airfoils with greatly reduced drag; in the 1970s he helped modify these methods for the design of efficient turbine blades; and in the 1980s his methods were being applied to the extraordinarily complex calculations associated with magnetohydrodynamics, the study of the behavior of plasma in the presence of electric and magnetic fields, which has found applications in fusion energy research.

The major world prize in mathematics is the Wolf Foundation award, which is given "for the promotion of science and art for the benefit of mankind." The 1983 prize of $100,000 was shared jointly by Shiing-Shen Chern of the University of California at Berkeley and Paul Erdos of the Hungarian Academy of Sciences in Budapest.

For several decades Chern has been the world's leading figure in global differential geometry—the study of calculus-like structures (integrals and derivatives) on higher dimensional curves and surfaces. His discovery of characteristic classes (now known as Chern classes) gave geometers an important tool for classifying these abstract surfaces and thereby launched global differential geometry on a period of unprecedented growth. Recently many of his results have proved important to theoretical physicists who have been using gauge field theories in attempts to arrive at a general unification theory of interactions among subatomic particles.

Paul Erdos is one of the most prolific mathematicians of our time. Nearly 40 years ago he gave (with Atle Selberg) an elementary proof of the famous prime number theorem, a statement that says that the density of prime numbers thins out in proportion to the number of digits in a number. Erdos virtually created the field of combinatorial mathematics, now a cornerstone of computer science. Recently he made major contributions to the partition calculus of set theory, thereby creating a whole new branch of mathematics at the interface of set theory and mathematical logic.

The 1983 Nobel Memorial Prize for Economics was awarded to the mathematician-economist Gerard Debreu of the University of California at Berkeley for his research in mathematical models of economic systems. Debreu's 1959 classic, *The Theory of Value: An Axiomatic Analysis of Economic Equilibrium*, represents the first major application of rigorous, theoretical mathematics to the uncertain world of economics. Debreu approached the theory of value "with the standards of rigor of the contemporary formalist school of mathematics"—a reference to the abstract French Bourbaki program under which he was educated.

Debreu's work substituted arguments from geometry (specifically, from convexity and topology) for those of classical calculus, thus giving economists a rigorous tool for analysis that did not presuppose the rigid standards of measurement and quantification of the Newtonian calculus. His study launched economics and, subsequently, other behavioral sciences into the world of abstract mathematical models where one gains both generality and conceptual simplicity.

—Lynn Arthur Steen

Medical sciences

General medicine

Advances in genetic research during the past year led to the discovery of both the defects that produce some serious diseases and the gene markers for others, while a new diagnostic procedure that might replace amniocentesis offered prospects of earlier prenatal diagnosis. Progress in understanding Alzheimer's disease, a degenerative ailment affecting nerve cells in the brain, came from the finding that a specific area of the brain appears to be selectively damaged in disease victims. More information about the role of cholesterol in heart disease and data supporting the efficacy of lowering cholesterol levels may change treatment approaches to this widespread problem. Attempts to find a cause for acquired immune deficiency syndrome (AIDS) produced a possible major breakthrough when researchers in the U.S. and France isolated a virus that they believed was responsible for the disease. Success in discovering the cause of a form of arthritis known as Lyme disease was reported. So-called low-tar cigarettes were branded as no safer than others.

Huntington's gene marker. Genetic research yielded clues to several serious disorders in 1983, raising hopes that prenatal diagnosis of such diseases and even treatment may not be far off. One team of investigators found a genetic marker for Huntington's disease. By using recombinant DNA (deoxyribonucleic acid) techniques to analyze blood and skin samples from two large family groups of affected individuals, they determined the location of the gene responsible for the ailment.

Huntington's disease, once known as St. Vitus' Dance and more recently prominent as the condition that affected noted U.S. folksinger Woody Guthrie, causes progressive motor abnormality and intellectual deterioration, often accompanied by depression and other psychiatric symptoms. Because its first symptoms do not appear until age 30 or later, affected people generally have had children before realizing that they have the disease. Any child of an affected parent has a 50% risk of developing Huntington's disease.

The application of the investigators' findings to research on Huntington's disease "is immediate," according to James Gusella, Nancy Wexler, and their associates. Wexler headed an expedition of investigators from 18 institutions that studied members of a Venezuelan population affected with Huntington's disease. More than 3,000 people near Lake Maracaibo in Venezuela are thought to be descendants of a woman who developed the disease in the 1800s, and blood and skin samples from 570 of them were obtained. Gusella and his colleagues then used re-

Huntington's disease victim in Venezuela was one of 570 subjects in a study that resulted in the discovery of a genetic marker for the ailment.

striction enzyme mapping techniques to analyze the samples and in so doing located the marker and localized it to chromosome 4.

"The discovery of a marker linked to the Huntington's disease gene makes it feasible to attempt the cloning and characterization of the abnormal gene on the basis of its map location. Understanding the nature of the genetic defect may ultimately lead to the development of improved treatments," reported Gusella, Wexler, and their colleagues. ". . . It is likely that Huntington's disease is only the first of many hereditary autosomal diseases for which a DNA marker will provide the initial indication of chromosomal location of the gene defect."

The findings indicate that individuals at risk of Huntington's disease will be able to discover whether they are indeed affected long before symptoms emerge. Prenatal diagnosis should also be possible. With further work investigators expect to identify the gene itself and perhaps develop methods of preventing its expression or prevent it from causing disease symptoms even if expressed.

Phenylketonuria. In another application of genetic research Savio Woo, Alan Lidsky, Flemming Güttler, T. Chandra, and Kathryn Robson reported that the cloning of the gene for liver enzyme phenylalanine hydroxylase allows prenatal diagnosis and carrier detection of phenylketonuria (PKU), an inborn error of amino-acid metabolism that causes severe mental retardation. Although PKU can be detected in newborns and treated by administering a diet low in phenylalanine, there has been no way to identify carriers of the phenylalanine hydroxylase deficiency that causes the disorder. Woo and his associates estimated that prenatal diagnosis and carrier status may now be determined in up to 75% of the people in families affected by PKU and in even more as the gene and nearby genetic material are more thoroughly mapped.

Sickle-cell disease and thalassemia. Success in the prenatal diagnosis of two disorders of hemoglobin production, sickle-cell disease and beta-thalassemia, was reported by Corinne D. Boehm and her colleagues at the Johns Hopkins University School of Medicine. They used a technique of analyzing DNA polymorphisms, which are normal inherited variations in DNA that can be used to document the inheritance of disease-producing genes even when the basic defect cannot be detected directly.

Amniotic fluid samples were studied for the presence of polymorphisms located very close to the abnormal gene on chromosome 11 that is responsible for defective hemoglobin production in these disorders, with additional information obtained in some from fetal blood studies. In a series of studies on 57 pregnancies in which the fetus was at risk for sickle-cell anemia, 32 at risk for beta-thalassemia, and 6 for other hemoglobin disorders, the prenatal diagnosis was shown to be correct in all of the 78 cases available for subsequent confirmation.

Lesch-Nyhan treatment. Yet another genetic disease, Lesch-Nyhan syndrome, was the subject of genetic manipulation involving the use of retroviruses (a family of animal viruses) as agents for gene transfer by a research team headed by A. Dusty Miller of the Salk Institute and the University of California at San Diego. Lesch-Nyhan syndrome, which produces severe retardation, spasticity, other neurological symptoms, and elevated levels of uric acid, is associated with defects in the gene that produces the enzyme hypoxanthine-guanine phosphoribosyltransferase (HGPRT). Miller's group cloned the HGPRT gene from a normal human cell, inserted it into a mouse retrovirus that acted as a transmitting agent, and infected human HGPRT-defective cells with the HGPRT-expressive virus produced. The defective human cells then began producing HGPRT protein.

The researchers planned to attempt gene transfer in mouse bone-marrow cells and, if that proved successful, to move on to human tests in which bone-marrow cells would be removed from patients, infected with the virus expressing the enzyme, and then transplanted back into the patients. Although they predicted that such treatment would alleviate the buildup of uric acid in affected individuals, it was too early to tell whether the neurologic symptoms associated with Lesch-Nyhan would be corrected. The technique, however, offers promise for other enzyme-deficiency disorders as well.

New prenatal test. Chorionic villus biopsy, developed in Europe, became available in the United States in 1983 and may replace amniocentesis for prenatal testing. The procedure involves removing early in pregnancy a small sample of tissue (the villi) from the chorion, the outer sac surrounding the fetus. The fetal cells thus obtained are then subjected to the same kinds of tests cytogeneticists use on samples of amniotic fluid.

The advantage of chorionic villus biopsy over amniocentesis is that it is done much earlier in pregnancy, 8 to 11 weeks after the last menstrual period, and results are available within a day or so because fetal cells divide so rapidly at that stage of pregnancy. As a result, if termination of pregnancy is considered necessary it could be done in the first, rather than the second, trimester. If fetal therapy is possible, it could be initiated early in pregnancy. Successful trials of the procedure were reported by groups in Italy, Great Britain, and the United States.

Diet and cancer. In 1983 Bruce Ames, of the University of California, Berkeley, observed that "laboratory studies of natural foodstuffs and cooked food are beginning to uncover an extraordinary variety

Chorionic villi, small samples of tissue from the outer sac surrounding a fetus, can be removed early in pregnancy and studied to determine whether or not the fetus is developing normally.

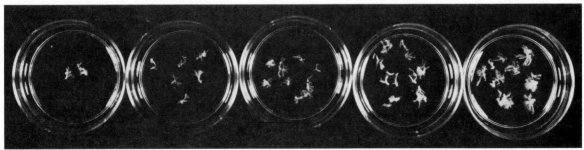

Michael Reese Hospital and Medical Center, Chicago

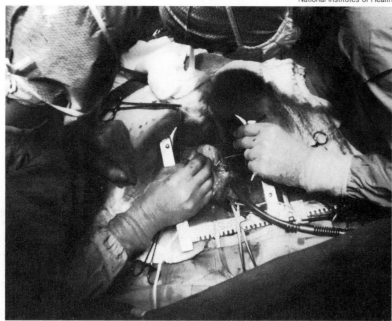

During a coronary bypass operation physicians use a rib retractor to separate the chest wall to provide room for them to work on a patient's heart. A heart-lung machine receives blood from the heart and returns it through two lines, one of which can be seen at the lower right.

of mutagens and possible carcinogens and anticarcinogens." Plants produce many toxic substances in large quantities to defend themselves against predators, and these toxins may be of more importance than synthetic chemicals in causing cancer.

Furthermore, mutagens (agents that tend to increase the frequency or extent of mutations) are produced when proteins are heated during cooking. When sugars are caramelized or interact with amino acids during the cooking process, agents that damage DNA are produced. In this way people may ingest several grams of browned and burnt food products each day; this is far more potentially harmful material than a two-pack-a-day smoker inhales. Cooking also speeds the reaction, causing fats to become rancid and thereby further increasing ingestion of mutagens and carcinogens (cancer-inducing substances).

Among the naturally occurring mutagens and carcinogens cited by Ames are safrole, found in oil of sassafras and in black pepper; hydrazines, present in edible mushrooms; furocoumarins, present in celery, parsnips, figs, and parsley; and nitrite, nitrate, and nitrosamines, present in beets, celery, lettuce, spinach, radishes, and rhubarb. Thus, diet may be a "major risk factor" for cancer, heart disease, and other degenerative disorders, perhaps because ingested carcinogens form free oxygen radicals that damage tissues.

On the other hand Ames noted that many enzymes protect cells from oxidative damage and that "a variety of small molecules in our diet are required for antioxidative mechanisms and appear to be anticarcinogens." Included in the latter category are vitamin E; beta-carotene and other carotenoids—which are

present in green and yellow vegetables; selenium, usually present in the diet as selenite; glutathione; and ascorbic acid (vitamin C). "The optimal levels of dietary antioxidants, which may vary among individuals, remain to be determined," Ames warned. He cautioned against attempts to protect oneself by consuming large amounts of these agents, because some, like selenium, are known to have harmful side effects at high doses.

Ames also noted that the body's defense mechanisms against mutagens and carcinogens include the continuous shedding of the surface layer of skin, stomach, cornea, intestines, and colon. He urged cancer, heart, and aging specialists to perform additional research on those mechanisms.

Diabetic guidelines. Nutritionist Phyllis Crapo and diabetologist Jerrold Olefsky called for changes in dietary recommendations for diabetics in the wake of research showing that biological responses to foods vary widely. Existing recommendations are based on the assumption that, in comparison with simple sugars, complex carbohydrates are absorbed and broken down into sugars more slowly and therefore produce smaller elevations of blood sugar levels. However, one group of investigators headed by John Bantle of the University of Minnesota, Minneapolis, found that the simple sugar sucrose did not produce significantly higher blood sugar levels in diabetics or normal individuals than did such complex carbohydrates as potato starch and wheat starch. The simple sugar fructose produced the smallest elevations.

Crapo, Olefsky, and Gerald Reaven showed that the responses of blood sugar levels to carbohydrates and sugars vary widely. Potatoes cause high eleva-

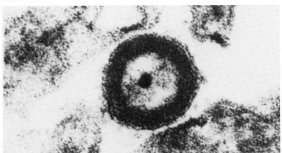

Human T-cell leukemia virus III, strongly associated with AIDS (acquired immune deficiency syndrome) and perhaps the cause of it, was discovered in 1984.

tions, while rice produces very little. Another group of investigators headed by David Jenkins of the University of Toronto found that legumes and pasta products produce much lower blood sugar elevations than do cereals. Foods also had different effects on blood sugar levels when given in different combinations.

"Diabetics may not need to fear a moderate amount of sucrose in a mixed meal," although fructose might be preferable, Olefsky and Crapo observed. They recommended working "toward a system that allows us to make dietary recommendations on the basis of the expected biologic response to a food," but noted that many foods had not been tested for blood sugar responses and that more must be learned about food–food interactions before accurate predictions of such responses could be made.

Cholesterol and heart disease. Progress in understanding the links between cholesterol and heart disease was reported on several fronts. A major study from the National Heart, Lung, and Blood Institute (NHLBI) confirmed that lowering cholesterol levels can prevent heart attacks. Conducted at 12 medical centers, the 10-year study involved more than 3,800 men who were placed on a moderate diet to reduce cholesterol. Half also received cholestyramine, a drug that removes cholesterol from the liver. The latter group suffered substantially fewer heart attacks than did the former, according to NHLBI researchers, although they emphasized that a strict cholesterol-lowering diet—on which none of the study participants was placed—could be expected to have the same effect as the drug. Those in the study were followed for at least 7.5 years and had initial cholesterol levels of at least 265 mg. By slowing the development of coronary artery disease, cholestyramine was also reported to benefit individuals with type II hyperlipoproteinemia, a familial disorder that is associated with elevated cholesterol levels, atherosclerosis (deposition of fatty substances in the inner layer of the arteries), and early myocardial infarction. A progression of coronary artery lesions was seen in significantly more members of the placebo

group than in the treated group, according to Robert Levy, who reported on the results of the ten-year NHLBI study.

Michael Brown, Joseph Goldstein, and associates at the University of Texas Health Science Center at Dallas and other research groups found that giving mevinolin, an experimental drug that blocks cholesterol synthesis, with cholestyramine dramatically lowered the levels in the bloodstream of low-density lipoproteins (LDL's) in affected patients. (High levels of LDL's are associated with atherosclerosis and myocardial infarction.) Similar results using cholestyramine and compactin were reported by Hiroshi Mabuchi and associates at Japan's Kanazawa University School of Medicine. In ten patients cholestyramine alone lowered serum cholesterol levels by 20% and LDL cholesterol by 28%. After compactin was given in addition, levels dropped by 39% and 53%, respectively. High-density lipoprotein, believed to protect against arterial disease, rose to a higher level during treatment with cholestyramine alone and remained there after compactin was added.

Brown and his associates used work done with a group of rabbits that develop very high cholesterol levels and coronary artery disease to learn more about how heart disease could be caused by a lack of receptors for low-density lipoproteins and subsequent high blood LDL levels. They found that LDL's are primarily taken up by the liver and adrenal glands and also discovered that patients with familial hypercholesterolemia (an excess of cholesterol in the blood) produce high levels of LDL, because, like the affected rabbits, they are deficient in LDL receptors on liver cells. As a result the precursors to LDL, known as very-low-density lipoproteins, remain in the plasma and are converted to LDL's, causing very high levels of the latter.

Although most individuals with high cholesterol levels at risk for heart attacks do not suffer from the genetic defect causing familial hypercholesterolomia, researchers believe that treatment with cholestyramine and mevinolin may be worthwhile for them

Spirochetes (below) are passed via the Ixoder dammini *tick to humans and are the bacteria responsible for the form of arthritis known as Lyme disease.*

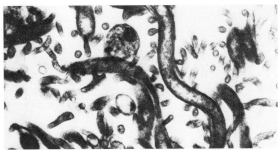

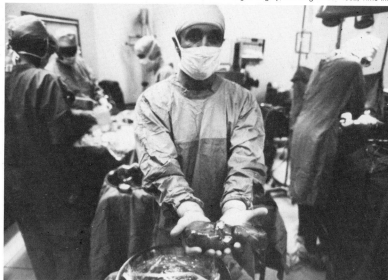

Ergun Cagaty, *Life* Magazine © 1982, Time Inc.

Surgeon holds liver just taken from a deceased donor. Before it was transplanted into a patient suffering from liver disease, the recipient was given the drug Cyclosporine in an effort to prevent transplant rejection.

too, since they suspected that dietary cholesterol accumulates in the liver and decreases LDL receptors, causing LDL buildup in the blood.

Bypass surgery. Yet another large-scale NHLBI study raised doubts as to whether coronary artery bypass surgery is necessary for patients with mild symptoms of heart disease, continuing the debate over whether surgical treatment is clearly preferable to medical management. Findings from the European Coronary Surgery Study, reported in 1982, indicated that bypass surgery was better than medical management for patients with triple-vessel coronary artery disease and those with double-vessel disease affecting the left anterior descending artery. The newer NHLBI (U.S.) Coronary Artery Surgery Study found no statistically significant advantage for patients treated surgically, although such patients had less chest pain and required less medical treatment.

In the five-year NHLBI study of 780 patients at 11 participating centers, patients were assigned to surgery or medical management on a randomized basis, and no significant differences in survival were seen. About 5% of those in the medical group underwent bypass surgery each year when their disease worsened.

Eugene Passamani, project director for the NHLBI-sponsored study, concluded that the study showed that those with mild heart disease symptoms need not have bypass surgery immediately but could wait until their disease worsens without risking death from a heart attack in the interim. Such a delay might eventually prove advantageous, because bypass grafts have been shown to close in up to 40% of patients within ten years, requiring repeat surgery, according to Passamani.

AIDS. The condition known as acquired immune deficiency syndrome (AIDS) was not conquered de-

spite a massive national and international research effort. By early 1984 more than 3,000 cases had been reported in the U.S., Europe, Canada, central Africa, and Haiti. Although most cases continued to be homosexual and bisexual males who had had large numbers of sex partners, apparent victims of AIDS were also reported to be spouses of bisexual men and drug addicts, infants with parents in high-risk groups, and Haitians.

As of early 1984 researchers had not yet found the cause of AIDS, although much attention was focusing on two retroviruses. One was the human T-cell leukemia virus (HTLV) isolated in 1980 by Robert Gallo of the U.S. National Cancer Institute and his associates. In 1983 they reported evidence of HTLV infection and detection of the virus in AIDS patients.

Because antibodies to HTLV were identified in only about one fourth of AIDS patients, the virus's role in the disease remained unclear, and the possibility that HTLV might only be one of the many opportunistic infections that AIDS patients develop could not be ruled out. Gallo pointed out, however, that the HTLV viruses, unlike the organisms causing opportunistic infections, are rare, although they are endemic in certain parts of the world where AIDS has also been observed. Furthermore, they are known to have a selective effect on helper T cells, which are diminished in AIDS patients, and to cause immune suppression in some animals. Gallo expected that at least another year's work would be required to rule out HTLV as a possible cause of AIDS and that even longer would be needed to develop clear-cut evidence that it is, in fact, the cause.

A French research group reported identifying a retrovirus similar to, but distinct from, HTLV in patients with lymphadenopathy, an enlargement of the lymph nodes that may be a precursor to full-blown AIDS.

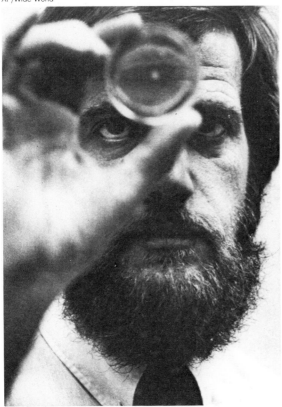

Enzo Paoletti, here examining cultures in a petri dish, worked with Dennis Panicali using genetic engineering techniques to develop a vaccine that has the potential to protect against herpes, hepatitis B, and influenza.

Luc Montagnier and other members of the French AIDS Working Group termed the agent "lymphadenopathy virus (LAV)" and began screening blood from AIDS patients for it, inoculating primates with it, and following the cases of those patients with lymphadenopathy to see if they eventually develop full-blown AIDS. In April 1984 Gallo and his colleagues found a retrovirus that also appeared to be strongly linked to AIDS. They named it HTLV III and began further testing to try to determine whether it was the cause of AIDS and also if it was the same virus as LAV.

Alzheimer's disease. The selective degeneration of a particular group of acetylcholine-releasing neurons in the brain appears to play an important role in Alzheimer's disease, a disorder that results in progressive loss of mental faculties. According to Donald Price, Joseph Coyle, and Mahlon DeLong, of the Johns Hopkins University School of Medicine in Baltimore, a group of neurons whose cell bodies lie in parts of the basal forebrain "appear to play an important role in cognitive functions, especially memory." The researchers observed the loss of these neurons in brains from patients who had died of Alzheimer's disease. A 60–90% decrease in activity of

the enzyme choline acetyltransferase had previously been observed in the brains of individuals who had died with Alzheimer's disease.

Price and his colleagues pointed out that destruction of these neurons is probably not the sole cause of Alzheimer's disease, because there was strong evidence of degeneration of other neuronal systems. However, loss of those neurons was also observed in other forms of dementia, such as that seen in Parkinson's disease. Consequently, the researchers concluded that "the identification of a transmitter-specific pathway selectively affected in a major form of dementia is an important step in the design of diagnostic studies, investigations of pathogenic mechanisms, and the development of therapeutic approaches to these debilitating neuropsychiatric disorders."

"Low-yield" cigarettes. Researchers studying a group of smokers reported that the tobacco in so-called low-yield cigarettes contains as much nicotine as tobacco from standard brands, and that people smoking the low-yield varieties consumed as much nicotine as do those smoking standard cigarettes. They also challenged the usefulness of the Federal Trade Commission's figures on tar and nicotine, which are derived from tests using cigarette-smoking machines, arguing that the test data do not correlate with blood measurements of the nicotine metabolite cotinine.

"Advertisements from cigarette manufacturers suggesting that smokers of low-yield cigarettes will be exposed to less tar and nicotine are misleading. Patients who smoke cigarettes should be so advised," recommended Neal Benowitz and his associates at San Francisco General Hospital Medical Center, Langley Porter Psychiatric Institute, and the University of California, San Francisco.

Lyme disease. In what was hailed as a success "for academia and the community," two groups of investigators reported the recovery from patients of a spirochete that had previously been found in the tick believed to transmit a form of arthritis known as Lyme disease. The condition was first identified in 1975 after a woman informed the Connecticut state health department that 12 children in Lyme had developed an illness diagnosed as juvenile rheumatoid arthritis. Within two years 39 adults and 12 children in three Connecticut communities were found to have the disease.

Investigators eventually linked Lyme disease to bites from a tick, *Ixodes dammini*. In 1982 a spirochete was isolated from *I. dammini* ticks that produced in rabbits a skin lesion similar to that characteristically seen in human patients with the disease. The isolation of the same organism in blood and tissue from affected patients, reported in 1983 by one group headed by Allen Steere and another headed by Jorge Benach, should allow researchers to determine the best method of treating the disease.

Organ transplants. Progress was reported on several fronts in transplant research. A panel convened by the U.S. National Institutes of Health (NIH) found that liver transplantation "is a promising alternative to current therapy in the management of the late phase of several forms of serious liver diseases," such as extrahepatic biliary atresia in children and chronic active hepatitis that causes liver failure. The panel noted, however, that substantial questions remain concerning the appropriate selection of patients and the stage of the disease at which the procedure should be performed, as well as problems in obtaining donor livers.

Two new approaches to the preparation of bone marrow for transplantation yielded promising results in 1983. In the past bone marrow transplants used to treat such conditions as leukemia and severe combined immunodeficiency (in which the body has little or no natural immunity to disease) could only be given if a donor whose cell tissue was compatible with that of the patient could be found. The odds of finding such donors are extremely small unless an affected individual has an identical twin or family member with matching marrow.

By treating partially matching marrow to remove mature T cells, however, a nonmatching graft can be administered without causing the symptoms of rejection known as graft-versus-host disease. Researchers of Boston Children's Hospital and the Sidney Farber Cancer Institute used genetic engineering techniques to develop antibodies to an antigen found on all mature T lymphocytes. The antibodies removed all of these mature T cells, and when immature cells matured in the host they did not provoke a rejection reaction.

A marrow transplant prepared in this way was administered to a 12-year-old boy who had spent his entire life in a plastic bubble under the care of physicians from Baylor College of Medicine. The boy had been placed in a germ-free chamber seconds after birth because he suffered from severe combined immunodeficiency (SCID). The marrow graft came from his 15-year-old sister. After several months, however, the boy's body rejected the transplant. He was removed from the chamber for treatment of the rejection, but his condition deteriorated and he died two weeks later.

In New York City researchers at Memorial Sloan-Kettering Cancer Center have been using another method of removing mature T lymphocytes from donor marrow, treating it with a protein derived from soybeans known as soybean agglutinin. They reported success when grafts treated in that manner were administered to several children with SCID and several with leukemia.

Vaccines and drugs. Two new approaches to the production of vaccines were reported in 1983. Virologists at the New York State Department of Health in Albany and the NIH began using genetic engineering techniques to create vaccines that offer protection against herpes, hepatitis B, and influenza. Dennis Panicali and Enzo Paoletti announced that they had modified the vaccinia virus used in the past to produce the antibody against smallpox so that it also would produce antibody responses in rabbits and mice against herpes simplex I, hepatitis B, and influenza. Another vaccine was developed that offers protection against herpes simplex II, but it awaited further testing.

A different approach to vaccine preparation was reported by Richard Lerner, of the Research Institute of the Scripps Clinic, La Jolla, Calif. Rather than using actual virus material in killed or attenuated form, Lerner and his associates began synthesizing peptides that mimic small regions of a virus's outer coat and appear to successfully stimulate the production of antibodies capable of neutralizing the virus.

"If virtually any surface region of a viral protein can elicit antibodies against that protein, the way is open for designing a vaccine rationally instead of injecting whole virus particles and in effect taking whatever the immune system offers," Lerner observed. After developing a vaccine against foot-and-mouth disease, he and his associates moved on to work on vaccines against influenza and hepatitis B. In other applications Massachusetts Institute of Technology researchers David Baltimore and Marie Chow tested a synthetic vaccine against polio virus in rats, and Baltimore and his associates also used synthetic peptides to learn more about how viruses reproduce themselves after infecting cells.

A genital herpes vaccine that uses a glycoprotein unit from herpes simplex II virus to stimulate antibody response but does not contain possibly infectious viral DNA was being tested in patients, with promising results. In a trial at the University of Washington 22 of 23 volunteers demonstrated immune response to injections of the experimental vaccine, and the side effects were mild. Further tests for vaccine efficacy were under way.

The U.S. Food and Drug Administration convened a special board of inquiry to assess Depo-Provera, a contraceptive agent used in many parts of the world, after its manufacturer, the Upjohn Co., asked the agency to reconsider its ban on the drug in the U.S. The company claimed that studies linking the drug to cancer in beagles and monkeys should be discounted because neither species is a good model for human response, but FDA officials disagreed and called epidemiological studies of Depo-Provera inadequate. At the year's end its ban on use in the U.S. continued.

—Susan V. Lawrence

Dentistry

During 1983 the dental profession in the United States undertook a critical self-examination of its long-range goals and identified the extension of needed dental services to more segments of the population as its highest priority. "Although remarkable strides have been made in the control of tooth decay through fluoridation and other preventive measures, there is still a significant level of unmet dental need—one half of the populace still does not visit a dentist in any given year," said a Special Committee on the Future of Dentistry of the American Dental Association (ADA). And while the U.S. public has become increasingly more sophisticated about the need for regular dental care, the ADA committee made specific recommendations to use recognized ethical marketing techniques and practices to motivate potential patients to seek such care. In approving the recommendation the ADA House of Delegates agreed to study institutional national advertising.

Implementation of steps to fill unmet dental care needs would, of course, also be influenced by the increase in the number of dentists. According to the U.S. Department of Labor this number was expected to rise by 24%, from the current 170,000 to 213,-000 by 1995.

In its drive to expand dental services "dentistry's record on cost restraint has been impressive," said Sen. Orrin Hatch (Rep., Utah), chairman of the Senate Labor and Human Resources Committee. "By emphasizing less expensive preventive care and requiring patient financial participation in prepaid dental plans, the cost of dental services has risen at a rate far below other segments of the health care sector," he said at committee hearings on health-care inflation.

Pill against tooth decay. Swallowing a capsule may one day prevent dental decay, Richard Gregory of the University of Alabama at Birmingham told the Federation of Experimental Biologies. In his study Gregory collected from a volunteer the bacterium most responsible for tooth decay, *Streptococcus mutans*. The bacterium was then cultured, killed, freeze-dried, and packaged into gelatin capsules. When a woman volunteer took a series of such capsules, the amount of cavity-causing bacteria in her mouth was reduced by more than 99% according to Gregory.

Previously, most other anticavity vaccine research had focused on therapy that requires injection. Gregory maintained that an oral vaccine may be more effective at circulating antibodies into the saliva of patients.

Gum disease and diabetes. For diabetics, a toothbrush and floss are almost as important as insulin, claimed M. Manouchehr-Pour, assistant professor of periodontics at Case Western Reserve University in Cleveland, Ohio. Periodontal, or gum, disease is more severe in diabetics than nondiabetics. "Diabetes doesn't cause periodontal disease, but once periodontal disease is established in diabetics, it progresses more rapidly, producing greater damage in a shorter period of time," he said.

Periodontal disease, the most frequent cause of adult tooth loss in the United States, results when bacterial plaque accumulates below the gum line, irritating the gum surface and creating pockets where infection can occur. Untreated, it leads to bone destruction and eventual tooth loss.

Smokeless tobacco. Millions of Americans chew tobacco, believing that they have found a safe alternative to smoking. What they have found instead is a good way to ruin their teeth, their gums, and their general health, warned H. William Hoge, assistant

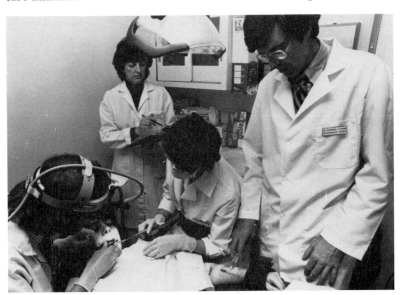

Nurse coordinator (standing at left) and clinical pharmacologist and dentist (standing at right) aid the staff of the National Institute of Dental Research in their study of the causes and treatment of acute and chronic pain.

National Institutes of Health

professor of periodontology at Marquette University School of Dentistry in Milwaukee, Wis. Since 1974 smokeless tobacco consumption has increased 11% annually in the U.S., bringing the number of habitual users in the nation to 22 million in 1984. "Many Americans have made the wise decision to quit smoking, only to replace it with another habit that can have disastrous consequences for their health—most notably their oral health," Hoge said.

Smokeless tobacco, like cigarette tobacco, contains irritants that can lead to the breakdown and permanent destruction of periodontal tissues. Repeated, prolonged use of smokeless tobacco can also lead to the formation of a whitish, callouslike thickening in the mouth known as hyperkeratosis, Hoge explained. "Though withdrawal of the smokeless habit will eliminate the hyperkeratotic region, continued use could produce a more serious condition called leukoplakia which is considered precancerous," he added.

Jaw surgery. A new surgical technique may aid patients suffering from temporomandibular joint (jaw) pain when its cause is a defective articular disk. The technique, which involves replacing dislocated or damaged articular disks with Silastic implants, won first place in an awards competition of the American Society of Maxillofacial Surgeons.

The articular disks normally act as cushions between upper and lower jaws, explained Joseph Natiella, professor of oral pathology, State University of New York at Buffalo. Natiella developed the method with the assistance of two plastic surgeons and a radiologist.

Vitamin C and gum disease. The notion that large doses of vitamin C will give one healthier gums may be nothing more than an old wives' tale, said Amid I. Ismail of the University of Michigan. A survey of a cross section of the U.S. population found little evidence to support the popular belief that periodontal disease is deterred by consumption of vitamin C in amounts greater than the U.S. Recommended Daily Allowances. Furthermore, the study revealed only a weak association between vitamin C deficiency and periodontal disease.

For the study, the vitamin C intake of more than 8,500 Americans was calculated based on the foods that each individual reported consuming within a 24-hour period. Subjects were also asked whether they were taking vitamins of any kind.

Sports and dental injuries. After gum disease and tooth decay the greatest threat to teeth could be a person's ten-speed bicycle or tennis partner, according to John Olmsted at the University of North Carolina at Chapel Hill. "We see increased dental injuries at the beginning of each sports season. Right after dental injuries from automobile accidents, sports-related injuries to the teeth are the most common," he added.

Joseph Natiella, State University of New York at Buffalo

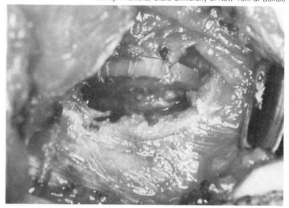

Silastic implant in a jaw joint (center) is a plastic replacement of a defective articular disk. It will act as a cushion between the upper and lower jaws.

For people who suffer such injuries Olmsted had specific advice. If a tooth has been knocked out, it should be put back in its socket and a dentist should be seen immediately. According to Olmsted, "If the tooth landed in the mud, you can rinse it off. But don't scrub it. You don't know what's important tissue and what's not. Let the dentist take care of the real clean-up. Hold the tooth in place in the mouth with finger pressure and head for the dental office. If for some reason the tooth cannot be put back in its socket—if the patient is unconscious, for example, or has other, more critical injuries—drop the tooth into a glass of water or milk or wrap it in a wet cloth."

After losing a tooth, a person should have it treated within 30 minutes. The dentist will gently take the tooth out, clean it, possibly clean out the root canals and place it back in the socket. Using a technique known as bonding, the dentist may place a splint very much like an orthodontic brace to hold the injured tooth in position until it stabilizes, which may require from seven days to eight weeks depending on the extent of the injury.

New extraction technique. Extracting a tooth usually means that it is gone forever. But extracting certain teeth could actually help save them, suggests Donald Arens, associate professor at the Indiana University School of Dentistry, Indianapolis. Speaking at the annual session of the ADA in Anaheim, Calif., in October, he advocated a deliberate extraction/reimplantation technique to save otherwise untreatable teeth. He likened the method to the repair of a faulty carburetor, which is removed by the mechanic, fixed, and then returned to the engine. The extraction/reimplantation technique should be offered as an alternative to extraction/dentures, said Arens.

While the deliberate extraction, repair, and replacement of teeth is not a common dental treatment, Arens remained convinced that it had great potential: "For those certain cases, this is going to be what saves the tooth. It requires a high degree of skill on the part of the dentist and a committed, understanding patient. It allows them, as a team, to salvage teeth that would otherwise be untreatable."

Canker sores. Many Americans are confusing canker sores, irritating but normally harmless lesions of the mouth, with herpes, an incurable disease, said Steven Budnick, associate professor of oral pathology at Emory University in Atlanta, Ga. This confusion can be easily avoided. As Budnick pointed out, "Recurrent canker sores only occur on movable tissues such as your tongue, cheeks, and throat. Oral herpes, on the other hand, only occur on nonmovable tissues atached to bone such as your gums. A classic feature of herpes is painful redness of the gums."

Primary herpes is a one-time occurrence common in children 12 and under. According to one study about half the population 18 and under contracts primary herpes. For children with primary herpes Budnick prescribed an analgesic to control pain and fever and also advocated considerable fluid intake because of possible dehydration. In regard to canker sores research thus far has indicated that, unlike herpes, they are not communicable and disappear by themselves with little or no treatment.

Plastic sealants. A thin plastic film painted over the grinding surface of molar teeth could safely, effectively, and economically prevent most tooth decay that afflicts children and teenagers, according to an 11-member panel of dental scientists. Commissioned by the U.S. National Institutes of Health, the panel urged dentists to increase their routine use of sealants in children and encouraged health insurance companies to include the plastic sealants in their dental coverage.

The first sealants of the 1960s were less effective than today's products, which may have discouraged widespread use in the past. But evidence from studies during the last decade indicates that the sealants now in use are 100% effective in protecting teeth as long as the plastic coating is retained. Studies showed that more than 80% of the newer sealants were still in place after seven years.

Not all teeth need the protection of sealants, according to James Bawden of the University of North Carolina. He suggested that parents consult their child's dentist about sealant application soon after the molars appear—at about age two or three for primary molars and six years for permanent teeth. The panel targeted children and adolescents as a group most likely to benefit from the treatment because of eating and oral-hygiene habits that tend to make them cavity-prone. Fluorides appear to provide the best protection to the smooth surfaces of teeth but leave vulnerable the crevices and pits of molars.

In turn, the plastic coating on the uneven surfaces prevents the entrapment of food and bacteria that produce enamel-eating acids. Sealants and fluorides "work best in concert," said Bawden.

Dentures and implants. Magnets made from the rare-earth elements (such as lanthanum and yttrium) and cobalt were being tested by Australian dental scientists to improve denture retention. The tiny, high-strength magnets that are incorporated into the denture are especially suitable for over-dentures used in patients with retention problems, said B.R.D. Gillings of Sydney, Australia. Following the removal of tooth nerves, the tooth is trimmed to be level with the gum line, and then special metal disks are attached to the roots. An over-denture is constructed, and tiny magnets grip the metal disks to hold the denture securely. This type of denture is comfortable because of the root support and added retention, Gillings told the Annual World Dental Congress of the Fédération Dentaire Internationale meeting in Tokyo.

New long-term studies indicate that porous titanium dental implants stabilized by bone ingrowth can be viewed as the most promising tooth implant system. In these studies, conducted on rhesus monkeys, Franklyn Young of the Medical University of South Carolina tested the function and longevity of the roots of titanium implants and found that they may provide long-term use without any harmful effects.

—Lou Joseph

Veterinary medicine

With the increasing availability of reasonably priced small computers, many veterinarians have begun to use this technology for such diverse purposes as maintaining medical records, generating scheduled vaccination reminders and monthly client statements, keeping drug inventories, and general bookkeeping. Food-animal practitioners were using computers to compile data on breeding, nutrition, and disease, information that is necessary in order to formulate complex health programs for dairy, beef, swine, and sheep herds. A veterinarian having a computer with a modem (a device for telephonic communication with other computers) can search for information stored in large computers at university and governmental or commercial agencies. Veterinarians at Cornell University in Ithaca, N.Y., and Auburn (Ala.) University developed computerized data bases to assist practitioners in diagnosing obscure disease or other problems.

As the first commercially produced genetically engineered vaccine for animal use, a bacterin to prevent colibacillosis (diarrhea caused by the bacterium *Escherichia coli*) in calves was marketed by Dellen Laboratories in early 1983. When given to a pregnant cow, the bacterin stimulates production of antibodies to *E. coli* that are transmitted to her

The product of the world's first embryo transplant among water buffalo stands with his surrogate mother at the University of Florida's Veterinary Medical Teaching Hospital.

calf via the colostrum (the first milk after calving). A similar bacterin for colibacillosis in baby pigs also became available. The first monoclonal antibody product licensed for livestock disease prevention was marketed by Molecular Genetics in Canada in 1983 and in the United States in early 1984. (Monoclonal antibodies are those that have been developed to combat specific disease agents.) Unlike bacterins this product is given by mouth to newborn animals for prevention of colibacillosis.

Concerning the approval of these and other genetically engineered drugs and hormones, Lester Crawford, director of the U.S. Food and Drug Administration's Bureau of Veterinary Medicine, said: "We want to give them high priority and get them on the market, especially if they will replace toxic compounds or resistance-causing compounds that are already in use. . . . We have a number of growth promotion products on the market now that are antibiotics. It appears that these will be replaced, at least in part, with bioengineered products that are not antibiotics and are therefore likely to be less toxic and less capable of causing resistance to disease."

The advantages of pet animals for elderly persons were summarized by Cindy Wilson and F. Ellen Netting, who noted: "Pets will not be the solution for the problems associated with aging. However, there are certain areas in which pets might be beneficial to some older individuals. . . . The roles pets can have in the lives of older people include (1) companionship, (2) something to care for, (3) tactile communication, (4) something to keep one busy, (5) focus of attention, (6) exercise, and (7) safety." A companion animal can function in pet-facilitated psychotherapy, they said, by serving as a substitute for close human relationships.

The decade-old debate over banning the use of penicillin and tetracycline as growth promoters in animal feeds was highlighted in late 1983 when former FDA commissioner Jere Goyan declared: "The indiscriminate use of these antibiotics in animal feeds will lead to a major national crisis in public health . . . . Unless we take action now to curb the use of these drugs in the livestock industry, we will not be able to use them to treat human diseases in the future." An FDA-funded study was reported to show that "not only do animal and human bacteria mix readily, but also that antibiotic resistance travels from animals to human beings." Such a ban would not affect the 18 antibiotics approved for animal feed use but which have no human use. These 18 drugs constitute half the total used in animal feeds, which in turn contain half of all antibiotics sold in the U.S.

Another problem raised during the past year was that of the extra-label use (use for purposes not listed on the label) of drugs by veterinarians and livestock owners. Previously, veterinarians had been permitted to use almost any drug for any presumably rational purpose whether or not it had been approved by the U.S. Food and Drug Administration for such use. The proposal to restrict usage to label indications was prompted in large part by the misuse of feed additives, especially by owners, with the result that drug residues in excess of those allowed were appearing in many slaughtered animals. Veterinarians protested that this would make treatment of certain diseases nearly impossible. After extensive discussion with representatives of veterinary organizations and producer groups, an FDA announcement in January 1984 indicated that most extra-label drug use would be permitted but only on written prescription by a veterinarian.

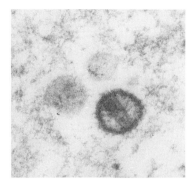

Virus (above) found in rhesus monkeys (left) triggers a disease in the monkeys that resembles AIDS (acquired immune deficiency syndrome) in humans.

In 1978 a survey by the Arthur D. Little organization indicated that the supply of veterinarians in the U.S. (about 32,000) was then in balance with the demand but projected a "significant" supply surplus—on the order of 25%—by 1990. A National Research Council committee report made available in 1983, however, indicated that supply and demand were "approaching a balance" and that only a "modest" surplus would accrue by 1990.

The committee recommended that "the colleges of veterinary medicine adjust their curricula, admissions criteria, and clerkship programs to meet societal needs in environmental health protection, food production and protection, economic productivity in animal-related industries, biomedical research, and animal welfare, as well as needs for clinical patient care of animals." The report also suggested that there would not be a surplus of veterinarians in private practice in the 1990s if more students were to receive specialized training for other branches of the discipline, including clinical medicine, epidemiology, laboratory animal science, microbiology, pathology, and toxicology.

The annual rate of increase in veterinary school enrollment continued to decline, from about 10% in the early 1970s to 4% during 1981–82 and 2% during 1982–83, despite the opening during that period of eight additional schools. Among the factors contributing to this change were a perceived surplus of veterinarians in some areas, increased student fees and living expenses, and reduced federal and, in some instances, state support of veterinary colleges. The lessened availability of scholarship and loan funds in relation to schooling costs apparently caused some potential applicants to enter other fields, and others may have been unwilling to incur a substantial debt burden. Upon graduation in 1983 the debt of the approximately 1,500 students averaged $18,897, and 26.4% had debts in excess of $20,000.

The devastating effects of the acquired immune deficiency syndrome (AIDS) on the human immune system led some medical researchers to postulate that the disease was due to a recently introduced animal virus against which the human body had no defense. Investigators at Johns Hopkins University in Baltimore, Md., reported having found antibodies to canine parvovirus (CPV) in the blood serum of AIDS patients. However, a leading veterinary authority on CPV, Leland Carmichael of Cornell University, considered this unlikely despite the fact that AIDS in persons was recognized about the same time (1979) as CPV infection in dogs. The manifestations of the two diseases are distinctly different, he pointed out, and in the latter "the degree of immunodepression is transient and minimal in comparison to AIDS." Also, in tests of more than 500 serum samples from persons working with infectious CPV material, there was no evidence of transfer of the virus.

A fatal disease resembling AIDS and discovered almost simultaneously affected monkeys at primate research centers in Massachusetts and California; it was termed simian AIDS (SAIDS). According to Roy Hendrickson, senior veterinarian at the University of California at Davis, in both the human and monkey diseases there is a high incidence of infection with cytomegalovirus (CMV), which is similar to herpesvirus. However, "It is not clear whether this is a secondary or opportunistic infection." At the New England Regional Primate Research Center Ronald Hunt reported that CMV had caused the death of some 30 monkeys in 1979, many with symptoms like those of SAIDS.

361

On the basis of circumstantial evidence Jane Teas of the Harvard University School of Public Health suggested that the virus of African swine fever may have caused outbreaks of AIDS in humans. The first cases of AIDS were reported in 1979 concomitantly with the diagnosis of African swine fever in Haiti. According to Teas, AIDS originated with a homosexual man who had eaten pork infected with African swine fever virus, a practice permitted during the African swine fever eradication program in Haiti. James Downard, a veterinarian with the U.S. Department of Agriculture, characterized the proposed link between AIDS and African swine fever as "not without some validity, but a highly improbable thing. . . . It's never been substantiated before in any countries which have had ASF and continue to have ASF." (For additional information on AIDS, *see* General Medicine, above.) After a four-year effort the last of 384,000 pigs was killed in Haiti in June 1983, and repopulation with pigs from the United States and Canada was begun.

—J. F. Smithcors

Optical engineering

Optical engineering, particularly electro-optics, continued to grow in importance during the past year, although the level of innovation did not appear to be as marked as in some previous years. (Electro-optics is the study of systems that contain both electronic components and optical components, such as video systems and visual display devices.) There were significant technical achievements involving laser sources and the control of complex active optical systems. Because of the worldwide economic recession only evolutionary development in optical devices of wide application occurred.

Development in the area of large telescopes appeared to move toward the application of combined electro-optical systems for the control of large mirrors. Two proposals for the United States National New Technology Telescope were being studied. The first was a multiple-mirror telescope consisting of an array of four telescopes, each with a diameter of 5 m. These four individual instruments would be capable of operating together as a single-phase array telescope. This approach would depend heavily upon technology already developed on the existing University of Arizona-Smithsonian Observatory 8-m-diameter telescope array in Arizona.

The other proposal was for a 15-m-diameter telescope having a large primary mirror made up of about 54 individual smaller segments. The technology needed for this instrument would be based largely upon that devised for the 10-m telescope design at the University of California.

Courtesy, AT&T/Bell Laboratories

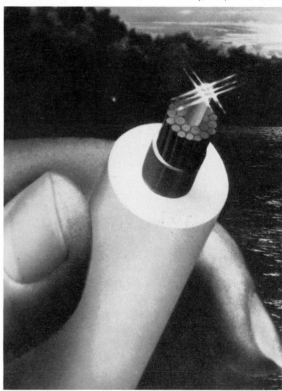

A cable made of optical fibers, promising swifter and virtually error-free transmission, was tested on the bottom of the North Atlantic.

The pointing, control, and phasing of either of these telescopes were designed to be accomplished by the use of an electro-optical sensor to record the image of a star. This stellar image would then be analyzed by a computer to produce electrical signals; these signals in turn, drive servomechanisms that keep the telescope mirrors in alignment. A decision on the type of telescope to be built was expected in mid-1984.

Several new products that had been expected to be major items in the consumer marketplace failed to attract the expected attention. The major disappointments were optical videodiscs and direct electro-optical miniature cameras. In the video image area the principal developments included the reduction in size of consumer-level cameras and recorders by the use of established videocassette formats. As a result it appeared that the electro-optical still camera as a replacement for the conventional 35-mm camera was not likely to be a significant entry in the marketplace in the near future. Amateur and home movies on film had virtually disappeared in favor of recording on videocassettes, and it appeared that the applications of electro-optical recording in the consumer area would be reserved for the recording of motion and sound.

In regard to conventional photography the design and fabrication of zoom lenses reached a new level of achievement with the introduction for 35-mm cameras of several zoom lenses that have 5:1 ratios of focal length. In addition, the use of automatic focus devices in relatively inexpensive cameras became quite commonplace, with standard electronic sensors and control chips being developed by some manufacturers. The introduction of new high-speed color films gave these cameras additional flexibility. No revolutionary innovations having the impact of Eastman Kodak's Disc cameras occurred during the past year, however.

Optical videodiscs virtually disappeared from the market except for specialized educational or catalog applications in which the ability to carry out a rapid search of an image catalog or to interact with a computer-driven educational process is important. Some applications as part of elaborate adventure video games appeared. In these cases scenes selected from a videodisc are mixed with computer-generated action figures that have been inserted in the foreground. While this is a sophisticated computer-driven electro-optical system, it is not expected to be sold in large quantities.

The introduction of digital data storage on videodiscs was just beginning, however. Huge volume and rapid access to such data bases were convenient for many applications. Magnetic recording developments made in recent years permitted information storage densities that were competitive with optical storage. However, most authorities believed that optical data storage devices would maintain a tenfold advantage over magnetic storage in the amount of information that could be stored within a unit area. Major gains in the widespread use of optical data storage were likely to occur as a result of the introduction of erasable, reusable media, which in 1984 were just becoming practical.

Optical audiodiscs appeared to be gaining in popularity as the catalog of available selections widened. The cost of players for the discs remained high, and no wide market could be expected until inexpensive portable players appear.

In terms of other applications the past year appeared to be one in which the laser machine shop grew and matured. A trade publication listed 35 shops in the United States that were equipped to provide services in the fabrication by laser of parts, made of various materials, to user specification. An even larger number of installations were likely to be found within large manufacturing concerns. Some of the work being done was obviously experimental, but the production of elaborate detailed structures in materials that cannot be worked in other ways, such as ceramics, seemed certain to produce new concepts in manufacturing. One of the principal advantages of laser working of materials is that the production of delicate, thin-sectioned components is possible.

The major component of the electro-optical market, at least in the United States, was the defense industry. Large quantities of laser trackers, range finders, target designators, and low-light-level or night-vision devices were being procured. This led to a major expansion in engineering areas and some growth in production. Optical fabrication was still an art to some extent, and the economic efficiencies that had been achieved in selected portions of the photographic lens industry had not yet penetrated into precision optics.

Analytical devices employing laser spectroscopy for the identification of minute impurities in various materials became widely used in industry in 1983. Several systems featuring a combined pump laser and a tunable dye laser in a single package became available. Such a device can be used to supply coherent laser radiation of a color or wavelength that can be continuously varied over a wide range. These sources make it simple to achieve high-speed spectral scanning of selected volumes of a material. Significant applications in the chemical industry and the improvement of such combustion devices as jet engines were recorded.

A combination of array detectors and microprocessors led to the development of "smart" sensors that have limited capabilities for analyzing an observed scene as an intrinsic part of the detector process. The future development of such devices has applications in the areas of robotic vision and the classification of objects in a complex field. The significance of this approach to the recording of images is that some level of intelligence can be built into the camera that initially records a scene. It is possible to detect the presence of specific objects and to determine the orientation of simple three-dimensional shapes almost as fast as the image is being collected. More sophisticated discrimination of objects will require larger computers than the microprocessors presently available. But even with a limited discrimination capability these sensors can be used as the primary detectors for robotic systems in manufacturing operations. Reductions in cost and hazards involved in factories can thus be achieved.

The most exciting applications of optical engineering that can be expected in the near future are based on the use of intelligent sensors. For example, electro-optical cameras that can make simple decisions concerning the objects observed on the chip that is collecting the image may appear. There will be considerable development of intelligent sensors as robot vision systems for use in industry. Other applications are expected to be increasingly elegant automatic focus devices and image motion trackers.

—Robert R. Shannon

Physics

Satisfaction, surprise, a philosophical unease placed high on the list of physicists' experiences during the past year. The long-awaited discovery of the W and Z particles, whose existence figures importantly in the present theory of subatomic particles, gave theorists and experimentalists the confidence to push ahead into unexplored territory. Likewise, the continued success of the shell model in explaining the observed behavior of the atomic nucleus served as a major driving force for a worldwide renaissance in nuclear physics. Two new and completely unexpected phenomena, the quantized Hall effect and the fractional quantized Hall effect, captured the attention of researchers seeking to understand the behavior of the carriers of electric current in two-dimensional solids. Finally, a peculiar and disquieting prediction of quantum theory—that well-defined properties of fundamental particles do not exist until they are measured—received some strong experimental support, thus contradicting the intuitive concept of an objective reality.

General developments

In recent months physicists exploring some of the peculiarities of quantum theory reported the strongest experimental evidence yet to challenge our commonsense notion that properties of objects exist independently of their measurement. Investigators

"Ohhhh. . . look at that, Schuster. . . . Dogs are so cute when they try to comprehend quantum mechanics."

Drawing by Gary Larson, reprinted by permission of Chronicle Features San Francisco

also succeeded in creating a mirrorlike device capable of automatically canceling optical distortions and established new limits on the rate at which the fundamental force of gravity could possibly be changing with time.

Quantum mechanical reality. In a careful experiment carried out by Alain Aspect, Jean Dalibard, and Gérard Roger at the University of Paris-South in Orsay, France, it finally seemed proved beyond all reasonable doubt that the "real" world—the world of physics on the smallest, most fundamental scale—is governed by the indeterministic logic of quantum mechanics and not by the deterministic logic of "common sense." For example, common sense says that things have well-defined properties whether anyone measures them or not. A tree in the middle of an impenetrable forest either is standing up or has toppled over. Common sense does not allow the answer "neither." By contrast, in describing the world of subatomic particles quantum mechanics says, for instance, that a photon of light, which is always found spinning either to the left or to the right, cannot be said to have either a left-hand spin or a right-hand spin until it is measured. For many years physicists have argued and tried to demonstrate whether such a statement could indeed describe reality or whether it reflected some sort of weakness in a theory that on the whole had proved amazingly successful in dealing with matter and energy.

In the experiment done by Aspect and his colleagues, two photons were made in a special way which insured that they would fly off in exactly opposite directions and with the same spin. In other words, both photons were made to be either left circularly polarized or right circularly polarized, although whether both were left or both were right occurred randomly. The photons traveled six meters (about 20 feet) to an analyzer of linear polarization—essentially a filter—that was randomly switched from a vertical orientation to a horizontal orientation. In either orientation, because the analyzer looked for linear polarization and the photon was circularly polarized, the photon would pass through the analyzer only half the time. (Circularly polarized light can be said to be made up of half vertically polarized light and half horizontally polarized light, so there is a 50–50 chance that a circularly polarized photon, be it left or right, will make it through the linearly polarized analyzer.)

When the experimental results at both ends were compared, it was found that if the two polarizers both happened to be oriented in the same direction, it was highly probable either that both photons made it through or that both photons were stopped. It was as if each photon knew what was happening to the other photon some 12 m away. What is most important about this experiment, the latest in a line

From J. Feinberg, *Optic Letters* 7, 486 (1982)

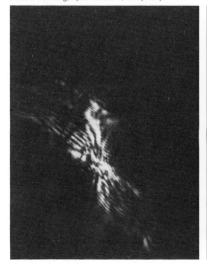 

Two reflections of the image of a cat, originally made in green-colored laser light, are compared. For the left photo the light making up the image was first passed through an optical distorter and then reflected from an ordinary mirror back through the distorter. For the right photo the mirror was replaced by a magic mirror, or optical phase conjugator. This device caused the light that was broken up by its first trip through the distorter to retrace its path as it made its return trip thereby canceling the distortion and correcting the image.

of several similar investigations, is that the two polarization analyzers were being switched randomly once every ten nanoseconds (ten billionths of a second). Since it takes 40 nanoseconds for the fastest possible signal to pass over 12 m of space (at the speed of light, the presumed universal speed limit), there was no way for one photon to know what was happening to the other photon even if there were some force yet unknown to science but limited by light speed that would allow them to communicate. Other experiments with the analyzers set at angles other than vertical and horizontal disagreed sharply with all possible deterministic theories and showed excellent agreement with the indeterministic predictions of quantum mechanics.

An oversimplified, but perhaps revealing, way of looking at this experiment is to imagine that a blind man sitting in New York opens a package of sandwich cookies, the kind with frosting in the middle. One after the other he twists the sandwiches apart to obtain two wafers, each with frosting on one side. The two wafers are put into separate boxes, either both frosting side up or both frosting side down. The boxes are closed, and relays of messengers carefully carry them off in opposite directions to Monte Carlo and Las Vegas. There, at each location, the boxes are opened and, without anyone looking inside, a croupier tosses the wafers into the air, making sure that they tumble thoroughly. A record is kept whether the wafer lands on the table frosting side up or frosting side down. Provided the frosting is thin and dry enough, the results will be completely random, no different than flipping a coin. It surely would be of great interest to the world's gamblers if it were found that the results of the two sets of tosses were correlated—if nearly every time a wafer fell frosting up at Monte Carlo its twin would land frosting up at Las Vegas, even though each half of the wafer

pair was tossed in a completely different way by a completely different person in a place thousands of miles away.

If one replaces the twisted-apart wafer pairs with quantum-correlated photon pairs, quantum mechanics predicts that there will be such a correlation. Even more "paradoxically," if anyone ever peeked in the boxes to determine if the wafers were frosting side up or frosting side down (measured whether the photons were right or left polarized), then the correlation would disappear, even though which side is up before the toss makes no difference in the results of the toss.

Scientists and nonscientists alike may find some mutual comfort in sharing a great sense of unease about these findings, but as Nobel laureate Richard Feynman once wrote, "There is no paradox . . . it is only a conflict between reality and your feeling of what reality 'ought to be.'"

Magic mirrors. Scientists at the Soviet Academy of Sciences, the Los Alamos National Laboratory in New Mexico, Bell Laboratories, the California Institute of Technology, the University of Southern California, and Hughes Research Laboratories, Malibu, Calif., uncovered a method of using lasers to create "magic mirrors." Technically called optical phase conjugators, these devices should one day revolutionize laser technology, optical communication, and optical computers.

Although there are many ways to make magic mirrors, one approach is to illuminate a special crystal with two laser "pump" beams from opposite directions. The crystal, typically barium titanate, is an electro-optical material that responds so strongly to light that its molecules store some of the lasers' energy. The laser beams thus "pump" up the energy in the molecules. If another light beam is passed through the crystal, it triggers the molecules

365

to release the stored energy and produce a copy of the input beam. The copy comes out of the crystal opposite in direction to that of the incoming beam in somewhat the same manner as a reflected beam from an ordinary mirror, but with a "magic" difference.

If a flashlight is aimed directly at a normal mirror, the light beam is reflected directly back to the flashlight. If the beam hits the mirror at an angle, it glances off the mirror and perhaps illuminates some distant object, spreading as it goes. Shine a flashlight into a magic mirror, however, and the light comes out the way it came in, no matter what the incoming angle. In addition, if the flashlight beam was spreading when it entered the magic mirror, the return beam would converge, ultimately focusing itself back on the filament in the light bulb. Such a mirror would be of little use for everyday purposes. If a person tried to see himself, no matter what part of the mirror he used or what angle he looked from, all he would see would be his eyes.

What is useful about these magic mirrors is their ability to correct for distortions. If a piece of shower glass is placed between a regular mirror and the viewer, the reflection is nothing but a distorted blotch. But if the mirror is a magic mirror, the viewer will see his eyes as if the shower glass were no longer there.

This distortion cancellation capability occurs because the magic mirror "reflects" light beams back on themselves, no matter what the original direction. When the viewer's eye is positioned in front of a piece of distorted glass, the light coming from the eye is broken up into many beams by the distortions. The beams emerge from the far side of the glass going in many different directions. But, as each beam strikes the magic mirror, the copy is sent back on itself and precisely retraces its path through the same portion of distorted glass. There the distortions bend each beam so that it lines up again with all the other beams and returns to the eye.

Magic mirrors are expected to play a significant part in the technological world of the future. For example, scientists at Los Alamos and elsewhere have been working to create controlled nuclear fusion by imploding tiny pellets of deuterium (hydrogen-2, a heavy isotope of hydrogen). The implosion, a violent inward compression, is obtained by hitting the pellets from all sides with powerful laser beams. One of the many problems with this technique is that the pellets are not perfectly round, so that the laser light does not strike them completely symmetrically. In addition, as the large laser amplifiers are driven to higher and higher power levels, they start to distort and heat up, and they no longer make a perfect laser beam that can be focused onto the tiny pellet. Then too, there are the creep in the focusing lenses and

warping in the mirrors that direct the beam to the pellet from the lasers many meters away.

Amazingly, all of these problems can be solved with the use of a magic mirror. After a pellet is put into place, a weak laser beam is used to illuminate the surface. The light reflects from the distorted pellet surface, is picked up by the creeping lenses, bounces off the warped mirrors, and passes through the distorted laser amplifiers where it becomes stronger. Finally this contorted version of the original beam strikes the magic mirror. The mirror reflects the contorted beam back through the laser amplifier where it becomes even stronger, and as the beam retraces its path it grows increasingly more uniform until it strikes the surface of the pellet with just the right amount of distortion to compensate for the imperfections on the pellet surface. Consequently the pellet implodes completely symmetrically. The same process can be used to send an entire picture through a tiny optical fiber many kilometers long or to turn a cheap low-quality laser into a cheap perfect laser.

Italian scientists ready a 2.3-ton gravitational wave antenna for testing at CERN in Geneva. The new detector will join international efforts in the search for gravitational field vibrations believed to be produced during stellar explosions, tightly co-orbiting stars, and other cosmic events.

By putting a pattern on the pump beams used to excite the magic mirror as well as a pattern on the incoming beam, one can produce an output beam in which the two patterns are "multiplied" together. If the patterns are arrays of bright spots and black spots representing numbers, then whole arrays of numbers can be added, subtracted, or multiplied at one time, thus forming the basis for a superfast optical computer. Scientists are only beginning to understand how these magic mirrors work, and they have found materials besides special electro-optical crystals that can be used. Many more uses should be found for them in the near future.

The constancy of gravity. In the past such theoretical physicists as Paul Dirac have wondered if the Newtonian gravitational constant G, the number relating the gravitational force experienced between two bodies to their masses and separation distance, might be variable and, in particular, if gravity is weaker now than it was billions of years ago. Recently, after analyzing data from the Viking landers on Mars, two teams of scientists, one from the Massachusetts Institute of Technology and the Harvard-Smithsonian Center for Astrophysics and the other from NASA's Goddard Institute for Space Studies and the Jet Propulsion Laboratory, put new limits on possible changes to G.

The basic idea of the experiment was to compare the time rates of a gravitational clock (the orbital period of Mars) with an atomic clock (which does not rely on the gravitational force for timekeeping) to see if they drift apart with time. Microwave signals were sent to the transponders on the Viking spacecraft, which echoed the signals back to Earth. The signals were strong enough so that the distance from the transmitting antenna on Earth to the lander antenna on Mars could be measured accurately to ten meters. A succession of these distance measurements were then used to calculate the orbital period of Mars over the years 1976–82. The time so obtained and the time measured by an atomic clock were found to be the same to less than a few parts in a trillion per year. This limit for variation is significantly less than the 50 parts per trillion predicted by Dirac in 1937. So, unlike old soldiers, it looks as though gravity will not just fade away.

—Robert L. Forward

High-energy physics

In 1983 high-energy physicists made experimental discoveries that confirmed some of the main features of the present theory of subatomic particles. They also worked to develop ideas that would account for some of the unexplained features of present theory and to develop new experimental methods to test these ideas.

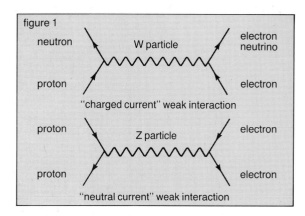

Weak interactions of a proton and an electron as mediated by a W particle (top) and a Z particle (bottom) are compared diagrammatically. The W exchange transfers electric charge between interacting particles (hence the term "charged current"), whereas the Z exchange ("neutral current") does not.

W and Z particles. The most important finds in 1983 took place at the proton-antiproton collider at the European Laboratory for Particle Physics (CERN) in Geneva. Within it protons and their antimatter counterparts, antiprotons, are accelerated to energies of 270 billion electron volts (GeV) each, stored for periods of several hours in order to accumulate large numbers of them, and made to collide while traveling in opposite directions. Under these circumstances all of the energy of the colliding particles is available to create new particles; for example, pairs of particles each having a rest energy as high as the energy of each beam can be produced.

During the past year this technique proved successful in creating two particles never before observed, the W and Z. Both had long been predicted, and specific values for their rest energies had been inferred in the 1960s as a consequence of the unified theory of weak and electromagnetic interactions proposed by Sheldon Glashow, Steven Weinberg, and Abdus Salam. This "electroweak" theory states that W and Z particles are exchanged between particles such as electrons and protons, mediating the weak interactions between them (figure 1). In the 1970s these weak interactions were studied, and their detailed properties were found to agree with the predictions of the electroweak theory. Nevertheless, the mediating W and Z particles were not observed because existing accelerators had insufficient energies to produce them. The situation at that time was somewhat like inferring the existence of an animal by observing its effect on the plants that it eats, without ever seeing the animal itself.

In the proton-antiproton collisions at CERN the W and Z are produced rarely, perhaps once in every million such collisions. When they are produced, they

Adapted from information obtained from CERN

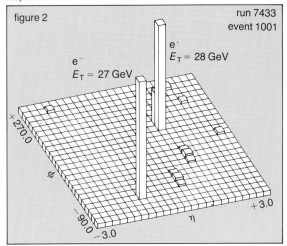

figure 2

run 7433
event 1001

e⁺
E_T = 28 GeV

e⁻
E_T = 27 GeV

+270.0

φ

−90.0

−3.0

η

+3.0

*The signature of a Z particle decay—an electron-positron
(e⁻e⁺) pair having high transverse energies (E_T; energy carried
perpendicular to the direction of the colliding beams)—
stands out in a plot of the energy deposited to detectors
arrayed around the collision site.*

occur together with a large number of other particles. The experimenters needed a distinctive signature to distinguish these rare events from all the others. The signature used is the nearly instantaneous decay of the W and Z into lighter particles such as electrons and positrons (antimatter electrons), which emerge with high momentum along directions perpendicular to the direction of the colliding beams. By employing sophisticated computer analysis of the data produced in each collision "event," that is, of the energy and direction of each visible particle that emerges, the experimenters found it possible to isolate the high-energy electrons that signal the production and decay of a W or Z (figure 2).

New theoretical frontiers. With the discovery in hand of the basic particles of the unified electroweak theory, physicists turned their attention to an important open question about this theory. The equations of the theory describe the behavior of a set of mathematical functions known as quantum fields. Certain solutions to these equations correspond to observed particles, such as the W and Z. But the equations for the fields impute to the particles some properties that have not been seen. These missing properties involve the fact that the equations are unchanged when certain mathematical operations, known as symmetry transformations, are performed on the quantum fields. The solution to the problem of explaining this difference between the behavior of the equations and of the particles that they describe has come to be known as the mechanism of symmetry breaking. One indication of the need for a partial loss of symmetry is that, if the W and Z particles displayed the full symmetry of the equations, their rest energies would be zero rather than 80 and 90 GeV.

In the original work by Weinberg and by Salam the symmetry breaking was achieved through the introduction of additional quantum fields. These additional fields have the strange property that their value is not zero in otherwise empty space. A property, such as rest energy, of a particle that is introduced into this region of space will be influenced by the nonzero value of the new quantum field and so will be different from what it would have been if this field was not present. It is believed that the nonzero value of these quantum fields is a consequence of the present state of the universe, in which the overall temperature is quite low, about three degrees above absolute zero. In early stages of the universe, when the temperature was extremely high, it is thought that the

Tracks of an energetic, oppositely directed electron-positron pair (arrows), identified in the record of a spray of debris from a proton-antiproton collision at CERN, provide evidence for the production and decay of the Z particle. Center horizontal lines indicate the paths of the colliding beams.

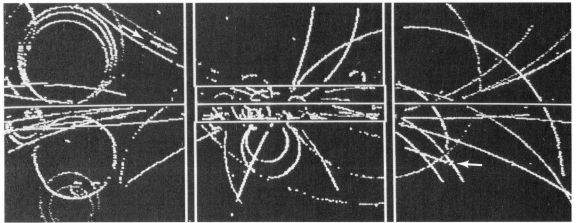

Courtesy, CERN

value of these fields was different; consequently the W and Z particles then in existence did have zero rest energy, and physical phenomena displayed the full symmetry of the underlying equations.

If this picture of symmetry breaking is correct, there should be other, yet undiscovered particles associated with the same quantum fields. These have come to be known as Higgs particles, after the British physicist who first proposed this approach to symmetry breaking. The rest energy of the Higgs particles is not known, but it is throught to be approximately a thousand billion electron volts (1 TeV).

Many physicists, however, have come to believe that the simple picture of symmetry breaking described above is unsatisfactory. For one thing, a large number of different quantum fields must be introduced for the purpose. Also, the interactions of these new fields with those fields representing known particles, including the quarks and leptons that make up ordinary matter, involve a large number of new and undetermined parameters. This circumstance substantially complicates the original theory, in which the interactions are almost completely determined by the symmetries of the theory.

Several new directions have been proposed for alternative symmetry-breaking mechanisms, which would avoid some of these difficulties. One such mechanism, which goes under the name of supersymmetry, involves a far-reaching extension of the types of symmetry transformation that physicists have been considering. In previous theories such transformations have always involved relations between quantum fields that describe particles of the same intrinsic spin. For example, in the electroweak theory symmetry transformations relate fields describing electrons to fields describing neutrinos, both of which particles have intrinsic spins of ½ unit. In supersymmetric theories additional transformations relate fields describing electrons to fields describing undiscovered particles of zero spin.

Theories with this type of symmetry differ in several ways from more conventional theories. They automatically imply the existence of certain particles, including the Higgs particles, whose existence in previous theories is an arbitrary feature rather than a necessary requirement. Furthermore, some features of the interactions of the Higgs particles with known particles are fixed by the new types of symmetry in the theory. In supersymmetric theories these interactions are related to those of the W and Z particles, whereas in previous theories these interactions were also arbitrary. In other words, supersymmetric theories leave much less to be determined by appeal to experiment because a great deal is fixed by the internal requirements of the theories. In this respect they represent a plausible extension of the direction that theoretical physics has followed for several

decades, in which various properties of subatomic particles, such as the ratios of their electric charges, have come to be seen as necessary consequences of a theory, rather than as arbitrary.

Supersymmetric theories also hold out the possibility of uniting gravity with the strong, weak, and electromagnetic interactions. In Einstein's general relativity theory, gravity is represented by a field that would be associated with particles having an intrinsic spin of two units. This requirement leads to severe mathematical problems in making a quantum field theory of gravity. A supersymmetric theory can be constructed in which the field representing gravity is related, via symmetry transformations, to fields associated with electromagnetism and weak interactions. In this type of "supergravity" theory some of the problems that have beset the quantum theory of gravity are avoided, and it may be that such a theory is the correct way to describe gravity and all the other interactions together.

Testing the new theories. Almost all of the ideas that have been proposed to understand symmetry breaking make predictions that can be examined experimentally, and it is clearly appropriate to consider such experiments. Probably the most direct experiment would be one designed to detect some of the new particles suggested by these mechanisms, such as those whose existence is implied by supersymmetry. It is not certain what the rest energies would be of the new particles—for example, the spin-zero partners of electrons—that must exist if supersymmetry is a correct property of quantum field theory. It is argued, however, that at least some would have rest energies not much greater than those of the W and Z particles; that is, around 1 TeV. Particles of this rest energy cannot be produced with existing accelerators or with any accelerators presently under construction, and so the interest of high-energy physicists has turned to the construction of new, more powerful machines. In view of the very successful experiments done at the CERN collider it is natural to consider more energetic proton-proton or proton-antiproton colliders. It is expected that if 1-TeV particles exist, they could be produced in reasonable numbers in collisions between protons each having an energy of 10–20 TeV. It is this consideration that has set the energy scale for the discussions of new accelerators that have taken place over the past year.

As of early 1984 the most energetic machine, producing protons of about 0.8 TeV, was at the Fermi National Accelerator Laboratory (Fermilab) in Illinois. A project to upgrade its energy to about 1 TeV was nearing completion. Nevertheless, a major new step in accelerator scale would be necessary to achieve 10–20 TeV. If the Fermilab accelerator ring, which has a circumference of several kilometers, were simply scaled up by a factor of 20, the resulting accelerator would enclose an area greater than New York City. In order to mitigate this space requirement somewhat, physicists are seriously considering the use of magnets that can produce fields as high as ten teslas, or some 200,000 times greater than the magnetic field of the Earth. With such high fields the ring needed for a 10–20-TeV collider can be several times smaller than a simple scaling would imply—but it would still need to be 15–30 km (about 10–20 mi) across. Such magnets require the use of superconducting materials to carry the electric currents that generate the large magnetic fields. The relevant technology is available in principle, although ten-tesla magnets have not yet been produced in large number. Upgrading the Fermilab accelerator to 1 TeV involves superconducting magnets of somewhat lower fields, and it is expected that the experience from this project will clarify the feasibility of the more powerful accelerator.

A specific proposal to build a 10–20-TeV proton-proton collider was put forward in 1983 by a group of physicists acting as an advisory committee to the U.S. Department of Energy. The proposed machine, known as the Superconducting Super Collider (SSC), would take 10–15 years and several billion dollars to build. Details of construction, including the site, are yet to be determined. Indeed, as of early 1984 there was no decision by the U.S. government to support this project. A high-level coordinating committee was appointed to oversee preliminary research efforts and to allocate funds among them, with a view toward producing a more definite plan within a few years for construction of the SSC. Most high-energy physicists are convinced that this project is essential for studying the new phenomena that are expected to occur in the energy range of a few TeV.

—Gerald Feinberg

Nuclear physics

The past year was characterized by a striking renaissance in nuclear physics worldwide and particularly in the United States. Activity, enthusiasm, and optimism abounded as new techniques, new concepts, and new instrumentation were being brought to bear on an understanding of the nuclear many-body problem. A parallel resurgence of activity occurred in the applications of nuclear physics to a wide variety of fields ranging from nuclear medicine to archaeology and art history.

The structure of nuclei. In recent years remarkable progress has been made in terms of understanding the structure and quantum spectra of nuclei in terms of the simple concepts of a nuclear shell model, in which the protons and neutrons (nucleons) in the nucleus fill a preassigned set of energy levels, or shells. During the past year these concepts were extended to situations in which the nuclei are spinning so rapidly that they might be expected to disintegrate spontaneously under centrifugal forces. For example, David Radford and his collaborators at the universities of Strasbourg and Paris and at Yale University succeeded in understanding, in microscopic detail, all the quantum (energy) states up to 12.5 MeV (million electron volts) of excitation of the isotope of holmium having mass 153. All states having spins up to 67/2 units of angular momentum were fully described in terms of a shell model involving a magic, closed core of 64 protons and 82 neutrons, plus 7 outer, or valence, nucleons. (In nuclei, when the number of neutrons or protons is 2, 8, 20, 28, 50, 82, or 126, the nucleus is said to be magic because it has a spherical shape and special stability.) In order to understand the additional states having spins of 69/2 to 81/2 units, a single nucleon

View along the tunnel of the main accelerator ring at Fermilab shows some of the 1,000 superconducting magnets, mounted just off the floor, that make up the facility's new Tevatron accelerator. The upper row of magnets belongs to Fermilab's older, conventional 400-GeV machine, which has been incorporated into the new system as a proton injector at an energy of 150 GeV. In a preliminary run in February 1984 the Tevatron accelerated a beam of protons to 0.8 TeV as it moved toward its final goal of 1 TeV.

D. Allan Bromley

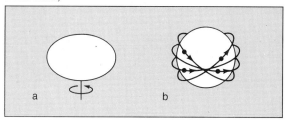

As an atomic nucleus is spun faster, its increasing angular momentum can be accommodated in only one of two ways. Either the entire deformed nucleus rotates faster in a collective fashion (a) or the individual nucleons, one after another, adjust their orbits so that they contribute more and more to the total nuclear spin (b).

must be promoted from inside the closed core into a valence orbit where it couples with the valence nucleons already there.

In parallel work Peter Kleinheinz and his colleagues in Jülich, West Germany, in detailed studies on gadolinium isotopes, found compelling evidence for quantum states that can be described in terms of a shell model, but one in which the closed core has been excited into a pear-shaped oscillation (octupole). In addition, for the first time, Kleinheinz and his collaborators found evidence for structures involving not only one but two units of this pear-shaped oscillation.

From numerous studies like these, carried out in laboratories around the world, it finally has been possible to understand in some detail how a nucleus responds to increasing spin. Walter Henning and co-workers at the Argonne National Laboratory in Illinois reported perhaps the most detailed such study of dysprosium isotopes having neutrons from 82, a magic number, to 94. As expected, the nuclei having a magic number of neutrons are essentially spherical; those having a small number of valence neutrons above this magic number, *i.e.*, 2–4, are rather soft vibrators; while those having a greater number of valence neutrons are polarized by these neutrons into a relatively rigid, deformed football shape.

As these nuclei are spun increasingly fast, they can respond in only two ways. Either the individual neutron and proton orbits can realign themselves to contribute more to the total spin, or the entire nucleus can spin faster in a collective fashion. What Henning's team found is that in the region from 10 to perhaps 40 units of angular momentum, those isotopes having few valence neutrons respond to increased spin by aligning individual valence nucleons with respect to a doorknob-shaped core. Those with an intermediate number of valence neutrons align the valence neutrons and protons relative to a football-shaped core. Those with the largest number of neutrons simply spin as a more or less rigid collec-

tive system. Above 40 units of angular momentum, however, all nuclei make a transition into a football shape, as might be anticipated on the way to eventual disintegration under centrifugal forces.

The reality of nucleons. Despite such successes of the nuclear shell model, there has always been substantial doubt as to whether neutrons and protons deep in the hearts of large nuclei really retain the characteristics that they display as free particles. This question has been answered in elegant fashion by Bernard Frois and colleagues of the Center for Nuclear Research at Saclay, France. Recognizing that lead-206 differs from thallium-205 only by a single proton occupying an orbit (3s) that gives the particle a high probability of being at the center of the nucleus (quantum mechanically, the proton has a maximum in its wave function at the center of the nucleus), they carried out precise inelastic electron-scattering studies on these two nuclei and attributed the observed differences to the 3s proton. They thus were able to determine the detailed shape of the wave function of this proton. In addition to showing that the wave function has the classic shape anticipated for such an orbit, the work demonstrated that a proton, even at the very center of a lead nucleus, retains its full character as a nucleon.

Three-dimensional plot, derived from inelastic electron-scattering data, depicts the probability density of the 3s proton in the lead-206 nucleus. The chance that the 3s proton will be found in a particular place is at its maximum for the center of the nucleus (center of grid).

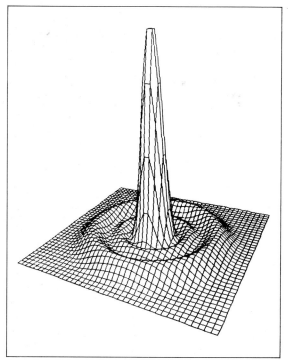

Bernard Frois, Saclay, France

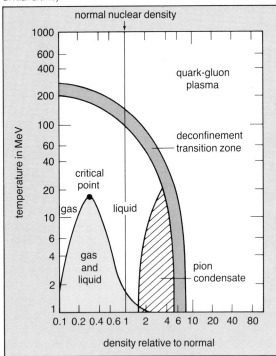

Schematic phase diagram for nuclear matter plots nuclear temperature against relative density. Above certain combinations of energy and density, demarcated by a deconfinement transition zone, individual nucleons are expected to melt together into a quark-gluon plasma.

Equation of state of nuclear matter. There is perhaps no more fundamental question in nuclear physics than that of determining the equation of state of nuclear matter; *i.e.*, the way it responds to changes in pressure and temperature or, in the language of nuclear physics, to changes in density and excitation energy. With the growing availability of high-energy, high-precision accelerators for electrons, protons, and heavy ions, scientists have been able to glimpse what the high-energy domain may hold in store. The very fragmentary data available from electron machines suggests that at low energies neutrons and protons are the dominant entities in nuclei, although even at the present level of precision it becomes essential to incorporate the quite visible effects of the currents of mesons that flow in even the simplest nucleus. As the available energy is increased, the neutrons and protons themselves can absorb energy and become promoted into their excited quantum states—the so-called isobars—beginning somewhere above 300 MeV. At this level begins a domain in which the observable phenomena are largely determined by the interactions of these excited nucleons. Finally at much higher energies, above 3–4 GeV (billion electron volts), it appears that the neutrons and protons (made up of three quarks each) effec-

tively melt into a plasma formed from their quarks and from the particles, called gluons, that mediate the force holding the quarks together in nucleons. This quark-gluon plasma seems to have existed in nature during the earliest moments following the big bang and possibly appears only in the very final moments of gravitational collapse of massive stars into black holes. Understanding its characteristics obviously poses a major challenge.

Electron accelerators are powerful probes in these studies because the electrons experience only point-like interactions with the quarks themselves. On the other hand, heavy-ion accelerators will be expected to play a very important role because only heavy-ion collisions can produce, if only for very short times, the greatly increased nuclear-matter densities that are required to probe the equation of state. It is currently believed that in collisions involving massive nuclei and energies beyond a few tens of GeV, it will be possible to "deconfine" the quarks and gluons to create conditions very similar to those in the earliest universe. For a variety of reasons, however, this de-

In an artist's rendering two uranium nuclei collide at very high energy. (Top) Incoming uranium projectile, traveling near the speed of light, is relativistically contracted to a thin disk as it nears a stationary target nucleus. (Center) Projectile has passed through part of the target, raising the temperature of that material above several hundred million degrees. (Bottom) Target, now a fireball possibly made of quark-gluon plasma, expands as the heated projectile flies on. Between the two lies a so-called fire tube that may be filled with a new form of mesonic matter.

Lawrence Berkeley Radiation Laboratory

372

confinement transition is not expected to be a sharp one, and as yet it has not been possible to predict a unique experimental signature for the creation of the quark-gluon plasma that would be expected to come into existence at densities several times that normal in nuclei. Furthermore, since it would be expected that the compression in a heavy-ion collision would be accompanied by an effective rebound or rarefaction, there is the possibility of a second phase transition in nuclear matter at densities substantially less than normal, corresponding to the change from liquid to gas in ordinary matter. This transition, in contrast to the quark-gluon one, should be very sharp and have the characteristics of a simple phase transition. A number of phenomena, particularly those involving the mass distribution of the collision fragments, have been suggested as signatures.

Finally, at densities above normal but below those necessary for deconfinement, it is theoretically possible that the nuclear system will develop a coherent field of pi mesons (pions, comprising two quarks each), which would be very much like the electromagnetic field in a laser and which would consist of a condensed phase of pions. Because pions can carry charge, the condensation could represent an entirely new form of superconductivity. Despite a few sporadic searches involving relatively low energies and relatively light colliding nuclei, there is no evidence to date for the existence of pion condensates in heavy-ion collisions. Nevertheless, this field presents a wealth of opportunities for entirely new phenomena and entirely new science.

Quark effects in nuclei. There was recent evidence from the inelastic scattering of mu mesons (muons) carried out by the European Muon Collaboration at the European Laboratory for Particle Physics (CERN) in Geneva and from the subsequent reanalysis of old electron inelastic scattering data obtained at the Stanford Linear Accelerator Center (SLAC) that the degree and character of the melting process involved in deconfining the quarks may depend upon the specific nucleus under study. It has been found, for example, that inelastic scattering of particles from the deuteron (hydrogen-2 nucleus) is significantly different from scattering from aluminum-27 or iron-58. R. L. Jaffe of the Massachusetts Institute of Technology and others interpreted these differences as implying that (1) there is a tendency for quarks to percolate from nucleon to nucleon in aluminum and iron, *i.e.*, that the confining "bags" which normally hold the quarks in nucleons "leak"; (2) there is a large increase in the number of quarks not associated with a specific nucleon in aluminum but possibly existing as pions or other mesonlike components; (3) the fraction of the momentum per nucleon carried by the gluons is significantly less in aluminum and iron than it is in the deuteron; and (4) there

is a small probability for the existence, in normal iron and aluminum, of entities that consist of more than three quarks and are therefore fundamentally different from either neutrons or protons. Again the studies were still fragmentary in character, but they provided unexpected and exciting new insight into what may lie ahead in the realm of higher energies.

—D. Allan Bromley

Solid-state physics

Solid-state physics is a fertile breeding ground both for new concepts in physics and for applications leading to new technologies. It is thus natural that the vigorous, pioneering research characterizing the field is being pursued in both industrial and university laboratories. Advances in solid-state physics may include new physical phenomena, new materials that often require highly sophisticated preparation methods, and new devices. Another important feature of solid-state physics is the intimate relationship between experiments and theory.

Of the many advances in recent months a striking example of the discovery of new phenomena is embodied in research involving a physical effect called the Hall effect, which has been known over a century. The observations were possible because of recent advances in materials-preparation techniques and the availability of devices developed in conjunction with semiconductor technologies.

The Hall effect. In 1820 Danish physicist Hans Christian Ørsted found that an electric current causes a magnetic field. A wire carrying an electric current and placed in a magnetic field will therefore experience a force as the field around the wire and the applied field interact. This discovery is the basis for the electric motor. A free electron moving perpendicular to a magnetic field in a vacuum will also experience a force since it also represents an electric current. This force is called a Lorentz force and is perpendicular to both the magnetic field and the line of motion of the electron (current flow). Similarly the negative or positive charge carriers (electrons or holes) in a current-carrying conductor that is placed in a magnetic field will experience a force. As figure 1 depicts, if the field is applied in the z spatial direction and the electric current flows along the x direction, the resulting force will be in the y direction, perpendicular to both the applied field and the current. This force will cause the charge carriers in the conductor to move in the y direction and accumulate along an edge of the conductor, producing an electric field across the conductor in the y direction. If a voltmeter is connected across the conductor in the y direction, it will measure a voltage, the Hall voltage. The effect was discovered by the U.S. physicist Edwin H. Hall in 1879.

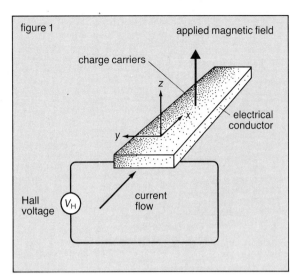

figure 1

applied magnetic field

charge carriers

z

x

y

electrical
conductor

Hall
voltage

V_H

current
flow

When a current-carrying conductor is placed in a magnetic field that is perpendicular to the current, the Lorentz force exerted on the charge carriers in the conductor will cause a transverse electric field across the conductor and a measurable voltage, the Hall voltage.

For a conductor like a simple metal, having free or nearly free electrons as charge carriers, one can define a constant, called the Hall coefficient, that depends on the concentration of free electrons. By sign convention the coefficient has a negative value. For metals like the alkali metals (*e.g.,* sodium or potassium), the theoretically predicted value of the Hall coefficient is very close to the experimentally measured values both in size and sign, indicating that the charge carriers behave very much like a gas of free electrons. For many materials, however, the measured values cannot be explained in such terms. In fact, the sign can be positive, indicating that the main mechanism for charge transport is by positive carriers; *i.e.,* holes. As is evident from many other transport mechanisms involving electrons in a solid, the "effective" mass of electrons in a solid is most often quite different from that of free electrons. Nevertheless, what can be called the ordinary Hall effect is quite well understood for various types of both metallic and semiconductor materials. It is used to measure the properties of materials when those properties relate to the concentration of charge carriers. Since the Hall voltage varies in direct proportion to the strength of the applied magnetic field (for moderate values), it is also used in magnetometers to measure field strengths.

A complication arises in materials for which one must consider the effect of the spin of the electron and the coupling of this spin to the orbits of the electrons around the atoms of the material. These factors give rise to an unusually large Hall effect, called the anomalous Hall effect. This effect is important

for magnetic systems and is particularly large for magnets incorporating noncrystalline (amorphous) rare-earth elements and transition metals. It is also finding practical applications, in magnetic recording, for example.

The quantized Hall effect. All of the above considerations are based on the assumption that the charge carriers move in three-dimensional space. However, just as the surface properties of a crystal prove to be very different from its bulk properties because of the two-dimensional character of a surface, the Hall effect for a two-dimensional system shows new and completely unexpected phenomena. Not until recently have investigators had access to a real system that is two-dimensional in character. Using a silicon semiconductor device called a MOS-FET (metal-oxide-semiconductor field-effect transistor), they have been able to study a two-dimensional sheet of mobile electrons called an inversion layer. A MOSFET transistor (figure 2) consists of a source and a drain separated by a gate, which is an electric contact on top of an insulating layer of silicon dioxide. Applying a positive voltage to the gate induces a thin layer of electrons beneath the silicon dioxide layer, which allows a current to flow between the source and the drain (*i.e.,* the transistor is on). If the polarity on the gate is reversed, no current will flow (the transistor is off). When the temperature of the device is lowered near absolute zero (below 1.5 K), the electrons generated in the inversion layer by a positive voltage on the gate electrode are confined to the potential well caused by the gate voltage and can only move laterally along the inversion layer but not in the z direction perpendicular to the layer and the surface.

If one applies a modest magnetic field in the z direction and an electric field in the x direction causing current to flow between the source and the drain, one observes the normal Hall voltage in the y direction. But, if the magnetic field is increased to very high values (above 150,000 gauss) the Hall voltage becomes much more puzzling and intriguing. In 1980 physicists Klaus von Klitzing of the University of Würzburg, West Germany, Gerhard Dorda of Siemens Research Laboratories, Munich, and Michael Pepper of the Cavendish Laboratory in Cambridge, England, discovered that, in a plot of the Hall voltage as a function of the applied gate voltage in a MOSFET exposed to low temperature and a high magnetic field, the curve showed very distinct plateaus (figure 3) instead of a smooth decline. The Hall effect appeared to be quantized. The steps occurred at very regular intervals, which could be described by the Hall resistance formula, $R_H = (h/e^2)n$, in which h is Planck's constant, e the unit charge of the electron, and n is an integer (1, 2, 3, . . .). In fact, the accuracy of h/e^2 determined in this way is better than

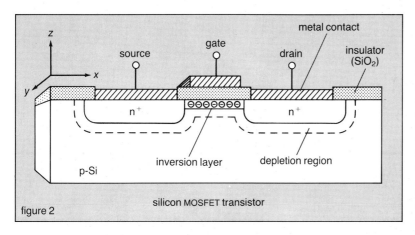

figure 2

silicon MOSFET transistor

one part in a million, and the possibility exists that this accuracy can be further increased with refined experimental methods. The unit h/e^2 has the dimension of electrical resistance (25,813 ohms). If the accuracy of the measurements can be increased as expected, the quantized Hall effect could provide an absolute standard of resistance defined in terms of fundamental constants.

The observation of the quantized Hall effect came

Hall voltage, as measured in a silicon MOSFET device exposed to a high magnetic field (above 150,000 gauss) and temperatures below 1.5 K, shows very distinct plateaus as a function of the gate voltage.

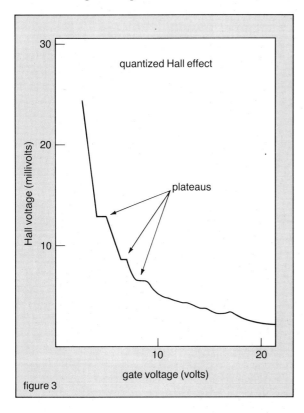

figure 3

as a surprise, and the intriguing puzzle is why the experimental results seem to be independent of the variation in the experimental conditions that is bound to occur in working with real solids. This spurred a great interest among theorists, and soon several of them produced plausible theories. Among them was Robert Laughlin, then a postdoctoral fellow at Bell Laboratories in the U.S., who reasoned that such an accuracy in nature cannot be dependent on specific models or materials systems but must be of a general nature. He and others developed a theory that takes into account the two-dimensional nature of the system and describes a way in which the high magnetic field can break the degeneracy of the electron gas into quantized energy states that are ultimately the reason for the appearance of the plateaus. The next question was what happens when the magnetic field is increased still further.

The fractional quantized Hall effect. As is often the case in science, another research group was at work on the same problem. David Tsui, Horst Störmer, and Arthur Gossard at Bell Laboratories were using a similar device but with another semiconductor material, gallium arsenide (GaAs). After confirming the results on the quantized Hall effect, they set out to seek experimental verification of another property of a two-dimensional electron gas, one predicted as early as 1934 by the U.S. theoretical physicist Eugene Wigner. Wigner had theorized that a two-dimensional electron gas should crystallize into a regular lattice at sufficiently low temperatures. The Bell group therefore went to very high magnetic fields (280,000 gauss) and even lower temperatures (0.5 K). But instead of observing the expected Wigner crystallization, in 1983 the physicists were astonished to see new Hall resistance plateaus corresponding to fractions in the formula. They found plateaus not only for $n = 1, 2, 3 \ldots$ but also for $n = \frac{1}{3}, \frac{2}{3}, \frac{4}{3}, \frac{5}{3}, \frac{2}{5}, \frac{3}{5}, \frac{4}{5}$, and $\frac{2}{7}$. For this discovery Tsui, Störmer, and Gossard were awarded the 1984 Buckley Prize for Solid State Physics.

Courtesy, Andrew Alimonda, Xerox Palo Alto Research Center

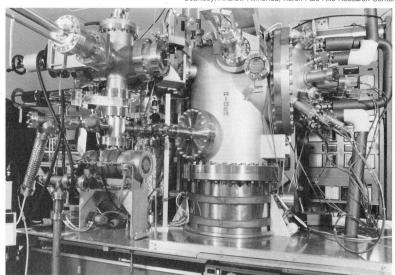

Complex molecular beam epitaxy (MBE) apparatus, designed around an ultrahigh-vacuum chamber, permits the deposition of desired elements one atomic layer at a time in order to achieve very precise crystal structures. Such degrees of sophistication and control in crystal growth were required for detection of the fractional quantized Hall effect.

The discovery of the fractional quantized Hall effect was even more challenging to the theorists, among them again Laughlin at the Lawrence Livermore National Laboratory in California. In the latest theory being developed, the interaction (correlation) between two electrons plays a very important role. Instead of a Wigner crystallization, there seems to exist a quantum-liquid state, a completely new condensed phase of matter consisting of electrons. If this picture is correct, the burden will again be on the experimentalists to hunt for other phenomena that would manifest this new condensed electron phase.

The observation of the fractional quantized Hall effect not only requires high magnetic fields and low temperatures but also the very cleanest interface between contacting surfaces to create the inversion layer. The last requirement was achieved by growing the material by means of a refined technique called molecular beam epitaxy (MBE). MBE involves the evaporation and subsequent condensation of the constituent elements—the GaAs device used gallium, arsenic, aluminum, and silicon—in an ultra-high vacuum system to assure purity. This growth technique had been developed to produce opto-electronic components for communications and other applications.

—Stig B. Hagstrom

Psychology

Two especially noteworthy events occurred during the past year. First, the American Psychological Association (APA) purchased the popular magazine *Psychology Today*. After having decided several years ago not to undertake publication of a new popular magazine, the APA yielded to the continuing pressure to produce a publication with a broader appeal than any

of its 17 scholarly journals. The decision to purchase was not without its critics, many of them vociferous, within the APA itself, and it remained to be seen how well the planned upgrading of the magazine would survive the crucial test of the marketplace.

Second, the International Council of Scientific Unions granted membership to the International Union of Psychological Science. Admittance to this prestigious organization permitted the 44 affiliated national psychology associations, of which APA was by far the largest, to take a more active role in the formation of international policy.

Mental health. In an unprecedented first step toward a comprehensive cooperative mental health program the APA agreed to undertake a number of joint activities with the American Psychiatric Association, the National Association of Social Workers, and the American Nurses Association. These organizations represent the four core mental health professions. Among the planned joint efforts was the establishment of an interdisciplinary mental health study group. The first topic to be attacked was to be chronic mental illness.

Washington, D.C., was the site of the biennial meeting of the World Congress on Mental Health. This week-long conference was attended by mental-health professionals from 39 countries. Its theme was the personality damage caused by pervasive violence and threats of violence throughout the world.

The largest foreign contingent was from Japan. A major address was delivered by Soedjatmoko, the rector of the United Nations University in Tokyo. He was especially concerned about the mental health of children exposed to considerable violence. "It is difficult to raise people with the mental strength to be peaceloving when they have been brought up surrounded by violence," he commented.

Supportive relationships. One answer to the above question was suggested by Michael Rutter, professor and head of the Department of Child and Adolescent Psychiatry at the University of London. He reported that supportive interpersonal relationships, along with social and academic success in school, helped children cope with adversity.

Rutter also reported some research results at a summer seminar sponsored by the National Institute of Mental Health. Two groups of children from the inner city of London were studied. Children from one group were raised mainly in institutions, and those in the other group in their own homes. Initially studied in 1964, the individuals were reevaluated as young adults beginning in 1978. The most important factor in their adjustment was identified as whether these children had at some time had partners or supportive associates, and not whether their initial social attachments had been interrupted (by the early institutionalization). Personality disorders were found in only 4% of females who had had a nondeviant partner (one without a record of alcoholism, drug abuse, psychiatric disorder, or crime). In contrast, disorders were found in 31% of females who had never had a partner and in 39% of those with a deviant partner.

Rutter concluded that instead of trying to produce fundamental personality changes therapists should focus on improving people's self-esteem and social skills. He also called for a much more fluid view of the developmental process to replace perspectives that emphasize fixed stages or structures in development.

The role of a supportive counselor in helping individuals accept and hold to stressful decisions (for example, to quit smoking or drinking) was intensively analyzed by psychologist Irving L. Janis of Yale University in a long-term research program. Among the many important conclusions that were reached was that there is a reliable increase in the acceptance of and adherence to a counselor's suggestions if the counselor signifies his or her acceptance of the counselee by means of consistent, positive feedback and if a moderate rather than a very high or very low amount of self-disclosure is elicited from the counselee.

Stress. The importance of social stress in the induction of atherosclerosis, or hardening of the arteries, was confirmed in a recent experiment on macaque monkeys. Researchers at the Bowman Gray School of Medicine in Winston-Salem, N.C., and the Yemassee Primate Center in South Carolina maintained 15 male monkeys in a stressful environment, compared with a control group of monkeys allowed to live without the special stress. Stress was manipulated by the periodic transfer of monkeys among the five-animal pens and by the addition of a sterilized

female to each pen group every two weeks during the last 9 months of the 21-month experiment. All of the monkeys in both the experimental and control groups were given a low-fat, low-cholesterol diet. The investigators concluded that social stress was a sufficient condition for atherosclerosis because of the greater accumulation of fatty materials in the inner walls of the arteries of the stressed monkeys.

There has been an increasing amount of attention paid to the various ways in which psychology can be applied to economic problems. Again, stress was seen as a major culprit. Stress was pointed out as the most pervasive and damaging "toxin" in the work environment by Leon Warshaw, executive director of the New York Business Group on Health. In economic terms it was estimated to cost U.S. industry $75 billion annually. This figure is ten times the annual cost of all strikes, according to Paul Rosch, president of the American Institute of Stress. Rosch also estimated that heart attacks, in which the role of stress is clearly indicated, are responsible for an additional $25 billion loss per year from premature deaths of business executives.

Controlled drinking. One of the most virulent controversies within psychology in recent years erupted over the issue of "controlled drinking" by alcoholics. Briefly, this term refers to a procedure whereby confirmed alcoholics are permitted a limited amount of alcoholic intake, as compared with the total abstinence that conventional professional wisdom has identified as the necessary treatment.

The suggestion that controlled drinking can be effective treatment, at least for some alcoholics, was first advanced by the late British physician R. L. Davies. In 1962 he reported that 7 patients out of a total of 93 being treated for alcoholism at Maudsley Hospital in London were able to drink normally for 7 to 11 years after the end of the hospital treatment. In 1970 Australian psychologists S. H. Lovibond and G. Caddy also reported a successful controlled-drinking program. Various behavioral treatments administered to 28 alcoholic patients resulted in 21 successes during a follow-up check.

Most of the recent controversy has surrounded results reported by the U.S. psychologists Mark and Linda Sobell. They directly compared controlled-drinking and total-abstinence therapies and found the former to be more effective. These results were vigorously challenged by psychologists Mary Pendery and Irving Maltzman, who, working with psychiatrist L. Jolyon West, reexamined the Sobells' original subjects. The Sobell follow-ups were done one and two years after the completion of therapy, and the Pendery-Maltzman-West reexaminations were performed ten years later. On the basis of alleged discrepancies between the Sobell surveys and the later reports, the Sobells were accused of misconduct. As a result a number of review committees were formed to look into the matter.

No evidence of professional misconduct by the Sobells was found by the independent committee organized by the Sobells' present employers, the Addiction Research Foundation of Toronto. This conclusion was confirmed in 1983 by a U.S. congressional committee (involved because of the federal funding given for the initial research). Addictive-behavior researcher G. Alan Marlatt interpreted the strong resistance of traditional researchers to controlled drinking as a reflection of their acceptance of a "disease model" for alcoholism, as contrasted with a behavioral perspective. (The controversy was reviewed extensively in the *American Psychologist* for October 1983.)

Experimental psychology. *Learning.* Intensive investigation of the behavioral process of learning continued, from the simplest to the most complex levels of behavior. At the former level, over the past year independent demonstrations of cellular "learning" mechanisms in the mollusk *Aplysia* were reported by investigators at Columbia University in New York; and at the University of Texas Medical School in Houston researchers were able to condition monosynaptic connections to tail motor neurons in individual sensory neurons.

At the more complex level, cognitive researchers were beginning to emphasize a new approach to mathematical and science learning. Lauren Resnick, co-director of the Learning Research and Development Center at the University of Pittsburgh, pointed out that students characteristically revert to pre-instructional ("naive") theories in their attempts to solve mathematical and scientific problems. For example, the naive meaning associated with such technical terms as "acceleration" has been found to inhibit problem solving that depends upon understanding more appropriate scientific meanings. Students seem especially to cling to their original, naive theories when problems that differ from their textbook examples are presented.

An important step in the resolution of this instructional problem, according to Resnick, is for teachers to recognize the need for students to use qualitative reasoning; teachers should not force students into premature application of new quantitative information (such as precise mathematical formulas) that has not been integrated into their working knowledge. The important goal is to encourage the students to make sense of the knowledge and skills provided by mathematics and science and then to use their new understanding to confront their naive theories directly.

Memory. A number of results have been reported that have implications for jury service, another relatively new area of research interest for psychologists. As one example, classroom witnesses of a staged theft were required to identify the thief from photographs and also to answer other questions in a videotaped cross-examination. The interesting result was an inverse relationship between accuracy for crucial and for trivial information: witnesses who did well on trivial questions tended to be inaccurate on thief identification, and vice versa. Moreover, mock jurors who were then shown the videotaped cross-examinations tended to discredit correct thief identifications when they were made by witnesses whose memory for trivia had been demonstrated to be relatively poor.

In another study the feasibility of using hypnosis for the enhancement of memory was questioned. Highly hypnotizable subjects were given the suggestion, during hypnosis, that they had been awakened by a loud noise during the past week. On subsequent posthypnotic examination more than half of those subjects (16 of 27) stated that the awakening event had actually occurred. If this result is generalizable, it raises some serious questions about the investigative use of hypnosis in legal situations.

Developmental psychology. Longitudinal developmental studies, those dealing with changes in an individual or a group over a period of years, are respected and sought after but seldom achieved, be-

Aplysia californica, a shell-less snail from the Pacific Ocean, was used to study physical changes that take place in response to learned behavior. After altering the snail's reflexes through training and conditioning, researchers found changes in the animal's cellular structure.

National Institutes of Health

cause of the great practical difficulties and costs that they entail. The persistence of one set of three such studies, initiated in California about 1930, is, therefore, a remarkable achievement. A progress report on these "Intergenerational Studies" recently appeared. One feature of the report is the surprisingly good predictability found, for those subjects at least, in their development over their full life spans.

The latter phases of the human life span have received a great deal of attention in recent years and may be expected to receive more in the near future as aged people constitute an increasingly high proportion of the general population. During recent months a traveling exhibit was assembled to demonstrate the diminished sensory capacities of people in their 70s and 80s. The exhibit was also designed to show that appropriate environmental modifications can alleviate sensory failures and that activity and even creativity can persist throughout those years. Developed by the University of Pennsylvania with financial support from a pharmaceutical company, the exhibit went on a two-year, 12-city tour of the United States.

Physiological psychology. The role of diet in behavior has long been a controversial topic, generally dominated by conventional folk wisdom rather than experimental data. By 1984, however, this picture was rapidly changing. Two conferences during the past year demonstrated the growing scientific maturity of diet-behavior research.

Brain biochemistry was emphasized in the conference held at the Massachusetts Institute of Technology under the auspices of its Center for Brain Sciences and Metabolism. Conference organizer Richard Wurtman and his associates started animal experimentation on this problem in the early 1970s. By 1984 they and other researchers had shown that several nutrients influence the synthesis of the important neurotransmitters. Although the behavioral effects thus far demonstrated are subtle, they are well established and, in at least one instance, were produced by a single meal.

As an example of the complexity of dietary relationships, one can consider the neurotransmitter serotonin. It seems to be dependent on the amino acid tryptophan, whose only bodily source is dietary protein. Because serotonin contributes to many important behaviors (such as feeding, locomotion, and aggression), the amount of tryptophan made available by meals is important. But the relationship is not a simple one. Merely increasing the level of protein in the meal does not increase the relative amount of tryptophan; eight other amino acids are also increased and compete for space on the carrier molecules that provide transport to the brain. A heavy carbohydrate meal, however, achieves that result, because the release of insulin facilitates the uptake of all the amino acids except tryptophan into body tissues.

The second conference, held at the University of Texas at Austin, concentrated on orthomolecular therapy, the attempt to restore disturbed biochemical balance by means of nutritional (in contrast to drug) treatment. This concept was first proposed three decades ago by Roger Williams, a pioneer in vitamin research at the University of Texas. Encouraging results were reported at the conference on such varied projects as improvement of intelligence in retarded people as measured by IQ tests and control of alcoholism.

Behavioral influences on physiological functions were also emphasized by psychologists in recent research. One demonstration involved the induction of autonomic nervous system effects by posed facial expressions. In research by Paul Ekman of the University of California at San Francisco, professional actors were instructed to move various sets of facial muscles, representing different emotions, while their physiological functions were monitored. Expressions associated with negative emotions (anger and fear) produced a greater increment in heart rate (8 beats per minute) than those related to positive emotions such as happiness (2.6 beats per minute).

Shepard Siegel of McMaster University in Hamilton, Ont., performed animal experimentation to test the hypothesis that heroin-overdose deaths are significantly influenced by classically conditioned drug-anticipation responses. Administering the drug in an environment that had not previously been experienced by the subject was predicted to result in a failure of the typical tolerance achieved by a chronically addicted individual. This prediction was supported in an experiment with rat subjects. Because of the prominence of heroin-overdose deaths, especially in large urban centers where it is among the leading causes of death in people under 35 years of age, this research promises to have important practical implications.

—Melvin H. Marx

Space exploration

One of the major achievements in space exploration took place during the past year when two U.S. astronauts became the first to walk in space without being tethered to their spacecraft. Other highlights included probes of Venus and the continued flight of Pioneer 10, which in June became the first manmade object to go beyond the known limits of the solar system. The Soviet Union continued to center its manned space program on the space station Salyut 7. A number of crews docked with and lived in the station during the past year.

Manned flight

The U.S. Space Transportation System (STS) shifted from engineering tests to commercial operations during 1983, as the space shuttle orbiter "Challenger" carried three payloads of commercial satellites into orbit. On another mission the shuttle orbiter "Columbia" was mother ship for the European scientific research habitat Spacelab 1. Operations in space with the Soviet Union's Salyut 7 space station were marred by a failure to rendezvous and dock a Soyuz to the space station and by an explosion on the launch pad during another Soyuz launch attempt.

Space shuttle. As commander of the STS—7 "Challenger," Robert Crippen was making his second orbiter space flight. This time he was accompanied by Frederick Hauck, John Fabian, Sally Ride (the first U.S. woman to fly on a space mission), and Norman Thagard. Crippen had flown aboard the first space shuttle orbital flight in April 1981. The "Challenger" lifted off from the Kennedy Space Center on June 18, 1983, and landed on June 24. Two communications satellites, the Telesat Canada Anik C-2 and Indonesian Palapa B-1, were deployed successfully from the "Challenger's" payload bay. The West German-built reusable free-flying Shuttle Pallet Satellite (SPAS) was deployed and later retrieved by the crew using the orbiter's robot arm. Cameras aboard SPAS yielded the first motion, still, and television pictures of an orbiter in space from a distance.

Scientific payloads aboard STS-7 included materials-processing experiments in the cargo bay and the McDonnell Douglas Corp./Johnson & Johnson prototype pharmaceutical factory, the Continuous-Flow Electrophoresis System (CFES), on the orbiter's middeck. The Kennedy Space Center's Shuttle Landing Facility was the planned STS-7 landing site, but turbulent weather and cloud cover forced the craft to land instead at Edwards Air Force Base after six days and two hours in orbit.

STS-8 carried another crew of five in the first space shuttle night launch on Aug. 30, 1983. Richard Truly, who had flown as STS-2 pilot, was "Challenger's" commander. Crewmen included Daniel Brandenstein, Guion Bluford, Jr. (the first U.S. black in space), Dale Gardner, and William Thornton. After deploying Insat 1-B for the government of India, the crew tested the orbiter's 15-m (50-ft) robot arm with a 3,380-kg (7,460-lb) "dumbbell" to simulate the handling of future large-mass payloads.

Tracking and Data Relay Satellite A (TDRSS-A), which had been deployed from STS—6, received extensive operational testing by the STS—8 crew, and the CFES was used to process live human kidney cells, rat pituitary cells, and dog pancreas cells in a further development of space pharmaceutical manufacturing techniques. Physician-astronaut Thornton used his crewmates and himself as test subjects in gathering data on space adaptation syndrome, or space motion sickness, which affects a high percentage of people when they first reach orbit. Extra lighting installed along the main runway of Edwards Air Force Base helped the shuttle accomplish its first night landing, as STS-8 "Challenger" landed in the early morning of September 5 after six days and one hour in space.

The shuttle orbiter "Columbia," which had undergone modifications since its use on STS—5, carried STS—9/Spacelab 1 into orbit for ten days of life sciences, astronomy, solar physics, Earth resources, and materials technology investigations in more than 70 European, U.S., Canadian, and Japanese experiments. A six-man crew of John Young; Brewster Shaw, Jr.; Owen Garriott; Robert Parker; Byron Lichtenberg; and West German physicist Ulf Merbold operated Spacelab experiments around the clock in two 12-hour shifts. Lichtenberg, an employee of the Massachusetts Institute of Technology, and European Space Agency payload specialist Merbold were the first persons to fly in the U.S. space program who had not been trained as astronauts.

STS-9/Spacelab was launched Nov. 28, 1983, and landed on December 8 at Edwards Air Force Base

Sally Ride, the first U.S. woman to fly on a space mission, communicates with ground controllers from the mid deck of the space shuttle "Challenger" in June 1983.

NASA/JSC

In Spacelab, situated in the cargo bay of the space shuttle "Columbia," Byron Lichtenberg performs an experiment at the fluid physics module. More than 70 Canadian, European, Japanese, and U.S. experiments were carried in Spacelab.

after a seven-hour delay caused by the failure of two of "Columbia's" five onboard computers—one of which was successfully restarted. Hydrazine fuel leaks in two auxiliary power units (APU's) in "Columbia's" tail section caused small flash fires during the landing and caused minor damage to the spacecraft. An investigating team found that residual hydrazine in APU feed lines between flights caused gradual erosion and metal fatigue of the valves and tubing.

Carrying a crew of five, "Challenger" was launched Feb. 3, 1984, from the Kennedy Space Center on the tenth mission. The flight brought bad news and good news. Two communications satellites that were launched from the shuttle failed to achieve their desired orbits and so were useless. A large rendezvous balloon exploded upon inflation in space, and the "Challenger's" 15-m robot arm failed to work properly. The good news was that Bruce McCandless and Robert Stewart successfully achieved the first walks in space without being tethered to the spacecraft by lifelines. Other crew members included Vance Brand, commander; Robert Gibson, pilot; and Ronald McNair. The "Challenger" landed at the Kennedy Space Center on February 11, the first shuttle mission to land there.

Soviet manned flight. Space station Salyut 7 remained in orbit but unoccupied from December 1982, when Anatoli Berezovoy and Valentin Lebedev completed 211 days in space, until June 1983. On March 2 the unmanned Cosmos 1443 was launched to dock with Salyut and await another crew to unload its cargo. The 20-ton Cosmos was described as a space tug for boosting Salyut to a higher orbit and for returning up to 500 kg (1,100 lb) of cargo to Earth from the space station.

An attempt to man Salyut failed after Soyuz T-8, with crew Vladimir Titov, Gennadi Strekalov, and

Aleksandr Serebrov, aborted a docking with the space station because of rendezvous guidance errors. Soyuz T-8 had been launched April 20, 1983, from Tyuratam Cosmodrome and returned to the Earth on April 22 near Arkalyk, Kazakhstan.

With his power source strapped to his back, Robert Stewart walks in space without being tethered to a spacecraft during the flight of the space shuttle "Challenger" in February 1984.

Soviet cosmonaut Vladimir Lyakhov, working in space on Nov. 3, 1983, attaches a new solar array (left) to the existing array (right) of the Salyut 7 space station.

Vladimir Lyakhov and Aleksandr Aleksandrov lifted off from the Cosmodrome on June 27 aboard Soyuz T-9 and docked with Salyut the following day. The crew performed experiments in semiconductor crystal growth, life sciences, plant growth, astrophysics, and Earth observations. After unloading cargo from Cosmos 1443, Lyakhov and Aleksandrov moved some 350 kg (770 lb) of experiment results and other cargo from Salyut into the Cosmos for return to the Earth. Cosmos 1443 separated from Salyut August 14 and landed in the U.S.S.R. on August 23.

Soyuz T-9 was moved by the crew from the docking port vacated by Cosmos 1443 to the opposite end of the space station to await arrival of the Progress 17 resupply vessel. Progress 17 was launched August 17, docked with Salyut August 19, undocked September 17, and vaporized during atmospheric reentry on September 18. A second resupply vessel, Progress 18, ferried fuel and other supplies to Salyut in October.

During an attempt to launch a Soyuz from Tyuratam September 27, the booster exploded on the launch pad. Crewmen Vladimir Titov and Gennadi Strekalov, both of whom had been aboard Soyuz T-8 during the aborted April docking, escaped unharmed when the Soyuz emergency escape rockets carried them away from the fireball.

Lyakhov and Aleksandrov made two space walks from Salyut in early November to install two additional solar panels for generating electrical power before preparing Salyut for unmanned operations. The crew returned to the Earth aboard Soyuz T-9 on November 23 after 150 days in space—the longest stay in space to date without a replacement Soyuz

having been brought up by a visiting crew.

The Soyuz T-10 was launched successfully on Feb. 8, 1984. Its three-man crew included Leonid Kizim, Vladimir Solovyev, and Oleg Atkov. On February 9 they docked with Salyut 7.

—Terry White

Space probes

The most significant event of 1983 took place on June 13 when the probe Pioneer 10 left the known limits of the solar system, the first man-made object to do so. It carried a specially designed plaque made by the astronomer Carl Sagan that illustrated the form of a man and a woman and revealed the Earth as the origin of the probe. The U.S. National Aeronautics and Space Administration (NASA) stated that it would be technically possible to track the probe for an additional decade. It would then be some eight billion km (five billion mi) from Earth. Scientists also stated that the closest approach to another star for Pioneer 10, over the next 850,000 years, would be the star Ross 248 and the distance from it would be 3.27 light-years. (One light-year equals 5,878,-000,000,000,000 mi.) Pioneer 10 had been launched on March 2, 1972.

As the year began, both Japan and the U.S. announced plans for future space probes. Japan's project involved launching a 638.6-kg (1,430-lb) spacecraft to map the geochemistry of the Moon in 1987. NASA, at the same time, began consideration of a second Galileo probe to Saturn. Composed of left-over parts and test components, it would be launched from the space shuttle, possibly using a Centaur upper stage for the boost from Earth orbit to the planet. Extensive observations of Saturn's satellite Titan would be planned, utilizing an imaging radar on the probe.

In January the Ukrainian Academy of Sciences of the U.S.S.R. released panoramic pictures of Venus made from data sent to it from the U.S. These data were from the Pioneer Venus probe. The pictures revealed rolling plains, extensive lowlands, and mountains higher than Everest. The area covered was more than 50,000,000 sq km (19,300,000 sq mi). The Soviet scientists developed a method for processing the data that involved the digital synthesis of images by a computer. The computer first developed a mathematical model of the Venusian surface, with the inclination of the surface and the estimated brightness of the planet taken into account. The computer then took the reconstructed landscape and put it onto the photographic film. Two stereoscopic, panoramic views resulted.

Probing Venus. Early in 1983 Soviet scientists reported on further studies of the Venera 13 and Venera 14 probes launched to Venus in 1981. Data received from them revealed bursts of gamma radiation and flares of solar X-radiation in the interplanetary medium.

In February NASA announced that its future Venus Radar Mapper probe, scheduled for launch in 1988 by the space shuttle, would cost only about half of the originally projected $300 million because the probe could utilize leftover components. For example, a spare antenna built for the Voyager probe could be used to both gather information and transmit it to the Earth. Other cost savings were expected to result from putting the probe into an elliptical orbit around Venus rather than the planned circular one. The Venus mapper will be able to resolve objects on the planet's surface as small as 999.1 m (3,278 ft) in diameter. It will map the entire planet from pole to pole.

On June 2 the Soviet Union launched Venera 15 toward Venus. It was followed on June 7 by Venera 16. Both craft were designed to continue the investigations of the Venusian surface and atmosphere as did predecessors in the Venera series that began in 1965. En route to Venus both probes made periodic measurements of cosmic rays of solar and galactic origin. Also measured were the intensity and energy spectrum of charged particles and the propagation of their flows.

Venera 15 went into orbit about the planet on October 10. It was followed by Venera 16 on October 14. Both were placed in elliptical orbits with periods of about 24 hours. The probes carried radar-imaging apparatus designed to penetrate the dense clouds of Venus. The radar had been tested in Soviet Il-18 aircraft flying at high altitudes over central Asia and the Kamchatka Peninsula when those regions were

The U.S. space probe Pioneer 10, shown below in an artist's rendition, became on June 18, 1983, the first man-made object to pass beyond the known limits of the solar system.

NASA

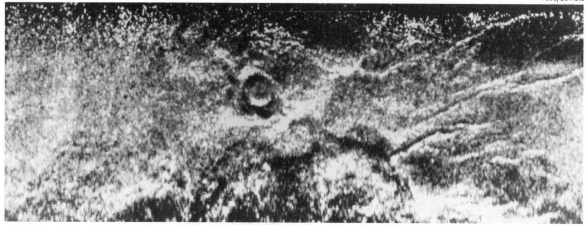

Surface of Venus is revealed in a radar photograph taken from a Soviet Venera space probe. Volcanoes and meander ridges of volcanic origin are seen at a surface resolution of 1 to 2 kilometers (0.6 to 1.2 miles).

covered with clouds. Initially, the two probes concentrated imaging on the northern polar regions of the planet.

A surface resolution of 1 to 2 km (0.6 mi to 1.2 mi) was claimed by Soviet scientists. One scientist reported that "The pictures show geological formations of different nature, pointing to a long period of active tectonics on the planet and the complexity of the geological processes taking place." These consisted of "impact craters, hills, major fractures, benches, mountain ridges." V. I. Barsukov, director of the Soviet Geochemistry and Analytical Chemistry Institute, examined the pictures and said that one of the images showed "a very deep powerful fracture with a width of about 1,493.5 to 1,999.5 m (4,900 to 6,500 ft), extended for something like 59.5 to 70.8 km (37 to 44 mi)."

Other scientific instrumentation aboard the probes included an infrared spectrometer-interferometer, developed jointly with scientists of the Academy of Sciences of East Germany. Data gathered by it established a vertical temperature profile of the planetary atmosphere as well as its content of ozone and water vapor. The instrument was designed to permit the determination of temperatures at altitudes of 65 to 90 km (38 to 56 mi), a region little studied previously.

At the 34th International Astronautical Federation congress in Budapest, Hung., during October the Soviets announced plans to release specially instrumented balloons into the Venusian atmosphere by their two Venus/Vega probes to be launched in 1984. Soviet scientists hoped that the two balloons would stay aloft for two days, transmitting data on wind currents. The two probes were also to send landing vehicles to the surface of the planet. The landers would begin taking measurements at an altitude above the planet's surface of about 60 km and

would continue to do so for about one hour during the descent, terminating before landing. Once the landers were on the surface, an X-ray fluorescent spectrometer and a gamma-ray spectrometer would make studies of the Venusian soil. The fly-by portion of the probes would continue on to a rendezvous with Halley's Comet in March 1986.

As 1983 drew to a close, the Soviet Union and France were nearing a final decision on a projected Venus probe to be launched in the 1990s. The project would be a follow-on to the Vega/Venus Halley's Comet probe. One concept of the sophisticated craft envisioned a large hot-air balloon inflated by the heat of the Sun that would float high in the Venusian atmosphere and release instrumented probes. The balloon would be approximately 20 to 30 m (65 to 100 ft) in diameter and have a mission duration of 10 to 20 hours. It would float at an altitude of about 65 km above the Venusian surface.

In describing the concept of using heat from the Sun an official of the French Centre National d'Études Spatials said, "In the U.S. studies for Vietnam, the balloon was first opened like a parachute, and the pilot then operated a heat source to keep the balloon aloft. In our studies, we found it was possible to eliminate the heat source, because there would be sufficiently strong solar-ray absorption for the balloon to stabilize itself at altitude."

During the year NASA also revealed information on Venus discovered with the ultraviolet spectrometer on Pioneer Venus. Nearly continuous observation of the atmosphere by the instrument since 1978 revealed great amounts of sulfur dioxide and sulfuric acid mist at the cloud tops. Radar imaging indicated that there also may be volcanoes. Still other data suggested lightning in the atmosphere near those regions. Lightning often occurs on the Earth near volcanic eruptions.

Farewell to Viking. In mid-November 1982 radio contact with the Viking 1 lander on Mars was lost. The attempts continued through Jan. 11, 1983. On that day the transmitting antenna of the probe was pointing in a direction that would permit it to send data as the Earth passed through its beam. Commands were sent to the Viking, but there was no response. On February 25 yet another attempt was made to revive the probe. After much study and further attempts to establish contact with the Viking, hope faded at the Jet Propulsion Laboratory. On May 5 an automatic transmitter within the probe should have sent signals to the Earth. It did not, and communications with the probe were switched off. Viking 1 was launched in August 1975 and landed on Mars on July 20, 1976.

Return to Mars. During the year both the U.S.S.R. and the U.S. continued plans for future probes to Mars. In the U.S. officials at NASA proposed a low-cost probe that would be launched in August 1990 and arrive at Mars in August 1991. Circling Mars in a polar orbit for two years at an altitude of 297.7 km (185 mi), it would gather climatic and soil chemistry data. Such data could then be compared with similar information gathered by probes some 15 years earlier. Primary scientific instrumentation would include a gamma-ray spectrometer, infrared reflectance spectrometer, radar altimeter, atmospheric sounder, and ultraviolet spectrometer/photometer.

Citing the relative amounts of data from Venus and Mars, Geoffrey A. Briggs, director of NASA's Solar System Exploration Committee, said, "We see Venus data that show a substantial loss of water on Venus through outgassing and on Mars we see dried-up river beds. We know Earth's present water state so we are trying to unravel what has happened on all three." He further added, "The mission will help us understand global circulation patterns, where the water is now and how it goes between atmosphere and surface. Then, having understood the situation today, we can go back and unravel the history."

The U.S.S.R. made known that it would launch a mission to Mars in 1986. It would be the first Soviet probe to that planet since 1973. A major mission would be to explore the Martian satellite Phobos. Placed in an orbit about Mars that would permit it to pass within a few thousand feet of Phobos, the probe would "fly in formation" with it, gathering data on the soil chemistry and taking high-resolution photographs of the surface.

Jupiter and Saturn. Tests made during the year on NASA's planned Galileo probe to Jupiter took place 30.8 km (19 mi) above the desert at White Sands Missile Range in New Mexico. A 50-story plastic balloon lifted the test component to that altitude and then released it for a nine-minute drop to the surface. The test proved that the main parachute would be fully open when the probe's heat shield separates from the instrument capsule. The success of the test was verified by visual observations from onboard cameras and also by telemetry.

As 1983 neared an end, NASA informed the European Space Agency that it needed to know by the end of the year if the latter wanted to participate in a cooperative mission to Saturn that would utilize backup components of a Galileo probe. Should no agreement be reached, then NASA would drop the option in favor of developing the Mariner MK 2 probe for a rendezvous with Comet Honda-Mrkos-Pajdusakova.

Preparing for Halley's Comet. A series of meetings throughout 1983 clarified plans for the multinational probing of Halley's Comet when it makes its nearest approach to Earth in 1986. The first conference took place in April in Kiev in the Soviet Union. It was attended by representatives of the U.S.S.R., Bulgaria, Hungary, Poland, Cuba, Czechoslovakia, East Germany, France, Japan, Austria, West Germany, ESA, and NASA. A meeting of the same group took place in Moscow in September, when the primary topic was the testing of instrumentation for probes that would investigate the comet. Key man in the discussions was A. R. Sagdeyev, director of the Soviet Academy of Sciences' Institute of Space Research and director of the U.S.S.R.'s Venus/Vega probe program. Among the information that he imparted was that the Venus/Vega probes, two of which were scheduled to be launched in 1984, would carry 130-kg (28 lb) payloads. The instrumentation was to be mounted on a special, stabilized platform developed by Czechoslovak engineers. It consisted of sensors to determine the structure of the comet's core, to identify primary molecules, to determine the elementary composition of dust particles, and to determine the chemical composition of the core.

NASA's contribution to the multinational effort continued to be minimal. The agency agreed to provide tracking service from its stations in the U.S., Spain, and Australia. However, work on NASA's cometary experiment with ISEE 3 (Interplanetary Sun Earth Explorer 3) continued throughout the year. Launched in 1978, ISEE 3 was later placed on a trajectory to make three swing-bys of the Moon in order to increase its acceleration for a rendezvous with Comet Giacobini-Zinner on Sept. 11, 1985. If all goes well with that encounter, the probe could move on to a rendezvous with Halley's Comet in the following year. The probe successfully made the critical swing-bys of the Moon, the last in December 1983, when it passed that body by only about 110 km (70 mi).

—Mitchell R. Sharpe

See also Feature Articles: SPACE: A NEW FRONTIER FOR INDUSTRY; THE SOVIET UNION IN SPACE; OCEANOGRAPHY IN ORBIT.

Transportation

Even though the economy of the United States was gradually pulling out of an extended recession during 1983 and 1984, the continuing high interest rates and cost of capital tended to put a damper on the introduction of new, technologically advanced transportation equipment and facilities. The impact of deregulation on transportation, including airlines, bus lines, railroads, trucking firms, and barge lines, resulted in a sharp increase in competition and, therefore, financial constraints in the area of research and development.

One common technological trend was the rapidly growing interest in computerization. This was taking place particularly in the administrative area in order to help facilitate the rate-making and rate-quoting processes for both passenger and freight services. Computerization for those purposes was being promoted in the U.S. by national transportation regulatory agencies such as the Civil Aeronautics Board, the Federal Maritime Commission, and the Interstate Commerce Commission.

Air transport. McDonnell Douglas Corp., citing the "continuing depressed state of the worldwide airline industry and the absence of evidence that the market for new aircraft is likely to improve significantly in the near term," canceled its proposed programs to develop and build three new commercial jet transports: MD-90, a two-engine, narrow-body, 100–125-seat craft to replace the DC-9; MD-100, a three-engine, wide-body, 270-seat, long-range plane to replace the DC-10; and D-3300, a 150-seat version not seriously considered during the past year. This decision left the two-engine, 150–170-seat, DC-9 Super 80 (now named MD-80) as the company's only active commercial transport aircraft.

The new PW4000 turbofan engine of Pratt & Whitney Corp. had been scheduled to be installed in the MD-100, but the company expressed optimism that it would be used in other new aircraft. The PW4000 was designed as a completely new engine and developed without any advance orders—a first according to Pratt & Whitney—as a replacement of the JT9D engine used on most wide-body air transports. Costing about $1.5 billion in research and development, the new engine should offer considerably better fuel economy through such improvements as faster engine rotational speeds, advanced compressor aerodynamics, reduced turbine cooling, and the use of electronic engine controls. Lower maintenance was expected because the PW4000 contains only half as many parts as the JT9D. Different versions were designed to provide thrust in the 21,790–27,000 kg (48,000–60,000 lb) range.

Boeing Co., the predominant U.S. builder of commercial air transports, delivered to the airlines its two new-generation transports, the wide-body B-767 and the narrow-body B-757. Both of these two-engine transports featured computerized cockpits and automated control of virtually all major flight operations and functions. Significant fuel savings were reported because of the extensive use of strong but light composite materials. Both aircraft, along with the European wide-body A310, also featured another technological innovation: All three used so-called fat wings, which generated less drag and thus permitted either higher speeds for the same power or higher payloads at the same speed. The wing also became a more efficient fuel tank, and its less-swept design could be built stiffer to withstand heavier flight loads.

Builders of general aviation aircraft for business purposes foresaw dramatic changes in the immediate future for both airframes and engines. Innovative designers and builders, such as Beech Aircraft Corp. and Gates Learjet Corp., announced that the newer craft would use turboprop engines—the propellers of which are driven by turbojet engines—that are far more fuel-efficient than are pure jets. Small wings would protrude from the nose of the fuselage, and the major wing would contain small vertical tipsails at each wingtip. The tipsails and ventral fin would replace a conventional vertical tail, with rudders on each tipsail providing direction control.

To provide more space for passengers the main wing would be located behind and above the cabin. To save weight and fuel, thus permitting higher speeds, the new craft would be built with extensive use of composites. The engines would be pushers, since they would be located behind the main wing, rather than pullers in front of the wing. With more powerful engines than the present ones the new-generation business transports—to be available in about three years—would cruise at about 645 km/h (400 mph), considerably faster than present aircraft.

The U.S. Federal Aviation Administration (FAA) began a $10 billion, ten-year modernization of the nation's air traffic control (ATC) system. The key to the program was to be the development and construction of a new generation of airport radar through a $480.5 million contract with the Westinghouse Electric Corp. The new, solid-state radar units were to replace the 20-year-old, vacuum-tube radar currently used at U.S. airports. Called ASR-9, the new Airport Surveillance Radar would provide weather data at six different levels of intensity, ranging from weak to extreme. It would thus give airway controllers information to help guide pilots away from severe weather conditions such as wind gusts, turbulence, lightning, and hail. The radar was designed to display both weather and aircraft simultaneously, which the old radar could only do separately. The new radar also would permit better detection of small, low-flying aircraft not equipped with transponders. Deliveries

The two new-generation commercial transports of the Boeing Co. include the narrow-body B-757 (top) and the wide-body B-767 (bottom). Each has two engines, computerized cockpits, and automated control of almost all major flight operations.

and installation at 137 U.S. airports were to begin in mid-1986.

IBM Corp. and Sperry Corp. were awarded competitive contracts—for $40.5 million and $35.6 million, respectively—to design new computers for the updated ATC system. The FAA was to select the better one after a 21-month test and award a $250 million contract to build the computers. The new computers would replace present hardware as well as modify software at the 20 centers that track aircraft along flight paths between airports. The old computers were based on 15-year-old technology.

Also planned for the future was a $2.5 billion program to replace the air traffic controllers' work stations and to design new software. Because the task is so complicated, corporate teams were formed to ensure technological capability. Competitive contracts were to be awarded in July 1984, with the final award for building the work stations and related software to be made in 1986.

Highway transport. Cubic Corp. of San Diego, Calif., a major provider of automatic fare collection systems for rail transit, developed a modular, fully integrated fare collection system for transit buses. Recognizing the financial constraints on local transit bus systems, the company adopted the "add-on" concept for its new product. By plugging in additional modules, transit firms could thus purchase a simple, basic system and then build up to a sophisticated one. This also provided flexibility to adjust to particular operational needs and to ensure that the transit company's fare system did not become obsolete.

Cubic's automated bus fare box was designed to do any, or all, of the following: accept both coins and paper money, even though a major objective was to minimize cash transactions; accept magnetically encoded fare cards, including those with stored value rides; accept special time-duration passes, along with inter-transit and intra-jurisdictional transfer passes; and provide data for audits, ridership analyses, route evaluations, and passenger volume counts. The fare box could also contain, if desired, a voice synthesizer to explain to riders the proper way to use the system if they insert cards incorrectly or with insufficient values to cover the fare. Cubic claimed that it had taken steps to ensure the reliability of the new fare box, which was scheduled to be ready for marketing to the transit industry by mid-1984.

Initial U.S. government testing of a fuel-saving device revealed that it failed to reach the expectations and claims of the inventors. A Chrysler Corp. test car equipped with the unique valve—which uses two bonded, wire-mesh screens that are designed to vaporize the fuel more thoroughly before it enters the cylinder—achieved 5% less fuel mileage than a duplicate car without the device. The test car also emitted 55% more hydrocarbons and 58% more carbon monoxide than it was reported to have done during initial trials. The inventors claimed that the government tests, carried out by the National Highway Traffic Safety Administration, were inconclusive and would support the initial findings before they were completed.

The Lubrizol Corp. claimed that extensive tests of 360 trucks traveling more than 92 million km (57 million mi) showed that operating efficiencies of 50% or more could be achieved by fleet operators who serviced their diesel engines with premium-

387

quality lubricants. The company was sending a two-vehicle caravan on a 80,000-km (50,000-mi) tour to demonstrate its findings and to allow interested truckers to inspect components—including cylinder liners, pistons, rings, and gear parts—from a sample of the vehicles participating in the road tests.

The Motor Vehicle Manufacturers Association reported on gains in heavy-duty truck efficiency and productivity through technological advances over the last several years. It said that the 4.5 miles per gallon generally accepted in the industry a short time ago for combination tractor-trailer units can now be raised to 6 miles per gallon. This has been made possible by new-generation, low-speed, fuel-saving diesel engines with drive trains and accessories that are designed to improve efficiency and also by advanced aerodynamic designs and the increased use of radial tires.

The association described the probable truck of the future as an "aerodynamic tractor-trailer made of lightweight, high-strength materials such as fiber-reinforced plastics or graphite fiber composites, powered by a sophisticated array of electronic controls to assure greatest fuel efficiency and minimum air pollution." Such a vehicle, it claimed, would contain onboard computers that control engine performance, shift gears, monitor engine and vehicle functions, and even give verbal instructions to the driver. The use of microprocessors would allow monitoring of tire pressure, brake systems, engine and exhaust temperatures, and oil and fuel levels. While these are relatively recent innovations for trucks, some were already in use in automobiles.

Pipelines. Marathon Pipe Line Co. began operating a centralized computer control system in Findlay, Ohio, that permitted 24-hour-a-day instant monitoring and control of movements of 1.5 million bbl per day of crude oil and refined products over a pipeline system 6,750 km (4,200 mi) long, extending from Wyoming and the upper Middle West to the Gulf of Mexico. Costing more than $3.5 million over three years of planning and building, the new center was designed to permit almost instantaneous control of movements throughout the network with the push of a few buttons.

The system provided monitoring and operation through three consoles, each with an analyst surveying one black-and-white and three color cathode-ray tubes. Marathon claimed that "if any event occurs at any of the status points across the network—every ticking meter, tank level, and valve opening—we know about it within 15 seconds," and that "within one second after the commands are given, the required action is initiated within the system, no matter how many hundreds of miles away the field device is from central control." Such capabilities are impressive, especially when it is recognized that the

Marathon Oil Company

Centralized computer system allows instant control of the movement of 1.5 million barrels of oil per day over 6,750 kilometers of pipeline.

company's network includes 11 trunk lines moving 65 different types of crude oil, 7 major refined-products lines moving 15 grades of products, and 100 shipment batches a day through pipelines ranging from 15–90 cm (6–36 in) in diameter.

Petroleum pipelines were finding that by mixing special polymer additives to the petroleum moving through their lines they could reduce the amount of drag sharply, thus allowing either greater flow without more pump pressures or the maintenance of existing flow with less operating pressures. Such an innovation—first tried successfully on a large-scale basis in commercial application on the 120-cm (48-in)-diameter Trans-Alaska Pipe Line System in mid-1979—provides a relatively inexpensive alternative to expanding capacity or upgrading the line's operating pressure limit.

According to pipeline spokesmen, drag is caused by frictional pressure from small particles in the petroleum flow that move in irregular, random motions transverse to the direction of the flow and create eddy currents at the pipe wall that move toward the center of the pipe. By injecting a drag-reducing additive—usually high-molecular-weight hydrocarbon polymers—these eddy currents are weakened and reduced, thereby also reducing the drag. The more turbulent the flow, the more effective the additive.

According to Continental Pipe Line Co. of Houston, Texas, a simple mechanical installation will permit the injection of the drag-reducing additive into the pipeline. The firm cautioned, however, that because flow through a mainline pump breaks up the polymer and eliminates the effectiveness of the drag reducer, the additive must be injected downstream of each pump station.

Despite rejection by the U.S. House of Representatives of another attempt to pass legislation that would give backers of coal-slurry pipelines the right of eminent domain to build interstate lines that cross railroad rights-of-way, advocates of such lines continued to voice optimism that they would be built soon. They claimed that the necessary technology had been developed and that such lines would reduce significantly the transport costs of utilities.

A new study by the Virginia Society of Professional Engineers reported that the cost of moving one ton of coal through a coal-slurry pipeline from mines in southeastern Virginia to Hampton Roads on the state's Atlantic coast would be about 40% less than the cost of transport by railroad. The study noted that the great need for water in such a line—a ton of water to move a ton of coal—was a potential drawback (especially in the water-sparse western portions of the U.S.), but pointed out that adequate water supplies were available in Virginia. Recycling of the water would be possible, where necessary, but at an increased cost of about 25%. Other advantages included a minimum of environmental disruption from an underground pipeline and virtually no operational noise.

In a related development the Electric Power Research Institute reported success in tests involving use of coal-water slurry as a new fuel, following completion of a 35-day continuous burn in an industrial boiler of a Memphis, Tenn., plant owned by the Du Pont Co. The slurry contained a mix of 70% crushed coal, 29% water, and 1% special additives that kept it stable during transportation and in storage tanks. Slurrytech Inc., a participant in the project along with the U.S. Environmental Protection Agency and Bechtel Corp., said that the additives proved so successful that it lost only 1% of the coal (from vibrations that cause the coal to "settle out" of the slurry) during the transport of 400 tons over the 1,600 km (1,000 mi) to the project site.

Rail transport. With financial assistance from both federal and state/local governments, as well as private business groups, high-speed passenger-train service was being seriously studied for a number of U.S. corridors, including Las Vegas–Los Angeles, Orlando–Tampa–Miami, Philadelphia–Pittsburgh, Montreal–New York City, and Chicago–Detroit. The First Boston Corp., under contract with the recently formed American High Speed Rail Corp., claimed that a $2.9-billion service between Los Angeles and San Diego could be financed without taxpayer aid.

The Budd Co., which had exclusive marketing rights to the West German Maglev high-speed system in the U.S., reported the beginning of full-scale tests with several 200-passenger Maglev vehicles on a 32-km (20-mi) track in Emsland, West Germany, as the "final step of a ten-year development program." According to Budd such a train—which travels along an elevated guideway through use of electromagnets that lift, guide, and propel the vehicles at speeds up to 400 km/h (250 mph)—could carry about 3.2 million passengers annually along the 370-km (230-mi) Los Angeles–Las Vegas corridor on 70-minute trips. (For additional information, *see* Feature Article: *Lightning on the Rails.*)

An advanced-technology, multipurpose locomotive simulator was built by the IIT Research Institute in Chicago for the purpose of offering the railroad industry a national center for training engineers and for generating data to provide safer, more fuel-efficient train handling. It consisted of a locomotive cab and separate control room, and it contained an audiovisual system providing realistic front, side, and rear views. It was capable of simulating one to ten head-end power units and one to five remote units for trains of up to 150 cars in length and operating at speeds up to 160 km/h (100 mph).

The deregulation of railroad trailer-on-flatcar and container-on-flatcar (TOFC/COFC) traffic stimulated the introduction and use of a variety of lightweight flatcars, including skeletonized, articulated, and drop-bottom versions—mostly to reduce weight for fuel economy. The growth in this traffic was impressive, with gains of 20% reported by U.S. railroads in 1983 compared with 3.5% for overall freight.

American President Lines, a major U.S.-flag ocean carrier operating in the Pacific, announced that it had become the first shipping company to purchase its own railroad cars. As a means of promoting and improving its international overseas container service, it ordered three train sets of new custom-designed, lightweight COFC cars to handle the U.S. domestic segment of the service. Each train was to be made up of 20 articulated, low-profile cars; each car would comprise 5 platforms able to carry 10 containers stacked two-high for a total of 200 containers per train. Since each car weighs 60% less than a conventional COFC car, fewer locomotives would be needed per train and major energy savings would be possible. APL planned to inaugurate the first new train set in early 1984 and phase in the other two a few months later. They were to provide service between Los Angeles and New York or Chicago.

Railroads were testing a new version of the "Glasshopper," a hopper car made of fiberglass-reinforced polyester to reduce weight and save fuel without loss of payload. Sponsored by Cargill, Inc., ACF Industries, Inc., and the Southern Pacific Transportation Co.,

Courtesy, IIT Research Institute

Multipurpose locomotive simulator is a training device that consists of a locomotive cab, separate control room, and an audiovisual system providing realistic front, rear, and side views.

the new version weighed 15,545 kg (34,200 lb) as compared with 19,545 kg (43,000 lb) for the old. This was accomplished largely by eliminating inside bulkheads, which could be done because the cars were to be used for handling only one commodity, such as coal or grain, and thus had no need for dividers to separate commodities.

The Chessie System announced that it was testing a new type of coal-carrying car especially designed to expedite unloading at ports. The 100-ton-capacity cars were built with a twin-pod, round bottom to permit rapid dumping of the entire load by rotary dumpers that can lift and turn the car—and which were already in service at most ports served by the Chessie. The cars were 10% lighter than conventional hoppers yet could handle 10% greater loads. The reduced weight resulted from the use of thinner body sheets and an interior free of cross bracing. The new car was 17.8 cm (7 in) lower in height than conventional models with a lower center of gravity, and its interior was coated with a polymer resin that reduced damage from corrosion and also inhibited coal from freezing in the cars during the winter. Another advantage of the coating was an expected five-year increase in car life.

Union Tank Car Co. was hoping to capture frozen fruit juice traffic from trucking firms through the use of a unique "Sandwich Car." It contained an inner tank surrounded by one foot of urethane-foam insulation to prevent loss of the freezing temperature and subsequent thawing of the juice. The test shipment from Lake Wales, Fla., to Fullerton, Calif., was received at the tank car at a temperature of −16 to −13° C (4 to 9° F), and it arrived ten days later at a temperature of −10° C (14° F) even though outside temperatures along the route were over 32° C (90° F).

Water transport. Economy of scale continued to be applied to ocean containerships, with major operators visualizing the "ideal" containership of the late 1980s as one able to transport 1,500 12-m (40-ft) containers at average speeds of 16–20 knots, using slow-speed diesel engines for economy; it would be operated with crews of 20–25 persons, about one-third of current manning levels. This would be possible because all operations and maintenance would be aided by automation and mechanization. In 1984 United States Lines had on order in South Korean shipyards 12 so-called super-containerships, each of which was designed to be able to handle 4,200 6-m (20-ft) units. The largest ships of U.S. liner carriers at present could carry only 1,800 such containers.

The U.S. Maritime Administration chose Farrell Lines to test four large open-top container frames for the handling in containerships of oversized cargoes such as cranes, pipe, and transport equipment. Each frame weighed 30 tons when empty and could carry 100 tons of cargo. The frames could be stacked four-high in a ship's hold and could support, through the use of adapter beams, 12-m containers on their tops.

Japanese shipowners and shipyards were cooperating with the Japanese Transport Ministry to develop high-technology ships that emphasized increased efficiency by means of automation and computerization. The top priority was the development of an experimental "supership" as the prototype for the 21st century. This project was expected to cost $83 million, and emphasis was to be placed on use of high-technology operating and maintenance equipment that would allow crew levels to be held to ten or less. The need for highly reliable, low-maintenance engines was considered vital to the success of the project, since low-quality oil must be used to hold down costs at the same time that the ships were operating under rigorous conditions at sea.

The first coal-fired steamship built in the U.S. since 1929 was launched and fitted at the Quincy, Mass., shipyard of General Dynamics Corp. for service between Norfolk–Baltimore–Philadelphia ports and power plants along the Massachusetts coast. The ship was built for the New England Electric System, which was converting some of its power plants from oil to coal and therefore decided to build such a ship as a means of transporting its coal. The $73 million "Energy Independence" is 200 m (665 ft) in length and transports 36,250 tons of coal. The coal is loaded and unloaded automatically through the use of two conveyor belts that extend the length of the vessel and feed the coal onto a covered boom 80 m (260 ft) in length. The 250 tons of coal needed for a round trip are fed into the engines from a separate hold. The clouds of black smoke that belched from stacks of old coal-fired ships are replaced by a gray plume, the builders claimed, and they foresaw no environmental problems. Other large coal-fired ocean ships were expected to be operating soon, with five under construction at shipyards in Japan and Italy.

The development of sail-rigged ships to complement engines and thus cut fuel consumption by as much as 50% for vessels of equal size and capacity continued to receive high priority in Japan, a nation almost fully dependent on foreign fuel supplies. One of the most recent projects was the construction by Japan Marine Equipment Development Association of the world's first large sail-rigged bulk carrier, at a cost of $11.7 million, for Tanaka Industries, Ltd. The new ship was to have a capacity of 26,000 deadweight tons and would be 25.2 m (83.2 ft) wide and 152 m (501.6 ft) long. Its two sails were to be computer-controlled and their use synchronized with the ship's main engines. No additional seamen would be required for handling the sails, since all furling, unfurling, and trimming would be done automatically by a microcomputer. The top speed of the ship was designed to be 13.5 knots.

The Canadian Coast Guard, in cooperation with maritime and petroleum interests, was planning the construction of "the world's most powerful icebreak-er ship" to permit year-round movements of oil and gas tankers in the Canadian Arctic by the end of the 1980s. The $340 million "Polar Eight" would be equipped with engines able to generate 100,000 hp, enough to enable the ship to break up ice 2.4 m (8 ft) thick with the specially designed steel plates on its bow. As of 1984 the Soviet Union had the largest icebreaker ships, with nuclear engines that generated 75,000 hp. The Canadian government planned to assist the project directly through its already established system of ice mapping—made possible by the use of satellites and radar-equipped survey aircraft that are able to transmit continuous, up-to-date information to both icebreakers and cargo ships utilizing the cleared shipping lanes.

—Frank A. Smith

U.S. science policy

The *Wall Street Journal*, in its issue of June 6, 1983, reported with satisfaction that a team of scientists studying the habits of the manatee, or sea cow, at the National Institute of Amazonian Research in Brazil, owed their discovery of an important fact about their specimens to the lack of sufficient financial support to purchase adequate holding facilities. Instead of making use of large filtered aquariums, the scientists were forced to improvise with large plastic swimming pools that had to be drained and cleaned weekly.

During one weekly scouring a member of the team discovered cast-off manatee teeth, from which the researchers were able to deduce that the manatee replaced its worn-down incisors from the rear, like a conveyor belt. That deduction led to still anoth-

The SS "Energy Independence," the first coal-burning steamship built in the U.S. since 1929, can transport 36,250 tons of coal. Cargo is loaded and unloaded automatically by means of two conveyor belts extending the length of the vessel. The coal needed to fuel the ship is supplied from a separate hold.

Courtesy, General Dynamics, Quincy Shipbuilding Division, Quincy, Mass.

er, this from the editors of the *Wall Street Journal*: "[T]hrowing money at science isn't always the way to make progress. Sometimes discovery comes about because funds are short."

That comforting view is not widely held within the research community; on the contrary, the prevailing view of the scientific leadership has been that the national scientific enterprise, in the words of the editor of *Science* magazine, would fall into "mindless disarray" without substantial and continuing federal funding.

Such fears were widely expressed after severe reductions in the support of academic research took place under the administrations of Presidents Lyndon Johnson and Richard Nixon. Encouraging restorations occurred during the presidencies of Gerald Ford and Jimmy Carter. (The federal funding of science has been remarkably insensitive to changes in political party.)

The arrival of Ronald Reagan as president in 1981, however, with his promises to slash federal budgets and bureaucracy, sent shivers of concern through most of academic science. There appeared to be ample justification for this reaction in the early Reagan budgets, but later the Reagan bark, at least as far as science was concerned, was proving to be far worse than its bite. For example, the proposed fiscal year 1984 federal budget called for a 17% increase over 1983 for research and development (R and D) funding, including a 10% increase in support for basic research. The growth since fiscal 1982 in funding R and D was 25%, and for basic research it was 22%.

The early apprehension about overall funding was by 1984 giving way to a different concern—the rapid shift of funding from civilian to military research. In fiscal 1980 civilian R and D funding exceeded that for the military, $16.6 billion to $15.1 billion. In fiscal 1984, however, the administration proposed to spend twice as much for defense-related R and D, $30 billion, with no significant change in the nonmilitary sector.

George E. Brown, Jr., a Democratic congressman from California who maintained a watchful eye over science funding, expressed the reservations of many of his constituents when the 1984 budget was revealed. "I don't want to be a spoiler," he said, "but I think we have to put the administration's proposals into perspective and take a critical look at overall trends and priorities."

He pointed out that even within the static budget for nondefense R and D, almost all the increases went into the so-called hard sciences and into science education and scientific instrumentation. By contrast, programs in health, energy, space, social sciences, and the environment either were cut or were held to the fiscal 1983 levels.

Finally, even within the civilian R and D sector there were important distinctions to be noted in the treatment accorded to R, research, and D, development. While the totals remained the same, there were significant currents moving from D toward R. The view of the administration was that civilian industry should be expected to assume more of the expense of applied research and development, while the government would retain primary responsibility for basic research, performed principally in academic institutions.

It must be noted that industry supported R and D at a rate higher than that of the federal government. Battelle Memorial Institute, in its year-end roundup, predicted that overall R and D expenditures for 1984 would reach $94.2 billion. Industrial funding was expected to increase more significantly than government support, so that it would account for more than half the total.

On the other hand, industry was also getting a bigger bite of the federal budget, mostly through huge military development programs. A report from the National Science Foundation (NSF), issued in April, showed that industry was receiving 56% of federal R and D funds, compared with less than 50% throughout most of the 1970s. Overall, private industry was expected to perform more than three-quarters of all U.S. R and D in 1984.

The politics of science. U.S. scientific bodies have historically sought to avoid any activity that smacked of lobbying, even though the practice is a major industry in the nation's capital. Some of the research community's best friends in Washington have despaired over the lack of organized political support that they receive when doing legislative battle. "Scientists and engineers treat politics as if it were some kind of social disease," observed Sen. Paul Tsongas (Dem., Mass.). Representative Brown of California, who may be one of the most effective friends of science on Capitol Hill, warned scientists to overcome their elitism: "They have to be aggressive in getting their message across to the political community. They can't act as if it's beneath them." Frank Press, president of the National Academy of Sciences and science adviser to Jimmy Carter, added, "When I compare it to the smooth operation of other lobbies, it's incoherent and disorganized."

A report from the *Congressional Quarterly*, issued in March, suggested that times were changing. Although individual scientists had organized successful lobbies in the past for new fields, such as high-energy physics and oceanography, it took the Reagan budgetary slashes into the social and behavioral sciences to give birth to the first successful disciplinary strike force. It was COSSA, the Consortium of Social Science Associations, formed in 1981 to campaign against a proposed 75% cut in the social-science budget of the

NSF and equally savage reductions aimed at social-science activities in the health agencies.

Social scientists found a handy and effective lever in the acknowledged value of economic data to government planners. When a director of the University of Michigan's renowned Institute for Social Research (ISR) was invited by the White House Office of Management and Budget (OMB) to assist in the analysis of ISR data, he took pains to point out that the president's budget did not provide for the data to be available next year.

OMB quietly sent word to the appropriations committees that it would not object vigorously to restoration of some of the funding cuts. COSSA maintained the pressure, and in fiscal 1984 the White House proposed a 12.5% increase in the NSF budget for the social and behavioral sciences. Since this increase still did not return the funding level to that of fiscal 1980, the social scientists were far from satisfied, but they had demonstrated beyond question that a well-organized lobby worked as well for scientists as it did for milk producers.

Before the year was over, however, it appeared to some as though the scientific community, despite its late entry into the political swim, was already in over its head. It all started in May, when the Washington lobbying firm of Schlossberg-Cassidy and Associates successfully engineered a floor amendment in Congress to a House authorizations bill for the Department of Energy. The amendment provided start-up funding for research facilities at Columbia and Catholic universities. The projects were not only unfamiliar to House members voting on the bill, they were also not even known to the Department of Energy.

This legislative technique was hardly new to Capitol Hill. What was new was its use for scientific research facilities. Traditionally, federal funding for such purposes is provided after some form of consultation with other scientists in relevant disciplines—

a peer review. One of the privileges historically accorded to the scientific enterprise by the federal government, the peer-review system allows scientists to decide which of its many pleas for support are most worthy. Catholic and Columbia had not only made an end run around peer review, they had apparently scored a touchdown.

By the end of the year, Schlossberg-Cassidy had similarly won preliminary approval for a $7.5 million library for Boston College and almost rang up $15 million for an engineering laboratory at Boston University. They also were receiving considerable business from other institutions.

At the same time, however, the lobbying firm had worked up a storm of indignation from nonclients who felt that a familiar but fragile mechanism for parceling out federal funds was about to be irreparably shattered. Even worse, the floor amendments authorizing funds for the Catholic and Columbia facilities identified several previously authorized projects of other institutions that were to be stripped in order to provide the necessary funds.

It was not long before the offended institutions went public with their outrage. In October a dean at the University of Maryland wrote to the *New York Times*, pointing out that Columbia University was already well provided for within the peer-review system and asking, "Is all this 'business as usual' or retrogressive? In the opinion of a number of observers in Washington, it is definitely the latter. . . . The Washington spokesmen for the scientific and educational communities must work to reverse the drift toward politicization of the process for supporting scientific research."

The first protests came before the month was over and, naturally enough, from those who had most to lose in any attack on the peer-review system. The Association of American Universities, whose members are the elite of U.S. research institutions, is-

Mitchell Wallerstein of the U.S. National Research Council speaks at the seminar "National Security and Scientific Communication: An Update." During the year scientists were urged to become more aggressive in expressing their views to the government.

Jeffrey Ruth

sued a carefully worded statement asking scientists, university administrators, and Congress "to refrain from actions that would make scientific decisions a test of political influence rather than a judgment on the quality of work to be done." Within a week the National Academy of Sciences added its voice, urging "vigilance" to protect "this informed evaluation and decision-making process." By the end of the year they were joined by the American Physical Society, the National Association of State Universities and Land Grant Colleges, and the American Association for the Advancement of Science.

Only Schlossberg-Cassidy spoke up for itself. Said Kenneth Schlossberg: "It ill behooves those who are rich in research resources to tell others, who are not, that they should not pursue the only legal, ethical route open to them to meet their pressing needs." Added Gerald S. J. Cassidy: "I don't believe members of Congress are going to sit by and watch that need [for funding of research facilities] be unfulfilled because of some ideal people have regarding this. It is not a research question at all; it is an economic question." Indeed, considering the scarcity of bricks-and-mortar money for university laboratories during the past decade, it may even be a question of survival, all around.

Academe and industry. A mutually beneficial relationship between industry and the major research institutions has existed since about 1900. Recently, however, that relationship has threatened to become a powerful determinant of university research. In the past university professors whose research had led them to promising technologies were encouraged to establish private corporations close to the campus. Thus developed such industrial money-makers as Hewlett-Packard Co. and Itek Corp.

But for more than a decade, as their own research funding began to shrink, universities have looked more and more covetously at the profits made by such spin-off groups. The result has been a growing body of multiyear, multimillion-dollar research agreements between corporations and university-based research.

The research universities have expressed their concern that these highly profitable arrangements might result in a loss of their independence. During the past year the National Science Board, chief policy apparatus of the NSF, also sounded a cautionary note:

If the university moves nearer to a partnership with industry, more resources become available, but the university may relinquish some of its unique capabilities for unrestricted exploratory research and freedom of action. There are no absolutes, and the issues become matters of degree and common sense. The primary requirement, therefore, is not so much increased partnership, but increased understanding of each other's role. That is the ultimate basis for a healthy strengthening of university and industry cooperation.

Just how close a university can come to a full entrepreneurial partnership with a private firm and how profitable that partnership can be to both parties were illustrated by two leading research institutions in early 1984. In February Harvard University announced that it had granted an exclusive license to one firm, Biogen, to use a genetic-engineering technique for the manufacture of insulin. The technique had been developed at Harvard by Walter Gilbert and had been one of the reasons that Gilbert received a Nobel Prize. Gilbert also had a part-time relationship with Biogen, one of the firms spawned by the development of recombinant DNA (deoxyribonucleic acid) technology. Biogen offered to pay the legal fees associated with obtaining a patent on the process. In 1981 Gilbert left Harvard to become chief executive officer of Biogen. The cost to Biogen of obtaining what may be one of the most lucrative licenses in genetic engineering was, according to the *New York Times*, about $500,000.

Across the continent Stanford University was also reaping the rewards of a first-class scientific department. As the result of a favorable decision by the U.S. Patent Office, Stanford and the University of California had licensed a genetic-engineering technique to 68 different companies; by Feb. 1, 1984, fees from those firms to the two universities had reached more than $3 million. Stanford was also eagerly awaiting the completion of a Center for Integrated Systems, the $14,250,000 cost of which was being met by a combination of 19 U.S. computer and electronics firms.

Other developments. As it has so often in the past, science once more followed science fiction in 1983. Not too long after the development of the first atomic bomb, an author conjured up the idea of a "doomsday machine." Buried in some secret place on the surface of the Earth, it was triggered to explode if any atomic bomb were detonated on the Earth. Its power was so great that it would destroy all life on Earth. Its message was all too clear: the first nation to use an atomic weapon would be committing suicide.

In October a worldwide group of scientists announced that the very size of modern nuclear arsenals had, in effect, created a real doomsday machine. According to their findings any moderate exchange of nuclear weapons would produce a "nuclear winter," a cloud of dust so impenetrable to solar radiation that all warm-blooded animals would perish in the frigid aftermath. (For an extended discussion of this subject *see* Year in Review: ENVIRONMENT.)

Futures somewhat less apocalyptic were offered by the Environmental Protection Agency and the National Academy of Sciences. In reports issued within a week of each other both organizations warned that new studies only served to confirm earlier predic-

"That's how Research and Development put the pressure on. First they hustle you to promise them results. Then they hustle you some more to promise them results in our lifetime!"

tions that the increasing burden of carbon dioxide in the atmosphere would indeed produce the so-called greenhouse effect, thus raising average global temperatures to an extent that severe worldwide flooding and an increase in the area afflicted by drought would result. The studies differed only in that the Academy study saw less need for hasty action.

On the other hand the Academy found it necessary to back off once again on the relationship between fluorocarbon use and a predicted decrease in the ozone layer that shields the Earth from the harmful effects of ultraviolet radiation from the Sun. In a report issued in 1979 it predicted a whopping 15 to 18% reduction—enough to seriously affect the U.S. market for the chemical. Three years later the Academy declared that the decrease would be more in the order of 5 to 9%. In 1984, in an effective demonstration that science progresses through a self-correcting process, the Academy predicted that the reduction would be more like 2 to 4%.

The Academy had occasion in 1983 to reexamine a study that it had completed in 1982. In this case the earlier study reported that, although there was some threat to national security in the uncontrolled leakage of high-technology data to the Soviet Union and its allies, virtually none of that leakage occurred in the conduct of university-based research. Therefore, the Academy had said, there was no need to impose severe restrictions on the exchange of scientific information, especially at the level of fundamental research, except in a few specific "gray areas."

By the end of 1983, however, it appeared that the Academy's advice had been largely ignored and that the government had imposed relatively severe restrictions on all levels of scientific communication. As the new year began, the leaders of academic science began to marshal their forces in opposition to the new policies.

A Louis Harris survey published near the end of the year had far better news for university research groups. According to the poll 68% of the U.S. public favored increased federal support for basic research, even at a time of budgetary stringency. Furthermore, about 70% of Capitol Hill agreed. On the other hand, some aspects of technology worried the respondents—specifically, the perceived threat to privacy in an increasingly computerized society. Three out of four found that worrisome on the eve of 1984.

A number of distinguished scientists found another cause of worry: a White House decision in March to go ahead with a massive plan to develop weapons aimed at protecting the U.S. against nuclear attack from satellites and strategic missiles. The most outspoken opposition came from a group of scientists who had been associated with both weapons development and arms control during previous administrations, but even the National Academy of Sciences declined to assist the White House in identifying scientists for membership on planning groups. Negative reactions were based chiefly on three factors: the domain of space is now free of weaponry and should be kept that way, the systems probably will not work, and history shows that every defensive weapon system will shortly be overcome by new—or simply more—offensive weapons.

The White House science office and the Department of Defense rejected these arguments, pointing out that their own study groups had found reason to be optimistic about the long-range potential of the development program. They believed that $18 billion to $27 billion could be spent through the end of the decade in pursuit of the president's goals.

Another White House project, a manned orbiting space station, was announced in President Reagan's state of the union message in February 1984. The administration favored the project despite negative reviews from many space researchers.

A final note was one of harmony. After strenuous complaints from the Palomar Mountain Observatory in California that San Diego's new high-pressure sodium street lights were virtually blinding their instruments, the city fathers reversed their previous position and agreed to use low-pressure lights despite the complaint that they made people "look like cadavers."

—Howard J. Lewis

Scientists of the Year

Honors and awards

The following article discusses recent awards and prizes in science and technology. In the first section the Nobel Prizes for 1983 are described in detail, while the second is a selective list of other honors.

Nobel Prize for Chemistry

The 1983 Nobel Prize for Chemistry was awarded to Henry Taube of Stanford (Calif.) University, who has devoted more than three decades to investigations of the structures and reactions of dissolved inorganic compounds, particularly oxidation-reduction reactions, in which electrons are transferred from one atom to another. He has been especially successful in developing general principles by which the patterns and rates of the reactions of metallic compounds can be correlated with their electronic structures. His interpretations of these phenomena have been widely adopted by other scientists as guides in selecting metallic compounds for such uses as catalysts, pigments, and superconductors and in understanding the essential functions of metal ions that are present in the molecules of many substances that are involved in biological processes.

Metals differ from the other chemical elements in that one or more of the electrons present in their atoms are only weakly attracted to the nucleus. In the compounds of metals some or all of these loosely bound electrons have been removed or shared with other atoms, and the originally neutral atom has been converted to a positively charged ion. The number of electrons lost is commonly designated the oxidation state of the element. Several metals form series of compounds in which the oxidation state has different

Henry Taube

values, each corresponding to the loss of a specific number of electrons. Iron, for example, forms two series of compounds in which the oxidation states are 2 and 3: the light green crystalline salt called ferrous chloride or iron(II) chloride, which has the formula $FeCl_2$, and the deep yellow salt called ferric chloride or iron(III) chloride, which has the formula $FeCl_3$, are members of the two series.

When metallic compounds are dissolved in water, the positive ions may form stable chemical bonds with several surrounding neutral molecules, such as those of the water itself or ammonia, or with negative ions, such as chloride, fluoride, or bromide. The ions or molecules attached to the central atom are called ligands, and the number of bonds they form with the central atom is called the coordination number. The aggregates of central atoms and clusters of ligands may be neutral or electrically charged, and many of them retain their identity in solution or even when they separate from the solvent during the formation of crystalline solids. When these complex or coordination compounds were first discovered, in the late 18th century, theories of the structures of chemical compounds had not yet been worked out, and their properties could not be explained by any recognized rules.

The Swiss chemist Alfred Werner studied the series of compounds formed when cobalt(III) chloride, $CoCl_3$, is dissolved in water and treated with ammonia. He could identify five distinct products, differing in color, in which the number of ammonia molecules per atom of cobalt ranged between three and six (two of the compounds contained four molecules of ammonia). His analyses of the firmness with which the ammonia molecules and chloride ions were bound to the cobalt atom led Werner to conclude that the cobalt(III) ion must have a coordination number of six; the existence of the two compounds containing four molecules of ammonia suggested to him that the bonds between the ligands and the cobalt ion are directed in space. Werner was awarded the Nobel Prize for Chemistry in 1913 for his interpretation of the structures of this class of inorganic compounds.

For a long time thereafter chemists suspected that water molecules could act as ligands in the same fashion as ammonia molecules or chloride ions, but direct proof was lacking because there was no way of distinguishing bonded water molecules from those present in the surrounding solvent. In the late 1940s Taube carried out experiments with isotopes, showing that in water solution the ions of metals do indeed form chemical bonds with several molecules of water and that the rates at which one ligand replaces another vary greatly, depending on the identity and oxidation state of the metal. He also helped to develop other techniques for studying coordination compounds that he and other inorganic chemists used in delineating the mechanisms by which they react—the individual collisions between atoms or molecules and the other elementary processes that take place simultaneously or in sequence during the course of transforming a given set of chemical species to another. Studies of reaction mechanisms must account for the rates at which the starting materials disappear and the products appear and for the geometrical arrangement of the constituents of complex substances.

Taube's initial investigations were summarized in a classic article, published in 1952, in which he interpreted the properties and reactions of a large number of coordination compounds in terms of the known distributions of the least tightly bound electrons of the metal ions.

In the oxidation or reduction of one metal ion by another, one or more electrons are exchanged between the two ions. Many such reactions occur rapidly, even when the ions are combined in coordination compounds. It might be expected that the cluster of water molecules or other ligands would keep the metal ions from getting close enough to one another for electrons to be exchanged directly. Taube's further research showed that, in an intermediate stage of many such reactions, a chemical bond forms between one of the metal ions and a ligand that is still bonded to the other. This ligand acts as a temporary bridge between the two ions, and its bond to the original metal ion later breaks in such a way as to bring about the transfer of the electrons.

Taube, who was born on Nov. 30, 1915, in Neudorf, Sask., earned bachelor's and master's degrees in chemistry at the University of Saskatchewan, Saskatoon, and in 1940 he gained his Ph.D. at the University of California, Berkeley. He taught for a year at Berkeley; from 1941 until 1946 at Cornell University, Ithaca, N.Y.; and from 1946 until 1961 at the University of Chicago. He joined the faculty of Stanford, where he is now Marguerite Blake Wilbur

Professor of Chemistry, in 1961. He became a U.S. citizen in 1942.

Nobel Prize for Physics

The Nobel Prize for Physics in 1983 was divided equally between two U.S. astrophysicists. Subrahmanyan Chandrasekhar of the University of Chicago and William A. Fowler of the California Institute of Technology, Pasadena, both of whom have devoted long and distinguished careers to the investigation of processes that take place during the evolution of stars. Their studies have been complementary rather than collaborative, focusing on classes of events that involve entirely different scales of magnitude but interact closely in affecting the overall history of individual celestial objects. Chandrasekhar clarified the macroscopic phenomena that influence the whole mass of a star during the successive periods of its existence; for example, his calculations have shown how the mass of a star controls its eventual transformation into one or another of the very dense bodies called white dwarf stars, neutron stars, and black holes. At the other extreme Fowler devoted his attention to the microscopic realm of the nuclear reactions that account for the generation of energy and the changes in the chemical composition of stars during successive stages of their lives. He and his co-workers developed a highly detailed scheme that provides a plausible account of the formation of all of the known chemical elements in their observed relative abundances.

The direct antecedents of Chandrasekhar's first major discovery extend back to 1844, when the German astronomer Friedrich Wilhelm Bessel reported that the nearby bright star Sirius follows a wavy path through the sky and concluded that it must be a member of a pair of stars that orbit each other in the same way that the Earth and the Moon are known to do. Bessel's telescopes were not powerful

Subrahmanyan Chandrasekhar
William A. Fowler

enough for him to see the second body, but from his measurements of the motion of Sirius itself he could calculate that the mass of its unseen partner must be about the same as that of the Sun.

The U.S. astronomer Alvan Clark (who with his sons supplied the lenses mounted in the largest refracting telescopes ever built) saw this very faint star—called Sirius *comes* (Latin for "companion") or Sirius B—in 1862. In 1915 another American, Walter Sydney Adams, used the 60-in reflecting telescope at Mt. Wilson, California, to measure the spectrum of Sirius B. The spectra of stars reveal a great deal of information about their chemical composition and also indicate their surface temperatures; Adams's results showed that Sirius B is hotter than the Sun, and so its surface must be very bright. Adams concluded that the star is faint only because its surface area is small; its volume must be similar to that of the Earth. For a star to have the same mass as the Sun but only the size of the Earth, its density must be about 100,000 times that of water. Thus, Sirius B was the densest object that had ever been observed.

Arthur Eddington of the U.K., one of the leading astronomers and physicists of that era, pointed out to Adams in 1924 that the gravitational field of an object as small and dense as Sirius B should be so intense that, according to Einstein's general theory of relativity, the light the star emits should have slightly longer wavelengths than light emitted by a body of the same temperature and composition but of ordinary density. Adams reexamined the spectrum and found that, indeed, the wavelengths were shifted to the extent required by Einstein's theory. This result led Eddington to pursue a theoretical investigation of the structure of matter under the physical conditions that exist in Sirius B.

Solids, liquids, and gases—the forms of matter common at the surface of the Earth—are composed of atoms in which most of the electrons remain confined within a region of space surrounding each nucleus. The volume of this region is millions of times greater than that of the nucleus itself, and under terrestrial conditions the atoms strongly resist being squeezed so closely together that their electron clouds overlap. But in flames and lightning bolts—and the interiors of stars—the motions of electrons and nuclei become so energetic (as indicated by the high temperatures) that the atomic structure disintegrates and the matter turns into a plasma, a chaotic assemblage of electrically charged particles.

Eddington had previously solved an important problem concerning the internal structure of giant stars, which are much less dense than white dwarfs, the name adopted for stars like Sirius B. He had assumed that the giant stars were composed entirely of plasma that has the mechanical properties of a gas. He further assumed that at every point within such stars there must be an exact balance between the contractive force of gravity and the expansive forces of gas pressure and radiation pressure. On these bases Eddington had derived a mathematical relationship (called an equation of state) expressing the dependence of pressure, density, and temperature upon the distance from the center of a star of given mass and chemical composition.

When Eddington applied his theory to the case of Sirius B, he found that the calculated density agreed with the value deduced by Adams. He then reasoned that a star in such a state would remain dense while it cooled, emitting electromagnetic radiation. The cooling process, however, would represent the loss of so much of the internal energy of the star that when the nuclei and electrons slowed down enough to recombine into atoms, the accompanying expansion—requiring the expenditure of further energy against the gravitational attraction—would not be possible. This state of affairs seemed to imply that the matter would be stable at low temperatures and extremely high densities.

Eddington was puzzled by this outcome, but he was reassured by an explanation offered in 1926 by one of his colleagues at Cambridge, Ralph Howard Fowler (no relation to the Nobel laureate of 1983). Fowler recognized that the classical physical principles underlying Eddington's analysis do not apply to extremely dense systems; he determined that quantum statistical mechanics should be valid. Fowler used the latter method, which had just been introduced by Enrico Fermi and Paul A. M. Dirac, to derive a new expression for the physical properties of matter in white dwarf stars. As Fowler had expected, his result differed from Eddington's; in particular, the Fermi-Dirac statistics indicated that the cooling of a white dwarf would not affect the density and pressure but would result in a cold plasma in which the electrons do not recombine with the nuclei. Fowler's calculations further suggested that a star of any mass could contract to a white dwarf.

Chandrasekhar, as an undergraduate in India, had studied Einstein's special and general theories of relativity and Fermi-Dirac statistics; he also had read the article in which Fowler presented his application of the Fermi-Dirac theory to the properties of dense stellar matter. In the summer of 1930, during the long sea voyage to England to begin graduate study at Cambridge, he undertook a detailed review of Fowler's derivation of the new equation of state. He realized that, at the densities of the interior of a white dwarf, the electrons must be so closely confined that the Fermi-Dirac statistics require their velocities to assume very great magnitudes—so great that, according to Einstein's special theory of relativity, their masses increase. This effect, which had been overlooked by both Fowler and Eddington, required a further modification of the equation of state to a form that imposed an upper limit on the mass of a star that could be stable against gravitational contraction even more severe than that observed for white dwarfs. The limiting mass—now called the Chandrasekhar limit—is 1.44 times the mass of the Sun. If Chandrasekhar's reasoning was correct, no star with a mass greater than this could end its life as a white dwarf.

It was necessary for Chandrasekhar to obtain independent verification of his results before he could proceed with assurance in the investigation of the final stages in the evolution of stars with masses greater than the limiting value he had deduced for white dwarfs. The obvious source of support was Eddington, who not only was the foremost authority on astrophysics but also had amassed a large popular audience by writing several books in which he explained scientific subjects in an engaging style. Although Eddington and Chandrasekhar quickly established a warm personal relationship, Eddington refused to acknowledge the value of Chandrasekhar's discovery. More than twenty years passed before the validity of the Chandrasekhar limit was generally recognized.

William Fowler's achievements, like Chandrasekhar's, rest on the foundation built by earlier scholars, who, mostly during the 20th century, contributed to the development of the present view of the sequence of events that take place during the life of a star. In the decade following the end of World War I the U.S. astronomers Harlow Shapley and Edwin Hubble made observations that gave rough estimates of the size of our Milky Way galaxy, the distances of other galaxies, and the rate at which the universe appears to be expanding. In 1927 the Belgian astronomer Georges Lemaître made those findings the basis of his hypothesis that the universe has evolved into its present condition in the aftermath of a gigantic explosion that occurred in the distant past.

Even though this Big Bang conjecture was refined by Walter Baade of Germany and Milton Humason of the United States in the 1940s and '50s, it was not taken seriously enough to lead other investigators to try to detect the cosmic background microwave radiation that should be present if the Big Bang had indeed occurred. In 1964, however, two U.S. radio astronomers, Arno Penzias and Robert Wilson, discovered this radiation; although they had been looking for something quite different, the cosmological significance of their finding was immediately recognized, and they were awarded half of the Nobel Prize for Physics in 1978. Partly because of their observations, the Big Bang theory has become the most widely accepted interpretation of the origin of the universe.

For some time after the Big Bang the largest objects would have been protons (the nuclei of hydrogen atoms) and alpha particles (helium nuclei); these positively charged particles would have been too hot—that is, moving too fast—to combine with electrons, which are negatively charged, to form atoms. Eventually the universe would expand and cool enough so that electrons and nuclei would unite, and in any region of space that happened to be densely populated with atoms, the force of gravity could begin to pull these thin clouds of gas together into galaxies and stars.

As Chandrasekhar and younger astrophysicists have shown, almost the entire future course of evolution of an individual star is determined at this early stage, because the possibility of alternative later developments depends very closely on the mass of gaseous matter involved in the initial condensation. The gravitational attraction exerted by a cloud of gas upon each of its component particles represents potential energy; as the attractive force acts on each particle and causes it to move toward the center of the cloud, the potential energy is converted into the kinetic energy of the motion. As the cloud contracts, it becomes denser and hotter as the kinetic energy of its particles increases. As the average distance between pairs of particles decreases, however, forces other than gravity cause them to repel one another, and the body of gas develops an internal pressure that opposes further gravitational contraction.

If the initial cloud of gas contained much less matter than our Sun, its shrinkage would stop when the internal pressure at every depth was just great enough to support the weight of the layers farther out. At the core the density, temperature, and pressure would become very high; the nuclei and electrons might become separated, but the nuclei would never attain sufficient kinetic energy to fuse with one another in reactions that yield additional energy. Eventually the heat at the core would flow out to the surface and into the surrounding space, and the stillborn star would glow briefly and feebly before growing dark and cold.

On the other hand, if the initial cloud were massive enough, its contraction would raise the core temperature to about 5 million degrees, and events would take a different course. Protons then move so fast that two of them, approaching head on, overcome the repulsive force arising from their similar electrical charges. They undergo nuclear fusion, combining into a single larger particle (a deuteron) and releasing two lighter particles, a neutrino and a positron. The neutrino escapes, carrying away some energy, but the positron soon encounters an electron in the plasma; both particles are annihilated, and their mass is converted into gamma radiation. The deuteron combines with another proton to form a helium-3 nucleus, and as these become abundant enough to find each other, a pair of them react to produce a helium-4 nucleus (an alpha particle) and two protons that reenter the sequence of fusions. This connected set of reactions, called the proton-proton chain, releases energy at each step and has the effect of converting four protons (hydrogen nuclei) into one alpha particle (a helium nucleus).

Astrophysicists refer to this nuclear process as hydrogen burning, regarding hydrogen as the fuel and helium as the residue, or ash. This kind of burning differs, of course, from the ordinary kind, which involves the chemical reaction of a fuel with an oxidizing agent (such as the oxygen in the air); the chemical burning of hydrogen produces water, not helium, and also yields energy, but only a tiny fraction of the amount released in nuclear fusion. Hydrogen burning in stars is the most important source of energy in the universe.

The suggestion that some sort of nuclear reaction involving the conversion of mass into energy might provide the energy radiated by stars was apparently first offered in 1917 by Eddington, who was a strong advocate of Einstein's theory of special relativity. This theory implies that the disappearance of a small amount of matter results in the appearance of a large amount of energy. Eddington's initial hypothesis, that electrons and protons might annihilate one another, was rejected by most other physicists, but he clung to the general idea. The tide began to turn in his favor in the mid-1920s, when the development of the new quantum mechanics provided theoretical justification for antimatter, which would annihilate ordinary matter in an energy-releasing process. The discovery of the positron and its annihilation by the electron, in 1932, was all the evidence needed to restore Eddington's hopes.

The first plausible mechanism for hydrogen burning was proposed in 1938 by Hans Bethe in the United States and Carl von Weizsäcker of Germany. Bethe, who also later proposed the proton-proton chain theory described above, won the Nobel Prize for Physics in 1967. The process outlined in 1938 is a cycle consisting of the six nuclear reactions represented by the following equations:

$$^{12}C + p \rightarrow {}^{13}N + \gamma$$
$$^{13}N \rightarrow {}^{13}C + e^+ + \nu$$
$$^{13}C + p \rightarrow {}^{14}N + \gamma$$
$$^{14}N + p \rightarrow {}^{15}O + \gamma$$
$$^{15}O \rightarrow {}^{15}N + e^+ + \nu$$
$$^{15}N + p \rightarrow {}^{12}C + \alpha$$

(The symbols in these equations have the following meanings: ^{12}C, nucleus of a carbon-12 atom; ^{13}N, nucleus of a nitrogen-13 atom; ^{13}C, nucleus of a carbon-13 atom; ^{14}N, nucleus of a nitrogen-14 atom; ^{15}O, nucleus of an oxygen-15 atom; ^{15}N, nucleus of a nitrogen-15 atom; p, proton [nucleus of a hydrogen atom]; γ, photon of gamma radiation; e^+, positron; ν, neutrino; α, alpha particle [nucleus of a helium-4 atom].)

The sum of the six equations is the same as the sum of the equations of the proton-proton chain, and the same amount of energy is released. These six equations make up the so-called carbon-nitrogen cycle, which is thought to take place in stars more massive than the Sun. In such stars the initial gravitational contraction is more rapid and can lead to a hotter core than that formed in small stars. The higher temperatures are necessary for the carbon-nitrogen cycle to operate, because more kinetic energy is required to bring about fusion of a proton with the highly charged nuclei of carbon-12, carbon-13, nitrogen-14, and nitrogen-15.

The onset of thermonuclear hydrogen burning, by either the proton-proton chain or the carbon-nitrogen cycle, is the beginning of the stellar fireworks, because this process sets free much more energy than gravitational contraction. It immediately raises the temperature and pressure at the core of the star. The increased pressure offsets the force of gravity, and so the star remains the same size for as long as its central hydrogen supply lasts; for the Sun this period of stability probably began about 5 billion years ago and should continue for about the same amount of time into the future.

By 1939 it was obvious to Fowler and his colleagues at the California Institute of Technology that their experience with particle accelerators could be valuable in the study of the nuclear reactions involved in the production of energy in stars. The necessary experiments were measurements of the relative probability of different reactions that might occur when a target containing a given species of atomic nuclei was bombarded with lighter particles that had been accelerated to kinetic energies typical of those imparted by the temperatures of stellar cores.

Measurements of the rates at which the reactions occurred would also be needed. As soon as nuclear weapons development slowed down after World War II, these experiments were started, and within ten years enough data had been collected to permit Fowler, in collaboration with Margaret and Geoffrey Burbidge and Fred Hoyle, to publish an article in which they presented a theory that accounts for the formation of all the chemical elements and their isotopes by reactions taking place in stars.

Their theory is based on the occurrence of nine distinct classes of nuclear reactions, each of which can take place under specific conditions. The proton-proton chain proceeds at the lowest temperatures; the carbon-nitrogen cycle of hydrogen burning takes place in hotter stars.

During the millions of years in which hydrogen burns at the center of a star, the temperature there remains quite steady and the proportion of helium rises while that of hydrogen falls. When the hydrogen is finally all used up, gravitational contraction resumes and raises the temperature again. If the mass of the star is great enough, the temperature will reach 100 million degrees (10^8 K), at which point helium nuclei will begin to combine, three at a time, into carbon nuclei. Under the same conditions carbon nuclei will combine with helium nuclei successively to form the nuclei of oxygen, neon, and magnesium. If nitrogen-14 nuclei are present, they will combine with helium nuclei to form fluorine-18; this isotope is unstable and decays to oxygen-18, which in turn absorbs a helium nucleus to form neon-22. All of these reactions are considered parts of the helium burning stage.

In successively hotter stars larger atomic nuclei are built up. In stars massive enough for the core temperature to reach about 5×10^8 K, two carbon-12 nuclei can combine to form the nuclei of neon, sodium, and magnesium. At temperatures of 10^9 K oxygen nuclei are converted to silicon, phosphorus, and sulfur; at still higher temperatures, about 3×10^9 K, nuclei of iron, cobalt, and nickel are the main products of the fusion reactions of smaller nuclei. The elements of this group are the heaviest that can be formed by fusions; beyond that point energy is consumed, rather than liberated, by such reactions.

Heavier nuclei are formed, but by a different class of reaction, in which neutron absorption alternates with the process of beta-decay. Neutrons, which are not electrically charged, do not have to overcome electrostatic repulsion when they approach an atomic nucleus. In supernova explosions so many neutrons are liberated that several of them may be captured by a nucleus before beta-decay has time to take place. These events are apparently responsible for the synthesis of several rare isotopes that are found in the crust of the Earth and can be detected in certain stars by their characteristic spectra.

Chandrasekhar was born on Oct. 19, 1910, in Lahore, India (now in Pakistan). He is the nephew of Sir Chandrasekhara Venkata Raman, who was awarded the 1930 Nobel Prize for Physics for the discovery of the Raman effect, the characteristic changes in the wavelength of light as it passes through transparent materials. Chandrasekhar graduated from Presidency College of Madras University, India, and received a doctorate from the University of Cambridge, England, in 1933. He remained at Cambridge as a fellow of Trinity College until 1937 and then accepted the position of research associate at the University of Chicago. He was named Morton D. Hull Distinguished Service Professor of Astrophysics in 1952 and was naturalized as a U.S. citizen in 1953.

Barbara McClintock

Fowler was born on Aug. 11, 1911, in Pittsburgh, Pa. He graduated from Ohio State University, Columbus, in 1933 and earned a doctorate in physics at the California Institute of Technology in 1936. He remained at that school as a member of the faculty and in 1970 was designated the first Institute Professor of Physics.

Nobel Prize for Physiology or Medicine

The 1983 Nobel Prize for Physiology or Medicine was awarded to Barbara McClintock of the Cold Spring Harbor Laboratory, Cold Spring Harbor, N.Y., a cytogeneticist who first explained the cellular mechanisms that account for the mutability of the hereditary traits of living things. She made her discoveries in the course of a lifelong study of the maize plant, or Indian corn, correlating the variations in outwardly visible properties, such as the pigmentation patterns of the kernels and leaves, with changes in the genetic elements of the cell nuclei. These elements, the chromosomes, can be seen with the aid of a microscope, using methods that McClintock perfected.

Her mastery of the details of the development of the corn plant so far surpassed the knowledge of other investigators that when she presented her complicated findings in 1951 scarcely anyone else in the world could comprehend what she had accomplished. Eventually, during the 1960s and '70s other geneticists became familiar with the behavior of chromosomes and found that McClintock's analysis applied to many organisms besides maize. In recent years widening recognition of the fundamental importance of her research brought her several other significant awards.

Barbara McClintock was born on June 16, 1902, in Hartford, Conn., and despite her mother's misgivings entered Cornell University, Ithaca, N.Y., in 1919. She had intended to study plant breeding, but

401

that curriculum was deemed unsuitable for women at the time, and so she earned her bachelor's, master's, and doctor's degrees as a botany major. As an undergraduate, again she overrode tradition by getting her hair shingled (the style became fashionable a few years later); as a graduate student, she decided that a pair of knickers would be more practical attire than a skirt while working in the cornfield. The cornfield in this case was the one tended by the members of Rollins Emerson's small plant-breeding group, which was studying the genetics of maize in a program similar to one carried out earlier by Thomas Hunt Morgan on the fruit fly. One of McClintock's colleagues in Emerson's company was George W. Beadle, who later studied with Morgan and won a Nobel Prize in 1958.

Emerson's investigation proceeded more slowly than Morgan's; one reason was that the maize plant takes a year to reproduce, while the fruit fly is sexually mature ten days after it hatches. A second reason was the lack of a technique for characterizing the chromosomes of the maize cells. The life cycle of the corn plant cannot be accelerated by human intervention, but McClintock made a major contribution to the study of its genetic mechanisms by developing the cytological procedures needed for visualizing the ten pairs of chromosomes in the somatic cells (those of the stems, leaves, and other structural parts of the plant) or the ten unpaired chromosomes of the germ cells (those involved in reproduction).

After receiving her doctorate in 1927, McClintock remained at Cornell until 1931 as an instructor. During this period she capitalized on her method of observing the maize chromosomes by carrying out field and laboratory experiments showing that trait-determining (genetic) information was transferred from the parent to the progeny in the crossing-over stage of meiotic cell division. In this process the paired chromosomes—one from each parent—intertwine and exchange segments; when the pairs separate at a later stage, each new chromosome, now containing elements from both parent plants, becomes part of a male or female germ cell, or gamete.

The article in which these results were published in 1931 became a cornerstone of cytogenetics. It provided the proof of a connection that had been assumed to exist between the processes that involve chromosomes within a cell and the transmission of traits from one generation of an organism to the next. McClintock's motivation in executing this piece of research was her perception of the necessity of establishing continuity in the chain of logical steps that underlay not only her own investigations but related projects being conducted by other geneticists in the United States and Europe. This insistence on making sure of the validity of her conclusions at each step remained a hallmark of her work.

For the rest of the 1930s McClintock continued her research on maize while holding brief appointments at the California Institute of Technology, Pasadena; the University of Freiburg, Germany; Cornell again; and the University of Missouri, Columbia. There was no doubt of her commitment to plant genetics, but the academic establishment during the depression of the 1930s extended scant hospitality to a female scientist working in any field, least of all to one whose reputation as a maverick and a loner was just as firmly established as were her credentials as a skilled, imaginative, and diligent researcher.

In 1942 McClintock accepted an appointment to the staff of the Cold Spring Harbor Laboratory, which then was operated by the Carnegie Institution of Washington. (It is now a self-governing organization supported by funds from Carnegie and from a group of sponsoring universities and individuals; its director in 1984 was James D. Watson, whose research on the structure of the genetic material DNA [deoxyribonucleic acid] brought him a share of the Nobel Prize in 1962.) Soon after joining the laboratory, McClintock observed a distinctive pattern of mutations in the pigmentation of the maize plant that revealed—to her practiced eye—a genetic anomaly waiting to be explained. Fox six years she spent the summers tending her crossbred corn plants and the winters analyzing the chromosomes and planning the next season's experiments. The mass of data built up in this solitary campaign satisfied her that the variations in the leaves and kernels resulted from a previously unsuspected instability of the chromosomes. She realized that two kinds of mobile elements in the chromosomes (called "jumping genes," "insertion elements," and "transposons" by a later generation of geneticists) participate in causing the changes.

One of McClintock's mobile elements, which she designated Ac, can spontaneously migrate within the chromosomes of maize. Its movement can cause the second element, Ds, to relocate; if Ds thereby becomes the neighbor of a pigment-forming gene, that gene's activity is suppressed, and pigment formation stops. If Ac causes Ds to move again, the gene's activity is resumed and a characteristically speckled kernel develops. Transposition of Ds or Ac can also cause breaks in the chromosomes.

The validity and generality of McClintock's conclusions did not become apparent until after the revolution in molecular biology that was initiated by Watson's and Francis Crick's discovery of the double-helix structure of DNA in 1953. The extension of their research led inevitably to the rediscovery of mobile elements in the chromosomes of many plants and animals and finally resulted in the acknowledgment of McClintock's astonishing insight.

—John V. Killheffer

AWARD	WINNER	AFFILIATION
ANTHROPOLOGY		
American Association for the Advancement of Science—Socio-Psychological Prize	Edmund J. Bourne	California State University, Long Beach
American Association for the Advancement of Science—Socio-Psychological Prize	Richard A. Shweder	University of Chicago, Ill.
ARCHAEOLOGY		
MacArthur Prize Fellow Award	David Stuart	Silver Spring, Md.
ARCHITECTURE		
Gold Medal of the French Academy of Architecture	Arthur Erickson	Arthur Erickson Architects, Vancouver, B.C.
Honor Award of the American Institute of Architects	Michael Graves	Princeton, N.J.
Honor Award of the American Institute of Architects	Hardy Holzman Pfeiffer Associates	New York, N.Y.
Honor Award of the American Institute of Architects	Hartman-Cox Architects	Washington, D.C.
Honor Award of the American Institute of Architects	Hoover Berg Desmond	Denver, Colo.
Honor Award of the American Institute of Architects	Richard Meier & Partners	New York, N.Y.
Honor Award of the American Institute of Architects	Skidmore, Owings & Merrill	Chicago, Ill.
Honor Award of the American Institute of Architects	Taft Architects	Houston, Texas
Honor Award of the American Institute of Architects	Urban Forms	Los Angeles, Calif.
Honor Award of the American Institute of Architects	Venturi, Rauch and Scott Brown	Philadelphia, Pa.
Honor Award of the American Institute of Architects	Welton Becket Associates	Santa Monica, Calif.
Honor Award of the American Institute of Architects	Wolf Associates Architects	Charlotte, N.C.
International Pritzker Architecture Prize	I. M. Pei	I. M. Pei & Partners
ASTRONOMY		
A. Cressy Morrison Award	Riccardo Giacconi	Space Telescope Science Institute, Johns Hopkins University, Baltimore, Md.
Gregory and Freda Halpern Award	Joel G. Levine	Langley Research Center, Hampton, Va.
Richtmyer Lecture	David N. Schramm	Enrico Fermi Institute, University of Chicago, Ill.
CHEMISTRY		
Alfred Stock Memorial Prize in Chemistry	Eugene G. Rochow (Retired)	Harvard University, Cambridge, Mass.

AWARD	WINNER	AFFILIATION
American Chemical Society Award in Analytical Chemistry	Allen J. Bard	University of Texas, Austin
American Chemical Society Award in Inorganic Chemistry	Malcolm Green	University of Oxford, England
American Chemical Society Award in Pure Chemistry	Eric Oldfield	University of Illinois, Urbana
Anachem Award	Roger G. Bates (Emeritus)	University of Florida, Gainesville
Arthur C. Cope Award	Albert Eschenmoser	Swiss Federal Institute of Technology, Zürich, Switz.
Benedetti-Pichler Memorial Award	Louis Meites	Clarkson College of Technology, Potsdam, N.Y.
Charles A. Thomas and Carroll A. Hochwalt Award	Denis Forster	Monsanto Co.
Charles H. Stone Award	George B. Butler	University of Florida, Gainesville
Charles N. Reilley Award in Electroanalytical Chemistry	Allen J. Bard	University of Texas, Austin
Cliff S. Hamilton Award in Organic Chemistry	Vladimir Prelog	Swiss Federal Institute of Technology, Zürich, Switz.
Earl K. Plyler Prize	William A. Klemperer	Harvard University, Cambridge, Mass.
Edgar M. Queeny Award	L. Stanley Eubanks	Monsanto Co.
Edgar M. Queeny Award	Walter R. Knox	Monsanto Co.
Edgar M. Queeny Award	Frank E. Paulik	Monsanto Co.
Ernest Orlando Lawrence Memorial Award	Nicholas Turro	Columbia University, New York, N.Y.
Garvan Medal	Martha L. Ludwig	University of Michigan, Ann Arbor
Gold Medal of the American Institute of Chemists	Mary Lowe Good	UOP Inc.
Gregory and Freda Halpern Award in Photochemistry	Mark S. Wrighton	Massachusetts Institute of Technology, Cambridge
Howard N. Potts Medal	George G. Guilbault	University of New Orleans, La.
Howard N. Potts Medal	Paul C. Lauterbur	State University of New York, Stony Brook
Huffman Award	Reed M. Izatt	Brigham Young University, Salt Lake City, Utah
Irving Langmuir Prize	Dudley R. Herschbach	Harvard University, Cambridge, Mass.
Jacob F. Schoellkopf Medal	Raymond Annino	Canisius College, Buffalo, N.Y.
James Flack Norris Award in Physical Organic Chemistry	Michael J. S. Dewar	University of Texas, Austin
Kaj Linderstrom-Lang Prize	Harold Scheraga	Cornell University, Ithaca, N.Y.
Kenneth A. Spencer Award	Peter Albersheim	University of Colorado, Boulder
Leo Hendrick Baekeland Award	Henry F. Schaefer III	University of California, Berkeley
MacArthur Prize Fellow Award	Richard S. Berry	University of Chicago, Ill.
National Medal of Science	F. Altert Cotton	Texas A & M University, College Station
National Medal of Science	Gilbert Stork	Columbia University, New York, N.Y.
Pauling Award Medal	Gilbert Stork	Columbia University, New York, N.Y.

AWARD	WINNER	AFFILIATION
Peter Debye Award in Physical Chemistry	B. S. Rabinovitch	University of Washington, Seattle
Priestley Medal	Linus C. Pauling	Linus Pauling Institute of Science and Medicine, Palo Alto, Calif.
Richard C. Tolman Medal	Donald T. Sawyer	University of California, Riverside
Senior U.S. Scientist Award	Edward C. Taylor	Princeton University, N.J.
Stephen Dal Nogare Award	Hamish Small	Dow Chemical Co.
Welch Award in Chemistry	Henry Taube	Stanford University, Calif.
Willard Gibbs Medal	John D. Roberts	California Institute of Technology, Pasadena
William Lloyd Evans Award	Vladimir Prelog	Swiss Federal Institute of Technology, Zürich, Switz.
Wolf Prize	Herbert S. Gutowsky	University of Illinois, Urbana
Wolf Prize	Herden M. McConnell	Stanford University, Calif.
Wolf Prize	John S. Waugh	Massachusetts Institute of Technology, Cambridge

EARTH SCIENCES

AWARD	WINNER	AFFILIATION
Arthur L. Day Medal	Harmon Craig	Scripps Institution of Oceanography, University of California, San Diego
Award for Outstanding Contribution to the Advance of Private Sector Meteorology	Paul B. MacCready, Jr.	AeroVironment Inc.
Carl-Gustaf Rossby Research Medal	Bert R. Bolin	University of Stockholm; International Meteorological Institute, Stockholm, Sweden
Charles Chree Medal and Prize	Sir Granville Beynon	University College, Aberystwyth, Wales
Clarence Leroy Meisinger Award	Robert A. Maddox	Environmental Research Laboratories, National Oceanic and Atmospheric Administration
Cleveland Abbe Award for Distinguished Service to Atmospheric Sciences	C. Gordon Little	Wave Propagation Laboratory, National Oceanic and Atmospheric Administration
Crafoord Prize	Edward Lorenz	Massachusetts Institute of Technology, Cambridge
Crafoord Prize	Henry Stommel	Woods Hole Oceanographic Institution, Mass.
Delmer S. Fahrney	Robert M. White	National Academy of Engineering, Washington, D.C.
Franklin Medal	Verner E. Suomi	University of Wisconsin, Madison
James B. Macelwane Award	Mary K. Hudson	Space Sciences Laboratory, University of California, Berkeley
James B. Macelwane Award	Raymond Jeanloz	University of California, Berkeley
James B. Macelwane Award	John H. Woodhouse	Harvard University, Cambridge, Mass.
Jule G. Charney Award	Peter V. Hobbs	University of Washington, Seattle
Maurice Ewing Medal	Xavier Le Pichon	University of Paris, France
Penrose Medal	G. Arthur Cooper (Emeritus)	Smithsonian Institution, Washington, D.C.

AWARD	WINNER	AFFILIATION
Robert E. Horton Medal	Charles V. Theis (Retired)	U.S. Geological Survey
Special Award of the American Meteorological Society	Henry T. Harrison	Climatological Consulting Corp.
William Bowie Medal	Marcel Nicolet	Brussels University, Belgium

ELECTRONICS AND INFORMATION SCIENCES

Ada Augusta Lovelace Award	Capt. Grace Murray Hopper	U.S. Naval Reserve
A. M. Turing Award	Dennis M. Ritchie	AT&T Bell Laboratories
A. M. Turing Award	Ken Thompson	AT&T Bell Laboratories
Distinguished Service Award of the Association for Computing Machinery	Capt. Grace Murray Hopper	U.S. Naval Reserve
Eckert-Mauchly Award	Tom Kilburn (Emeritus)	University of Manchester, England
John Price Wetherill Medal	Eugene Garfield	Institute for Scientific Information, Philadelphia, Pa.
Outstanding Contribution Award of the Association for Computing Machinery	Richard Austing	University of Maryland, College Park
Outstanding Contribution Award of the Association for Computing Machinery	Seymour Wolfson	Wayne State University, Detroit, Mich.
Paterson Medal	John M. Shannon	Philips Research Laboratories, Redhill, England
Richard E. Merwin Award	Merlin G. Smith	IBM
Software System Award	Dennis M. Ritchie	AT&T Bell Laboratories
Software System Award	Ken Thompson	AT&T Bell Laboratories
Stuart Ballantine Medal	Adam Lender	GTE Network Systems
W. Wallace McDowell Award	Daniel L. Slotnick	University of Illinois, Urbana

ENERGY

Enrico Fermi Award	Herbert L. Anderson	Los Alamos National Laboratory, N.M.
Enrico Fermi Award	Seth H. Neddermeyer	University of Washington, Seattle
National Medal of Science	Donald L. Katz (Emeritus)	University of Michigan, Ann Arbor

ENVIRONMENT

Audubon Medal	Margaret Wentworth Owings	Big Sur, Calif.
Ernest Orlando Lawrence Memorial Award	Raymond E. Wildung	Battelle Memorial Institute, Pacific Northwest Laboratories, Richland, Wash.
F. J. Zimmermann Award in Environmental Science	Irwin H. Suffet	Drexel University, Philadelphia, Pa.
Gairdner Foundation International Award	Bruce N. Ames	University of California, Berkeley
J. Paul Getty Wildlife Conservation Prize	Mario Andres Boza	Costa Rica
J. Paul Getty Wildlife Conservation Prize	Alvaro Ugalde	National Park Service of Costa Rica
Tyler Prize in Ecology and Energy	Harold Johnston	University of California, Berkeley

AWARD	WINNER	AFFILIATION
Tyler Prize in Ecology and Energy	Mario J. Molina	University of California, Irvine
Tyler Prize in Ecology and Energy	F. Sherwood Rowland	University of California, Irvine

FOOD AND AGRICULTURE

AWARD	WINNER	AFFILIATION
Bio-Serv Award in Experimental Animal Nutrition	John A. Milner	University of Illinois, Urbana
Borden Award in Nutrition	Richard Forbes	University of Illinois, Urbana
Borden Award in Nutrition	Herta Spencer	Veterans Administration Hospital, Hines, Ill.; Loyola University Stritch School of Medicine, Chicago, Ill.
Conrad A. Elvehjem Award for Public Service in Nutrition	James S. Dinning	University of Florida, Gainesville
John Deere Medal	Marvin E. Jensen	U.S. Department of Agriculture— Agricultural Research Service
Lederle Award in Human Nutrition	James D. Cook	University of Kansas, Lawrence
Massey-Ferguson Medal	Gustave E. Fairbanks	Kansas State University, Manhattan
Mead Johnson Award for Research in Nutrition	Barry Shane	Johns Hopkins University, Baltimore, Md.
National Medal of Science	Glenn W. Burton	U.S. Department of Agriculture
Osborne and Mendel Award of the Nutrition Foundation	Mark R. Haussler	University of Arizona, Tucson
Osborne and Mendel Award of the Nutrition Foundation	John Wesley Pike	University of Arizona, Tucson
Senior U.S. Scientist Award	John S. Boyer	U.S. Department of Agriculture— Agricultural Research Service
Wolf Prize	Don Kirkham	Iowa State University, Ames
Wolf Prize	Cornelis T. de Wit	Agricultural University of Wageningen, Neth.

LIFE SCIENCES

AWARD	WINNER	AFFILIATION
Alan T. Waterman Award	Corey S. Goodman	Stanford University, Calif.
Balzan Prize	Ernst Mayr (Emeritus)	Museum of Comparative Zoology, Harvard University, Cambridge, Mass.
Biological Physics Prize	Howard C. Berg	California Institute of Technology, Pasadena
Biological Physics Prize	Edward M. Purcell	Harvard University, Cambridge, Mass.
Ciba Medal	George Rada	University of Oxford, England
Colworth Medal	Eric Oldfield	University of Illinois, Urbana
Eli Lilly Award in Biological Chemistry	David Goeddel	Genentech, Inc.
Enrico Fermi Award	Alexander Hollaender (Retired)	Washington, D.C.
Gairdner Foundation International Award	Susumu Tonegawa	Massachusetts Institute of Technology, Cambridge
Kihara Prize	Susumu Ohno	City of Hope, Los Angeles, Calif.
Linnean Medal	Cecil T. Ingold	Birkbeck College, University of London
Linnean Medal	Michael J. D. White	Australian National University, Canberra

Scientists of the Year

AWARD	WINNER	AFFILIATION
Louisa Gross Horwitz Prize	Stanley Cohen	Vanderbilt University, Nashville, Tenn.
Louisa Gross Horwitz Prize	Viktor Hamburger (Emeritus)	Washington University, St. Louis, Mo.
Louisa Gross Horwitz Prize	Rita Levi-Montalcini	Washington University, St. Louis, Mo.
National Medal of Science	Seymour Benzer	California Institute of Technology, Pasadena
National Medal of Science	Mildred Cohn	University of Pennsylvania, Philadelphia
Novo Biotechnology Award	Kei Arima (Emeritus)	Tokyo University, Japan
Pfizer Award in Enzyme Chemistry	Robert Tjian	University of California, Berkeley
Rosenstiel Medallion	Keith R. Parter	University of Colorado, Boulder
Rosenstiel Medallion	Alexander Rich	Massachusetts Institute of Technology, Cambridge
Wellcome Trust Award	Robert Williamson	St. Mary's Hospital Medical School, London
Willem Meindert de Hoop Prize	Kenneth Murray	University of Edinburgh, Scotland

MATERIALS SCIENCES

AWARD	WINNER	AFFILIATION
American Physical Society International Prize for New Materials	J. P. Remeika	AT&T Bell Laboratories
Arthur Frederick Greaves-Walker Award	James I. Mueller	University of Washington, Seattle
Carl Wagner Prize	Manfred Rühle	Max Planck Institut für Metallforschung, Stuttgart, West Germany
Copeland Award	Sidney Diamond	Purdue University, West Lafayette, Ind.
Francis J. Clamer Medal	Louis F. Coffin	General Electric Co.
Francis J. Clamer Medal	S. Stanford Manson	Case Western Reserve University, Cleveland, Ohio
Gold Medal of the Acta Metallurgica	Charles S. Barrett	University of Denver, Colo.
International Prize for New Materials	David Turnbull	Harvard University, Cambridge, Mass.
John Jeppson Medal	Girard W. Phelps	Rutgers, The State University of New Jersey, New Brunswick
Ross Coffin Purdy Award	William H. Rhodes	GTE Laboratories Inc.

MATHEMATICS

AWARD	WINNER	AFFILIATION
George David Birkhoff Prize in Applied Mathematics	Paul R. Garabedian	New York University, New York
Leroy P. Steele Prize	Shiing-Shen Chern (Emeritus)	University of California, Berkeley
Leroy P. Steele Prize	Paul R. Halmos	Indiana University, Bloomington
Leroy P. Steele Prize	Stephen C. Kleene (Emeritus)	University of Wisconsin, Madison
National Medal of Science	Marshall Stone (Emeritus)	University of Massachusetts, Amherst
Wolf Prize	Paul Erdos	Hungarian Academy of Sciences
Wolf Prize	Shiing-Shen Chern (Emeritus)	University of California, Berkeley

AWARD	WINNER	AFFILIATION
MEDICAL SCIENCES		
Albert Lasker Basic Medical Research Award	Eric R. Kandel	College of Physicians and Surgeons, Columbia University; New York State Psychiatric Institute, New York
Albert Lasker Basic Medical Research Award	Vernon B. Mountcastle, Jr.	Johns Hopkins School of Medicine, Baltimore, Md.
Albert Lasker Clinical Medical Research Award	F. Mason Sones, Jr.	Cleveland Clinic Foundation, Ohio
Albert Lasker Public Service Award	Maurice R. Hilleman	University of Pennsylvania School of Medicine, Philadelphia; Merck Sharp & Dohme Research Laboratories
Albert Lasker Public Service Award	Saul Krugman	New York University School of Medicine, New York
Alfred P. Sloan Jr. Medal	Raymond L. Erikson	Harvard University, Cambridge, Mass.
Banting Medal for Distinguished Service	Irving L. Spratt	I. L. Spratt, M.D. Diabetes Medical Clinic, Inc., San Bernardino, Calif.
Banting Medal for Scientific Achievement	Arthur H. Rubenstein	University of Chicago School of Medicine, Ill.
Charles F. Kettering Award	Emil Frei III	Dana-Farber Cancer Institute, Boston, Mass.
Charles F. Kettering Award	Emil J. Freireich	M. D. Anderson Hospital, Houston, Texas
Charles S. Mott Award	Bruce N. Ames	University of California, Berkeley
Distinguished Service Award of the American Medical Association	Merrill O. Hines	New Orleans, La.
Dr. Charles H. Best Medal for Distinguished Service	Harlan L. Hanson	Thermo-Serv, Inc.
Dr. Charles H. Best Medal for Distinguished Service in the Cause of Diabetes	J. William Flynt, Jr.	Atlanta, Ga.
Dr. William Beaumont Award	William H. Foege	Centers for Disease Control, Atlanta, Ga.
Duddell Medal	Ian Young	GEC Hirst Research Centre, England
Eli Lilly Award	Howard S. Tager	Diabetes Research and Training Center and Pritzker School of Medicine, University of Chicago, Ill.
Elliott Cresson Medal	Elizabeth F. Neufeld	National Institutes of Health, Bethesda, Md.
Enrico Fermi Award	John H. Lawrence	Donner Laboratory, University of California, Berkeley
Gairdner Foundation International Award	Gerald D. Auerbach	National Institutes of Health, Bethesda, Md.
Gairdner Foundation International Award	John A. Clements	University of California Medical Center, San Francisco
Gairdner Foundation International Award of Merit	Donald A. Henderson	School of Hygiene and Public Health, Johns Hopkins University, Baltimore, Md.

AWARD	WINNER	AFFILIATION
Gregory Pincus Medal and Award	Robert Edwards	University of Cambridge, England
Gregory Pincus Medal and Award	Patrick Steptoe	University of Cambridge, England
Hammer Prize	Michael J. Bishop	University of California, San Francisco
Hammer Prize	Raymond L. Erikson	Harvard University, Cambridge, Mass.
Hammer Prize	Robert A. Weinberg	Whitehead Institute for Biomedical Research, Massachusetts Institute of Technology, Cambridge
Hammer Prize	Harold E. Varmus	University of California, San Francisco
Howard Taylor Ricketts Award	Maurice R. Hilleman	University of Pennsylvania School of Medicine, Philadelphia; Merck Sharp & Dohme Research Laboratories
Joseph B. Goldberger Award in Clinical Nutrition	Maurice E. Shils	Cornell University Medical College, New York, N.Y.
Lita Annenberg Hazen Award	Robert J. Lefkowitz	Duke University, Durham, N.C.
Pfizer Award for Outstanding Clinician in the Field of Diabetes	Harvey C. Knowles, Jr. (Retired)	Juvenile Diabetes Clinic, University of Cincinnati, Ohio
Scientific Achievement Award of the American Medical Association	Maurice R. Hilleman	University of Pennsylvania School of Medicine, Philadelphia; Merck Sharp & Dohme Research Laboratories

OPTICAL ENGINEERING

AWARD	WINNER	AFFILIATION
Adolph Lomb Medal	Edward H. Adelson	RCA David Sarnoff Research Center
Albert A. Michelson Medal	Hyatt M. Gibbs	University of Arizona, Tucson
David Richardson Medal	Erwin G. Loewen	Bausch & Lomb
Edgar Tillyer Award	Mathew Alpern	University of Michigan, Ann Arbor
Frederic Ives Medal	Herwig Kogelnick	AT&T Bell Laboratories
Joseph Fraunhofer Award	Donald R. Herriott	Norwalk, Conn.
R. W. Wood Prize	Otto Wichterle (Retired)	Institute of Macromolecular Chemistry, Czech.
Thomas Young Medal	James M. Burch	National Physical Laboratory, Teddington, England

PHYSICS

AWARD	WINNER	AFFILIATION
American Physical Society High Polymer Physics Prize	Frank E. Karasz	University of Massachusetts, Boston
American Physical Society High Polymer Physics Prize	William J. MacKnight	University of Massachusetts, Boston
American Physical Society Prize in Fluid Dynamics	George Currier	Harvard University, Cambridge, Mass.
Annual Medal of the International Academy of Quantum Molecular Science	John P. Simons	University of Utah, Salt Lake City
Apker Award	Raymond E. Goldstein	Massachusetts Institute of Technology, Cambridge
Beams Award	Ivan A. Sellin	University of Tennessee, Knoxville; Oak Ridge National Laboratory, Tenn.

AWARD	WINNER	AFFILIATION
Charles Hard Townes Award	Veniamin P. Chebotayev	Soviet Institute of Thermodynamics
Charles Hard Townes Award	John L. Hall	Joint Institute for Laboratory Astrophysics, University of Colorado, Boulder
Charles Vernon Boys Prize	Roger Cashmore	University of Oxford, England
Dannie Heineman Prize for Mathematical Physics	Robert B. Griffiths	Carnegie-Mellon University, Pittsburgh, Pa.
Davisson-Germer Prize	Manfred A. Biondi	University of Pittsburgh, Pa.
Davisson-Germer Prize	Gordon H. Dunn	Joint Institute for Laboratory Astrophysics, University of Colorado, Boulder
Elliott Cresson Medal	Herbert B. Callen	University of Pennsylvania, Philadelphia
Ernest Orlando Lawrence Memorial Award	George Chapline, Jr.	Lawrence Livermore National Laboratory, Calif.
Ernest Orlando Lawrence Memorial Award	Mitchell J. Feigenbaum	Los Alamos National Laboratory, N.M.; Cornell University, Ithaca, N.Y.
Ernest Orlando Lawrence Memorial Award	Michael J. Lineberry	Argonne National Laboratory, Ill.
George E. Pake Prize	Arthur G. Anderson	IBM
Glazebrook Medal and Prize	Alan F. Gibson	Rutherford Appleton Laboratory, Chilton, England
Gold Medal of the Acoustical Society of America	Martin Greenspan	National Bureau of Standards
Gold Medal of the British Society of Rheology	Arthur S. Lodge	University of Wisconsin, Madison
Guthrie Medal and Prize	Jeffrey Goldstone	Massachusetts Institute of Technology, Cambridge
Hewlett-Packard Europhysics Prize	Isaac F. Silvera	University of Amsterdam, Neth.
Irving Langmuir Award in Chemical Physics	Robert W. Zwanzig	University of Maryland, College Park
James Clerk Maxwell Prize for Plasma Physics	Harold P. Furth	Princeton University, N.J.
Maxwell Medal	Alastair Bruce	University of Edinburgh, Scotland
National Medal of Science	Philip W. Anderson	Princeton University, N.J.; AT&T Bell Laboratories
National Medal of Science	Yoichiro Nambu	Enrico Fermi Institute, University of Chicago, Ill.
National Medal of Science	Edward Teller	Hoover Institution on War, Revolution and Peace, Stanford University, Calif.
National Medal of Science	Charles H. Townes	University of California, Berkeley
Oersted Medal	Frank Oppenheimer (Emeritus)	University of Colorado, Boulder
Oliver E. Buckley Condensed Matter Physics Prize	A. C. Gossard	AT&T Bell Laboratories
Oliver E. Buckley Condensed Matter Physics Prize	H. L. Stormer	AT&T Bell Laboratories
Oliver E. Buckley Condensed Matter Physics Prize	D. C. Tsui	Princeton University, N.J.

AWARD	WINNER	AFFILIATION
Physical and Mathematical Sciences Award	Irwin Shapiro	Smithsonian Astrophysical Observatory, Cambridge, Mass.
Tom W. Bonner Prize in Nuclear Physics	Harald A. Enge	Massachusetts Institute of Technology, Cambridge
Trent-Crede Medal	Eric E. Ungar	Bolt Beranek and Newman Inc.
Vannevar Bush Award	Frederick Seitz (President Emeritus)	National Academy of Sciences; Rockefeller University, New York, N.Y.
William F. Meggers Award	Robert D. Cowan	Los Alamos National Laboratory, N.M.
Wolf Prize	Erwin L. Hahn	University of California, Berkeley
Wolf Prize	Theodore H. Maiman	TRW Inc.
Wolf Prize	Sir Peter Hirsch	U.K. Atomic Energy Authority; University of Oxford, England

PSYCHOLOGY

Distinguished Scientific Award for the Applications of Psychology	Donald E. Super	Gainesville, Fla.
Distinguished Scientific Contribution Award	John W. Thibaut	University of North Carolina, Chapel Hill
Distinguished Scientific Contribution Award	Endel Tulving	University of Toronto, Canada
Distinguished Scientific Contribution Award	Hans Wallach	Swarthmore College, Swarthmore, Pa.

SPACE EXPLORATION

Boris Pregel Award	Bruce Murray	California Institute of Technology, Pasadena; Jet Propulsion Laboratory, Pasadena
Distinguished Public Service Medal of the National Aeronautics and Space Administration	Charles A. Barth	University of Colorado, Boulder
Distinguished Public Service Medal of the National Aeronautics and Space Administration	Eugene H. Levy	University of Arizona, Tucson
Distinguished Public Service Medal of the National Aeronautics and Space Administration	James A. Michener	NASA Advisory Council
Distinguished Public Service Medal of the National Aeronautics and Space Administration	Warren D. Nichols	Hughes Aircraft Co.
Distinguished Public Service Medal of the National Aeronautics and Space Administration	Allan M. Norton	Martin Marietta Aerospace Corp.
Goddard Award	Krafft A. Ehricke	Space Global Co.
Wright Brothers Memorial Trophy	John Leland Atwood (Retired)	Rockwell International Corp.

TRANSPORTATION

Collier Trophy	U.S. Army/Hughes Helicopters Inc. Industry Team	Culver City, Calif.
Frank G. Brewer Trophy	John V. Sorenson (Retired)	Montgomery, Ala.

AWARD	WINNER	AFFILIATION
James Watt International Gold Medal	Sir Christopher Cockerell	Wavepower Ltd.
National Medal of Science	Edward F. Heinemann	Heinemann Associates, Calif.

SCIENCE JOURNALISM

AWARD	WINNER	AFFILIATION
American Association for the Advancement of Science-Westinghouse Science Journalism Award	Timothy Ferris	*New York Times Magazine*
American Association for the Advancement of Science-Westinghouse Science Journalism Award	Robert Richter	WNET-TV, New York, N.Y.
American Association for the Advancement of Science-Westinghouse Science Journalism Award	John N. Wilford	*New York Times*
American Institute of Physics-U.S. Steel Foundation Science Writing Award in Physics and Astronomy	Martin Gardner	*Discover* magazine
James T. Grady Award for Interpreting Chemistry for the Public	Cristine Russell	*Washington Post*
Washburn Award	David Attenborough	British Broadcasting Corporation

MISCELLANEOUS

AWARD	WINNER	AFFILIATION
Midgley Award	Hans Wirtz	Bayer AG, West Germany
Westinghouse Science Talent Search	1. Christopher R. Montanaro	Oxford Hills High School, South Paris, Maine
	2. Sandy Chang	Bronx High School of Science, New York, N.Y.
	3. Michael Tai-ju Lin	LaJolla High School, San Diego, Calif.
	4. Roger C. Hayward	Falmouth High School, Falmouth, Mass.
	5. Eva L. Assimakopoulos	Bronx High School of Science, New York, N.Y.
	6. Atom Sarkar	Stuyvesant High School, New York, N.Y.
	7. Lisa B. Szubin	Ramaz School, New York, N.Y.
	8. Peter A. Mead	Greenwich High School, Greenwich, Conn.
	9. Jessica G. Riskin	Stuyvesant High School, New York, N.Y.
	10. Mark C. Hamburg	H. H. Dow High School, Midland, Mich.

Obituaries

Bloch, Felix (Oct. 23, 1905—Sept. 10, 1983), U.S. physicist, shared the 1952 Nobel Prize for Physics with Edward Mills Purcell for the discovery of nuclear magnetic resonance (NMR) and its development into a powerful technique for studying the atoms and molecules that make up solids and liquids by measuring the magnetic behavior of their atomic nuclei. In the mid-1940s Bloch found that a strong stationary magnetic field applied to certain kinds of atomic nuclei caused them to align with the field like tiny bar magnets; when probed with weak, carefully tuned external radio waves, the nuclei could be made to resonate, or ring like a bell, absorbing and reemitting characteristic amounts of energy that could be used to evaluate the immediate chemical environment. In the early 1980s NMR emerged as a promising tool for medical diagnosis in the form of a device that produces cross sections of the human body similar to those made by computerized axial tomographic (CAT) scanners. During his scientific career Bloch also made many contributions to solid-state physics and devised a method for polarizing neutrons, separating them according to the clockwise or counterclockwise direction of their intrinsic spins. Bloch, who earned a Ph.D. from the University of Leipzig in Germany, immigrated to the U.S. when the Nazis came to power in 1933, and in 1934 joined the faculty of Stanford University. There he held the post of Max H. Stern professor of physics until his retirement in 1971. Bloch had also served (1954–55) as the first director general of the European Commission for Nuclear Research, a project set up in Geneva by 12 European governments for large-scale nuclear research.

Bok, Bart Jan (April 28, 1906—Aug. 5, 1983), Dutch-born astronomer, rocked the astronomical world in 1936 when he challenged cosmologist Sir James Jeans's estimate of the universe's age of 10 trillion years; Bok calculated that the universe was much younger, with an upper age limit of 20 billion years, a figure that is now widely accepted. Bok's enchantment with astronomy began when he was a Boy Scout, and his fascination with the Milky Way Galaxy became a lifelong passion. Bok, who earned a Ph.D. in 1932 (with a dissertation on the southern emission nebula, Eta Carinae) from the State University of Groningen in The Netherlands, was associated with Harvard University from 1929 to 1957, and from 1946 to 1952 served as associate director of Harvard College Observatory. In 1957 he went to Australia to serve as professor of astronomy at the Australian National University in Canberra and to direct Mount Stromlo Observatory. While there he was instrumental in obtaining major additions to the observatory facilities and was successful in attracting

News and Publications Service, Stanford University

Felix Bloch

Australian students to the field of optical astronomy. He returned to the U.S. in 1966 to become professor of astronomy at the University of Arizona, Tucson, and director of the Steward Observatory the same year. During the 1940s Bok gained distinction by calling attention to a class of dark compact nebulae that he referred to as "globules"; he described their importance to star formation in the Galaxy. The nebulae are now universally known as Bok globules. Besides contributing more than 150 articles to scientific journals such as *Sky and Telescope, American Scientist,* and *Scientific American,* Bok was the author of *The Distribution of Stars in Space* (1937), *The Astronomer's Universe* (1958), and his classic, *The Milky Way* (1941; with his wife, Priscilla F. Bok). He had just completed working on the 5th edition of the latter book shortly before his death.

Bond, George F. (1915—Jan. 3, 1983), U.S. physician, was a U.S. Navy captain and medical officer whose pressure-chamber studies demonstrated that men could live in an artificial helium-oxygen atmosphere at a simulated depth of 60 m (200 ft) for prolonged periods and not experience any harmful effects. His studies led to the Navy's sponsorship of Sealab, an experimental underwater laboratory established to determine whether man could live and work successfully for long periods of time at the bottom of the ocean. During the Sealab I and II experiments teams of aquanauts lived for days in the Sealab, a 17-m (57-ft)-long capsule anchored about 60 m below the ocean surface off California. Bond became an internationally recognized expert on saturation diving; he developed a process in which the body's tissues are saturated with a mixture of helium and oxygen so that divers can endure the prolonged pressure of deep ocean dives. In 1969, however, the Sealab III project was aborted when an aquanaut died in a 180-m (600-ft) dive. Bond served in the Navy for 25 years (1953–78).

Boyd, William Clouser (March 4, 1903—Feb. 19, 1983), U.S. immunochemist, while conducting studies on blood types during the 1940s discovered lectins, any of a number of plant proteins that induce clumping of red blood cells; the finding was significant because it resulted in the detection of several new blood types and the further subdivision of those already known. In 1956, using data that he had compiled from his studies on mummies and from his extensive travels during the 1930s when he blood-typed masses of people, Boyd was able to divide mankind into 13 groups and was able to establish patterns of prehistoric migration. His work in blood chemistry and immunology also proved that a person's blood group is inherited and cannot be altered. After earning a Ph.D. in chemistry from Boston University in 1930, he joined the faculty of the medical school as professor of biochemistry. In 1948 he was named the university's first professor of immunochemistry, a post he held until his retirement in 1968. Boyd, an expert in many disciplines, wrote textbooks in both immunology and anthropology, including *Genetics and the Races of Man* (1950), *Biochemistry and Human Metabolism* (1952; with B. S. Walker and Isaac Asimov), *Races and People* (1955; with Asimov), and *Introduction to Immunochemical Specificity* (1962). He also published works of science fiction.

Claude, Albert (Aug. 24, 1898—May 22, 1983), Belgian-born scientist, shared the 1974 Nobel Prize for Physiology or Medicine with Christian René de Duve and George Emil Palade for their research on structural and functional organization of cells. Claude, who never graduated from high school, was given special dispensation by the Belgian government to begin university studies in 1922 after his valorous service during World War I. In 1928 Claude earned his medical degree at Liège University and pioneered the use of the electron microscope and the centrifuge as essential tools in the study of cell structure. In 1933 he became the first to isolate and chemically analyze a cancer virus and to identify it as a ribonucleic acid (RNA) virus. After he became a U.S. citizen in 1941, Claude revolutionized modern cell biology with the publication in 1945 of the first detailed view of cell anatomy. While working at Rockefeller University in New York City, Claude and his colleagues not only found that cells contain a variety of specialized internal organs but also discovered the function of such cell constituents as ribosomes and lysosomes. Claude also discovered the presence of mitochondria, which store the cell's energy. In 1950 he left the United States to become head of the cytology department at the Free University of Brussels. He later served as director of the Institut Jules Bordet and founded a cancer research laboratory in Brussels.

Clegg, Hugh Anthony (June 19, 1900—July 6, 1983), British physician, as editor of the *British Medical Journal* (BMJ) from 1947 to 1965 enhanced the journal's layout and contents and guided its course during the controversies that arose during the formative years of Britain's National Health Service. He also played an active and influential role in international relations in the medical field. Clegg, the son of a clergyman, was educated at Westminster School and at the University of Cambridge. After qualifying at St. Bartholomew's Hospital, London, in 1925, he served as house physician there and at the Brompton Hospital for Diseases of the Chest and later as medical registrar at Charing Cross Hospital. Lacking the funds then needed to become a consultant, in 1931 he became a subeditor of the BMJ, the journal of the British Medical Association (BMA), advancing to deputy editor in 1934 and editor in 1947. In 1953 Clegg organized in London the World Medical Association's (WMA's) First World Conference on Medical Education. As a member of the WMA council and chairman of its Committee on Medical Ethics, he drafted the code of ethics on human experimentation adopted in modified form as the Declaration of Helsinki (1964; revised 1975). Clegg later set up the Royal Society of Medicine's Office for International Relations in Medicine and was its first director (1967–72). He also founded and edited (1971–72) *Tropical Doctor*. He was awarded the BMA's Gold Medal in 1966 and the same year was made Commander of the Order of the British Empire.

Crohn, Burrill B. (June 13, 1884—July 29, 1983), U.S. gastroenterologist, became renowned for identifying and treating ileitis (Crohn's disease), a chronic inflammation of the intestine that, in its classic form, is confined to the terminal portion of the ileum, the section of the small intestine farthest from the stomach. After earning his M.D. from the Columbia University College of Physicians in 1907, Crohn joined the staff of Mount Sinai Medical Center in New York City, where he conducted his pioneering work on ileitis and spent most of his professional career. In 1932, together with Leon Ginzburg and Gordon Oppenheimer, Crohn published the landmark report "Regional Ileitis: A Pathological and Clinical Entity." The study illuminated the cause and identity of the ailment that had mistakenly been diagnosed as a form of tuberculosis. Crohn was also one of the first physicians to correlate anxiety and stress with gastric and intestinal disorders. He was the author of more than 100 articles for professional journals and of such volumes as *Affections of the Stomach* (1927), *Understand Your Ulcer* (1943), and *Regional Ileitis* (1947; second edition 1958). In 1982

415

Crohn was named consultant emeritus in gastroenterology at Mount Sinai.

Crowther, J. G. (1899?—March 30, 1983), British science journalist, in effect created his own profession when, in 1929, he applied for a post as a science writer on the *Manchester Guardian* and was told by the editor, C. P. Scott, that no such branch of journalism existed. Scott, however, hired him, and over the next 24 years Crowther pioneered the treatment of topical scientific developments in the daily press with special attention to their social and political repercussions. He traveled to Germany, the Soviet Union, and the U.S. and was able to report such significant developments as the state of scientific research in Germany during the 1930s and the impact of nuclear physics. During World War II, while still on the staff of the *Manchester Guardian,* he served as director of the science department of the British Council. In later years he published biographies and an autobiography and was a contributor to *Encyclopædia Britannica.*

Debus, Kurt Heinrich (Nov. 29, 1908—Oct. 10, 1983), German-born electrical engineer, was a pioneer in the development of modern rocketry and a member of the German research team, headed by Wernher von Braun, which developed the V-1 missile and the V-2 liquid-propellant rocket that devastated London in 1944–45. Debus, who earned a Ph.D. in electrical engineering from the Technical University of Darmstadt in 1939, taught at his alma mater before becoming chief engineer in the V-2 program in 1943. As flight test director of the V-2 he developed instruments and techniques for missile guidance and control and for in-flight stress measurements. After the surrender of Nazi Germany in World War II, Debus joined von Braun and other scientists in the U.S. to develop the U.S. space program. During the 1950s Debus helped create the U.S. Army's first missiles that could be armed with nuclear warheads, and he was then named director of operations of what became the Kennedy Space Center, a launch facility for missile testing and for space vehicles. Debus, who probably launched more large missiles than any other person in the West, oversaw the launches of Explorer 1, the first U.S. earth satellite; Pioneer 1, the first U.S. deep-space probe; and the first space flight of primates, in 1959. He also supervised the 1961 flight that made Alan B. Shepard, Jr., the first American in space, and he made possible the 1969 lunar landing with his ingenious conception of the vertical vehicle assembly installation and the mobile rocket launching equipment needed for the Apollo lunar landing missions. Debus, who was inducted into the National Space Hall of Fame in 1969, retired from the space program in 1974.

Dee, Philip Ivor (April 8, 1904—April 17, 1983), British physicist, was professor of natural philosophy at the University of Glasgow from 1945 to 1972 and performed experiments with cloud chambers during the 1930s. His findings were important contributions to the study of nuclear physics. Dee studied at Sidney Sussex College, Cambridge, and became a research student at the Cavendish Laboratory, where he conducted cloud chamber studies that helped lead to the discovery of tritium and where he developed a million-volt high-tension set. During World War II, at the Telecommunications Research Establishment in Swanage, he helped to develop radar for use by bomber pilots in scanning their targets. At Glasgow, where he was recognized as an outstanding teacher, he oversaw the construction of his department's new building, which was equipped with an electron synchrotron, and he later obtained funds for the installation of an electron linear accelerator. Dee was elected a fellow of the Royal Society in 1941 and was awarded the society's Hughes Medal in 1952. He was made Commander of the Order of the British Empire in 1946.

Du Plat Taylor, (Frederica Mabel) Joan (1906—May 21, 1983), British archaeologist, was librarian at the Institute of Archaeology of the University of London from 1945 to 1970 and played a leading role in encouraging the development of underwater archaeology. During the 1930s she was assistant curator at the Cyprus Museum, Nicosia, and excavated several sites on the island. Du Plat later directed the excavation of Iron Age sites in Italy. In 1960 she helped in the excavation of a Bronze Age vessel wrecked off Cape Gelidonya in Turkey and further promoted this branch of archaeology by making amateur divers aware of underwater opportunities. For eight years she edited the *International Journal of Nautical Archaeology,* published by the Council for Nautical Archaeology, which she helped to found. She was also first president of the Nautical Archaeology Society, a fellow of the Society of Antiquaries, and editor of *Marine Archaeology.* She lived to see the successful raising, in 1982, of Henry VIII's ship "Mary Rose," a symbolic tribute to her pioneering work in directing attention to the importance of underwater sites.

Euler (-Chelpin), Ulf Svante von (Feb. 7, 1905—March 9, 1983), Swedish physiologist, shared the 1970 Nobel Prize for Physiology or Medicine with Julius Axelrod and Bernard Katz for discoveries concerning the chemistry of nerve transmission. Euler was honored for his discovery in 1946 of the compound noradrenaline, the key neurotransmitter (or impulse carrier) in the sympathetic nervous system. He also confirmed that noradrenaline was stored within nerve fibres themselves. These discoveries laid the groundwork for Axelrod's determination of the role of enzymes in nerve activity and led to the development of drugs for the treatment of Parkinson's disease and mental illness. Euler's father, Hans von Euler-Chelpin, was the Nobel laureate in chemistry in 1929, and in the following year Euler earned his M.D. from Karolinska Institute. He served as professor of physiology at his alma mater from 1939 to 1971 and from 1966 to 1975 was president of the prestigious Nobel Foundation. Euler also conducted research on prostaglandins, hypertension, and arteriosclerosis. Besides the Nobel Prize, he was recipient of the Swedish Order of the North Star and the Stouffer Prize.

Fuller, R(ichard) Buckminster (July 12, 1895—July 1, 1983), U.S. inventor, was a visionary Renaissance man who was best known as the designer of the geodesic dome and as a tireless preacher who advocated "synergetic" methods of seeking solutions to mankind's problems. Fuller, who was a self-described engineer, inventor, mathematician, architect, cartographer, comprehensive designer, and choreographer, was twice expelled from Harvard University by his own design (he cut classes and deliberately got into trouble). He was then dispatched to Canada by his family to work in a factory that made machinery—and was fascinated by the experience. He held a variety of jobs before joining the U.S. Navy and marrying Anne Hewlett in 1917. After his discharge from the Navy in 1919 Fuller worked for a meatpacker and as a sales manager for a trucking company before starting a business with his father-in-law in 1922. In the same year Fuller's life was shattered when his daughter died on her fourth birthday. He went on a five-year drinking binge, was forced out of business, and was contemplating suicide in 1927. He rejected the idea, however, and decided to dedicate his life to discovering principles that are operative in the universe and applying them to benefit his fellow man. His determination to prove that tech-

R. Buckminster Fuller

Tom Munk—R. Buckminster Fuller Archives

nology could "save the world from itself, provided it is properly used," led him to turn to construction, the industry for which he was best suited. In his early career Fuller was viewed as a lovable crackpot, the creator of a prefabricated Dymaxion House that had rooms hung from a central mast and had outer walls of continuous glass and of an omnidirectional Dymaxion three-wheeled automobile that used a standard 90-hp engine and could reach a speed of 193 km/h (120 mph). Both inventions were commercial failures. In 1943, though, he captured the serious attention of scientists when he designed the Dymaxion Airocean World Map, which showed the Earth's entire surface in a single flat view without a visible distortion. In 1947 Fuller patented his geodesic dome, constructed of light, straight structural elements in tension, arranged in a framework of triangles to reduce stress and weight. The dome was innovative because, unlike other large domes, it could be placed directly on the ground as a complete structure. Some of the finest examples of his more than 200,000 domes include the Union Tank Car Co. maintenance shop in Baton Rouge, La., and the U.S. exhibition dome at Expo 67 in Montreal. Fuller was also a prolific author of 25 books, including *Operating Manual for Spaceship Earth* (1969). Though he never formally studied architecture, he was awarded the prestigious Gold Medal of the American Institute of Architects in 1970 and in 1983 was presented with the Presidential Medal of Freedom in recognition of his many innovations.

Gibson, Reginald Oswald (1903—July 22, 1983), British industrial chemist, was working with E. W. Fawcett at Imperial Chemical Industries Ltd. (ICI) in 1933, studying the properties of gases at high pressures, when the two men discovered the first polythene (polyethylene) while experimenting on the reaction of ethylene and benzaldehyde. The new substance, commercially manufactured by 1939, played an important role in the application of radar during World War II and became one of the most widely used plastics in electrical goods, the building industry, and a vast range of consumer products after the war. Gibson studied chemistry at the University of Leiden. In 1926 he joined Brunner, Mond & Co., which in 1927 became part of ICI. He left ICI in 1948 and worked with Associated Octel Co. on antiknock gasoline additives, later becoming its technical director. In 1983 he attended the conference in London marking the 50th anniversary of the discovery of polythene.

Hartline, Haldan Keffer (Dec. 22, 1903—March 17, 1983), U.S. biophysicist, shared the 1967 Nobel Prize for Physiology or Medicine with George Wald and Ragnar Granit for discoveries about chemical and physiological visual processes in the eye. Hartline, who earned an M.D. from Johns Hopkins Univer-

Haldan Keffer Hartline

sity in 1927, conducted research at the universities of Leipzig, Munich, and Pennsylvania, before serving as professor of physiology at Cornell University Medical College and as professor of biophysics at his alma mater. In 1953 he joined Rockefeller University, where he did research in the electrophysiology of the retina. By studying the optic nerve of the horseshoe crab and other marine animals, he came to understand the integrative action of the retina. His basic research laid the foundation for nearly every advance in the neurophysiology of vision. Hartline retired from Rockefeller University in 1974.

Hildebrand, Joel Henry (Nov. 16, 1881—April 30, 1983), U.S. chemist, as a faculty member at the University of California at Berkeley for 69 years instructed some 40,000 freshman students in the rudiments of chemistry, and as the dean of U.S. chemists served as a pioneer in the field of physical chemistry. While still a high-school student Hildebrand proved that the molecular structure of nitrous oxide gas was NO rather than N_2O_2; his findings thus debunked the theory set forth in a book by a Harvard chemistry professor. After earning a Ph.D. in chemistry from the University of Pennsylvania, Hildebrand spent a year in Berlin studying the newly emerging field of physical chemistry under J. H. van't Hoff and Walter Nernst. When Hildebrand returned to the U.S., he was the first to teach this new science at the University of Pennsylvania before joining the faculty of the University of California in 1913. During his long and distinguished career his most important contribution to chemistry was his investigation of the chemistry of solutions. He was the author of *Solubility* (1924; later editions, *Solubility of Non-Electrolytes*), a classic reference for more than 50 years. He was an expert on intermolecular forces, and on solubility and the structure of liquids. Besides writing more than 300 scientific papers, Hildebrand also was the author of several textbooks, including the classic *Principles of Chemistry* (1918), which went through seven editions. During the week-long celebration of his 100th birthday he received the first Joel Henry Hildebrand Award in the Theoretical and Experimental Chemistry of Liquids, and a Joel H. Hildebrand Chair in Chemistry was established at the University of California in his honor. Though he formally retired from teaching in 1952, he continued to instruct graduate students at the University of California until a few months before his death at the age of 101.

Hinton of Bankside, Christopher Hinton, Baron (May 12, 1901—June 22, 1983), British engineer, as chairman of the Central Electricity Generating Board (CEGB) from 1957 to 1964 strongly influenced the British nuclear power industry at a crucial stage in its development. Trained as an engineer, Hinton designed and oversaw the construction of the first generation of nuclear power plants in Britain, notably Calder Hall (opened 1956), the world's first large-scale nuclear power station. He also supervised the construction of a second generation of reactors under the Dounreay program, which made Britain one of the leading exploiters of nuclear power for peaceful purposes. Hinton studied at Trinity College, Cambridge, before joining Imperial Chemical Industries Ltd. (ICI). During World War II he was on loan from ICI to the Ministry of Supply, and in 1946 he was appointed the ministry's deputy controller for atomic energy production. He continued to work on the design problems associated with nuclear reactors as managing director (1954–57) of the industrial group of the U.K. Atomic Energy Authority at Harwell. His abilities as both an engineer and an administrator led to his appointment as chairman of the CEBG when it was formed in 1957. Knighted in 1951, he was made Knight Commander of the Order of the British Empire in 1957 and a life peer in 1965.

Kahn, Herman (Feb. 15, 1922—July 7, 1983), U.S. futurist, was recognized as a brilliant and influential thinker, one who provoked controversy with his distinctive ideas on nuclear war. Kahn attracted national attention in 1960 with the publication of *On Thermonuclear Warfare*. In this book he claimed that thermonuclear war was not only a possibility but a probability; that the U.S. should be prepared to defend itself against a nuclear onslaught; and that a nuclear war would not necessarily mean the annihilation of civilization. He was severely criticized by those who believed that any minimizing of the dangers of nuclear war made such a war more likely. After receiving an M.S. in 1948, Kahn worked as a mathematican and physicist for the Rand Corp., a research organization that worked on contract for the U.S. Air Force. In 1961, however, he founded his own think tank, the Hudson Institute, at Crotonon-Hudson, N.Y., where he concerned himself with problems of national security and international order. He made predictions on a wide range of subjects and advocated thinking "unthinkable" thoughts. A zealous optimist, Kahn stated his views on nuclear war in *Thinking About the Unthinkable* (1962). In *The Coming Boom* (1982) he prophesied a bright future for the U.S., with median family income reaching $65,-000 by the year 2033, an attractive public education system, a rise in productivity, and an abundance of resources. He foresaw a bright future for the world's long-term prospects in *The Next Two Hundred Years* but tempered his original projection, set forth in *The Emerging Japanese Superstate* (1970), of Japanese economic ascendancy over the U.S. by the end of the century. In *The Japanese Challenge* (1979) Kahn maintained that Japan could achieve economic superiority only if it strengthened its domestic economy and curbed its exports. Though his unequivocal pronouncements raised the ire of unbelievers, his influence was substantial and far-reaching. At the time of his death Kahn was contemplating such diverse issues as the prospects for electronic transmission of mail, strategies for winning a war in El Salvador, alternatives to the U.S. federal income tax, and the future of Australia.

Liley, Sir (Albert) William (March 12, 1929—June 15, 1983), New Zealand obstetrician, was professor in perinatal physiology at the University of Auckland and a pioneer in the treatment of erythroblastosis fetalis (hemolytic disease of the newborn). Liley's experimental work concentrated on rhesus factor incompatibility (incompatibility of blood group between mother and fetus). By the use of amniocentesis he was able to diagnose and treat afflicted fetuses who might otherwise have been stillborn. He administered blood transfusions to the fetus in utero—an innovative step because such transfusions previously had only been given after birth. His findings also provided an invaluable first step toward the diagnosis and treatment of a variety of other conditions in the unborn child. Liley studied at the University of Auckland, at the Australian National University, and at Columbia University in New York City before joining the New Zealand Medical Research Council Postgraduate School of Obstetrics and Gynecology in Auckland. His accomplishments were recognized by his appointment as Companion (1967) and Knight Commander (1973) of St. Michael and St. George. Other honors included fellowship of the Royal Society of New Zealand and of the Royal College of Obstetricians and Gynecologists.

Massey, Sir Harrie Stewart Wilson (1908—Nov. 27, 1983), Australian nuclear physicist, was a world authority on the theory of atomic collisions and the joint author of a standard work on the subject, published in 1933. He served as Quaim professor of physics at University College, London, from 1950 to 1975 (afterward emeritus) and became the first chairman of the British National Committee for Space Research in 1959. He studied at the University of Melbourne, writing a dissertation on the field of wave mechanics, and went to the Cavendish Laboratory in Cambridge, where he contributed to the understanding of the wave nature of electrons. In 1933 he was appointed lecturer at Queen's University, Belfast, and in 1938 professor of applied mathematics at University College. During World War II he was chief scientist at the naval Mine Design Department and made a substantial contribution to the field. During 1943–45 he worked in Berkeley, Calif., on the development of the nuclear fission bomb. On his return to Britain he continued his research into atomic theory and at the same time established his reputation as a leading expert in other fields, including space physics and astronomy. His publications included *Negative Ions* (1938), *Electronic and Ionic Impact Phenomena* (with E. H. S. Burhop, 1952), *Atomic and Molecular Collisions* (1979), and numerous research articles. He was elected to the Royal Society in 1940 and served as its vice-president and physical secretary. His other honors included the Royal Society's Hughes Medal and Royal Medal, and he was knighted in 1960.

Melicow, Meyer (Dec. 25, 1894—June 3, 1983), Russian-born physician, specialized in the identification and treatment of urological cancer. He was dubbed the "father of uropathology" for his research and teaching, which encompassed ailments associated with the urinary tract. Melicow received his M.D. in 1920 from the College of Physicians and Surgeons, Columbia University, and served as a faculty member there for more than 30 years. He was a founding member of the Squier Urological Clinic and served as its first pathologist when Columbia-Presbyterian Medical Center was formed in 1928. He served as director of the clinic from 1930 to 1957. During his career Melicow was credited with being the first to identify specific characteristics of several urological cancers. His accomplishments were recognized in the form of awards, including the Hektoen Gold Medal given by the American Medical Association in 1949 for his work on adrenal tumors and the Lattimer Medal from the American Urological Association in 1977. In 1960 he became the first Given Professor of Uropathology Research, a chair that Columbia University established in his honor, and he became professor emeritus in 1963. Melicow, who wrote more than 200 papers on cancer and other medical topics, published "The Three Steps to Cancer: A New Concept of Cancerigenesis" in 1982.

Mikhailov, Aleksandr Aleksandrovich (April 26, 1888—October 1983), Soviet astronomer, was director of the Pulkovo Observatory from 1947 to 1964 and enjoyed an international reputation for his work in the fields of positional astronomy and eclipses. He was educated at Moscow University, where he taught from 1918 to 1948. The Pulkovo Observatory was completely destroyed during World War II, and he played an important role in the rebuilding and reequipping that allowed it to open again in 1954. His knowledge of telescope design helped to make Pulkovo one of the most advanced observatories. Mikhailov was vice-president of the International Astronomical Union in 1947 and 1967, an associate of the Royal Astronomical Society, and a corresponding member of the Bureau des Longitudes. His many awards included four Orders of Lenin and the Polish Order of Merit.

Monroe, Marion (Feb. 4, 1898—June 25, 1983), U.S. child psychologist and author, together with William Gray had a profound influence on three decades (1940s to 1970s) of schoolchildren as the author of the classic "Dick and Jane" primers that instructed beginning readers to "see Spot . . . see Spot run." Monroe, who earned a Ph.D. from the University of Chicago, also developed the Monroe Reading Aptitude Tests and was the author of such other books as *Children Who Cannot Read, My First Picture Dictionary,* and *The First Talking Alphabet.* The "Dick and Jane" textbooks were eventually discarded in the early 1970s because some educators advocated a stronger phonics approach to the learning of reading and because others felt that the books were racist and sexist.

Nachmansohn, David (March 17, 1899—Nov. 2, 1983), Russian-born biochemist, conducted extensive research on the nervous system and was especially noted for his studies on the chemical and molecular basis for nerve activity. Though he was born in Russia, Nachmansohn grew up in Germany and earned an M.D. from the University of Berlin in 1926. He was a research scientist at the Kaiser Wilhelm Institute of Biology until Hitler came to power in 1933 and then spent six years at the University of Paris before accepting a post in 1939 at the Yale School of Medicine in the U.S. In 1942 he joined the faculty of Columbia College of Physicians and Surgeons, where he served as professor of biochemistry until his retirement in 1967. While there he and his colleagues shed new light on Nachmansohn's 20-year-old theory of the biochemical reaction that prompts a nerve to carry an electric current and then shut it off. Their studies, which proved that if the current were not shut off, the nerve would wear out, also led to the development of safer and more effective local anesthetics. Nachmansohn had also conducted secret research for the U.S. during World War II on toxic nerve gases developed by Germany. Together with Irwin B. Wilson he developed effective antidotes for the poisons called PAM. While analyzing the complex process by which nerve impulses are generated along nerve and muscle fibers, Nachmansohn used eels and other electric fish as models of gigantic nerves. His pioneering studies led to a greater understanding of the human nervous system, especially of Parkinson's neuromuscular disease. Nachmansohn's investigations led to the publication of some 400 papers on nerve transmission.

Pagel, Walter T. U. (Nov. 12, 1898—March 25, 1983), German-born pathologist, was the author of a standard work on pulmonary tuberculosis and an outstanding writer on the history of medical science. Pagel published scholarly studies of the works of Paracelsus, William Harvey, and Jan Baptist van Helmont. The son of Julius Pagel, professor at Berlin University, he studied at the Friedrich Wilhelm University, Berlin, and the Robert Koch Institute before specializing in the study of tuberculosis. Research into the history of that disease led him to the investigation of the philosophical context of medical science, especially in the 16th and 17th centuries. In 1930 his first major work, on van Helmont, was published, but with the accession to power of the Nazis he was forced, as a Jew, to leave Germany. Pagel went to France and then England, where he worked first at the Papworth Village Settlement laboratory near Cambridge and then at the Central Middlesex Hospital and the Clare Hall Sanatorium, Barnet. His contributions to the study of tuberculosis and to the history of medical science were recognized in such honors as the Dexter Award of the American Chemical Society and the Sarton, Julius Pagel, William H. Welch, and Robert Koch medals. His last book. *The Smiling Spleen,* was on press at the time of his death.

Reichelderfer, Francis W(ilton) (Aug. 6, 1895—Jan. 26, 1983), U.S meteorologist, as chief (1938–63) of the U.S. Weather Bureau (now the National Weather Service), built the agency into one of the most effective and sophisticated national meteoro-

Francis W. Reichelderfer

logical services in the world. After graduating from Northwestern University, Reichelderfer studied advanced meteorology at the Blue Hill Observatory of Harvard University before joining the U.S. Navy and earning his aviator wings. His expertise in the field of meteorology was recognized when he was assigned to Lisbon, Portugal, to provide weather information for the Navy's flying boat NC-4 during its transatlantic flight. In 1921 he was promoted to lieutenant and served (1922–28) as director of the Naval Meteorological Organization at the Bureau of Aeronautics in Washington, D.C. Reichelderfer then studied at the Geophysical Institute in Bergen, Norway, and while serving (1935–36) as executive officer at the U.S. naval air station in Lakehurst, N.J., made four transatlantic flights on the German dirigible "Hindenburg." In 1938, after the death of Willis Gregg, Reichelderfer was named acting weather chief of the U.S. Weather Bureau, and in the following year the position was made permanent. During his tenure at the bureau, Reichelderfer introduced the analysis of weather fronts, 5-day and 30-day forecasts, and the Earth-orbiting weather satellite program. He also helped develop the bureau's own advanced meteorological radar system. For many years he also wrote the article "Meteorology" for the *Britannica Book of the Year.*

Russell, Dorothy Stuart (June 27, 1895—Oct. 19, 1983), British neuropathologist, wrote definitive studies of brain tumors and hydrocephalus and was recognized as a world authority in her field. She was professor of morbid anatomy at the London Hospital Medical College from 1946 until her retirement in 1960. Russell studied at Girton College, University of Cambridge, and London Hospital Medical College, where she won the Sutton Prize in Pathology. Her research for her thesis was concerned with glomerulonephritis, a kidney disorder, and it was only when studying in Boston and Montreal on a Rockefeller scholarship that she turned to neuropathology. She became a pioneer in the field in Britain, her work eventually leading to the publication in 1959 of *Pathology of Tumours of the Nervous System.* She joined the Medical Research Council in 1933, and in 1939 she went to Oxford to work with Hugh Cairns, a professor of surgery there. Russell was a member, then fellow, of the Royal College of Physicians and the first woman member of the Medical Research Club. Her publications included *Observations on the Pathology of Hydrocephalus* (1949) and many research articles. On her retirement she was appointed professor emeritus. Russell's awards included the John Hunter Medal and Triennial Prize of the Royal College of Surgeons.

Sert, José Luis (July 1, 1902—March 15, 1983), Spanish-born architect, was a disciple of Le Corbusier and under his tutelage became a leading proponent

José Luis Sert

of modernism in architecture. Sert was celebrated for his accomplishments in city planning and urban development and for softening the edges of modernist architecture's austere cement-and-glass structures. He frequently added colorful Mediterranean touches to his structures and in his designs of large buildings was famous for his trademark semicircular light scoops, which made maximum use of natural light. After graduating from the Escuela Superior de Arquitectura, Barcelona, in 1929, Sert formed his own architectural firm and devoted himself primarily to town planning. Two years after he designed the Spanish pavilion at the 1937 Paris World's Fair, he immigrated to the U.S. and in 1941 joined Town Planning Associates, an organization that provided planning and urban design for South American cities. Sert's experience in town planning was utilized in his work for the campuses of Harvard and Boston universities (1958–65) and was evidenced in his designs for the Fondation Maeght at Saint-Paul-de-Vence, France (1964), and for the Joan Miró Foundation at Barcelona. Sert, who was president of the International Congress of Modern Architecture from 1947 to 1956, served as dean of the Graduate School of Design at Harvard University from 1953 to 1969. In 1980 he was awarded the Gold Medal of the American Institute of Architects, the highest award given by that organization.

Simons, Joseph H. (May 10, 1897—Dec. 30, 1983), U.S. chemist, while conducting a routine experiment at Pennsylvania State College (now Pennsylvania State University) found one of the first practical ways to synthesize fluorocarbons; the discovery was instrumental in the development of the atomic bomb. Simons, who received a B.S. in chemistry from the University of Illinois in 1919, earned a Ph.D. from the University of California, Berkeley, in 1923. He later served as assistant professor (1926–32) of chemistry at Northwestern University and as professor (1934–50) of chemistry at Pennsylvania State College. There he discovered that by passing fluorine through an arc of carbon gas, a few drops of fluorocarbon were produced. He put the bottle of clear liquid into a filing cabinet, where it remained until Harold Urey, who was working on the top-secret Manhattan Project to develop the atomic bomb, presented Simons with a dilemma: the project was at a standstill because scientists were unable to produce enough fissionable uranium-235. Simons retrieved the bottle containing the fluorocarbon and pronounced, "Here is a chemical the world has never seen before. . . . It may do the trick." Urey then reacted the fluorocarbon with uranium to produce gaseous uranium hexafluoride; in this form the uranium isotopes could be sufficiently separated to produce the uranium-235 needed to make an atomic bomb. Simons later invented a process for large-scale producton of fluorocarbons, which led to the development by the mid-1950s of more than 800 new compounds containing those substances. In 1950 he joined the faculty of the University of Florida, Gainesville, where he served as professor of chemical engineering and chemistry.

Spiegelman, Solomon (Dec. 14, 1914—Jan. 21, 1983), U.S. microbiologist, was internationally renowned for his research on deoxyribonucleic acid (DNA) and ribonucleic acid (RNA) and for his studies on the links between viruses and human cancer. Spiegelman, who in 1944 earned a Ph.D. in cellular physiology from Washington University in St. Louis, Mo., found that only one of the two strands of molecules that make up DNA carried the message that generated genetic information for the production of new substances. He showed that RNA carried life's hereditary coding, and in 1962 he developed a technique (nucleic acid hybridization) that made apparent the detection of specific DNA and RNA molecules in cells. This breakthrough helped lay the foundation for genetic engineering. During his career he was associated with several universities, most notably the University of Illinois, where he was professor of microbiology from 1949 to 1969, and then the Institute of Cancer Research and the Comprehensive Cancer Center at Columbia University's College of Physicians and Surgeons, where he served as director and conducted research on the molecular basis of cancer. At the time of his death Spiegelman was trying to perfect a blood test for the diagnosis of breast cancer.

Sulzberger, Marion Baldur (March 12, 1895—Nov. 24, 1983), U.S. dermatologist, was a founding member of the Society for Investigative Dermatology in 1937 and was credited with helping to establish the modern field of dermatology in the U.S. Sulzberger, who earned a B.A. in medical science from the University of Geneva, received an M.D. from the University of Zürich in 1926. Three years later he opened a private practice in New York City and became an innovator in administering cortical steroids directly to the skin as a treatment for various skin diseases. His specialty was dermatologic immunology, and Sulzberger was especially noted for his studies of contact allergies. Besides serving as chairman of the department of dermatology at the New York University School of Medicine from 1949 to 1960, he was the author of hundreds of articles and textbook chapters devoted to dermatology. He also served as mentor to dozens of physicians, some of whom later headed departments of dermatology. After serving as a medical adviser to the U.S. Army surgeon general from 1961 to 1964, Sulzberger founded a research hospital in San Francisco which later became known as the Letterman Army Institute of Research.

Tank, Kurt (Feb. 24, 1898—June 5, 1983), German aircraft designer, was technical director of the Focke-Wulf company and designer of some of the most successful German planes used during the 1930s and World War II. His aircraft included the Fw-200 Condor, which established a record in 1938 for the first nonstop transatlantic crossing by a passenger aircraft in both directions, and the Fw-190 and Ta-152 fighters, which scored notable successes against British planes. The Ta-152 had a top speed of 760 km/h (472 mph) and was a night fighter of outstanding potential. But by the time it was in full production, the German economy was unable to produce sufficient planes to challenge Allied bombers. Tank also designed a jet aircraft, the plans for which may have been captured by the Soviets and used as a prototype for the MiG-15. After the war Tank lived in Argentina and India before returning to West Germany in the late 1960s.

Thompson, Frederick Roeck (July 20, 1907—April 13, 1983), U.S. orthopedic surgeon, in 1950 developed the Thompson Vitallium Hip Prosthesis, a forerunner of the full artificial hip that was frequently used in hip surgery to treat fractures and in plastic surgery of the joints. The device was revolutionary because, though it was made of metal, it was compatible with human tissue and useful in making hip joints. Thompson received his M.D. (1927) from the University of Texas and a Ph.D. in medical science from Columbia University in 1938. After his residency (1934–39) at the New York Orthopedic Dispensary, he studied in Europe. He later served as a clinical professor of orthopedic surgery (1946–72) at the New York Polyclinic Hospital and Postgraduate School and director and chief (1961–72) of the orthopedic staff at St. Luke's Medical Center in New York City. He spent his last years in private practice.

Contributors to the Science Year in Review

C. Melvin Aikens *Archaeology*. Professor and Chairman, Department of Anthropology, University of Oregon, Eugene.

D. James Baker *Earth sciences: Oceanography*. President, Joint Oceanographic Institutions Inc., Washington, D.C.

Fred Basolo *Chemistry: Inorganic chemistry*. Morrison Professor of Chemistry, Northwestern University, Evanston, Ill.

Keith Beven *Earth sciences: Hydrology*. Hydrologist, Institute of Hydrology, Wallingford, Oxon, United Kingdom.

Eric Block *Chemistry: Organic chemistry*. Professor of Chemistry, State University of New York, Albany.

David F. Bond *Defense research*. Senior Associate Editor, *Aerospace Daily*, Washington, D.C.

David Boore *Earth sciences: Geophysics*. Consulting Professor, Department of Geophysics, Stanford University, Stanford, Calif.

Harold Borko *Electronics and information sciences: Information systems and services*. Professor, Graduate School of Library and Information Science, University of California, Los Angeles.

Robert Boylestad *Electronics and information sciences: Electronics*. Professor of Electrical Technology, City University of New York, New York, N.Y.

D. Allan Bromley *Physics: Nuclear physics*. Henry Ford II Professor of Physics, Yale University, New Haven, Conn.

John Davis *Architecture and civil engineering*. Supervisor, Casement Seal Inc., Alexandria, Va.

Warren D. Dolphin *Life sciences: Zoology*. Professor of Zoology and Executive Officer, Biology, Iowa State University, Ames.

F. C. Durant III *Electronics and information sciences: Satellite systems*. Aerospace Historian and Consultant, Washington, D.C.

Robert G. Eagon *Life sciences: Microbiology*. Professor of Microbiology, University of Georgia, Athens.

Gerald Feinberg *Physics: High-energy physics*. Professor of Physics, Columbia University, New York, N.Y.

Lawrence E. Fisher *Anthropology*. Adjunct Associate Professor of Anthropology, Northwestern University, Evanston, Ill.

Robert L. Forward *Physics: General developments*. Senior Scientist, Hughes Research Laboratories, Malibu, Calif.

David R. Gaskell *Materials sciences: Metallurgy*. Professor of Metallurgical Engineering, Purdue University, West Lafayette, Ind.

Richard L. Gordon *Energy*. Professor of Mineral Economics, Pennsylvania State University, University Park.

Stig B. Hagstrom *Physics: Solid-state physics*. Laboratory Manager, Xerox Palo Alto Research Center, Palo Alto, Calif.

Robert Haselkorn *Life sciences: Molecular biology*. F. L. Pritzker Professor and Chairman of the Department of Biophysics and Theoretical Biology, University of Chicago.

John Patrick Jordan *Food and agriculture: Agriculture*. Administrator, Cooperative State Research Service, U.S. Department of Agriculture, Washington, D.C.

Lou Joseph *Medical sciences: Dentistry*. Senior Science Writer, Hill and Knowlton, Inc., Chicago.

George B. Kauffman *Chemistry: Applied chemistry*. Professor of Chemistry, California State University, Fresno.

John V. Killheffer *Scientists of the Year: Nobel prizes*. Associate Editor, *Encyclopædia Britannica*.

David B. Kitts *Earth sciences: Geology and geochemistry*. Professor of the History of Science, University of Oklahoma, Norman.

Mina W. Lamb *Food and agriculture: Nutrition*. Professor emeritus, Department of Food and Nutrition, Texas Tech. University, Lubbock.

Susan V. Lawrence *Medical sciences: General medicine*. Free-lance medicine and science writer, Chevy Chase, Md.

Index

This is a three-year cumulative index. Index entries to feature and review articles in this and previous editions of the *Yearbook of Science and the Future* are set in boldface type, *e.g.,* **Astronomy.** Entries to other subjects are set in lightface type, *e.g,.,* Radiation. Additional information on any of these subjects is identified with a subheading and indented under the entry heading. The numbers following headings and subheadings indicate the year (boldface) of the edition and the page number (lightface) on which the information appears.

Astronomy 85–256; **83**–256
    cosmic voids **85**–48
    honors **85**–403; **84**–404; **83**–402
    optical engineering **85**–362;
    physics research **83**–363
    quasars **84**–160

All entry headings, whether consisting of a single word or more, are treated for the purpose of alphabetization as single complete headings and are alphabetized letter by letter up to the punctuation. The abbreviation "il." indicates an illustration.

Acknowledgments

33	Based on information obtained from William A. Cassidy, John O. Annexstad, and Edward J. Olsen
48–49	Photograph, © 1976 AURA, Inc., Kitt Peak National Observatory
53, 61	From *The Poetry of Robert Frost*, edited by Edward Connery Lathem. Copyright 1923, © 1969 by Holt, Rinehart and Winston, copyright 1951 by Robert Frost. Reprinted by permission of Holt, Rinehart and Winston, Publishers
67–78	Illustrations by Kathy Goss
78–79	Additional assistance by Robert Laemle, Communication Arts Department, Abbott Laboratories
86–88	Illustrations by Richard A. Roiniotis
118	Adapted from "Slurry Pipelines," Edward J. Wasp, © November 1983 Scientific American Inc. All rights reserved
130–131	Illustrations by Anne Hoyer Becker
144	(Top) Additional audiovisual assistance and research by Thomas J. Veltre, Audio-Visual Specialist, New York Zoological Society
146, 150	Illustrations by Inez Smith
159–171, 229, 230	Illustrations by John L. Draves
193	(Top) NASA/JSC; (center) NASA; (bottom) from "Visual Observations of the Ocean," R. E. Stevenson, *Skylab Explores the Earth*, NASA, SP-380, 1977
203	(Top) NASA
206–207	(Left) James Mason—Black Star; (right top, bottom) for further information see Aden and Marjorie Meinel, *Sunsets, Twilights, and Evening Skies*, Cambridge University Press, New York, 1983
224	© Aldana/Garrett—Woodfin Camp & Associates
226–242	This article is New Jersey Agricultural Experiment Station Publication no. D-32506-2-84 supported by state funds and by National Science Foundation grant OCE-80-24897, OCE-83-10891, and INT-83-12858
230	(Bottom) Adapted from "Hot Springs on the Ocean Floor," John M. Edmond and Karen Von Damm, © April 1983 Scientific American Inc. All rights reserved
234	(Top) From "Morphological Survey of Microbial Mats Near Deep-Sea Thermal Vents," Holger W. Jannasch and Carl O. Wirsen, *Applied and Environmental Microbiology*, vol. 41, no. 2, pp. 528–538, February 1981; (center) from "Growth of 'Black Smoker' Bacteria at Temperatures of at Least 250°," John A. Baross and Jody W. Deming, *Science*, vol. 303, pp. 423–426, June 2, 1983, © 1983 AAAS; (bottom) from "Prokaryotic Cells in the Hydrothermal Vent Tube Worm *Riftia pachyptila* Jones: Possible Chemoautotrophic Symbionts," *Science*, Colleen M. Cavanaugh, S. L. Gardiner, M. L. Jones, H. W. Jannasch, and J. B. Waterbury, *Science*, vol. 213, pp. 340–342, July 17, 1981 © 1981 AAAS

BRITANNICA HOME LIBRARY SERVICE, INC.

IN THE BRITANNICA TRADITION OF QUALITY...

Now, there's a way to give your baby a headstart in life, with the Better Baby Reading Program. This remarkable, at-home reading program has been designed for you to teach your baby how to read in just two weeks.

No matter how young your babies are, just a few minutes a day will open up a whole new world for your child...and your child will be happier because of it.

Thousands of parents and their children are using the Better Baby Reading Program everyday...instilling in their children a life-long love for learning.

PLEASE SEE OTHER SIDE FOR ORDERING INFORMATION.